INTERNATIONAL ENCYCLOPAEDIA OF FOOD AND NUTRITION

EDITORIAL BOARD

E. J. BIGWOOD, *Brussels*   R. S. GOODHART, *New York*
J. MASEK, *Prague*   A. A. POKROVSKY, *Moscow*
V. RAMALINGASWAMI, *New Delhi*

EDITOR IN CHIEF, H. M. SINCLAIR, *Oxford*

VOLUME 5

FOOD CONSUMPTION AND PLANNING

VOLUME EDITOR
the late K. K. P. N. RAO, MSC, BSC, *India*.

INTERNATIONAL ENCYCLOPAEDIA OF FOOD AND NUTRITION

HONORARY EDITORIAL ADVISORY BOARD

M. AUTRET, *Rome*
V. BASNAYAKE, *Colombo*
C. H. BEST, *Toronto*
F. W. CLEMENTS, *Sydney*
E. H. CLUVER, *Johannesburg*
SIR DAVID CUTHBERTSON, *Glasgow*
W. J. DARBY, *Nashville, Tenn.*
M. J. L. DOLS, *The Hague*
M. VAN EEKELEN, *The Hague*
E. FERBER, *Zagreb*
F. FIDANZA, *Naples*
A. GHONEIM, *Cairo*
G. A. GOLDSMITH, *New Orleans, La.*
P. GÖMÖRI, *Budapest*
H. GOUNELLE DE PONTANEL, *Paris*
F. GRANDE, *Minneapolis, Minn.*
C. DEN HARTOG, *The Hague*
J. HAWTHORN, *Glasgow*
R. JACQUOT, *Bellevue*
G. J. JANZ, *Lisbon*
W. J. E. JESSOP, *Dublin*

E. AAES-JØRGENSEN, *Copenhagen*
H. D. KAY, *Reading*
H. KRAUT, *Dortmund*
J. KÜHNAU, *Hamburg*
R. A. MORTON, *Liverpool*
R. NICOLAYSEN, *Oslo*
R. PAOLETTI, *Milan*
SIR RUDOLPH PETERS, *Cambridge, Eng.*
J. V. SANTA MARIA, *Santiago*
F. B. SHORLAND, *Wellington, N.Z.*
B. SIMIČ, *Belgrade*
J. C. SOMOGYI, *Zurich*
E. H. STOTZ, *Cambridge, Mass.*
A. SZCZYGIEL, *Warsaw*
R. TARJÁN, *Budapest*
T. TASHEV, *Sofia*
K. TÄUFEL, *Potsdam*
J. TRÉMOLIÈRES, *Paris*
B. VAHLQUIST, *Uppsala*
J. VERZÁR, *Basel*
R. WENGER, *Vienna*

S. ZUBIRAN, *Mexico*

FOOD CONSUMPTION AND PLANNING

VOLUME EDITOR

the late K. K. P. N. RAO, MSC, BSC, *India*

PERGAMON PRESS

OXFORD . NEW YORK . TORONTO . SYDNEY

PARIS . FRANKFURT

U.K.	Pergamon Press Ltd., Headington Hill Hall, Oxford OX3 0BW, England
U.S.A.	Pergamon Press Inc., Maxwell House, Fairview Park, Elmsford, New York 10523, U.S.A.
CANADA	Pergamon of Canada, P.O. Box 9600 Don Mills, M3C 2T9 Ontario, Canada
AUSTRALIA	Pergamon Press (Aust.) Pty. Ltd., 19a Boundary Street, Rushcutters Bay, N.S.W. 2011, Australia
FRANCE	Pergamon Press SARL, 24 rue des Ecoles, 75240 Paris, Cedex 05, France
WEST GERMANY	Pergamon Press GmbH, 6242, Kronberg-Taunus, Pferdstrasse 1, Frankfurt-am-Main, West Germany

Copyright © 1976 Pergamon Press Ltd.

All Rights Reserved. No part of this publication may be reproduced, stored in a retrieval system, or transmitted, in any form or by any means, electronic, mechanical, photocopying, recording or otherwise, without the prior permission of Pergamon Press Ltd.

First edition 1976

Library of Congress Cataloging in Publication Data

Main entry under title:

Food consumption and planning.

(International encyclopaedia of food and nutrition v. 5)
1. Nutrition policy. 2. Food consumption.
3. Food supply. I. Sinclair, Hugh Macdonald,
1910– . II. Rao, K. K. P. N., 1918–1972.
III. Series.
TX359.F66 1975   338.1'9   75–9534
ISBN 0–08–016459–5

Photosetting setting by
Thomson Press (India) Limited, New Delhi and
Printed in Great Britain by A. Wheaton & Co., Exeter

CONTENTS

LIST OF CONTRIBUTORS	vii
PREFACE	ix
GENERAL INTRODUCTION	xi

CHAPTER 1   Food Consumption: Food Balance Sheets, Food Supplies   1
            W. SCHULTE, K. BECKER, and L. NAIKEN, *Statistical Analysis Service, Food and Agriculture Organization, Rome, Italy*

CHAPTER 2   Food Consumption: Food Consumption Surveys—Methods and Results   31
            EMMA REH, 4320 *Old Dominion Drive, Arlington, Virginia, 22207, United States*

CHAPTER 3   Food Consumption: Levels and Patterns-Variation by Geographical Regions and Socio-economic Groups   63
            MARINA FLORES, *Institute of Nutrition of Central America and Panama (INCAP), Guatemala, CA*

CHAPTER 4   Nutritional Requirements: Dietary Allowances and Requirements for Calories and Nutrients   139
            CONRADO R. PASCUAL, CARMEN Ll., INTENGAN, JOSEFINA BULATAO-JAYME, RODOLFO F. FLORENTINO, and LEON G. ALEJO, *Food and Nutrition Research Center, National Science Development Board, Manila, Philippines*

CHAPTER 5   Nutritional and Physiological Basis of Military Rations   221
            C. FRANK CONSOLAZIO, *Chief, Bioenergetics Division, Department of Nutrition, Letterman Army Institute of Research, Presidio of San Francisco, California 94129*

CHAPTER 6   Industrial Feeding in European Countries   315
            E. N. BENNETT, *Catering Consultant*

CHAPTER 7	Alimentation in Communities of Old People and in Hospitals H. GOUNELLE DE PONTANEL and L. BÉRARD, *Centre de Recherches Foch, 4 Av. de l'Observatoire, Paris, France*	339
CHAPTER 8	Special Feeding: Sports and Athletics, Mountaineering, and Other Expeditions MARTTI J. KARVONEN, *Institute of Occupational Health, Helsinki, Finland*	371
CHAPTER 9	Food Control: Legislation, Standards, Hygiene, and Inspection L. I. PUGSLEY, *Consultant, Food and Drug Directorate, Department of National Health and Welfare, Ottawa, Canada*	425
NAME INDEX		467
SUBJECT INDEX		479

LIST OF CONTRIBUTORS

ALEJO, LEON, G., *Food and Nutrition Research Center, National Science Development Board, Manila, Philippines*
BECKER, K., *Statistical Analysis Service, Food and Agriculture Organization, Rome, Italy*
BENNETT, MISS E. N., *Catering Consultant*
BÉRARD, MADAM L., *Centre de Recherches Foch, 4 Av. de l'Observatoire, Paris, France*
BULATAO-JAYME, JOSEFINA, *Food and Nutrition Research Center, National Science Development Board, Manila, Philippines*
CONSOLAZIO, C. FRANK, *Chief, Bioenergetics Division, Department of Nutrition, Letterman Army Institute of Research, Presidio of San Francisco, California 94129*
FLORENTINO, RODOLFO F., *Food and Nutrition Research Center, National Science Development Board, Manila, Philippines*
FLORES, MARINA, *Institute of Nutrition of Central America and Panama (INCAP), Guatemala, CA*
INTENGAN, CARMEN LL., *Food and Nutrition Research Center, National Science Development Board, Manila, Philippines*
KARVONEN, MARTTI J., *Institute of Occupational Health, Helsinki, Finland*
NAIKEN, L., *Statistical Analysis Service, Food and Agriculture Organization, Rome, Italy*
PASCUAL, CONRADO R., *Food and Nutrition Research Center, National Science Development Board, Manila, Philippines*
PONTANEL, H. GOUNELLE, DE, *Centre de Recherches Foch, 4 Av. de l'Observatoire, Paris, France*
PUGSLEY, L. I., *Food and Drug Directorate, Department of National Health and Welfare, Ottawa, Canada*
REH, EMMA, *4320 Old Dominion Drive, Arlington, Virginia 22207, U.S.A.*
SCHULTE, W., *Statistical Analysis Service, Food and Agriculture Organization, Rome, Italy*

PREFACE

DURING the Sixth International Congress of Nutrition in Edinburgh in August 1963, Mr. Robert Maxwell, the Publisher at Pergamon Press, gave a luncheon to thirty-two persons from seventeen countries for discussion of my draft plan of the *International Encyclopaedia of Food and Nutrition*, and for the selection of editors of the volumes. As editor-in-chief I had planned the contents of the different volumes and suggested editors. Dr. K. K. P. N. Rao agreed at the luncheon to be editor of Volume 5, dealing with *Food Consumption*, and this he confirmed in a letter dated 5 December 1963. He was then Chief, Food Consumption and Planning Branch of the Nutrition Division of FAO; and both he and Dr. Autret (Director of the Nutrition Division) suggested the volume should be called *Food Consumption and Planning*. He and I decided to include fourteen chapters, and for these authors were obtained. Dr. Rao himself intended to write a chapter entitled "Nutrition in food policy and planning for development: short-term and long-term nutritional targets for food supplies, and policies and measures required to attain them". It was never completed, and Dr. Rao was tragically killed in an air accident in India on 14 June 1972 when travelling from Bangkok for a meeting in New Delhi where he was to represent the FAO, of which he was then Senior Nutrition Officer, Regional Office for Asia and the Far East.

He was born in India on 7 July 1918, the son of a well-known lawyer, and he studied at the Benares Hindu University and at the Andrah University, from which he obtained the degrees of BSc and MSc. From 1940 to 1943 he worked at the Parlakimedi Research School, Nutrition Research Laboratories, Coonoor, which had been founded by Sir Robert McCarrison and were then directed by his successor, Dr. W. R. Aykroyd. From 1943 for four years he worked in the Department of Food of the Indian Government; in 1947 he joined the FAO in Washington, moving to Rome in 1951. He had particular concern for the welfare of staff, and for several years was chairman of the FAO Staff Council; this arose from his intense interest in people, and he was not really interested in the technical aspects of nutrition. He was strict in his vegetarianism, and he never drank alcohol though he provided it for his guests. He was survived by a widow, a daughter, and a son.

At the time of his death, half of the fourteen chapters had been completed. I took over the editorship and obtained two further ones, but reluctantly had to abandon four since the correspondence Dr. Rao had with the authors showed they were unlikely to fulfil their promises to him; Dr. Rao's chapter is also missing. But it has been possible to include in the chapters now published much of the material that would otherwise have been part of the abandoned chapters. And I am therefore confident that the volume appears much as Dr. Rao would have wished, and makes a valuable contribution to the *International Encyclopaedia of Food and Nutrition*.

HUGH SINCLAIR

GENERAL INTRODUCTION

THE three primitive instincts of all higher animals including man are nutrition, self-preservation, and sex. Of these nutrition is the earliest since all animals and plants ingest and metabolize food. Hence the science of nutrition and the practical application of that science interest those engaged in a wide variety of disciplines. For instance, the chemist studies the composition of foodstuffs, the biochemist their transformations in the body with consequent growth and energy-production, the physiologist the normal processes of metabolism, and the pathologist the changes that result from abnormalities of those processes. The clinician must recognize the disorders produced by faulty or insufficient food, and the dietist helps to correct these; agriculturalists and economists are concerned with the production and distribution of food whether animal or vegetable; sociologists and politicians with the national and international aspects of that production and distribution.

There are two factors that have made desirable the collection and integration of existing knowledge of food and nutrition at the present time. First, this knowledge has been advanced very rapidly in the past few years largely by the great discoveries in biochemistry. Secondly, there is no more urgent problem in the world today than the nutritional disasters that are now present amongst us and will increase with the explosive rise in the population of the world. Hundreds of thousands of years have been needed to reach our present population of 3400 million, but another 3400 million persons will probably be produced in the next 35 years. And it is alleged that two-thirds of the present population is underfed. Whatever the proportion, we have a food deficit that is certain to increase and must be met by increased production of food whether by more efficient methods, bringing new lands into cultivation, or by the use of new types of foodstuffs, for instance from oil.

Nor need the other third be complacent about its present food and nutrition, for the rapid developments in food technology have created new problems as foods are increasingly processed and sophisticated. We now treat foods with a variety of chemicals. Such additives are essential for two reasons. First, the housewife increasingly demands partially cooked foods in plastic wrappers which she merely warms at home; she no longer prepares and cooks what she gathered from her garden. Secondly, we have to produce the maximum amount of food from the land and then store it and transport it over long distances. Therefore we very properly use chemical fertilizers, pesticides, hormones, antibiotics, and improvers (such as vitamins A and D in margarine). All these activities create problems.

An encyclopaedia is a work that contains exhaustive information on a branch of knowledge, arranged systematically and not necessarily alphabetically. The aims, scope, and purpose of this one were discussed with Mr. Robert Maxwell, the publisher, at the International Congresses of Nutrition in Washington, Edinburgh, and Hámburg in 1960, 1963, and 1966. The plan is to provide an authoritative and comprehensive presentation of knowledge in the whole field of nutrition of man and lower animals, with brief reference to the nutrition of plants and micro-organisms. Each volume is written primarily for nutritional scientists, but is of value to others such as chemists, biochemists, medical practitioners, dietists, veterinary surgeons, agriculturalists, and economists. Experimental details of an essentially practical nature are not emphasized in the *Encyclopaedia*; but a thorough background of the theoretical basis of techniques is included so that these may be understood and applied at the fullest extent. The *Encyclopaedia* provides for investigations in the fundamental biological sciences—biophysics, biochemistry, physiology, pathology, psychology, experimental therapeutics, experimental zoology, and related fields—data which will help each in his own field. Further, the advanced student in both the basic medical sciences and clinical specialities will find these volumes an invaluable guide and an authoritative source of reference to literature.

As editor-in-chief I have been supported by five regional editors and by an Honorary Editorial Advisory Board composed of the world's leading nutritional scientists and under the chairmanship of the publisher, Mr. Robert Maxwell. We regret that the authorship of the articles has not been as widely international as is desirable, but while in some volumes there is a preponderance of articles from the English-speaking countries, greater emphasis on international authorship has been achieved in many parts of the *Encyclopaedia*. Perhaps it is inevitable that in multi-author works delays in one or two chapters should affect a whole volume, but we believe that this has not detracted seriously from the usefulness of the work as a whole. Indeed, the rapid advances in the science of nutrition create a problem. To meet it an annual review will be published entitled "Progress in the Science of Nutrition and Food Technology" which will report advances in the respective fields covered by the *Encyclopaedia* and give full bibliographical details of recent works for easy reference.

The *International Encyclopaedia* is now assisted by being associated with the recently created International Institute of Human Nutrition. This Institute, registered as a charity, is located between the Universities of Oxford and Reading, England, and exists to do fundamental research on human nutrition and to be a centre for information. Both the late Lord Boyd Orr and the late Earl of Woolton (wartime Minister of Food in Britain) gave support and encouragement to the creation of this Institute which is governed by a Council of Management to ensure its permanence and objectivity.

H. M. SINCLAIR
Oxford

CHAPTER 1

FOOD CONSUMPTION: FOOD BALANCE SHEETS, FOOD SUPPLIES

W. Schulte, K. Becker, and L. Naiken

Statistical Analysis Service, Food and Agriculture Organization, Rome, Italy

CONTENTS

1. History and Development	1
2. Food Balance Sheets—What they are and how they can serve	4
3. Accuracy of Food Balance Sheets	5
4. Concepts and Definitions used in Food Balance Sheets	6
4.1. Commodity Coverage	6
4.2. Supply and Utilization Elements	7
4.2.1. Production	7
4.2.2. Changes in Stocks	8
4.2.3. Gross Imports	9
4.2.4. Supply	9
4.2.5. Gross Exports	9
4.2.6. Feed	9
4.2.7. Seed	10
4.2.8. Manufacture	10
4.2.9. Waste	10
4.2.10. Food (Gross), Food (Net), and Extraction Rate	11
4.2.11. *Per Caput* Consumption	11
5. Global Levels and Trends of Food Supplies and Nutrition	12
Appendix IA. Food Balance Sheet Format at Present used by the FAO	18
Appendix IB. Food Balance Sheet Format previously used by the FAO and still used by Many Countries	20
Appendix II. *Per Caput* Food Supplies, Average 1964–6—Quantity	21
Appendix III. *Per Caput* Food Supplies, Average, 1964–6—Calories	22
Appendix IV. *Per Caput* Food Supplies, Average 1964–6—Proteins	24
Appendix V. *Per Caput* Food Supplies, Average 1964–6—Fat	26
Appendix VI. Classification of Countries According to Economic Class and Region	28
References	29

1. HISTORY AND DEVELOPMENT

First attempts at preparing food balance sheets date back to World War I. The technique was refined in the 1920s and 1930s, particularly by the Berlin Institute for the Study of Business Cycles. Food balance sheets served as a major source of data for the work of the International Institute of Agriculture, which in 1936 carried out a systematic international comparison of food consumption data at the request of the League of Nations Mixed Committee on the Problem of Nutrition and its sub-committee on Nutritional Statistics.

The interest in food balance sheets was substantially increased during World War II. In 1942 the Inter-Allied Committee on Postwar Requirements, through the use of food balance sheets, made a number of studies on post-war food requirements in European countries. The following year a joint committee of experts from Canada, the United States of America, and the United Kingdom published its first report, *Food Consumption Levels in the United States, Canada and the United Kingdom*, in which a more detailed technique of food balance sheets was employed and developed. In Germany also, on the other side of the front, *'Ernährungs Bilanzen'* (food balance sheets) were prepared for Germany and the occupied countries. Immediately after the war, food balance sheets played an important role in the work of the International Emergency Food Council established to deal with problems of food allocation and distribution during that period of worldwide shortages of food.

The Food and Agriculture Organization of the United Nations (FAO) has from its very beginning given considerable importance to the further development of the technique of food balance sheets—as a useful tool for the analysis of progress made in improving the food position in all countries. The technique was extensively employed in FAO's first *World Food Survey* (1946). The fourth session of the FAO conference adopted a resolution recommending *inter alia* that governments should be encouraged to develop their own food balance sheets and that the FAO should be prepared to assist those governments which find it difficult to do so. The conference also recommended that food balance sheets be published as soon as possible for those countries with adequate data after consultation with the governments concerned, and that, in the future, food balance sheets for as many countries as possible be published regularly. As regards food balance sheets for OECD member countries, work is co-ordinated with the OECD. In accordance with this recommendation, FAO in 1949 published food balance sheets for 41 countries covering the pre-war period and 1947/8, with a supplement in 1950 giving 1948/9 data for 36 countries. The *Handbook for the Preparation of Food Balance Sheets* was also published in 1949. In 1955 food balance sheets giving 1950/1 and 1951/2 data were published for 33 countries, together with revised data for the pre-war period. Supplements were issued in 1956 giving 1952/3 data for 30 countries, and in 1957 giving 1953/4 and 1954/5 data for 29 countries.

For methodological reasons, it was decided in 1957 to discontinue the publication of annual food balance sheets and to publish instead three-year average food balance sheets. The first set of three-year average food balance sheets for 30 countries was issued in 1958, covering the period 1954–6; the second for 43 countries in 1963, covering the period 1957–9 and the third, for 63 countries in 1966, covering the period 1960–2. In 1960, time series covering average periods 1935–9, 1948–50, 1951–3, and 1954–6 were published showing data for 32 countries on production, available supply, feed and manufacture, as well as *per caput* food supplies available for human consumption in quantity, caloric value, and protein and fat content.

In recent years the geographic coverage of the FAO's regular work on food balance sheets has been progressively extended to meet the statistical needs of the FAO'S contribution to the review and appraisal studies for the Second UN Development Decade of the FAO's *Agricultural Commodity Projections 1970–1980* and of work initiated under the FAO'S Perspective Study of World Agricultural Development. This has led to the establishment of an interlinked computer storage and processing system of food and agricultural commodity data and related statistics on an up-to-date basis including all major countries of the world. Accordingly, it has been possible to include in the publication of 1964–6 average food balance sheets data for as many as 132 countries. A publication of 1969–71 average food balance sheets is in preparation. In addition to the special publications of complete food balance sheets, the FAO publishes annually in its *Production Yearbook* data on *per caput* supply by major food groups as obtained from food balance sheets.

Food balance sheets were the main source of data used in the assessment and appraisal of the world food situation which the FAO made for the pre-war period in its first *World Food Survey* (1946), for the early post-war period in the *Second World Food Survey* (1952), and for the late 1950s in its *Third World Food Survey* (1963b). For the purposes of these surveys, food balance sheets were prepared on an *ad hoc* basis for many more countries than had been included in the regular publications on the subject referred to earlier. Thus, the first *World Food Survey* was based on pre-war data for 70 countries, representing about 90 % of the world population at that time, and the *Third World Food Survey* on data for over 80 countries relating to the late 1950s covering some 95 % of the world's population. Food balance sheets also provide a major source of information for establishing the statistical base of the FAO's *Indicative World Plan for Agricultural Development,* for which purpose 1961–3 average food balance sheets were prepared for all the 64 developing countries included in the study.

2. FOOD BALANCE SHEETS—WHAT THEY ARE AND HOW THEY CAN SERVE

A food balance sheet presents a comprehensive picture of the pattern of a country's food supply during the specified reference period. The food balance sheet shows for each food item, i.e. each commodity potentially available for human consumption, the sources of the supply, and its utilization. The total quantity of foodstuffs produced in a country added to the total quantity imported and adjusted to any change in stocks that may have occurred since the beginning of the reference period gives the *supply* available during that period. On the *utilization* side a distinction is made between the quantities exported, fed to livestock, used for seed, put to industrial and other non-food uses, losses during storage and transportation and food supplies available for human consumption at the retail level, i.e. as the food leaves the retail shop or otherwise enters the household. The *per caput* supply of each such food item available for human consumption is then obtained by dividing the food supplies available for human consumption by the related data on the population actually partaking of it. Data on *per caput* food supplies are expressed in terms of quantity and by applying appropriate food composition factors also in terms of caloric value and protein and fat content.

Annual food balance sheets tabulated regularly over a period of years will show the trends in the overall national food supply, disclose changes that may have taken place in the types of food consumed, i.e. the structure of the diet, and reveal the extent to which the food supply of the country, as a whole, is adequate in relation to nutritional requirements.

By bringing together the larger part of the food and agricultural data in each country, food balance sheets also serve for a detailed examination and appraisal of the food and agricultural situation in a country. A comparison of the quantities of food available for human consumption with those imported will indicate the extent to which a country is depending upon imports to provide its supplies (self-sufficiency ratio). The amounts of food crops used for feeding livestock in relation to total crop production indicate the degree to which primary food resources are being utilized to produce animal foods, which is useful information when analysing livestock policies or patterns of agriculture. Data on *per caput* food supplies serve as a major element for the projection of food demand together with other elements such as income elasticity coefficients, projections of private consumption expenditure, and of population.

It is important to note that the quantities of food available for human consumption as estimated in the food balance sheet relate simply to the quantities of food reaching the consumer but not necessarily to the amounts of food actually consumed by the population. Wastage on the farm during distribution and processing is taken into consideration as an element in the food balance sheet. However, the amount of food actually consumed may be lower than the quantity shown in the food balance sheet depending on the degree of losses of edible food and nutrients after the retail level in the household, e.g. during storage, preparation, and cooking, as plate-waste or quantities fed to domestic animals and pets or thrown away.

Food balance sheets do not give any indication of the differences that may exist in the diet consumed by different population groups, e.g. different socio-economic groups, ecological zones, and geographical areas within a country. They do not provide information on seasonal variations in the total food supply. In order to obtain a complete picture, food consumption surveys showing the distribution of the national food supply at various times of the year among different groups of the population should be conducted. In fact, the two sets of data are complementary. There are commodities for which a production estimate could best be based on estimated consumption as obtained from food consumption surveys. On the other hand, there are also commodities for which production, trade, and utilization statistics could give a better nationwide consumption estimate than the data derived from food consumption surveys.

3. ACCURACY OF FOOD BALANCE SHEETS

The accuracy of food balance sheets, being in essence a derived statistic, is, of course, dependent on the reliability of the underlying basic statistics of population, supply, and utilization of foods and of their nutritive value. These vary a great deal between countries both in terms of coverage as well as in accuracy. In fact, there are many gaps, particularly regarding the statistics of utilization for non-food purposes such as feed, seed, and industrial use, as well as those of farm, commercial, and even government stocks. To overcome the former difficulty, estimates were prepared in the FAO, while the effect of the absence of statistics of stocks is considered to be reduced by preparing the food balance sheets as an average for a three-year period. But even the statistics of production and trade, on which the accuracy of food balance sheets depends, are in many cases subject to considerable improvement through the organization of appropriate statistical field surveys.

The available statistics being what they are, considerable use had to be made in the preparation of the food balance sheets of evaluation techniques provided by consistency checks. Internal consistency checks are inherent in the accounting technique of the food balance sheet itself. Even more important are external consistency checks based on related supplementary information such as the results of food consumption and dietary surveys taken in various parts of the world as well as relevant technical, nutritional, and economic expertise. For this purpose, interdisciplinary meetings are organized within the FAO to consider the food balance sheets prior to submitting them to countries for review, comments, and approval before publication.

It is believed that the food balance sheets so prepared, while often being far from satisfactory in the proper statistical sense, provide an approximate picture of the overall food situation in the countries that may be used for economic and nutritional studies, the preparation of the development plans, and the formulation of related projects, as, in fact, is being done in the FAO. It is also hoped that through identification of major gaps in the available data, the improvement of national statistics at the source will be stimulated.

4. CONCEPTS AND DEFINITIONS USED IN FOOD BALANCE SHEETS

4.1. COMMODITY COVERAGE

As already indicated, all commodities that are potentially edible should in principle be taken into account in preparing food balance sheets whether they are actually eaten or used for non-food purposes. This principle is kept in mind in the FAO's current work on food balance sheets, but has not been strictly adhered to in the past, when often the commodity coverage of food balance sheets was limited to foods actually eaten. Furthermore, the definition of a complete list of potentially edible commodities presents virtually insurmountable difficulties—both conceptual and statistical. For practical purposes, therefore, some pragmatic list of commodities will have to be adopted. The FAO, for example, at present works with about 800 basic items which in the FAO's statistical computer system are reduced into some 350 individual or aggregate items. The following classification of commodities has been prepared by FAO for food balance sheet purposes:

CLASSIFICATION OF COMMODITIES FOR FOOD BALANCE SHEET PURPOSES

Cereals
  Wheat
  Rice (paddy)
  Course grains:
    Maize
    Barley
    Oats
    Millet and sorghum
    Rye
    Others n.e.s.

Starchy food
  Potatoes
  Sweet potatoes
  Cassava
  Yams
  Plantains and bananas
  Others n.e.s.

Sugar
  Sugar, centrifugal
  Sugar, non-centrifugal
  Syrups
  Others n.e.s.

Pulses, Nuts, and Oilseeds
  Pulses
  Nuts and kernels
  Oilseeds

Vegetables

Fruit
  Citrus fruit:
    Oranges and tangerines
    Lemons and limes
  Bananas
  Others fresh fruit
  Dried fruit

Meat (carcass weight)
  Beef and veal (including buffalo)
  Mutton, lamb, and goat meat
  Pigmeat
  Poultry meat
  Other meat n.e.s.
  Offal

Eggs

Fish
  Finfish
  Shellfish

Milk and Milk Products
  Milk, whole
  Milk, skimmed
  Cheese

Fats and oils
  Butter (including ghee)
  Vegetable oils
  Animals fats (including marine oil)

Miscellaneous vegetable
  Spices
  Cocoa

Beverages and beverage Crops
  Coffee
  Tea
  Soft beverages
  Alcoholic beverages

Under each item, primary as well as derived commodities, up to specified levels of processing, are considered as appropriate, e.g. wheat, wheat flour, wheat-flour preparations, bran, etc., or milk, butter, ghee, skim milk, cheese (from whole milk and skim milk), whey, casein, dried and condensed milk (from whole milk or skim milk), etc.

4.2. SUPPLY AND UTILIZATION ELEMENTS[†]

4.2.1. *Production*

For primary commodities production relates to the total domestic

[†]Reference may be made to the sample forms of the most common types of food balance sheets at present in use which are given in Appendix IA and IB, pp. 18–20.

production whether inside or outside the agricultural sector, i.e. it includes non-commercial production and production in kitchen gardens. Unless otherwise indicated, production is reported at the farm level for primary crop and livestock items (i.e. excluding harvesting losses for crops) and in terms of live weight (i.e. the actual ex-water weight of the catch at the time of capture) for primary fish items. Production of processed commodities relates to the total output of the commodity at the manufacture level (i.e. it comprises output from domestic and imported raw materials of originating products). Reporting units are chosen accordingly, e.g. cereals are reported in terms of grain or paddy rice. As a general rule, all data on meat are expressed in terms of carcass weight. Usually the data on production relate to that which takes place during the reference period. In the absence of information on changes in stocks, however, production of certain crops may relate to the harvest of the year preceding the consumption period if harvesting takes place late in the year, as in such cases the production of a given year is largely moving into consumption in the subsequent year. In the first of the two food balance sheet formats attached, a distinction is made between "output" and "input". The production of primary as well as of derived products is reported under "output". For derived commodities amounts of the originating commodity required for obtaining the output of the derived product are indicated under "input", expressed in terms of the originating commodity.

4.2.2. Changes in Stocks

In principle this comprises changes in stocks occurring during the reference period at all levels between the production and the retail levels, i.e. it comprises changes in government stocks, in stocks with manufacturers, importers, exporters, other wholesale and retail merchants, transport and storage enterprises, and in stocks on farms. In actual fact, however, the information available often relates only to stocks held by governments, and even this is not available for a number of countries and important commodities. It is for this reason that food balance sheets are usually prepared as an average for several years, as this is believed to reduce the degree of inaccuracy contributed by the absence of information on stocks. Net increases in stocks are generally indicated by the + sign and net decreases by the − sign.

4.2.3. *Gross Imports*

In principle this covers all movements of the commodity in question into the country as well as of commodities derived therefrom and not separately included in the food balance sheet. It therefore includes commercial trade, food aid granted on specific terms, donated quantities, and estimates of unrecorded trade for any of the types of utilization accounted for in the food balance sheet. As a general rule, figures are reported in terms of net weight, i.e. excluding the weight of the container.

4.2.4. *Supply*

There are various possibilities to define "supply" and, in fact, various concepts are in use. The elements involved are production, imports, exports, and changes in stocks (increases or decreases). There is no doubt that production, imports, and decreases in stocks are genuine supply elements. Exports and increases in stocks might, however, be considered to be utilization elements. Accordingly, the following possibilities exist for defining "supply":

(a) Production + imports + decrease in stocks = total supply.
(b) Production + imports + changes in stocks (decrease or increase) = supply available for export and domestic utilization.
(c) Production + imports − exports + changes in stocks (decrease or increase) = supply for domestic utilization.

4.2.5. *Gross Exports*

In principle this covers all movements of the commodity in question out of the country during the reference period. Remarks made above under imports apply by analogy. A number of commodities are processed into food and feed items. Therefore, there is a need to identify the components of processed material exported in order to arrive at a correct picture of supplies of food and feed in a given country in a given time reference period.

4.2.6. *Feed*

This comprises amounts of the commodity in question and of edible commodities derived therefrom not shown separately in the food balance sheet (but excluding byproducts such as bran and oilcakes) fed to livestock during the reference period, whether domestically produced or imported.

4.2.7. Seed

In principle, this comprises all amounts of the commodity in question used during the reference period for reproductive purposes, such as seed, sugar-cane planted, eggs for hatching, and fish for bait, whether domestically produced or imported.

4.2.8. Manufacture

A distinction can be made between manufacture for food and manufacture for industrial use. The amounts of the commodity in question used during the reference period for manufacture of derived commodities for which separate entries are provided in the food balance sheet, including alcoholic beverages, are shown under "manufacture for food". Quantities of the commodity in question used for manufacture for non-food purposes, e.g. oil for soap, are shown under "manufacture for industrial uses".

4.2.9. Waste

This comprises amounts of the commodity in question and of the commodities derived therefrom, not further pursued in the food balance sheet, lost through wastage during the reference period at all stages between the level at which production is recorded and the retail level, i.e. wastage in processing, storage, and transportation. Losses occurring during the pre-harvest and harvest stages are excluded. The waste of both edible and inedible parts of the commodity occurring after the retail level, e.g. in the kitchen, is also excluded.

Post-harvest losses in most of the countries are considered to be substantial due to the fact that most of the grain production is retained on the farm so as to provide sufficient quantities to last from one harvest to the next. Farm storage facilities in most of the developing countries are usually primitive and inadequately protected from the natural competitors of man for food.

The losses tend to become even more serious in countries where the agricultural products reach the consumers in urban areas only after passing through several marketing stages. In fact, one of the major causes of wastage of foods in some developing countries is the lack of adequate marketing systems and organizations. Much food remains unsold because of the imbalances of supply and demand. This is particularly true of perishable foods such as fresh fruit and vegetables. Post-harvest losses of fruit and vegetables of between 25 and 40% occur in developing countries and are mainly due to harvesting at the wrong time and improper packing.

4.2.10. *Food (Gross), Food (Net), and Extraction Rate*

These are concepts which also are used in food balance sheets. "Food (gross)" comprises the amounts of the commodity in question and of any commodities derived therefrom, not further pursued in the food balance sheet, available for human consumption during the reference period. For example, if an entry is provided for wheat only, "food (gross)" of wheat relates to the amounts of wheat, wheat-flour, and any other derived product in terms of grain, available for human consumption during the reference period. "Food (gross)" of milk relates to the amounts of milk available for human consumption during the reference period as milk, but not as butter, cheese, or any other milk product provided for in the food balance sheet. Where the data in these food balance sheets are recorded for primary commodities only, but where the commodities derived therefrom appear at the retail level in a different form (e.g. cereals which usually appear at the retail level in the form of flour or milled rice), the column "extraction rate" indicates the average national rate at which these commodities are converted from the original form into the form in which they appear at the retail level. The corresponding amount of the derived commodity is then shown under "food (net)".

4.2.11. Per Caput *Consumption*

The columns under this heading give estimates of *per caput* food supplies available for human consumption during the reference period in terms of quantity, caloric value, and protein and fat content. *Per caput* food supplies in terms of quantity are given both in kilograms per year and grams per day, calorie supplies are reported in kilocalories (Calories) per day, and protein and fat supplies in grams per day respectively. *Per caput* supplies in terms of quantity are derived from the total supplies available for human consumption, through dividing by the total population actually partaking of the food supplies during the reference period, i.e. the present in-area (*de facto*) population within the present geographical boundaries of the country in question at the mid-point of the reference period. In other words, nationals living abroad during the reference period are excluded but foreigners living in the country are included. Adjustments are made wherever possible for part-time presence or absence, such as temporary migrants and tourists, and for special population groups not partaking of the national food supply such as aborigines living under subsistence conditions (if it has not been possible to include subsistence production in the food balance sheets) and refugees supported by special schemes such as UNRRA and CARE (if it has not been possible to allow for the amounts provided by such schemes under imports).

For the purpose of calculating the caloric value and the protein and fat content of the *per caput* food supplies, considerable research was carried out to obtain additional information regarding the specifications of the foods required for the choice of the appropriate food composition factors. For example, the choice of the food composition factors for wheat-flour, among other factors, depends on the water content, the variety, and the degree of milling. The choice of the corresponding factors for cheese depends on whether cheese is derived from whole milk, partly whole milk, or skim milk from cows, sheep, goats, buffaloes, camels, and whether the cheese is hard, semi-soft, or soft. First-hand expert knowledge available in the FAO, both in the fields of nutrition and food technology, and available national, regional, and international food composition tables, proved to be of particular value in this respect. For reasons of international comparability, once the commodities have been sufficiently specified the FAO's international food composition tables are generally used in the food balance sheets prepared by the FAO. Totals of the caloric value and the protein and fat content are shown by commodity groups. In addition, a grand total is given excluding the contribution of alcoholic and soft beverages, which is shown separately.

5. GLOBAL LEVELS AND TRENDS OF FOOD SUPPLIES AND NUTRITION

The purpose of this section is to present a picture of global levels of food supplies and nutrition as they emerge from the FAO 1964–6 average food balance sheets. Some reference is also made to trends since the pre-war period.

TABLE 1 *Per Caput* Daily Food Supplies in Terms of Calories and Protein
—World and Economic Classes

Economic class	Cal (No.)				Total protein (g)				Animal protein (g)			
	1934–8	1948–52	1957–9	1964–6	1934–8	1948–52	1957–9	1964–6	1934–8	1948–52	1957–9	1964–6
Developed market economies	2870	2760	2880	2960	81	80	85	86	37	38	45	49
Developing market economies	2060	1940	2180	2120	57	53	57	55	12	10	11	11
Centrally planned economies	2460	2280	2430	2370	76	69	71	68	12	12	15	17
World	2380	2240	2420	2380	69	64	68	66	18	18	20	21

Note. The data in this table may be used as indicators of the overall food supply situation in the areas referred to. They are not, however, sufficient for appraising the adequacy of food supplies within these areas as they do not give any indication of the food distribution between and food consumption by different socio-economic and age and sex groups.

Appendix II presents data on the quantity of *per caput* food supplies available during 1964–6 classified by major food groups, economic classes, and regions. Appendices III, IV, and V show the corresponding calorie, protein and fat content, indicating also the percentage contribution of each major food group. Appendix VI shows the country coverage of the economic classes and regions.

The appendices show that during 1964–6 the world average *per caput* supply of calories was 2380 and those of protein and fat were 66 and 55 g/day respectively. In Table 1 these data are compared with the corresponding findings of the FAO's *Third World Food Survey*, together with data for the developed and developing market economies and the centrally planned economies.

Although the data in Table 1 are not fully consistent, it is believed that they provide a broad indication of trends in *per caput* food supplies during the three decades covered.

Table 1 shows that there was a steady improvement in the food situation of the developed market economies since the post-war period, both in terms of quantity (calories) and nutritional quality (proteins), and that during 1964–6 *per caput* supply levels were well above those of the pre-war period. Also in the developing market economies and the centrally planned economies, consumption levels increased as compared to the post-war period, but the increase was mainly in the quantity of *per caput* food supplies. Furthermore, the increase largely took place during the 1950s. Thereafter the situation remained more or less static. In fact, owing to the poor harvests in 1965 and 1966, *per caput* supplies in 1964–6 were somewhat below those in 1957–9.

Table 1 also brings out the wide gap in the *per caput* food supply levels between the developed and developing market economies and shows that this gap has widened further during the period under review. These disparities do, however, not necessarily imply nutritional inadequacy. To throw further light on this point the average daily calorie and protein requirements and the 1964–6 available supplies as a percentage of these requirements are shown in Table 2.

Table 2 shows that *per caput* calorie supplies are considerably in excess of requirements in the developed market economies and in Eastern Europe and the USSR. On the other hand, they fall well below requirements in the developing market economies (except Latin America) and the Asian centrally planned economies, indicating the continued existence of undernutrition on a considerable scale.

With respect to protein, Table 2 would suggest a surplus of protein

TABLE 2 *Per Caput* DAILY CALORIE AND PROTEIN REQUIREMENTS AND SUPPLIES

Economic class and region	*Per Caput* daily requirements		1964–6 *per caput* supplies as percentage of requirements	
	Cal (No.)	Protein (g)	Cal	Protein
Developed market economies	2560	39.2	116	219
Developing market economies	2280	38.4	93	143
Africa	2340	41.5	92	140
Latin America	2380	37.7	104	170
Near East	2460	45.5	96	147
Asia and Far East	2220	36.6	90	134
Asian Centrally Planned Economies	2360	38.3	87	151
USSR and Eastern Europe	2570	40.0	122	228
World	2380	38.7	100	170

Note: The data in this table may be used as indicators of the overall food supply situation in the areas referred to. They are not, however, sufficient for appraising the adequacy of food supplies within these areas as they do not give any indication of the food distribution between and food consumption by different socio-economic and age and sex groups.

availability. However, the evidence available suggests a very uneven distribution of the protein supplies among the population aggravated by seasonal imbalances in supplies; in addition, protein from different sources differs in nutritive value. Furthermore, wherever calories are in short supply, proteins are diverted from their primary function of providing for growth and maintenance of tissues to the supply of energy for other vital functions. This explains the widespread incidence of protein calorie malnutrition in spite of the apparent excess in protein supplies.

The appendices bring out the relative importance of the various food groups in the diet.

Cereals evidently are the major source of calories and protein. At the world level, their contribution to the total calorie and protein supply is 52% and 48% respectively. Their role is even more important in the diets of the developing market economies and the centrally planned economies, and they contribute as much as two-thirds to the calorie and protein supplies in certain areas. Against this, their contribution to the calorie and protein supplies is only about one-third in the developed market economies and as low as one-fifth in northern America.

It is interesting to note the important role of cereals as a source of fat which is often not fully recognized. For the world as a whole about 10% of *per caput* fat supplies are derived from cereals and the percentage is as large as 18 in Africa.

Starchy and other staple foods are more important for calories than for protein and fat contributing 8% of calories, 4% of protein, and 1% of fat at the world level. The importance of this food group is greatest in Africa, where it provides 23% of the calorie supply.

Sugar and sweets are mainly a source of energy. They provide about 9% of the world's calorie supplies. There are, however, pronounced differences between the developed and developing regions. With the exception of Latin America, the developing regions derive less than 10% of their calories from this food group, whereas in the case of the developed regions the percentage is between 10 and 20%.

Pulses, nuts, and seeds are predominantly consumed in the developing regions. They are an important source of protein. At the world level about 12% of protein and 5% of calories are derived from this food group. The highest contribution to protein is in the Asian centrally planned economies (20%) and the lowest in the developed countries of Oceania (2%).

Vegetables and fruit are usually considered as sources of minerals and vitamins. It should, however, not be overlooked that they also provide energy, protein, and small amounts of fat. In fact, at the world level they contribute to calories twice as much as eggs and fish together. Their contribution to the protein supplies is as large as that of fish and twice that of eggs, and their contribution to the fat supply is as large as that of fish.

Meat contributes 7% of calories, 14% of protein, and 26% of fat for the world as a whole. There are considerable disparities in meat supply levels between the regions. About 13% of calories, 26% of protein, and 28% of fat are derived from this product in the developed market economies, while the corresponding percentages are 3, 8, and 15 for the developing market economies and 7, 12, and 34 for the centrally planned economies.

The main importance of *eggs and fish* is for animal protein. At the world level about 7% of protein is derived from these two food groups. The range at regional levels is between 21% for the other developed market economies and 2% for the Near East.

Milk is after meat the second most important source of animal protein; its percentage contribution to total protein supply at the world level being 11%. Here again considerable disparities exist between regions, the percentage contribution to protein supplies ranging from 25% for Western Europe to about 1% in the Asian centrally planned economies.

Milk is also important for its fat and calorie content: 11% of fat and 5% of calories are derived from milk for the world as a whole.

Oils and fats are the major single source of fat. Nevertheless, they only contribute 41% of world *per caput* fat supply, indicating the considerable amount of invisible fat from other food groups in the diet. There are no wide regional disparities although the percentage contributions are generally somewhat higher for the developed regions.

APPENDIX 1A. FOOD BALANCE SHEET FORMAT AT PRESENT USED BY THE FAO

COUNTRY _____ YEAR _____
POPULATION _____ (thousands) (thousand metric tons unless otherwise specified)

| COMMODITY | PRODUCTION | | Changes in STOCKS | Gross IMPORTS | SUPPLY | Gross EXPORTS | DOMESTIC UTILIZATION | | | | MANUFACTURE for | | WASTE | PER CAPUT CONSUMPTION | | | | |
	Input	Output					TOTAL	FEED	SEED		Food	Industrial use		FOOD Kilogr. per year	Grams per day	CALORIES per day number	PROTEINS per day grams	FAT per day grams

Food Consumption: Balance Sheets

ASSUMPTIONS UNDERLYING PRODUCTION AND UTILIZATION STATISTICS (supporting table to food balance sheet format, Appendix 1A)

COUNTRY ——————   YEAR ——————

CROPS	SEED rate kg/ha	FEED % of supply	WASTE % of supply	MAIN DERIVED PRODUCTS		BY-PRODUCTS		DAIRY PRODUCTS	POPULATION PRODUCING %	YIELD/year No of eggs and gr/egg or kg/animal	HATCHING or FEED % of supply	WASTE % of supply	MAIN DERIVED PRODUCTS		BY-PRODUCTS	
				Derived product	Extr. rate %	By-product	Extr. rate %						Derived product	Extr. rate %	By-product	Extr. rate %

	LIVESTOCK	TAKE-OFF rate %	CARCASS WEIGHT kg/animal		OFFALS % of carcass weight	SLAUGH-TER FATS	DERIVED MEAT PRODUCTS extraction rate: %			
			Domestic	Imported			Cured	Canned	Meal	De-hydrated	Extract

APPENDIX 1B. FOOD BALANCE SHEET FORMAT PREVIOUSLY USED BY THE FAO AND STILL USED BY MANY COUNTRIES

COUNTRY _____ YEAR _____
POPULATION _____
(thousand metric tons unless otherwise specified)

COMMODITY	PRODUCTION	Changes in STOCKS	FOREIGN TRADE		Available SUPPLY	DISTRIBUTION						PER CAPUT CONSUMPTION				
			Gross EXPORTS	Gross IMPORTS		Animal FEED	SEED	Manu-facture	WASTE	FOOD (Gross)	Extr. Rate	FOOD (Net)	Kilogr. per year	Grams per day	CALORIES per day number	PROTEINS per day grams	FAT per day grams

Food Consumption: Balance Sheets

APPENDIX II. PER CAPUT FOOD SUPPLIES, AVERAGE 1964-6 — QUANTITY

Economic class and region	Population in Millions	Cereals[a]	Starchy and other staple foods[b]	Sugar and sweets[c]	Pulses, nuts, and seeds[d]	Vegetables[e]	Fruit[e]	Meat[f]	Eggs[g]	Fish[h]	Milk[i]	Fats and oils[j]
						grams per day						
Developed market economies	691	264	199	100	24	274	214	174	36	29	489	53
Northern America, developed	214	179	148	131	21	294	240	279	49	16	670	59
Western Europe	342	269	249	93	20	257	233	148	31	25	496	61
Oceania, developed	14	226	140	139	13	199	219	290	37	17	641	42
Other developed market economies	121	403	156	61	40	295	111	47	25	67	130	20
Developing market economies	1530	354	190	49	43	104	89	31	4	9	119	14
Africa, developing (excluding Near East in Africa)	247	325	524	19	44	57	49	33	3	7	54	13
Latin America	244	274	314	100	52	67	156	95	12	8	217	20
Near East, developing	144	440	83	46	23	175	211	40	4	4	167	20
Asia and Far East, Developing	895	370	81	43	43	115	62	11	2	10	102	12
Centrally planned economies	1129	398	275	36	33	164	33	67	12	14	139	16
Asian centrally planned economies	796	389	245	9	39	150	16	47	8	10	10	7
USSR and Eastern Europe	333	418	346	99	17	196	75	116	20	23	448	36
WORLD	3350	350	220	55	36	159	96	73	13	15	202	23

[a] In terms of flour and milled rice.
[b] Including plantains, bananas, and dates when considered staple foods.
[c] In terms of refined sugar; including crude sugar, syrups, honey, and other sugar products.
[d] Shelled equivalent for nuts; including cocoa beans.
[e] In terms of fresh.
[f] In terms of dressed carcass-weight; including edible offals.
[g] In the shell, in terms of fresh.
[h] Estimated edible weight.
[i] Including milk products in terms of fresh milk; excluding butter.
[j] Fat content.

APPENDIX III. PER CAPUT FOOD SUPPLIES, AVERAGE 1964-6—CALORIES

Economic class and region	Cereals	Starchy [and other staple foods](a)	Sugar and sweets(b)	Pulses, nuts, and seeds(c)	Vegetable	Fruit	Meat(d)	Eggs	Fish	Milk(e)	Fats and oils	Total(f)	Alcoholic beverages
						Number per day							
Developed market economies	942 (31.8)	142 (4.8)	390 (13.2)	94 (3.2)	67 (2.3)	96 (3.2)	385 (13.0)	51 (1.7)	38 (1.3)	286 (9.6)	472 (15.9)	2960 (100)	115 (3.9)
Northern America, developed	651 (20.6)	100 (3.2)	514 (16.3)	100 (3.2)	72 (2.3)	101 (3.2)	600 (19.0)	70 (2.2)	26 (0.8)	395 (12.5)	526 (16.7)	3160 (100)	(...)
Western Europe	961 (32.0)	179 (6.0)	362 (12.0)	78 (2.6)	60 (2.0)	111 (3.7)	344 (11.5)	45 (1.5)	34 (1.1)	286 (9.5)	545 (18.1)	3000 (100)	138 (4.6)
Oceania, developed	820 (25.7)	101 (3.2)	550 (17.3)	61 (1.9)	47 (1.5)	102 (3.2)	655 (20.5)	52 (1.6)	23 (0.7)	403 (12.6)	377 (11.8)	3190 (100)	(...)
Other developed market economies	1421 (57.4)	116 (4.7)	236 (9.5)	130 (5.2)	77 (3.1)	42 (1.7)	90 (3.6)	34 (1.4)	74 (3.0)	79 (3.2)	178 (7.2)	2480 (100)	268 (10.8)
Developing market economies	1253 (59.0)	175 (8.2)	187 (8.8)	152 (7.2)	24 (1.1)	41 (1.9)	66 (3.1)	6 (0.3)	14 (0.7)	73 (3.4)	126 (5.9)	2120 (100)	21 (1.0)
Africa, developing (excluding Near East in Africa)	1133 (53.0)	501 (23.4)	73 (3.4)	165 (7.7)	13 (0.6)	24 (1.1)	61 (2.9)	4 (0.2)	13 (0.6)	35 (1.6)	116 (5.4)	2140 (100)	36 (1.7)
Latin America	990 (40.1)	262 (10.6)	385 (15.6)	186 (7.5)	16 (0.6)	66 (2.7)	218 (8.8)	17 (0.7)	14 (0.6)	133 (5.4)	179 (7.3)	2470 (100)	64 (2.6)

Food Consumption: Balance Sheets

Region													
Near East, developing	1508 (64.2)	76 (3.2)	183 (7.8)	88 (3.7)	41 (1.7)	98 (4.2)	74 (3.2)	5 (0.2)	5 (0.2)	90 (3.8)	177 (7.5)	2350 (100)	17 (0.7)
Asia and Far East, developing	1317 (66.3)	78 (3.9)	165 (8.3)	150 (7.6)	26 (1.3)	30 (1.5)	24 (1.2)	3 (0.2)	15 (0.8)	65 (3.3)	106 (5.3)	1990 (100)	5 (0.3)
Centrally planned economies	1424 (60.0)	228 (9.6)	137 (5.8)	112 (4.7)	36 (1.5)	16 (0.7)	173 (7.3)	17 (0.7)	16 (0.7)	74 (3.1)	139 (5.9)	2370 (100)	38 (1.6)
Asian Centrally Planned Economies	1390 (67.9)	222 (10.8)	34 (1.7)	134 (6.5)	33 (1.6)	7 (0.3)	133 (6.5)	12 (0.6)	14 (0.7)	6 (0.3)	63 (3.1)	2050 (100)	(...)
USSR and Eastern Europe	1505 (47.9)	243 (7.7)	384 (12.2)	58 (1.9)	43 (1.4)	36 (1.1)	270 (8.6)	29 (0.9)	19 (0.6)	236 (7.5)	322 (10.2)	3140 (100)	128 (4.1)
WORLD	1246 (52.4)	186 (7.8)	212 (8.9)	127 (5.3)	37 (1.6)	44 (1.9)	168 (7.1)	19 (0.8)	20 (0.8)	117 (4.9)	202 (8.5)	2380 (100)	46 (1.9)

(a) Including bananas, dates, and plantains when considered staple food.
(b) Including crude sugar, syrups, honey, and other sugar products.
(c) Including cocoa beans.
(d) Including edible offals.
(e) Including milk products; excluding butter.
(f) In certain cases the percentages do not add up to 100 because the totals shown include spices of other unspecified food products. Total does not include calories from alcoholic or non-alcoholic beverages.

APPENDIX IV. PER CAPUT FOOD SUPPLIES, AVERAGE 1964–6 – PROTEINS

Economic class and region	Cereals	Starchy and other staple foods[a]	Sugar and sweets[b]	Pulses, nuts, and seeds[c]	Vege- tables	Fruits	Meat[d]	Eggs	Fish	Milk[e]	Fats and oils	Animal protein	Total[f]
Developed market economies	24.9 (28.8)	3.1 (3.6)	—	4.8 (5.5)	3.6 (4.2)	1.2 (1.4)	22.3 (25.8)	3.9 (4.5)	5.5 (6.4)	17.0 (19.7)	0.1 (0.1)	49 (56.5)	86 (100)
Northern America, developed	16.0 (17.1)	2.3 (2.4)	0.1 (0.1)	4.2 (4.5)	3.6 (3.8)	1.2 (1.3)	34.2 (36.5)	5.3 (5.7)	3.2 (3.4)	23.5 (25.1)	0.1 (0.1)	66 (70.8)	94 (100)
Western Europe	28.4 (33.0)	4.3 (5.0)	—	3.3 (3.8)	3.5 (4.1)	1.5 (1.7)	19.7 (22.9)	3.4 (3.9)	4.6 (5.3)	17.3 (20.1)	0.2 (0.2)	45 (52.4)	86 (100)
Oceania, developed	22.7 (24.1)	2.3 (2.4)	—	2.3 (2.4)	2.5 (2.6)	1.2 (1.3)	34.2 (36.2)	4.1 (4.4)	3.1 (3.3)	21.7 (23.0)	0.3 (0.3)	63 (67.2)	94 (100)
Other developed market economies	31.0 (42.2)	1.1 (1.5)	—	10.6 (14.4)	4.0 (5.4)	0.5 (0.7)	6.9 (9.4)	2.8 (3.8)	12.5 (17.0)	4.1 (5.6)	—	26 (35.8)	74 (100)
Developing market economies	31.1 (56.9)	2.0 (3.7)	0.2 (0.4)	8.4 (15.4)	1.4 (2.6)	0.4 (0.7)	4.2 (7.7)	0.4 (0.7)	2.2 (4.0)	4.3 (7.9)	—	11 (20.3)	55 (100)
Africa, developing (excluding Near East in Africa)	32.3 (56.0)	5.9 (10.2)	—	9.2 (15.9)	0.8 (1.4)	0.2 (0.4)	4.8 (8.3)	0.3 (0.5)	2.2 (3.8)	2.0 (3.5)	—	9 (16.1)	58 (100)
Latin America	24.1 (37.6)	3.1 (4.8)	0.2 (0.3)	11.0 (17.2)	0.8 (1.3)	0.9 (1.4)	13.1 (20.4)	1.3 (2.0)	2.0 (3.1)	7.5 (11.7)	0.1 (0.2)	24 (37.4)	64 (100)

Near East, developing	44.9	0.9	—	4.9	2.3	1.0	5.4	0.4	0.8	6.4	—	13
	(66.9)	(1.3)	—	(7.3)	(3.4)	(1.5)	(8.1)	(0.6)	(1.2)	(9.5)	—	(19.4)	67 (100)
Asia and Far East, developing	30.4	0.8	0.3	8.0	1.6	0.3	1.4	0.2	2.4	3.7	—	8	49
	(61.7)	(1.6)	(0.6)	(16.2)	(3.3)	(0.6)	(2.8)	(0.4)	(4.9)	(7.5)	—	(15.6)	(100)
Centrally planned economies	35.3	3.9	—	9.2	2.3	0.2	8.0	1.3	2.5	4.8	0.2	17	68
	(52.1)	(5.8)	—	(13.6)	(3.4)	(0.3)	(11.8)	(1.9)	(3.7)	(7.1)	(0.3)	(24.8)	(100)
Asian Centrally Planned Economies	32.4	3.1	—	11.6	2.1	0.1	5.2	0.9	2.4	0.3	0.1	9	58
	(55.7)	(5.3)	—	(19.9)	(3.6)	(0.2)	(8.9)	(1.6)	(4.1)	(0.5)	(0.2)	(15.3)	(100)
USSR and Eastern Europe	42.1	5.9	—	3.3	2.8	0.6	14.9	2.2	2.8	15.6	0.3	36	91
	(46.5)	(6.5)	—	(3.7)	(3.1)	(0.7)	(16.5)	(2.4)	(3.1)	(17.2)	(0.3)	(39.5)	(100)
WORLD	31.2	2.9	0.1	7.9	2.2	0.5	9.2	1.4	3.0	7.1	0.1	21	66
	(47.6)	(4.4)	(0.2)	(12.0)	(3.3)	(0.8)	(14.0)	(2.1)	(4.6)	(10.8)	(0.2)	(31.7)	(100)

(a) Including plantains, bananas and dates when considered staple food.
(b) Including crude sugar, syrups, honey and other sugar products.
(c) Including cocoa beans.
(d) Including edible offals.
(e) Including milk products; excluding butter.
(f) In certain cases the percentages do not add up to 100 because the total shown include some other spices or other unspecified food products.

APPENDIX V. PER CAPUT FOOD SUPPLIES, AVERAGE 1964-6—FAT

Economic class and region	Cereals	Starchy and other staple foods[a]	Sugar and sweets[b]	Pulses, nuts, and seeds[c]	Vegetables	Fruit	Meat[d]	Eggs	Fish	Milk[e]	Fats and oils	Total
					Grams per day							
Developed market economies	3.6	0.2	—	4.4	0.5	0.6	32.2	3.7	1.5	15.8	53.1	116
	(3.1)	(0.2)		(3.8)	(0.4)	(0.5)	(27.9)	(3.2)	(1.3)	(13.7)	(45.9)	(100)
Northern America, developed	2.4	0.3	—	6.1	0.6	0.7	50.3	5.0	1.2	21.4	59.4	147
	(1.6)	(0.2)		(4.2)	(0.4)	(0.5)	(34.1)	(3.4)	(0.8)	(14.5)	(40.3)	(100)
Western Europe	3.6	0.2	—	3.4	0.5	0.7	28.7	3.3	1.5	16.1	61.2	119
	(3.0)	(0.2)		(2.8)	(0.4)	(0.6)	(24.1)	(2.8)	(1.3)	(13.5)	(51.3)	(100)
Oceania, developed	3.4	—	—	4.2	0.2	0.2	56.9	3.8	0.9	22.3	41.9	134
	(2.5)			(3.1)	(0.2)	(0.2)	(42.5)	(2.8)	(0.7)	(16.7)	(31.3)	(100)
Other developed market economies	5.5	—	—	4.1	0.5	0.3	7.0	2.5	2.3	4.4	20.0	47
	(11.8)			(8.8)	(1.1)	(0.6)	(15.0)	(5.4)	(4.9)	(9.5)	(42.9)	(100)
Developing market economies	6.1	0.4	—	4.5	0.2	0.3	5.2	0.4	0.3	3.9	14.2	36
	(17.2)	(1.1)		(12.7)	(0.6)	(0.8)	(14.7)	(1.1)	(0.8)	(11.0)	(40.0)	(100)
Africa, developing (excluding near East in Africa)	9.7	1.2	—	5.7	0.1	0.2	4.5	0.3	0.4	1.8	13.1	37
	(26.2)	(3.2)		(15.4)	(0.3)	(0.5)	(12.2)	(0.8)	(1.1)	(4.9)	(35.4)	(100)
Latin America	5.6	0.5	—	3.9	0.1	0.7	18.0	1.2	0.5	6.8	20.1	57
	(9.7)	(0.9)		(6.8)	(0.2)	(1.2)	(31.4)	(2.1)	(0.9)	(11.8)	(35.0)	(100)

Food Consumption: Balance Sheets

Region									
Near East, developing	7.8	—	2.8	0.6	5.7	0.4	0.1	4.6	20.0	43
	(18.2)	—	(6.5)	(1.4)	(13.3)	(0.9)	(0.2)	(10.7)	(46.6)	(100)
Asia and Far East, developing	4.9	—	4.6	0.1	1.9	0.2	0.3	3.6	11.9	28
	(17.5)	—	(16.4)	(0.4)	(6.8)	(0.7)	(1.1)	(12.9)	(42.5)	(100)
Central planned economies	4.9	—	3.4	0.2	15.4	1.3	0.4	3.2	15.7	45
	(10.8)	—	(7.5)	(0.4)	(33.9)	(2.9)	(0.9)	(7.0)	(34.6)	(100)
Asia Centrally Planned Economies	4.8	—	4.3	0.1	12.2	0.9	0.5	0.2	7.0	31
	(15.5)	—	(13.9)	(0.3)	(39.3)	(2.9)	(1.6)	(0.6)	(22.6)	(100)
USSR and Eastern Europe	5.1	—	1.3	0.3	23.0	2.1	0.3	10.5	36.4	80
	(6.4)	—	(1.6)	(0.4)	(28.8)	(2.6)	(0.4)	(13.2)	(45.6)	(100)
WORLD	5.2	—	4.1	0.3	14.2	1.4	0.6	6.1	22.7	55
	(9.4)	—	(7.4)	(0.5)	(25.7)	(2.6)	(1.1)	(11.0)	(41.1)	(100)

(a) Including plantains, bananas, and dates when considered staple food.
(b) Including crude sugar, syrups, honey, and other sugar products.
(c) Including cocoa beans.
(d) Including edible offals.
(e) Including milk products; excluding butter.
(f) In certain cases the percentages do not add up to 100 because the total shown include spices or other unspecified food products.

APPENDIX VI. CLASSIFICATION OF COUNTRIES ACCORDING TO ECONOMIC CLASS AND REGION

Economic class and region	Countries covered by classification
Developed market economies	
Northern America, developed	Canada, United States
Western Europe	Austria, Belgium, Denmark, France, Finland, Germany (Federal Republic and West Berlin), Greece, Iceland, Ireland, Italy, Luxembourg, Malta, Netherlands, Norway, Portugal, Spain, Sweden, Switzerland, United Kingdom, Yugoslavia
Oceania, developed	Australia, New Zealand
Other developed market economies	Israel, Japan, Southern Africa (including Botswana, Lesotho, Namibia, South Africa, Swaziland)
Developing market economies	
Africa, developing (excluding Near East in Africa)	Algeria, Angola, Burundi, Cameroon, Central African Republic, Chad, Congo, Dahomey, Ethiopia, Gabon, Gambia, Ghana, Guinea, Ivory Coast, Kenya, Liberia, Madagascar, Malawi, Mali, Mauritania, Mauritius, Morocco, Mozambique, Niger, Nigeria, Rhodesia, Rwanda, Senegal, Sierra Leone, Somalia, Tanzania, Togo, Tunisia, Uganda, Upper Volta, Zaire, Zambia
Latin America	Argentina, Bolivia, Brazil, Chile, Colombia, Costa Rica, Cuba, Dominican Republic, Ecuador, El Salvador, Guatemala, Guyana, Haiti, Honduras, Jamaica, Mexico, Nicaragua, Panama, Paraguay, Peru, Puerto Rico, Surinam, Trinidad and Tobago, Uruguay, Venezuela
Near East, developing	Afghanistan, Cyprus, Egypt, Iran, Iraq, Jordan, Lebanon, Libya, Saudi Arabia, Sudan, Syrian Arab Republic, Turkey, Yemen Arab Republic, Yemen (People's Democratic Republic of)
Asia and Far East, developing	Burma, Hong Kong, India, Indonesia, Khmer Republic, Korea (Republic of), Laos, Malaysia, Nepal, Pakistan, Philippines, Singapore, Sri Lanka, Thailand, Viet-Nam (Republic of)
Centrally planned economies	
Asian centrally planned economies	Korea (Democratic People's Republic of), Mongolia, Viet-Nam (Democratic Republic of)
USSR and Eastern Europe	Albania, Bulgaria, Czechoslovakia, Germany (Democratic Republic and East Berlin), Hungary, Poland, Romania, USSR

REFERENCES

ADVISORY COMMITTEE ON NUTRITION (1937) *First Report*, Ministry of Health, London.

AGOSTINUCCI, D., BECKER, K., and SCHULTE, W. (1971) Problems involved in the preparation of food balance sheets on the basis of a set of accounts of supply/utilization statistics for primary and derived agricultural commodities (paper prepared for the FAO/UNDP-TA Seminar on Supply/Utilization Balances for Food and Agricultural Commodities for the Near East Region).

DECKEN, H. VON DER (1933) *Deutschlands Nahrungs- und Futtermittelversorgung*, p. 88, Sonderheft, Berichte über die Landwirtschaft, Reichministerium für Ernährung und Landwirtschaft, Berlin.

FARNSWORTH, H. C. (1961) Defects, uses and abuses of national food supply and consumption data, *Bull. Inst. Statist. Int.* 33 Session, Paris.

FOOD AND AGRICULTURE ORGANIZATION OF THE UNITED NATIONS (FAO)
- (1946) *World Food Survey*, Washington DC.
- (1949a) *Handbook for the Preparation of Food Balance Sheets*, Washington DC.
- (1949b) *Food Balance Sheets* (with a supplement in 1950), Washington DC.
- (1949c) *Report of the Fourth Session of the Conference*, Washington DC.
- (1952) *Second World Food Survey*, Rome.
- (1954) *Food Composition Tables (Minerals and Vitamins) for International Use*, FAO Nutritional Studies No. 11, Rome.
- (1955) *Food Balance Sheets* (with supplements in 1956 and 1957), Rome.
- (1958) *Food Balance Sheets, 1954–56 Average*, Rome.
- (1960) *Food Supply*, Times Series, Rome.
- (1963a) *Food Balance Sheets, 1957–59 Average*, Rome.
- (1963b) *Third World Food Survey*, Rome.
- (1966) *Food Balance Sheets, 1960–62 Average*, Rome.
- (1967) Food balance sheets (paper presented at the 3rd Session of the FAO Statistics Advisory Committee).
- (1969a) Preparation of utilization balances for agricultural commodities—review and recommendations regarding methods, concepts, definitions (paper presented at 1969–72 round of sessions of FAO Regional Commissions on Agricultural Statistics).
- (1969b) Provisional indicative world plan for agricultural development (document C69/4 presented to the 15th Session of the FAO Conference, Rome).
- (1971a) *Food Balance Sheets, 1964–66 Average*, Rome.
- (1971b) *Agricultural Commodity Projections, 1970–1980*, Rome.
- (1972) Preparation of supply utilization accounts in selected countries in Asia and the Far East (paper prepared for the 4th Session of the Asia and Far East Commission on Agricultural Statistics).
- *Production Yearbook* (annual), Rome.

HAHN, W. (1933) *Die Versorgung Deutschlands und seiner Wirtschaftsgebiete mit Nahrungs- und Futtermitteln*, Berichte über die Landwirtschaft, Reichministerium für Ernährung und Landwirtschaft, Berlin.

LEAGUE OF NATIONS (1937) *The Relation of Nutrition to Health, Agriculture and Economic Policy*, final report of the Mixed Committee on the Problem of Nutrition, Geneva.

ORGANIZATION FOR ECONOMIC CO-OPERATION AND DEVELOPMENT (OECD)
- (1970) *Food Consumption Statistics 1960–1968*, Paris.
- (1973) *Food Consumption Statistics 1955–1970*, Paris.

SCHULTE, W., BECKER, K., NAIKEN, L., and CHINAPPI-FAVILLI, A. (1973) Food balance sheets on world food supplies, *FAO Nutrition Newsletter* **11**, No. 2.

SMIT, C. P. G. J. (1962) International comparison of food consumption data, *Mon. Bull. Agric. Econ. Statist.* **11**, No. 12.

SPECIAL JOINT COMMITTEE SET UP BY THE COMBINED FOOD BOARD (1944) *Food Consumption Levels in the United States, Canada, and the United Kingdom*, US Dept. of Agriculture, War Food Administration, Washington DC.

ZARKOVICH, S. S., SAID, E. E., and KHAMIS, S. H. (1961) Statistics of food and nutrition, *Bull. Inst. Statist. Int.* 33 Session, Paris.

CHAPTER 2

FOOD CONSUMPTION: FOOD CONSUMPTION SURVEYS—METHODS AND RESULTS

Emma Reh

4320 Old Dominion Drive, Arlington, Virginia, 22207, United States

1. Introduction	32
2. Kinds of Information Needed	34
3. Types of Food Consumption Surveys	35
3.1. The Population Unit	35
4. The Use of Sampling Methods	39
5. Time Coverage	40
6. The Reporting Period	41
7. Pilot Surveys	42
8. Training the Investigators	42
9. Equipment	43
10. Data on the Population	43
10.1. Household Characteristics	43
10.2. Definition of Household	44
10.3. Household Size	44
10.4. Age–Sex Composition	44
10.5. Economic Status	44
10.6. Farm, Non-farm, and Urbanization Status	45
10.7. Other Population Characteristics and Environmental Conditions	46
11. Data on the Foods	47
11.1. Sources of Foods	47
11.2. Processed Foods and Prepared Dishes	48
11.3. Food Wastage in the Home	48
11.4. Cost or Money Value of Foods	49
11.5. Classification of the Foods	49
12. Food Composition Tables	52
12.1. Description of the Foods	53
12.2. The Role of Alcohol	55
13. Nutritional Requirements	55
13.1. Losses of Edible Food and Nutrients	56
13.2. Adjustments for Food Obtained and Eaten Away from Home and Food Eaten by Visitors in the Home	57
13.3. Uses and Limitations of Comparisons of Intake with Requirements	58

14. Tabulation of the Results	58
14.1. Population Groups for which Consumption Data should be Tabulated	59
14.2. Food Consumption Statistics to be Shown	59
14.3. Other Information on the Households in Each Population Group Distinguished	60
14.4. The Food Items and their Classification	60
14.5. Additional Tabulations and Useful Information	61

INTRODUCTION

As knowledge of the relation between diet, health, and disease has increased, countries have become more concerned with the food supplies available for their people and the extent to which the supplies meet the nutritional needs. A tool for assessing a country's food supply is the food balance sheet, which some 50 countries of the world now compile at various intervals of time from national statistics of food production, food stocks on hand, food imports and exports, food expended in industry or in seed, food losses in marketing or storage, etc. The foods available for consumption are expressed in amounts per person per day by the use of population census figures. The calorie and nutrient content of the foods is calculated by means of food composition tables. The proportions of the total calories and nutrients which are derived from different foods or food groups can be shown. The nutritional requirements of the population per person per day are estimated in accordance with standards defined in nutrition science. The nutrient value of the food supply is compared to the nutritional requirements to show its overall adequacy. The data reveal which nutrients may be deficient and which foods might best correct the inadequacies found. Food balance sheets prepared periodically show the movements of consumption levels over the years and indicate adjustments which may be required in the supplies.

Food balance sheets, however, give only the average amounts of foods available per person in a country and do not tell how the supplies are actually distributed among different social and economic classes, various geographic or political subdivisions, urban or rural areas, and at various times of the year. Supplies which might be adequate for a country if appropriately distributed among the people are usually more available to some population groups or areas than to others. Over- and underconsumption may coexist and hunger occur in the presence of plenty. When national supplies are marginal or deficient, maldistribution of the meager supplies may have serious consequences for a country.

Food consumption surveys, on the other hand, show how food supplies are distributed within a country, in different population groups, and areas. They indicate the sectors of a population where nutrition problems may exist, the kind and degree of dietary deficiencies, and their prevalence in a country. Surveys repeated at intervals of years detect changes in food habits and consumption levels which may follow population movements, industrialization, famine, educational programs, welfare activities, and other events in different areas of a country. Social and economic information customarily collected in food consumption surveys reveals factors associated with differences in consumption levels and may signal obstacles which impede planned improvements. Such information is useful to workers in the fields of health, social welfare, agricultural extension, etc. The knowledge gained about food habits, food preferences, prejudices, and consumption patterns is of value to food industries in their production and marketing plans.

In addition, food consumption surveys complement food balance sheets, providing data not obtainable from national statistics, such as foods derived from home gardens, hunting, fishing, etc. They improve national statistics of the food supply. Food balance sheets combined with food consumption surveys have helped developed countries to identify and correct their most important nutrition problems. In these countries the general health, longevity, and productivity of the population have increased greatly. Developing countries, on the other hand, often lack proper national statistics of food production, trade, etc., necessary for compiling food balance sheets. Food consumption surveys in these areas are also few, small in scale, or lacking, and no basis exists for national food policy and planning. Health conditions in these areas are usually poor, nutrition problems often great, and longevity and productivity in the population low.

In the absence of national statistics, food consumption surveys offer the earliest possibility of obtaining factual information on food consumption and nutrition in these areas. Such surveys are, however, expensive and difficult for developing countries to carry out alone at this time. They require statistical organization, trained personnel, and other facilities lacking in most of these areas. In recent years, international agencies and certain individual countries and scientific institutions have aided some developing areas in carrying out food consumption surveys. These surveys were usually of limited or local scale. Since 1959, the United States has collaborated with a number of developing countries in nutrition surveys of national scale which included food consumption surveys.

2. KINDS OF INFORMATION NEEDED

Data needed for determining the adequacy of the diet in a population group include the quantity and kinds of different foods consumed, the chemical composition of the foods, and the nutritional requirements of the people consuming them. The information about the foods is often difficult to obtain and involves great detail, as discussed in another section. Information on the calorie and nutrient content of foods is given in food composition tables. Data on human nutritional requirements have been brought together by the Food and Agriculture Organization of the United Nations and the World Health Organization, from available scientific sources, and are subject to continuing review and investigation. Since nutritional requirements vary with sex, age, height, and weight of individuals, pregnancy and lactation status in women, environmental temperature, and physical activity, information on these subjects is also needed in a survey. Since clothing and housing may modify the effective environmental temperature, observations on these matters must be made. The physical activity of a population, general working conditions, topography, and other factors influencing energy requirements, should be described.

Information on socio-economic conditions associated with differences in consumption levels is also collected in food consumption surveys. The kind of supplementary data needed depends on the purpose of a survey. Surveys may be made to determine the adequacy of the diet in a population and improve the food habits in the light of current knowledge of nutrition. Survey may be made to define the effects on consumption levels of changing social or economic conditions, population movements, public welfare programs, disasters, or other conditions. Food consumption surveys may form part of broader studies such as investigations of household living costs to provide information for computing cost-of-living indices for a country. Food consumption surveys are incorporated in medical nutrition investigations together with clinical and biochemical studies in population groups. The clinical and biochemical findings reflect the nutritional status of the persons examined, while the data on food intake attest to the part which diet may have had in the findings.

In addition to the data on the age, sex, height, weight, etc., of household members, needed for estimating nutritional requirements, various supplementary data on household characteristics are desired in accordance with the scope and purpose of a food consumption survey. The supplementary data may include: relation of members to the household head; educational level of the household head and spouse; ethnic or religious affiliations, if these are likely to be associated with food habits or consumption levels; occupation of the household head and other members; income or other indicators of economic level; housing; facilities for preparing or storing food, etc.

In addition to data on amounts and kinds of foods consumed, certain supplementary information on foods may be required, depending on the purposes of a survey. This may include: cost or money-value of the various foods; their origin, whether produced, purchased, or otherwise obtained; food habits; preferences, prejudices and attitudes regarding foods, etc. In medical nutrition investigations, information on weaning habits and feeding practices in relation to infants, pre-school children, pregnant and lactating women, and other vulnerable groups, is considered important.

3. TYPES OF FOOD CONSUMPTION SURVEYS

3.1. THE POPULATION UNIT

The family or household is the population unit most often employed in food consumption surveys. The family is an economic unit ordinarily sharing a common food supply. Information on quantities and prices of foods consumed is most easily obtained on a family basis. The family is also the unit through which practical nutrition programs eventually adopted would be applied in a population.

When the family is the survey unit, the results are necessarily stated as averages per person, and the actual distribution of foods and nutrients among the family members is not known. When a family-type food consumption survey forms part of a medical nutrition investigation, the clinical and biochemical findings for the individuals examined can only be related to the average intake in the corresponding families. Family food consumption surveys do not lend themselves to estimating the number of malnourished individuals in a population. The distribution of the family diets by level of adequacy can, however, be shown, and for most practical purposes family food consumption surveys do indicate the prevalence or severity of nutrition problems in a population. When the average intake of calories and nutrients in a family is low or deficient, it is certain that few members of that family will have diets substantially superior to that average.

Food consumption surveys in which the individual is the unit studied are preferred in medical nutrition investigations, and they are indispensable in strict scientific nutrition studies. They are, however, difficult under field conditions and not feasible on a large scale. Whereas the different food items brought into the home for the family meals can be weighed or recorded with some accuracy, it is hard to measure or estimate the amounts of the different ingredients which each member of the family finally consumes. Replica meals may be analyzed in laboratories, but this procedure is costly and also impractical on a large scale. Interview and weighing techniques, using food composition tables in the analysis of the foods, often employed in surveys of school or pre-school children, pregnant or lactating women, the elderly, etc., provide results sufficiently accurate for planning practical nutrition programs for those groups. A food consumption survey of individuals sufficiently large to represent the total population of a country would be an almost insurmountable task at this time. The family type of survey is therefore generally used in the study of large populations.

Three principal methods have been used for obtaining the information on amounts and cost of the different foods consumed.

1. The housewife or person preparing the food is asked in a single interview to recall the quantities and cost of the various items used during the day, the week, or other reporting period preceding the interview. A list of foods common to the area is used as an *aide mémoire*.

2. By keeping a current day-by-day account of the amounts and cost of all foods purchased or otherwise brought into the house during the reporting period. Foods already on hand at the beginning of the reporting period and those remaining at the end are properly taken into account. Foods eaten outside the home by household members are included, and foods given away or otherwise leaving the house are excluded. Either the housewife or the field worker in daily visits keeps the records.

3. By weighing all food items before they are prepared for meals or otherwise eaten by household members. Foods already on hand at the beginning of the reporting period and those remaining at the end are duly taken into account. Foods eaten by family members outside the home are included, and foods given away or otherwise not eaten are excluded. Either the housewife weighs the foods with scales left in the house for the purpose or the field worker does this during daily visits.

In theory any of the three methods can be used alone, but in practice they are usually combined. The field worker arriving at a home to weigh the foods may find some articles already eaten. The housewife then describes the amounts already eaten, or shows the amounts in household measures. Similar items still remaining can be weighed. Foods eaten by family members outside the home can only be described. In the food accounting method, fruits, vegetables, and other items may be reported in numbers, bunches, heaps, or other measures. These must be translated into weight by weighing corresponding samples in the home or market. The same holds true for the interview technique.

The comparative merits of the several survey techniques have not been fully determined by proper statistical methods. The large number of surveys already carried out have, however, shown that the interview technique is the simplest and least expensive. Its demands on the respondent are less and nonresponse is likely to be smaller. The errors of observation can, however, be greater than by the other techniques, since major dependence is on memory, even when the interviewer is armed with a food list as an *aide mémoire*. The longer the reporting period extends into the past the greater the errors can be. Foods consumed before the reporting period may easily be included and items consumed within the period forgotten. Marketing or food procurement patterns differ from place to place and may affect responses. Major food staples may be obtained weekly, biweekly, or monthly, and not coincide with reporting periods. Where much food is home produced, as in rural or developing areas, housewives may be less able to estimate weights or other quantities. False information may be given by the respondent whatever the survey technique used. Differences exist in the interviewers' skill and in ability to establish good relations with the informant. Informants in turn vary in their dispositions. The single interview provides a limited opportunity for an effective explanation of the work or for crosschecking or verifying the data obtained.

The food accounting technique extends over a period of time, and the various visits of the field worker to each home make better understanding possible and provide opportunities for reviewing the data and rectifying errors. The food accounting technique puts less dependence on memory and should result in greater accuracy. In developing areas where the educational level of the population may be low, the investigator is usually the one who records the foods. This increases the number of workers needed and raises the survey costs. When the recording is left to the respondents the work is likely to overburden some busy housewives and decrease the cooperation in the survey. This may introduce bias in the results since noncooperating families may differ importantly from the others.

The method of weighing all foods which enter the home each day should be the most accurate of all. As in the food accounting technique, supplies already on hand at the beginning of the reporting period are added and those remaining at the end deducted, as are foods leaving the house or not eaten by family members. In some countries housewives have been furnished with scales for weighing their own foods. This system is burdensome to many housewives and requires a certain educational level in the survey population. Moreover, scales left in homes have been found irresistible to some children and to incur damage. Furthermore, although weighing is a simple task, errors are easily made by those not accustomed. In surveys in developing countries, trained field workers are generally used to weigh the foods in home visits. This requires adequate personnel and is expensive. Easier and more economical techniques for obtaining reliable information on food consumption are continually being sought. In recent surveys in Central American countries, where the interview and the food weighing techniques were carried out simultaneously in comparable population groups, the interview technique gave results consistently higher than the weighing technique.

As mentioned before, the weighing technique can rarely be used in its purest form. To weigh all foods consumed by household members, a survey worker would need to remain in a home for 24 hours a day in the reporting period, clearly undesirable either for the family or the survey worker. The worker must usually survey more than a single family each day and tries to reach each home after the foods for the day have been brought from the field or market, but before they are prepared for cooking or have been eaten. The worker can, however, rarely arrive before some foods, as in early breakfasts, have been eaten. The information on these is then obtained by interview. The housewife may show the worker the amounts or measures of the different items consumed. Items similar to those already eaten sometimes remain in the house and can be weighed. Means for making good estimates of quantities of foods which can no longer be weighed must be devised during surveys.

Whatever the technique used, reliable information on food consumption is obtained only with the good will and understanding of the respondent. An adequate explanation of the purpose of the survey and of the information needed is essential. Proper permission must be sought for the invasion of the family privacy which a food consumption survey involves. In rural and developing areas, the visits of the field worker are likely to be welcome, and the meticulous attention to details about the foods in the home are interesting to the housewife and to others in the family. In urban and industrialized areas, where diversions are numerous and women may have outside work, housewives may be found at home only irregularly and with difficulty. The visits of the field worker may be inconvenient and less welcome than in other areas.

4. THE USE OF SAMPLING METHODS

The complex nature of food consumption surveys makes the use of sampling methods the only practical procedure in the study of a population. Sampling methods other than random should be avoided, since they may produce bias and preclude the use of scientific techniques for estimating the error in the results. Statistical manuals describe the various sampling methods which are available.

Random sampling in developing areas may encounter practical difficulties. A census of population, useful as a sampling frame, may be lacking, and communication and transportation difficult. In such cases multistage sampling devices may serve for the construction of a sampling base. A sample of villages or other places is first selected, and households in these localities are then listed. In listing the households, the investigators have the opportunity for collecting additional information needed for stratification of the households. They also become acquainted with the families and prepare the ground for the survey and improving the possibility of securing good cooperation and reliable information. By limiting the survey to selected localities, travel and overall costs are decreased.

In using multistage sampling devices, the smaller variability expected in food consumption patterns in comparable households within limited areas should be taken into account. Sampling designs in each country should consider the specific requirements of the survey, the local conditions, and budget and personnel available. If the weighing technique, for example, appears too expensive, the interview method can be applied in a large-scale study and the weighing technique in a subsample of the total sample, permitting the calculation of a correction factor to apply to the total sample.

The value of a sample is affected by the proportion of the total households which may be unwilling or unable to give the information sought. No general method has been devised to correct fully for non-response in a survey. All means must therefore be used to ensure full cooperation. The investigators must be properly selected and trained. They must be mindful of the lines of authority in a community or a family and make adequate explanations of the purposes of a survey and of the information needed. Experience has shown that with proper attention to such details, nonresponse tends to be less important as a problem in rural and underdeveloped areas than elsewhere.

When the aim of a food consumption survey is to obtain information on certain specific topics, the size and composition of the sample are particularly involved. If estimates are needed for geographic areas or for socio-economic groups, for instance, the sample should be selected from a population stratified according to these characteristics. Otherwise the sample should be large enough to ensure the representation of the most important population groups, for which estimates are then obtained by post-survey classification.

The sample size is determined by various factors. These include the precision desired in the results; the sample design adopted; the tabulation plans; and the budget, personnel, and other facilities available. No fixed sample size can be recommended for all countries or all purposes. Experience has, however, indicated that in a survey of national scale, requiring information on a minimum of major topics, the households are more likely to number in the thousands than in the hundreds.

5. TIME COVERAGE

A food consumption survey should properly represent an entire year, since this cycle of time is marked by various fluctuations in levels and in patterns of consumption due to many factors among which seasonal influences are of particular importance. A maize or rice crop may have one, two, or even more harvests in a year. Jobs available in plantation areas at harvest or other times in the year may temporarily boost the purchasing power of people in the area. Religious and traditional holidays punctuating the year are also recurring events affecting food consumption. Wages, prices and other economic factors influence consumption, particularly in urban areas where modern development in storage and marketing has leveled many seasonal differences. Seasonal effects, on the other hand, are important in rural or subsistence farming areas where dependence on produced foods is greater.

No one day, week, month, or other part of a year will necessarily be representative of the year as a whole. A survey made in a single season may overestimate or underestimate rural-urban differences. A survey repeated in several seasons, at time intervals believed to be representative of each season, will improve the annual average, but the accuracy of each seasonal average, and of the annual average, will nevertheless be unknown.

To study a large group of households over an entire year would be an impractical undertaking because of cost and other reasons. A valid annual average can, however, be obtained by applying the principles of random sampling to the year. Various devices for this purpose are available. One scheme is to take the seasons as strata, giving attention also to other periods when food consumption differs markedly from the ordinary. Stratification by season requires careful consideration. The pattern of food consumption may vary greatly within a country, as, for example, in mountainous regions where altitudes modify the effects of latitude and produce a variety of climates. Unless stratification of the year, using seasons as strata, is based on adequate knowledge of local conditions, unstratified sampling of time may be preferable. A simple design would be to spread the sample of households uniformly over the year.

6. THE REPORTING PERIOD

The reporting period is the space of time during which individual families in the sample furnish information on foods consumed, at the selected intervals in the year. The reporting period is preferably a span during which consumption follows a certain pattern which is constantly repeated. A week is such a span of time which is a characteristic of many countries. Fridays, Saturdays, or Sundays—depending on the particular country or culture area—are traditional holidays, religious in origin, on which food consumption, among other things, may depart significantly from the ordinary. Fixed market days in some areas and paydays in others are also associated with differences in food consumption. Food consumption surveys should include at least one consumption cycle in each season or other interval into which the year may be divided for purposes of the survey. This is necessary for estimating average food consumption patterns for different population groups, and also when frequency distributions comparing intakes with requirements are needed. When the information collected in a food consumption survey refers to food acquired rather than to food consumed, a buying cycle would be the proper reporting period.

Techniques selected for obtaining food consumption data should be suitable for the length of the reporting period. When data for a long reporting period are collected in a single interview, possibilities for error exist. Pressures continually exist for combining the least expensive survey method with the shortest reporting period in order to reduce the high survey cost. In various medical nutrition investigations, food consumption surveys using the interview technique have been carried out concurrently with medical studies having much smaller time requirements. Consumption cycles were ignored. Data collected were often considerably at variance with information obtained by objective methods and over longer reporting periods. In one country using the longer weighing technique, the reporting period was shortened by omitting several of the weekdays but weighting the data afterwards to represent a week. Researchers are continually seeking reliable food consumption survey techniques faster and less expensive than those now available. The use of computers in the processing of the data has facilitated that phase of survey work.

7. PILOT SURVEYS

A valuable device in the planning stage of a food consumption survey is a pilot survey in a small group of families in the area, for pre-testing proposed procedures and techniques. The pilot survey provides an objective basis for estimating survey costs and requirements of personnel and equipment. Knowledge gained about the population will be helpful in securing cooperation. Data collection methods and questionnaires can be tested and improved and reporting periods defined. On the basis of consumption data collected a food list for the area can be compiled and components of variation indicated. Key personnel can be trained during the pilot survey, including local interpreters where needed.

8. TRAINING THE INVESTIGATORS

Whatever the survey technique used, the value of the data obtained depends largely on the competence of the investigator. The investigators should be selected taking into consideration their facility with figures and capacity for friendly relations with people. They should be given theoretical training in different aspects of survey operations and information on foods, nutrition, and statistical techniques. Experience has shown that a permanent staff of investigators facilitates survey work and is preferable to local recruits trained for each particular place. The permanent investigators cannot only be better selected and trained, but they improve with each experience. They are also available for all the improtant phases of the survey, from planning to editing data collected. Local recruits, however, make invaluable assistants, guides, and interpreters for the permanent investigators.

9. EQUIPMENT

Adequate equipment is essential for the success of a survey. When data are collected by the weighing technique, there should be a sufficient number of food scales, easy to use under field conditions. Transportation during field work and provisions for sleeping, cooking, etc., may have to be provided under some conditions. At survey headquarters calculating equipment speeds the preparation of the field data.

10. DATA ON THE POPULATION

The particular purpose of a survey determines the scope of the data to be collected. If the aim is to assess the nutritional levels in a population the emphasis is on foods consumed and the household members' personal characteristics which have a bearing on nutritional requirements. If the information is needed for other purposes as well, as, for example, in constructing cost of living indices, data on food and other living costs are required. For use in demand analysis, information on income is most important. If the ultimate aim of a survey is to improve nutritional levels in a population through the introduction of new foods or by other changes in food habits, information on the cultural environment and micro-economic factors is necessary. The successful introduction of new elements into a cultural system may prove as difficult to bring about as the acceptance of a foreign tissue in a transplant. The specific purpose of a survey has a bearing on all phases of the project from the sample design and collection of data to the tabulation and analysis of the results. The data collected are of two general kinds: (1) data on the social, economic and personal characteristics of the household members, and (2) data on the characteristics of the foods consumed, food habits, food technology, etc.

10.1. HOUSEHOLD CHARACTERISTICS

Whatever the purpose of a survey, it is always useful to classify the households according to the characteristics known or believed to affect their food consumption. Not all factors are equally important in all areas, and some have little relevance in most places. Certain household characteristics which are consistently associated with differences in food consumption are:

> Number of members and age-sex composition.
> Economic status as measured by income or other quantity.
> Farm or nonfarm and urban–rural status.

10.2. DEFINITION OF HOUSEHOLD

For purposes of food consumption studies the household is defined as the group of persons sharing a common food supply. The household may consist of a single person, a family, or a larger group including relatives of the family head, boarders, servants, and other unrelated persons sharing the meals. Some members of this food consumption group, farm workers for example, may live under another roof but share the same food. Some persons under the same roof may eat elsewhere, and are therefore not members of the food consumption group. This definition of household differs from that in population censuses, especially with regard to household size, but this does not usually create important problems in selecting sample families from census rolls.

10.3. HOUSEHOLD SIZE

For calculating average consumption levels for whole populations or broad groups thereof, the number of persons in the household may be taken as those obtaining most of their food from the common supply during the reporting period. Visitors to the home for a few meals are not counted. This definition of household size is not sufficiently accurate for comparing food intake of individual households with requirements. Still other definitions of household may be used for calculating *per caput* income, etc.

10.4. AGE–SEX COMPOSITION

For estimating the nutritional requirements of individual households, information is required on age and sex and height and weight of household members, and the pregnancy and lactation status in women.

10.5. ECONOMIC STATUS

Household income or total living expenditure may be used as an indicator of economic status. Information on income is often difficult to obtain for a number of reasons. The definition of income itself varies. There is gross income; net income; cash income; cash income plus imputed value of food, housing, and other goods obtained without direct expense, definitions which are applicable in developing and some other areas. There is also income before or after taxes or other fixed deductions, income with or without inventory changes or depreciation allowances, etc., definitions which would be applicable in industrialized areas. Income may also refer to that of the household head or to the total income of all the household members. Because conditions differ widely among countries, a single definition of income for all areas is difficult to select.

Practical difficulties in obtaining information on income also exist. In rural and developing areas there is the problem of assessing the value of foods and other goods which are home-produced. Moreover, in all parts of the world, people are reluctant to disclose their income. The inclusion of questions on income may decrease participation in a survey, especially if this information is requested at the beginning of the study. Questions on income are often better asked at the end of a survey, when good relations with the respondents have been established and the purpose of the survey is well understood. Experience in many countries has shown that income tends to be underestimated.

For these reasons, total living expenditures, which are closely correlated with income, are often taken as an indicator of economic status of a household. People are more willing to talk about their living costs than about their income. The reporting period for income or living costs should preferably be a year. A shorter period, such as a week or a month, may be used for salaried people or wage workers.

Where no information on income or living costs can be obtained, other indicators of economic status are sometimes used. These may be: size of agricultural holdings, livestock numbers, occupation and status within the occupation, etc. The information on economic status is used for classification of households and analysis of the results. If the food consumption survey is made in conjunction with a family living study, the definition of income or other indicator of economic status may be determined by the broader purposes of the total study rather than by those pertaining to the food consumption survey alone.

10.6. FARM, NON-FARM, AND URBANIZATION STATUS

The availability of foods is important in determining differences in consumption levels among population groups. The home-produced foods of farm and rural households, and the products of hunting, fishing, and collecting, are usually unavailable to urban households. The more expensive products of rural areas often go to town or city markets, and supplies in urban areas often tend to be more plentiful and varied than in rural areas. Because of differences in food consumption levels and patterns which have distinguished farm and nonfarm households and rural and urban classes, households should be classified according to these characteristics. The classification of farm and nonfarm and urbanization status may follow the definitions used in the world census of agriculture and population. A farm household may be defined as one in which at least one member operates an agricultural holding. An agricultural holding should be defined in accordance with the most recent world census of agriculture. The class of farm households may be broken down by size of holding, type of land tenure, or other characteristics. Urbanization status may be defined by size of city, town, village, or other settlement.

10.7. OTHER POPULATION CHARACTERISTICS AND ENVIRONMENTAL CONDITIONS

Religion is another characteristic associated with differences in food consumption levels and patterns, e.g. Muslims do not eat pork, Hindus avoid beef, Catholics were forbidden meat on Fridays until recently, and orthodox Jews are not allowed shellfish, certain other fish, and pork. A number of the religious have long fasting periods which modify food consumption.

Every culture, including the Western, has its own concept of what is a food. Westerners do not eat worms or insects, regardless of their nutritive value; the American Indians abhorred milk when first introduced to it and many still do so; the French consider as a delicacy snails which others abhor; etc. Unscientific beliefs and prejudices, not based on religion, dictate foods which pregnant or lactating women, infants, the sick, and others, should or should not eat. Traditions deeply rooted in culture systems inhibit quick adoption of new foods or changes in food habits, however beneficial. Individuals emigrating from their culture area tend to make changes more readily than those remaining within their environment.

Some of the cultural factors operating in food habits are microeconomic. A new food must fit into the local economy. It must not be too expensive compared to the habitual foods, and it must be easy to use with the home equipment, etc. The wider economic studies often carried out in conjunction with food consumption surveys in developing areas omit minutiae which are important in practical nutrition programs.

Also important to record in food consumption surveys are the educational level of the household head and spouse and the languages spoken, since these affect communication. Some characteristics may be strongly correlated, as, for example, educational and economic level, so that their relative influence is difficult to judge.

Material conditions may affect calorie requirements. The customary housing and clothing of population groups may modify to varying degrees the effect of environmental temperature. Although energy needs of a population cannot be determined by observation, it is useful to describe the customary physical activities of a population surveyed. Villagers cultivating mountain slopes by hand, walking long distances from home to fields, conveying produce on their backs, would be expected to have greater calorie needs than farmers living on the plain, plowing with animals, and carrying crops in wagons. In medical nutrition studies it is desirable to describe environmental conditions of the household which may bear on health and whose effects might otherwise be thought related to nutritional factors.

11. DATA ON THE FOODS

The information on the weight of the foods is obtained by one or the other of the survey techniques described. The quantities recorded in the field must often be translated from a variety of terms into metric weight in order to conform to the food composition data in the available tables. Foods may be weighed in the home as they come, fresh from the field or market, i.e. as gross or as purchased weight; or as edible portion ready for cooking or eating, with inedible material removed. This distinction must be specified.

11.1. SOURCES OF FOODS

The differences noted in food consumption patterns between urban and rural households are explained to a large extent by the ready availability of home produced foods in rural areas. Information on the sources of food—whether purchased, produced, or otherwise obtained—provides helpful checks for national food balance sheets, and it is also important statistically for market analysis. As already indicated, foods not purchased or produced may include foods received as gifts, obtained in barter, as school meals or milk for children, meals in part pay for labor in farms or industry, and products of hunting, fishing, or collecting in the wild.

11.2. PROCESSED FOODS AND PREPARED DISHES

In the industrialized countries processed and prepared foods of various kinds are continually increasing in importance. In the industrialized countries, for example, wheat is available in the form of dark or light flour, pastes, prepared breakfast foods, bread, etc. Fruits and vegetables may be had fresh in season but also canned, dried, frozen, etc. The less developed areas also have a variety of traditional prepared food products in their markets. Soybeans, important in various Asian countries, may be had as the dry seed, soy "milk", soy "cheese", soy cake fermented with fungus, etc. In reporting foods in a survey, information on the form of the food is essential both for the nutritional analysis as well as for market analysis. Additional descriptive data needed for the nutritional analysis are indicated in a later section.

11.3. FOOD WASTAGE IN THE HOME

While waste in food supplies occurs at all stages—in the field, in transportation, in storage, and in the kitchen—only the wastage in the home is of concern in food consumption surveys. Much of the food is recorded at the "as purchased" or "retail level", as it comes into the home from the market or field for preparation of meals or immediate consumption. Besides the loss of inedible parts such as peel and seeds in fruits or vegetables, bone in meat, etc., edible food is sometimes left on the plate, discarded as spoiled later, or fed to domestic animals. Information on the amount lost is important for both economic and nutritional analysis but is extremely difficult to obtain in a large scale survey. Food losses in the home vary in accordance with a number of factors. Among the well-to-do, where food is plentiful, plate waste may be high. The garbage pail is often an indicator of economic level. At the same time there may be good storage facilities for saving choice leftover foods. At low income levels, plate waste may be almost nonexistent, but some foods may nevertheless be lost in spoilage through lack of storage facilities. Domestic pets get some left-over food at almost all economic levels. Measuring the food waste in the home is necessary for determining the real or physiological consumption. Since this type of food waste is extremely difficult to assess in a large-scale survey, the problem could be studied in a subsample in a special investigation. Averages obtained from the smaller studies can be applied to the total survey.

11.4. COST OR MONEY VALUE OF FOODS

Information on food costs is usually obtained without great difficulty, but imputing money value to foods produced or obtained without direct expense involves various questions. Money value can be imputed to foods in accordance with producer or retail prices, depending on the type of household or the specific purpose of the survey. The retail price concept is considered reasonable for nonfarm households or for comparing consumption levels of farm and nonfarm households. For comparison with national expenditures calculations, or for demand analysis, the producer price is considered more reasonable. Imputing money value to foods is questionable in areas where a subsistence economy predominates and where no meaningful market prices exist at either the producer or retail level.

11.5. CLASSIFICATION OF THE FOODS

1. Cereals and cereal products
    Whole grains (wheat, rice, maize, millet, sorghum, barley, oats, etc.).
    Meal, flour (from wheat, rice, maize, etc.).
    Pastes (macaroni, noodles).
    Commercially baked goods (bread, etc.).
    Other cereals and products.
2. Starches and starchy roots
    Potatoes (fresh, canned, dehydrated, flour, etc.).
    Sweet potatoes (fresh, flour, etc.).
    Cassava (fresh, meal, flour, etc.).
    Other starchy roots and products (yautia, taro, yam, etc.).
    Pure dry starches (from wheat, maize, rice, potato, cassava, sago, etc.).
3. Sugars and sweets
    Sugar; crude, refined (cane, beet, palm, maple, etc.).

Sirups and molasses (cane, beet, etc.).
Honey.
Others (jam, marmalade, candy).
4. Pulses (dry seed)
    Beans (kidney, lima, broad, mung, etc.).
    Peas (lentils, peas, chickpeas, etc.).
    Soybeans and products (whole beans, soy sauce, soy curd, soy paste, soy milk, etc.).
5. Nuts
    Groundnuts (in shell, shelled, roasted, salted, groundnut butter, etc.).
    Coconuts (mature, green, coconut milk, etc.).
    Other tree nuts (almonds, pistachios, cashew, walnuts, etc.).
6. Oily seeds (sesame, sunflower, squash, etc.)
7. Vegetables (fresh unless otherwise specified)
    Roots, bulbs, tubers (beets, carrots, onions, parsnips, radishes, turnips, etc.).
    Leaves (cabbage, celery, chard, kale, lettuce, spinach, turnip leaves, cress, etc.).
    Other (cauliflower, chayote, eggplant, green beans, green peas, tomatoes, squash).
8. Fruits (fresh unless otherwise specified)
    Bananas and plantains.
    Citrus fruits.
    Fat-rich fruits (avocados, olives, etc.).
    Other (apples, breadfruit, grapes, guavas, mangoes, melons, papayas, plums, etc.).
    Dried fruits (dates, figs, prunes, raisins, etc.).
9. Meat and meat products
    Fresh and frozen (beef, veal, pork, mutton, lamb, goat, horse, camel, etc.).
    Offal (liver, kidney, heart, brain, etc.).
    Meat products (bacon, ham, dried beef, canned beef, sausage, etc.).
    Poultry and wild birds (chickens, ducks, geese, turkeys, etc.).
    Insects—adult and larvae (ants, caterpillars, locusts, etc.).
10. Eggs (hen, duck, goose, turtle, etc.)
11. Fish and shellfish
    Fish, fresh:
        Fat-rich (herring, mackerel, pompano, salmon, tuna, etc.).
        Medium-fat (barracuda, bream, flatfish, mullet, perch, etc.).

Fat-poor (cod, haddock, etc.).
Fish, salted, smoked (fat-rich, fat-poor types).
Fish, canned, in oil, not in oil (fat-rich, fat-poor types).
Shellfish—fresh and canned (lobster, crabs, crawfish, shrimp, oysters, etc.).
Other aquatic animals (alligators, frogs, turtles, etc.).

12. Milk and dairy products
    Milk, fluid, whole (cow, goat, sheep, buffalo, camel, etc.).
    Skim milk, buttermilk.
    Cream (specify fat content if possible).
    Cheese (hard, soft, semi-soft):
        From whole, partly skimmed or wholly skimmed milk.
        From whey (hard, soft or semi-soft).
    Processed milk:
        Evaporated whole, unsweetened.
        Condensed, whole, sweetened.
        Condensed, skim.
        Dried milk, whole, skim.
        Yoghurt, etc.
    Ice cream.

13. Oils and fats
    Vegetable oils (olive, sesame, sunflower, cottonseed, etc.).
    Vegetable oils, hardened.
    Animal fats (butter, ghee, lard, suet, tallow, etc.).
    Marine oils.
    Mixed products of vegetable, animal and marine oils.
    Other (mayonnaise dressing, sandwich spreads, etc.).

14. Table salt

15. Miscellaneous (spices, cooking chocolate, cocoa, yeast, etc.)

16. Prepared foods and meals obtained outside the home and eaten at home

17. Beverages
    Alcoholic (beer, wine, spirits, etc.).
    Bottled soft drinks with sugar.
    Other beverages (tea, coffee, yerba mate, etc.).

18. Purchased foods eaten away from home
    Meals, snacks.
    Alcoholic drinks.
    Ice cream, candy, soft drinks, etc.

12. FOOD COMPOSITION TABLES

The nutritive value of the foods consumed is calculated with the use of food composition tables. National tables are more likely to have the most appropriate values for the foods in a country. The differences in the chemical composition of the same foods among neighboring countries are, however, often unimportant, especially if allowances are made for variations in water content, and food composition data compiled on a regional basis are usually satisfactory. Various countries now have food composition tables of their own. Many of these tables are, however, still incomplete, lacking values for many local foods and food preparations.

In 1961 the US Interdepartmental Committee on Nutrition for National Defense, in collaboration with the Institute of Nutrition of Central America and Panama, published *Food Composition Table for Use in Latin America*. In 1968 the US Department of Health, Education, and Welfare, in collaboration with the Nutrition Division of the Food and Agriculture Organization of the United Nations, published a second regional table, *Food Composition Table for Use in Africa,* based on analyses of foods from the respective areas. These tables likewise lack values for many foods in these areas. In 1972, a similar table for East Asia was published, under the same auspices.

Before regional food composition tables existed, the FAO of the United Nations, in 1954, published *Food Composition Tables for International Use,* based on data from wherever in the world original analytical data had been produced. These tables were intended for use in countries which had as yet no food composition tables of their own, as well as for international comparison of the nutritive value of the food supplies in the different countries.

The FAO international tables give average values for the following: calories, protein, fat, carbohydrate, calcium, iron, vitamin A value including carotene, thiamine, riboflavine, niacin, ascorbic acid, water, fiber, ash, and percent inedible material or refuse. The food composition values are presented, first, in terms of the edible portion, the form in which the data come from the laboratory; and, second, in terms of the gross or as purchased weight of the foods. The data in terms of gross or as purchased weight are applicable directly to the weight of the foods as they enter the home. The figures are derived from the values obtained in the laboratory analysis of the edible portion of the foods by applying correction factors based on the proportion of refuse and water content. However, since proportion of refuse and water content in similar foods may vary under different conditions, direct information on those factors should be obtained during surveys. Moisture in cereal grains, for example, may vary from wet to dry season or according to length of time and conditions of storage after harvest. Moisture content can be determined in the field with simple apparatus. Information on proportion of refuse in foods should be obtained in a subsample of households or in a special study. Food composition values in terms of gross weight should be recalculated when necessary.

Many of the national food composition tables, and regional tables as well, express the food values in terms of the edible portion only. Gross weights recorded in surveys are then converted to net weights on the basis of the percentages of refuse determined in the field and the food composition figures for edible portion applied.

The regional food composition tables include values for phosphorus in addition to the components given in the FAO international tables. The regional table for Africa distinguishes between different sources of vitamin A, and also gives values for tryptophan, an amino acid convertible to nicotinic acid. Various national food composition tables include figures for additional vitamins and minerals as well as for amino acids and fatty acids.

Food composition tables rarely have data for all the foods recorded in food consumption surveys. When no analysis of a food exists, and original laboratory analyses cannot be made, values for some similar food may be used as a temporary expedient.

12.1. DESCRIPTION OF THE FOODS

The correct use of food composition tables makes an adequate description of the foods at the field stage of a survey necessary. In addition to information on refuse in foods, considerable other detail may be needed. A cereal meal or flour varies in composition according to the amount of bran or germ removed. In developing areas, grains are often milled at home and the extraction rate, or portion of the gross weight which is recovered, may be determined experimentally in the field. Food composition tables usually contain analyses of cereal products at different levels of extraction. Many ways of refining grain are used in developing areas. The grain is sometimes pounded and winnowed to remove the bran; or it is tossed in a flat container to separate the different fractions by gravity. The pounded grain may be dropped into water and the floating bran skimmed off by hand. Dampened whole grain is sometimes buried in a sack in wet sand and processed when it is on the verge of sprouting, or is soft. In certain areas maize is soaked over night in hot lime water or infusion of wood ashes, washed free of hulls in the mornings, and ground into dough for baking. This lime treatment enriches the grain with calcium and produces other effects. In other places maize is soaked for days in water until it sours or is easy to grind. The processes should be described and the fraction of the whole grain utilized determined. If no analysis of similar items exist in food composition tables, samples of the product should be obtained for laboratory analysis.

The starchy root, cassava, a staple food in certain areas, also undergoes a variety of treatments. The root is sometimes simply peeled and boiled. The raw flesh of some varieties is grated and leached in water for its starch. Or the peeled root is roasted and ground into a meal ready for eating. The root is sometimes fermented and dried. Each resulting product varies in chemical composition and yield.

Large differences occur in the edible proportion of certain products such as bananas or plantains, which are also staple foods in some areas. Depending on variety and degree of maturity, bananas may have peels varying from 20 to 60% of the gross weight. Varieties of Andean potatoes, a staple food in that area, differ greatly in average size and vary from 15 to 30% in the amount of peel. When such foods are eaten in large quantities, correct percentages for edible portion are needed.

Color in maize, sweet potatoes, and some other foods is associated with the vitamin A value of those foods, and should be recorded in surveys.

The meat of cattle, hogs, sheep, and other animals differ in chemical composition, and the meat of a single animal may also vary by cut. In the industrialized countries, beef and other meats are marketed and priced by cut, but in developing areas all meat may be sold unclassified and designated only as meat with bone and meat without bone. In any community the amount of bone, fat, tendons, etc., sold with the lean meat is likely to form a customary proportion of the total. In some places all beef bought is lean because the fat is trimmed away for making into soap. In developing areas beef and other meats may be lean because livestock there is poorly fed. In poultry, the blood, intestines, feet, and head parts may be utilized so that "edible portion" forms a larger proportion than where these parts are thrown away. Edible portion varies to some extent with local custom.

Cooking oils and fats should be classified as of animal or vegetable origin, and the particular source specified if possible, e.g. olive oil, coconut oil, hog lard, rendered beef fat, butter, etc., because of the importance of fatty acids in human nutrition.

Industrialized areas have different but not fewer problems in regard to food composition data. Processed and prepared foods constantly increase in variety. The food list shows that milk may be liquid, evaporated (sweetened or not), or dried, partly or wholly defatted, and supplemented with vitamins or not. Flour and meals may be enriched with minerals and vitamins. Bread may contain dry skim milk, soybean flour, and other products. Such details should be recorded in food consumption surveys.

12.2. THE ROLE OF ALCOHOL

Fermented drinks are made throughout the world and may contain B-vitamins and sugar in addition to alcohol. The WHO recommended in 1954 that the calories provided by alcohol be counted in the total calorie value of a diet. The FAO of the United Nations in 1957 suggested that calories from alcohol be counted as part of the dietary calories to the extent of 10% of the total calories from food. The additional calories from alcohol, above the 10%, should, however, be reported.

13. NUTRITIONAL REQUIREMENTS

Knowledge of nutritional requirements accumulated in a number of countries before the end of the nineteenth century. Before the beginning of World War II the Technical Committee of the League of Nations published a table of nutritional requirements based on the knowledge available up to that time. Various countries used this table as a model for national tables of their own, adapted to local conditions and food policies. In 1949 the FAO of the United Nations convened an international committee to recommend methods for estimating calorie needs for different countries and population groups and published the *Report of the Committee on Calorie Requirements, Washington 1950* FAO Nutritional Studies, No. 5.

The approach in this undertaking was based on the intake in healthy men and women for whom accurate information was available. These reference persons were between 20 and 30 years old and averaged 65 kg in body weight for the men and 55 kg for the women. They lived under an environmental mean annual temperature of 10° Centigrade, and their physical activity was considered moderate, e.g. neither very light nor very heavy. From these reference individuals, the recommended calorie intake levels were extrapolated, on the basis of available information, for other types of persons varying in body size, age, and environmental conditions of temperature. Although the degree of physical activity is the most important factor influencing calorie requirements, it was considered difficult to apply the existing knowledge to determine the energy need of different population groups. The recommendations in these reports were tentative and subject to review as additional knowledge became available. Areas for further research were indicated. The first report on calorie requirements was revised and expanded by a second FAO international committee in Rome in 1957.

The reports on calories were followed by reports of subsequent international committees convened by FAO and the WHO, on protein, calcium, vitamin A, thiamine, riboflavine, niacin, ascorbic acid, and iron. Requirements for certain of these nutrients appear to be related to calorie intake but others to body size or protein intake. Food consumption surveys with emphasis on nutritional aspects thus require information on age, sex, height–weight, and environmental temperature for the people studied. While it is difficult to judge energy expenditure of household members in a population sample, field workers should observe their physical activity, describing this as light, moderate or heavy. Observed differences in calorie intake in otherwise comparable population groups can be looked at in the light of observed differences in physical activity.

The recommended levels of calories and nutrients are applicable to large population groups. When used in relation to smaller numbers, individual differences should be taken into consideration. The intakes recommended by the international committees on calories and nutrients are calculated at the "physiological level", i.e. they refer to actual food intake, exclusive of food waste or losses.

13.1. LOSSES OF EDIBLE FOOD AND NUTRIENTS

The deduction of inedible portions of foods, such as rind, pits, bone in meat, etc., has been discussed, as have losses of edible material such as plate waste and edible food shared with pets or otherwise not eaten, which should be deducted, since food intake, in order to be compared with nutritional requirements, should be at the physiological level as well. Losses between food prepared for meals and that actually eaten are difficult to estimate or measure in large scale surveys and should be the subject of special studies in subsamples of households.

The FAO International Committee on Calorie Requirements estimated that plate waste, edible food given to pets, and other losses of edible foods are likely to form from 10 to 15% of the total edible material. It was thought that 15% might be too low for some affluent population groups and 10% too high for many developing areas and for poor classes. These estimates were designed to apply to calories, without considering which kinds of foods would more likely be wasted than others. Observation suggests that carbohydrate foods including cereal products and starchy roots, where the latter are the staples, are more likely to be given to pets or otherwise not eaten than expensive protein foods such as meat or eggs, so that the estimated percentage losses would not apply equally to all nutrients.

Other kinds of losses not susceptible of measuring or estimating during surveys are losses of nutrients destroyed by heat in cooking, in storage, in technological processes to which foods may be subjected, etc. Water-soluble vitamins and minerals suffer loss when cooking water is discarded. The various vitamins and minerals differ in the proportions lost during the various processes. Calorie values may remain relatively unchanged, since protein, fat, and carbohydrate, the energy-yielding components of food, are little affected. Fat in meat may of course be lost in broiling or frying. The percentage loss of vitamins in storage, in cooking, or in other treatment of foods can be measured only in the laboratory. Correction factors to vitamin intake are sometimes applied to survey results on the basis of general knowledge available.

13.2. ADJUSTMENTS FOR FOOD OBTAINED AND EATEN AWAY FROM HOME AND FOOD EATEN BY VISITORS IN THE HOME

All the foods obtained and eaten outside the home by family members form part of the total intake which should be compared to the nutritional requirements. It is, however, most difficult to obtain quantitative information on all such items. In the industrialized countries many meals are eaten in school, at work, and elsewhere, and it may be impossible to obtain information on the quantities of the different foods which should be added to the household totals. When this is the case, it is customarily assumed that the food eaten away from home will be of approximately the same nutritive value as that at home, and adjustments are then made on the basis of the number of meals, taking into account the age and sex of the persons concerned. In some cases, sample surveys of public eating places may be made in order to obtain a rough estimate of the nutritive value of the meals on the basis of their cost. In food consumption surveys in less developed areas, adjustments may be made in other ways. The number of meals customarily eaten per day in a cultural group or geographic area may vary from two to four or more per day, and the meals differ greatly in their relative size. In all food consumption surveys adjustments should be made for foods or meals eaten in the home by visitors. Estimates of the amounts are not difficult to obtain, and these can be deducted from the household totals.

13.3. USES AND LIMITATIONS OF COMPARISONS OF INTAKE WITH REQUIREMENTS

Although the *per caput* values for calorie and nutrient intake for a country or population give a picture of the situation, a better idea is gained from the comparison of the intake with the requirements. These comparisons, expressed as percentages, take into consideration the various factors which affect nutritional requirements, such as age–sex distribution and other differences in the population. These percentages are estimates of the adequacy of the calories and nutrients in the foods consumed. The percentages for calories and protein are considered fairly reliable, but those for minerals and vitamins may be on less firm ground. The percentages, nevertheless, indicate the characteristics and value of the diet and signal defects likely to be important. The national averages conceal important differences in the estimated adequacy of the diets between the rich and poor, the rural and urban, ethnic groups, geographic areas, etc. The tabulation of the data by such population groups indicates the sectors within a country which may need special attention with regard to food and nutrition. When individual households are classified by level of adequacy in calories and nutrients, the kind and size of the nutritional problems are more clearly revealed. The results of the survey provide a basis for food policy and programs. Although household averages are not related directly with the clinical and chemical data on individual members of the household in medical nutrition surveys. the data are, nevertheless, correlated and indicative.

14. TABULATION OF THE RESULTS

Minimum tabulation plans should include tables essential for establishing national food and nutrition policy as well as for international comparisons. Although the tabulation of the data is a final stage in a survey, the tabulation plans are made in the initial stages since decisions on sample size and on information to be collected depend upon these.

14.1. POPULATION GROUPS FOR WHICH CONSUMPTION DATA SHOULD BE TABULATED

1. The country as a whole.
2. Urban–rural and farm–nonfarm classes, depending on their importance in the country.
3. Economic groups, defined by the most appropriate indicators of economic status available. Information on income or on total living costs, if available, may be expressed on a *per caput* or per household basis, depending on the purpose of the survey and on the conditions in the country. *Per caput* figures may be a better indicator of economic status of the household in comparison with the economic level of the country, whereas per household figures permit a more detailed analysis of the effect of household size. Fractile classifications aid in defining economic groups, obtained by first ranging the households by income or total living costs. When no numerical data on economic status are available, and households are classified as low, medium, and high in the economic scale, an attempt should be made to define the limits of these classifications.
4. Households classified by size.

14.2. FOOD CONSUMPTION STATISTICS TO BE SHOWN

The following statistics, per person or per household, per week or per other specified time period, should be given for each separate population group distinguished and for the total population:

1. Average amounts of different foods eaten at home, with separate averages for foods purchased, produced, or otherwise obtained, if such data are available and important.
2. Amounts of different foods eaten away from home, if data are available and amounts important.
3. Money value of different foods, and of all foods, eaten at home, with separate averages for foods purchased, produced, or otherwise obtained without direct expense, if these data are available and important.

60   *Food Consumption and Planning*

4. Expenditure on foods eaten away from home.
5. Average content of food consumed per person per day, in calories, protein, fat, carbohydrate, calcium, iron, vitamin A, thiamine, riboflavine, niacin and ascorbic acid.
6. Percent contribution of each food group to the total calorie and nutrient intake.
7. Percent of total calories in the food, derived from protein, fat, and carbohydrate.

14.3. OTHER INFORMATION ON THE HOUSEHOLDS IN EACH POPULATION GROUP DISTINGUISHED

1. Number of households in the sample. (This shows the relative importance of each group, if a self-weighting sample design is used. Depending on the sample design, it also provides a rough basis for judging the reliability of the estimates for the various groups.)
2. Average household size. (The averages are needed for interpreting the food consumption patterns of these groups and for computing per person averages.)
3. The measure of economic status used for classifying the households. (Where households are classified into qualitative economic groups, an effort should be made to assess the average income or family living expenditure for each group. Such averages are needed for demand analysis and other types of economic calculations.)

14.4. THE FOOD ITEMS AND THEIR CLASSIFICATION

The separate food items recorded in a survey are likely to make a very long list except in populations where the diet comprises a few staples and a limited number of other foods. A single food like wheat may have many derivative items, as seen in the food list already shown on p. 49. Each item varies in chemical composition and must be accurately named so that the proper nutrient values may be applied. The classification used in the list should be followed in the statistical tables dealing with the foods, in reporting the survey results.

Food items of small relative importance (or with large standard errors) should not be omitted from the list, for many reasons. They may be grouped in different ways for analytical purposes. The average for a group may be sufficiently reliable even when that of an individual item is not. The averages for certain individual wild greens consumed by some rural populations may be individually highly unreliable, but the average of wild greens as a group may be reliable and important. Expenditures for individual items of canned or frozen fruit and vegetables may be unreliable, but as a group they may be of considerable interest for purposes of market analysis. There are additional justifications for showing the complete list of items. The position in a welfare program of an individual item such as milk for children may be of importance. Also, benchmark information may be needed for certain items in initiating programs aimed at changing food habits.

When food patterns of different economic groups, rural–urban classes, and others, are compared, the list of foods must be strictly comparable, even if a given item is highly variable in the different population groups compared. For international comparisons, the broad groupings proposed should be followed.

14.5. ADDITIONAL TABULATIONS AND USEFUL INFORMATION

Depending on the ultimate aims of a survey and resources available, other information on the households may make additional tabulations possible. However, the more elaborate the tabulations, the larger the sample must be and the costlier the survey becomes. To the extent that sample size permits, food consumption data can be further classified by some of the following household characteristics, often associated with differences in food habits, consumption levels, and nutrient value of the diets:

> Ethnic affiliation.
> Religious groups.
> Social status.
> Educational level.
> Status of the household head within his occupation.
> Land tenure.
> Geographic or administrative area of residence.
> Size of city of urban households.
> Season of the year.

Cross-tabulation by so many factors is, however, rarely possible and often unnecessary. Various factors may be related among themselves or to the economic factor. The following additional food statistics can be shown for the population groups distinguished:

- Distribution of households by *per caput* intake of calories and nutrients.
- Distribution of households by percent "adequacy" of calorie and nutrient intake.
- Proportion of households in each population group using or purchasing specified foods.
- Average consumption of specified foods by households consuming those foods.
- Distribution of households by total expenditure (or money value) *per caput*, for all foods or for specified foods.
- Proportion of total expenditure attributed to food, or to each food group, in the different population groups distinguished and also at different levels of total expenditure.
- Percent contribution of each food group to the total calorie and nutrient intake.
- Percent of total calories derived from protein, fat and carbohydrates in the diet.

Although it is rarely possible to cross-tabulate the food data by all the factors or household characteristics observed, insight may be gained of the importance of these factors by the percentage of the households having the specified characteristics. Information on the attitudes and concepts concerning food problems gained during a survey may provide valuable guidance for the implementation of action programs. The success of an action program may depend as much on human factors, whose relation to food problems are not easily perceived, as on the correct technical diagnosis of the nutrition problem.

CHAPTER 3

FOOD CONSUMPTION: LEVELS AND PATTERNS-VARIATION BY GEOGRAPHICAL REGIONS AND SOCIO-ECONOMIC GROUPS

Marina Flores

Institute of Nutrition of Central America and Panama (INCAP), Guatemala, CA

CONTENTS

1. Introduction	63
2. Factors Involved in Food Selection	64
2.1. Geographical Location	64
2.2. Cultural Factors	65
2.3. Economic Factors	67
3. The Static and Dynamic Aspects of Food Patterns	70
4. Present Food Patterns in the World	75
4.1. Countries of the Far East	76
4.2. Countries of the Near East	79
4.3. African Countries	86
4.4. European Countries	96
4.5. American Countries	102
4.6. The Caribbean	117
4.7. Oceania	120
5. Present Dietary Levels in the World	123
References	135

1. INTRODUCTION

Nature offers the human being an enormous variety of foodstuffs. Men usually select them according to the quantity in which they are produced and give preference to those that will satisfy their basic needs. The main cultures and civilizations of the world have flourished in areas where the efforts of man were rewarded by the land with an abundance of a certain indigenous cereal. Through the centuries, rice, wheat, and maize have represented the source of life for the civilizations of the Far East, the Mediterranean (Egypt and Rome), and America, respectively, during the development of their societies. Teff, sorghum, and other cereals have constituted the basic food for other cultures. The opening of frontiers and routes across the world brought those grains to the rest of the world, where they combined with other products and formed special dietary designs called food patterns.

When man was able to control nature without competing with his neighbors for space, his wisdom was sufficient to establish the amounts in which all food products could be consumed by him and his family.

At present, man is no longer able to eat as he wants, owing to factors, inherent in the environment where he must survive, that limit food availability. In some areas of the world, the majority of people enjoy plentiful food sources, while in others low production limits food availability drastically, and only a minority satisfies its needs. The amounts in which different items are consumed by people in each area, and the customary treatment given to them, determine the levels reached by calorie and nutrient intake in every population group.

2. FACTORS INVOLVED IN FOOD SELECTION

Differences in types of foods and combinations in which they are consumed have been determined by several ecological factors, which could be defined as follows:

2.1. GEOGRAPHICAL LOCATION

The territory where man happens to live will lead him to select the staple, as well as other, food products, with which to build his diet. In the highlands or near the sea, close to the rivers or lakes, in the tropical or temperate zones, in hot or cold climates, land and water will offer him different foods. The topography of the land will make it either easy or difficult for him to cultivate the foods selected; whether he is living in a plateau or on the slopes of a mountain, in a place where there is scarcity or abundance of water resulting in dry or fertile soil, will make all the difference. Degree of humidity as well as amount of sunshine will offer suitable conditions for a given product or products.

In general, most cereals, as wheat and maize, and legume grains, such as beans or chickpeas, grow better in the high altitudes and temperate climates, while roots and oily seeds, like yams, cassava, sesame or cotton, are native of the warm lowlands. The sea shores, usually shaded by palm trees, provide foods rich in protein and fats. In addition, a variety of marine products are available to the inhabitants of such an area. The extensive plains, where cattle or other domesticated animals can feed on all kinds of grasses, provide their inhabitants with meat and milk. Thus, great differences in food patterns may exist not only between one country and the next, but also within each country itself. Roots and tubers, like sweet potatoes and cassava, and plantains or bananas, will predominate in the diets of people living in hot climates or near the sea (Grant and Groom, 1958). In addition, some fish will complement the diets of the latter. Wheat and maize will constitute the basic sustenance of people living in the highlands of a given country, with the addition of beans and greens; while, within that same country, starchy roots, rice, and bananas will feed coastal families (Thomason *et al.*, 1957). Sorghum will be the only cereal providing a source of energy for people in the dry regions (Aylward, 1966), while rice will predominate in the diets of families living in the tropical climates and regularly flooded areas (Hauck and Hanks, 1959). Beef constitutes the main food of people living in Australia, New Zealand, and Argentina, where great extensions of pasture land propitiate the breeding of large animals. In the Arctic, meat and fat from seals, whales or polar bears are the major dietary items, with berries and sea algae added as vitamin sources. Potatoes in Peru and Bolivia, and goats and sheep in Iran or Teheran, are other examples of the adoption of food patterns by man as he is forced to adapt to the geographical environment in which he lives.

2.2. CULTURAL FACTORS

Throughout the centuries cultures have developed around the principal indigenous foods of a given area. Man learned to cultivate and domesticate the plants and animals necessary to obtain his food. After many generations he inherited a special technology which told him how to prepare appropriately those products for human consumption. Each society disseminated its own culture and, consequently, foods which originated in one place appeared in different areas also, following the same routes taken by the other elements of an expanding civilization. As Aykroyd (1961) mentioned in one of his lectures, "wheat, which may have originated in what is now Ethiopia, has become a major food crop in the U.S.A., Canada, Argentina, and Australia. The maize of the new world reached Africa and Europe in the 15th century and the potato, originated in the highlands of Central and South America, crossed the Atlantic and progressed eastwards at about the same time." Aykroyd (1961) also indicated the place taken by sugar, originally from India, as the main crop of all tropical countries of the world. The animals domesticated in Asia or Europe to yield meat and milk traveled to America and constitute at present the wealth of many farmers and countries. Optimum climatic and soil conditions found in differing areas for certain products have favored the adoption of foreign articles. Thus, in addition to the constant migration of human beings there has been a real exchange of foods between the continents. The oily seed fruits of cacao used to prepare chocolate, which was regarded as the beverages of the gods in the Middle American civilization, emigrated to other lands, and coffee, from Ethiopia and the Near Eastern countries, has replaced that ancient product. Now chocolate is a favorite of both children and adults in European countries. Undoubtedly, India has been the motherland of many products which are cultivated now in African, European, and tropical American countries, and which were introduced by the seamen who discovered these new lands.

Nevertheless, each society is strongly attached to certain products which are part of its own culture. All possible mechanisms are utilized by men to increase their availability and to ensure their daily supply. How well foods reaching other areas were accepted by the people has been a matter of time, prestige, production, and the essential needs of the people. If local conditions were suitable for the new, well accepted foods, they became a part of the food patterns. If the new food was inadaptable to local conditions, it was not considered an important item, even though its prestige may have been great. Besides, experience gained by previous generations in adopting new food products resulted in favorable or unfavorable social attitudes toward the foods in the following generations. In this matter not only prestige and agricultural conditions were playing important roles; ease in preparation, good preservation as well as flavour, appearance, and other qualities were important for the adoption of the new product as part of their own food patterns.

The happy or unhappy experience of the people with new native or imported food drew an arbitrary division in food patterns, separating foods into two classes: the good and the bad ones. If the introduction of the new food is associated with an unhappy event, like disease or a change in the social organization, it is considered effectively taboo and is avoided at least by certain groups. In other instances, religious or other kinds of beliefs force the people to avoid important foods. Foods with high nutritive value, but with associated religious meaning, may be consumed only during local festivities; but for the rest of the year they are not considered appropriate as part of the customary diets. In some countries profound changes in dietary patterns are observed among certain Christian groups during Lent periods, involving the avoidance of all kinds of products of animal origin. In recent years there are several examples of misleading beliefs or unfortunate experiences with new products. When powdered skim milk was introduced in different parts of the world, and prepared with contaminated water, people deduced that children became ill from the new kind of milk. In several impoverished areas, where fruits are abundant, natives prevent their children from eating them because previous experience has taught them that some fruits produce worms. Meat and eggs may be considered as luxury items or as very strong foods to be avoided for the duration of certain physiological conditions. Fish, considered as a holy food by several societies, is eaten only during Lent and is not regarded by many groups as an important item which should be incorporated into the daily food pattern. In many instances, flavour is the quality that has guided people in the formation of an attitude towards a certain food, under which they attribute ill effects or medical properties to it.

2.3. ECONOMIC FACTORS

Food availability and traditional food patterns lead different groups of people to eat the same type of diet through the generations. However, new foods with more prestige may gradually replace indigenous products partially or totally if the economic condition of the people allows such a change. Every dietary survey carried out in any country of the world, and even in groups of small towns with the same culture and more or less homogenous social status, has always revealed differences in consumption, which are closely related to the economic status of the families. The common picture in a poor locality shows a large portion of families with diets in which the staple food amounts to almost the total volume of daily consumption. At the same time, a smaller portion with a larger income is consuming new products and less staple food, which improve the quality of the diet. Of course, differences within a town are not great, but differences between towns in a given country are remarkable when there are economic differences from one town or area to the next. Since calories constitute the primary necessity, poor families will be satisfied with a sufficient amount of calorie sources as cereals or tubers and very small quantities of other food products, while families in higher income brackets will be able to obtain a more varied diet and greater quantities of other expensive foods. Differences between countries, poor and rich, are painful to conceive, especially in regard to expensive foods of animal origin.

The classification of food products in three groups is characteristic of all countries where the economy is predominantly agricultural. Cereals, roots or tubers, plantains, and sugar, constitute the first group as the main calorie sources because they are produced with relatively less effort and in much greater quantities than the other foods, and consequently their value in currency is low. The second group are pulses, fresh vegetables, and fruits, which require efficient cultivation practices, more work and time, better field conditions, and good seeds, all of which increase their money value. A third group of foods are the animal products: milk, eggs, and meat. They are the most expensive items because good production requires optimum field conditions, a great deal of time and space, well developed techniques for sanitation, and efficient care of the animals. Furthermore, those animals may require concentrate grains which constitute the staple foods for humans.

In agricultural countries, particularly those with high population density per unit of arable land, it is inevitable that the major segment of the population may be poor, and that they have to obtain not only calories but almost all nutrients from their staple food, which is generally either cereals or tubers. In such areas, differences in food patterns among the economic groups are more defined than in other countries. For instance, in the rural communities of India the food pattern of the low income groups consists of rice, a small amount of pulses, and some vegetables, while the upper class families replace part of the rice with wheat, part of the pulses with milk and eggs, and they eat a greater variety of vegetables (Devadas and Easwaran, 1967). At the same time, it was found that although caste, occupation, and education do not influence food practices in these areas, income does; and, therefore, the scarcity of animal protein is felt only by low income groups.

In certain impoverished countries of Africa (Walker, 1966) or Latin America (Flores, 1961), where the sole occupation of men in the rural area is farming, the comparison between rural and urban areas in food consumption is paradoxical. The main farming products of the rural areas daily reach the city markets. Urban families with a regular cash income are able to buy a great variety of products. The families in the rural area have to be satisfied with a monotonous diet, under which a basic cereal is combined with beans or peas and some wild green leaves. In those countries, food supplies—especially animal products—are insufficient to feed the entire population; only the city families, a small segment of the population, enjoy the privilege of good diets. In any dietary survey of these cities, a long list of tropical fruits or fresh vegetables and meat, milk, and eggs will be part of the usual food pattern. Sugar, fats, and tea or coffee will complete the list. The diets enjoyed by a privileged few are rich in vitamins and animal protein, and are more comparable with the diets of families living in rich or well developed countries.

In the high income countries where the economy no longer relies on agriculture, where industry and technology are sufficiently developed to offer the people a high standard of living, we may observe quite a different state of affairs. The purchasing power of the people is sufficient for them to obtain a wide variety of commodities. Foods in these areas may be classified in different ways according to different purposes. Dietary differences between economic groups are of less magnitude owing to a diminished contrast in economic level. A major segment of the population enjoys good diets, and families are able to obtain all kinds of local or imported products and processed or unprocessed food in the necessary amounts. In these countries, the education level and size of the family (Hollingsworth, 1955), or perhaps the type of occupation in which the parents are involved rather than the family's degree of urbanization or economic level, influences its food pattern. Only very large families are limited in their consumption of adequate or varied diets, when their budget is not sufficient to cover the needs of each member. The differences among the upper, middle, or lower classes, in regard to food intake, exist only in the grading or quality of the products purchased by each group, as local products are abundant and a very small portion of the population is involved in farming. Economic factors, in combination with seasonal variation, may exert small or great influence on the availability of food products in each area of the world, including the staple food (Rao, 1961). In countries with marked seasons, severe winters, or very dry summers, animals and plants cannot resist the extreme temperatures, and survival is impossible if no special measures are taken to protect those food sources. Some food products will be scarce or will disappear temporarily from the market. It follows that low availability, due to an increased difficulty in production or to the high prices that must be paid for imported products, will render the product very expensive.

Some decades ago, the spring sickness was a yearly hazard in Europe owing to poor winter diets. At present, the devastating famines in countries of the Far East, such as India and China, are due to extreme shortage of the staple food for certain periods of the year. The tropical countries are free of marked seasonal differences, and their climate is not extremely hot or cold but, mild all the year round, the only variation is provided by heavy rains for several months. A majority of agricultural products are available at all times, and more than one staple crop is harvested because irregular topography provides a diversity of climates and altitudes. Dietary surveys carried out in these areas during the dry or rainy seasons, for instance those conducted in Central America, show no significant differences in nutrient intake although the products themselves may change. Some products are abundant during the dry season, and they are substituted by others during the period that follows; nutritionally, however, they are of the same nature. The principal markets in those countries are supplied with every type of product throughout the year. Food prices do not change significantly except for those of certain seasonal fruits.

Food technology, and advances in preservation, storage, and transportation, have made it possible for people in the high income countries to have all products at their disposal during the entire year and without interruption. Seasonal fluctuations no longer exist in the diets of people living in countries with a highly developed technology.

3. THE STATIC AND DYNAMIC ASPECTS OF FOOD PATTERNS

It was mentioned that soil, climate, and geographical location, as well as cultural factors, play the principal role in keeping populations on the same food pattern for generations. On the other hand, a changing economic status, increasing education, and the advent of technology or industrialization, will modify food patterns. The degree of modification will depend on the intensity with which societies succeed in following their plans for economic advancement, urbanization, agricultural development, and industrialization.

The more static area in food patterns corresponds to staple foods consumed by the people, mainly in the low income countries where farming systems are strongly traditional (Rao, 1967). The tendency of staples to survive through different conditions increases with the danger of changing farming systems. In such areas it is essential to secure the production of the main local food owing to the urgency of basic needs. It is easier to change the systems for other agriculture products, not essential to the diets, through different means, such as the introduction of new seeds, new implements, or new methods of cultivation. The main difficulty in changing staple foods resides mainly in the fact that they are deeply embedded in the system of cultural values of a society. In the rural areas of Central America, for instance, the same staple food, maize, has persisted for many centuries, and it has always been the principal farming product. For the cultivation of maize, people are still using the same implements and following the same methods employed by their ancestors. Furthermore, the process for converting maize into food has not changed since the ancient time of the Mayan civilization. In Indonesia, where tubers like yams and taro, supplemented with breadfruit and bananas, have remained as the principal food items, people still use the same implements and methods for cultivation. No changes in their preparation have been observed for centuries; prolonged boiling or roasting of tubers and bananas continue, undisturbed by any innovation.

A good illustration of the static mechanism of the staple food in a society may be found in a relatively recent project, launched in New Mexico with the purpose of helping the Navaho Indians. The basic diet of this group was maize, beans, squash, and potatoes (Apodaca, 1952). The agent paid great attention to the relationships between agricultural technology and the environmental condition of farming practices, as well as social organization within that people. With excellent field demonstration methods, the hybrid maize was planted and a successful yield followed, drawing enthusiastic response from the people. A good percentage of families adopted and planted the new seeds instead of the indigenous maize, and the desired improvement was obtained. However, the program collapsed completely when families failed to use the maize for their daily bread. The agent forgot to investigate food habits among the women, who discovered that the qualities of the new maize differed from those of common maize when "tortillas" were prepared, changing the original flavor and texture.

On the other hand, economic changes have such an impact on the behavior and social attitudes of people that even changes in the staple food may be produced, and new products adopted. Very often, the proximity of large urban centers to small rural groups and the opening of new roads, promote sophistication in developing countries. As families gradually derive better incomes, they start changing their food habits and introducing new products or replacing some of the local ones.

A small portion of rural families from small communities close to the main cities in Central America (Flores, 1961), will begin to use lard in their diets if their income increases, mainly for the preparation of beans and rice. The use of rice with lard has prestige value because the so-called "ladinos" (natives with some Spanish blood) eat rice in that way as one of their main dishes. Changes due to social status or prestige may bring beneficial effects, but sometimes this is not the case. One of the main sources of carotene in the Indian diets of Central America is constituted by yellow maize and wild green leaves. As a result of sophistication these foods, lacking prestige, are dropping from the diets of this population group and being replaced by white corn and other cereals and vegetables of low vitamin content. Soon after these changes, the diets become deficient. The same problem is observed in different parts of India, where some fermented foods (cereals or pulses) were used by the inhabitants, but urbanization or community development has introduced undesirable changes, causing them to drop the fermented foods and exchange them for imported flours with lower nutritive value. The obvious result is a marked decrease in daily vitamin intake.

The most dynamic area in food patterns is constituted by items generally utilized to complement the main calorie source, like new cereals, fats, and sugars. These are easily incorporated into the diets to improve flavor, and they may gradually replace the basic food or give more variety. If the new products can be prepared with less work, and if their flavor is accepted, adoption is more rapid. Thus, sugar sweets, and pancakes or biscuits made from wheat flour, for example, all have a high degree of acceptability among such people as the inhabitants of the colonies in the Polynesian Islands (Fry, 1957), the Eskimo in Canada (Sinclair, 1953) or the Indians from the reservations in the United States (Darby et al., 1956). The products are brought by white people, missionaries, or other visitors belonging to what is regarded as an upper class group, so that articles used by them are accepted because of their prestige value. Before the Eskimos came into contact with foreigners, their diets, compared to the diets of the white people, were rich in protein with low carbohydrate intake. However, a dietary survey in 1950–2 (Sinclair, 1953) showed that the proportion of protein, fat, and carbohydrates to total calorie intake in their diet was similar to that of American soldiers. Changes brought by the acquisition of mission food habits increased carbohydrates at the expense of fat, the main source of calories for the

Eskimo originally being marine animal fat. The primitive Eskimos used most of the soft parts of the animals, including organs rich in vitamins and iodine. Plants from land and sea were likewise consumed. At present, canned meat and canned vegetables have replaced them. In addition, there has been an increase in the consumption of sweets, refined flours, and soft drinks, which resulted in a pronounced deterioration of their teeth.

It is clear, therefore, that prestige provides a definite guideline for changes in food patterns promoted by socio-economic factors. As already mentioned, foods that belong to a group which is considered as belonging to a superior social class acquire prestige value, attracting people with an improved socio-economic status. The latter prefer to use foods consumed by groups with more political or social power. The use of wheat bread in the rural communities of Latin America or the Far East makes the people feel that they are eating like city people. The use of water with sugar by some of the rich families in the Polynesian Islands, instead of the unfashionable but more nutritious coconut sap, is another example (Parkinson, 1961). Indian communities in Guatemala use yellow corn. If they move to a Spanish community or to the western part of the country, yellow maize is fed to the animals, and white maize is used for the preparation of daily bread. It is fortunate that milk and meat rank high in the food social scale of Latin America and many other areas, and thus are able to benefit at least those families who can afford them. Cultural or religious beliefs no longer count in some groups of India and Africa when money is available to obtain expensive milk or meat products because they are eaten by European people (Devadas and Easwaran, 1967). It is unfortunate that fish does not enjoy the same prestige as beef or poultry in any part of the world; on the contrary, it is regarded in some areas as food eaten only by low class groups.

The role of agricultural extension in the improvement of food patterns is unquestionable. In some areas, advances in food science and technology have run parallel with advances in socio-economic research. There are countries, for instance in Africa, where population groups are more susceptible to changing patterns, not only because they are more receptive but because they are upholding no ancient tradition left behind by great civilizations. If some remnant traits of old cultures happen to exist, they are easily changed if the people are offered a proper substitute and the means of smooth adjustment to it. This is the reason why several African communities are undergoing rapid social, economic, and political changes as a result of successful educational programs.

Food technology and industrialization have been extremely influential in changing food patterns, not only in the well developed countries but also in countries where a certain amount of progress has been achieved in different disciplines. For instance, canned foods like fruit juice or ready-to-eat breakfast cereals, where no labor is needed and preservation is easy, also acquire certain prestige because they have been used first by the rich families. These products are replacing indigenous seasonal fruits or whole grain cereals which have to be cooked. In some Caribbean areas, and in Panama, the daily main dish at noon was always prepared with meat bone and some fresh vegetables. Now this typical preparation is disappearing because the dehydrated soups from the United States, which can be obtained at low prices and need only the addition of some water and a short time for boiling, are becoming more popular. Of course, their nutritive value is very low compared to that of the traditional meat soup. Sweet condensed milk, imported from the United States, is the only dairy product in the diets of people living on the Atlantic coast because it keeps for a long time in hot climates. Nevertheless, there are cases in which industrialization or advances in food technology have brought profound beneficial effects to prevailing food patterns, even when the early introduction of changes in processing may have had opposite results. In the case of cereals that have to be milled, machines substitute the domestic implements originally used to prepare the flours. In the beginning, nutrients were lost because the product made by the new machines did not retain them in its refined form; subsequently, however, the enrichment of those cereals or the improvement of the machines has yielded products with more B-complex vitamins, thereby abolishing the incidence of malnutrition problems.

Usually, one of the ultimate goals of industrialization is to improve the national economy. At the same time, large-scale production causes lower priced goods to reach more homes. Under certain other circumstances, industrialization means definite changes in life patterns for the population. These do not only affect working-hour schedules, but also food habits; those pertaining to meal times, for instance. In many developing countries, where the noon meal is most important, housewives have always had the entire morning to cook a whole meal for the family. However, industrialization eventually makes it necessary for them to change their cooking hours from morning to afternoon because the men must work a continuous 8-hour shift. At the same time, some industries install their own cafeterias, but only the most sophisticated societies are able to adopt them successfully because it is difficult to provide an attractive atmosphere and palatable and hygienic meals.

It is ironical that improved living standards have been accompanied in some societies by an increase in the employment of women. This, in turn, brings about changes in food patterns which are due not only to an increase in the family income but also to the fact that fresh food and home-cooked meals must be substituted by manufactured food, which can be preserved and prepared easily.

Advances in food science and technology tend to improve not only the quality of food products but make them uniform in nutrient content. Large-scale manufacturing and good preservation methods significantly decrease the price of foods, making them available everywhere at all times of the year and abolishing seasonal food shortage.

Another aspect of development that influences food patterns in any community is an improved system of communications. New roads and new transportation facilities gradually do away with cultural isolation. Food exchange and distribution is encouraged by numerous new facilities, and greater variety is incorporated into the diets. At present, highly developed countries can consume different products from remote places. Furthermore, they are eaten not as an infrequent treat; these items sometimes appear daily on the table. For instance, any family in the United States can enjoy a Californian orange, Florida avocado, or a Hawaiian pineapple, even if they live in New York. Often, in underdeveloped countries, new roads and transportation facilities may bring plentiful amounts of milk or other products from areas where these supplies are sufficient to satisfy both local needs and those of less favored regions. For instance, in Ethiopia the opening of roads could be very beneficial for the increase of milk consumption in the central towns because there are other areas where milk is abundant.

Unexpected social events have also made the breakdown of food patterns possible, introducing new foods and even rendering those with no prestige acceptable. American potatoes were incorporated into European diets, and African lentils traveled to France. In the history of food patterns, changes have been precipitated by the destruction of people, animals, and property by natural disasters or wars. New products rejected under normal circumstances were immediately accepted. Thus, through unexpected chains of events, new and modified food patterns may suddenly appear in the most unlikely places.

4. PRESENT FOOD PATTERNS IN THE WORLD

As part of the technological revolution at the core of the present era, food products, old and new, natural or processed, are swiftly traversing oceans and continents to be accepted or rejected by peoples around the world. Nevertheless, certain basic products are common to several countries, and important food habits recur in a given area, by virtue of a similarity in climatic condtions or socio-economic structure. Food patterns will be described by regions, keeping in mind that there are similarities of this type in countries and areas which are geographically apart or, conversely, there are dissimilarities within the same region.

4.1. COUNTRIES OF THE FAR EAST

All the Asiatic countries where rice is the staple food have to make use of their southern tropical flood areas to grow this cereal. India, Thailand, China, and Korea cultivate rice to ensure sufficient domestic supplies (Oshima, 1967; US Interdepartmental Committee on Nutrition for National Defense (US ICNND), 1962a, 1961c, 1957a). The northern mountainous area of India and Pakistan (US ICNND, 1956b), usually very poor, is dedicated to the cultivation of wheat, barley, or to the raising of sheep or goats. The central plains are good for vegetables, fruits, sugar cane, and are also suitable for raising cattle, buffalo, or other animals. The tropical and subtropical areas of these countries have two distinct seasons—the rains from April or May to October, and the dry months for the rest of the year. Soils are usually fertile and appropriate not only for rice but for other cereals like millet or corn, pulses, and tubers. The entire coastal plain is appropriate for the cultivation of coconuts and pineapple, and potentially rich because of the great availability of fish, shrimp, and other marine foods. Fish is also abundant in the many rivers and canals running through some of these countries, but this resource is not fully exploited because these waterways represent the most important means of transportation and communication. Railway systems and highways connect the principal cities, but they are not well developed, so that cattle and water buffalos have to be used for transportation as well as for working in the field.

The economy in this region relies mainly on agriculture, and around 80% of the population is engaged in farming rice and other food products (US ICNND, 1956b). Fishing takes the second place: fresh and dry fish are used locally and also exported in great numbers. Japan is exceptionally different owing to its degree of industrialization. In this case, fishing is one of the well developed industries. All these countries are great importers of wheat flour, dairy products, dry legumes, meats, sugars, fats, and oils, as a complement to their rice diets. With the exception of Taiwan they grow only one rice crop during the year. Nevertheless, in normal conditions, production is generally sufficient for local needs. Only in the poor areas of India is rice complemented with other cereals, like millet or wheat; during the dry season, rice is substituted there by other cereals. In countries like Thailand or Vietnam (US ICNND, 1960b), people cultivate more than 10 different kinds of rice for their daily sustenance. In Thailand, people prefer milled rice, and under-milled rice is not popular; but in the rural areas of India, China, or the Philippines (US ICNND, 1957c), the latter, which is richer in vitamins and minerals, has greater acceptance. The popularity of parboiled rice, also with higher nutritive value, is likewise irregular in the area. Rice is prepared in many ways, the most common of which is boiling; sometimes it is milled and converted into flour which is subsequently prepared as a soup or gruel. The grain is frequently washed two or three times and the water discarded; water after boiling is also thrown out. Occasionally, rice is only soaked in water and left over-night, then cooked until soft.

Pulses, mainly chickpeas, lentils, soya beans, and groundnuts, constitute the second most important item in the diets of some of these countries. Among the poor, beans or nuts are incorporated into the curries or soups, increasing the amount of protein in cereal diets. In the diets of the more prosperous economic classes, fresh and dry fish, or meats like beef, pork, chicken, or duck, rank second in the place of pulses (Datta *et al.*, 1963). An important traditional food preparation, extensively used throughout the area, but not in India, is a sauce made with fish or shrimp, which is added to different foods for flavor improvement. For the preparation of the sauces, small fish are placed in large wooden tanks containing brine and left soaking for several days. The fish layer which remains at the top is pressed and later allowed to ferment for periods of almost a year. Finally, the sauce is dried in the sun and mixed with other batch of fish sauce, then filtered and bottled. Shrimps are prepared in a similar way. These products represent an important industry, supplying all Far Eastern countries with fish or shrimp paste, which raises the nutritive value of their cereal diets.

Vegetables, mainly leafy greens consumed in the whole area, take third place in these diets. Some are merely gathered in the fields, while others are cultivated (Advaney *et al.*, 1967; Jyothi *et al.*, 1963). The pattern of food intake in the Far East can be labeled as a rice–fish–vegetable diet. In some areas of India or China the diversity of vegetables is such that when a dietary survey is made, more than 50 different kinds may be listed. In the highlands of these countries, especially in Vietnam, may be found the most beautiful gardens in the world, where all kinds of vegetables are grown. Cabbage, bamboo shoots, red peppers, pumpkins, and tomatoes are among the more common vegetables eaten by these populations.

Another dietary characteristic of considerable importance in these countries is seasoning, which they use in large quantities. Red and black peppers, garlic, onions, vinegar, salt, sugar, curry, mustard, soya sauce, ginger, and many others are all traditional seasoning ingredients utilized by every family. Several fresh vegetables may be processed for fermentation, or pickled in spices and canned. Tomatoes are used to prepare a paste which is also very popular. A more typical sauce is prepared with roasted chili and garlic, mixed with either dry shrimp, soya beans, or peanuts; fish sauce, sugar, and watery tamarind pulp or lime juice are added. The curries can be prepared with fish or shrimp, in combination with a pounded mixture of onion, garlic, dried hot peppers, turmeric, and salt. Sometimes they are prepared with coconut milk and, after cooking, tamarind is added, after which the whole blend is boiled. Beef curry is also prepared with chili, onion, garlic, and shrimp. Bamboo shoots are commonly added to the beef curry, and beef is also replaced by chicken or frog meat. Bamboo shoots and pumpkins are made into soups, sometimes with coconut milk, or else they are prepared with fermented fish or fermented soya beans and salt. Seasonal fruits are available in all the tropical zones of the Far East, but consumption is low even in the rural areas. Among the fruits very common to these countries are citrus fruit, guavas, bananas, mangoes, papaya, pineapple, and coconuts in the coastal area. Coconut cream is used in some areas for cooking rice and fish or for other preparations; coconut oil is also extracted for frying.

In island countries like Ceylon, the Philippines, and Malaysia, tubers and starchy roots are very important as a third item in the inhabitants' diets. For some areas, tubers constitute the staple food; for instance, yams or potatoes in Ceylon, sweet yellow potatoes in Taiwan (Chen and Huang, 1960), sweet white potatoes in the Philippines (Quiogue *et al.*, 1969), and cassava in some towns of Indonesia. Traditional methods of preparation for these products remain unchanged. They are sometimes combined with green plantains, which are treated in a similar way, and used in place of daily bread, because cereals are scarce. Tubers are also consumed though in smaller amounts in countries where rice or other cereals are the staple food. Their contribution to the nutritive value of the diet is not substantial. The contribution of oil to calorie intake is important, as groundnut, coconut, or soya bean oil are used in many local preparations. Several concerns produce oils on a large scale, not only for local consumption, but for exportation as well.

In general, the people of the Far East are able to ingest sufficient amounts of calories during the rainy season, but the rest of the year brings hunger to certain areas. Insufficient calorie intake results in weight reduction and a diminishing working capacity for the inhabitants of the poorer towns. In addition, rice availability decreases; cassava, potatoes, or maize—poorly treated—replace it and cause great deterioration in the diets. For instance, in the cassava area of Indonesia the hunger oedema is endemic (Bailey, 1962). On the other hand, in countries that are improving economically, such as Japan, consumption of rice is declining as industrialization progresses. The demand for wheat bread and more polished rice is growing, and beri-beri increased slightly among the low income groups. For the other economic groups, consumption of livestock and vegetables have increased rapidly during the last few years (Jones, 1965). In some countries, striking reduction in the incidence of beri-beri has been achieved with rice enrichment programs (for instance, in the Philippines (Salcedo et al., 1950) where there was a serious problem some years ago). This disease has affected children and infants in a few areas only. In addition to beri-beri, ariboflavinosis, goitre, anemia, and vitamin A deficiencies are relevant in this part of the world. Because of the infrequent consumption of dairy products, vitamin A and calcium intakes are very low. A great proportion of vitamin A is derived from green vegetables and fruits, but carotenes are not always beta-carotene. Calcium intake is at its lowest in the Philippines and other similar countries. However, the use of whole small fish or shells may provide more calcium than is suspected. In terms of quantity and in relation to the people's body size protein intake, may be adequate; but due to the lack of animal products some essential amino acids may be present in very little amounts. Vitamin C sources are abundant in the whole region.

A few countries were selected to illustrate the combination of foods in the diets of the different areas of the Far East (Fig. 1; Table 1). For each country, a list of the most common products are given according to the frequency with which they are used.

4.2. COUNTRIES OF THE NEAR EAST

From Pakistan to Lebanon and from Turkey to the southernmost

TABLE 1 FAR EASTERN COUNTRIES

Pakistan (US ICNND 1956b)		Thailand (US ICNND 1962a)		Philippines (Quiogue, 1966a, b)		Taiwan (FAO, 1966)	
Food	g/person/day	Food	g/person/day	Food	g/person/day	Food	g/person/day
Rice	505	Rice	440	Rice	423	Rice	371
Wheat	18	Cassava	3	Sweet potato	326	Wheat	60
Potatoes	50	Sweet potato	6	Sugar	19	Sweet potato	157
Sugar	7	String beans	8	Beans	31	Sugar	26
Chickpeas and other pulses	25	Bamboo shoots	7	Cabbage	23	Peanuts	11
Vegetables	102	Chinese cabbage	14	Green vegetables	49	Soya	49
Fruits	10	Cucumber	5	Banana+		Vegetables	65
Meats	6	Green vegetables	9	Guava +		Banana	13
Fish	32	Peppers	4	Papaya+		Citrus	11
Milk	15	Fruits	6	Pineapple	11	Pineapple	21
Ghee	1	Beef	8	Chicken	1	Pork	38
Seed oil	6	Chicken	7	Pork	6	Fish	63
		Frog	5	Eggs	1	Snails	4
		Eggs	4	Fish	9	Lard	5
		Fish	39	Snails	9	Oils	8
		Coconut products	18	Fats	4		
				Rice wine	27		

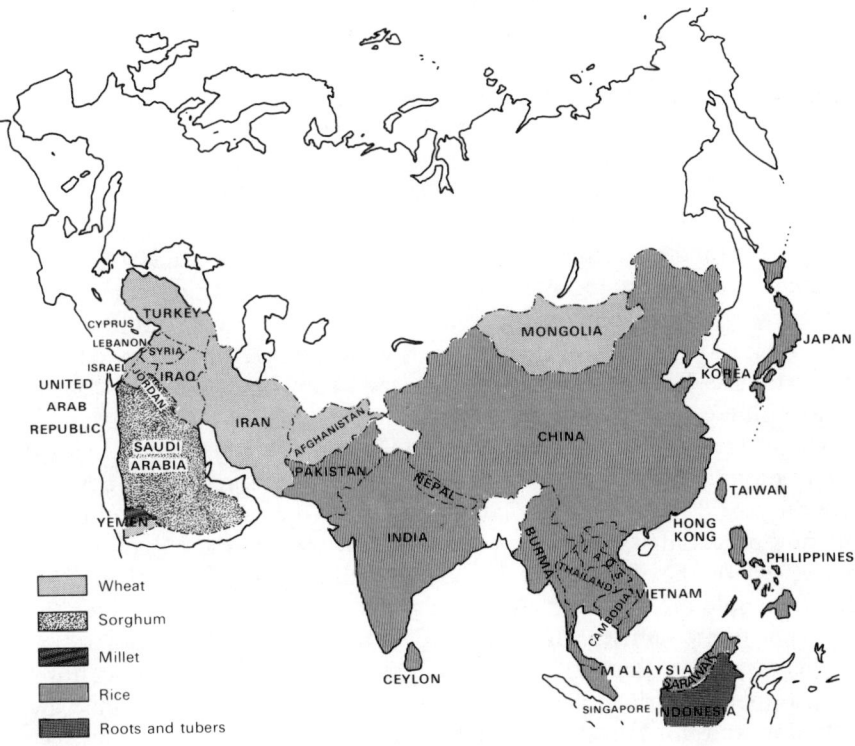

Arab countries, wheat has been the basic food item since the great legendary civilizations appeared in the eastern part of Asia. At present it is still the most important agricultural product used in the preparation of the universal daily bread consumed by the people of the Near East. To the north, the winters are very cold in the mountainous areas of Afghanistan, Iran, or Syria, and the otherwise dry soil absorbs sufficient humidity from the spring rivers to provide appropriate conditions for the cultivation of wheat and barley (US ICNND, 1956a). The tropical belt in these countries, where hot climates and low rainfall prevail during the summer, includes arid stretches—veritable desert areas—which force the inhabitants to use the land surrounding the oases or the fertile terrain near the lakes with the utmost efficiency. In these privileged spots they cultivate fruits and vegetables, which constitute the second most important product of the Near East, they are grown not only for the family diets, but also as a means of obtaining cash. Yemen and its neighboring areas make up the only portion of the Near East with really fertile soil, and production of fruits and vegetables is abundant. In the dry areas of Iran, Iraq, Syria, and Saudi-Arabia, the tribes are forced into a nomadic existence by the need to move from lands where the soil is quickly depleted to others with more appropriate conditions for their farming. Furthermore, they do not follow any system for enriching the soil. They keep animals, like sheep, goats, or camels, for food or transportation, but manure is used for fuel. The most common fruit cultivated near the oases is the date, which constitutes the growers' main source of income. In addition to wheat and barley, they may grow some millet, corn, and coffee, as well as oily seeds for domestic use. Rice is also cultivated in the swamplands near the coastal areas of these countries, mainly in Iraq.

The existence of petroleum in certain sections of this region has led the Food and Agriculture Organization (FAO) economists, for descriptive purposes, to divide these countries into two groups; one comprises the non-oil countries, including Afghanistan, Jordan, the Lebanon, and Syria, where the economy relies on agriculture and more than 70% of the people are involved in farming. The second group includes the oil-exporting countries, for instance Iran, Iraq, and Saudi-Arabia. In this case, more than 50% of the people are still engaged in agriculture. Iraq, Iran, and Syria are considered the main cereal producers, while the Lebanon and Jordan are the fruit growers. In all these countries, the raising of livestock has been an important activity, but production is not sufficient, even for local needs. Cotton is the most important cash product, and it accounts for more than half of the total agricultural exportation. The raising of sheep and goats represents the main activity in livestock production; they provide milk and also skins as raw material for the local industries. Although some members of the second group are rich from oil exploitation, Iraq and Iran must be considered poor, as the standard of living of most of their inhabitants is very low. On the other hand, the Lebanon, one of the non-oil countries where 50% of the people farm and the rest are engaged in trading and industry, is better off economically than any other Arab country (US ICNND, 1962b).

The basic diet in the entire region, where wheat is the staple food, includes also some barley, and small amounts of corn and rice, which increase caloric intake. The protein from these cereals is supplemented by the consumption of pulses and nuts, milk and meat from goats, camels, and fish. Fruits and vegetables are consumed very frequently where they are available like the Lebanon or Iran, but during winter those products are relatively rare in the diets. The most common fruits are dates, citrus fruit, grapes, apricots, peaches, figs, bananas; and, among the vegetables, tomatoes, beets, chard, lettuce, or cabbage. Olive oil in large amounts is almost universally used for cooking; ghee is also used very frequently. In addition to olives, the most important oily seeds are cottonseed, sesame, almonds, and peanuts. The consumption of sugar is high in these countries, in tea, coffee, or in sweets. Sugar cane is imported, but sugar beet is grown locally and it is also becoming an important article for exportation. There is a certain amount of poultry raising in all these countries, but in Israel, which is a special case, barnyard fowl provide the main animal protein source, amounting to twice the quantity of any other meat in the diet (Bavly, 1966). In this country, the consumption of fruits and vegetables is high owing to their great availability. Nevertheless, a considerable percentage of the fruit produced, for instance dates, raisins, apricots or figs, is dried or preserved in pickles for exportation. This kind of processing constitutes a very important industry in these countries.

Where cows are available, most of the milk is converted into different kinds of cheese, or into yoghurt and sour cream, both very popular. In the poor areas, the basic diet is reduced to large amounts of bread, some pulses, or fish and dates. In those areas, each family uses from 2 to 4 kg, approximately, of wheat flour per day. Certain regions are very dry and, lacking food and water for goats and sheep, their impoverished inhabitants are able to consume neither meat nor milk each day, their diet being thus limited to a small amount of pulses or nuts. To complement these diets, sugar is added to different kinds of leafy teas, taken with great frequency. On the other hand, city diets include a great variety of vegetables and fruits, less wheat bread, different kinds of cheese, and the meat of sheep, goats, mutton, or beef. In the coastal area surrounding the Caspian Sea, many products, like maize, tea, citrus fruit, figs, olives, and grapes, are grown. They also cultivate oily seeds, like sesame, flax, olives, and nuts. The production of sugar from beets is also very important. Onions are grown in abundance in this area; they are used in many local dishes and they are exported to Europe. Cheese, butter, or yoghurt appear in the daily diets, and lamb and mutton are used more than goat meat. The carpet weaving industry, well known throughout the world, is responsible for the fact that goats and sheep are neglected as meat sources while their skins and wool are considered all-important.

Compared to other underprivileged parts of the world, the Near

Eastern countries have better diets, and judging by the results of food consumption studies at least, the caloric and protein needs of the people are covered in adequate amounts. Low intake of food from animal origin appears only in some countries, and it represents a serious problem mainly in dry areas and among nomadic groups. The amounts in which milk from goats, camels, or cows, is consumed in the form of yoghurt, cheese, or cream, are not sufficient to meet the requirements for calcium, vitamin A, or riboflavin in low-income groups. Therefore, deficiency of those nutrients is revealed by surveys of those countries. Fruits and vegetables, abundant in Iran and the southernmost tip of the Arabian peninsula, may be short in other areas, and as they are sources of vitamins A and C, a deficiency of those vitamins may appear among the poorer groups. Some consumption of pulses or nuts increases protein intake in poverty-stricken areas, but greater amounts may be available to families

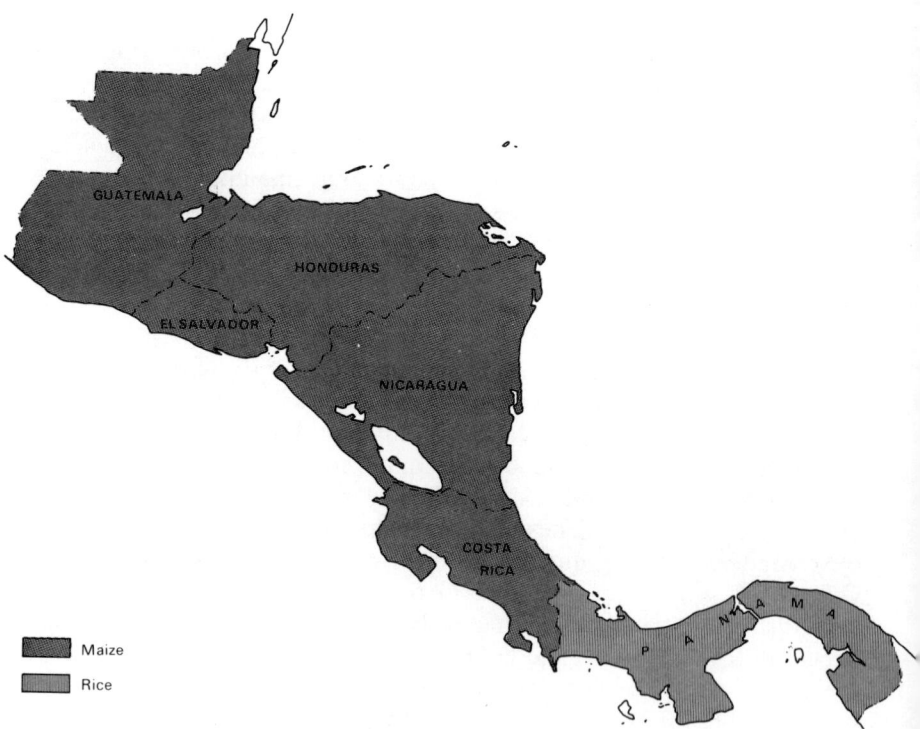

TABLE 2 NEAR EASTERN COUNTRIES

Lebanon (Cowan et al., 1964; US ICNND 1962b)		Iran (FAO, 1966)		Iraq (Demarchi, 1962; FAO 1966)		Israel (Bavly, 1966)	
Food	g/person/day	Food	g/person/day	Food	g/person/day	Food	g/person/day
Wheat	387	Wheat	308	Wheat	259	Wheat	250
Burghul + rice	90	Barley	9	Barley	46	Tubers	69
Potato	65	Rice	59	Rice	47	Sugar	60
Sugar	26	Sugar	52	Sugar	81	Carrot	18
Chickpeas + lentils	30	Dry beans	8	Broad beans	5	Cucumber	25
Leafy greens + yellow vegetables	114	Nuts	3	Dry beans	3	Onion	18
		Oil seeds	11	Lentils	4	Tomato paste	62
Citrus	55	Fresh vegetables	22	Cucumber	18	Apples	39
Olives	19	Dates	16	Onion	30	Citrus	127
Beef + mutton	41	Grapes	16	Tomato	62	Melon	11
Milk + yoghurt (laban)	157	Melon	45	Apples	14	Plums	11
		Beef	9	Dates	50	Poultry	37
		Mutton	22	Grapes	17	Eggs	49
		Cheese	10	Melon	21	Fish	26
		Curdled milk	94	Pommes-granates	11	Cheese	22
		Milk	35	Beef + veal	14	Sour cream	15
		Tea	2	Goat	6	Milk	175
				Lamb + mutton	14	Margarine	17
				Cow's milk	72	Oil	21
				Goat's milk	29		
				Sheep's milk	81		
				Oil	7		

with little access to animal protein. The consumption of fat, an important item in these diets, supplies about 12% of the calorie intake, mainly from olive oil, ghee, and sesame oil. With urbanization, the consumption of more sugar and soft drinks may diminish that of other important calorie sources. There is also a high incidence of anemia, perhaps due to iron deficiency brought about by parasitic infestations, which are very common in these countries. Severe winters in some areas produce rickets in infants owing to vitamin D deficiency; lack of calcium-rich foods is responsible for osteomalacia in pregnant and lactating women.

Certain countries were selected in order to illustrate the combination of foods in the diets of the different areas of the Near East (Fig. 2; Table 2). For each country, a list of the most common products is given according to the frequency in which these articles are used.

4.3. AFRICAN COUNTRIES

The vast territory of the African continent, divided into many different countries and mostly colonized by Europeans, offers a very heterogeneous picture in regard to food patterns and behavior. The diets are similar to those of certain Asiatic civilizations, except when environmental conditions determine the adoption of products from other continents. In Egypt, the northern parts of Ethiopia and the Sudan, wheat is the staple food owing not only to the influence of the Arabic countries but to similarities in climate and type of soil. America has provided Africa with certain products, like manioc (cassava), sweet potatoes, cacao, beans, leguminous seeds, tomatoes, and potatoes, all of which adapted well to the tropical areas of Africa (Aylward, 1966). Some of these products have been incorporated into the diets of different groups. In general food patterns in these countries rely greatly on the indigenous crops and animals available in each locality. This great dependence on the local food product generates changes on the staple food; crops abundant during one season result in great scarcity during the following one, and diets have to be supplemented by other different crops. In the northern part of Nigeria, Ghana (Collis, et al., 1962; Perisse, 1966) or Dahomey, millet, sorghum, and maize are the staple food, while in the southern part, where climate is hot and humid, yams or cassava constitute the basis of the diets.

This kind of subsistence area whose diet is based on roots, is also observed in the Congo or in the Guinea coast where yams, manioc, taro, and sweet potatoes appear daily on the tables of the families.

The whole continent of Africa has a great variation in physical environment and also in the ethnological structure of the population, presenting dramatic contrasts in the backgrounds, histories, and ways of life of the different societies. After many years of being economically and politically dependent on European countries, the new states are now rapidly emerging and are developing in many different ways with an intensive interchange with the rest of the world.

Geographically Africa falls into two distinct major divisions: North Africa which presents similarities with the Mediterranean countries and Africa south of the Sahara which includes tropical Africa and the rest of the countries which have become independent from Europe relatively recently. Compared with the other continents, Africa is geologically and topographically uniform. The litoral line around the continent is very regular, and the whole continent, except for the extreme northwest and extreme south, consists of one vast rigid block where bays or gulfs on which to build seaports are almost nonexistent. Along the coastal line the terrain rises to great elevations, beyond which are the plains. Inland transportation from the sea is almost impossible in many areas, and few rivers can be used for purpose of communication. For a long time the isolation of many African groups was due to the absence of roads. Immigrants into the continent were unable to endure the climate, and the inaccessibility of many regions has kept them away for centuries. There is an extensive plateau surface in east Africa that can be traced from the Dead Sea through Ethiopia to the valley of the Shire River in the south, and there are some parts of greater elevations. On the other hand, in the same area there is a vast depression in the land where the main lakes such as Rudolph, Naivasha, Natron, Tanganyka, Edward, and Albert are found. There are relatively few lowlands in Africa except for two basins in the western Sahara, so the bulk of the continent consists of a plateau with some marked differences between the areas north and south of the equator.

The African climate is mild to the north, near the Mediterranean, but the equator runs practically through the heart of the continent so that a great part of it is tropical. A vast area of dry, hot wasteland, the Sahara Desert, stretches across the entire continent from the Atlantic Ocean to the Red Sea. Most of intertropical Africa is hot throughout the year with relatively small changes in temperatures between the seasons, but the effect of the plateau upon the temperatures modifies the equatorial conditions. Rainfall is the most significant element also to change the climate and temperature. There is a wide range from the vast deserts of the Sahara, where there is no rainfall at any time in the year, to the very extensive area within the tropics where the rainfall averages are more than 80 inches annually. Intertropical Africa may be sectioned into different parallel zones running from north to south. The first two zones including part of the Sahara and "sub-Sahara" deserts, have scarce rainfall, and agriculture is possible only around the small fertile places where there is some water. Dates, wheat, and some leguminous seeds are grown there. The wandering populations consume their own products, including milk, from the animals they raise (Yousif, 1967). Toward the south, agriculture becomes more sedentary, and people lose their nomadic characteristics. There is a dense equatorial forest which is becoming important from the economic point of view due to the exploitation of hardwoods which has been increased with the improving of communications in countries such as Ghana, Nigeria, and the Ivory Coast.

According to their use of the land, farmers in Africa may be divided into cultivators and pastoralists; the latter have to move from place to place searching for food or water as the needs of their animals demand. They are forced, therefore, to use extensive areas especially when the dry season is long and intense, while the cultivators are directly dependent upon the climate and soil conditions of their own land. There still prevails a simple primitive system of shifting cultivation farming after the burning of fresh bushes. Where there is sufficient land, soils are more fertile, and where animal manure is available for the fields, a most permanent cultivation exists. In those areas it is possible to cultivate groundnuts like in the northern part of Nigeria or cocoa like in Ghana, or coffee in the farms of the Chaga tribe.

Even though there are large numbers of livestock in the different parts of Africa, few Africans depend upon their cattle for food, and among some tribes are those who only drink milk or use the blood of the animals instead of the meat. In many parts of Africa the possession of animals is regarded as indication of wealth, and the exchange of the animals is an essential part of many social events. Consequently, the quantity of cattle is more important than its quality, and in many areas the land has to support more livestock than it should because of the overgrassing and the decrease of water supply. Nevertheless, at present there are some African tribes who try to improve their methods of rearing the animals, increasing the markets for meat and milk as well as hides and skins, especially in South Africa, Southern Rhodesia, and Kenya.

As was mentioned, there are many racial types in Africa, but these could be divided into two indigenous groups: the Bushmanoid types, who are short and whose skins are light brown, and the Negroid people. In the southern part of the Sahara and extending to Ethiopia and Somalia, people have some Caucasian features but generally dark skin. North Africans are almost of Caucasian extraction—Arabs or some European groups. Due to the varied racial types there are great differences between the customs and the diets of the people. Some groups occasionally hunt and gather wild plant food like the Bushmen of the Kalahari Desert. Several people along the West coast primarily live by fishing rivers or lakes, as in the upper part of the Niger or in the Congo, but the great majority of Africans depend upon their agriculture products, especially where rainfall is sufficient during 6 months of the year.

People in East Africa, which includes Somalia, Ethiopia, Kenya and Uganda, subsist upon the basic products of their diets, that is to say maize and sorghum. Most of the grains in these countries are ground in mills to produce flour, which is cooked into a thick and heavy porridge, which becomes the bread of these people, providing most of the caloric intake. In the other areas like the Congo or on the Guinea coast, diets are based on roots like yams, manioc, taro, and sweet potatoes which appear daily, providing most of the caloric intake. In eastern and central African countries, besides the grains, there is a production of oily seeds, even though consumption of fat is low in rural areas. In the southern part of Africa, which is the principal zone for the exploitation of minerals, agriculture is very important and the rainfall is sufficient for the production of various crops such as corn, beans, pumpkins, and potatoes. In this area there are vast grasslands for the raising of cattle or sheep (Abramson, et al., 1960; Abramson, 1961). In urban areas of all these countries some imported foods—such as sugar and wheat flour—are becoming very important as sources of calories.

The most remarkable feature of the African diet is the modification which takes place according to the latitude of each zone. As a whole it is basically a cereal diet with the exception of what is consumed in the lowlands. For instance, in the river valley of Senegal 77% of calories are derived from cereals and about 2% from pulses, while in Bouake Ivory Coast 15% comes from cereals and leguminous seeds, but nearly 80% from tubers and plantains. From the equatorial zone to the tropical dry zone the amount of cereals increases while tubers and plantains are consumed in small quantities. The leguminous seeds are also important, but they are consumed in small quantities. In the eastern countries such as Ethiopia or Kenya, where the altitude favors the cultivation of all kind of grains, consumption of leguminous seeds is higher. In countries like Uganda and Ruanda the consumption of leguminous seeds is as high as 400 grams per person per day, providing most of the calories in the diets of these people.

The topography of these countries is so irregular that one of them may encompass high mountains or plateaus with elevations of 6000 to 10,000 ft above sea level, and the corresponding mild climates, together with a hot lowland area including jungles and dry desert regions. In the zones with high altitudes, wheat, barley, or teff, and different kinds of beans are abundant; in the warmer zones sorghum, maize, or cotton, some fruits, and oily seeds are grown; in the hot and very humid areas, corn, sugar cane, and plantains are cultivated.

Ethiopia is unique in growing the cereal called teff (US ICNND, 1959b), which is its basic food. The preparation of teff as the daily bread is typical of the treatment used in different parts of Africa for other cereals. It is milled into flour, then soaked in water and fermented for several days until finally it is baked in a large clay dish in the form of a large, round, and very thin pancake, called "injera". Millet, sorghum, and maize are also used to prepare "injera". Besides cereals, Ethiopia produces all kinds of pulses, like lentils, chickpeas, dry peas, peanuts, beans, and a great variety of oily seeds like "nuge" (Niger seed), sesame seed, cottonseed, linseed, rape seed, safflower, and flax. The oil extracted industrially from these seeds is consumed locally as well as exported.

Vegetables are grown in the African countries, even though their consumption is low in that continent, except the green leaves of cassava or sweet potatoes which are important in the diets of certain intertropical countries. During the last few years there has been some garden development in the cultivation of vegetables for the urban centers. Certain groups of Europeans settlers have introduced the cultivation of carrots, broccoli, beets, artichokes, cauliflower, and other vegetables, and also of fruits like peaches, pineapples, plums, apples, and even grapes in some north-eastern areas.

In some countries of the west coast, rice is grown extensively, and is the staple food in Sierra Leone (Thomas, 1972). Yields from these lowlands are large, about 930 kg per acre. Cassava is widely consumed next to rice, especially during the hungry months. It is cheaper than rice and available all the year around. These countries also use roasted groundnuts, sometimes mixed with sugar. In this area fish is used in small amounts for the preparation of the sauces and is cheaper than meat, but fresh fish is distributed in several markets where there are refrigeration facilities, but the price is very high. The consumption of vegetables is also low and they are used to prepare sauces, which may be mixed with oil, salt, and pepper. The most common vegetables are cassava leaves, sesame leaves, or spinachs. In this area sesame seed is grown not only for domestic use, but also for export; the small amount consumed is fermented to prepare sauces. Fish is available in some coastal areas in this continent and is generally well accepted by the people, mainly in the form of dry fish. People living inland are not able to obtain fish or any other marine product except in regions around the lakes or near the rivers. In the western area, large quantities of fish are produced for local consumption and also for exportation (Sai, 1969).

Meat production is very low because cattle suffer from many diseases and there is no local method for drying or conserving the meat, as in other parts of Africa. Consequently, the consumption of meat is low, as in most of African countries, appearing in the diets sporadically and usually associated with family or social festivities. High prices and limited availability of beef is due to several factors. Even though cattle is important, to sell it as food it is necessary to walk hundreds of miles to market centers. On the other hand, goats and sheep are very common in many parts of Africa, and people are very partial to their meat. It may be due to several factors, as Aylward (1966) pointed out: "Their relatively low cost makes them suitable for a family feast; their small size ensures that there is no problem of long term storage of meat." In addition, possession of those animals is also regarded as a sign of wealth. Pork is also consumed in certain areas, although not by the Moslem groups; in general, however, its consumption is very low. Among the Ethiopians and Egyptians who belong to the Coptic Church, animal products disappear from the diets during the long Lenten fasting periods.

Milk consumption is low in all African countries except for the nomadic groups of the deserts who drink camel or goat milk in addition to cow's milk. There is no consumption of cheese except among certain nomadic groups; only butter and ghee appear in the diets of different groups in the eastern part of Africa. In urban and semiurban areas the consumption of meat and milk is higher and more frequent. In Nigeria fresh milk is used abundantly by the pastoral tribes and the owners of the farms near Lake Chad, but milk is usually kept until it is sour. A considerable amount of canned milk is consumed in southern Africa, but only among urban families. In Sierra Leone some groups produce milk to make ghee which is eaten with rice and sour milk, and sometimes this food is given to the small children.

In many villages of these countries families raise their own chickens, but the consumption of eggs is very low. They sell the eggs because they have good market prices and, of course, there is more consumption of chicken and eggs in the towns among urban families. Guinea fowls are the most common animals that the families keep, but in many cases each family has only few animals.

In general, African communities subsisting upon agriculture, where they process and consume their own products, are able to function with a minimum of available cash (Quin, 1964). Nevertheless, cash is certainly beginning to have a very marked influence on nutrition in this Continent. All major food movements tend to be into large urban centers to ensure rapid cash. The quality of food consumed in the towns is very much influenced by the cash available in the home for food. The urban poor groups may be in the worst position because they need to buy all their foods and the quantity and quality of these is dictated by what other expenditures they have to make.

The food preparation process at the domestic level only requires the use of pestle and mortar for the manual grinding of grains. Recently, however, all African countries have introduced mills to convert the grains into flour, thus reducing to a great extent the amount of time and energy that the African women used to dedicate to processing the grains. Manioc, on the other hand, needs a great deal of processing before it is fit for human consumption. For the removal of hydrogen cyanide, the classical method followed by Africans consists of grating the manioc and then exposing it to air for a long time until it is ready for conversion into flour.

Cooking in most of the towns is not a complicated process, and usually involves boiling the different kinds of flours from starchy roots or cereal products or boiling the meat and vegetables together. Tubers and plantains are baked and mashed, and grains may be toasted as a feast dish. On the other hand, the preparation of local beverages, which are common to all African countries, needs a long and complicated process. Such is the case of "tala" in Ethiopia, beer in the Congo, which is prepared from bananas or manioc flour, wines from palms in the West countries, as well as all kinds of alcoholic beverages from cereals. Of late, European influence in the urban areas has led to the consumption of more wheat bread or rolls, white sugar, and sweets; and the establishment of slaughterhouses in the main cities has enabled their dwellers to purchase meat for their meals.

An assessment of the adequacy of calorie and nutrient intake in the

African people, would require a more complete study because of the great differences among the tribes and locations with respect to body size, climate, altitude, and type of working activity. In most cases, caloric and protein needs are probably met where cereal is the basic food. Where roots or tubers constitute the basic food, protein–calorie intake is so low that great deficiencies are bound to afflict the populations. In the countries with tropical areas and high altitudes, consumption of leguminous seeds, in combination with cereals, improves the quality of the proteins, which is also true of the coastal area, where fish is available. Where roots or tubers are consumed and no animal products are available, very serious deficiencies may be taken for granted, mainly among the small children. Where milk is available no calcium deficiencies are encountered; but in the rest of Africa, calcium levels reported in different surveys show deficiencies in many groups. The most serious deficiency brought to light by the surveys is in vitamin A intake, when neither milk nor eggs are consumed, and green vegetables are not important in the diets. Iron deficiencies are widespread in many African areas where requirements are extremely high owing to parasitic infestations. Among special groups, however, hemosiderosis has been found, but nutritional anemia is likely to be found in the same areas. All these deficiencies increase during the dry season in areas where production of cereals is limited to one seasonal crop. In the tropical humid zones, where the basic diet relies on tubers and roots, seasonal variations are less influential because these products are available all the year around. The consumption of animal products may change according to the periods or seasons in which ceremonies or festivities are celebrated. In industrial areas, consumption increases during certain periods when more cash is available, thus the demand for these products does not follow a seasonal fluctuation. Where fish is consumed, changes may also depend upon exportation, and sometimes there is a month-to-month fluctuation. In some eastern countries, or among the Moslem groups, intake levels decrease markedly during Lent because no animal products can be consumed then. In Ethiopia, for instance, butter is used for cooking at all times, except for those two months when animal products should not be consumed. During this period the dry red pepper, very rich in beta-carotene, constitutes almost the sole source of vitamin A in the diets. The consumption of vitamins of the B-complex among the adults, mainly the men, is probably improved by their daily drinking of large quantities of fermented beverages.

Cultural aspects in regard to the family life are important in the economy of the people and also in the consumption of food. The large extended family is still the rule with many hands available for farm work, but usually there are many children who are nonproductive elements, which affect the food intake. In Africa about 60% of the population is rural; nevertheless, some of the major cities are growing very rapidly. In few societies monogamy is the usual norm and sometimes the ideal, but in many other groups polygamy is a general characteristic of several tribes. The secret of the successful polygamous family is the social coexistence of the several wives who share farm work and care for the

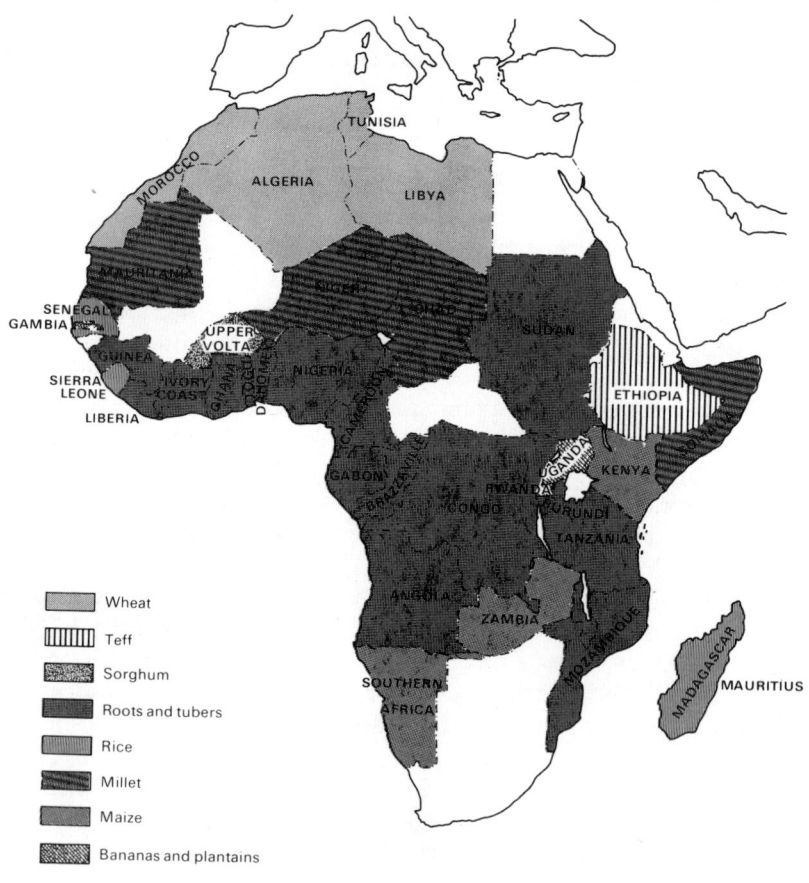

TABLE 3 SOME AFRICAN COUNTRIES

Ethiopia (US ICNND, 1959b)		Libya (US ICNND, 1957b)		Nigeria (Western Region) (US OIR, 1967)		South Africa (FAO, 1966)	
Food	g/person/day	Food	g/person/day	Food	g/person/day	Food	g/person/day
Teff	365	Wheat	583	Maize	117	Maize	318
Barley	152	Macaroni	161	Rice	19	Sorghum	22
Maize	29	Sugar	26	Cassava	86	Wheat	112
Sorghum	45	Beans	45	Taro	33	Potato	34
Wheat	27	Lentils	7	Yam	567	Sugar	72
Potato	4	Onion	22	Cowpea	40	Dry peas	9
Yam	9	Red pepper	10	Locust beans	12	Leafy greens + pumpkin	100
Sugar	4	Tomato paste	42	Melon seeds	3		
Chickpeas	5	Melon	44	Chillies—fresh	30	Citrus	33
Dry peas	12	Plum	42	Leafy greens	29	Beef	84
Lentils	7	Beef + mutton	53	Okra	25	Mutton	25
Onion	100	Fish	7	Plantain	48	Fish	18
Red pepper	3	Evaporated milk	16	Fish	7	Condensed milk	23
Beef + goat	45	Butter	17	Red palm oil	25	Fluid milk	186
Butter	30	Ghee	16	Palm wine	118	Oils	8
Oil	30	Olive oil	27			Kaffir (beer)	76
		Tea	4				

children. They may alternate cooking days or each wife has her own kitchen and her own house, but receives the same treatment and help from the husband. Such a social system works well in indigenous African societies, but with the pressure of foreign missions or colonialist governments, many difficulties exist at present since polygamy leads to a different form of family structure (*Encyclopedia Americana*, 1964).

A few countries were selected to provide an illustration of the combination of foods in the diets of the different areas of Africa (Fig. 3; Table 3). For each country, a list of the most common products is given according to the frequency with which they are used.

4.4. EUROPEAN COUNTRIES

From the Baltic to the Mediterranean, Europe is constantly swept by sea winds that maintain a humid climate over the entire region. The great irregularity of its shorelines has facilitated the opening of seaports throughout the centuries. Several sea inlets are perfect harbours, providing the rest of the world with access to many European countries. There are many rivers that keep the soils fertile, some of them large enough for use in transportation, connecting the principal commercial centers. The mountain ranges across Norway, Sweden, France, and Germany consist only of low hills; but, further south, high-mountain chains traverse Switzerland, France, Spain, Italy, and the east European countries. On the other hand, there is a belt running from France to Russia with no accidental topography, which has greatly favored communication and transportation among the central European countries. Winters are very severe in the north but, in the continental part of Europe, milder climates prevail, and the south, mainly the Mediterranean coastal area, is characterized by a long dry summer. Large sections of Spain, the country with the gravest agricultural problems, are characterized by lack of rainfall and poor soils.

Since Europe has been the point of convergence of all the great civilizations, its food patterns contain some characteristics contributed by the old Asiatic cultures. Selected local products, combined with countless imported items from other continents, mainly America, produce different types of diets. Most of the countries are agricultural, and ideal conditions of soil and climate have helped the people to produce all kinds of selected foods. In countries like Spain (US ICNND, 1958a), Portugal or Italy, more than 30% of the economically active population is engaged in agriculture; in the eastern countries, like Yugoslavia, Bulgaria, and

Rumania, more than 50% of the population is dedicated to this same activity according to the figures given in the *Production Year Book* (FAO, 1967). The economies of all the eastern European countries rely mainly on agriculture, but in England, with its great industrial centers, commerce has predominated for many centuries. In the twentieth century, food production has been greatly increased in order to diminish dependency on colonial supplies. In Germany and England, as well as Poland, the exploitation of mines is the backbone of the economy. At the same time, great industrial advance and the swift development of energy sources, mainly of electricity, have acquired primary importance in the economic structure of both countries. Ireland, England, Germany, and the Baltic countries have been responsible for great advances in cattle raising and the production of meat and milk. The well-known first class dairy products of Denmark, Holland, and Switzerland have required a high degree of technological development in the milk production industry. There are some areas in Germany and the south-eastern countries, where goats, sheep, and hogs are raised to obtain milk and meat. Fishing represents one of the principal industries in many European countries with extensive coasts, like Iceland, the Baltic countries, France, and Spain. In Norway, Sweden, and Finland, fish and marine products are produced in large quantities and processed for exportation to all parts of the world.

In all European countries, the main crop cultivated for food on a large scale is wheat, followed by other cereals like rye, barley, oats, maize, and some rice in the Mediterranean area. Second in importance are potatoes and sugar beets. France, Spain, Italy, and Greece are highly specialized in the cultivation of grapes for wine and, in the same countries, olives are grown on a large scale for consumption as fruit and for the production of the most popular comestible oil. In Yugoslavia, Bulgaria, and Hungary, grapes are also cultivated for wine production. In Yugoslavia, maize predominates as the main product, but they also grow other cereals, and a great variety of fruits, like plums, apples, or grapes. Italy has increased production of all kinds of vegetables, mainly artichokes, tomatoes, onions, peppers, eggplants, and lettuces. Other items grown in these countries, mainly in the south, are leguminous seeds, like lentils, broad beans, chickpeas, white beans, and also oily seeds. In the south-eastern countries, where cattle is raised only on a small scale, goats and sheep provide milk, but people prefer to consume it as yoghurt or cheese (US ICNND, 1958b). Yoghurt is made by boiling milk to reduce its water content, then cooling and fermenting it by means of a bacterium. It can be preserved for a long time if kept in covered containers. The poultry industry is well developed in many of the European countries, as this kind of meat is popular in many areas. Furthermore, animal feeds are highly industrialized.

The geographical location of each European country has a great deal of influence on its food pattern in spite of the generalized availability of most existing food products in large quantities. For instance, in Norway, Sweden, and Finland, people are great consumers of fish and marine products. Exploitation of mines and forestry are the main industries in these countries, and, in addition to the heavy work that men have to put into these activities, they must endure very low temperatures, They require concentrated caloric sources in their diets, and thus have to consume large quantities of fats and cereals or potatoes. For the Lapps in Sweden who are still nomadic, reindeer is the main source of meat (Mellbin, 1962). In Great Britain and other highly industrialized countries, people are able to consume adequate amounts of beef and fish, milk and milk products, eggs, and cereals, from the abundant national supplies. In addition, they are able to import fruits, vegetables, coffee, tea, and all kinds of meat in large amounts to supply the local markets. In general, all the northern countries of Europe produce enough milk, but in the south and west, consumption of milk and milk products is lower. Less milk and meat have caused the people in these areas to evolve a different food pattern from the one existing in the neighboring countries. The Spaniards consume great quantities of leguminous seeds, which come from their African neighbors. Almost all the arable land in Spain is used to grow wheat for bread. The fish supply in this country is sufficient for local demand but, as people prefer it fresh, consumption is low in the inland areas, and a great deal is exported. In the eastern and Mediterranean countries, diets in general are quite monotonous, and whole wheat and rye bread makes up most of their bulk. In rural Greece (Halley, 1946; Miller and Kaumvakali, 1955), for instance, the consumption of bread amounts approximately to a daily portion of 680 g per person. These populations consume some meat from goats, sheep, or cows, prepared in soups or stews and combined with vegetables like tomatoes, onions, or green leaves. During the spring they have fruits like melons, peaches, or strawberries, but the main dishes are prepared with leguminous seeds like lentils or chickpeas and combined with rice. Yoghurt is used very often to prepare local dishes.

Even in the southern countries of Europe, the intake levels surveyed do not show marked dietary deficiencies, except during the war periods.

Only in the immigrant groups of the northern countries, for instance in Great Britain, are certain nutrients. mainly vitamins A, D, and C, calcium and iron, deficient in their diets (Hollingsworth, 1955). In general, very few sources of iron appear in diets of those groups, but enrichment programs have partially solved this problem.

In some European countries, depending to a great extent on the world market, the food supply may change from year to year, and this in turn will influence food patterns. For instance, in 1961 fresh milk and eggs increased in the United Kingdom, while fish and wheat flour dropped. The meat supply rose because of an increase in home production of beef, lamb, and poultry; on the other hand, there was a decrease in margarine, lard, and other imported fats. There was a slight increment in potatoes in comparison with the previous year, but fresh vegetables, fruits, and leguminous seeds declined.

In countries like the Netherlands, Germany, Austria, and the United Kingdom, a considerable industrialization has been developed, producing great migration of the rural population to the cities, and mechanization of agriculture has become necessary. The diets of the rural people in these countries tend to be more conservative using the same natural local products, but the food pattern of the city people has undergone great changes. An overall decline in the consumption of cereals and a steep increase in sugar consumption has been observed in most of the eastern countries. In the Netherlands the consumption of high carbohydrate products as potatoes and bread has greatly decreased, while margarine has increased significantly. The consumption of fruits and vegetables has not changed, but citrus fruits are consumed in double amounts as compared to the pre-war periods. In Sweden, also, consumption of flour and potatoes has declined, and there is greater consumption of milk, meat, fats, eggs, vegetables, and fruits. In the United Kingdom, besides those changes in the food patterns in regard to the increase of milk, cheese, meat, eggs, and sugar consumption, another significant change has occurred which consists of a greater consumption of manufactured foods (Hollingsworth, 1955). Those food products are more expensive as nutrient sources, compared with natural foods, but they relieve the housewives of a long, cooking process.

In summary, for most of the European countries the post-war food patterns have changed toward a great improvement in the nutrient intake of the people, using more liquid or processed milk, butter, or margarine, and fresh or canned fruits and vegetables. The two main nutritional findings in many of these countries are, first, that the young generation has shown accelerated growth, and, second, blood levels of vitamin A in all groups have increased mainly among children with the vitaminization of margarine. Nevertheless, there are still some rural areas and low social groups in the cities where consumption of milk is low or subjected to seasonal variations because distribution or manufacturing of milk products is not organized or low consumption of vegetables and fruits resulting in low intakes of iron and vitamin C.

Food Consumption: Levels and Patterns Variation 101

TABLE 4 EUROPEAN COUNTRIES

Norway (Michell and Joffe, 1944; FAO, 1966)		Denmark (FAO, 1966)		Spain (FAO, 1966)		Italy (Michell and Joffe, 1944; FAO, 1966)		Rumania (Michell and Joffe, 1944; FAO, 1966)	
Food	g/person/day	Food	g/person/day	Food	g/person/day	Food	g/person/day	Food	g/person/day
Wheat	172	Wheat	118	Wheat	286	Macaroni +		Wheat	340
Rye	30	Rye	72	Potato	315	Wheat	331	Maize	191
Oats	4	Oats	13	Sugar	51	Potato	138	Potato	194
Potato	245	Potato	306	Beans +		Sugar	63	Sugar	35
Sugar	110	Sugar	135	Chickpeas +		Chickpeas	15	White beans	27
Carrot +		Brussels +		Lentils	22	Lettuce +		Cabbage	60
Cabbage +		Cabbage +		Lettuce +		Onion +		Onion	27
Tomato	92	Tomato	182	Peppers +		Peppers	380	Pimientos	14
Berries	17	Beef	49	Tomato	356	Citrus	38	Tomato	54
Beef	35	Pork	103	Citrus	59	Pears + others	200	Turnip	15
Pork	42	Fish	44	Olives	4	Beef	41	Plum	8
Eggs	24	Cheese	24	Peaches + others	173	Pork	19	Apple + others	92
Fish	111	Milk	394	Beef	17	Fish	20	Goat meat +	
Cheese	22	Butter	24	Fish	72	Cheese	21	Sheep meat	11
Milk	481	Oils	35	Olive oil	43	Olive oil	24	Pork	46
Butter	9	Beer	200	Wines	160	Wines	303	Veal	24
Vegetable oil	52							Milk	258
								Oils	22

To illustrate the combination of foods that appear in typical diets, some of the European countries were selected (Fig. 4; Table 4). A list of foods is presented for each country and given according to frequency with which they appear in the daily diets.

4.5. AMERICAN COUNTRIES

The tropics crossing the American continent, which extends from the Arctic to Antarctic, make three natural divisions: North, Central, and South America. The three regions are very different, not only geographically but culturally and socioeconomically.

North America, with Alaska, Canada, and the United States, encompasses some of the coldest places in the world. Near the Arctic there are regions where the soil is sterile, bare of vegetation, and where only a few Eskimos live by trapping. The winters are long, from November to May, and the rain falls during spring and summer. There are also great extensions covered with forests, very important economically as a source of many kinds of woods. The ethnic group living in the Arctic zone consists of Indians and Eskimos, and their culture has been based on hunting and fishing, from which they obtain food, clothing, and fuel (Sinclair, 1953). Communication is either by boat, through the many rivers and lakes, or by dog sled during the winter. During that season, they move north for trapping and they spend their summers fishing or working temporarily in the cities. The Indians live mainly near the forest in the mountainous area, where they also hunt for a living. The families living near the coastal area hunt seals and utilize their skins for certain household uses, their meat for food, and their fat for cooking.

The basic items in the diets among the Eskimos are meats from marine animals or from small furred animals, and during the spring the meat of inland animals like the caribou, wolf, or bear. In addition to meat they consume different kinds of berries, algae, and nuts during certain seasons. Since the time when white men invaded the Arctic zone, the food habits of Indians and Eskimos have changed a good deal. At present, the stores provide them with different products, like cereals, flours, rice, sugar, hydrogenated fats, sweets, milk, coffee, tea, and canned vegetables and fruits. Sometimes they can get fresh vegetables from countries farther to the south, for instance, onions, potatoes, carrots or citrus fruits, apples, and peaches; but this type of consumption is limited to a small group of families. The average calorie intake of the Eskimo males is below the recommended allowances, around 1855 calories; and their protein intake is higher than the allowances, almost 130 grams daily from meat and fish. There is a great variation in the individual mean intakes because the food supply fluctuates greatly from season to season. At present, about 30% of the total calories comes from fat, owing to the introduction of sugar and starchy products (US ICNND, 1959a). Before the white man came, the percentage was about 75% of calories from fat. Other changes have been observed in their food habits. The consumption of Arctic Ground Willow leaves and different kinds of berries and the organs of game animals has almost disappeared, with the consequent onset of serious dietary deficiencies. Mothers have left off breast-feeding their children for prolonged periods, while, at the same time, their beliefs forbid the feeding of meat at an early age. Thus, the weanling is left at the mercy of a starchy diet. Nevertheless, welfare programs now cover a great majority of children, improving their diets with the distribution of milk, vitamins, and minerals.

In Canada there are great areas of fertile soil, where climate and local conditions offer an adequate environment for the cultivation of cereals like wheat, oats, rye, barley, and buckwheat, making that country the second largest wheat exporter in the whole world. In the south, cattle raising has advanced to the point where meat and milk are produced in abundance, both for local consumption and for exportation. Fishing is a well developed industry on the Atlantic and Pacific coasts, as well as in the great lakes. The economy in this country is also amply supported by its natural resources, including considerable quantities of gold, silver, iron, nickel, zinc, and huge petroleum deposits. The production of electric power is also highly developed and is a prime force in the swift development of Canadian industry.

Food practices and nutrient levels in Canada are at present very similar to those found in the United States (Johnson and Feniak, 1965). The principal food item in the diets is meat, followed by enriched wheat bread, potatoes, and milk. Consumption of eggs, fresh vegetables, and fruits is low; but canned foods are reaching all the markets at low prices and are becoming very popular. The main meat is fish, followed by beef, pork, and poultry, and their use or preparation mode varies according to the preferences of people with different European backgrounds. Among the low income groups and immigrants (Roberston, 1962), food intake is not always adequate, and dietary deficiencies are found in certain age groups. For instance, the incidence of rickets in infants among the Italian families has been observed, vitamin D deficiency being responsible. Iron deficiency has also been found in small children. In many groups, teenagers have poor dietary habits and their consumption of milk, vegetables, and fruits is low. In the studies carried out in Ontario (Trenholme and Milne, 1963), a combination of meat, bread, potatoes, and sweets was found to be a common meal pattern among the children. The consumption of eggs, milk, whole grain, vegetables, and fruits, on the other hand, was very low.

The United States, with its vast expanse of territory and great industrial development, is one of the richest and most advanced countries of the world. Nature has endowed this country with a very regular topography, which renders communication and transportation extremely easy for its people. A few mountain ranges in the north east, the west, and along the Pacific coast, form certain accidental divisions. Extensive and fertile plains, irrigated by great lakes and rivers, or by artificial systems make up the rest. The climate in the northern part of the country is characterized by cold winters and very hot summers. In the south, temperatures are milder, and in the south-west certain areas enjoy almost tropical climates. The country has abundant mining riches in the Atlantic coast, petroleum wells in the south, and boundless electric energy from the great lakes and rivers everywhere.

Agriculture has been the main concern of all the national programs, and the production of all foods, aided by a high degree of mechanization, has advanced to an unexpected point. In the first place, meats, milk, and cereals are produced in volumes sufficient to feed the entire population. Leguminous and oily seeds are also grown on a large scale, and many are the industries connected with their processing. Cereals, vegetables, and fruits have been industrialized for broad coverage of domestic needs, and the surplus is such, mainly in cereals, that it is possible to distribute those products all over the world.

In the United States most families eat a variety of foods for their three daily meals, and it was found that, on the average, 50 different food items are consumed during a week (Clark, 1958). Usually, three or four servings of vegetables and fruits, the equivalent of two or three cups of milk, one egg, two or three ounces of meat, poultry or fish, potatoes, and bread, with other grain products, make up the daily food amount corresponding to each person. Seasonal variation in the diets is practically nonexistent because, although some spring products cannot be obtained during other seasons, other similar items with the same nutritive value replace them, or else they are substituted by processed articles. Surveys have shown a few small differences in dietary intake when families from different income levels are compared. It is only possible to find deficient food intake among large families, in which all members are unable to fill the requirements or among small immigrant groups, not yet fully integrated into the country's way of life and economic system. Although some regional variation may be observed in food patterns because certain food preferences persist in special groups, significant differences are present only in the amount of money spent for food (US Dept. of Agriculture, 1968). In the southern states, people with larger families spend less money, consuming more home produced foods. They prepare food more economically and there is less waste; in addition, families consume all meals at home. The upper class groups, mainly in the north, have a tendency to spend more money for food because they buy processed, ready-made products. It was found that if a poor city family should for any reason acquire $1000 in addition to their regular income, 28% of the extra money would be used for food, while a wealthy family in the same situation would spend only 5% of the $1000 for additional food (Murray and Blake, 1959).

In general, the national diet is adequate in the United States. Food supplies in all its markets are very generous and varied. Only in exceptional cases, involving very low income or lack of knowledge, do families consume inadequate diets, but these cases account for less than 10% of the population of the whole country (Boek, 1956; Grant and Groom, 1959). With the possible exception of calcium, and also ascorbic acid in some city groups, intakes of all nutrients exceed the recommended allowances. Improvement in the diets of the entire United States population has been excellent over the past few decades, especially among the low income families. In families with a high consumption of grain products, nutrient intake increases owing to effective enrichment programs. Wives working away from their homes may find it difficult to plan adequate menus, but their increased income allows them to buy more nutritious foods.

During recent years (1968–72) the nutritional surveys carried out in the different states are revealing some results which suggest that the consumption levels in this country have suffered a deterioration. A greater proportion of the population is malnourished compared to the past decade, but the severity of the problem is higher only in some segments of the population, especially among Latin Americans or the low income level like the Mexicans or the Puerto Ricans, and also among Negroes. In general the conditions of the whites remain more or less adequate in regard to the diets (*Nutrition Today*, 1972).

In these surveys the most clear evidence is that cases of malnutrition increase when income level decreases. Consequently, income is a major determinant factor in the food intake of these groups. A general finding was that adolescents between 10–16 years have the highest prevalence of inadequate nutritional status and also elderly persons over 60 years. The results again suggest that as the educational level of the mother increases, the evidence of nutritional inadequacies in the children decreases. In the analysis of the food consumption there is a heavy emphasis on meat in most of the diets and poor food choices in regard to the products rich in vitamin A. School lunch programs were found to be a very important part of the nourishment for many children. In regard to anthropometric measurements, they found that a large proportion of children were underweight and undersized according with their own standards. In regard to iron a high prevalence of low hemoglobin and hematocrit values were found in all segments of the groups that belong to the low income levels.

Middle America, comprising Mexico, Central America, and Panama, presents the other side of the coin with regard to food consumption. The topography is very irregular in these countries; a chain of mountains runs from north to south along the Pacific and Atlantic coastal areas. Very high elevations in Mexico and Central America, including active volcanoes, are combined with low areas and valleys with fertile soils. Mexico has all kinds of climates, from the desert heat and dryness to the humidity of lands covered with a great deal of vegetation. Very cold highland areas are close to hot regions with arid soils.

In Central America the climates are mild and the temperature ranges between 20° and 35°C, modified by winds and rains. Throughout the entire region there is only one seasonal variation in the whole year, irrespective of temperature, and that is the change from the dry to the rainy season. The latter period begins in May and lasts until October. Three ethnic groups live in Middle America; the two most numerous are the Indians of Aztec and Mayan descent, in Mexico and Guatemala, respectively, and the Mestizos (a mixture of Spanish and Indian). The Carib and Negro population of the Atlantic coast and Panama make up the third important group.

Divided into food and cash crops, the principal agricultural products of Middle America include mainly maize, beans, rice, and bananas as food crops; and coffee, sugar cane, and cotton as cash crops, on which the economy of the entire region relies. About 50% of the population is dedicated to farming. In addition, Mexico has abundant natural resources, including petroleum and other minerals and some well developed industries. In Central America, more than 60% of the people, considered the rural population, are involved in agricultural work. The data presented by Zubirán and Chávez (1963) on the basic diet in Mexico, which were derived from 26 surveys carried out in urban and rural areas, show that the most common food products are: maize tortillas, beans, vegetables, mainly chile, tomatoes, and leafy greens; some fruits, principally bananas; coffee and pulque. Preparation of food in Mexico is characterized by the use of many spices, among which chile (hot pepper) and cacao take first place. Sporadically, the diets include meat, milk, spaghetti, sugar, and fats. Differences between the rural and urban areas are very great (Zubirán et al., 1964); the urban population eat more wheat bread and rice (instead of maize tortillas), a greater variety of vegetables and fruits, about five times as much milk, and twice as much meat and eggs than their rural counterparts. Surveys show that consumption of sugar and fats in the rural area is 45 and 15 g, per person per day, respectively; while in the cities it is 83 and 27 g.

In the first four countries (Guatemala, El Salvador, Honduras, and Nicaragua) of Central America, as in Mexico, the staple food is maize tortilla. For its preparation, maize is treated with lime water or with ashes dissolved in water, depending upon the locality (Flores, 1961). Rice replaces maize as a staple in Costa Rica and Panama. The Negro and Carib groups use wheat flour instead of maize to prepare their tortillas. The second important food item in the Central American diet is constituted by different colored varieties of the common bean, mainly the black and red ones. The Indians prefer to prepare beans by boiling, with the addition of some herbs for flavor, while the Mestizos boil the beans and add lard, or else mash and fry them, also in lard. Vegetables constitute the third item in the diets of Central America, especially in Guatemala, where consumption of leafy greens and tomatoes is remarkably high among the Indians. In general, the wild leaves are eaten by Indians, and the cultivated vegetables, like cabbage, carrots, and kales are preferred by the Mestizos; the Negro–Carib group consumes the starchy roots and tubers. Fruit is not important to Central Americans except for the city families, and, even in this group, only citrus fruits and bananas are eaten with any degree of frequency. In all these countries, meat is consumed in very small amounts. The exception in this case is Panama, where consumption is about twice that of any other Central American country. The meat most commonly used is beef, but fish also appears in some population groups of Panama, Nicaragua, and Costa Rica. In the highlands there is some consumption of goat's meat or pork, but they do not count as an important contribution to the daily diets. All Central American groups drink small quantities of milk, and the Indians only consume it in insignificant amounts as cheese. Nicaragua and Costa Rica have more dairy products than the other countries, and surveys show that milk consumption is higher in those countries. A great majority of Indians and rural Mestizo families raise poultry and eat eggs, but chicken meat is strictly a feast day treat. Sugar availability is high, as all these countries cultivate the sugar cane; some rural groups prefer raw sugar, while urban dwellers favor the white refined product. Fat consumption in Guatemala is one of the world's lowest, and its only source for the Indian population is the tortilla with its maize oil content. On the other hand, in the Atlantic coast and in Panama, large quantities of vegetable oil, lard, or coconut cream prepared especially for cooking, are used. There are some processing industries for cottonseed and sesame oil, but production is sufficient only for local needs. In Mexico and in Central America there are traditional local dishes on Sundays or feast days, like "tamale" (maize dough with fat, wrapped in banana leaves and boiled with a filling of pork, tomatoes, and chile), stuffed meat peppers, or mashed fried plantains, stuffed with beans.

In general, animal production in these countries is low, and in some of them it is not sufficient to cover even the minimum food requirements of the population. In Costa Rica and Nicaragua there has been some development in dairy cattle raising, and in Panama meat cattle herds are sufficient only for local needs; nevertheless, large quantities of meat are exported from this area. Central American topography, which is almost uniformly accidental, combined with the lack of knowledge, technology, and mechanization, have slowed down agricultural development to a point where it is far behind the advances made in other areas of the world.

In countries like Guatemala, with a great variety of climates due to a range of different altitudes surprising for so small a territory, grains, vegetables, and fruits are exceptionally abundant, and production is sufficient to cover the demands of the Central American common market. Unfortunately, consumption of those products is low due to the lack of communication, storage, and transportation facilities.

All over Central America there is a serious calorie–protein deficiency among the preschool children, which becomes more severe among the Indian groups. A second serious problem is the lack of vitamin A, which is ingested in carotene-rich vegetables and fruits, but in insufficient amounts, except among the Indians of the highlands. Since dairy products in the area leave much to be desired in both quantity and quality, riboflavin levels are very low in the diets of all groups. Low thiamine intakes have also been found in some countries. Other nutritional problems which prevail in this region are anemias and goitre.

South America is likewise extremely irregular in topography, especially in its western part, where the Andes run from the north of Colombia to the south of Chile. The high mountains and great rivers leave valleys with fertile soils in many areas. The western countries, regardless of size, are sectioned by the towering mountain ranges into three well defined areas: the coast, the "sierra" (mountainous region) and the "selva" (jungle) (White *et al.*, 1954). The "selva" is on the Amazon river basin in Colombia, Ecuador, Peru, and Bolivia (US ICNND, 1961b, 1960a, 1959c, 1964a). In Venezuela the lowlands correspond to the Atlantic coast, but low areas also exist in the vicinity of the Amazon (US ICNND, 1964b).

The people in South America ethnically belong to the so-called "mestizo" group (Spanish and Indian), with small numbers of pure whites, blacks, and Indians scattered throughout the continent. The pure Indian population of Colombia and Chile are very small, and there are almost none in Argentina and Uruguay. In Ecuador, Peru, and Bolivia, however, where the Inca civilization once flourished, more than 50% of the total population belongs to this ethnic group. The economies of all these countries rely on agriculture, and for some of them, as is true in the Central American countries, it provides most of national revenues. In Colombia, Chile, Argentina, and Uruguay, part of the economy is supported by the textile industry and the exportation of food products (US ICNND, 1961a; 1963). Venezuela is an exceptional country in this region, because its economy is based mainly on the exploitation of petroleum. A part of Bolivia's national income comes from the mining industry, but not enough to change its status as an agricultural country. In Brazil (US ICNND, 1965) and the Guianas, diamonds, other precious stones, gold, and other minerals are mined in addition to farming.

The main agricultural products of South America are cereals, the kind and variety grown in each country depending upon climate and altitude. In the northern region, maize takes first place, followed by wheat and barley; in addition, oats and rye are grown in Colombia; maize is also the chief source of food in many areas of Colombia and Venezuela, and in combination with wheat in the highlands and rice in the lowlands the three cereals provide the largest percentage of calories in the diets. In

Ecuador, Peru, and Bolivia, in addition to maize, rice, wheat, and barley, quinoa is also produced and consumed in different localities. In the south, Chile, Uruguay, and Argentina, produce wheat in greater amounts than maize, but other cereals are also cultivated for local needs. In these countries wheat supplies the major portion of calories in the daily intake of the people. In the lowlands they cultivate rice, sugar, and tubers (i.e. potatoes or sweet potatoes), and they appear as essential components of the diets. In Paraguay the cultivation on mandioca takes first place and is consumed in high quantities as daily bread (about 500 g per person per day) (US Dept. of Health, Education, and Welfare, 1967). In certain coastal areas and near the Amazon River, bananas and plantains grow in abundance, constituting one of the main products for exportation, and they are also consumed in great amounts. Coffee is cultivated in the entire region except for the southern countries, and it represents a very important cash crop.

A great deal of beef is produced in Colombia, as its vast lowland areas are suitable for grazing. Milk is also abundant in certain parts of this country. Nevertheless, consumption of meat and milk in low quantities have been reported. In Ecuador, irregular topography within a relatively small territory prevents the raising of cattle, but sheep and goats provide meat and milk for local consumption in the sierra. Venezuela and Brazil raise some beef and dairy cattle, but only in small areas. The Bolivian high plains raise sheep, llama, and alpaca, and these animals provide food (especially sheep) and wool for the textile industry, but meat consumption is low. In Paraguay according to the dietary survey (US Department of Health, Education and Welfare, 1967), consumption of meat is high (about 137 g per person per day) and it is mainly beef. Chile has dedicated a good deal of its agricultural activity to the production of beef and dairy product for national consumption. The main food product, which has been highly industrialized in Chile and Peru is fish, owing to the very long coast-line that these countries possess. Grasslands abound in Argentina, Uruguay, and Paraguay, where cattle is raised for beef production. Milk is produced in a very limited scale in Paraguay, while in Uruguay the dairy industry has been well developed; the production in Argentina falls between those countries.

In all South American countries, fresh vegetables and fruits are produced on a large scale. The tropical or temperate climate and topography help these countries to cultivate a great variety of vegetables, including peppers, onions, cabbages, carrots, tomatoes, and leafy greens in the west countries. Nevertheless, consumption of fresh vegetables other than starchy roots is very limited in countries like Colombia, Venezuela, or Ecuador. In the southern countries, tomatoes, cucumbers, eggplants, and others are grown, but fruits are more important than vegetables; as in certain European regions, grapes take first place in some wine-producing areas of Chile, Argentina, and Uruguay. Different kinds of citrus fruit, peaches, apples, pears, plums, apricots, avocados, and cherries are also cultivated and consumed in this section of the continent.

The most important feature of the South American diet is constituted by the great differences existing from one area to the next, even within each country. This peculiarity is not only due to geographical location, but also to the fact that the predominant cultural group gives preference to different products in each case. In countries with European influence, like Argentina, Uruguay, and Chile, inhabitants eat mainly wheat bread, spaghetti, or macaroni, for which they have well developed industries. Barley, oats, or rye are also consumed sporadically. Maize prevails in the diets of Colombia, Venezuela, Ecuador, Peru, and Bolivia because their populations are faithful to the native Indian food pattern. In Brazil, the Guianas, parts of Venezuela and of Colombia, African, or Caribbean, dietary traits predominate in the food patterns, and tubers, roots, rice, bananas, and plantains are preferred. Fish is consumed only in the cities and in the coastal areas of Ecuador, Peru, and Chile. Fishing industries in these countries has taken place so that marine products reach the main cities of South America; but a significant portion of the fish is utilized for production of fish meal which is exported. In certain areas of Brazil and Venezuela there is some consumption of fish mainly where difficulties are great to get other kind of meats. In Argentina, Paraguay, and Uruguay, where beef is available, fish is unimportant and hardly eaten. For instance, in Paraguay the consumption of beef is as high as 145 g per person per day in the urban area, and about 88 g in the rural area while fish consumption is practically nil. In the lake regions of countries like Bolivia, people prefer the meat of sheep or goats to fish. Thus, as a whole, the latter is not a popular food item in Latin America.

A typical breakfast in South America consists of coffee and a roll of wheat bread or else and "arepa" (pancake or patty made of maize dough); sometimes coffee may be substituted by chocolate. In Chile people prefer tea and a sweet roll, and in Argentina and Paraguay bread and "mate" (a bitter brew of local herbs). In Uruguay, as in Italy, toast or pastry and coffee with milk are favored. For lunch, all South Americans have a common local dish, the preparation of which is subject to some variation in each region, consisting of a stew of meat and vegetables, called "puchero" in Colombia or "cazuela" in Chile. Potatoes, tomatoes, and other fresh vegetables go into this stew. It is eaten with bread or corn "arepa", or sometimes with green bananas, boiled and mashed. The evening meal consists of beans, chickpeas, or lentils as a main dish, with rice or spaghetti. City diets are different from those in the rural areas, as they are more varied and include more milk, meat, and eggs. White sugar is universally used to sweeten coffee, tea, or other beverages. In Colombia, however, raw sugar dissolved in water constitutes the typical beverage of the rural population. In Chile and Uruguay, where sugar beet is grown, beet sugar is used, although cane sugar is also consumed.

The rural areas in most of these countries have diets which are monotonous and in many instances deficient in minerals and vitamins, such as those of Ecuador, Peru, or Bolivia. The scarcity of meat and milk, which cannot be remedied by raising sheep, goats, or llamas, presents the same nutritional problem as in Central America: lack of good quality proteins in the diets, mainly among the preschool children. As a result of the many political problems afflicting all of these countries, agriculture has suffered a great deal. Countries that used to produce sufficient milk or cereals at present need to import large amounts of wheat and corn from the United States and dairy products from Europe. In Venezuela the food situation is very serious. Many products must be imported in huge quantities because agriculture has been abandoned, partly as a result of the oil industry's monopoly of manpower. There is some cultivation of oily seeds, like cottonseed, sesame, safflower, soya bean, or sunflower seeds, in Colombia and Venezuela. In Brazil they produce different kinds of nuts, not only for oil extraction but also for exportation. The oily seed industry has been developed for domestic consumption, and coconut oil has been industrialized also but on a smaller scale.

In areas where maize is the staple food, such as Colombia, Venezuela, and some sections of Peru and Ecuador, calorie, thiamine, and niacin intakes do not show marked deficiencies, and calorie intake ranges between 1200 and 2000 daily, per person. A higher caloric intake, of around 2800 is found in the sierra area of Ecuador and Peru. Calorie and protein deficiencies are found in poor groups of countries where tubers, plantains, and limited amounts of cereals such as rice or wheat rather than significant quantities of maize constitute the main sources of calories. For example, in Bolivia, the average diet covers only 80% of the requirements (US ICNND, 1964a); in Chile, caloric intake, about

2200 throughout the whole country (US ICNND, 1961a), which is lower than their requirements. In Uruguay (US ICNND, 1963) and Argentina, however, caloric intake surpasses the requirements. Protein intake presents the same picture; for instance, in Colombia, intake ranges from 25 to 42 g daily per person, but one-third is of animal origin (US ICNND, 1961b). In Venezuela (US ICNND, 1964b) intake ranges from 54 to

94 g, but animal protein is very low in several localities compared to that in Colombia. In Ecuador, total protein intake is 58 g and animal protein about 23 g (US ICNND, 1960a). In Peru (US ICNND, 1959c) and Bolivia, protein intake is about 54 g and animal protein from 10 to 18 g. In Uruguay and Argentina, protein intake is high, and the percentage of animal protein is about 50%.

There is a great difference between intakes in the northern part of

TABLE 5 NORTH AND CENTRAL AMERICA

United States (FAO, 1966; Clark, 1958)		Mexico (Zubiran and Chavez, 1963)		Guatemala (INCAP/OIR, 1969; Flores, unpublished data)		Panama (INCAP/OIR, 1969; Flores, unpublished data)	
Food	g/person/day	Food	g/person/day	Food	g/person/day	Food	g/person/day
Wheat (bread)	149	Maize tortilla	480	Maize tortilla	491	Rice	186
Maize (flakes)	17	Wheat bread	62	Wheat bread	40	Wheat bread	37
Potato	119	Potato	18	Sugar	53	Cassava	35
Sugar	111	Sugar	59	Black beans	50	Name	40
Fresh vegetables	182	Cacao	2	Green leaves	12	Sugar	51
Canned vegetables	55	Beans	48	Tomato	24	Beans	20
Fruits	136	Chile +		Other vegetables	27	Tomato	7
Canned fruits	29	Leafy greens +		Citrus	5	Orange	33
Beef	87	Tomato	104	Plantain	26	Green plantain	41
Chicken	49	Orange +		Beef	23	Mature plantain	58
Pork	73	Plantain		Eggs	17	Beef	47
Eggs	52	Meats	54	Milk	125	Fish	24
Fish	13	Eggs	64	Lard	5	Milk	73
Cow's milk	382	Cheese	9	Coffee	9	Coconut milk	21
Cheese	18	Milk	152			Oil	20
Butter	9	Fats	19				
Margarine	12						
Other fats	39						
Ice cream	32						

TABLE 6 SOUTH AMERICA

Colombia (US ICNND, 1961)		Ecuador (US ICNND, 1960a)		Bolivia (US ICNND, 1964a)		Brazil (US ICNND, 1965)		Chile (US ICNND, 1961a)	
Food	g/person/day	Food	g/person/day	Food	g/person/day	Food	g/person/day	Food	g/person/day
Maize (arepa)	53	Rice	96	Maize	23	Maize	65	Wheat bread	311
Rice	44	Maize	71	Quinoa	12	Rice	16	Spaghetti	40
Wheat bread	18	Barley	8	Rice	43	Wheat	30	Rice	23
Cassava	23	Wheat bread	38	Spaghetti	15	Cassava	80	Potato	153
Potato	160	Potato +		Wheat	13	Cassava flour	176	Sugar	49
Raw sugar	60	Cassava	215	Wheat bread	110	Sweet potato	34	Beans	27
Beans	16	Sugar	63	Chuño	36	Sugar	83	Leafy greens	97
Chocolate	17	Beans	26	Potato	294	Common beans	40	Apples +̱	
Vegetables	35	Leafy greens	46	Sugar	36	Vegetables	18	Grapes +	
Fruits	6	Tomato	16	Faba beans	31	Banana	142	Peaches	96
Plantains	74	Citrus	16	Carrot	19	Citrus	22	Beef	78
Beef	50	Plantain	51	Onion	14	Coconut	19	Fish	33
Milk	70	Beef	47	Banana	23	Mango	37	Milk	91
Fats	10	Fish	9	Beef	53	Beef	53	Oils	19
Coffee	2	Milk	193	Milk	22	Other meats chicken, mutton, pork	19	Wine	11
		Coffee	5	Lard	5	Fish	5		
				Coffee	142	Milk	65		
				Tea	66	Lard + oil	8		
						Coffee	4		

Brazil and those in the section to the south of the Amazon river.

A few countries were selected to illustrate food combinations in the diets of the different areas of America (Figs. 5 and 6; Tables 5 and 6). For each country, a list of the most common products is given according to the frequency with which they are used.

4.6. THE CARIBBEAN

The Caribbean countries are spread over numerous islands in the expanse of sea that begins at the southern Atlantic coast of North America and ends on the shores of Venezuela and the Guianas. Many are so small that their only resource is the tourist industry, but others are larger and very important in the international trading market. All are characterized by warm tropical climates consisting of a rainy season from May to November and a dry season for the rest of the year. Some have irregular topography dividing them into different areas. Their coastal belt is generally followed by a mountainous section and then by fertile plateaus or valleys in the middle, usually irrigated by rivers. Basically, two ethnic groups live on the islands: the Carib Indians and the Negroes. In addition, there is a minority of whites scattered throughout the area. Most of the islands are densely populated, in some at a ratio of about 500 persons per square mile, while in others the proportion is more than 1000 persons per square mile (Aykroyd, 1965). Their main problems are the lack of good roads, the very high percentage of illiteracy, and, in addition, innumerable illegitimate children with no means of support; all of which contribute to hold back economic development.

Petroleum wells and some mining resources like amber in the Dominican Republic are found in some areas of the Caribbean, but, in all its countries, the economy is mainly geared to agriculture. In the large islands, unfortunately, the land is used mostly to grow cash crops for exportation, like sugar cane, cacao, banana, coconut, coffee, and cotton. Jamaica, Puerto Rico, and Trinidad produce some foods for local consumption, while other islands are cultivating cereals like rice or sorghum, which are gradually becoming staples. As the climate is very humid in many islands, the land is able to produce great amounts of roots and tubers, which in general constitute the basic item of the diets. Most of these countries have to import many food products, mainly from the United States, among which are wheat flour, rice, processed milk, carbonated beverages, and sweets. In all islands there are some fishing industries, but they are not well organized and sometimes do not operate on a sufficiently large production scale, so that even local demand is not fully satisfied.

Traditional Spanish cooking predominates in the food patterns of Puerto Rico, though some influence from the United States has modified those patterns, mainly among the urban groups. The chief product in the diet is rice (Plough, *et al.*, 1963), followed by leguminous seeds, tubers, roots, and fish. There is some consumption of fruits like avocados, bananas, plantains, citrus fruit, mangoes, papaya, and pineapple. The main beverage is coffee with some milk, which may be occasionally substituted by chocolate or sweet drinks. Pork, beef, or poultry are consumed in limited amounts. In Haiti (Sebrell *et al.*, 1959), the basic product for daily consumption is plantain, followed by maize, sweet potatoes, roots, rice, beans, and nuts. There is also some consumption of meat and milk, since livestock is produced on a small scale. Goat milk is also used, as these and other small animals are raised in the highlands (Grant and Groom, 1958). Leafy greens are consumed very frequently by Indians in the highlands of Haiti. Fruits are not important, with the exception of plantains, which are combined with roots in the preparation of soups. In Haiti and other southern islands, the common method of cooking consists of placing all the ingredients in one pot and, while the mixture is boiling, adding oil or lard; when these fats are not available, coconut milk is used. Spices are not generally used; for flavoring purposes, fruit juice, for instance that of the sour orange or lemon, may be added. Condensed sweet milk is very popular everywhere, and in some areas it is practically the only dairy product in the diets of the Carib or Negro group. In the islands close to Venezuela (US ICNND, 1962c) there are many immigrant groups from India who try to keep up their homeland food habits, using rice, split peas, some vegetables, like eggplant or spinach, spices, mainly hot pepper and garlic, and their traditional curries. Among these groups, tea with some milk takes the place of coffee. Fish is not popular among them whereas the natives and Negroes eat fish every day, be it fresh, dried or canned (imported sardines are very popular). For drinking, Caribs use many different kinds of teas prepared with wild leaves.

In most islands, with the exception of Puerto Rico, there is a great incidence of protein–calorie malnutrition among children. Feeding practices are poor and, of late, lactation periods have been shortened from a year or more to 3 or 4 months. To replace mother's milk they use some evaporated milk dissolved in large quantities of water and combined with starchy flour from cassava or cereals, the nutritive value of which is almost nonexistent. Most of the native groups suffer from deficiencies of vitamin A, riboflavin, thiamine, and iron. Even total protein is low in different groups where fish or leguminous seeds are consumed in limited amounts. Lately the production of staple foods, mainly tubers and roots, has tended to decrease because people prefer to use imported flours.

Two countries were selected to illustrate the combination of foods in the diets of the Caribbean Islands (Fig. 7; Table 7). For each country, a list of the most common products is given according to the frequency with which they are used.

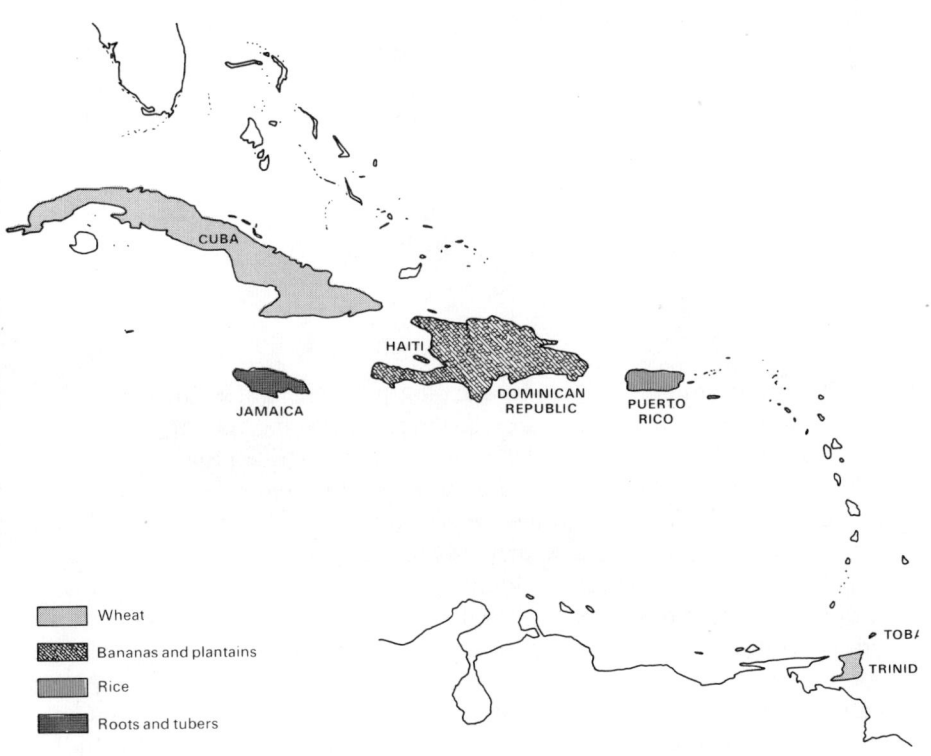

TABLE 7 CARIBBEAN ISLANDS

Trinidad (US ICNND, 1962c)		Dominican Republic (Flores, 1969)	
Food	g/person/day	Food	g/person/day
Rice	119	Rice	132
Wheat bread	60	Spaghetti	7
Wheat flour	143	Wheat bread	18
Potato	23	Cassava	
Sugar	46	Potato	
Dry peas	20	Sweet potato	67
Eggplant	10	Sugar	30
Leafy greens	18	Chocolate	3
Onion	9	Red beans	38
Tomato	18	Ahuyama (squash)	10
Avocado	9	Onion	4
Banana	19	Tomato paste	5
Citrus	29	Citrus	3
Plantain	8	Mango	28
Beef	10	Plantain (green)	145
Poultry	20	Beef	18
Fish	57	Salami	3
Milk: condensed	18	Dry fish (cod)	15
Milk: fresh	19	Milk: fresh	78
Coconut oil	14	Coconut milk	3
		Oil	26
		Coffee	5

4.7. OCEANIA

The multitudinous islands of the South Pacific differ greatly in size and economic development. For instance, Australia, the largest island, is a rich and highly developed country. Like the United States, its topography is very uniform and its coastal lines quite unbroken. Its tropical northern belt of land is characterized by a great deal of rainfall, while in the western and central parts there are arid or semiarid desert-like areas. There are some not very high mountains to the west and east. The climate ranges from mild to wet to very dry in the south. There are certain physical and chemical limitations in the Australian soil with respect to cultivation, these being mainly the lack of water and minerals. Nevertheless, great agriculture development has been possible by the tapping of underground water resources and intensive soil enrichment projects. Australia is one of the countries where dairy and meat cattle are raised in very large quantities, sufficient not only for local needs but also for exportation.

At the same time, the production of cereals is undertaken on a great scale, and Australia is an important wheat exporter. The cultivation of sugar cane and the exploitation of forest resources are other elements of their economy. Mineral deposits, for instance those of coal, iron, gold, as well as petroleum, make the country one of the richest in the world. Another country with ample resources is New Zealand, with two large main islands. On both, a chain of mountains runs from north to south, providing different altitudes and climates. The temperature in this part of the world is rather cold with prevailing constant humidity, which is adequate for pasture growth. Cattle raising is the most important source of income in this country. People in Australia and New Zealand enjoy very nutritious diets, including sufficient amounts of milk and meat. On the other hand, on islands like New Guinea (Bailey and Whiteman, 1963) or the Polynesian islands (Ferro-Luzzi, 1962), agricultural and economic development is advancing at a very low rate. Nevertheless, their inhabitants are fortunate in having access to both land and sea resources, for their activities include exploitation of corals and pearls, and the cultivation of spices, sugar cane, copra, and fruits (Fry, 1957). The climate is rather hot in the entire area. Staple foods include tubers, roots, and fruits, like sweet potatoes, taro, arrowroot, green bananas, and breadfruit. In places like the Cook Islands (Faine and Hercus, 1951), some imported products have been incorporated into the diets; some of these are wheat flour, sweets, biscuits, meats, jam, tea, and condensed milk. Fish is very important in most island diets, and *per caput* consumption is between 100 and 250 g daily (Fry, 1957), Coconut cream or oil is used for cooking (Parkinson, 1961). In New Guinea, leafy greens and beans are also quite common. Meat from certain birds and game animals is occasionally eaten. Part of the land in these islands is dedicated to the cultivation of cereals like corn or sorghum, but production is very low. Different kinds of soups prepared with cereal or tuber flours are common among the islanders. In some areas, coffee is also produced for local consumption, but it is not as important as tea made from different kinds of bush leaves.

In the Melanesian islands, the principal crops are cassava, taro, yam, different kinds of plantains, breadfruit, and sweet potatoes, according to prevailing soil and climate conditions. Taro and other green leaves are cooked with meat or fish and coconut cream. Some islands are growing cassava instead of other tubers at the present time. However, its disadvantage is that it is slow in growing and requires a great deal of cultivation work. In addition, the value of its protein is very poor, and thus its effects on a diet, especially on that consumed by small children, are deleterious.

Wheat

TABLE 8 .OCEANIA ISLANDS

New Guinea (Bailey and Whiteman, 1963)		Australia (FAO, 1966)	
Food	g/person/day	Food	g/person/day
Maize	28	Wheat	215
Taro	89	Potato	127
Yam and sweet potato	1656	Tubers	40
Beans and peas	3	Sugar	136
Bamboo tips	23	Leafy greens	98
Dark green leaves and cassava leaves	309	Tomato	36
		Citrus	52
Pale green leaves	4	Raisins	24
Pitpit (*Setaria* sp.)	34	Beef	120
Pumpkin	60	Mutton	123
Green banana	22	Pork	26
Pork lean	4	Fresh fish	11
		Milk	363
		Butter	30
		Margarine	12

In the entire south Pacific region, considerable consumption of roots and tubers provides sufficient amounts of calories as well as iron and vitamin C; with the introduction of carbohydrates like flour, bread, rice, or sugar into the urban areas, calorie deficiency is inevitable since they are imported products of higher price. Malnutrition, with attendant growth retardation, has been encountered among the children of New Guinea and other islands.

Two countries were selected to illustrate the combination of foods in the diets of the oceanic islands (Fig. 8; Table 8). For each country a list of the most common products is given according to the frequency with which they are used.

5. PRESENT DIETARY LEVELS IN THE WORLD

The degree of economic and technical development achieved by each country is in part responsible for the presence of new and adequate diets among its inhabitants or else for the persistence of traditional food patterns. The rural population of slowly developing countries will probably keep the same, markedly deficient diets for several more decades. Within these same countries, small urban groups, privileged by ample incomes, will continue to consume rich diets. In the well developed countries, on the other hand, with abundant food supplies and populations with high purchasing power, a great majority are able to enjoy diets, fully covering the daily nutritional requirements. Within these countries, only small groups, for instance poorly adapted immigrants, suffer from dietary deficiencies.

It is a fact that countless different consumption levels exist within the boundaries of each country, depending upon diverse ecological and socio-economic conditions. Thus a comparison between regions in terms of food consumption or nutrient intake is not possible. Thorough information covering all countries of highly advanced areas is not available, and, for developing areas, large number of reports are limited to small localities which do not represent the main areas of a given country. Therefore, an illustration will be given only on the basis of selected information comparing food consumption and nutrient intake levels in some countries that may be representative of the different regions of the world. Tables 9 and 10 present food consumption by food groups, and also daily intake levels, per person, obtained from different family dietary surveys. Some represent the whole country and others only one or two important areas.

On the basis of quantities in which they are consumed, cereals cons-

TABLE 9 AVERAGE FOOD CONSUMPTION (IN GRAMS) PER PERSON PER DAY IN SOME COUNTRIES OF THE WORLD

Countries	Cereals	Roots and tubers	Sugars	Pulses	Vegetables	Fruits	Meats	Eggs	Fish	Milk[b]	Fats
FAR EAST											
Philippines (Quiogue, et al., 1962)	298	11	29	7	102	85	43	11	55	74	14
Thailand (US ICNND, 1962a)	440	9	1	1	73	6	22	4	41	—	1
India (FAO, 1966)	382	29	54	70	8	48	4	1	6	129	10
NEAR EAST											
Lebanon (US ICNND, 1962b)	477	65	26	30	162	95	41	19	—	157	29
Israel (Urban) (Bavly, 1966)	253	69	67	16	197	321	89	49	20	328	36
AFRICA											
Ethiopia (US ICNND, 1959b)	450	25	4	50	130	6	40	6	0	90	60
Nigeria (US OIR, 1967)	310	739	6	50	—	91	17	3	10	32	20
EUROPE											
England (FAO, 1966)	224	270	145	16	160	129	193	40	26	604	63
Spain (US ICNND, 1958a)	317	315	52	39	356	237	57	20	72	220	56
AMERICA											
United States (FAO, 1966)	181	130	32	22	270	208	227	52	13	701	60
Guatemala (Flores, 1961)	494	5	47	58	61	25	34	4	0	10	1
Panama (Flores, 1961)	189	35	53	54	6	72	60	8	23	47	35
Bolivia (FAO, 1966)	267	332	50	8	116	202	64	3	1	108	13
Colombia (FAO, 1966)	206	333	132	16	32	105	96	6	9	294	16
Chile (US ICNND, 1961a)	379	153	50	27	143	107	100	8	33	91	27

[a] Amounts of edible portion
[b] In terms of liquid milk.

TABLE 10 CALORIE AND NUTRIENT INTAKE LEVELS PER PERSON PER DAY IN SOME COUNTRIES OF THE WORLD

Countries	Calories	Total protein (g)	Animal protein (g)	Calcium (mg)	Iron (mg)	Vitamin A (IU)	Thiamine (mg)	Riboflavin (mg)	Niacin (mg)	Ascorbic acid (mg)
FAR EAST										
Philippines (Quiogue, et al., 1962)	1727	50	22	350	10	2278	0.9	0.7	14.8	63
Thailand (US ICNND, 1962a)	1821	49	15	278	10	1781	0.5	0.4	15.0	34
India (Rao, 1956)	2588	70	7	310	24	582	1.3	0.8	15.9	11
NEAR EAST										
Lebanon (US ICNND, 1962b)	2312	73	18	574	11	3843	0.8	1.1	18.3	63
Israel (Urban) (Bavly, 1966)	2220	75	37	819	12	4460	1.2	1.4	12.7	87
AFRICA										
Ethiopia (US ICNND, 1959b)	2512	65	15	640	—	2901	2.4	0.7	12.2	14
Nigeria (Lagos) (US OIR, 1967)	2176	56	4	654	21	5345	0.6	0.4	6.5	32
EUROPE										
England (Baines and Hollingsworth, 1963)	2674	77	43	1064	14	4457	1.2	1.7	13.5	52
Spain (US ICNND, 1958)	2553	68	19	491	11	2205	1.2	1.0	12.0	113
AMERICA										
United States (Clark, 1958)	3200	103	69	1200	18	8500	1.6	2.3	19.0	106
Guatemala (Flores, 1961)	2243	66	7	1320	23	2273	1.4	0.7	12.2	35
Panama (Flores, 1961)	1927	55	20	200	12	438	0.7	0.6	10.2	48
Bolivia (US ICNND, 1964a)	1870	58	23	221	15	2671	0.8	0.7	14.1	84
Colombia (US ICNND, 1961b)	1306	33	13	220	10	1264	0.5	0.6	7.2	65
Chile (US ICNND, 1961a)	2280	72	25	700	18	6980	1.4	1.7	16.4	50

titute the main product in most of the countries. In some areas like Central America, Ethiopia, or the Asian countries, amounts range from 250 to 500 g per person per day. The high income countries show a *per caput* consumption of 180 or close to 200 g of cereals per day. In some African or South American countries, as well as the Pacific and Atlantic islands, roots and tubers take the place of cereals in importance. There are some countries, like England or Colombia, where sugar consumption is high, while in Africa or the Far East the amounts consumed are negligible. Pulses are eaten in substantial amounts in the Near East, East Africa, Central America, and in some areas of India. A great variety of fresh vegetables are consumed in the Far East, in Central America, and in a few countries of west South America. Fruit is more important in east South America, the United States, and Europe. Some countries in Central America and in the Far East have the lowest consumption of fat, while in some African groups, Europe and North America the consumption of fat is remarkable.

In the United Kingdom and the United States people consume more than 600 g of milk per person, daily, while in the Far East and in some African and Central American countries, practically no milk is consumed. Meat is eaten in the United States, England, and some countries of South America at the rate of 85–170 g daily, per person. In the remaining countries, the average figure appears to be from 28–56 g. Consumption of eggs or poultry appears only in high income countries, and a considerable amount of fish is consumed only in some European countries in North America, and in the Pacific islands.

The nutritive value of the average diet is given in Table 10 for the same areas. For the low income countries, the calorie intake figures are misleading because they are averages for the whole group surveyed. It is necessary to consider that the distribution of food is extremely uneven, which means that there is a great number of people with values lower than the average. In addition, in those diets the percentage of calories derived from carbohydrates is as high as 75% approximately. In high income countries, the average calorie intake is more representative because food is distributed uniformly, and calories are derived from more nutritive sources. Protein levels are very low in poor countries where tubers or roots are the staple foods. Such levels increase in countries where the staple is a cereal, yielding average figures for total protein which are quite close to the high income countries. However, the essential amino acid content is likely to be limited, and adequacy, in terms of nutritive value, is quite different from that in the high income countries.

GRAPH 1 CONTRIBUTION OF FOOD GROUPS TO TOTAL CALORIE INTAKE IN SOME LOW-INCOME COUNTRIES OF THE WORLD

	Calories (%)							
	Cereals	Roots and tubers	Sugar and syrups	Pulses	Vegetables and fruits	Meat and eggs	Milk and cheese	Oils and fats
Afghanistan	82	—	2	0	3	3	9	1
Ceylon	60	5	9	15	3	2	2	4
India	67	1	9	11	1	0	5	5
Iran	67	0	10	2	4	4	5	8
Jordan	58	1	11	5	9	2	3	11
Pakistan	72	0	7	2	3	1	7	6
Turkey	69	2	6	4	5	2	4	6
United Arab Republic	72	1	6	4	6	3	4	5
Guatemala	68	1	13	4	4	4	3	3
Surinam	54	3	15	4	2	5	4	13

GRAPH 2 CONTRIBUTION OF FOOD GROUPS TO TOTAL CALORIE INTAKE IN SOME HIGH-INCOME COUNTRIES OF THE WORLD

	Calories (%)							
	Cereals	Roots and tubers	Sugar and syrups	Pulses	Vegetables and fruits	Meat and eggs	Milk and cheese	Oils and fats
Australia	26	3	18	2	4	24	11	11
New Zealand	25	3	14	2	4	22	16	14
Denmark	22	7	16	2	5	17	11	20
France	31	6	11	2	6	17	10	18
Germany	26	8	12	2	5	16	10	21
England	25	6	17	2	3	19	11	17
Canada	21	4	17	3	5	22	13	16
United States	21	3	16	3	5	22	13	16
Argentina	32	7	13	1	4	23	6	13
Uruguay	31	5	13	1	3	23	12	12

128 Food Consumption and Planning

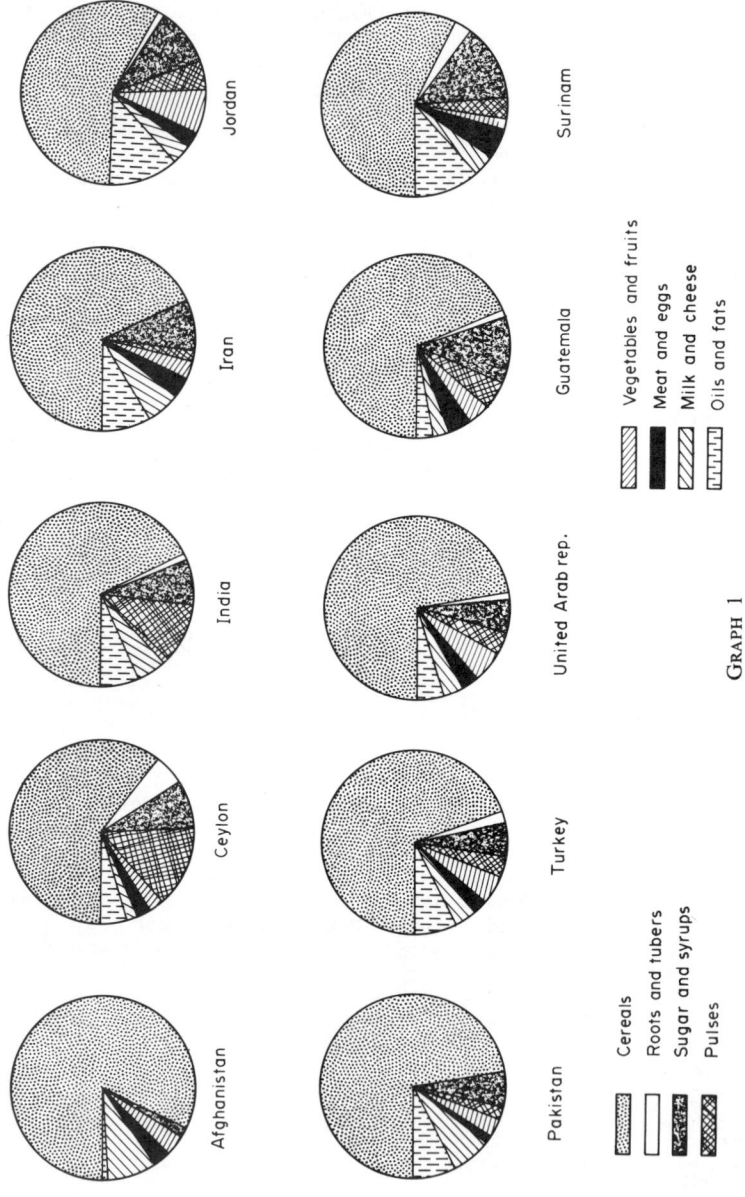

GRAPH 1

Food Consumption: Levels and Patterns Variation

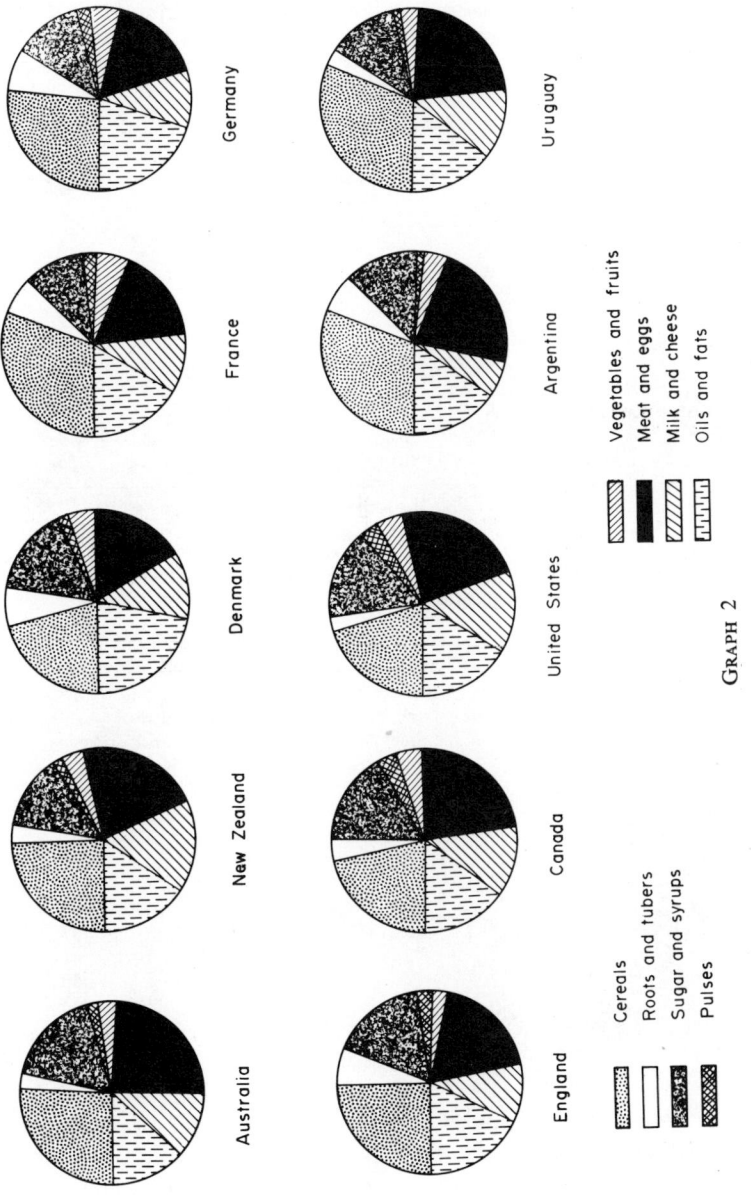

GRAPH 2

GRAPH 3 CONTRIBUTION OF FOOD GROUPS TO TOTAL PROTEIN INTAKE IN SOME LOW-INCOME COUNTRIES OF THE WORLD

	Protein (%)						
	Cereals	Roots and tubers	Sugar and syrups	Pulses	Vegetables and fruits	Meat and eggs	Milk and cheese
Afghanistan	75	—	—	0	2	8	15
Ceylon	60	2	0	16	4	14	3
India	60	1	1	26	1	2	9
Iran	71	0	—	4	2	12	11
Jordan	64	1	—	9	9	10	7
Pakistan	69	0	1	7	2	5	16
Turkey	70	2	—	7	4	7	10
United Arab Republic	69	1	—	9	6	10	6
Guatemala	70	0	0	10	4	9	6
Surinam	54	2	—	9	2	25	9

GRAPH 4 CONTRIBUTION OF FOOD GROUPS TO TOTAL PROTEIN INTAKE IN SOME HIGH-INCOME COUNTRIES OF THE WORLD

	Protein (%)						
	Cereals	Roots and tubers	Sugar and syrups	Pulses	Vegetables and fruits	Meat and eggs	Milk and cheese
Australia	25	3	—	2	3	45	21
New Zealand	24	2	—	2	4	41	27
Denmark	25	6	—	3	3	37	26
France	30	5	—	2	7	36	20
Germany	25	7	—	2	4	37	24
England	28	5	—	4	3	37	23
Canada	23	3	—	4	4	41	25
United States	17	2	—	4	5	45	26
Argentina	26	5	—	2	3	52	12
Uruguay	28	3	—	2	2	46	20

From 40 to 70 g of animal protein are consumed by each person in Europe or the United States every day, while in poor countries like India or some areas of Latin American countries, the average figure amounts only to 7 g. Another striking difference relates to vitamin A intake levels, amounting to approximately 4000 or 8000 international units per person,

Food Consumption: Levels and Patterns Variation

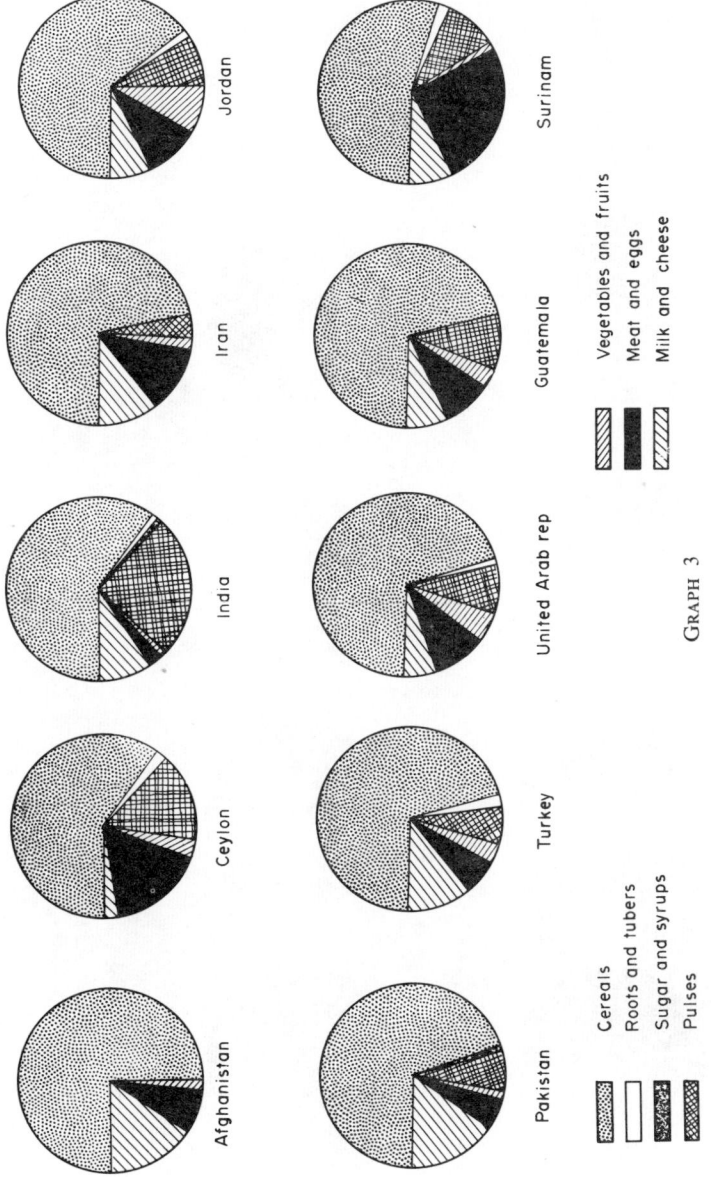

GRAPH 3

132 Food Consumption and Planning

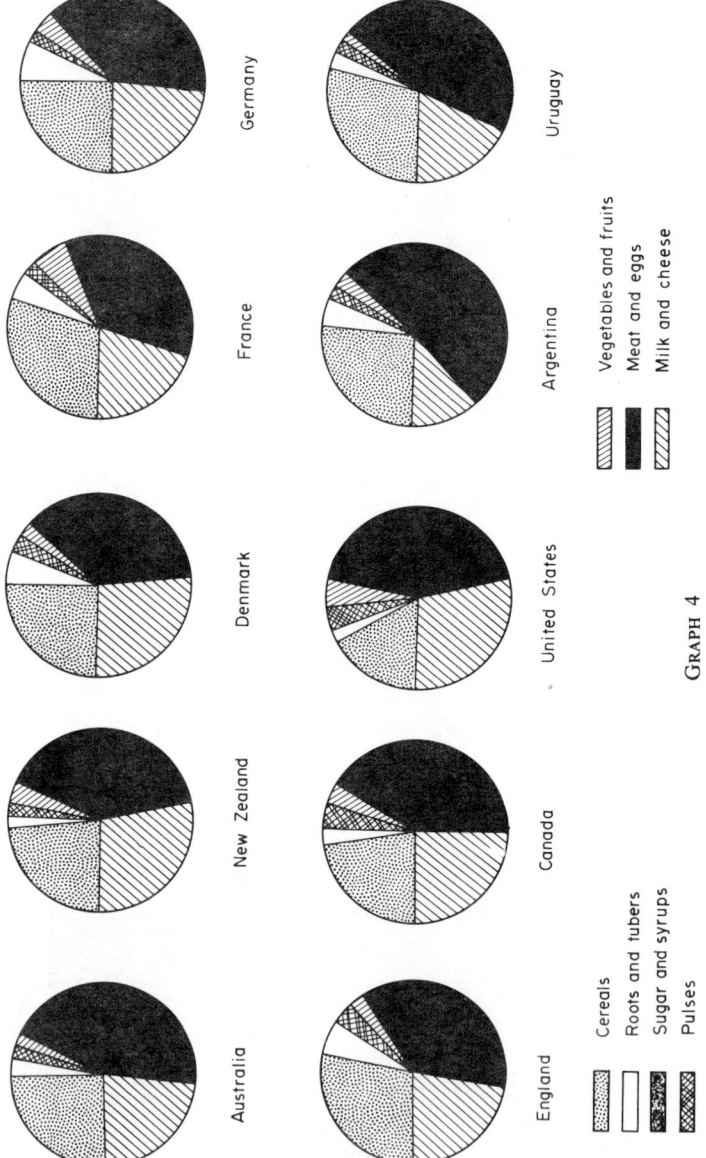

GRAPH 4

per day in wealthy countries, while in underprivileged areas the average figures range from 500 to 3000 I.U., at the most. In certain rural areas of Nigeria or of any other developing country high intake levels are due to the consumption of abundant vegetables rich in carotene. However, availability, as well as absorption, are probably low, and the high figure does not really represent high levels of vitamin A.

Food balance sheet data (FAO, 1966) may have great limitations, but they offer a unique way to compare countries by giving figures at the national level. Thus data given in FAO food balance sheets 1960-2 have been used to prepare Graphs 1-4 showing the percentage contribution of food groups to total calorie and protein intake.

Those figures reveal quite clearly the role of each food group in the different types of diets of the 20 selected countries which have been divided into low income and high income to show the striking differences in calorie and protein sources, according to food patterns.

For calories, cereals provide more than 50% of total intake in the diets of low income countries, while in the high income countries they contribute only 20 or 30% at the most. In the wealthy areas, meat, milk, sugar, and fat provide the rest of the calories.

The main protein sources in low income countries are cereals, contributing more than 60% to the total intake, followed by pulses and milk products with a contribution of around 10%. In contrast, the main sources of protein in high income countries are meats, milk, eggs, and fish, in combination providing more than 60%, while cereals contribute 25%. If the calorie and protein contribution of cereals in one group of countries is more than 50%, it is clear that all the rest of the nutrients are provided by the same food group, while animal products constitute the main source of all nutrients in the other group of countries. Given the present situation, it can be judged easily and without any further analysis that malnutrition will remain an affliction common to all groups with a low income and limited food supply.

It has been confirmed (Collis et al., 1962; Kleevens, 1966; Oshima, 1967; Quiogue et al., 1969) that any change in the economic level of a population group is reflected on the type of diet and nutritional status of the individuals. Dietary surveys carried out among low income groups show that the nutrient intake levels are always related to the economic status of the individual family. Several studies found in the literature also show that increments in the income of the family result in improvement of the nutritive value of the diets and consequently in the nutritional status of all members of the family. A good illustration is the study of

Abramson (1961) among African labourers working in a manufacturing industry in South Africa. All workers coming from the same socio-economic environment, with the same ethnic composition and all with practically no knowledge of the nutritive value of the foods, were divided into low and better paid workers. The nutritional state of the latter group appeared to be better than that of the low paid laborers of the same age, sex, and family size. The diets were considerably better among the better paid groups, especially with respect to consumption of milk, meat, eggs, and green vegetables. Some dietary studies in India yielded similar information when results are given by economic or caste groups (Devadas and Easwaran, 1967). The dietary pattern in the low income groups in one of the studies appear different from the rest of the population. The staple food consumed by low income groups were mainly millet and a small amount of pulses, neither milk nor vegetables, while the upper income groups used mainly rice, more pulses and, in addition, they consumed milk and green vegetables. The prevalence of nutritional diseases appeared to be higher in the low income groups when compared with the high income groups. Another common finding in these type of studies refers to the percentage of the total expenditure assigned to food which is very high among the lower income groups. In high income countries dietary surveys also show similar differences in dietary patterns due to income levels. In the United States the diets of higher income families, in general, include larger amounts of nearly all nutrients than those of lower income groups (Clark, 1958), especially in relation to vitamin C intake. The data given in the 1965 report from the US Department of Agriculture show that with increasing income a greater percentage of households had diets that met the allowances, nevertheless, high income did not always ensure good diets. The Bureau of Agriculture Economics in Canberra (1967) reported, in regard to a household meat consumption in Sydney, that for every 10% increase in income among families, expenditure in foods rose by 2.2% and expenditure for meats 2.5%. With such increase the quantity of beef bought rose 1.5%, but also higher expenditures in meats were taken up by the purchase of more expensive meat cuts.

Studies in food consumption in the United Kingdom have shown that the high income groups have greater consumption of liquid milk, cheese, meat, vegetables, and fruits than the rest of the population (Greaves and Hollingsworth, 1966). Since there is an indication that the gap between classes, in regard to food consumption has been narrowing considerably in this country since the pre-war periods, it may be possible that food patterns of the whole population, in the future, will approach more closely that of the high income groups. The same situation, of course, would be desirable for the rest of the world.

REFERENCES

ABRAMSON, J. H. (1961) *S. Afr. med. J.* **35**, 268–272.
ABRAMSON, J. H., SLOME, C., and WARD, N. T. (1960) *Am. J. clin. Nutr.* **8**, 875–884.
ADVANEY, M., VENKATARAMAN, A., and RAO, N. R. (1967) *J. Nutr. Dietet.* **4**, 110–115.
APODACA, A. (1952) In *Human Problems in Technological Change, A Casebook*, pp. 35–39 (E. H. Spicer, ed.), Russell Sage Foundation, New York.
AYKROYD, W. R. (1965) *J. Hyg.* **63**, 137–153.
AYKROYD, W. R. (1961) *Nutrition, Lond.* **15**, 65–70.
AYLWARD, F. (1966) *Chemy Ind.* No. 39, 1624–1627.
BAILEY, K. V. (1962) *Trop. geogr. Med.* **14**, 1–10.
BAILEY, K. V. and WHITEMAN, J. (1963) *Trop. geogr. Med.* **15**, 377–388.
BAINES, A. H. J. and HOLLINGSWORTH, D. F. (1963) *Nutr. Abstr. Rev.* **33**, 653–668.
BAVLY, S. (1966) *Levels of Nutrition in Israel 1963–64 Urban Wage and Salary Earners*, Ministry of Education and Culture, College of Nutrition and Home Economics, and Central Bureau of Statistics, the Jerusalem Post Press, Jerusalem.
BOEK, J. K. (1956) *Am. J. clin. Nutr.* **4**, 239–245.
CANBERRA, BUREAU OF AGRICULTURE ECONOMICS (1967) *Household Meat Consumption in Sydney*, Beff Res. Rep. No. 3.
CHEN, J. S. and HUANG, C. S. (1960) *Metabolism* **9**, 594–603.
CLARK, F. (1958) *J. Am. diet. Ass.* **34**, 378–382.
COLLIS, W. R. F. DEMA, I., and OMOLOLU, A. (1962) *Trop. geogr. Med.* **14**, 201–229.
COWAN, J. W., CHOPRA, S., and HOURY, G. (1964) *J. Am. diet. Ass.* **45**, 130–133.
DARBY, W. J., ADAMS, C. M., POLLARD, M., DALTON, E., and MCKINLEY, P. (1956) *J. Nutr.* **60**, suppl. 2, 19–33.
DATTA, S. P., KUTTY, V. J., and GOPALAN, T. K. (1963) *Indian J. med. Sci.* **17**, 148–156.
DEMARCHI, M., MOHANTY, M., ALI, M., AL-AZZAWEE, M., AL-SAIDI, S., and ISA, A. (1962) *J. Fac. Med. Baghdad* **4**, 140–149.
DEVADAS, R. P. and EASWARAN, P. P. (1967) *J. Nutr. Diet.* **4**, 156–161.
Encyclopedia Americana (1969) US American Corporation, pp. 219–223.
Evaluación Nutricional de la Población de Centro América y Panamá. Guatemala (1969) Instituto de Nutrición de Centro América y Panama (INCAP), Oficina de Investigaciones Internacionales de los Institutos Nacionales de Salud (EEUU), Ministerio de Salud Pública y Asistencia Social, Instituto de Nutrición de Centro América y Panamá, Guatemala.
Evaluación Nutricional de la Población de Centro América y Panamá. Panamá (1969) Instituto de Nutrición de Centro América y Panamá (INCAP), Oficina de Investigaciones Internacionales de los Institutos Nacionales de Salud (EEUU), Ministerio de Salud Pública, Instituto de Nutrición de Centro América y Panamá, Guatemala.
FAINE, S. and HERCUS, C. E. (1951) *Br. J. Nutr.* **5**, 327–343.
FERRO-LUZZI, G. (1962) *Am. J. clin. Nutr.* **11**, 299–311.
FLORES, M. (1961) In *Tradition Science and Practice in Dietetics, Proceedings of the 3rd International Congress of Dietetics, London*, 1961, pp. 23–27, Wm. Byles, Bradford, Yorkshire, United Kingdom.
FLORES, M. (1969) Unpublished data.

Food and Agriculture Organization of the United Nations (FAO) (1966) *Food Balance Sheets* 1960–62 *Average,* Rome.
Food and Agriculture Organization of the United Nations (FAO) (1967) *Production Yearbook* 1966, Rome.
Fry, P. C. (1957) *Am. J. clin. Nutr.* **5**, 42–50.
Grant, F. W. and Groom, D. (1958) *J. Am. diet. Ass.* **34**, 708–716.
Grant, F. W. and Groom, D. (1959) *J. Am. diet. Ass.* **35**, 910–918.
Greaves, J. P. and Hollingsworth, D. F. (1966) *Wld Rev. Nutr. Diet.* **6**, 34–89.
Halley, H. (1946) *J. Am. diet. Ass.* **22**, 977–983.
Hauck, H. M. and Hanks, J. R. (1959) *J. Am. diet. Ass.* **35**, 1143–1148.
Hollingsworth, D. F. (1955) *Proc. Nutr. Soc.* **14**, 71–77.
Johnson, B. and Feniak, E. (1965) *Can. Nutr. Notes* **21**, 61–65.
Jones, G. T. (1965) *Fm. Economist* **10**, 435–445.
Jyothi, K. K., Dhakshayani, R., Swaminathan, M. C., and Venkatachalam, P. S. (1963) *Trop. geogr. Med.* **15**, 403–410.
Kleevens, J. W. L. (1966) *Singapore Med. J.* **7**, 202–208.
Mellbin, T. (1962) *Acta paediatr.* **51**, suppl. 131.
Miller, C. and Kaumvakali, T. (1955) *J. Am. diet. Ass.* **31**, 269–272.
Mitchell, H. S. and Joffe, N. T. (1944) *J. Am. diet. Ass.* **20**, 676–687.
Murray, J. and Blake, E. (1959) In *Food: The Yearbook of Agriculture* 1959, US Department of Agriculture, Washington.
National Nutrition Survey (US) (1972) *Nutr. Today* **7** (4), 4–11.
Oshima, H. T. (1967) *Econ. Devel. cult. Change* **15**, 385–397.
Parkinson, S. (1961) In *Tradition Science and Practice in Dietetics, Proceedings of the* 3rd *International Congress of Dietetics, London,* 1961, pp. 16–22, Wm. Byles Bradford, Yorkshire, United Kingdom.
Périssé, J. (1966) L'Alimentation en Afrique Intertropicale. Étude Critique a Partir des Données des Énquetes de Consommation 1950–1965, these (Docteur, Mention Pharmacie) presentée a la Faculté de Pharmacie de l'Université de Paris.
Plough, I. C., Fernández López, N. A., Angel, C. R., and Roberts, L. J. (1963) *Boln Asoc. med. P. Rico* **55**, 12A, suppl., 1–51.
Quin, P. J. (1964) *S. Afr. med. J.* **38**, 969–971.
Quiogue, E. S. (1966a) *Philipp. J. Nutr.* **19**, 173–193.
Quiogue, E. S. (1966b) *Philipp. J. Nutr.* **19**, 272–293.
Quiogue, E., Salvosa, C. B., Palma, E. M., and Espinas, O. E. (1962) *Nutrition Survey of Metropolitan Manila. I. Dietary Survey,* pp. 5–50, Republic of the Philippines, National Science Development Board, National Institute of Science and Technology, Food and Nutrition Research Center, NSDB Printing Press, Manila.
Quiogue, E. S., Villavieja, G. M., and Ramos, V. (1969) *Philipp. J. Nutr.* **22**, 61–78.
Rao, B. R. H., Klontz, C. E., Rao, P. S. S., Begum, A., and Dumm, M. E. (1961) *Indian J. med. Res.* **49**, 316–329.
Rao, K. V. (1967) *J. Nutr. Dietet.* **4**, 79–87.
Rao, M. V. R. (1956) *Diet and Nutrition Studies in Rural Areas in Bombay State,* I: *Sirur Health Unit, Sirur (District Poona);* II: *Karjat Community Project Area (District Kolaba),* Government Central Press, Bombay.
Robertson, E. C. (1962) *Can. Nutr. Notes* **18**, 13–18.
Sai, F. T. (1969) *Wld Rev. Nutr. Diet.* **10**, 77–99.
Salcedo, J., Jr., Bamba, M. D., Carrasco, E. O., Chan, G. S., Concepción, I., José, F. R., de León, J. F., Oliveros, S. B., Pascual, C. R., Santiago, L. C., and Valenzuela, R. C. (1950) *J. Nutr.* **42**, 501–523.
Sebrell, W. H., Smith, S. C., Severinghaus, E. L., Delva, H., Reid, B. L., Olcott, H. S., Bernadotte, J., Fougere, W., Barron, G., Nicolas, G., King, K., Brinkman, G. L., and French, C. E. (1959) *Am. J. clin. Nutr.* **7**, 538–584.

SINCLAIR, H. M. (1953) *Proc. Nutr. Soc.* **12,** 69–82.
THOMAS, H. M. (1972) *Wld Rev. Nutr. Diet.* **14,** 48–58.
THOMASON, M. J., TOBAR, R., OLMEDO, R., SÁNCHEZ, M., and VARGAS, C. (1957) *Am. J. clin. Nutr.* **5,** 295–304.
TRENHOLME, M. and MILNE, H. (1963) *Can. J. publ. Hlth* **54,** 455–462.
US DEPARTMENT OF AGRICULTURE (1968) *Dietary Levels of Households in the United States, Spring 1965. A Preliminary Report*, US Department of Agriculture, ARS 62–17, Washington, DC.
US DEPARTMENT OF HEALTH, EDUCATION AND WELFARE (1967) *Republic of Paraguay — Nutrition Survey, May–August*, 1965, Bethesda, Md.
US Interdepartmental Committee on Nutrition for National Defense (1959a) *Alaska, an Appraisal of the Health and Nutritional Status of the Eskimo, March–April, 1958*, Department of Defense, Washington, DC.
US INTERDEPARTMENTAL COMMITTEE ON NUTRITION FOR NATIONAL DEFENSE (1964a) *Bolivia, Nutrition Survey, May–July 1962*, Department of Defense, Washington, DC.
US INTERDEPARTMENTAL COMMITTEE ON NUTRITION FOR NATIONAL DEFENSE (1961a) *Chile, Nutrition Survey, March–June 1960*, Department of Defense, Washington, DC.
US INTERDEPARTMENTAL COMMITTEE ON NUTRITION FOR NATIONAL DEFENSE (1961c) *Republic of China, Nutrition Survey of the Armed Forces, September–October, 1960*, Department of Defense, Washington, DC.
US INTERDEPARTMENTAL COMMITTEE ON NUTRITION FOR NATIONAL DEFENSE (1961b) *Colombia, Nutrition Survey, May–August,* **1960,** Department of Defense, Washington, DC.
US INTERDEPARTMENTAL COMMITTEE ON NUTRITION FOR NATIONAL DEFENSE (1960a) *Ecuador, Nutrition Survey, July–September, 1959*, Department of Defense, Washington, DC.
US INTERDEPARTMENTAL COMMITTEE ON NUTRITION FOR NATIONAL DEFENSE (1959b) *Ethiopia, Nutrition Survey, September–December, 1958*, Department of Defense, Washington, DC.
US INTERDEPARTMENTAL COMMITTEE ON NUTRITION FOR NATIONAL DEFENSE (1956a) *Iran, Nutrition Survey of the Armed Forces, 1956*, Department of Defense, Washington, DC.
US INTERDEPARTMENTAL COMMITTEE ON NUTRITION FOR NATIONAL DEFENSE (1962a) *The Kingdom of Thailand, Nutrition Survey, October–December, 1960*, Department of Defense, Washington, DC.
US INTERDEPARTMENTAL COMMITTEE ON NUTRITION FOR NATIONAL DEFENSE (1957a) *Korea, Nutrition Survey of the Armed Forces, 1957*, Department of Defense, Washington, DC.
US INTERDEPARTMENTAL COMMITTEE ON NUTRITION FOR NATIONAL DEFENSE (1962b) *Republic of Lebanon, Nutrition Survey, February–April, 1961*, Department of Defense, Washington, DC.
US INTERDEPARTMENTAL COMMITTEE ON NUTRITION FOR NATIONAL DEFENSE (1957b) *Libya, Nutrition Survey of the Armed Forces and Civilians, June–August, 1957*, Department of Defense, Washington, DC.
US INTERDEPARTMENTAL COMMITTEE ON NUTRITION FOR NATIONAL DEFENSE (1956b) *Pakistan, Nutrition Survey of the Armed Forces, January–April, 1956*, Department of Defense, Washington, DC.
US INTERDEPARTMENTAL COMMITTEE ON NUTRITION FOR NATIONAL DEFENSE (1959c) *Peru, Nutrition Survey of the Armed Forces, February–May, 1959*, Department of Defense, Washington, DC.
US INTERDEPARTMENTAL COMMITTEE ON NUTRITION FOR NATIONAL DEFENSE (1957c) *Philippines, Nutrition Survey of the Armed Forces, 1957*, Department of Defense, Washington, DC.

US INTERDEPARTMENTAL COMMITTEE ON NUTRITION FOR NATIONAL DEFENSE (1958a) *Spain, Nutrition Survey of the Armed Forces, April–June,* 1958, Department of Defense, Washington, DC.

US INTERDEPARTMENTAL COMMITTEE ON NUTRITION FOR NATIONAL DEFENSE (1958b) *Turkey, Nutrition Survey of the Armed Forces, April–June,* 1957, Department of Defense, Washington, DC.

US INTERDEPARTMENTAL COMMITTEE ON NUTRITION FOR NATIONAL DEFENSE (1963) *Republic of Uruguay, Nutrition Survey, March–April,* 1962, Department of Defense, Washington, DC.

US INTERDEPARTMENTAL COMMITTEE ON NUTRITION FOR NATIONAL DEFENSE (1960b) *Republic of Vietnam, Nutrition Survey, October–December,* 1959, Department of Defense, Washington, DC.

US INTERDEPARTMENTAL COMMITTEE ON NUTRITION FOR NATIONAL DEFENSE (1962c) *The West Indies, Trinidad and Tobago, St. Lucia, St. Christopher, Nevis and Anguilla, Nutrition Survey, August–September,* 1961, Department of Defense, Washington, DC.

US INTERDEPARTMENTAL COMMITTEE ON NUTRITION FOR NATIONAL DEFENSE (1964b) *Venezuela, Nutrition Survey, May–June,* 1963, Department of Defense, Washington, DC.

US INTERDEPARTMENTAL COMMITTEE ON NUTRITION FOR NATIONAL DEVELOPMENT (1965) *Northeast Brazil, Nutrition Survey, March–May,* 1963, Department of Defense, Washington, DC.

US OFFICE OF INTERNATIONAL RESEARCH (1967) *Republic of Nigeria Nutrition Survey, February–April,* 1965, a report by the Nutrition Section Office of International Research, National Institutes of Health, US Department of Health, Education, and Welfare, Washington, DC.

WALKER, A. R. P. (1966) *S. Afr. med. J.* **40,** 814–852.

WHITE, H. S., COLLAZOS, C., C., WHITE, P. L., HUENEMANN, R. L., BENITES, R., CASTELLANOS, A., BRAVO, Y., MOSCOSO, I. I., and DIESELDORFF, A. (1954) *J. Am. diet. Ass.* **30,** 856–864.

YOUSIF, M. (1967) *Trop. geogr. Med.* **19,** 192–198.

ZUBIRÁN, S. and CHÁVEZ, A. (1963) *Boln Of. sanit. pan-am.* **54,** 101–103.

ZUBIRÁN, S., CHÁVEZ, A., and SOBERÓN, G. (1964) *Prensa med. Méx.* **29,** 95–107.

CHAPTER 4

NUTRITIONAL REQUIREMENTS: DIETARY ALLOWANCES AND REQUIREMENTS FOR CALORIES AND NUTRIENTS

Conrado R. Pascual, Carmen Ll. Intengan,
Josefina Bulatao-Jayme, Rodolfo F. Florentino, and
Leon G. Alejo

Food and Nutrition Research Center, National Science Development Board, Manila, Philippines

CONTENTS

1. Introduction	141
2. Calorie Requirements	145
2.1. Basal Metabolism	145
2.2. Energy Cost of Physical Activities	146
2.3. Specific Dynamic Effect of Foods	148
2.4. Total Caloric Requirements	149
3. Protein	155
3.1. Roles	155
3.2. Bases of Requirement	156
3.2.1. Blood Levels, Total Serum Protein, Serum Albumin, and Albumin Globulin Ratio	158
3.2.2. Urinary Excretion	158
3.3. Estimates of Requirements	159
3.3.1. Other Protein Standards	162
3.4. Factors Affecting Requirements	163
3.4.1. Quality and Quantity of Dietary Protein	164
3.4.2. The Protein–Nutrient Interrelationships	165
3.4.3. Minor Factors	167
4. Calcium	167
4.1. Food Sources	167
4.2. Roles	168
4.3. Absorption from the Intestine	168
4.4. Requirements	169
4.4.1. Methods of Estimation	169
4.4.2. Recommendations on Calcium Needs	171

- 5. Iron — 173
  - 5.1. Role and metabolism — 173
  - 5.2. Requirement — 175
    - 5.2.1. Adult — 175
    - 5.2.2. Pregnancy and Lactation — 175
    - 5.2.3. Infants — 176
    - 5.2.4. Children — 177
    - 5.2.5. Adolescents — 177
  - 5.3. Factors Affecting Absorption — 177
    - 5.3.1. The size of Iron Stores Influence the Absorption of this Mineral — 177
    - 5.3.2. Form of Iron — 177
    - 5.3.3. Composition of the Diet — 178
    - 5.3.4. Effect of Phytates — 178
    - 5.3.5. Erythropoeisis Rate — 179
    - 5.3.6. Iron Absorption — 179
    - 5.3.7. Reducing Compounds — 179
    - 5.3.8. Gastrointestinal Disturbances — 179
    - 5.3.9. Iron Requirement — 180
- 6. Retinol — 180
  - 6.1. Vitamin Intake and Sources — 181
  - 6.2. Role — 181
  - 6.3. Assessment — 181
  - 6.4. Terminology — 182
  - 6.5. Estimation of Requirement — 182
    - 6.5.1. Adults — 183
    - 6.5.2. Pregnancy — 183
    - 6.5.3. Lactation — 183
    - 6.5.4. Infants — 184
    - 6.5.5. Age Groups — 184
  - 6.6. Factors Influencing Requirement — 184
    - 6.6.1. Biological Activity — 184
    - 6.6.2. Dietary Fat — 185
    - 6.6.3. Protein Nutriture — 185
    - 6.6.4. Vitamin Interrelationship — 186
    - 6.6.5. Infection — 186
    - 6.6.6. Preparation and/or Preservation of Food — 186
- 7. Thiamine — 187
  - 7.1. Metabolic Function — 187
  - 7.2. Methods of Estimating Requirement — 187
    - 7.2.1. Urinary Excretion — 187
    - 7.2.2. Blood Pyruvic Acid — 188
    - 7.2.3. Red Cell Transketolase Activity — 188
    - 7.2.4. Urinary Thiamine "Metabolites" — 189
    - 7.2.5. Dietary Intake — 189
  - 7.3. Estimates of Requirements — 189
  - 7.4. Factors Affecting the Requirement — 190
    - 7.4.1. Composition of the Diet — 190
    - 7.4.2. Dietary Practices — 190
    - 7.4.3. Thiaminase — 191
- 8. Riboflavin — 191
  - 8.1. Assessment of Riboflavin Nutriture — 192
    - 8.1.1. Urinary Excretion — 192
    - 8.1.2. Red Cell Concentration — 194

8.1.3. Tissue Saturation	194
8.2. Bases of Requirement	194
8.3. Estimate of Requirement	196
8.3.1. Recommended Dietary Allowances	196
8.3.2. Urinary Excretion	197
8.3.3. Biochemical/Clinical Assessment	197
8.4. Factors Affecting Riboflavin Requirements	197
8.4.1. Composition of the Diet	197
8.4.2. Effect of Protein and Other Vitamins	198
8.4.3. Climate, Physical Activity, and Other Pathological Stresses	199
9. Nicotinic Acid or Nicotinamide	199
9.1. Roles	199
9.2. Principles and Methods of Estimating Requirements	199
9.3. Estimation of Requirement	201
9.3.1. Adults	203
9.3.2. Pregnancy and Lactation	203
9.3.3. Infants and Children	203
9.4. Factors Affecting Requirements for Nicotinamide	203
9.4.1. Composition of the Diet	203
9.4.2. Pregnancy	204
9.4.3. Absorption	204
9.4.4. Climate, Body Weight, and Physical Activity	205
9.4.5. Interrelationship Among the Vitamins	205
10. Ascorbic Acid	205
10.1. Food Sources	205
10.2. Roles	206
10.3. Requirements	207
10.3.1. Methods of Estimation	207
10.3.2. Dietary Standards	209
References	211

1. INTRODUCTION

The study of nutrient requirements and allowances, while fascinating to nutritionists and related workers, is still replete with many difficulties. Despite the rapid advances in the science of nutrition during the last few decades, the subject of nutrient requirements and allowances still remains speculative. The term "minimum requirement" is generally defined as the least amount of a nutrient needed to support good health or prevent signs and symptoms of nutritional deficiency. Actually there should be only one such level for a healthy individual at a given time, but this normally varies from one person to another. On the other hand, the "optimum requirement" is a level that should not go beyond the needs for optimum health. However, the criteria for the assessment of what constitutes optimal health are still insufficient. There is also the uncertainty of whether higher levels promote greater functional efficiency or whether harmful effects may be produced. All this means that there is a need for defining nutritional requirements with more accuracy—defining the limit at the top being just as important as what is reasonably possible at the bottom. It appears, therefore, that there is still a wide gap in our knowledge of nutritional requirements. Hence it becomes necessary to introduce a "safety allowance" to cover this gap of insufficient nutritional information as well as variation in individual requirements.

Safety allowances vary depending upon the nutrient under consideration. In the case of protein, for example, the quality ordinarily consumed by the population group will be a major determining factor in estimating the allowances that can be given. The generous allowance for iron is based on various reports that there is poor absorption of this mineral from many foodstuffs. In the allowance given for vitamin A, the percentage of carotene in the diet is an important factor to be considered in arriving at the amounts to be allowed for the vitamin.

Since the basis used in the formulation of dietary allowances may vary from one country to another, there is a need for clearly stating its objectives. If the goal is the attainment of health of a normal individual, clarification should be made on whether optimum health is desired or just the average or the usual. Thus some countries like the United States (Food and Nutrition Board, NAS–NRC, 1968) have set their dietary allowances at optimum amounts to cover the needs of nearly all healthy people of that country; others, like Canada (Canadian Council on Nutrition, 1964), have drawn up a set of standards which is the lowest that will prevent a deficiency, thus setting the amount at a level below which maintenance of good health cannot be assumed.

When the term "allowances" is used, it is meant to imply that a certain percentage has been given over and above the minimum and that this amount is subject to change depending on newer findings and knowledge in food and nutrition. Such allowances have been termed "practical allowances" and are designed to cover the dietary needs of nearly all the population. Practical allowances and optimum allowances as currently used in the literature seem to connote the same meaning.

There is still a need for more studies on nutrient requirement. To begin with, the number of so-called "essential" nutrients can be expected to increase as our knowledge in the chemistry of life broadens. In recent years the role of some of the trace elements in human nutrition has been elucidated; and in the case of vitamins the function of some of them still remains to be clearly understood.

In estimating requirements for nutrients there are other factors which may account for variability in experimental results besides those inherent in biology. Sources of such variability are the differences in experimental design, number of subjects, analytical methods used, difficulties in collection of samples, and the extent of cooperation of the subjects. In many cases, such conditions as the nutritional status of the subject used for the particular nutrient under study would affect the response of the individual to balance studies. Likewise psychological factors or emotional stress could distort the data obtained from such studies.

In view of these various factors affecting nutritional requirements, some nutritionists have even suggested that values be given as a range and not as a single figure. By so doing, interpretation of results and evaluation of individual intake could be placed on a more accurate basis, or closer to the individual's particular nutritional status. The Interdepartmental Committee on Nutrition for National Defense (ICNND, 1963) of the United States has suggested such a range of nutritional standards (Table 1) and is designed to provide a definition of various degrees of adequacy of dietary intake. However, for general use specially in the evaluation of intakes of whole population groups, a single dietary standard is more convenient and less confusing.

TABLE 1   SUGGESTED GUIDE TO INTERPRETATION OF NUTRIENT INTAKE DATA FOR REFERENCE MAN[a]

	Deficient	Low	Acceptable	High
Calories	—	—	—	—
Protein (gm/kg body weight)	< 0.5	0.5 –0.9	1.0–1.4	≥ 1.5
Calcium (gm/day)	< 0.3	0.30–0.39	0.4–0.7	≥ 0.8
Iron (mg/day)	< 6	6–8	9–11	≥ 12
Vitamin A (IU/day)	< 2000	2000–3499	3500–4999	≤ 5000
Ascorbic and (mg/day)	< 10	10–29	30–49	≥ 50
Thiamine (mg per 1000 Cal)	< 0.2	0.20–0.29	0.3–0.4	≥ 0.5
Riboflavin (mg/day)	< 0.7	0.7 –1.1	1.2–1.4	≥ 1.5
Niacin (mg/day)	< 0.5	5–9	10–14	≥ 15

[a] From Interdepartmental Committee on Nutrition for National Defense (1963), *Manual for Nutrition Surveys*, National Institute of Health, Bethesda, Md, 2nd edn.

There is also a need for more precise knowledge on nutrient interrelationships and their effect on the requirement. While it is true that there has been some progress in this direction, we have barely scratched the surface, and there possibly remains much more to be done before enough appreciation of their complex relationship can be made to bear on the problem of nutrient requirements and allowances. Moreover, there are a great number of environmental factors—socio-cultural, economic, educational, technological, climatic, etc.—which vary from one geographic area to another and which may significantly affect recommendations for certain nutrients.

The adaptation of the human body to changing environmental conditions is of great interest to nutritionists. It is reassuring to know that when the body is subjected to nutritional stress, such as an inadequate or excessive supply of one or more of the nutrients, the body can somehow adapt itself by regulating its metabolic processes.

In the light of all these findings, dietary requirements and allowances so far have been set only in tentative terms and subject to a fuller understanding of the human physiological needs for specific nutrients, the nature and extent of their interrelationships, the improvements in methods of research and technology, the interplay of adaptation and homeostasis, etc. There are, of course, limitations in setting up dietary standards which have to be clarified if intelligent use is to be made of such standards.

Results of well conducted nutrition surveys can be very helpful in arriving at more practical dietary standards. The occurrence or absence of clinical signs and symptoms of deficiency conditions, and the levels of nutrients in biological samples, when related with the intake of the nutrient under study, can serve as guidelines in arriving at nutritional requirements.

Recommended nutrient requirements and allowances are usually formulated to provide a guide in planning for the nutrient needs of the average healthy individual or, more appropriately, of a particular population group. Unless an individual meets the criterion of the "average" man, such dietary standards should not be used as a yardstick for nutritional assessment without making the necessary adjustments. At best, dietary standards are useful in checking the nutrient intake of population groups as guidelines in setting up goals for food production and the country's food supplies and as essential tools in drawing up food policies in national and international programs on food and nutrition.

Generally, each country formulates its own dietary standards that are practical and suitable for its needs. Developing countries cannot afford to set up optimal estimates, and although the majority of people could be benefited by such standards, this may remain unattainable.

It would be a simple matter to assess the world's need for food and the global food situation if a universal dietary standard could be formulated. However, this is too complex and difficult even to attempt at this time, and it imposes a heavy burden of responsibility on anyone who will attempt to do so. While there is no question as to its desirability, at the most it would be a better idea to have this on a regional basis.

This chapter tries to set the bases and the general concepts used in the formulation of nutrient requirements and recommended allowances. It is hoped that these concepts can lead to a more reasonable understanding and appreciation of dietary standards.

2. CALORIE REQUIREMENTS

The energy expenditure of an adult individual largely consists of three components, namely, energy for basal metabolism, energy for physical activities, and specific dynamic effect of food. During period of growth, including pregnancy and lactation, additional energy is needed for the synthesis of new tissues and for milk secretion. Mental activity requires such a small expenditure of energy that it is usually ignored for all practical purposes in the estimation of energy requirements.

2.1. BASAL METABOLISM

Basal metabolism represents the energy needed to maintain the vital life processes of the body such as heart and respiratory function, maintenance of body temperature, etc. It is usually determined by indirect calorimetry, that is, by measuring the oxygen consumption of the individual as he breathes through an apparatus, such as the Benedict-Roth respirometer. This is taken under conditions of physical and mental rest, while the subject is awake, between 12–18 h after a meal and at a comfortable environmental temperature. These conditions, however, are merely intended to standardize the procedure, so that the rate of metabolism obtained is relatively constant and low. It is therefore not necessarily "basal" or the lowest for the individual, since lower values may be obtained under other conditions such as profound sleep and chronic undernutrition. For this reason, Krogh (1916) proposed the term "standard metabolism" to erase the erroneous impression that basal metabolism is the least resting metabolism, i.e. the lowest that could be obtained from an individual. This view was supported by other authors (Boothby et al., 1936; Du Bois, 1936; Keys, 1950). Although the term "standard metabolism" has not gained universal usage, the meaning of basal metabolism is taken as such.

Basal metabolism is usually expressed in terms of surface area since this parameter is a better indicator of body size than either height or weight. When expressed in this manner, basal metabolic rate (BMR) is more or less constant for all normal individuals of the same sex and age. In fact the BMR of normal adults varies only slightly: for males, it ranges from 36 to 41 Cal/m²/h and for females, from 34 to 36 Cal/m²/h (Boothby et al., 1936). The BMR, however, is much higher in infancy, and it diminishes as age advances (except possibly for a slight rise at the time of puberty) until it reaches a relatively stationary level during adulthood. The apparent difference between the male and female values in standard BMR tables is actually not a physiological difference; it is merely due to the fact that women are, in general, fatter than men. Thus, when basal metabolism is expressed on the basis of "metabolically active tissue" or lean body mass, the sex difference disappears (Passmore, 1966). Nevertheless, because of difficulty in estimating "metabolically active tissue," surface area (computed from the formula of Du Bois and Du Bois, 1916), as modified to suit particular populations (Banerjee, 1962), continue to be used in standard BMR tables.

Many standards on BMR have been formulated such as the Mayo Foundation Standards (Boothby et al., 1936) and those of Robertson and Reid (1952), Fleisch (1951), Vogelius (1945), Lewis et al., (1943), etc., but their differences lie mainly in the manner in which the standards were derived. Sargent (1961) gives an excellent evaluation of the voluminous BMR data in children and youth in the United States. The influence of race on the BMR is still open to question; while some have found a lower BMR for people living in the tropics than those in the temperate regions, others have found practically no difference. Thus, while studies in India (Sen and Banerjee, 1958) have shown a lower BMR when compared to Western standards, the difference is more apparent than real. It has been shown that the BMR of Indians is the same as that of people of the West when cell mass, cell solid, or lean body mass—rather than surface area—is used as the basis for expression (Banerjee, 1962). Studies in the Philippines have shown that the slightly lower BMR of Filipinos when compared to the Mayo Standards are probably due to the differences in the manner in which BMR data were selected rather than to any intrinsic difference (Florentino, 1966).

2.2. ENERGY COST OF PHYSICAL ACTIVITIES

The body spends a large proportion of its energy needs for physical activities. Even the simple and usually unconscious act of keeping oneself in a sitting position involves energy which is added to the basal caloric needs. Since the advent of indirect calorimetry, particularly with the use of the Muller–Franz gasmeter, thousands of measurements of the caloric cost of various types of activities have been made, from lying at rest to swimming and coal mining. The subject, while performing the activity under test, is made to breathe into a gas meter which measures pulmonary ventilation (Durnin and Brockway, 1959; Insull, 1964). The expired air, or an aliquot of it, is analyzed for oxygen and carbon dioxide. An extensive compilation of the results of such work conducted by Western investigators over the past 50 years is that of Passmore and Durnin (1955). In this treatise, as in other more recent work, results are expressed in gross calories per minute without subtracting values for BMR (Table 2). However, in the application of these results to individuals

TABLE 2   ENERGY EXPENDITURES OF SELECTED ACTIVITIES[a]

Subject	Age	Sex	Weight (kg)	Activity	Cal/min
Average of 12	32	M	66	Lying at ease	1.3
Average of 16	34	M	66	Sitting at ease	1.6
Average of 5	26	M	69	Standing at ease	1.7
1	28	M	68	Washing and dressing	2.6
Average of 6	20–25	M	62	Dressing	3.0
Average of 3	19	M	64	Driving a car	2.8
Average of 4	22	F	50	Sweeping floor	1.7
1	43	F	84	Washing small clothes	2.3
7	19	M	70	Tennis	7.1

[a]From Passmore and Durnin (1955).

or populations of different body size, the figures are best expressed in terms of body weight (Durnin, 1959) or, perhaps more accurately, in terms of "metabolic size" which, according to Kleiber (1947), may be taken as the three-quarter power of body weight (in kilograms). Passmore (1966) gives tables for predicting energy cost of sitting quietly and of walking (Tables 3 and 4). In order to facilitate the estimation of energy expenditure in different occupations, they are classified into light, moderate, heavy, or very heavy work according to arbitrarily chosen ranges of caloric cost (Table 5). It is recognized that there is a wide variation in the energy cost of a physical activity as performed by different individuals and, in fact, even by the same individual at different times (Booyens and McCance, 1957; Durnin and Namyslowski, 1958). In

TABLE 3   NORMAL VALUES FOR THE ENERGY EXPENDITURE OF ADULTS SITTING QUIETLY[a]

Age (years)	Men no.	Cal/min per 65 kg		Standard deviation
		Mean	Range	
20–39	30	1.39	0.97–1.79	0.25
40–64	30	1.37	0.87–1.94	0.29
65+	23	1.29	0.91–1.94	0.25
		Cal/min per 55 kg		
20–39	30	1.15	0.75–1.68	0.28
40–59	30	1.07	0.78–1.56	0.19
60	23	1.09	0.77–1.62	0.31

[a] From Passmore (1966).

TABLE 4   NORMAL VALUES FOR THE ENERGY EXPENDITURE WHEN WALKING (CAL/MIN)[a]

Weight (kg)	45	55	65	75	85	95
Speed (km/h)						
3	2.1	2.5	2.8	3.2	3.5	3.8
4	2.7	3.2	3.6	4.0	4.3	4.6
5	3.2	3.7	4.2	4.7	5.1	5.5
6	3.8	4.4	4.9	5.4	5.9	6.4
7	4.4	5.0	5.5	6.1	6.6	7.1

[a] From Passmore (1966).

estimating the total energy expenditure of an individual, however, determining the exact energy cost of the individual's activities is less important than accurate determination of the time spent in each of these activities (Passmore and Durnin, 1955).

2.3.   SPECIFIC DYNAMIC EFFECT OF FOODS

The specific dynamic effect (SDE) of food represents the increase in heat production after the ingestion of food. Owing to the lack of knowledge on the exact cause of this effect of nutrients to metabolism (Johnson, 1967), in addition to the lack of agreement as to how it may be expressed (whether as maximum rise above basal metabolism, average rise for a period of time, or total increment after ingestion of food), confusion

TABLE 5 EXAMPLES OF THE ENERGY EXPENDITURE OF VARIOUS PHYSICAL ACTIVITIES [a]

Light work at 2.5–4.9 Cal/min		Moderate work at 5.0–7.4 Cal/min	Heavy work at 7.5–9.9 Cal/min	Very heavy work at over 10 Cal/min
Assembly work	Building industry	General laboring (pick and shovel)	Coal mining (hewing and loading)	Lumber work
Light industry	Bricklaying			Furnace men (steel industry)
Electrical industry	Plastering	Agricultural work (non-mechanized)	Football	Swimming (crawl)
Carpentry	Painting	Route march (rifle and pack)	Country dancing	
Military drill	Agricultural work (mechanized)	Ballroom		Cross country
Most domestic work with modern appliances	Driving truck	Gardening		
	Golf	Tennis		
Gymnastic exercises	Bowling	Cycling (up to 10 mph)		Hill climbing

[a] From Passmore (1966).

still prevails on the magnitude of this component of energy expenditure. For practical purposes, however, it is usually taken as between 6–10% of the total calories ingested from a mixed diet. Keys (1950) suggests an average figure of 10%. At any rate, its contribution to the total caloric expenditure is quite small.

2.4. TOTAL CALORIC REQUIREMENTS

Theoretically, the total caloric requirement of an adult individual is the sum of the three components of energy expenditure discussed above: basal metabolism, net energy cost of activities, and SDE. In practice, however, the estimation of the daily energy requirement may be facilitated by collecting two sets of data—the time spent in each of the various activities performed by an individual from day to day, and the gross energy cost of these activities per unit of time as actually determined by indirect calorimetry or estimated from previously published tables. As pointed out above, greater errors arise in determining the time involved rather than the energy cost of the activity.

Alternatively, the caloric requirement of a normal adult with a steady weight or of a child with normal rate of growth may also be determined by measuring his caloric *intake*. This method has been used as a check to the simpler time–motion studies. Besides being technically difficult, however, it has the disadvantage in that the intake may not be the actual requirement such as in times of food abundance or scarcity. Besides, the method gives no information on how the energy in the diet is spent, so that it would be difficult to make adjustments when these figures are applied to other individuals.

For population groups, standards of caloric requirements have been devised mainly as a guide for the formulation of adequate diets. The Food and Agriculture Organization of the United Nations has come out with such standards for use in an international scale (FAO, 1957). The recommendations are based on Reference Man and Woman who are assumed to require, on an average for the entire year, 3200 Cal and 2300 Cal per day, respectively. The FAO defines the Reference Man and Woman as follows:†

> The Reference Man is 25 years of age. He is healthy, that is, free from disease and physically fit for active work. He weighs 65 kilograms. He lives in the temperate zone at a mean annual temperature of 10°C. He consumes an adequate well balanced diet and neither gains nor loses weight. On each working day he is employed 8 hours in an occupation which is not sedentary, but does not involve more than occasional periods of hard physical labor. When not at work, he is sedentary for about 4 hours daily and may walk for up to $1\frac{1}{2}$ hours. He spends about $1\frac{1}{2}$ hours on active recreation and household work.
>
> The Reference Woman is a similarly healthy woman aged 25 years and weighing 55 kilograms. She lives in the same environment as the Reference Man. She may be engaged either in general household duties or in light industry. Her daily activities include walking for about 1 hour and 1 hour of active recreation, such as gardening, playing with children, or non-strenuous sport.

Formulas are given for adjustments for people of different age, weight, or living in a different climate compared with that of the Reference Man and Woman. Thus to allow for variations in body size, the following formulas are given:

$$E = 152(W)^{0.73} \text{ (man)},$$

$$E = 123.4\,(W)^{0.73} \text{ (woman)},$$

†Compare the definitions of Reference Man given by the International Commission on Radiological Protection, ICRP Publication 23, *Reference Man*, Pergamon Press, Oxford (to be published).

TABLE 6 CALORIE REQUIREMENTS OF ADULTS ACCORDING TO BODY WEIGHT IN REFERENCE TEMPERATURE AND AGE[a]

Weight (kg)		Cal/day	
Men	Women	Men	Women
	35		1654
	40		1823
45	45	2447	1987
50	50	2643	2146
55	55	2833	2300
60	60	3019	2451
65	65	3201	2599
70	70	3379	2743
75		3553	
80		3725	

[a]From FAO (1957).

TABLE 7 CALORIE REQUIREMENTS OF ADULTS ACCORDING TO AGE AT REFERENCE TEMPERATURE AND BODY WEIGHT[a]

Age (years)	Percentage of reference	Cal/day	
		Men	Women
20–30	100.0	3200	2300
30–40	97.0	3104	2231
40–50	94.0	3008	2162
50–60	86.5	2768	1990
60–70	79.0	2528	1817
70+	69.0	2208	1587

[a]From FAO (1957).

where W is the weight in kilograms. As age advances beyond 25 years, a reduction in the caloric requirement is recommended. For the decades 30–40 and 40–50, a reduction for each decade of 3% of the requirement at 25 is suggested. For decades 50–60 and 60–70, a decrement of 7.5% for each decade is applied, and for ages beyond 70, a further decrement of 10% is used. For people living at a mean annual temperature above 10°C, the FAO recommends a reduction of the caloric requirement assigned to the Reference Man and Woman by 5% for every 10°C above the reference temperature. On the other hand, requirements are increased by 3% for every 10°C of mean annual external temperature below the

TABLE 8 CALORIE REQUIREMENTS OF ADULTS ACCORDING TO MEAN ANNUAL EXTERNAL TEMPERATURE AT REFERENCE AGE AND BODY WEIGHT[a]

Mean external annual temperature (°C)	Percentage of reference	Cal/day Men	Cal/day Women
−5	104.5	3344	2404
0	103.0	3296	2369
5	101.5	3248	2335
10	100.0	3200	2300
15	97.5	3120	2243
20	95.0	3040	2185
25	92.5	2960	2128
30	90.0	2880	2070

[a]From FAO (1957).

reference temperature of 10°C. Tables 6–8 illustrate these adjustments that may be made on the requirements of the Reference Man and Woman.

Pregnancy entails an increase in energy requirement for the building of new fetal and maternal tissues and for the rise in the BMR. The FAO recommends that for calculating the caloric requirements of countries, an allowance of 40,000 Cal per pregnancy be added. For the lactating woman, assuming an average nursing period of 6 months and a daily milk output of 850 ml, an extra 1000 Cal/day is recommended in calculating national average requirements.

The caloric requirements for infants and children have to take into account the needs for growth as well as the high degree of physical activity common to children. The FAO recommends the following for infants:

<pre>
1–3   months   120 Cal/kg weight
4–9   months   110 Cal/kg weight
10–12 months   100 Cal/kg weight
Yearly average   110 Cal/kg weight
</pre>

Mainly in the light of food consumption data, the FAO recommends the following for children and adolescents:

<pre>
1–3   years inclusive children   1300 Cal
4–6   years inclusive children   1700 Cal
7–9   years inclusive children   2100 Cal
10–12 years inclusive children   2500 Cal
</pre>

13–15 years	inclusive	boys	3100 Cal
		girls	2600 Cal
16–19 years	inclusive	males	3600 Cal
		females	2400 Cal

The FAO further recommends that the requirements for adolescents (aged 16–19) be assessed as 113 and 104%, respectively, of requirements at 25 years for males and females. Similar adjustments for environmental temperature as are applied for adults are applied also for adolescents when called for.

What is much more difficult to assess than the changes on the caloric requirement brought about by differences in climate, age, and body size, is the wide variation in physical activities not only among individuals but also among population groups. Here is where energy and time–motion studies are necessary to provide first-hand assessment of the caloric needs of individual population groups.

Thus a number of countries have come out with their own recommendations applicable to their respective populations. The Food and Nutrition Board of the National Research Council (US) issued in 1968 its seventh revision of the *Recommended Dietary Allowances* for healthy persons in the United States under contemporary conditions. The recommendations for calories are based, like that of the FAO, on a Reference Man and a Reference Woman except that they are 22 years old with respective weights of 70 kg and 58 kg, and both are living in an environment with a mean temperature of 20°C. The Reference Man is assumed to require 2800 Cal and the Reference Woman 2000 Cal/day. In adapting allowances for difference in body size for adults, the use of the so-called desirable body weight (defined as the average weight of individuals of given sex and height at age 22) is employed. It is likewise proposed that caloric allowances be reduced by 5% between ages 22 and 35, by 3% per decade between ages 35 and 55, and by 5% per decade from ages 55 to 75. A further decrement of 7% is recommended for age 75 and beyond. No simple procedure has been derived for estimating allowances in relation to expenditure of physical energy. Little adjustment appears to be necessary for change in environmental temperature between 20° and 30°C, but under condition of increased physical activity, an increase in caloric allowance by 0.5% per degree of temperature rise between 30° and 40°C is recommended. On the other hand, an average individual with average caloric need working in a high temperature may even reduce his caloric requirement because of the tendency to reduce activity.

The Nutrition Committee of the British Medical Association published in 1950 its dietary recommendations for people in the United Kingdom. For adult males, six grades of activities are described and for adult females, five, ranging from grade 0 (no work, lying in bed) to grade 5 (very heavy work) and grade 6 (extremely heavy work). The man, 20 years or over, weighing 65 kg and performing medium work, is assumed to require 3000 Cal/day, while the woman of the same age, weighing 56 kg and doing medium work, 2500 Cal/day.

The Canadian Dietary Standards (1964) recommend 2850 cal/day for a moderately active man, 25 years old and weighing 75 kg, and 2400 Cal for a moderately active woman of the same age weighing 57 kg. The Dietary Allowances for Australians (1965) provide 2900 Cal for the Reference Man who is 25 years old and weighs 70 kg and 2100 Cal for the Reference Woman of the same age and weighing 58 kg. It has the advantage in that adjustment for different grades of activities from grade 0 to grade 3 are defined.

The caloric allowances that have been recommended for populations of smaller stature than, for example, Americans or Europeans, are different mainly because of smaller body size rather than any intrinsic differences between races. The Japanese recommendations (1960), for example, call for 2500 Cal and 2100 Cal for a man (55.5 kg) and woman (48.5 kg), respectively, belonging to the 20–29 year age group, both performing "light work".

In 1958 the Nutrition Advisory Committee of the Indian Council of Medical Research revised its 1944 recommendations for calories based on the results of energy studies in India and elsewhere as well as on FAO recommendations (Patwardhan, 1960). The Indian Reference Man, 25.5 years of age, weighing 55 kg, and engaged in light industrial occupation (moderate activity) is assumed to require 2800 Cal while the Reference Woman, 21.5 years of age, weighing 45 kg, and of the same activity classifications, is assumed to require 2300 Cal.

Prior to 1963, very few studies on energy expenditure of Filipinos have been published. Thus the caloric allowances recommended by the National Research Council of the Philippines (subsequently revised by the Food and Nutrition Research Center) have been based mainly on foreign figures and a few local studies on BMR. In the Philippine RDA (FNRC, 1960), the caloric allowance for a moderately active man, 25 years of age and weighing 53 kg, is taken as 2600 Cal and that of a moderately active woman of the same age, weighing 45 kg, is taken as 2300 Cal. Recent work on energy expenditure of Filipinos, however, indicate that these allowances are probably overestimated, especially for the average woman (Florentino, 1966). The actual figures would probably come nearer to FAO recommendations adjusted according to body size and higher environmental temperature.

Because of the great many differences among population groups throughout the world such as in body size, environmental temperature, and activity pattern, it becomes, indeed, a formidable task to formulate caloric allowances on an international scale. The recommendation set by the FAO is a giant step towards such a task. Still, there is a great need for further research on such aspects as the caloric requirements of various types of occupations as performed in different countries, activity pattern of population groups, the effect of climate and aging on energy needs, and so on. As the results of such studies come in and are evaluated, more practical allowances can be formulated which can serve not only as a general yardstick by which national diets can be gauged but as an instrument of food planning on worldwide scale.

3. PROTEIN

Proteins are complex macro molecules made up mainly of amino acids combined in peptide chains. Nearly half of the dry weight of the human body is protein (Longenecker, 1963). Every living cell and all body fluids, except bile and urine (normally), contain protein. The cellular protein is synthesized by the body from the dietary protein which has been broken down through digestive processes into its component amino acids.

Protein deficiency manifests itself as a complex syndrome probably due to the fact that a diet low in proteins may also provide inadequate amounts of vitamins.

Recent reviews on protein deficiency or protein malnutrition point out to the following factors related to the pathogenesis of the deficiency: (a) caloric intake, (b) age of the subjects, and (c) quantity and duration of the deficient diet (Waterlow *et al.,* 1960; Hansen, 1961; Viteri *et al.,* 1964). Like most other nutritional deficiencies, protein deficiency in man may result from defective intake (either in quantity or quality), poor absorption, excessive loss or destruction, or faulty synthesis.

3.1. ROLES

Dietary proteins serve as a source of nitrogen and amino acids for the synthesis of body protein and other nitrogen containing substances such as creatinine, histamine, certain hormones, and enzymes. The human body proteins contain some 20 amino acids eight of which are classified as indispensable or "essential" in the adult, and the rest as dispensable or nonessential. Essential amino acids have to be supplied in adequate amount by the dietary protein because they are not synthesized by the body. For the human adult, the essential amino acids are: isoleucine, leucine, lysine, methionine, phenylalanine, threonine, tryptophan, and valine; besides these, the infant also needs histidine. Growth in experimental animals and nitrogen balance in adult man can be maintained on diets with minimal requirements of essential amino acids when the nonessential amino acids are supplied by glycine, glutamic acid, or ammonium citrate (Sprinson and Rittenberg, 1949; Swendseid et al., 1960).

To allow for the most effective synthesis of body protein, the amino acids should be in a definite pattern at the moment of synthesis. If all the amino acids necessary are not present at the proportion needed, production is limited by the one least available (called the limiting amino acids), and the rest of the amino acids not thus utilized are lost for that purpose. The latter are retained in a general metabolic pool for use in the construction of other nitrogenous substances or to be eventually deaminated and transformed into sugar or fats which are then burned up or are deposited as carbohydrate or lipid reserves. It should be mentioned that an imbalance in the intake of amino acids which results from an excess, rather than a shortage of any of them may likewise have an adverse effect on the efficiency of the protein synthesis. It should also be realized that under certain conditions it may be the amount of nonessential nitrogen in the diet that is limiting. The Joint FAO/WHO Expert Group (1965) cited the case of both cow's milk and egg, where the minimal quantity that will maintain nitrogen balance in the adult provides more than double the estimated requirement of each essential amino acid (Allison, 1958). It was therefore suggested that after the required pattern of the essential amino acids has been specified, the proportion of the total nitrogen intake which these amino acids form must also be indicated.

3.2. BASES OF REQUIREMENT

Hegsted (1969) defined the two problems involved in the estimation of protein requirements:

(1) protein quality, its method of measurement and why proteins differ in quality;

(2) defining the minimal protein needs for different ages and sexes, environmental conditions, etc.

The usual approach to these problems is to define protein requirements in terms of one protein and then relate the quality of the protein with other protein of interest. By said process, one can decide the requirement for any protein.

There are, however, limitations to the methods of evaluating protein quality. Protein efficiency ratio (PER) is not an adequate method (Hegsted and Chang, 1965). It merely indicates the differences among proteins compared. The method uses weight gain *per se* as sole criterion of protein value. Methods that precisely define protein retention are likely to give more accurate results.

Biological value (BV), as defined by Mitchell (1963), is a measure of nitrogen retained for growth or maintenance and is expressed as nitrogen retained divided by nitrogen absorbed. However, the method is hard to execute and is likely to overestimate the quality of protein of poor nutritional quality (Hegsted, 1964).

Net Protein Utilization (NPU) represents the proportion of food nitrogen retained whereas BV represents the proportion of absorbed nitrogen retained. NPU therefore is related directly to dietary intake of nitrogen and therefore one of the better methods (Miller and Bender, 1955; Miller, 1963). The technique, nevertheless, has been criticized (Miller and Payne, 1961, and Hegsted and Worcester, 1967). Several investigators (Hegsted and Chang, 1965; Hegsted and Worcester, 1967; Hegsted *et al.*, in press) have recommended a "slope ratio" technique since it has a better statistical base than the original method (Miller and Bender, 1955).

The nutritional quality of proteins may be measured by any of several methods, some of which can only be carried out by animal experimentation. Among these may be mentioned nitrogen balance, carcass analysis, chemical score, changes in liver nitrogen, and ratio of urinary nitrogen to urinary creatinine.

Laboratory determinations have been widely used in appraising nutritional status with respect to protein. Since the plasma proteins are in dynamic equilibrium with the proteins of the body, fluctuations in one should be reflected in others (Holman *et al.*, 1934). Hemoglobin levels have also been found valuable in several studies on protein deficiency. The basis for the determination of hemoglobin assumed that the volume of the circulating fluids of the body is constant. But the volume of circulating plasma is subject to considerable variation in relation to growth, age, health, and acute and chronic disease. Therefore, the expanding and contracting blood volume may affect the values for concentration. This makes plasma protein or hemoglobin levels not a very good criterion for protein status (Albanese et al., 1958). Yoshimura (1961), however, suggested that total hemoglobin or total albumin or both in circulating blood may be taken as a tentative measure of adequate protein store. In his paper, he cited that there is much evidence to show that blood protein, including hemoglobin, acts as a reserve protein to replace disintegrated substance in protein deficiency.

3.2.1. Blood levels, Total Serum Protein, Serum Albumin, and Albumin Globulin Ratio

A level of total serum proteins above normal does not always indicate good protein nutrition for there are numerous reports of elevated total serum protein concentrations in people living in tropical and subtropical regions with inadequate intakes (Arroyave, 1962). The high levels are believed to be due to an increase in the concentration of the γ-globulin fraction. However, the measurement of serum albumin level is a more sensitive biochemical index even in marginal protein deficiency. The effects of protein depletion and repletion upon serum albumin and globulins are reviewed by Chow et al. (1945), Scrimshaw and Behar (1961), and Arroyave (1962). These reviews report reduction of serum albumin associated with protein deficiency in man. The significance of the test may be demonstrated by the regeneration of serum albumin levels to the normal range under the influence of good protein feeding in the cure of kwashiorkor (Brock, 1961). Serum albumin is sensitive to declining protein reserves. There is a level called "marginal hypo-albuminaemia" which indicates declining reserves without other manifest evidence of protein deficiency. Studies that have been conducted to define marginal serum albumin on children (Schendel et al., 1960; Yoshimura, 1961; Waterlow et al., 1960) found no change in the distribution of albumin in the tissues and commented on the possible changes in man.

The ratio of albumin to globulin has been used and should give a better index. Ratios below 1.0 have been used to indicate protein deficiency and those above 1.0 are considered normal.

3.2.2. Urinary Excretion

A reduced protein intake causes a decrease in protein turnover. The excretion of nitrogen after fasting is high when the protein intake has been high, and the excretion is low when the protein intake has been low. Urea excretion follows the same trend except during extreme protein depletion as in starvation. Platt (1954) presented data on the ratio of urea/total nitrogen to show the relation between the total output of nitrogen in the urine and the amount excreted as urea. He also found low ratios of urea per total nitrogen in a small group of lactating women with poor nutrition (Platt, 1958). He further suggested the ratio of urea per gram creatinine which is more meaningful. Arroyave (1962) studied low income rural localities and upper income urban groups and confirmed the applicability of relating the ratio to protein intake. The study of Luyken and Luyken-Koning (1960) on children in Surinam and the Netherlands likewise confirm the above findings.

Creatinine excretion per unit time per kilogram body weight. This is based on the constancy of creatinine excretion which is a measure of the muscle mass and thereby reflects the protein status of an individual.

Urinary sulfate sulfur/creatinine ratio. Recently the sulfate sulfur/creatinine ratio was suggested as a good index of the quality and quantity of dietary protein (National Academy of Sciences, National Research Council, 1963). This is based on the demonstration of Miller and Naismith (1953) that the sulfur content of mixed diets was a more reliable index of net dietary protein value than earlier indexes. Miller and Donoso (1963) proposed that the ratio of sulfur to nitrogen in a diet serve as a direct index for protein quality. Since the urinary S/N ratio may be an approximate indicator of the quality of the protein consumed and the N/creatinine ratio may be the index of protein quantity (Powell *et al.*, 1961) then

$$\frac{N}{creatinine} \times \frac{S}{N} = \frac{S}{creatinine}$$

The ratio may therefore be used to express quality and quantity of dietary protein intake.

3.3. ESTIMATES OF REQUIREMENTS

There are two approaches to the estimation of protein requirements. One consists of determining the minimum intakes of protein that support normal growth of infants and children and maintain nitrogen equilibrium in adult man. The second method (Joint FAO–WHO Expert

Group, 1965) makes use of the balance technique. Thus, the requirements for nitrogen may be estimated as follows:

$$R = (U_B + F_B + S + G) \times 1.1,$$

TABLE 9   THE AVERAGE NITROGEN REQUIREMENTS OF CHILDREN AND ADULTS[a]

Age (years)	Weight (kg)[b]	mg N/kg/day			
		Basal urinary N[c]	Total basal loss[d]	Requirement for growth[e]	Total requirement[f]
Children:					
Both sexes:					
1	11.3	74	114	20	148
2	13.5	70	110	13	136
3	15.5	68	109	13	134
4– 6	18	66	106	13	130
7– 9	27	59	99	13	123
10–12	36	54	94	10	114
Boys:					
13–15	49	50	90	10	110
16–19	63	46	86	7	102
Girls:					
13–15	49	49	89	10	110
16–19	54	48	88	3	100
Adults:					
Men	65	46	86	—	95
Women	55	46	86	—	95

[a] From *Report of a Joint FAO/WHO Expert Group on Protein Requirements* (1965).

[b] The weights of children up to 4 years are taken from table 9 in Nelson's *Textbook of Pediatrics* (1959) and represent mean weights for the age intervals 1–2, 2–3, and 3–4 years for boys and girls, 50th percentile. The weights of older children are those given in the report *Evaluation of Protein Nutrition*, National Academy of Sciences—National Research Council, 1959. For adults the weights taken are those of the Reference Man and Woman given in the report of the FAO Second Committee on Calorie Requirements (FAO, 1957a).

[c] The basal urinary nitrogen loss has been taken as 2 mg N per basal kcal. The basal metabolic rate of children was computed from the formula given by Smuts (1935):

$$BMR = 70.4 \times N\ 0.734,$$

where the BMR is in kcal and W is the weight in kg. For adults the figures are those for the FAO Reference Man and Woman (FAO, 1957a).

[d] The figures are those for basal urinary nitrogen loss with the addition of 20 mg N/kg for endogenous faecal loss and 20 mg N/kg for dermal loss.

[e] For children up to 4 years, the nitrogen requirement for growth and maturation is taken from table 1 in Holt *et al.* (1960). For older children, to calculate the nitrogen retained during growth, it is assumed that 18% of the weight gain is protein, with a nitrogen content of 16%. The rates of gain at each age are those cited in the report *Evaluation of Protein Nutrition*, National Academy of Sciences—National Research Council, 1959.

[f] The figures are the sum of the basal requirement plus the requirement for growth with an addition of 10% to cover the effects of everyday stresses.

where: R is the requirements of nitrogen per kilogram body weight per day,

U_B the basal urinary nitrogen loss per kilogram body weight per day,
F_B the basal fecal nitrogen loss per kilogram body weight per day,
S the nitrogen lost from the skin per kilogram body weight per day (integumental + minimum sweating), and
G the nitrogen increment during growth per kilogram body weight/day.

In this formula, 1.1 represents an addition of 10% to allow for the stress of ordinary life.

$R \times 6.25$ gives the requirement in terms of reference protein (g per kilogram body weight per day), 6.25 being the conventional conversion factor.

TABLE 10 THE PROTEIN REQUIREMENTS OF CHILDREN AND ADULTS IN TERMS OF REFERENCE PROTEIN[a]

Age (years)	g per kg body weight per day		
	Average	−20%	+20%
Children:			
1–3	0.88	0.70	1.06
4–6	0.81	0.65	0.97
7–9	0.77	0.62	0.92
10–12	0.72	0.58	0.86
Adolescents (boys and girls):			
13–15	0.70	0.56	0.84
16–19	0.64	0.51	0.77
Adults	0.59	0.47	0.71

Additional allowance for pregnancy: 6 g/day in the second and third trimesters.
Additional allowance for lactation: 15 g/day.
[a] From report of a Joint FAO–WHO Expert Group on Protein Requirements (1965).

TABLE 11 THE PROTEIN REQUIREMENTS OF INFANTS IN TERMS OF REFERENCE PROTEIN[a]

	0–3 months (mg N/kg)	9–12 months (mg N/kg)
Gram reference protein per kg	1.48	0.77
Plus 20% for individual variation	1.78	0.93

[a] From report of a Joint FAO–WHO Expert Group on Protein Requirements (1965).

The resulting requirements thus calculated are shown in Table 9.

In terms of the reference protein, the requirements are estimated in Table 10.

Using the same approach in the case of infants, their requirements are shown in Table 11.

For pregnant women in the second and third trimester, who do not normally consume liberal quantities of protein in the nonpregnant state, an additional 6 g reference protein (or 8 g protein with NPU 70–80) per day was recommended by the FAO–WHO Expert Group. This was increased to 15 g reference protein per day for lactating women.

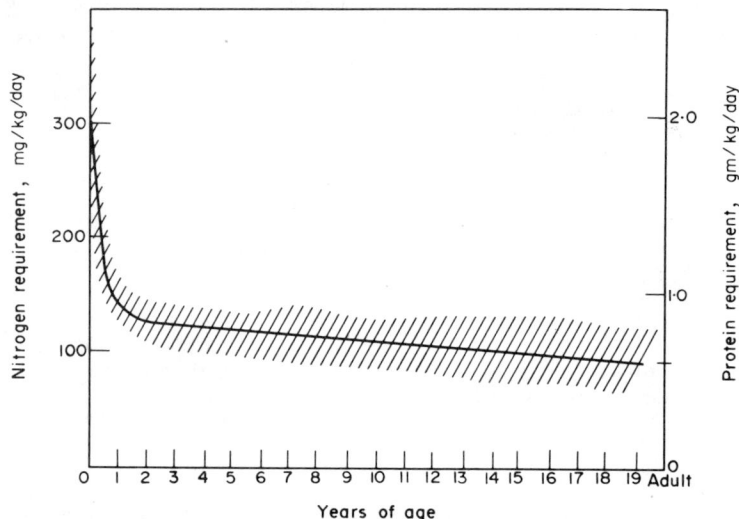

FIG. 1. Nitrogen requirement at different ages in terms of reference protein. The solid line represents average figures and the shaded zone the requirements of 95% of the population. Taken from Holt and Snyderman (1965).

Figure 1 illustrates the requirements of man for reference protein computed from the above formula. The graph indicates levels 20% below and above the average based on the estimate of the expected range of individual variation. The upper level covers the requirements of all but a very small proportion of the population. The lower level is that below which protein deficiency may be expected to occur in all but a very few individuals.

3.3.1. *Other Protein Standards*

Mention was already made of the US–NRC allowance. The Canadian

Dietary Standard was set at a level below which nutritional adequacy cannot be assumed. The British standard for protein was based on evidence that growth and health were well sustained at levels of protein intakes between 10 and 14% of the total calories. The British protein allowances were therefore recommended at dietary levels of not less than 11% of the energy allowance for adults while 14% of the same was deemed sufficient during growth, pregnancy, and lactation. A comparison of these standards is shown in Table 12.

TABLE 12 A COMPARISON OF THE PROTEIN ALLOWANCES FOR ADULTS

Country	Sex	Age (years)	Weight (kg)	Protein (g)
Australia	M	18–75	70	70
	F	18–75	58	58
Canada	M	—	65.5	46
	F	—	50.5	35
India	M	25.5	55	55
	F	21.5	45	45
Japan	M	25	55.5	70
	F	25	48.5	60
Philippines	M	25	53	55
	F	25	45	45
United Kingdom	M	20+	65	87
	F	20+	56	73
United States	M	18–75	70	70
	F	18–75	58	58

3.4. FACTORS AFFECTING REQUIREMENTS

The question of defining the reference protein is still pursued by several investigators. According to Cresta *et al.* (1969), the amino-acid pattern of milk protein appears to be more suitable than egg protein in maintaining nitrogen balance (BV) while the pattern of egg protein appears to be more suitable than that of milk protein in meeting growth requirements (PER). But not one of the reference protein at present in use seems to give a good correlation of the chemical score simultaneously with both biological value and PER. The multiple regression analysis used by the above authors, moreover, shows that the amino acids vary in importance accordingly as to whether they are to meet maintenance or growth requirements. The solution of the problem of assessing protein quality may be approached by a series of biological experiments (BV, PER, NPU) carried out on a sufficiently extensive number of foods and diets. It is also essential that the amino-acid pattern of these foods be ascertained by column chromatography. Some laboratories are already implementing programs of this kind (Kofrányi and Jekat, 1966). Revision of protein requirements should follow the determination of the existing interrelationship between the amino-acid composition of foods and their protein quality.

The review and studies of Mitchell and Edman (1962) have contributed much to give the estimates for requirements more meaning. However, analysis of their data by others showed that estimates for protein requirements must be based on studies on those people for whom the requirements are intended.

3.4.1. *Quality and Quantity of Dietary Protein*

Biological assays have been employed to assess protein quality. The successful application of the method depends on several factors: (1) the accuracy of knowing the protein requirements of the experimental animal, (2) relationship between protein requirements and energy expenditure, and (3) variability among groups and individuals.

The evaluation of protein quality from the amino-acid content of a protein food is another approach to the problem of amino-acid requirements, and consequently to protein requirements. Holt and Snyderman (1965) reviewed several studies on amino-acid requirements of humans. In spite of the enormous effort involved in gathering the voluminous data, it now appeared to be of very limited value. Requirements of essential amino-acids vary greatly under different experimental conditions. Harper (1964) discussed the relation between chemical score[†] and amino-acid imbalance. He pointed out the adverse effect on growth of experimental animals subsisting on diet containing an imbalance protein. The effect is more pronounced when the protein intakes are marginal or low.

The above findings do not discredit the practical significance of amino-acid supplementation on diets which are deficient in one or more amino-acids. They merely emphasize the fact that the "law of minimum" applies to amino-acid supplementation (Rosenberg *et al.*, 1959, 1960).

[†]Chemical score represents the percentage content of each of the essential amino acids of a protein based in a standard weight on score of 100.

3.4.2. The Protein–Nutrient Interrelationships

Protein occurs with other nutrients which in one way or another affect the efficiency of utilization of the protein. The mechanisms and interrelations involved have been explored, and Munro (1964) reviews aspects of protein metabolism and diet. Important nutrient interrelationships are discussed below, particularly as nitrogen balance is affected.

3.4.2.1. Sparing Effect of Carbohydrate and Fat

The nitrogen balance of an adult who is subsisting on an adequate protein intake is sensitive to changes in calorie intake (Munro, 1964). An increase in the energy intake beyond requirement leads to nitrogen retention, whereas a reduction in the energy value of the diet leads to nitrogen loss from the body. There seems to be a certain level below which the response becomes impaired. The basic mechanism on the effect of carbohydrates may involve the secretion of insulin (Munro, 1963) which induces the deposition of the incoming amino-acids from dietary protein and those that come from endogenous metabolism (amino-acids in the "metabolic pool") into muscle protein (Munro et al., 1959). The deposition may deprive the other tissues of their amino-acid supply particularly the liver. This effect is more pronounced when the protein intake is marginal.

Carbohydrate present in foodstuffs can react chemically with free amino groups in the food protein (Lea and Hannan, 1950). This makes amino-acids, particularly lysine, unavailable to the body (Henry and Kon, 1950).

The type of carbohydrate probably influences the efficiency of absorption of protein consumed in the same food (Harper and Katayama, 1953; Munro, 1964).

Work on animals suggests that a deficiency of essential fatty acids leads to inefficient utilization of body protein (Naismith, 1962). This observation may have relevance to the nutrition of human infants in an undernourished population where fat consumption is negligible.

3.4.2.2. Protein-Vitamin Interrelationship

Proteins and their constituent amino-acids affect vitamin metabolism. Protein levels have to be maintained for the retention of some vitamins which act as coenzymes, or form a constituent part of some body proteins.

Bro-Rasmussen (1958a) discussed in detail that the urinary excretion of riboflavin increases during negative nitrogen balance.

It has been shown that the tryptophan intake increases the amount of nicotinamide equivalent in man. Besides being needed for protein synthesis, tryptophan is therefore metabolized to form nicotinamide, and so there is a compromise as to which pathway has the priority. There is a dearth of studies conducted along this line, although available information seems to suggest that tryptophan is preferentially used to maintain nitrogen balance first and later for nicotinamide conversion. Brown et al. (1958) found that the levels of 10 urinary tryptophan metabolites decreased when low levels of tryptophan were fed to human adults. The level of 2–pyridone remained low until the blood pyridine nucleotide levels were restored with the addition of tryptophan to the diet.

Campbell (1963) believes that protein depletion seems to interfere with the absorption and utilization of carotene. Depletion may also retard utilization of liver reserves of retinol because the vitamin cannot leave the liver without the protein carrier.

When there is an excess of protein or amino-acid in the diet, the activities of many of the enzyme required for their catabolism is increased (Rosen et al., 1959). Since the transaminases contain vitamin B_6 as coenzyme, and the activity of the transaminases increases with excess protein, therefore, a high protein diet may induce a higher requirement for B_6.

3.4.2.3. Protein–Mineral Interrelationship

Protein-deficiency anemia has been decribed by Yoshimura (1961). The importance of protein is just as great as iron and some B-vitamins in the formation of hemoglobin.

Some enzymes need iron and other mineral elements as co-factors. The flavo-protein contain molybdenum in the molecule.

In studies on experimental animals, high levels of dietary protein offer great protection against excessive tissue accumulation and toxic effect of some trace elements like copper (Mills, 1963).

3.4.2.4. Nutritional Status and Protein Reserves

Labile body protein or storage protein is the amount of protein store which the body can draw upon during emergency. The nature, magnitude, place of storage and the metabolic function are factors that affect in turn protein requirement. It may be important to consider whether the presence of labile body protein plays a significant role in the well-being of an individual.

3.4.3. *Minor Factors*

Timing in the feeding of interrelated foodstuffs (Munro, 1964), degree of subdivision of food, and the presence of other nonprotein nitrogen sources like purine, pyrimidine, urea, and amines can affect protein requirements to a limited degree.

4. CALCIUM

Calcium is a major mineral constituent of the body. It makes up about 0.8% of the body weight in the newborn as against 1.5–2.0% in adults. The body is constantly losing some of this essential mineral nutrient, and it therefore becomes necessary to replace the loss through diet if health is to be maintained. For adults, whose tissues are fully formed, it is only necessary to make good such losses, but for the young children there must be an additional allowance for growth.

4.1. FOOD SOURCES

The major calcium salt ingested is calcium phosphate, since it is in this form that calcium is present in materials which serve as food. Calcium also occurs in nature as the carbonate, tartrate, and oxalate, and— together with magnesium—as the highly insoluble mixed salt of phytic acid (hexaphosphoric acid ester of inositol) present in cereals.

Milk and milk products are the richest sources of easily assimilable calcium for the human diet. Animal tissues, except bone, supply easily available calcium but not much of it. Fish bones, and bones of pork cooked with vinegar, supply considerable amounts of calcium.

People in developed countries derive most of their calcium from milk and milk products, while those in many developing countries get their calcium mainly from plants. In plant foods calcium is enclosed within cells whose cellulose walls are not so readily digested. Seeds of legumes and certain millets are high in calcium. Most of the calcium of cereal grains are in seed coats; in the outer coats, it is in association with phytic acid. Green leafy vegetables are good sources of calcium although some contain enough oxalic acid to interfere with its absorption.

4.2. ROLES

Calcium plays several important functions within the human body. Of all the calcium in man (25–30 g at birth and 850–1400 g at completion of growth), all but only a fraction of 1 % is in the skeleton (Leitch, 1964). This serves as a supporting structure and a buffer protecting the body against sudden change in the calcium content of the soft tissues and body fluids. The more easily mobilized calcium is in the trabeculae. Hard tissues of the teeth, dentine, and enamel are more metabolically stable (Hegsted, 1968).

The remaining less than 1 % of the body calcium serves a number of fundamental roles, unrelated to bone structure. The concentration of calcium in intracellular fluid is approximately 20 mg per 100 g of tissue. Its presence is essential for the activity of a number of enzyme systems, including those responsible for the contractile properties of muscle and for the transmission of nerve impulse. The concentration of calcium also appears to be essential in extracellular fluid, particularly for the response of muscle to neural stimuli and for the functioning of the blood-clotting mechanism.

4.3. ABSORPTION FROM THE INTESTINE

The most important single factor in the absorption of calcium is vitamin D. *In vitro* tests with segments of rat intestine confirmed that during vitamin D deficiency, the transfer of calcium from the mucosal to the serosal surfaces was small and took place mainly by diffusion; in the intestines of animals supplied with the vitamin, there was an active transport, even against a concentration gradient (Harrison and Harrison, 1960).

To be absorbed, the calcium of food must be separated from the complexes in which it occurs in food and be made soluble and ionizable (Leitch, 1964). The absorption of calcium from the intestine and the ebb and flow between blood and bone, and between blood and urine, are under the influence of the parathyroid hormone and vitamin D. Vitamin D aids calcium absorption from the gut, increasing with vitamin D supply. On the other hand, vitamin D in moderate amounts increases calcification of bone; but at high doses it mobilizes bone salt. Thus, excessive vitamin D causes withdrawal of calcium from bone and a consequent hypercalcemia. Parathyroid hormone, acting synergistically with vitamin D, appears to affect the rate at which calcium moves across the intestinal membrane and in and out of the bone (Pike and Brown,

1967). It appears that the integrated action of vitamin D and parathyroid hormone is the means whereby the total amount and the ratio of calcium and phosphate ions are maintained in the internal environment.

The ultimate control of calcium absorption resides with the rate of new growth or remodeling of bone which determines the demand for calcium and the absolute need to maintain the concentration of ionized calcium in plasma within the necessary narrow limits.

The plasma calcium is present in three different forms. (1) Approximately 50% of the calcium (2.5 m-eq/l) is combined with plasma proteins and consequently is nondiffusible through the capillary membrane. (2) Approximately 5% of the calcium (0.2 m-eq/l) is diffusible through the capillary membrane but is combined with other substances of plasma and intestinal fluids in such a manner that it is not ionized. (3) The remaining 45% of the calcium in the plasma is both diffusible through the capillary membrane and ionized. Thus, the plasma and intestinal fluids have a normal calcium ion concentration of approximately 2.3 m-eq/l. This ionic calcium is important for most function of calcium in the body, including the effect of calcium on the heart, on the nervous system, and on bone formation (Guyton, 1966).

Absorption is affected also by the ease with which calcium is liberated in digestion from different foods and the presence or absence of certain nutrients. Calcium absorption is enhanced by the presence of lactose, citrates, tartrates and amino acids 1-arginine and 1-lysine; and retarded by phosphates, oxalates, phytates, and fatty acids. There appears to be no evidence from long term studies to suggest that the usual amounts of these substances in everyday diets require serious consideration in the estimates of normal calcium requirement.

4.4. REQUIREMENTS

4.4.1. *Methods of Estimation*

Several methods have been used to determine calcium requirements; namely, accretion method, balance technique, growth studies, X-ray and bone density studies, epidemiological studies, and radioisotope tracer technique.

The balance technique has been the most widely used method. The greatest loss of dietary calcium occurs through the feces rather than the urine, and represents calcium that is not absorbed from the intestinal lumen and that secreted into the lumen in intestinal juices. Urinary excretion of calcium tends to vary less than fecal loss for the individual subject so that differences in balance reflect chiefly the degree of absorption of dietary calcium. Losses of calcium through the skin, hair, and nails have to be taken into account also. Calcium balances are likely to be poor estimates of actual retention, however, because they are influenced by previous calcium intakes, by adaptation response, or emotional disturbances, or by physiological states like growth, pregnancy, and lactation. Furthermore, underestimation or overestimation during short balance periods when multiplied for long periods of time may lead to gross misestimations.

In the accretion method, human cadaver of various ages are analyzed for calcium. To obtain the amount of calcium required per day, the difference in calcium content from adulthood minus that in infancy is divided by the number of days of their age difference and later multiplied by the percentage absorption of calcium from food. Calcium absorption varies from roughly 15–35% or more. The usual value used is 40% in the case of cow's milk or any other food, and 70% for breast milk. The weakness of this method stems from the fact that growth does not proceed at a uniform rate and there is more need for calcium during spurts of growth (0–2, and 12–18 years); also, the concentration of calcium in bone is not the same in infancy and maturity.

In the case of growth studies, estimates of the calcium requirement for infants and children have been derived by calculation of the rates of skeletal growth from body weight changes. Direct changes as to the rate of growth of the skeleton at different ages is, however, both meager and unsatisfactory.

X-ray measurements of bone structure and bone density have also proved available in experimental studies. However, quantitative bone density measurements can conveniently be made only on certain bones of the extremities; furthermore, density changes can only be studied directly when there is at least 15–30% change in bone mass.

Radioactive calcium (^{45}Ca) has been used to derive estimates of both intestinal absorption and endogenous fecal calcium. Its use is limited in humans because of its hazards. Only a few studies have been made on diseased individuals since the rate of calcium turnover is long.

Careful epidemiological studies in populations with widely different calcium intakes, utilizing appropriate clinical and laboratory techniques, could contribute to current knowledge of the calcium needs of man. So far, the existence of a clear-cut calcium deficiency disease has not yet been clearly established. Walker (1954) found no conclusive evidence that low calcium intakes significantly reduced growth rate or resulted in altered structure or composition of bone, provided vitamin D was available. On the other hand, habitually low calcium intakes appear to be implicated in the etiology of senile osteoporosis (Whedon, 1959; Nordin, 1960; Bernstein et al., 1966).

Whedon (1964) believes that the application of a combination of the metabolic balance and isotopic techniques whenever possible is both reasonable and necessary in the estimation of actual true absorption and endogenous calcium losses among various populations of the world. Such application could be useful in showing whether or not the maintenance of adequate mineral balance is more critical than heretofore realized.

4.4.2. Recommendations on Calcium Needs

The FAO–WHO Expert Group on Calcium Requirements (1962) defined the minimum requirement of calcium for adults as the smallest amount of that nutrient which will maintain health and keep the body in calcium balance over a period of years when the diet is otherwise adequate and the vitamin D status of the body is satisfactory.

Cognizant of the inadequacy of present knowledge, the Expert Group found it impossible to specify the amounts of calcium required under different physiological and environmental conditions. However, it is considered that current knowledge could be useful in suggesting tentative calcium allowance to be used in practical program pending future consideration of the problem when more research data would be available.

Table 13 shows the recommended daily allowance for calcium by the US Food and Nutrition Board (NAS–NRC, 1968).

The recommended dietary allowances of calcium for adults and lactating women in the present revision are unchanged from 1963. However, the allowances for infants, young children, and pregnant women have been modified. The allowance of 800 mg calcium for adults assumes absorption of approximately 40% of ingested calcium (320 mg) and further assumes that this amount is required to replace the daily endogenous loss of approximately 124 mg in feces, 175 mg in urine, and 20 mg in sweat.

An FAO–WHO Expert Group established standard for calcium, calories, and protein intended for international use and, therefore, for many varied population groups. The standards were defined as safe practical allowances, compatible with health but not so high as to be

TABLE 13 UNITED STATES RECOMMENDED DIETARY ALLOWANCES FOR CALCIUM (1968)

	Age	Calcium (g/day)
Infants	0–2 months	0.4
	2–6 months	0.5
	6–12 months	0.6
	(years)	
Children	1– 2	0.7
	2– 3	0.8
	3– 4	0.8
	4– 6	0.8
	6– 8	0.9
	8–10	1.0
Males	10–12	1.2
	12–14	1.4
	14–18	1.4
	18–22	0.8
	22–35	0.8
	35–55	0.8
	55–75	0.8
Females	10–12	1.2
	12–14	1.3
	14–16	1.3
	16–18	1.3
	18–22	0.8
	22–35	0.8
	35–55	0.8
	55–75	0.8
Pregnancy	additional	0.4
Lactation	additional	0.5

TABLE 14 FAO–WHO SUGGESTED PRACTICAL ALLOWANCES FOR CALCIUM (1962)

Age (years)	Calcium (mg/day)
0–12 months (not breast fed)	500–600
1– 9	400–500
10–15	600–700
16–19	500–600
Adults	400–500
Pregnancy (third trimester and lactation)	1000–1200

unattainable by many people of the world. Calcium needs were defined in terms of dietary intakes known to be compatible with health and obtainable in many areas of the world. These practical allowances are shown in Table 14.

The allowances advocated by the FAO–WHO Expert Group are much lower than the US National Research Council's recommended dietary allowances for calcium, which is fortunate because large allowances above minimal needs can create nutritional problems which may not really exist and, where resources are limited—as they are in most developing countries—can be detrimental to the development of sound nutrition programs.

5. IRON

Iron deficiency represents a major public health problem involving population groups throughout the world. At the first World Food Congress (FAO–WHO), deficiency anemia has been ranked second to protein malnutrition in the number of people affected. Results of nutrition surveys in many developing countries have reported that the problem is caused not only by limitations in total food supplies but is also complicated by the lack of naturally rich food sources of iron, as well as by the high prevalence of parasitism. Nevertheless, even in the more affluent countries like the United States of America where food supply is not a problem at present, iron deficiency has been reported by the American Medical Association (1968) to be high among infants and pregnant women. White and White (1968) attribute this to current practices in food processing, handling and home preparation which have tremendously reduced available iron arising from "contamination", and also from the decreased consumption of fortified cereal products.

About 35–60 mg of iron per kilogram body weight are found in the body of a normal adult and which is distributed roughly as follows: 35–45 mg as "essential" iron (in hemoglobin, myoglobin, cellular enzymes, and plasma) and 10–12 mg in storage forms. The total body iron (2 to more than 6 mg) in normal men and women depends largely on body size, the hemoglobin level, and the quantity stored (Moore, 1968).

5.1. ROLE AND METABOLISM

Early studies have shown that the body excretes iron very sparingly, that is, whatever is released in hemoglobin breakdown, if not excreted, can be utilized again for hemoglobin synthesis (Heath and Patek, 1937; McCance and Widdowson, 1938). The great majority of the iron turnover is accounted for by hemoglobin and to a lesser extent by myoglobin of muscles, cytochrome, ferritin, and hemosiderin.

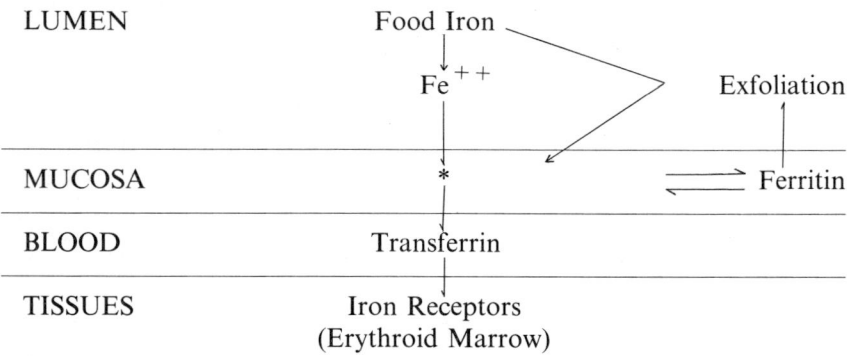

Fig. 2. Scheme of iron absorption from Bothwell and Finch, *Iron Metabolism* (1962), p. 94.

The main pathway by which iron gains access to the body is shown in Fig. 2. As soon as food iron becomes suitable for absorption it enters the mucosal cells in the intestinal lumen either in ionic form or bound to a low molecular weight nonprotein substance. This iron complex is transferred across the cell membrane into the plasma. Whatever is not transported complexes with apoferritin to form ferritin. In the plasma, the mineral is transported bound to a protein called transferrin or siderophilin, and is cleared into the erythroid precursors of the bone marrow (about 90% of iron absorbed), or into storage complexes. The total iron turnover in the body is about 25–40 mg/day (Peden, 1967).

A balance between the amount of iron absorbed and the amount excreted determines the adequacy of iron intake. Dubach *et al.* (1955) reported that the body needs only small amounts of iron for replacement of about 0.1 mg lost in urine and 0.3–0.5 mg lost in the feces. There is controversy about the amounts of iron lost from the skin. Using radio-iron, the same workers found a minimum loss of 0.13 mg/day by insensible perspiration. Adams *et al.* (1950) found an average iron content of 0.3 mg/l in sweat low in cells and of 7.1 mg/l in sweat high in cells. However, other workers (Johnston *et al.*, 1950; Foy and Kondi, 1957) reported higher losses of 0.24–0.28 mg per kilogram body weight. In areas where excessive sweating occurs, this may be an important source of iron loss. Further investigations are therefore needed to evaluate critically the iron lost through sweat. FAO (1969)[†] considers that the total daily iron losses for an adult man amount to 0.91 mg (65 kg × 14 mcg).

5.2. REQUIREMENT

5.2.1. Adult

From evidence given above it would seem justifiable to assume that the average normal healthy male requires 1.0 mg iron daily. By the use of isotope techniques, however, it has been found that the total daily exchange of iron represented by the daily excretion averages 0.6 mg/day.

In the female, additional losses are incurred during menstruation. Johnston et al. (1949) suggested an intake of 1.2 mg iron to meet daily requirement and replace menstrual losses. The menstrual loss was estimated by Hytten et al. (1964) to average about 12 mg per period. Finch (1965) reported that in some women, menstrual losses may be in excess of 1 mg/day. Because of the wide variability of menstrual loss from one woman to another, FAO estimated such losses to be 2.2 and 2.8 mg/day in young and mature women respectively.

To attain a retention of 1.2 mg on a normal mixed diet, it was found that a daily intake of 10–11 mg iron was sufficient. Likewise, for the adult male, a 10 mg daily allowance can safely give a retention of 1.0 mg.

5.2.2. Pregnancy and Lactation

Pregnancy results in maternal losses to the fetus and in bleeding at the time of delivery. To some extent, this loss is offset by the absence of menstruation so that the net deficit as calculated by Bothwell and Finch (1962) is approximately 230 mg of iron; if this amount is spread out during the period of pregnancy and external loss included as well, the daily deficit is 2 mg or 0.8 mg more than the average nonpregnant female. The net cost of pregnancy as estimated by FAO (1969) is shown in Table 15.

According to FAO (1969) iron requirements are not evenly distributed throughout pregnancy (Table 16). During the first half, iron is primarily needed to cover basal losses, but in the second half it also takes care of

[†]FAO, Rome, 1969. Private communications.

TABLE 15 IRON REQUIREMENTS FOR PREGNANCY (mg)[a]

	First half of pregnancy	Second half of pregnancy	Total	Net cost of pregnancy
Expansion of red cell mass	—	500	500	—
Blood loss at and after delivery	—	—	—	250
Fetal iron	—	290	290	290
Fetal iron in placenta	—	25	25	25
Basal losses (skin, etc.)	120	120	240	—
Total	120	935	1055	565

[a] FAO (1969), private communications.

TABLE 16 DISTRIBUTION OF IRON REQUIREMENTS DURING PREGNANCY AND LACTATION (FAO, 1969)[a]
(Assuming a loan from a 500 mg iron store in the body)

Period	Requirements (mg)	
	Total	Daily average
First half of pregnancy	120	0.8
Second half of pregnancy (935–500 mg)	435	2.9
Lactation [b]	440	2.4
Repayment of blood loss 250		
Milk iron loss 45		
Basal losses 145		

[a] Estimates are based on available evidence reviewed in the text.
[b] Assuming a 6 month lactation period.

the increase in red cell mass and the iron contents of fetus and placenta.

During lactation the need for iron is also estimated at 2 mg since about 1 mg/day is secreted in milk.

5.2.3. *Infants*

Babies at birth contain about 80 mg of iron per kilogram body weight of which 25 mg/kg is present as storage iron. During the first few weeks of life, much iron is drawn from these stores due to increase in blood volume and rapid growth of tissues. Normally, enough iron stores are present to satisfy requirements up to 6 months. Additional amounts of iron are obtained from milk. The relatively large proportion of iron (ranging from 43 to 53%) absorbed from milk by infants, makes up for the low concentration of the element in this foodstuff (Wadsworth, 1959).

At 6 months, infants receiving iron only from milk were observed by Niccum *et al.* (1953) to show a slow decrease in hemoglobin levels and if the store is poor or at a low ebb, an iron-deficiency anemia will occur in late infancy. Based on optimal hemoglobin concentration of the infant (Schulman, 1961), the requirement was established to be 0.8 mg/day. Since the finding of Schulz and Smith (1958) indicates that approximately 10% of iron available in milk, enriched cereals and eggs was absorbed by infants, an 8 mg daily allowance for infants, 6 months of age, should be adequate.

5.2.4. *Children*

Between ages 4 and 12 years, the iron requirement ranges from 0.4 to 1.0 mg/kg/day. Children subsisting on a mixed diet should be able to maintain iron balance easily at 10 mg or 12 mg intake or allowance.

5.2.5. *Adolescents*

There is an increase in the iron requirement for adolescents since extra hemoglobin is being formed during growth. For the male, a requirement of 1 mg will be sufficient. The adolescent female has the added burden of menstruation which was assumed to be 0.01 mg/kg/day (Bothwell and Finch, 1962). Requirement is set at approximately 1.5 mg/day or a daily dietary allowance of 15 mg.

5.3. FACTORS AFFECTING ABSORPTION

5.3.1. *The Size of Iron Stores Influence the Absorption of this Mineral*

It was observed by Pirzio-Biroli and Finch (1960) that iron-depleted subjects averaged 19% absorption as compared to 4% in the iron-loaded group. The higher absorption is comparable to the average value of 22% found in iron deficient subjects with anemia. Similar findings were reported by Fisher and Price (1963).

5.3.2. *Form of Iron*

At low levels of iron intake (5 mg) there was no difference in the absorption between ferrous and ferric compound unlike at high dosage (equivalent to 30 mg of elemental iron). Brise and Hallberg (1963) found that about 3–7 times more iron was absorbed from ferrous sulfate than from ferric sulfate.

5.3.3. *Composition of the Diet*

Much variation in the availability of iron from foodstuff has been reported. Iron in green vegetables have been found by Hussain *et al.* (1965) to be absorbed by less than 5% in normal subjects. Higher absorption is obtained from animal tissues.

Isotopic-iron studies on absorption revealed that iron absorption varied in the presence of different foods. FAO (1969) has recommended intakes on a basis of these types of diets: those with (1) high, (2) medium, or (3) low content of animal foods as shown in Table 17.

TABLE 17 IRON ABSORPTION AS RELATED TO TYPES OF DIET [a]

Type of diet	Assumed upper limit for iron absorption by normal individuals (%)
Less than 10% of calories from foods of animal origin	10
10–25% of calories from foods of animal origin	15
More than 25% of calories from foods of animal origin	20

[a] FAO (1969), private communications.

5.3.4. *Effect of Phytates*

The proportion of phosphorus as phytates to total phosphorus in the diet has been shown by Hussain and Patwardhan (1959) to influence iron retention. Thus on an average intake of 22 mg iron by healthy male adults, the retention was 2.483 mg iron when phytate phosphorus was 8% of total phosphorus, but only 0.173 mg iron was retained when the proportion of phytate was 40%. Since 50–70% of the phosphorus in tubers occurs as phytic acid, 30–60% in cereals, and 20–30% in fruits, this problem becomes serious in countries where large amounts of cereals and tubers are consumed (Oke, 1965).

The presence of other ions like calcium has priority in binding with phytates. It has been reported that anemic patients can utilize some of the iron from very large doses of iron phytates. The degree of absorption of iron from food varies not only with the food, but among people also. Some disagreements and conflicting results from observations on iron absorption can reasonably be regarded as reflections of differences in balance of influence among the various factors involved. Difference in the iron stores of the subjects could be important (Hawkins, 1964).

5.3.5. *Erythropoiesis Rate*

The rate of erythropoiesis also influences the absorption of iron. In most children, for example, iron was absorbed by at least five times more than by adults as shown by studies of Schulz and Smith (1958). Again, in pregnancy, three or more times iron was absorbed at 30 weeks gestation and over than during the period before the 15th week of gestation (Hahn *et al.*, 1951).

5.3.6. *Iron Absorption*

The absorption of iron, although small, increases with dosage, but not linearly (Coons, 1964).

5.3.7. *Reducing Compounds*

Reducing compounds like ascorbic acid when administered orally in sufficient amounts (200 mg) was reported by Brise and Hallberg (1962) to increase the absorption of 30 mg iron. The reducing action of the ascorbic acid was shown to occur within the gastrointestinal lumen, delaying the formation of insoluble ferric compounds. The simultaneous presence of large amounts of ascorbic acid and sulphydryl groups facilitate the absorption of iron (WHO, 1959).

5.3.8. *Gastrointestinal Disturbances*

Gastrointestinal disturbances such as diarrhea, deficient gastric secretion, and intestinal disease will interfere with the absorption of iron even though it is present in the food. Iron losses may likewise occur in the presence of intestinal parasites, such as hookworm.

TABLE 18 RECOMMENDED INTAKES FOR IRON (FAO, 1969)

	Absorbed iron required (mg)	Type of diet		
		Animal foods below 10% of calories (g)	Animal foods 10–25% of calories (g)	Animal foods over 25% of calories (g)
Infants:				
0– 4 months	0.5	(a)	(a)	(a)
5–12 months	1.0	10	7	5
Children 1–12 years	1.0	10	7	5
Boys 13–16 years	1.8	18	12	9
Girls 13–16 years	2.4	24	18	12
Adult women menstruating	2.8	28	19	14
Adult men [b]	0.9	9	6	5
Pregnancy [c]				
Lactation [a]				

[a] Breast feeding is assumed to be adequate.
[b] For nonmenstruating women the recommended intakes are the same as men.
[c] For women whose iron intakes throughout life has been at level recommended herein, the daily intake during this stage should be the same as that recommended for women (nonpregnant, nonlactating) of child-bearing age.

5.3.9. Iron Requirement

As shown in Table 18, FAO has based its recommended intakes for iron at various ages for either sex, on the type of diet habitually consumed. Present information on the effect of environment upon iron requirement are neither sufficient nor precise to consider it as a factor in making recommendation.

6. RETINOL

In many developing countries today, the adequacy of dietary retinol presents a serious problem if not the foremost among the vitamin needs. Nutrition surveys in India, Pakistan, and Indonesia, for example, have shown a wide prevalence of retinol deficiency as manifested by skin abnormalities, xerophthalmia, and night blindness in less serious cases. Oomen et al. (1964) undertook a global survey of xerophthalmia and found hypovitaminosis A of varying degrees of severity in a large number of developing countries, especially in East Asia.

6.1. VITAMIN INTAKE AND SOURCES

Where the available supply of animal foods and their byproducts is inadequate, the source of preformed retinol is limited and becomes even more so to the underprivileged. The report of a joint FAO–WHO Expert Group (1967) gives some information on the level of retinol intake in different regions and countries of the world as shown below:

Intake of retinol (IU)	*Per caput* per day
Europe, majority	3000–7000
USA, average	9000
Latin America, majority	1500–3000
Asia and the Far East, majority	1000–2500
Near East, majority	500–2000
Africa, majority	1500–4000

The lowest intakes are found in the Near East followed by Asia and the Far East. The principal sources of retinol in these countries are the naturally occurring plant pigments called carotenes which are present in fruits and vegetables and in red palm oil. Among these carotenoid pigments, of importance for human nutrition are α-carotene, β-carotene, γ-carotene and cryptoxanthin. These are present in appreciably large amounts in green leafy and yellow vegetables. β-Carotene is the most important precursor, first, because its concentration greatly exceeds those of the other pro-vitamins in most foods, and, second, its biological activity is at least twice that of the other carotenoids. The carotenes are converted into retinol mostly in the intestinal wall and to a much less extent in the liver. Other tissues are also capable of carrying out this process.

6.2. ROLE

Our present knowledge on the role of retinol in vision was made possible according to Moore (1957) by the investigations of Wald (1953) and Ball and Morton (1949). Functions of the vitamin outside the retina are not well understood. Roels (1966) points toward the role of the vitamin in the synthesis of the mucopolysaccharide moiety of the muco-protein molecule. In retinol deficiency, formation of these mucus-secreting cells is depressed and results in keratinization of epithelial tissues.

6.3. ASSESSMENT

The assessment of retinol nutriture, although dependent mostly on clinical examination, is at best only suggestive of the early and even moderate stage of retinol deficiency except when xerophthalmia has developed, in which case it represents advanced stage of the deficiency. While night blindness is generally accepted as an early sign of deficiency, its use for routine examination, especially in surveys, is subject to experimental errors.

Serum levels have been used to detect inadequacy of the vitamin before clinical signs become manifested. However, in the case of retinol, the interpretation of serum levels is done with caution since it has been shown in animal studies that even at low intakes of the vitamin, serum levels can be maintained when liver stores are high (Lewis, *et al.*, 1941; High, 1954).

The levels of excretory products of retinol can also be used in its assessment. These excretory products were reported by Masek (1962) to have appeared as carbon dioxide (5.2%) and as water-soluble fraction (11.6%) when labeled retinol was given to animals. Garbers *et al.* (1960) also reported the findings of the water soluble product(s) but whether they are the active intermediate(s) or merely a breakdown product(s) of the vitamin is not known. These gaps in knowledge make an early diagnosis of retinol deficiency difficult.

6.4. TERMINOLOGY

In most food composition tables, the retinol value in foods expressed in international units (IU) represents their content of the preformed vitamin and its precursors, if both are present. The equivalent of 1 IU is 0.3 mcg retinol, or 0.344 mcg retinyl acetate; in the case of provitamin, the equivalent is 0.6 mcg β-carotene, or 1.2 mcg of other biologically active carotenoids. It has been suggested that since retinol is now available as a reference standard, the practice of expressing retinol values in terms of international units is no longer necessary (FAO–WHO Report, 1967).

6.5. ESTIMATION OF REQUIREMENT

Some of the methods used in establishing requirement are the following: (a) animal studies where relationship of serum retinol level has been related to intake and where it has been shown that liver storage occurs only after maximum serum level has been reached; (b) nutrition surveys where a wide range of intake can be correlated with clinical findings; and (c) controlled human depletion–repletion studies such as the Sheffield experiment (Hume and Krebs, 1949).

The well-documented Sheffield study reported a dose of 6 mcg of retinol per kilogram body weight per day to correct or prevent visual symptoms of retinol deficiency in the adult. However, the amount was not sufficient to raise the serum retinol level to that found before the subjects were depleted. On an intake of 11.5 mcg/kg/day of retinol, plasma retinol can be maintained at desirable levels. This level was also found before the subjects were depleted. On an intake of 11.5 mcg/kg/day of retinol, plasma retinol can be maintained at desirable levels. This level was also found to maintain liver stores. From the above finding, the FAO–WHO Expert Group that deliberated on vitamin requirements in 1965 recommended an intake of 12 mcg per kilogram body weight per day of retinol for the normal adult. It is noted, however, that despite the difference of 10 kg in weight, the recommendation for the average man is the same as for the average woman. The group adopted the previous practice of using body weight as basis for estimating retinol requirements in view of the absence of evidence of other factors by which the requirement could be influenced or related.

6.5.1. *Adults*

Using an allowance of 12 mcg retinol per kilogram body weight, a normal adult weighing 55 kg will need 660 mcg of retinol per day.

6.5.2. *Pregnancy*

The liver stores of retinol of newborn infant was used as basis for estimating needs during pregnancy. The liver of infants weighs about 120–160 g and contains approximately 45 mcg retinol per gram. The mother will therefore need approximately an additional 25 mcg retinol per day throughout pregnancy.

6.5.3. *Lactation*

It is accepted that during lactation the average milk secretion of a well-nourished mother is around 850 ml/day, with a retinol content of 45 mcg%. This additional need for the vitamin secreted in the milk amounts to 417 mcg retinol per day and should be provided in the diet of the mother in addition to the recommended intake of 12 mcg per kilogram body weight daily.

6.5.4. *Infants*

From reports reviewed it has been estimated that an infant will need an intake of 65 and 50 mcg per kilogram body weight per day at the end of 3 and 5 months of life, respectively. It is assumed that infants breastfed by well-nourished mothers are provided with sufficient retinol to maintain health, promote normal growth, and provide adequate liver stores. In areas where poor diet prevails, the retinol content of milk is reduced by one-third to half of that found in well-nourished mothers. Although these levels may promote growth in infants, they are probably not sufficient to provide adequate liver stores.

6.5.5. *Age Groups*

The requirement at various age groups of both sexes shown in Table 19 are based on weight increment per kilogram body weight as recommended by the FAO–WHO (1967).

TABLE 19 RECOMMENDED INTAKE OF RETINOL AT VARIOUS AGES

Age	Recommended intake (mcg retinol per day)	Age	Recommended intake (mcg retinol per day)
0– 6 months	(a)	7– 9 years	400
6–12 months	300	10–12 years	575
1– 3 years	250	13–15 years	725
4– 6 years	300	above 15 years	750

Note: for diets containing both carotene and retinol, adjustment must be made.

(a) For infants 0–6 months it is accepted that breast feeding by a well-nourished mother is the best way to satisfy the nutritional requirements for vitamin A.

6.6. FACTORS INFLUENCING REQUIREMENT

6.6.1. *Biological activity*

The requirement for retinol will be much influenced by the proportion of carotene to the total vitamin value in the diet. The joint FAO–WHO Expert Group (1967), after reviewing the availability and conversion of the carotene in both animal and human studies, "recommends that in the absence of more specific data for foods, the availability of β-carotene be taken as one third and that the efficiency of conversion in the body be accepted as one half of the available β-carotene; hence the utilization of efficiency in the human is taken as one sixth." Thus 1 mcg β-carotene is equivalent to the biological activity of 0.167 mcg retinol.

The retinol intake for a 55 kg man whose recommended intake of retinol is 660 mcg (§ 6.5.1), but where the source is 90% β-carotene and 10% retinol would thus be adjusted as follows:

Recommended intake of mixed vitamin active compounds
$$= \frac{\text{recommended intake of retinol}}{0.167 K^* + (1-K)}$$
$$= \frac{660}{(0.167 \times 0.9) + (1-0.9)}$$
$$= 2640 \text{ mcg}$$

where K is the proportion of beta carotene in the diet

Other considerations agreed upon by the said Group are: (a) The activity of other carotenoids be taken as one-half of that of β-carotene, and (b) The biological activity of dehydroretinol, which is found in fresh water fish and in fish liver oils, is approximately 40% of the activity of retinol. Special consideration is therefore needed in estimating requirements in areas where fresh-water fish is the major source of protein.

6.6.2. *Dietary Fat*

A low content of fat in the diet hinders the availability of the carotene. Roels *et al.* (1958) has shown by balance studies in humans that addition of some fat in the diet markedly increases the absorption of dietary carotene accompanied by corresponding increases in serum carotene and retinol levels. On the other hand, diets containing high amounts of unsaturated fatty acids may be destructive to retinol especially when other anti-oxidants like vitamin E and ascorbic acid are low in the diet.

6.6.3. *Protein Nutriture*

Manifestations of retinol deficiency have been associated with protein malnutrition. In acute kwashiorkor cases, Arroyave *et al.* (1961) reported that administration of protein without added retinol has been shown to result in an increase in the serum level of the vitamin. It was suggested that the protein therapy mobilized tissue stores of the vitamin.

The effect of protein deprivation on carotene utilization is shown by animal studies. Working with rats given a protein-free diet, Mathews and Beaton (1963) were able to demonstrate the impaired conversion of the carotenes to retinol and adversely affected its absorption. Earlier, Friend et al. (1961) have reported that storage of retinol in the liver of pigs is dependent on the dietary adequacy of protein. Gronowska-Senger and Wolf (1968) analyzed the enzyme which converts carotene to retinol in rat intestinal mucosa and concluded that the activity of this enzyme is dependent on the dietary protein intake.

6.6.4. Vitamin Interrelationship

The dietary levels of other vitamins influence the utilization of carotene. Thus Mayfield and Roehm (1956) report that small levels of ascorbic acid increased the utilization of carotene while larger amounts may have no effect or decrease its utilization. Similarly, low levels of α-tocopherol favor the utilization of carotene and retinol (Herbert and Morgan, 1953) while high levels lowered the storage of retinol in livers and kidneys of rate (Swick and Baumann, 1951). It is felt that further data on this aspect is needed for practical application in the estimation of retinol requirements for humans.

6.6.5. Infection

The relation of infection to retinol was demonstrated by Rogers et al. (1968) in germ-free vitamin A deficient rats. After 64 days on the deficient diet, the germ-free female rate were still gaining weight whereas the ex-germ-free deficient rats lost weight after 44–48 days.

Although enough evidence is still lacking, Oomen et al. (1964) suggested that roundworms may be a predisposing cause of xerophthalmia.

6.6.6. Preparation and/or Preservation of Food

Processing and preservation of foods affect the retinol value. Although the vitamin is relatively stable to heat, the length of cooking and such factors as presence of moisture, pH of medium, and the influence of light and air, would cause some losses.

The degree of availability of carotene is also dependent on the manner in which food is prepared. Thus the more ruptured the plant cells are, the higher or more efficient is the utilization of its carotene content.

Excess of retinol could have serious effects on both man and animals.

Acute forms of vitamin intoxication have been noted in persons taking massive single doses. Severe cases of hypervitaminosis A have been found among faddists who include excessively large doses of vitamin in their diet. However, its deficiency is still the most serious problem related to this vitamin.

7. THIAMINE

The disease beriberi was recognized some half a century ago. In 1927, approximately a decade after, the anti-beriberi factor was isolated to which the term "thiamine" received international acceptance. It took another decade before Williams and co-workers could synthesize thiamine. Thus its use, for clinical purposes and as a public health measure, was made possible. Although beriberi has not been completely eradicated, its rate of mortality and morbidity has gradually decreased in many areas. Meanwhile, studies have continued to evaluate its nutritional role and clarify its biochemical function.

7.1. METABOLIC FUNCTION

The most important role generally accepted for thiamine is its participation in carbohydrate metabolism. It constitutes an essential component of the co-enzyme of the enzyme carboxylase which catalyses the oxidative decarboxylation of pyruvic acid to acetic acid (acetyl co-enzyme A):

$$CH_3COCOOH + O_2 \xrightarrow[\text{cocarboxylase}]{\text{carboxylase}} CH_3COOH + CO_2$$

This coenzyme, known as cocarboxylase, was identified by Lohmann and Schuster (1937) as thiamine pyrophosphate. There are over 24 enzyme systems reported in the literature (Williams, 1961; Beaton and McHenry, 1964; Shimazono and Katasure, 1965) where thiamine pyrophosphate serves as the coenzyme. The reactions in which thiamine pyrophosphate is involved are classified by Sauberlich (1967) as (a) oxidative decarboxylation, (b) nonoxidative decarboxylation, and (c) phosphoroclastic cleavage of α-keto acids, where a phosphate ester bond is cleaved in the reaction.

7.2. METHODS OF ESTIMATING REQUIREMENT

7.2.1. *Urinary Excretion*

The estimation of thiamine requirement is generally based on the urinary vitamin excretion in relation to intake (Melnick, 1942; Mason and Williams, 1942; Williams *et al.*, 1943; Mickelson *et al.*, 1947; Louhi *et al.*, 1952; Oldham *et al.*, 1951; Pearson, 1962). By correlating intake with excretion, a critical point is reached below which the excretion level approximates those associated with signs and symptoms suggestive of thiamine deficiency. Beriberi patients have been reported by the Advisory Board on Quartermaster Research (1954) to have a urinary thiamine excretion range of 0–14 mcg per 24 h; and among experimental subjects, early signs of deficiency showed up when 24 h excretion levels fall below 40 mcg. However, this approach has its limitation since urinary excretion levels are influenced by recent intakes of the vitamin and are therefore not an accurate reflection of the thiamine nutriture of the individual. The load test or retention of a known dose of thiamine has been of value in evaluating the tissue stores.

7.2.2. Blood Pyruvic Acid

Another approach in the estimation of requirement is the measurement of blood pyruvic and α-ketoglutaric acids. One biochemical abnormality when thiamine is not present in adequate amounts is the accumulation of pyruvic acid in the tissues and its concentration rises in the circulating blood (Williams *et al.*, 1943). Although estimation of blood pyruvate level can help in evaluating thiamine nutrition, this should be correlated with other tests.

7.2.3. Red Cell Transketolase Activity

More recently the estimation of red cell transketolase activity has been reported (Brin *et al.*, 1960; Brin, 1964) to be a more sensitive test for early thiamine deficiency. Transketolase is a coenzyme of thiamine pyrophosphate (TPP) which activity decreases as thiamine deficiency progresses. Addition of TPP *in vitro* enhances enzyme activity and TPP effect increases with thiamine deficiency.

Although the above tests were found to be adequate for the detection of a developing and impending thiamine deficiency, they are all dependent in the final analysis on a correlation between biochemical levels and the appearance of clinical deficiency symptoms. Inasmuch as such symptoms appear slowly and gradually, it is somewhat difficult for the clinician to draw the line between adequacy and deficiency.

7.2.4. *Urinary Thiamine "Metabolites"*

A new approach to the assessment of thiamine requirement which does not suffer from the above weakness has been offered; measurement of urinary thiamine "metabolites" (signifying those compounds excreted in urine which, when incubated with dried active baker's yeast, form a compound which behaves like thiamine in the USP or AOAC fluorometric assay for thiamine). Studies reported by Ziporin *et al.* (1965) indicate that thiamine metabolite excretion may represent a measure of the rate at which body stores of thiamine are depleted, thereby reflecting the daily requirement. Over 20 metabolites of thiamine have been established to be found in the human urine, eight of which appear to be major metabolites (Baker *et al.*, 1966; Neal and Pearson, 1964). Further investigations are needed on the excretion of metabolites of patients with beriberi or of subjects subsisting on suboptimal levels of thiamine.

7.2.5. *Dietary Intake*

Results of nutrition surveys and epidemiological findings can also give additional information concerning thiamine requirement on the premise that if signs and symptoms of the vitamin are absent, then the dietary intake of the population for the particular nutrient can be considered sufficient to meet their requirement.

7.3. ESTIMATES OF REQUIREMENTS

Various approaches and different experimental procedures have been reported in the literature and used to determine thiamine requirement. The most widely used are measurements of thiamine excretion as related to controlled intake of the vitamin. More recently, Ziporin *et al.* (1965) measured the pyrimidine and thiazole moieties of thiamine, besides urinary excretion of thiamine, to arrive at minimum daily requirement.

Shown hereunder are some data which were considered by FAO–WHO (1967) in arriving at the recommended vitamin intake:

0.20 mg per 1000 Cal: not adequate (Horwitt *et al.*, 1948).
0.23 mg per 1000 Cal: minimum amount (Keys *et al.*, 1943).
0.27–0.33 mg per 1000 Cal: minimum amount (Ziporin *et al.*, 1965).
0.33–0.35 mg per 1000 Cal: minimum amount (Melnick, 1942).
0.30 mg per 1000 Cal: not adequate for South and East Asia (Cruickshank, 1961).

From the above data it was the consensus that a value of 0.33 mg thiamine per 1000 Cal represents the requirement. An allowance of 20% was made for individual variation so that the recommended intake for thiamine is 0.4 mg per 1000 Cal. The British recommendation is also 0.4 mg per 1000 Cal. The American allowance is higher, and 0.5 mg per 1000 Cal is recommended.

The FAO–WHO expert group (1967) that went through the available experimental information found little evidence to indicate that thiamine need is increased in the vulnerable group except the increase in the amount needed to maintain the ratio of thiamine to calorie during pregnancy, lactation, and growth. In a similar manner, physical activity and climate would have an effect on the thiamine requirement only as they relate to an increase or decrease in the caloric requirement.

7.4. FACTORS AFFECTING THE REQUIREMENT

Other factors besides caloric intake may have to be considered in arriving at requirements.

7.4.1. *Composition of the Diet*

As has been previously mentioned, the primary role of thiamine is its participation in carbohydrate metabolism. In relatively more affluent countries where carbohydrates constitute about 50% of the diet, only 0.4 mg thiamine per 1000 Cal is the recommended amount. In countries where 75–80% of the calories in the diet comes from carbohydrates 0.4 mg thiamine may be at most the minimum requirement. Controlled human studies reported by Caasi *et al.* (1965) have shown that on a rice diet where carbohydrates contributed 78% of the caloric intake, acceptable thiamine excretion level is reached at an intake of 0.38 mg thiamine per 1000 Cal. On the other hand, high amounts of fats have been known to exert a sparing action on thiamine.

7.4.2. *Dietary Practices*

Dietary practices indigenous to population groups can influence the thiamine requirement. Thus, the lime treatment of corn practices in most Latin American countries, the use of baking soda in vegetable cookery, the prolonged heating or reheating of foods, etc., are some practices which cause considerable destruction of the vitamin. Likewise, prolonged dehydration, sterilization, and irradiation of foods would have to be considered since they would cause appreciable thiamine loss. Milling of cereals, particularly rice, has reduced the thiamine source in population groups where polished rice is the staple of preference. This can be compensated for, without change in palatability, by enrichment. On the other hand, parboiling of rice has increased the retention of the vitamin in the grain.

7.4.3. *Thiaminase*

Fish, especially those from fresh water, as well as other sea foods, are known to contain several enzymes referred to as thiaminases. Hilker and Peter (1966) reported its presence in 21 to 30 species studied in squid, shrimp, and clam, in dried tuna and herring and in salted salmon. Thiaminase destroys a part or most of the dietary thiamine when eaten raw (Fruton and Simmonds, 1958). It acts by replacing the pyrimidine or thiazole moiety with structurally similar but biologically inactive moieties present in fish tissues.

8. RIBOFLAVIN

Riboflavin is a yellow water-soluble pigment with green fluorescence. In neutral aqueous solution it is relatively heat stable as in ordinary cooking procedures like roasting, braising, or broiling. It is also quite stable in strong mineral acids and oxidizing agents but sensitive to alkali. It is decomposed on irradiation in the ultraviolet rays or visible light.

Riboflavin is an essential growth factor for man as well as for animal species and some types of bacteria. It is presently recognized as a component of the active prosthetic group of enzymatically active compounds called flavo-proteins which are concerned with tissue oxidation and reduction (Conn and Stumpf, 1963). This is chiefly in the form of flavine-adenine dinucleotide (FAD) and a few flavo-proteins contain flavine mononucleotide (FMN).

If the young growing rat is readily depleted of riboflavin, growth ceases and death ensues. It is interesting and quite puzzling, however, that a lack of this vitamin does not result in a discrete deficiency syndrome in the human. It is always present in conjunction with some other forms of deficiency states like protein deficiency. It seems that the adult human is not easily depleted of the vitamin. The fact that riboflavin is technically a prosthetic group, i.e., the riboflavin is bound to the enzyme protein, may lend a stability that the more loosely bound coenzyme vitamins do not enjoy. Since riboflavin is associated with protein in foods it seems likely that if a riboflavin deficiency developed it would occur in conjunction with a protein deficiency, and that the symptoms might merge into a variable syndrome such as is observed in kwashiorkor (Pike and Brown, 1967).

The vitamin is readily absorbed from the small intestine in its naturally occurring free form. Some riboflavin is synthesized by the bacterial flora of the intestinal tract depending on the character of the diet, and there is evidence that the intestinal flora is of importance in furnishing riboflavin to man (Bro-Rasmussen, 1958b). Apparently, a high carbohydrate low-fat diet seems to encourage synthesis of riboflavin by intestinal bacteria. Studies have been reported by Najjar et al., (1944) which indicate that riboflavin synthesized by bacteria can be absorbed by man.

Tissue stores of riboflavin increase with the intake. The stores, however, are not great, and the utilization of the extra riboflavin is poor because of the low renal thresholds for this vitamin. A riboflavin–protein retention relationship has been demonstrated wherein protein breakdown is associated with a concomitant loss of riboflavin from the tissues (Goldsmith, 1964).

8.1. ASSESSMENT OF RIBOFLAVIN NUTRITURE

8.1.1. *Urinary Excretion*

The method of evaluation of riboflavin nutriture now in wide application is primarily based, like that of thiamine, on the urinary excretion of the vitamin. Fasting urine samples, 24 h or even 6 h urine collection as well as casual or random samples have been utilized for this purpose.

The experiments of Horwitt *et al.* (1948) have demonstrated under carefully controlled conditions that the amount of riboflavin excreted in the urine can be correlated with the dietary intake. Urinary riboflavin excretion of less than 50 mcg day were found among those exhibiting chronic symptoms of the deficiency of the vitamin. At intake levels of 1.1 mg/day or less, the average excretion of riboflavin was found to be 10% of the intake, and at levels of 1.6 mg the average excretion was found to be 30%. Since riboflavin excretion increased markedly when intake was 1.6 mg as compared to 1.1 mg, these investigators concluded that tissue saturation could be reached at some point between 1.1–1.6 mg/day.

Bro-Rasmussen (1958a) suggested an excretion of 20% of the intake to indicate tissue saturation.

The minimum riboflavin requirement for 10 normal Filipinos (Caasi et al., 1967) was found to be 0.013 mg/g of protein or 0.72 mg riboflavin per day for the males, and 0.012 mg/g protein or 0.54 mg riboflavin per day for the females. The minimum requirement was found to be 0.4 mg riboflavin per 1000 Cal for all the subjects studied.

Another way of assessing riboflavin nutritional status in many population groups is to get the riboflavin excretion per gram creatinine (ICNND, 1963). However, although convenient and practical, it is acknowledged that more should be known about this parameter of vitamin excretion. This procedure of relating urinary excretion of vitamins and creatinine assumes that creatinine is relatively constant for short-term collection periods. In the study of Clark et al. (1966) it was found that there was much less variation in the hourly excretion of creatinine than in that of either thiamine or riboflavin.

Schaefer (1966) gives the following criteria of the interpretation of urinary riboflavin excretion data:

I. In adult males and nonpregnant, nonlactating females

	Deficient	Acceptable
mcg per 6 h	< 10	30–99
mcg per gm creatinine	< 27	80–269

II. In children

mcg per gm creatinine		
Age 1–3	< 150	500–900
4–6	< 100	300–600
7–9	< 85	270–500
10–15	< 70	200–400

III. In pregnant women

mcg per gm creatinine		
1st trimester	< 27	80–269
2nd trimester	< 39	120–399
3rd trimester	< 30	90–299

There are several limitations to this method of assessing riboflavin status: riboflavin levels have been found to be elevated during short periods of fasting (Windmueller et al., 1964). The excretion rate was 10–15 times that for the control. This confirms the report of Bro-Rasmussen (1958a) that riboflavin excretion increased during negative nitrogen balance which is a consequence of fasting. This makes the urinary excretion of the vitamin very difficult to evaluate.

8.1.2. Red Cell Concentration

The general consensus now is that plasma levels of riboflavin in the human may be more related to riboflavin consumed just before sampling than to the body riboflavin reserves. Red cell riboflavin stores are but slowly filled after deprivation, they are less susceptible to dietary influences and should therefore be a reasonable index of riboflavin stores (Burch et al., 1948).

Bessey et al. (1956) found a correlation between the intake and the levels in the red blood cell in eight subjects who consumed a diet providing 0.50 mg riboflavin per day for one day. These authors observed that red cell concentration below 14 mcg per 100 ml will lead to deficiency symptoms if continued for sometime. Studies by Pargaonkar and Srikantia (1964) reported red cell riboflavin levels of 20 mcg per 100 ml among the high income group of their subjects, 11.7 mcg for pellagrins and 12.0 mcg for subjects with signs of deficiency. Few data are available for assessing the usefulness of the technique for the determination of the levels of riboflavin in the red cell in healthy women and children and with some exhibiting clinical sign of mild or gross deficiency.

8.1.3. Tissue Saturation

Load tests have also been employed to assess tissue saturation with respect to riboflavin. Measurement of urinary excretion or blood level following a test dose of the vitamin can also give additional information on the requirement of population groups.

At the present time, no enzymic level approaches have been proposed for the measurement of riboflavin status. The metabolic products of riboflavin present in normal urine have not been investigated.

8.2. BASES OF REQUIREMENT

The Food and Nutrition Board (1964) reported the computed allowance of riboflavin to be 0.6 mg per 1000 Cal. In previous reports (1958) the recommended allowance was based on protein and a factor of 0.025 mg of the vitamin per gram protein was used.

Bro-Rasmussen (1958b) critically analyzed the relation of growth and other clinical data to be used in establishing riboflavin requirement. He concluded that since flavo-protein enzymes are concerned with the utilization of energy, the requirement should be related to the oxygen consumption of the body and therefore should be stated in terms of milligram per 1000 Cal consumed. He pointed out that whenever dietary protein is adequate, a deficiency of riboflavin does not occur in adult human subjects with daily intakes above 0.5–0.8 mg. Problems arise in very low and high calorie intakes. In order to compromise the theoretical consideration to experimental observation, the Food and Nutrition Board suggested that adult requirement intakes of less than 2000 Cal should be considered as if they were 2000 Cal.

Horwitt (1966) claimed that although the flavo-proteins are sometimes concerned with the utilization of energy, it does not follow that riboflavin is consumed at the same rate as the energy is utilized. This has been demonstrated by Bessey et al. (1958) in the growing rat that little or no direct destruction of riboflavin is associated with its function in metabolism. The same investigators also showed that increasing the calorie expenditure in rats by cold or by tyrosine administration did not increase the utilization of riboflavin. These investigators concluded that it is unnecessary to supply extra riboflavin when the calorie consumption is increased, as, for example, by physical exercise.

The protein to riboflavin relationship during growth is well summarized by Kaunitz et al. (1954) in their report on the effect of varying both protein and riboflavin intake on growth, food consumption, survival time, and corneal vascularization in the rat. They concluded that riboflavin and protein are limiting factors and that a high level protein may become toxic in riboflavin deficiency.

Horwitt further argued that although some flavo-proteins are involved in energy utilization, he emphasized that other flavo-protein, such as mono-oxidase, xanthine oxidase, etc., may have other functions not directly related to calorie utilization. He said that a differentiation must be made between the various levels of protein recommended and the amount actually utilized in relation to body size. He recommended the use of a factor of 0.025 on the protein allowance which, in a moderate sized inactive adult, will be found to be slightly higher than his "critical intake" of 1.1 mg of riboflavin per day.

According to Horwitt, this recommendation has special bearing in population groups in which the adult is small on a genetic basis and less protein is considered necessary and riboflavin requirement can be related more easily to the need.

8.3. ESTIMATE OF REQUIREMENT

The estimation of the need for this vitamin, like thiamine, can be assessed by relating vitamin intake to urinary excretion, clinical signs and symptoms, depletion–repletion studies and/or from survey data.

8.3.1. Recommended Dietary Allowances

The following levels of riboflavin intake have been reported by various workers and considered by the Food and Nutrition Board, the National Research Council, the National Academy of Sciences. Washington, DC, in formulating the allowances:

0.25 mg per 1000 Cal, not adequate for adults.
0.30 mg per 1000 Cal, minimum requirement for adults.
0.30–0.50 mg per 1000 Cal, can maintain body stores in adults.

More recently, studies have indicated that the requirement for riboflavin is related to body size, metabolic rate, and rate of growth. Consequently, the parameter used in the 1968 revision of the RDA is metabolic body size referred as kilograms of body weight taken to the 0.75 power. This includes the measure of body size and metabolic rate and ignores the rate of growth.

In the said revision it is assumed that infants require 0.1 and adult 0.07 mg/kg$^{0.75}$ to maintain tissue saturation. Riboflavin retention was considered to represent the difference between dietary intake and urinary excretion. Due to the lack of sufficient data to permit better estimates of the vitamin in the transitional period between childhood and adulthood, an arbitrary age-grouping adjustment was made. Children in the age group of 10–12 and 13–14 were considered to require 0.09 and 0.08 mg of riboflavin per kg$^{0.75}$, respectively. To provide for the envisioned demand for growth, a bigger allowance is made for children than adults.

Pregnancy: the factor 0.07 mg/kg$^{0.75}$ was considered adequate for pregnant women (Oldham *et al.*, 1950). An increase of 0.3 mg/day was made to allow for increase in metabolic body size owing to growth of the fetus and accessory cells. Thus, the recommended allowance is 1.8 mg/day.

Lactation: the mean riboflavin content of human milk is approximately 40 mcg per 100 ml (Roderuck *et al.*, 1946; Food and Nutrition Board, 1950) and the mean daily excretion over an average lactation period of 6 months (WHO Technical Reprint Series No. 362, 1965) is 850. A 70% utilization of the additional riboflavin for milk production is assumed

(Bro-Rasmussen, 1958a; Horwitt, 1966) thus an additional daily intake of approximately 0.5 mg or a total of 20 mg is recommended.

Infants: the value used for infants is 0.1 mg/kg$^{0.75}$.

8.3.2. *Urinary Excretion*

The FAO–WHO report (1965) reviewed depletion–repletion studies and cited the following range of intake as related to urinary excretion and/or clinical findings:

0.15–0.25 mg per 1000 Cal, ariboflavinosis is clinically evident.
0.31–0.36 mg per 1000 Cal, urinary excretion is less than 50 mcg/day but clinical signs are not clear.
0.41 mg per 1000 Cal, no clinical signs are evident.
0.44 mg per 1000 Cal, significant increase in urinary excretion.

From the above data it was assumed that the requirement of the body is met at an intake of 0.44 mg per 1000 Cal. Allowing 20% for individual variation, an intake of 0.55 mg per 1000 Cal is recommended for all age groups including pregnant and lactating women.

8.3.3. *Biochemical/Clinical Assessment*

From survey studies, levels of intake can be correlated with biochemical and/or clinical assessment:

0.70 mg/day, ariboflavinosis was manifested (ICNND, 1963).
0.45–0.54 mg per 1000 Cal, urinary excretion was over 160 mcg/day (Pargaonkar and Srikantia, 1964).
0.23–0.33 mg per 1000 Cal, deficiency symptoms were observed.

8.4. FACTORS AFFECTING RIBOFLAVIN REQUIREMENTS

There are nutritional factors and other conditions which affect riboflavin requirement:

8.4.1. *Composition of the Diet*

Several investigations on animal requirement have shown the effect of diet on the intestinal synthesis of riboflavin. De and Roy (1951) found that excretion of riboflavin in feces and urine rose because of greater intestinal synthesis when lactose or starch replaced sucrose. Czaczkes and Guggenheim (1946) suggested that excess carbohydrate reduces the riboflavin requirement and, conversely, excess fat increases the need for the vitamin. Excretion was also observed to be much greater during the week that a diet high on meat was consumed than when a diet low in meat was fed.

Animal experiments have shown that intestinal synthesis may be expected to increase when the main constituent of the diet is a slowly absorbed carbohydrate such as starch, cellulose, or ketose. Replacement of these carbohydrates by fat or protein inhibits synthesis and increases requirement. There are, however, no supporting data for man showing the effect of altering the ratio of carbohydrate to fat on the riboflavin requirement.

It might be that the difference in the intestinal micro-flora of the different test animals used could be the factor influencing riboflavin requirement. As pointed out by Bro-Rasmussen (1958b), the composition of the diet has little effect on the intestinal microflora of dogs and poultry and thus does not affect the requirement for these animals. On the other hand, for other animals, e.g. the rat and cat, intestinal synthesis of the vitamin may be markedly influenced by the composition.

Najjar et al. (1944) observed in human subjects that the urinary excretion and fecal excretion was two and five times the intake which furnishes only 60–90 mcg riboflavin per day. No clinical signs of deficiency were noted. This indicates that synthesis of riboflavin by intestinal micro-flora may be sufficient to take care of the riboflavin need. This finding suggests that the intestinal flora may be of importance also for man's riboflavin supply.

8.4.2. *Effect of protein and other vitamins*

A high riboflavin excretion was observed during a prolonged state of negative nitrogen balance.

There also exists a possible interdependence of thiamine and nicotinic acid with riboflavin. Sure and Ford (1942) observed thiamine deficiency may increase riboflavin excretion and reduce the riboflavin content of most tissues.

The relationship between riboflavin, on the one hand, and thiamine and ascorbic acid, on the other, has been recognized from animal experiments.

8.4.3. Climate, Physical Activity, and other Pathological Stresses

Mitchell and Edman (1962) observed no significant influence of climate on riboflavin requirement. Rodahl (1954) found no increase in riboflavin requirement in American soldiers in Alaska. Ershoff (1948) reported reduced physical activity and less food. FAO (1967) cited a publication of Scrimshaw (in press) and noted that there is no clear evidence in man to establish the effect of infection on riboflavin requirements.

9. NICOTINIC ACID OR NICOTINAMIDE

Liver, yeast, most legumes, and whole cereals are rich sources of nicotinamide. In cereals, most of this vitamin occurs in a "bound" form, i.e. available only when it is hydrolyzed (Krehl and Strong, 1944; Kodicek *et al.*, 1956; Pearson *et al.*, 1957). It is possible that the unavailability of cereal niacin may play a role in the pathogenesis of pellagra although a firm conclusion cannot yet be made. Since the discovery in the rat of the conversion of tryptophan to niacin (Krehl *et al.*, 1946), any consideration of nicotinamide metabolism must include this potential source of the vitamin. The enzymatic aspects of the biosynthesis of tryptophan to niacin in man and in many other species are now well established (Jones, 1965). Thus, the daily requirement for niacin is influenced by the amount and kind of dietary protein available (Sarett and Goldsmith, 1949; Vilter *et al.*, 1949). It is not known how much the conversion of tryptophan to niacin is affected when tryptophan is the limiting factor in the diet.

9.1. ROLES

Nicotinamide functions in the body as a component of the pyridine nucleotide coenzymes (nicotinamide adenine dinucleotide (NAD) or coenzyme I and nicotinamide adenine dinucleotide phosphate (NADP) or coenzyme II) that are primarily concerned with electron transfer reactions in the respiratory chain and oxidative phosphorylation. These functions provide some justification for considering the requirement in relation to calorie intake.

9.2. PRINCIPLES AND METHODS OF ESTIMATING REQUIREMENTS

The evaluation of biochemical tests for niacin nutriture becomes complicated because tryptophan may serve as its precursor and the metabolic products of niacin in man are many. The main end product, however, is N^1methyl nicotinamide (NMN) and its pyridone (N^1methyl 2-pyridone-5-carboxylamide or commonly called 2-pyridone).

Goldsmith et al. (1952) and Horwitt et al. (1956) found that NMN value reach a minimum at about the time of the deficiency. The original method was described by Huff et al. (1945) and subsequently modified by Huff and Perlzweig (1947) and Carpenter and Kodicek (1950). Pelletier and Campbell (1962) described a rapid method for the determination of NMN with better sensitivity and good reproducibility which can be suitable for survey work.

Questions still remain unanswered on the reliability of the above methods for assessing nicotinamide nutriture. Joubert and de Lange (1962) demonstrated that a low NMN excretion in the urine runs parallel to a reduced excretion of creatinine which means that the per gram creatinine value of NMN is not reduced even in severe nicotinamide deficiency. They say that urinary excretion of 2-pyridone per gram creatinine may be a better index. The same authors (de Lange and Joubert, 1964) proposed that the ratio of pyridone to NMN may be of more use as a criterion for nicotinamide status than methods currently employed. They were able to show a correlation between the ratio of 2-pyridone to NMN excretion and the dietary tryptophan and nicotinic acid intake.

Some workers have tried to relate NAD concentrations in plasma and in red blood cells to nutritional status (Burch et al., 1955; Morley et al., 1957). Vivian et al. (1958) reported that whole blood values of NAD decreased almost 40% in human subjects after 3 weeks on a diet insufficient in niacin and tryptophan, and subsequently returned to normal after supplementation with tryptophan.

Intakes of less than 7.50 mg nicotinamide per day have been associated with the occurrence of pellagra (Goldsmith et al., 1952; Goldberger and Wheeler, 1920), but these studies were made before the role of tryptophan as nicotinamide precursor was acknowledged. Tryptophan had been used to ameliorate symptoms of pellagra (Bean et al., 1951; Vilter et al., 1949; Sarett and Goldsmith, 1950). Duncan and Sarett (1951) observed that the increases in erythrocyte pyridine nucleotide after the administration of 1 g of nicotinic acid were approximately equal to those observed after 10 g of DL-tryptophan. Studies of the efficiency of tryptophan conversion to nicotinamide indicate that an average of 60 mg of dietary tryptophan is equivalent to 1 mg nicotinamide (Goldsmith et al., 1961; Horwitt et al., 1956; Vivian, 1964; Wertz et al., 1958). Thus, one niacin

TABLE 20 NIACIN EQUIVALENT IN REPRESENTATIVE FOODS[a]

Food	Niacin	Tryptophan	Niacin equivalent per 1000 Cal
	mg per 1000 Cal		
Cow's milk	1.2	673	12.4
Human milk	2.5	443	9.8
Beef, round	24.7	1280	46.0
Whole eggs	0.6	1150	10.8
Salt pork	1.2	61	2.2
Wheat flour, white	2.5	297	7.4
Corn grits	1.8	70	3.0
Guatemalan corn	5.0	106	6.7

[a] Reproduced from Horwitt (1958).

equivalent is defined as 1 mg of nicotinamide or 60 mg dietary tryptophan (Horwitt, 1955). There is some evidence that pregnant women can convert tryptophan to nicotinamide (Wertz et al., 1958; Lojkin et al., 1952). Table 20 shows the nicotinamide equivalent of foods like milk and eggs, which provide very little preformed nicotinamide but are not pellagragenic.

9.3. ESTIMATION OF REQUIREMENT

The minimum requirement for nicotinamide equivalent to prevent pellagra has been estimated at 4.4 per 1000 Cal/day (Horwitt et al., 1956; Goldsmith et al., 1952, 1955, 1956; Goldsmith, 1965) or at a minimum of 9 equivalents when the caloric intake is less than 2000 Cal. Table 21 shows that 4.4 nicotinamide equivalents per 1000 Cal approximate the minimum requirement for the prevention of clinical deficiency in adult subjects. The recommended allowance expressed in nicotinamide equivalents is 6.6 per 1000 Cal and not less than 13 equivalents at calorie intakes of less than 2000 Cal.

The idea of relating nicotinamide and tryptophan requirements as one does for thiamine to calories consumed has been suggested by Horwitt (1968). The dependence was illustrated by comparing the experimental pellagra-producing diet used by Goldberger (1920) with those used by Goldsmith et al. (1952) and the Elgin studies (Horwitt et al., 1956). The Goldberger diet provided 6.7 mg nicotinamide and 330 mg tryptophan in 3000 Cal, or 4.1 nicotinamide equivalent per 1000 Cal, whereas diets in the other studies which provided 5.2 mg of nicotinamide plus 235 mg tryptophan in 2000 Cal, or 4.4 nicotinamide equivalent per 1000 Cal did not produce pellagra. In the Tulane studies (Goldsmith et al., 1952),

TABLE 21 RELATIONSHIP BETWEEN NIACIN INTAKE AND CLINICAL SYMPTOMS IN CONTROLLED EXPERIMENTS[a]

Diet	Cal	Niacin[b] (mg)	Tryptophan (mg)	Niacin equivalents	Niacin equivalents per 1000 Cal[c]	Proportion with symptoms of pellagra
Tulane "corn"[d]	1700–2100	4.4–5.4	170–207	7.3–8.7	3.7–4.4	10/10
Tulane "wheat"[e]	1600–1900	4.2–5.0	177–200	7.3–8.3	3.7–4.2	3/5
Goldberger[f]	3000	6.7	330	12.2	4.1	6/11
Elgin	2070	5.2	238	9.2	4.4	0/1
Elgin	2300	5.8	265	10.2	4.4	0/11
Elgin	2530	6.4	292	11.3	4.4	0/1
Elgin	2760	7.0	318	12.3	4.4	0/2
Tulane "corn"[g] + Niacin	1970	6.7	190	9.9	4.9	0/1

[a] Reproduced from Horwitt (1958).
[b] Includes bound niacin.
[c] Diets providing less than 2000 Cal are arbitrarily calculated as containing 2000 Cal.
[d] Calculated from Goldsmith et al. (1956).
[e] Three of these subjects, two of whom consumed the most niacin-equivalents 8.7, were considered to have "mild niacin deficiency". The other seven, who consumed from 7.3 to 8.6 niacin equivalents, had "severe niacin deficiency".
[f] Calculated from Frazier and Friedmann (1946).
[g] Same as "Tulane corn" above plus 2 mg niacinamide per day.

diets which provided less than 4.4 nicotinamide equivalents per 1000 Cal even at levels of intake of 2000 Cal did produce pellagra.

9.3.1. *Adults*

On the basis of calorie requirements for adults (Food and Nutrition Board, NRC, 1968), the recommended intake of 6.6 nicotinamide equivalents per 1000 Cal/day would provide 18 nicotinamide equivalents for Reference Man (2800 Cal) and 13 nicotinamide equivalents for Reference Woman (2000 Cal).

9.3.2. *Pregnancy and Lactation*

Wertz et al. (1958) reported an increased conversion of tryptophan to nicotinamide during pregnancy. Lojkin et al. (1952) believed that ovarian hormones increased the catabolism of protein thereby liberating tryptophan for its conversion to nicotinamide. Although this does not necessarily indicate that nicotinamide needs are increased during pregnancy, the recommended allowance provides an increase of 2.0 equivalents/day based on the recommended increase in calorie intake. For lactation, an additional daily allowance of 7 nicotinamide equivalents is recommended consistent with the additional allowance of 1000 Cal.

9.3.3. *Infants and Children*

For infants 0–2 months, the recommended allowance is 5 mg nicotinamide mg equivalent per day; for 2–6 months, 7 mg equivalents; and for 6–12 months, 8 mg equivalents. Human milk contains an average of 0.17 mg of nicotinamide and 22 mg of tryptophan per 1000 ml, i.e. a nicotinamide equivalent of around 0.5 per 100 ml or 8 equivalents per 1000 Cal (Food and Nutrition Board, 1950). Holt (1956) reported that the daily requirement of infants fed a purified diet devoid of nicotinamide may apparently be met by 6 nicotinamide equivalents derived from tryptophan.

9.4. FACTORS AFFECTING REQUIREMENTS FOR NICOTINAMIDE

9.4.1. *Composition of the Diet*

The well-known unavailability of nicotinamide from maize is a factor that must be considered not only in populations consuming large amounts of this cereal but also in populations consuming large amounts of any cereal. Kodicek and Wilson (1960) and Das and Guha (1960) reported the isolation of a nicotinamide-containing alkali-labile factor from wheat bran, rice bran, and maize, but the reasons for its unavailability have not been determined.

Research with animals (Krehl et al., 1946) reported the possibility that certain amino-acid imbalance may increase the requirement for nicotinamide or may interfere in its formation from tryptophan. In diets where the tryptophan intake is limiting, the usual conversion to nicotinamide may not occur (de Lange and Joubert, 1964).

Data on leucine–nicotinamide–protein relationship has been presented by Gopalan and Srikantia (1960). When diets containing an excess of leucine but marginal in protein are fed to individuals, an increased urinary excretion of NMN results. Exaggeration of the symptoms of pellagra is concomitant with this observation. When rice diets containing an equivalent amount of nicotinamide and a lower leucine are substituted for the millet diet, the urinary excretion of the metabolite is restored to normal. An amino-acid imbalance occurs with the millet diet which explains the observation on the abnormal increase in the N-methyl nicotinamide excretion. The increased excretion probably depletes nicotinic acid in the tissues. This shows how an unbalanced protein affects the retention of the vitamin in the body.

9.4.2. *Pregnancy*

Elevated excretions of NMN and free nicotinamide are seen in pregnancy particularly in the last trimester. Increased excretion of NMN have been recorded repeatedly in pregnant women examined during ICNND nutrition surveys. It has been linked to an alteration in pyridoxine metabolism, but Lojkin (1962) considers that it may be related to the general amino acidosis known to occur in pregnancy. Wertz et al. (1958) supported the view that the conversion of tryptophan to nicotinamide is more efficient in the pregnant than in the nonpregnant woman.

9.4.3. *Absorption*

In vitro work of Hughes and Turner (1962) suggests that nicotinamide is absorbed in the intestinal wall by free diffusion. Mickelsen (1956) is doubtful if nicotinamide is available in synthesis by intestinal bacteria.

9.4.4. *Climate, Body Weight, and Physical Activity*

Climate *per se* has not been associated with change in the requirement for nicotinamide. No adjustment has been made for body weight and physical activity except that automatically provided for with an increase on calorie needs.

9.4.5. *Interrelationship Among the Vitamins*

Charconnet-Harding *et al.* (1953) and Henderson *et al.* (1955) showed the importance of riboflavin-containing enzymes for the conversion of tryptophan to nicotinic acid. No quantitative relation was mentioned, but it appears that riboflavin deficiency might increase the requirement of nicotinic acid. Sarett (1950a, b), however, observed no extra excretion of NMN after *DL*-tryptophan administration when the same diet was supplemented with thiamine, riboflavin, pyridoxine, folic acid, and pantothenic acid.

10. ASCORBIC ACID

The dietary prevention of scurvy, a disease due to a deficiency of *L*-ascorbic acid, was well-documented by Lind in 1753. Ascorbic acid, previously purified by several workers, was crystallized from orange juice, cabbage juice, and ox adrenal glands, and chemically identified as "hexuronic acid" by Szent-Györgyi in 1928—the same year that Waugh and King showed its identity to an antiscorbutic substance vitamin C which they isolated from lemon juice. Its structure was established by Karrer and others and confirmed by synthesis by Reichstein and co-workers, both in 1933 (Woodruff, 1964). It is an essential vitamin only in the case of man and other primates, guinea pig, and Indian fruit bat, because they are genetically deficient in the enzyme *L*-gulonolactone oxidase. Other animals synthesize ascorbic acid from glucose (chiefly) and galactose, via glycuronic acid and gulonic acid lactone.

10.1. FOOD SOURCES

The supply of ascorbic acid comes mainly from plant sources. Ascorbic acid occurs predominantly in the reduced form in most fresh fruits and vegetables, but upon storage, variable amounts of dehydro-ascorbic acid are formed. There is good evidence that the entire ascorbic acid content of food is available for absorption. In the United States and other Western countries, fresh potatoes, sweet potatoes, apples, parsnips, and cabbage are used to supply most of the vitamin C needs. Lately greater reliance is given on citrus fruits and juices and tomatoes as its main source. Cantaloupes and strawberries, as well as green peppers and broccoli, are also reliable sources. It is also common practice in developed countries to add synthetic ascorbic acid to foods to protect natural flavors and colors by serving as an antioxidant. Ascorbic acid is quite perishable in foods, especially under adverse conditions of storage and processing.

In general, the ascorbic acid content of meats is relatively low, and cooking of meat destroys the vitamin. However, it is widely distributed in animal tissues. Muscle tissue is relatively low in content compared with glandular tissues; pancreas, kidney, liver, thymus, salivary, spleen, and brain tissues are intermediate. Pituitary, adrenal cortex, corpus luteum embryonic tissue, leucocytes, and glandular cells of the intestinal tract are high in ascorbic acid. Since it is an essential nutrient only in the case of primates and guinea pig, ascorbic acid probably plays an important role in animal metabolism.

10.2. ROLES

Ascorbic acid is a strong reducing compound and it probably can be reversibly oxidized and reduced within the body. It is believed that ascorbic acid functions in the body either as a reducing agent in specific metabolic processes or as an oxidation-reduction system, reversibly exchanging electrons with other oxidation-reduction systems (Guyton, 1966). It appears to serve as a coenzyme or cofactor where the rate of reaction is critical. Its mechanism of action, however, remains obscure. If a coenzyme form exists for the vitamin, it must be a highly unstable molecule since it has eluded the investigators. It has been shown to be a reducing coenzyme for many hydroxylations like that of proline to form hydroxyproline (an unusual amino acid which occurs almost exclusively in collagen); and those of aromatic compounds like p-hydroxyphenylacetic acid from phenylalanine and tyrosine to form homogentisic acid, tryptamine to 5-hydroxytryptamine (serotonin), the formation of corticosterone and 17-dehydrocorticosterone, and the conversion of tryptophan to 5-hydroxytryptophan. Staudinger *et al.* (1961) report that ascorbic acid participates between NADH and cytochrome b_5 in the electron transport chain of mammalian microsomes, and suggested that this reaction may be coupled with hydroxylation.

As a reducing agent (Pike and Brown, 1967) it is known to protect the oxidase of tyrosine metabolism and in the reduction of the ferric ion to the more easily transported ferrous ion, as well as in the reduction of folic acid to folinic acid (citrovorum factor).

Physiologically, the major function of ascorbic acid appears to be the maintenance of normal intercellular substances throughout the body. These include the formation of collagen and intercellular cement substances between the cells, formation of bone matrix, and formation of dentine.

In children, symptoms of scurvy include tender, swollen joints, limitation of motion, petechial hemorrhages, inadequate tooth development, arrested skeletal development with characteristic bone disease, impaired wound-healing, and anemia. Except in anemia, impaired formation of collagen and chondroitin sulfate is the basis for all these changes. The collagen that is deposited is said to be poor in hydroxyproline. In severe cases, there is failure of formation of new ground substance and extensive depolymerization and solution of existing cement material, leading to breakdown of old, healed wounds. The anemia of scurvy may relate to impaired ability to utilize stored iron as well as to a secondary impairment in folic acid metabolism.

Ascorbic acid has also been reported (King, 1967) to afford a significant sparing action on the requirement for several B-vitamins including thiamine, riboflavin, folic acid, and pantothenic acid, and on vitamins A and E. The effects appear to depend on its reducing or antioxidant action. In rats, the sparing action on requirements for these B-vitamins appear to be caused by changes in the intestinal flora, with resultant synthesis of available quantities of the B-vitamins.

10.3. REQUIREMENTS

10.3.1. *Methods of Estimation*

The usual methods used to assess ascorbic acid requirement rely mainly in the evaluation of response to controlled dietary intake of the vitamin. These are clinical evaluation of subjects, measurement of urinary excretion of ascorbic acid or its metabolites, measurement of blood level of the vitamin, and the use of radioisotopes.

Clinical evaluation provides an estimate of minimum requirement to prevent deficiency symptoms like hyperkeratotic papules, petechiae, perifolliculosis, swollen spongy gums, and poor wound-healing. Here, one establishes the clinical course of vitamin C deficiency in subjects maintained on carefully controlled ascorbic acid intakes, and thus dietary levels that will prevent physical deterioration is determined. These studies are usually carried out over a period of several months since intakes that appear adequate for a short period may result in deficiency symptoms over longer periods of time as tissue supplies of the vitamin are gradually depleted.

Measurement of urinary excretion of ascorbic acid is commonly used to determine the requirement for the vitamin. Carefully controlled studies in which dietary intake is correlated with urinary excretion and/or appearance or absence of deficiency symptoms have formed the basis for evaluation of dietary intakes compatible with a "desirable" state of nutrition. Adjustments of urinary excretion of ascorbic acid to changes in dietary intake occurs fairly rapidly, within 10–15 days.

Measurement of ascorbic acid level in both plasma and white cells also tend to follow dietary intake. Ascorbic acid level of white cells declines later and at a much lower rate, and therefore appears to be a much better method of evaluating deficiency.

One other method used recently is to trace the metabolites of ascorbic acid resulting from its breakdown. Catabolism of ascorbic acid usually results in carbon dioxide, oxalate, or urinary excretion. By the use of C14-labeled ascorbic acid Baker *et al.* (1962) showed that 50% of the daily oxalate excretion results from the breakdown of ascorbic acid. They further found in six men studied that ascorbate utilization in terms of C14-oxalate excretion occurred at the rate of 0.207 mg/kg of fat-free weight. This implies that the greatest quantity of ascorbate that could be metabolized by the largest healthy man is only 18 mg/day.

Abt *et al.* (1963), also using C14-labeled ascorbic acid, determined the vitamin C requirement of adult man based on a new excretory pathway of ascorbic acid—the respiratory tract. They established that in man the major portion of ascorbic acid is excreted within the first few hours following ingestion through the expired air and the urine in a manner similar to their earlier findings in the guinea pig and the monkey. From their data, they reported the minimum human adult requirement of ascorbic acid per day to be 1.0–3.0 mg/day, a figure within the range obtained in 1944–6 by the British Medical Research Council.

10.3.2. Dietary Standards

Recommended dietary allowance may be aimed at any of the following:

(a) Preventing nutritional deficiencies to occur (minimum physiological requirement).
(b) Promoting good nutrition in the average healthy individual (minimum requirement plus one standard deviation to cover 68% of the population).
(c) Promoting good nutrition in essentially all healthy individuals (minimum requirement plus two standard deviation to cover 95% of the population).
(d) Promoting good nutrition in all members of the population.

The dietary standard formulated by the British Medical Association is based on quantities of nutrients believed to be sufficient to maintain good nutritional status in representative individuals in the population and thus refers to an average of the population; that of the United States, in contrast, is intended for essentially all of the population (Pike and Brown, 1967).

An investigation conducted by the British Medical Research Council from 1944 through 1946 led to the conclusion that the minimum requirement for ascorbic acid in adults must be below 10 mg/day (White *et al.*, 1968) and in the neighborhood of 5 mg/day.

Braestrup (1939) reported that the minimum requirement for infants may be greater in some instances than the 3–6 mg daily amounts obtained from raw cow's milk formulas. It is recognized that unless the mother's diet has been deficient for a markedly long period, the ascorbic acid content of human milk is three to four times that of cow's milk (King, 1967).

FAO[†] has considered that there is sufficient evidence that a daily ascorbic acid intake of around 10 mg will prevent scurvy in most individuals. But due to biological variations between individuals, and since there seems to be some evidence that the ordinary stresses of daily life may increase the need for ascorbic acid, a recommended intake of 30 mg for the normal adult of either sex was therefore adopted. FAO also considered that women in their second and third trimesters of pregnancy (despite insufficient evidence), and during lactation, require an additional

---

[†] Food and Agriculture Organization of the United Nations, Rome, 1969, Private communications.

TABLE 22 RECOMMENDED INTAKES OF ASCORBIC ACID (MALE AND FEMALE)[a]

Age	Recommended daily intake (mg)
0– 6 months (bottle fed)[b]	20
7–12 months	20
1– 3 years	20
4– 6 years	20
7– 9 years	20
10–12 years	20
13–15 years	30
16–19 years	30
Adult	30
Pregnancy (second and third trimester)	50
Lactation	50

[a] Food and Agriculture Organization of the United Nations, Rome (1969) private communications.

[b] For children 0–6 months it is accepted that breast feeding by a well-nourished mother is the best way to satisfy the nutritional requirements for ascorbic acid.

TABLE 23 COMPARATIVE DIETARY STANDARDS OF ASCORBIC ACID IN SELECTED COUNTRIES[a]

Country	Sex	Ascorbic acid (mg/day)
United States	M	60
	F	55
Australia	M	30
	F	30
Canada	M	30
	F	30
Central America and Panama	M	60
	F	50
Japan	M	65
	F	60
Netherlands	M	50
	F	50
Norway	M	30
	F	30
Philippines	M	75
	F	70
South Africa	M	40
	F	40
United Kingdom	M	20
	F	20
USSR	M	70
	F	70

[a] Food and Nutrition Board, NRC–NAS (1968).

20 mg of ascorbic acid in their daily diet. There is insufficient evidence to recommend additional amounts to meet unusual stresses and heavy physical activity.

Table 22 shows the recommended allowances for ascorbic acid. The RDA of the vitamin in selected countries is shown in Table 23.

The recommended allowance of 60 mg ascorbic acid for adults in the United States is greatly in excess of that required to prevent scurvy (10 mg) and twice that necessary to maintain relatively low blood levels of the vitamin (30 mg). In practice, this amount of ascorbic acid may be obtained easily by most people in the United States. Their average intake per day has risen from 69 to 117 mg/day during the past 50 years.

The heat-labile character of the vitamin, the individual variation in needs and in utilization, storage capacity in man (being water soluble it is not stored in large amounts), and adequate body stores to meet emergency conditions in times of stress (temperature, infection, surgical operations), are some of the reasons for aiming at higher allowances for adults. Whether this line of reasoning is justified, can be questioned.

Lower intakes recommended by some workers in other countries are based on the lack of evidence that the higher tissue levels provide added protection to health and the practical difficulty of providing more than the 30–50 mg of ascorbic acid on diets customarily eaten by the people. The 1968 revision of the United States recommended dietary allowances for ascorbic acid gives lower values in most age groups. For the adults, 60 and 55 mg/day was recommended for the adult male and female respectively (NAS–NRC, 1968).

It would therefore be expedient to re-evaluate allowance for this nutrient in some countries inasmuch as the higher standards are not easily met in many areas of the world, and the safety margin derived therefrom may be considered a luxury.

REFERENCES

INTRODUCTION

FOOD AND NUTRITION BOARD, NATIONAL RESEARCH COUNCIL (1968) *Recommended Dietary Allowances,* 7th rev. edn., National Academy of Sciences Publication 1694, Washington DC.

CANADIAN COUNCIL OF NUTRITION (1964) *Dietary Standard for Canada,* Canadian Bull. Nutr. No. 6, Queen's Printer, Ottawa.
INTERDEPARTMENTAL COMMITTEE ON NUTRITION FOR NATIONAL DEFENSE (1963) *Manual for Nutrition Survey,* 2nd *edn.,* US Government Printing Office, Washington DC.

CALORIES

BANERJEE, S. (1962) *Studies in Energy Metabolism,* Ind. Council Med. Res. Sp. Rep. Ser. No. 43, New Delhi.
BOOTHBY, N. M., BERKSON, J., and DUNN, A. L. (1936) *Am. J. Physiol.* **116,** 468–484.
BOOYENS, J. and MCCANCE, R. D. (1957) *Lancet* **i,** 225–229.
CANADIAN COUNCIL OF NUTRITION (1964) *Dietary Standard for Canada,* Canadian Bull. Nutr. No. 6, Queen's Printer, Ottawa.
DU BOIS, E. F. (1936) *Basal Metabolism in Health and Disease,* 3rd edn., Lea & Febiger, Philadelphia.
DU BOIS, D. and DU BOIS, E. F. (1916) *Archs intern. Med.* **17,** 863–871.
DURNIN, J. V. G. A. (1959) *Br. J. Nutr.* **13,** 68–71.
DURNIN, J. V. G. A. and BROCKWAY, J. M. (1959) *Br. J. Nutr.* **13,** 41–53.
DURNIN, J. V. G. A. and NAMYSLOWSKI, L. (1958) *J. Physiol.* **143,** 573–578.
FLEISCH, A. (1951) *Helv. med. Acta* **18,** 23–44.
FLORENTINO, R. F. (1966) *Philipp. J. Nutr.* **19,** 50–71.
FOOD AND AGRICULTURE ORGANIZATION (1957) *Caloric Requirements,* FAO Nutritional Studies No. 15, Rome.
FOOD AND NUTRITION BOARD, NATIONAL RESEARCH COUNCIL (1968) *Recommended Dietary Allowances,* 7th rev. edn., National Academy of Sciences Publication 1694, Washington DC.
FOOD AND NUTRITION RESEARCH CENTER (1960) *Recommended Daily Allowances for Specific Nutrients,* Table 1, revised 1965 FNRC Publication No. 75, Manila.
INSULL, W. (1964) *Indirect Calorimetry by New Techniques. A Description and Evaluation,* USA Army Med. Nutr. Lab. Rep. No. 146, Denver.
JOHNSON, O. C. (1967) *Nutr. Rev.* **25,** 257–261.
KEYS, A. (1950) *J. Am. med. Ass.* **142,** 333–338.
KLEIBER, M. (1947) *Physiol. Rev.* **22,** 511–541.
KROGH, A. (1916) *The Respiratory Exchange of Animals and Man,* Longmans, New York; cited by A. Keys (1950).
LEWIS, R. C., DUVAL, A. M., and ILIFF, A. (1943) *J. Pediat.* **23,** 1–18.
NATIONAL HEALTH AND MEDICAL RESEARCH COUNCIL (1965) *Dietary Allowances for Australians,* Canberra.
NUTRITION COMMITTEE, BRITISH MEDICAL ASSOCIATION (1950) *Dietary Recommendations.*
NUTRITION SECTION, BUREAU OF PUBLIC HEALTH, MINISTRY OF HEALTH AND WELFARE (1960) *Nutrition in Japan,* Tokyo.
PASSMORE, R. (1966) *Nutritio Dieta* **8,** 161–167.
PASSMORE, R. AND DURNIN, J. V. G. A. (1955) *Physiol. Rev.* **35,** 801–840.
PATWARDHAN, V. N. (1960) *Dietary Allowances for Indians, Calories and Protein,* Ind. Council Med. Res. Sp. Rep. Ser. No. 35, New Delhi.
ROBERTSON, J. D. and REID, D. D. (1952) *Lancet* **i,** 940–943.
SARGENT, D. W. (1961) *An Evaluation of Basal Metabolic Data for Children and Youth in the United States,* Home Econ. Res. Rep. No. 14, Agricultural Res. Services, US Dept. Agriculture, Washington DC.
SEN, R. N. and BANERJEE, S. (1958) *Ind. J. med. Res.* **46,** 759–765.
VOGELIUS, H. (1945) *Acta Med. scand.,* Suppl., **165,** 1–160.

PROTEIN

ALBANESE, A. A., ORTO, L. A., and ZAVATTARO, D. N. (1958) *Metabolism* **7**, 256–265.
ALLISON, J. B. (1958) *Ann. N Y Acad. Sci.* **69**, 1009–1024.
ARROYAVE, G. (1962) *Am. J. clin. Nutr.* **11**, 447–461.
BROCK, J. F. (1961) *Recent Advances in Nutrition,* pp. 84–86, J. & A. Churchill, London.
BRO-RASMUSSEN, F. (1958a) *Nutr. Abstr. Rev.* **28**, 1–23.
BROWN, R. R., VIVIAN, V. M., REYNOLDS, M. S., and PRICE, J. M. (1958) *J. Nutr.* **66**, 599–606.
CAMPBELL, J. A. (1963) *Proc. Nutr. Soc.* **23**, 31–38.
CHOW, B. F., ALLISON, J. B., COLE, W. H., and SEELEY, R. D. (1945) *Proc. Soc. exp. Biol. Med.* **60**, 14–17.
CRESTA, M., PÉRISSÉ, J., AUTRET, M., and LOMBARDO, E. (1969) *FAO Nutrition Newsletter* **7**, 1–15.
FOOD AND AGRICULTURE ORGANIZATION (1957) *Protein Requirement,* FAO Nutritional Studies No. 16, Rome.
FOOD AND AGRICULTURE ORGANIZATION (1957b) *Committee on Protein Requirement,* FAO Nutritional Studies No. 16, Rome.
GOPALAN, C. and SRIKANTIA, S. G. (1960) *Lancet* **i**, 954–957.
HANSEN, J. D. L. (1961) *Recent Advances in Human Nutrition* (J. F. Brock, ed.), pp. 267–281, J. & A. Churchill, London.
HARPER, A. E. (1964) *Fedn Proc.* **23**, 1087–1092.
HARPER, A. E. and KATAYAMA, M. C. (1953) *J. Nutr.* **49**, 261–275.
HEGSTED, D. M. (1964) *Nutrition—A Comprehensive Treatise,* vol. 1, pp. 116–173 (G. H. Beaton and E. W. McHenry, eds.), Academic Press, New York.
HEGSTED, D. M. (1969) *Protein-enriched Cereal Foods for World Needs,* vol. 7, pp. 4–15, (M. Milner, ed.), American Association of Cereal Chemist.
HEGSTED, D. M. and CHANG, Y. O. (1965a) *J. Nutr.* **85**, 159–168.
HEGSTED, D. M. and CHANG, Y. O. (1965b) *J. Nutr.* **87**, 19–25.
HEGSTED, D. M. and WORCESTER, J. (1967) *Proceedings of the Seventh International Congress of Nutrition, Hamburg,* vol. 4, pp. 1–8, Pergamon Press, Oxford.
HEGSTED, D. M., NEFF, R., and WORCESTER, J. (1968) *J. Agric. Food Chem.* **16**, 190–195.
HOLMAN, R. L., MAHONEY, E. B., and WHIPPLE, G. (1934) *J. exp. Med.* **59**, 251–267.
HOLT, L. E. JR. and SNYDERMAN, S. E. (1965) *Nutr. Abstr. Rev.* **35**, 1–13.
JOINT FAO–WHO EXPERT COMMITTEE ON PROTEIN REQUIREMENTS (1965) *Protein Requirements,* FAO Nutr. Meet. Rep. Ser. No. 37, WHO Tech. Rep. Ser. No. 301, Rome.
KOFRÁNYI, E. and JEKAT, F. (1966) The minimum N-requirement of man, *Proceedings of the Seventh International Congress Nutrition,* Hamburg, Pergamon Press, Oxford.
LEA, C. H. and HANNAN, R. S. (1950) *Biochim. biophys. Acta,* **4**, 518–531.
LONGENECKER, J. B. (1963) *Newer Methods of Nutritional Biochemistry,* pp. 113–144 (A. A. Albanese, ed.), Academic Press, New York and London.
LUYKEN, R. and LUYKEN-KONING, F. W. M. (1960) *Trop. geogr. Med.* **12**, 229–242.
MATHEWS, J. and BEATON, G. H. (1963) *Can. J. Biochem. Physiol.* **41**, 543.
MILLER, D. S. (1963) A procedure for determination of NPU using rats body N-technique, in *Evaluation of Protein Quality,* Publication No. 1100, National Academy of Sciences, National Research Council, Washington DC.
MILLER, D. S. and BENDER, A. E. (1955) *Br. J. Nutr.* **9**, 382–388.
MILLER, D. S. and DONOSO, G. (1963) *J. Sci. Fd Agric.* **14**, 345–349.
MILLER, D. S. and NAISMITH, D. J. (1958) *Nature, Lond.* **182**, 1786–1787.
MILLER, D. S. and PAYNE, P. R. (1961) *J. Nutr.* **74**, 413–419.
MILLS, C. G. (1963) *Proc. Nutr. Soc.* **23**, 38–45.
MITCHELL, H. H. (1923) *J. biol. Chem.* **58**, 470–476.
MITCHELL, H. H. and EDMAN, M. (1962) *Am. J. clin. Nutr.* **10**, 163–172.

MUNRO, J. N. (1963) *Proc. Nutr. Soc.* **23,** 1–53.
MUNRO, H. N. (1964) *Mammalian Protein Metabolism*, vol. 1, pp. 382–481 (H. N. Munro and J. B. Allison, eds.), Academic Press, New York.
MUNRO, H. N., BLACK, J. G. and THOMPSON, S. T. (1959) *Br. J. Nutr.* **13,** 475–485.
NAISMITH, D. J. (1962) *J. Nutr.* **77,** 381–386.
NATIONAL ACADEMY OF SCIENCES, NATIONAL RESEARCH COUNCIL (1963) *Evaluation of Protein Quality,* Publication No. 1100, Washington DC.
PLATT, B. S. (1954) *Malnutrition in African Mothers, Infants and Young Children,* report of the Second Inter-African Conferences on Nutrition, Gambia; cited by Arroyave, 1962.
PLATT, B. S. (1958) *Fed. Proc.* **17,** 8–18.
POWELL, R. C., PLOUGH, I. C., and DAKER, E. M. (1961) *J. Nutr.* **73,** 47–52.
ROSEN, F., ROBERTS, N. R., and NICHOL, C. A. (1959) *J. biol. Chem.* **234,** 476–480.
ROSENBERG, H. R., CULIK, R., and ECKERT, R. E. (1959) *J. Nutr.* **69,** 217–228.
ROSENBERG, H. R., ROHDENBURG, E. L., and ECKERT, R. E. (1960) *J. Nutr.* **72,** 415–422.
SCHENDEL, H. E., HANSEN, J. D. L., and BROCK, J. F. (1960) *S. Afr. med. J.* **34,** 791.
SCRIMSHAW, N. S. and BEHAR, M. (1961) *Science* **133,** 2039–2047.
SPRINSON, D. B. and RITTENBERG, D. (1949) *J. biol. Chem.* **180,** 707–714.
SWENDSEID, M. E., HARRIS, C. L., and TUTTLE, S. G. (1960) *J. Nutr.* **71,** 105–106.
VITERI, F., BEHAR, M., ARROYAVE, G., and SCRIMSHAW, N. S. (1964) *Mammalian Protein Metabolism* (H. N. Munro and J. B. Allison, eds.), Academic Press, New York.
WATERLOW, J. C., CRAVIOTO, J., and STEPHEN, J. M. L. (1960) *Adv. Protein Chem.* **15,** 131–238.
YOSHIMURA, H. (1961) *Fedn Proc.* **20,** 103–110.

CALCIUM

BERNSTEIN, D. S., SADOWSKY, N., HEGSTED, D. M., GURI, C. D., and STARE, F. J. (1966) *J. Am. med. Ass.* **198,** 499–504.
BOURNE, G. H. and WILSON, E. M. R. (1965) *World Review of Nutrition and Dietetics,* vol. 5 (S. Karger, Ed.), New York.
FAO–WHO Expert Group (1962) *Calcium Requirements,* FAO Nutrition Meetings Report Series No. 30, WHO Technical Report Series No. 230, Rome.
GUYTON, A. C. (1966) *Textbook of Medical Physiology,* 3rd edn., W. B. Saunders, Philadelphia.
HARRISON, H. E. and HARRISON, H. C. (1960) *Am. J. Physiol.* **199,** 265–271.
HEGSTED, D. M. (1968) *Nutr. Rev.* **26,** 65–70.
LEITCH, I. (1964) *Nutrition—A Comprehensive Treatise,* vol. 1, pp. 261–307 (G. H. Beaton and E. W. McHenry, Eds.), Academic Press, New York.
NATIONAL ACADEMY OF SCIENCE,–NATIONAL RESEARCH COUNCIL (1968) *Proceedings of the Food and Nutrition Board,* **XXVIII,** 23 pp., Washington DC.
NORDIN, B. E. C. (1960) In *Bone as a Tissue* (K. Rodahl, J. T. Nickelson, and E. M. Brown, Jr., eds.), pp. 46–66, McGraw-Hill, New York.
PIKE, R. L. and BROWN, M. L. (1967) *Nutrition: An Integrated Approach,* pp. 240–248, Wiley, New York, London, and Sydney.
WALKER, A. R. P. (1954) *Am. J. clin. Nutr.* **2,** 265–271.
WHEDON, G. D. (1959) *Fedn Proc.* **18,** 1112–1118.
WHEDON, G. D. (1964) In *Proceedings of the Sixth International Congress of Nutrition* (D. P. Cutbertson, C. F. Mills, and R. Passmore, eds.), pp. 425–438, Livingston, Edinburgh.
WHITE, A., HANDLER, P. and SMITH, E. L. (1964) *Principles of Biochemistry,* 3rd edn., McGraw-Hill, New York.

IRON

ADAMS, W. S., LESLIE, A., and LEVIN, M. H. (1950) *Proc. Soc. exp. Biol. Med.* **74**, 46-48.
BOTHWELL, T. H. and FINCH, C. A. (1962) *Iron Metabolism,* 1st edn., I. & A. Churchill, London.
BRISE, H. and HALLBERG (1962) *Acta med. Scand.,* Suppl. 376, **171**, 7-22.
COONS, C. M. (1964) (F. Gross, ed.), Heidelberg, Springer-Verlag, Berlin and Cottingen, 459-480.
COMMITTEE ON IRON DEFICIENCY, COUNCIL ON FOOD AND NUTRITION, AMERICAN MEDICAL ASSOCIATION (1968) *J. Am. med. Ass.* **203**, 119.
DUBACH, R., MOORE, C. V., and CALLENDER, S. (1955) *J. Lab. clin. Med.* **45**, 599-615.
FINCH, C. A. (1965) *Nutr. Rev.* **23**, 129-131.
FISHER, D. S. and PRICE, D. C. (1963) *Proc. Soc. exp. Biol. Med.* **112**, 228-229.
FOY, H. and KONDI, A. (1957) *J. trop. Med. Hyg.* **60**, 105-118.
HAHN, P. F., CAROTHERS, E. L., DARBY, W. J., MARTIN, M. SHEPPARD, C. W., CANNON, R. O., BEAM, A. S., DENNEN, P. M., PETERSON, J. C., and MCCLELLAN, G. S. (1951) *Am. J. Obstet. Gynec.* **61**, 477-486.
HAWKINS, W. W. (1964) *Nutrition—A Comprehensive Treatise,* vol. 1, pp. 309-372 (G. H. Beaton and E. W. McHenry, eds.), Academic Press, New York.
HEATH, C. W. and PATEK, JR., A. J. (1937) *Medicine* **16**, 267-350.
HUSSAIN, R. and PATWARDHAN, V. N. (1959) *Indian J. med. Res.* **47**, 464-682.
HUSSAIN, R., WALKER, R. B., LAYRISSE, M., CLARK, P., and FINCH, C. A. (1965) *Am. J. clin. Nutr.* **16**, 462-471.
HYTTEN, F. E., CHEYNE, G. A., and KLOPPER, A. I. (1964) *Am. J. Obstet. Gynec.* **71**, 255-259.
JOHNSTON, F. A., FRENCHMAN, R., and BOROUGHS, E. D. (1949) *J. Nutr.* **38**, 479-487.
JOHNSTON, F. A., MCMILLAN, F. J., and EVANS E. R. (1950) *J. Nutr.* **42**, 285-296.
MCCANCE, R. A. and WIDDOWSON, E. M. (1938) *J. Physiol.* **94**, 148-154.
MOORE, C. V. (1968) *Modern Nutrition in Health and Disease,* 4th edn., pp. 339-364 (M. G. Wohl and R. S. Goodhart, eds.), Lea & Febiger, Philadelphia.
NICCUM, W. L., JACKSON, R. L., AND STEARNS, G. (1953) *Am. J. Dis. Child* **86**, 553.
OKE, O. L. (1965) *Indian J. med. Res.* **53**, 417-420.
PEDEN, JR., J. C. (1967) *Nutr. Rev.* **25**, 321-324.
PIRZIO-BIROLI, G., and FINCH, C. A. (1960) *J. Lab. clin. Med.* **55**, 216-220.
SCHULMAN, IRVING (1961) *J. Am. med. Ass.* **175**, 118-123.
SCHULZ, J. and SMITH, N. J. (1958) *Am. J. Dis. Child* **95**, 109-119.
WADSWORTH, G. R. (1959) *World Review of Nutrition and Diet,* vol. 1, pp. 149-175 (G. H. Bourne, ed.), Pitman Medical Publication.
WHITE, H. S. and WHITE, P. L. (1968) *Fd Nutr. News* **39**, 1-4.
WHO STUDY GROUP (1959) *Report on Iron Deficiency Anemia,* WHO Tech. Rep. Ser. No. 182, Geneva.

RETINOL

ARROYAVE, G., WILSON, D., MENDEZ, J., BEHAR, M., and SCRIMSHAW, N. S. (1961) *Am. J. clin. Nutr.* **9**, 180-185.
BALL, S. and MORTON, R. A. (1949) *Biochem J.* **45**, 298.
FRIEND, C. J., HEARD, C. R. C., PLATT, B. S., STEWART, J. J. C., and TURNER, M. D. (1961) *Br. J. Nutr.* **15**, 231-240.
GARBERS, C. F., GILLMAN, J., and PEISACH, M. (1960) *Biochem. J.* **75**, 124-132.
GRONOWSKA-SCNGER, A. and WOLF, G. (1968) *Fed. Proc.* **27**, 310 (Abstract No. 534).
HIGH, E. G. (1954) *Archs Biochem.* **49**, 19-29.
HERBERT, J. W. and MORGAN, A. F. (1953) *J. Nutr.* **50**, 175-190.
HUME, E. M. and KREBS, H. A. (1949) Medical Research Council, Spec. Rep. Ser. No. 264, cited in Moore (1957), pp. 368-372.

JOINT FAO–WHO EXPERT GROUP (1967) *Requirements of Vitamin A, Thiamine, Riboflavin and Niacin,* FAO Nutr. Meet. Rep. Ser. No. 41, WHO Tech. Rep. Ser. No. 362, Rome.
LEWIS, J. M., BODANSKY, O., FALK, K. G., and MCGUIRE, C. J. (1941) *J. Nutr.* **23,** 352–363.
MASEK, J. (1962) *World Review of Nutrition and Diet,* vol. 3, pp. 171–177 (Bourne, G. H., ed.), Pitman Medical Publications.
MATHEWS, J. AND BEATON, G. A. (1963) *Can. J. biochem. Physiol.* **41,** 543–549.
MAYFIELD, H. L. and ROEHM, R. A. (1956) *J. Nutr.* **58,** 203–217.
MOORE, T. (1957) *Vitamin A,* Elsevier, Amsterdam.
OOMEN, H. A. P. C., MCLAREN, D. S., and ESCAPINI, H. (1964) *Trop. geogr. Med.* **16,** 271: cited in Joint FAO–WHO Expert Group (1967); FAO Nutr. Meet. Rep. Ser. No. 41; WHO Techn. Rep. Ser. No. 362, Rome, p. 3.
ROELS, O. A. (1966) *Nutr. Rev.* **24,** 129–132. Also in the Nutrition Foundation, Inc. (1967) *Present Knowledge in Nutrition,* pp. 51–54, New York.
ROELS, D. A., TROUT, M., and DUJACQUIER, R. (1958) *J. Nutr.* **65,** 115–127.
ROGERS, W. E., JR., MCDANIEL, E. G., and BIERI, J. C. (1968) *Fedn Proc.* **27,** 309 (Abstract No. 527).
SWICK, R. W. and BAUMANN, C. A. (1951) *Archs Biochem. Biophys.* **36,** 120–126.
WALD, G. (1953) *An. Rev. Biochem.* **22,** 497.

THIAMINE

ADVISORY BOARD ON QUARTERMASTER RESEARCH AND DEVELOPMENT (1954) *Methods for Evaluation of Nutritional Adequacy and Status,* US Department of the Navy, Washington DC.
BAKER, E. M., BALAGHI, M., PARDINI, R. S., and SAUBERLICH, H. F. (1966) *Fedn Proc.* **25,** 245 (Abstract No. 320).
BRIN, M. (1964) *J. Am. Med. Ass.* **187,** 762–766.
BRIN, M., TAI, M. OSTASHENER, A. S., AND KALINSKY, H. (1960) *J. Nutr.* **71,** 273–281.
CAASI, P., LUNA, Z. G., and CAMCAM, G. A. (1965) *Philipp J. Sci.* **44,** 23–42.
CRUICKSHANK, E. K., quoted by R. R. Williams (1961) *Toward the Conquest of Beriberi,* Harvard University Press, Cambridge.
FOOD AND NUTRITION BOARD, NATIONAL RESEARCH COUNCIL (1948) *Investigations of Human Requirements for B-Complex Vitamins,* Bull. 116, Washington DC.
FRUTON, J. and SIMMONDS, S. (1958) *General Biochemistry,* 2nd edn., p. 983, Wiley, New York.
GOLDSMITH, G. (1964) *Nutrition—A Comprehensive Treatise,* vol. 2, pp. 110–145 (G. H. Beaton and E. W. McHenry, eds.), Academic Press, New York and London.
HILKER, D. M. and PETER, O. F. (1966) *J. Nutr.* **89,** 419–421.
JOINT FAO–WHO EXPERT GROUP (1967) *Requirements of Vitamin A, Thiamine, Riboflavin and Niacin,* FAO Nutr. Meet. Rep. Ser. No. 41, WHO Techn. Rep. Ser. No. 362, Rome.
KEYS, A., HENSCHEL, A. F., MICKELSON, O., and BROZEK, J. M. (1943) *J. Nutr.* **23,** 399–415.
LOHMANN, K. AND SCHUSTER, P. (1937) *Biochem. Z.* **294,** 188–214.
LOUHI, H. A., YU, H. H., HAWTHORNE, B. E., and STORVICK, C. A. (1952) *J. Nutr.* **48,** 297–316.
MASON, H. L. AND WILLIAMS, R. D. (1942) *J. clin. Invest.* **21,** 247–259.
MELINICK, D. (1942) *J. Nutr.* **24,** 139–150.
MICKELSON, O., CASTER, W. O., and KEYS, A. (1947) *J. biol. Chem.* **168,** 415–430.
NEAL, R. A. and PEARSON, W. N. (1964) *J. Nutr.* **83,** 351–357.
OLDHAM, H. G., DAVIS, M. V., and ROBERTS, L. J. (1951) **45,** 213–223.
PEARSON, W. N. (1962) *J. Am. med. Ass.* **180,** 49–55.
SAUBERLICH, H. E. (1967) *Am. J. clin. Nutr.* **20,** 528–542.
SHIMAZONO, N. and KATASURA, E. (1965) *Review of Japanese Literature on Beri-beri and Thiamine,* p. 308, Vitamin B Research Committee of Japan, Clin. Nutr. Faculty Med., Kyoto Univ., Sakyo-ku.

WILLIAMS, R. D., MASON, H. L., SMITH, B. F., and WILDER, R. M. (1943) *J. Nutr.* **25**, 361–377.
WILLIAMS, R. R. (1961) *Toward the Conquest of Beri-beri*, Harvard Univ. Press, Cambridge, Mass.
ZIPORIN, Z. Z., NUNES, W. T., POWELL, R. C., WARING, P. P., and SAUBERLICH, H. E. (1965) *J. Nutr.* **85**, 297–304.

RIBOFLAVIN

BESSEY, O. A., HORWITT, M. K., and LOWRY, O. H. (1956) *J. Nutr.* **58**, 367–383.
BESSEY, O. A., LOWRY, O. H., DAVIS, E. B., and DOWN, J. L. (1958). *J. Nutr.* **64**, 185–202.
BURCH, H. B., BESSEY, O. A., and LOWRY, O. H. (1948) *J. biol. Chem.* **175**, 457–470.
BRO-RASMUSSEN, F. (1958a) *Nutr. Abstr. Rev.* **28**, 1–23.
BRO-RASMUSSEN, F. (1958b) *Nutr. Abstr. Rev.* **28**, 369–386.
CAASI, P. I., CAMCAM, G. A., MARZAN, A. M., EVA, T. C., and BELTRAN, P. G. (1967) *Philipp. J. Sci.* **96**, 273–293.
CLARKE, R. P., COSGROVE, L. DE G., and MORSE, E. H. (1966) *Am. J. clin. Nutr.* **19**, 335–341.
CONN, E. E. and STUMPF, P. M. (1963) *Outline of Biochemistry*, Wiley, New York and London.
CZACZKES, J. W. and GUGGENHEIM, K. (1946) *J. biol. Chem.* **162**, 267–274.
DE, H. N. and ROY, J. K. (1951) *Indian J. med. Res.* **39**, 73–82.
ERSHOFF, B. H. (1948) *Physiol. Rev.* **28**, 107–137.
FOOD AND NUTRITION BOARD, NATIONAL RESEARCH COUNCIL (1950) Bull. 123, National Academy of Sciences, Washington DC.
FOOD AND NUTRITION BOARD, NATIONAL RESEARCH COUNCIL (1964) *Recommended Dietary Allowances*, 6th rev. edn., Publication 1146, National Academy of Sciences, Washington DC.
FOOD AND NUTRITION BOARD, NATIONAL RESEARCH COUNCIL (1968) *Recommended Dietary Allowances*, 7th rev. edn., Publication 1694, National Academy of Sciences, Washington DC.
GOLDSMITH, G. (1964) *Nutrition—A Comprehensive Treatise*, vol. 2, pp. 146–152 (G. H. Beaton and E. W. McHenry, eds.), Academic Press, New York and London.
HORWITT, M. K. (1966) *Am. J. clin. Nutr.* **18**, 458–466.
HORWITT, M. K., LIEBERT, E., KREISLER, O., and WITTMAN, P. (1948) National Research Council Bull. 116, Washington DC.
INTERDEPARTMENTAL COMMITTEE ON NUTRITION FOR NATIONAL DEFENCE (1963) *Nutrition Survey Reports*, Washington DC.
JOINT FAO–WHO EXPERT GROUP (1967) *Requirement of Vitamin A, Thiamine, Riboflavin and Niacin*, FAO Nutr. Meet. Rep. Ser. No. 41, WHO Techn. Rep. Ser. No. 362, Rome.
KAUNITZ, A., WIEGSINGER, H., BLODI, F. G., JOHNSON, R. E., and SLANETZ, C. A. (1954) *J. Nutr.* **52**, 467–482.
MITCHELL, H. H. and EDMAN, M. (1962) *Am. J. clin. Nutr.* **10**, 163–172.
NAJJAR, V. A., JOHNS, G. A., MEDAIRY, G. C., FLEISCHMANN, G., and HOLT, L. E., JR. (1944) *J. Am. med. Ass.* **126**, 357–358.
OLDHAM, H. G., SHIFT, B. B., and PORTER, T. (1950) *J. Nutr.* **41**, 231–245.
PARGAONKAR, V. U. and SRIKANTIA, S. E. (1964) *Indian J. med. Res.* **52**, 1202–1206.
PIKE, R. L. and BROWN, M. L. (1967) *Nutrition: An Integrated Approach*, pp. 51–55, Wiley, New York, London, and Sydney.
RODAHL, K. (1954) *J. Nutr.* **53**, 575–588.
RODERUCK, C., CORYELL, M. N., WILLIAMS, H. H., and MACY, I. C. (1946) *J. Nutr.* **32**, 267–283.
SCHAEFER, A. E. (1966) *Proceedings of the Seventh International Congress of Nutrition, Hamburg*, vol. 3, pp. 1–8, Pergamon Press, Oxford.

SCRIMSHAW, N. S., TAYLOR, C. E., and GORDON, J. G. (1975) *Interactions of Nutrition and Infection,* WHO Geneva (in press).
SURE, B. and FORD, Z. W. (1942) *J. biol. Chem.* **146**, 241–250.
WINDMUELLER, H. G., ANDERSON, A. A., and MICKELSEN, O. (1964) *Am. J. clin. Nutr.* **15**, 73–76.

NICOTINIC ACID OR NICOTINAMIDE

BEAN, W. B., FRANKLYN, M., and DAUM, K. (1951) *J. Lab. clin. Med.* **38**, 167–172.
BURCH, H. B., STORVICK, C. A., BECHNELL, R. L., KUNG, H. C., ALEJO, L. G., EVERHART, W. A., LOWRY, O., KING, C. G., and BESSEY, O. A. (1955) *J. biol. Chem.* **212**, 897–907.
CARPENTER, K. J. and KODICEK (1950) *Biochem. J.* **46**, 421–426.
CHARCONNET-HARDING, F., DALGLIESH, C. E., and NEUBERGER, A. (1953) *J. biol. Chem.* **53**, 513–521.
DAS, M. L. and GUHA, B. C. (1960) *J. biol. Chem.* **235**, 2971–2976.
DUNCAN, M. and SARETT, H. P. (1951) *J. biol. Chem.* **193**, 317–324.
FOOD AND NUTRITION BOARD, NATIONAL ACADEMY OF SCIENCES (1950) *Maternal and Child Health,* Bull. 123, Washington DC.
FOOD AND NUTRITION BOARD, NATIONAL RESEARCH COUNCIL (1968) *Recommended Dietary Allowances,* 7th rev. edn., Publication 1964, National Academy of Sciences, Washington DC.
GOLDBERGER, J. and WHEELER, G. A. (1920) *Archs intern. Med.* **25**, 451–471.
GOLDSMITH, G. A. (1965) *J. Am. med. Ass.* **194**, 167–173.
GOLDSMITH, G. A., SARETT, H. P., REGISTER, U. D. and GIBBENS, J. (1952) *J. clin. Invest.* **31**, 533–542.
GOLDSMITH, G. A., ROSENTHAL, H. L., GIBBENS, J., and UNGLAUB, W. G. (1955) *J. Nutr.* **56**, 371–386.
GOLDSMITH, G. A., GIBBENS, J., UNGLAUB, W. G., and MILLER, O. N. (1956) *Am. J. clin. Nutr.* **4**, 151–160.
GOLDSMITH, G. A., MILLER, O. N., and UNGLAUB, W. G. (1961) *J. Nutr.* **73**, 172–176.
GOPALAN, C. and SRIKANTIA, S. G. (1960) *Lancet* **i**, 954–957.
HENDERSON, L. M., KOSHI, R. E., and D'ANGELI, F. (1955) *J. biol. Chem.* **215**, 369–376.
HOLT, L. E., JR. (1956) *Archs Dis. Child.* **31**, 427–438.
HORWITT, M. K. (1955) *Am. J. clin. Nutr.* **3**, 244–245.
HORWITT, M. K. (1958) *J. Am. diet. Ass.* **34**, 914–919.
HORWITT, M. K. (1968) *Modern Nutrition in Health and Disease,* 4th edn., pp. 247–259 (Wohl, M. G. and Goodhart, R. S., eds.), Lea & Febiger, Philadelphia.
HORWITT, M. K., HARVEY, C. C., ROTHWELL, W. S., CUTLER, J. L., and HAFFRON, D. (1956) *J. Nutr.* **60**, Suppl. 1, 1–43.
HUFF, T. W., and PERLZWEIG, W. A. (1947) *J. biol. Chem.* **167**, 157–167.
HUFF, J. W., PERLZWEIG, W. A., and TILDEN, N. W. (1945) *Fed Proc.* **4**, 92–93.
HUGHES, D. E. and TURNER, J. B. (1962) *Q. J. exp. Physiol.* **47**, 107–123.
JONES, M. E. (1965) *An. Rev. Biochem.* **34**, 381–418.
JOUBERT, C. P. and DE LANGE, D. J. (1962) *Proc. Nutr. Soc. S. Afr.* **3**, 60–65.
KODICEK, E., BRAUDE, B., KON, S. K., and MITCHELL, K. G. (1956) *Br. J. Nutr.* **10**, 51–66.
KODICEK, E. and WILSON, P. W. (1960) *Biochem. J.* **76**, 278–280.
KREHL, W. A. and STRONG, F. M. (1944) *J. biol. Chem.* **156**, 1–19.
KREHL, W. A., SARMA, P. S., TEPLY, L. S., and ELVEHJEM, C. A. (1966), **31**, 85–106.
LANGE, D. J. DE and JOUBERT, C. P. (1964) *Am. J. clin. Nutr.* **15**, 169–174.
LOJKIN, M. E. (1962) *J. Nutr.* **78**, 287–294.
LOJKIN, M. E., WERTZ, A. W., and DIETZ, C. G. (1952) *J. Nutr.* **46**, 336–352.
MICKELSEN, O. (1956) *Vitams Horm.* **14**, 1–95.
MORLEY, N. H. and STORVICK, C. A. (1957) *J. Nutr.* **63**, 539–554.

PEARSON, W. N., STOMPFEL, S. J., VALENZUELA, J. S., HUTLEY, M. H., and DARBY, W. J. (1957) *J. Nutr.* **62**, 445–463.
PELLETIER, O. and CAMPBELL, J. A. (1962) *Analyt. Biochem.* **3**, 60–67.
SARETT, H. P. (1950a) *J. biol. Chem.* **182**, 659–679.
SARETT, H. P. (1950b) *J. biol. Chem.* **182**, 691–697.
SARETT, H. P. and GOLDSMITH, G. A. (1949) *J. biol. Chem.* **177**, 461–475.
SARETT, H. P. and GOLDSMITH, G. A. (1950) *J. biol. Chem.* **182**, 679–690.
VILTER, R. W., MUELLER, J. F., and BEAN, W. B. (1949) *J. Lab. clin. Med.* **34**, 409–413.
VIVIAN, V. M. (1964) *J. Nutr.* **82**, 395–400.
VIVIAN, V. M., CHALOUPKA, M. M., and REYNOLDS, M. S. (1958) *J. Nutr.* **66**, 587–598.
WERTZ, A. W., LOJKIN, M. E., BOUCHARD, B. S., and DARBY, M. B. (1958) *J. Nutr.* **64**, 339–353.

ASCORBIC ACID

ABT, A. F., SCHUCHING, S. V., and ENNS, T. (1963) *Am. J. clin. Nutr.* **12**, 21–29.
BAKER, E. M., SAUBERLICH, H. E., WOLKSKILL, S. J., WALLACE, W. T., and DEAN, E. E. (1962) *Proc. Soc. exp. Biol. Med.* **109**, 737–741.
BRAESTRUP, P. W. (1939) C-Vitamin Studier Hos Spaud Born, Copenhagen, Dissert., Hass Son.
FOOD AND NUTRITION BOARD, NATIONAL RESEARCH COUNCIL (1964) *Recommended Dietary Allowances*, 6th rev. edn., Publication 1146 (National Academy of Sciences), Washington DC.
GUYTON, A. C. (1966) *Textbook of Medical Physiology*, 3rd edn., W. B. Saunders, Philadelphia.
KING, C. G. (1958) *Nutr. Rev.* **26**, 33–36.
NATIONAL ACADEMY OF SCIENCES, NATIONAL RESEARCH COUNCIL (1968) *Proceedings of the Food and Nutrition Board*, **XXVIII**, 23 pp., Washington DC.
PIKE, R. L. and BROWN, M. L. (1967) *Nutrition: An Integrated Approach*, Wiley, New York.
STAUDINGER, H., KRISCH, K., and LEONHAUSER, S. (1961) *Ann. NY Acad. Sci.* **92**, 195–207.
WHITE, A., HANDLER, P., and SMITH, E. L. (1968) *Principles of Biochemistry*, 4th edn., McGraw-Hill, New York. Edition.
WOODRUFF, C. W. (1964) In *Nutrition—A Comprehensive Treatise*, vol. 2, pp. 265–298 (G. H. Beaton and E. W. McHenry, eds.), Academic Press, New York.

CHAPTER 5

NUTRITIONAL AND PHYSIOLOGICAL BASIS OF MILITARY RATIONS

C. Frank Consolazio

Chief, Bioenergetics Division, Department of Nutrition, Letterman Army Institute of Research, Presidio of San Francisco, California 94129

CONTENTS

1. Introduction	222
2. Responsibility of Nutritional Adequacy of Rations	222
3. Nutritional Adequacy of Allowances	224
4. Difference Between Allowances and Minimal Requirements	230
5. Maintenance of Physical Efficiency	230
6. Dietary Allowances and Climatic Stress	232
7. Salt	234
8. Water	236
9. Ketosis	239
10. Rations	239
11. History of US Army Feeding	241
12. K-Ration	248
13. Rations and Food Packets (TM 8–501, 1961)	249
13.1. Ration	249
13.2. Ration Supplement	249
13.3. Food Packets	250
13.4. Garrison Rations	251
13.5. Field Rations	256
13.6. Operational Rations	259
13.7. Combat Rations	263
13.8. Combat Individual Rations	264
14. Combat Rations for Group Feeding	268
15. Limited Warfare Ration (2000 Cal)	284
16. Limited Warfare Rations: 10-day Starvation and Caloric Restriction Below 1000 Cal/Day	291
17. Survival Rations	294
18. Survival at Sea	304
19. Future Concepts of Military Feeding	306
20. New Feeding Systems	307
21. Summary	310
References	311

1. INTRODUCTION

When I accepted the invitation to prepare a manuscript on military rations, little did I realize the monumental task that I had undertaken since practically every country in the world has its own version of garrison, combat, and survival rations. As a result, an attempt has been made to discuss the nutritional and physiological basis of rations and the problems related to ration planning and development in which some comparisons can be made between rations of the various countries. In some instances, examples are presented to emphasize the results of the adequacy or deficiencies in the rations. Since the field trials for evaluation of rations are too numerous to compare, the US rations will be used to illustrate the history of ration development, the present-day ration, and the future concepts of feeding troops.

The preparation of this manuscript would have been an impossible chore without the excellent studies and reviews on ration development, field trials of combat, survival rations, and water deprivation. These include the work of Stevenson on survival feeding (1958), the field ration studies by Johnson and Kark in hot and cold environments (1947b); studies by Sargent and Johnson on the physiological basis of survival rations (1957); work by the US Army Medical Research and Nutrition Laboratory in the fields of energy requirement, field ration trials, mineral metabolism, and caloric restriction; the various US Army technical manuals on rations and nutrition; and the history of US ration development by the former Armed Forces QM Food and Container Institute in Chicago (1949).

The great world conquests might never have been accomplished by the eminent Greek and Roman legions without adequate provision of food supplies for the armies of troops. The logistics of military feeding in combat has always been a major problem long before Napoleon stated that "an army travels on its stomach". There is no question that nutritionally adequate foods are highly essential for the maintenance of an optimal state of nutrition that in turn will preserve morale, discipline, and the military effectiveness of troops at all times.

2. RESPONSIBILITY OF NUTRITIONAL ADEQUACY OF RATIONS

In the United States, the Office of the Surgeon General (OTSG) has the responsibility for the supervision of the evaluation of the nutritional

TABLE 1 US ARMY BASIC DIETARY STANDARDS

Nutrients	Physically active[a] AR 40–5,	Relatively sedentary 1964[a]	AR 40–25[b] Moderately active 1972
Calories	3600	3000	3400
Protein (g)	100	100	100
Calcium (g)	0.70	0.70	0.80
Iron (mg)	—	—	20
Vitamin A (IU)	5000	5000	5000
Thiamine (mg)	1.7	1.5	1.7
Riboflavin (mg)	2.0	2.0	2.0
Niacin (mg)	16	16	22
Ascorbic acid (mg)	75	75	60

[a] Troops in basic or advanced training, including paratroopers, ski troops, etc. (1964).
[b] The fat calories should not exceed 40% of the total issued in planned menus. Carbohydrate will provide those calories not furnished by protein and fat.

status of military populations. Army regulations state that the OTSG is "also responsible for prescribing basic standards of diet for the Army under various conditions of its operation, reporting nutritional deficiencies wherever they occur, and recommending the necessary corrective measures" (Army Regulations, 1972). The U.S. military nutritional standards are the same for all of the services. In the past (AR 40–5), the Army allowances were designed for two groups—the relatively sedentary and the physically active individual living in a temperate environment. The new major changes are for increased calcium intakes to 0.80 g/day, the increase in niacin from 16 to 22 mg/day and a decrease in ascorbic acid intake from 75 to 60 mg/day. The present nutritional standards are designed for the moderately active individual living in a temperate environment (AR 40–25, 1972).

The military services now recommend daily intakes of 3400 kcal for moderately active men living in a temperate environment (Table 1). The daily protein allowances are 100 g, calcium 0.8 g, iron 14 mg, vitamin A 500 IU, thiamine 1.7 mg, riboflavin 2.0 mg, niacin 22 mg and ascorbic acid 60 mg. There are no recommended allowances for fat or carbohydrate, however the desirable proportion of fat calories to total calories should not exceed 40% in planned menus and carbohydrate will be provided by those calories not furnished by protein or fat.

The OTSG also has the responsibility for field testing all rations, under simulated conditions, for their nutritional adequacy and for maintenance of maximal physical efficiency prior to being placed in the millitary ration system.

3. NUTRITIONAL ADEQUACY OF ALLOWANCES

In the development of any type ration, the daily recommended allowances for calories, minerals, and vitamins must be strongly adhered to, since only under these conditions will the nutritional adequacy of the rations (field, combat, and survival) be effective in maintenance of optimal mental and physical efficiency of the combat soldier (Johnson, 1943). Although some of the criteria may be difficult to attain, these rations must be adequate in weight, cubage, packaging, field utility, density, acceptability, palatability, and nutrient composition. United States Army Regulation 40–25 (1972) recommends that a ration must supply the minimal allowances of the various nutrients that are considered to be nutritionally adequate. The ration must contain sufficient essential nutrients so that consumption of less than recommended allowances for short periods of time will not result in serious nutritional deficiencies.

Some modifications have been made in the latest revision of the NRC Recommended Dietary Allowances. The allowances for age groups between 23–50 and 50+ years have been combined. In the 1968 NRC edition the age groups were classified at 20 year intervals after age 35 years. The new calorie allowances for the 18–22 year group have been increased from 2800–3000 kcal/day, although the body weights are less— 67 kg vs the 70 kg man in 1968.

However, the protein allowances for the same age group were decreased

TABLE 2 Recommended Dietary Allowances, National Research Council[a] and Food and Nutrition Board 1968[b] and 1974

Nutrients	Year & age groups (men)				
	1968 18–22 yrs	1974 19–22 yrs	1968 22–35 yrs	1974 23–50 yrs	1968 35–55 yrs
Calories	2800	3000	2800	2700	2600
Protein (g)	65	54	65	56	65
Calcium (g)	0.8	0.8	0.8	0.8	0.8
Iron (mg)	10	10	10	10	10
Vitamin A (IU)	5000	5000	5000	5000	5000
Thiamine (mg)	1.4	1.5	1.4	1.4	1.3
Riboflavin (mg)	1.7	1.8	1.7	1.6	1.7
Niacin (mg)	18	20	18	18	17
Ascorbic acid (mg)	60	45	60	45	60

[a] The greatest changes were the decreases in the daily caloric intake, protein and ascorbic acid.
[b] The standard man weighs 70 kg, is 175 cm in height, moderately active and lives at 20°C.

to 54 g/day and ascorbic acid reduced to 45 mg/day in the same group. The other changes in this age group were negligible. The same approximate changes were noted in the other age groups.

The National Research Council's Dietary Allowances (1974) [Table 2], have been modified to suit the military needs.

Although the military have recommended these calorie allowances for the two groups, every soldier eating at the US military mess is given an issue of 4200–4400 Cal/day as prescribed by the "Master Menu" (Dept. of Army, 1967). In addition, the military requirements also provide for an increase in the food allowances when the situation arises, since it is the prerogative of the local post surgeon to increase the daily allowances by 10% under conditions of growth, heavy physical activity, and to maintain energy equilibrium. These daily allowances are actually designed to serve as a guide in the planning of an adequate diet for the normal, healthy soldier. One should keep in mind that to be considered nutritionally adequate, the dietary allowances should be the quantity of food actually consumed—not issued.

An excessive and increased caloric intake above the daily energy expenditure can be harmful since it results in an increased deposit of fat (as obesity) with a subsequent increase in body weight, which presents a greater work load to the heart. One must keep in mind that a positive caloric balance of only 100 Cal/day will result in a body weight gain of approximately 4.8 kg/year.

Although the recommended protein allowances are 0.8 g/kg body weight (NRC, 1974), adults with normal calorie intakes can maintain a nitrogen balance on protein intakes of approximately 0.5 g/kg/day; however, one must remember that nitrogen balances may not necessarily reflect all of the functions of protein in maintaining normal body metabolism and health. The additional increase in protein up to 100 g/day by the military is to provide some margin of safety for the individual soldier's requirement and be sufficient to provide new tissue for growth.

The normal American diet contains at least 12% of the calories as protein, which if consumed will supply sufficient quantities of the essential amino acids. On intakes of 3600 Cal/day, this would amount to 108 g of protein per day. The British recommend 11% of the calories consumed from protein (Dept. of Health, 1970), but the Russians feel that athletes in training should consume 17% of the calories from protein, which at the 3600 Cal/day level amounts to 154 g of protein per day or 2.3 g/kg of body weight (Jakovlev, 1961).

There is no question that individuals prefer high animal protein diets, but this is due to psychological rather than physiological factors and to taste rather than to sound physiology. This is based on information that since muscle is built of protein, then an increased intake of protein will stimulate excessive muscle growth and in turn improve muscle strength. It has been shown that an increased protein intake also increases the water requirements, due to the fact that additional fluid is required to eliminate the nitrogen byproducts in the urine. This would be an additional problem under combat conditions.

A considerable amount of work has been done on the effects of high protein intakes and performance. In studies by Pitts *et al.* (1944a) and Darling *et al.* (1944), no changes in physical fitness and work performance were observed or attributable to the dietary protein level which ranged from 75 to 150 g/day. In fact, the metabolic rate (oxygen uptake) in the high protein group was actually increased by 4% in men performing the same work, indicating a greater energy requirement to utilize the excess protein. Gontzea (1956) also observed that during bicycling, higher protein intakes at breakfast resulted in higher energy expenditures, which decreased muscular efficiency appreciably.

At the present time, there is no conclusive evidence that muscular activity results in an increased destruction of cellular protein in individuals receiving adequate food intakes, and it is the general feeling that protein requirements are not increased with increased physical activity. A well-balanced diet will provide the necessary daily protein requirements. Increased physical activity will result in an increased caloric intake, with a subsequent increase in protein. An excessive protein intake will only serve as an expensive source of energy, due to the increased SDA, and will also increase the water requirements.

The National Research Council (1968) has not made any recommendation for the daily allowances of fat, but it has been shown that diets containing above 50% of calories from fat are usually intolerable, since they could result in nausea and ketosis. The high consumption of saturated fats, which results in elevated plasma cholesterol and triglycerides, have been shown to influence the prevalence of coronary heart disease. This has resulted in an increase of unsaturated fatty acids in the American diet, which have been known to decrease the plasma cholesterol levels.

Fat is a very important source of food energy, and is very essential since it creates a feeling of satiety, increases the palatability of the diet, is the carrier of all the fat soluble vitamins including A, K, D, and E, and is the source of supply of the essential unsaturated fatty acids. Practically all of the body tissues require these fatty acids as an energy source, the only exception being the central nervous system. These EFA requirements appear to be greatly influenced by several factors including age, sex, and possible physical activity.

Although the daily EFA allowances are low (2% linoleic acid in the total diet), a dietary deficiency of the EFA (primarily arachidonic and its precursor linoleic acid) has been shown to result in an impairment of growth and reproductive capacity; in a decrease in the efficiency of energy utilization; and a decrease in the resistance to stress. It appears that a normal daily intake of the unsaturated fats would be sufficient to provide the necessary EFA requirements.

Carbohydrate is required in the ration because it is an essential nutrient for cardiac and neurological activity, and that it is readily available and easily utilized as a quick source of energy. Astrand (1967) has reviewed the effects of diet upon sustained strenuous performance by athletes engaged in cross-country skiing. In one study, the maximal work times of cross-country skiers averaged 57 min after consuming a high protein (or a low carbohydrate) diet; 114 min after a normal mixed diet, and 167 min after a high carbohydrate diet. Based primarily on the work of Hermansen *et al.* (1967) and Bergstrom *et al.* (1967), he concluded that: (a) nitrogen excretion was not affected by the physical activity level, (b) an increase in muscular activity increased the relative metabolism of carbohydrate, and (c) high carbohydrate diets improved work capacity. Hermansen *et al.* (1967) reported the capacity to continue work at 75–80% of maximal capacity was related to muscle glycogen stores, and that when these stores were depleted, the subjects were unable to continue working. The RQs indicated that the major source of energy throughout the exercise period was carbohydrate. Bergstrom *et al.* (1967) reported that muscle glycogen content can be increased with high carbohydrate diets and reduced with low carbohydrate diets. In this study, the RQ dropped, indicating an increased energy yield from free fatty acids. Christensen and Hansen (1939) also observed a greater efficiency in bicycle endurance that averaged two to three times greater on a high carbohydrate versus a high fat diet. They concluded that carbohydrates are readily available for metabolism, and are more easily metabolized than fat or protein, particularly in short strenuous work where quick energy is required. The feeding of high carbohydrate diets appear to give the best energy yield/liter of oxygen (5.05 Cals as compared to 4.87 Cals for fat, and 4.48 Cal for protein). It would also increase CO_2 production to maintain pCO_2 because one liter of carbon dioxide is produced for each liter of oxygen consumed in carbohydrate metabolism, while only 0.7

liters of CO_2 is liberated for each liter of oxygen consumed in the metabolism of fat.

These observations on high carbohydrate diets (70% of the calories) indicate that additional research should be performed in this area to have a better understanding of the mechanisms involved. This would result in a clearer understanding of the beneficial effects of increasing work performance with high carbohydrate diets.

TABLE 3A TAIWAN RATION TEST—WINTER 1954–55
COMPARISON OF ENERGY EXPENDITURE FOR VARIOUS ACTIVITIES

Activity	Control diet		Enriched diet	
	Cal/h	Cal/h/m²	Cal/h	Cal/h/m²
Basal metabolic rate	68.6	43.2	61.0	38.8
Sitting after breakfast	81.8	51.5	77.6	49.4
Standing at ease	84.8	53.2	80.1	50.9
MR after lunch	80.2	50.4	76.9	49.0
Resting position (squat)	89.0	56.0	82.3	52.4
Regular road march	315.0	198.0	309.0	200.0
Rest period, regular march	101.8	63.8	93.0	60.3
Marching, full pack and rifle	343.0	216.0	343.0	217.0
Walking 110–120 paces/min	259.3	163.0	221.2	141.0
Walking 110–120 paces + 10 kg load	286.7	180.0	263.6	168.0
Walking + 20 kg load	318.6	199.0	288.0	183.0
Walking + 30 kg load	344.0	218.0	324.0	206.0
Walking + 40 kg load	371.4	234.0	373.7	238.0
Labor details, moderate	227.7		236.5	

TABLE 3B ENERGY BALANCE—TIME MOTION, ENERGY EXPENDITURE, AND FOOD CONSUMPTION

Day of week	Control	Cal expended per day	
		Enriched	Difference
1	3529	3354	175
2	3529	3354	175
3	3490	3317	173
4	3413	3243	170
5	3490	3317	173
6	3376	3208	172
7	2322	2179	143
Mean per day	3307	3138	169
Body weight loss (120 days)	1.0 kg		58 Cal
Total			227
Food intake per body weight changes	3610	3380	230

Although the daily NRC allowances for vitamins are quite adequate for any given situation, one must keep in mind that marginal nutritional deficiencies could impair performance, decrease resistance to diseases, and slow down rehabilitation from wounds. An exceptional example of deficient-to-marginal intakes and performance was observed in a study of Chinese Nationalist troops in Taiwan (Consolazio et al., 1956). At the beginning of the study, 80% of the men were deficient in thiamine, riboflavin, and niacin. These 1100 men were divided into two groups; one-half to receive the same deficient diet and the other half to receive the same diet and the daily NRC allowances of thiamine, riboflavin, niacin, vitamin A, and iron. After 3 months of supplementation, a significant improvement was observed in the performance efficiency of the group receiving the recommended daily allowances (a 5% significant decrease in oxygen uptake). It was suggested that there was a direct relationship between vitamin deficiency states and the efficiency of utilizing calories in the performance of daily physical activities (Tables 3A and 3B).

On the other hand, massive doses of vitamins will not improve physiological performance. This concept was based on some earlier work, which was never substantiated and later disproved by Keys et al. (1944), that considerable quantities of vitamins and minerals were lost in sweat and needed to be replaced. Other investigators have shown that B-vitamin supplementation did not improve (a) static and dynamic work tests (Simonson et al., 1942), (b) muscular endurance tests (Karpovich and Millman, 1942), (c) heavy work in industry (Bransby et al., 1944), and (d) oxygen uptake during standardized work tests (Keys and

TABLE 4   UK RECOMMENDED DIETARY ALLOWANCES[a]

	Sedentary		Active		Very active	
	1950	1970	1950	1970	1950	1970
kcalories	2500	2700	3000	3000	4250	3600
Protein (g)	69	68	82	75	117	90
Calcium (g)	0.8	0.5	0.8	0.5	0.8	0.5
Iron (mg)	12	10	12	10	12	10
Vitamin A (IU)	5000	3750	5000	3750	5000	3750
Thiamine (mg)	1.0	1.1	1.2	1.2	1.7	1.4
Riboflavin (mg)	1.5	1.7	1.8	1.7	2.6	1.7
Niacin (mg)	10	18	12	18	17	18
Ascorbic acid (mg)	20	30	20	30	20	30

[a] The 1950 data was prepared by the British Medical Council on Nutrition. The latest 1970 data was prepared by the Dept. of Public Health. There are some differences between the new UK and US dietary allowances, i.e., ascorbic acid 30 vs 20 mg; vitamin A 3750 vs 5000 IU, and calcium 0.5 vs 0.8 g/day.

Henschel, 1942). In a 6-week study, designed to evaluate the possible beneficial effects of high vitamin intakes, it was concluded that these high intakes did not improve performance. The Harvard step test and the Army physical fitness test was improved in the supplemented and control groups, indicating a training effect for both (Ryer *et al.*, 1954).

The recommended dietary allowances for the US (NRC, 1974), and the British (BDH, 1970) are approximately the same with the exception of the allowances for protein and ascorbic acid. The US allowances of 60 mg/day for ascorbic acid are based on estimates of ascorbic acid plasma levels and consideration of general health, while the British feel that 10 mg/day will prevent scurvy, 20 mg or less may be adequate for adults, and that 30 mg/day will provide a safety margin (Table 4). The US allowance for protein, based on body weight, is 0.8 g/kg body weight per day, while the British standard is based on 11% of the calories being protein. This means that the higher the caloric allowance, the higher the daily protein intake.

4. DIFFERENCE BETWEEN ALLOWANCES AND MINIMAL REQUIREMENTS

The minimal nutrient requirements are defined as the smallest quantity of nutrients that will maintain an individual in balance when the daily intake is essentially adequate in other respects. One must keep in mind that the recommended daily allowances are not the daily minimal requirements. They actually represent not only the minimal requirements of an individual, but the nutrient intakes selected to allow for variations in body size of a large segment of a population with an added safety margin. The recommended allowances are designed to provide an excess of nutrients that will permit some storage for emergencies that may be encountered such as periods of caloric restriction during survival or increased requirements during recovery from diseases. The optimal allowances are designed to permit optimal body function, and should include adequate quantities of the nutrients to enable the body stores or reserves to be established.

5. MAINTENANCE OF PHYSICAL EFFICIENCY

As mentioned previously in the text, in addition to being acceptable, a field ration must also maintain physical efficiency in troops. Johnson and Kark (1947a) have defined the basic conditions that are required to maintain maximal physical efficiency, and have also presented examples

TABLE 5 PHYSICAL EFFICIENCY AND INEFFICIENCY IN SOLDIERS
THE BASIC CONDITIONS FOR MAINTENANCE OF PHYSICAL EFFICIENCY
ILLUSTRATED BY EXAMPLES OF DETERIORATION (JOHNSON AND KARK, 1947a)

Basic condition to maintain physical efficiency	Examples of deterioration
1. General	
a. Freedom from chronic or acute debilitating diseases	a. Australian casualties in Owen Stanley campaign
b. Good general physical and phychological training and condition for the job at hand	b. Deteriorated US troops in rear areas, Pacific
2. Adaptation to environment	
a. Acclimatization for the particular environment and work	a. Inefficient mountain troops on first day at 9000 ft (2743 m); desert heat exhaustion in British troops
b. Preventive measures against environmental stresses and avoidance of exceeding limits of physiological endurance	b. Deteriorated Indian Army muleteers; ill US troops in New Guinea
c. Good clothing, personal equipment, and protective devices against injury from the environment	c. Collapse of troops from carbon monoxide poisoning in the Arctic; improperly clothed US troops on Attu
3. Nutrition	
a. Maintenance of water balance	a. US troops exhausted by limitation of water in the desert
b. Maintenance of adequate intake of calories	b. Caloric deficiency in theaters of war and in various ration trials
c. Maintenance of salt balance	c. Salt deficiencies in British troops in Iraq
d. Maintenance of adequate intake of other important nutrients such as protein and vitamins	d. Vitamin deficiency diseases among Allied troops
e. Insurance of a, b, c, and d by adequate planning, supply, catering, and indoctrination	e. Examples quoted by many observers at Food Conference, April 1–30, 1946

of deterioration in troops when these basic conditions are not carried out (Table 5). As examples, they cite (a) studies on water deprivation resulting in the exhaustion of desert troops, (b) studies on caloric deficiencies in various theaters of war and in ration trials, (c) studies on salt deficiencies in British troops in Iraq, and (d) studies on various marginal vitamin deficiency diseases among Allied troops. There is no question that some of these deficiencies could have been prevented with proper planning and indoctrination. One must never forget to protect the individual against the environmental stresses that include (a) acclimatization for the particular environment and physical work, (b) preventive measures against the environmental stresses, especially in not exceeding the limits of physiological endurance, and (c) protection against the environment with good clothing, personal equipment, and other protective devices against injury from the environment.

In the hot, humid environment of tropical areas, the greatest problem is the prevention of physical deterioration, which is usually due to a caloric deficit caused by the loss of appetite. Anorexia is quite common during the initial heat acclimatization phase, and it is not unusual for an individual to have anorexia during his entire tour in a hot environment. Psychological factors tend to aggravate this condition, and it is the general feeling of experts that it is the individual's reaction to an undesirable environment over which he has no control. In addition to ameliorating the psychological factors, a great deal of research should be done to increase the individual's appetite. For example, whenever practical, the packaged rations used in feeding the troops in the tropics should be replaced with fresh foods (Dept. of Army, 1961).

6. DIETARY ALLOWANCES AND CLIMATIC STRESS

The daily energy requirements are affected by many factors including age, sex, physical activity, body size and composition, and environmental temperature. Recently, the NRC's (1974) daily allowances were revised and decreased for Reference Man from 2800 to 2700 Cal/day. This was primarily due to the decreased physical activity of modern-day Americans and to the fact that a large percentage of the population is overweight.

Prior to the publication of the new NRC's *Recommended Dietary Allowances* (1974), the general concept had been that the caloric requirements were inversely proportional to the environmental temperature (Johnson and Kark, 1947b). This meant that the energy requirements were increased in an extremely cold environment and decreased in an extremely hot environment. The increased requirements in the cold could not be explained in terms of body size or different physical activities, but were at least partially due to the increased requirements for maintaining thermal equilibrium and to the binding or "hobbling" effect of the clothing worn.

These allowances for extreme environmental conditions were controversial for quite some time, but work by Welch *et al.* (1957) in an extremely cold environment showed that the caloric requirements were not increased over the requirements of men living in a temperate environment, except for the 2–5 % due to wearing heavy clothing and foot wear.

These authors concluded that if the men were adequately clothed there was no reason for the energy requirements being increased in the cold unless (a) enough time is spent in the cold to make a man shiver, (b) wearing extra-heavy clothing which would impose a resistance to body movement, or (c) an individual wearing heavy foot wear which would result in an increase in energy expenditure.

The work in extremely cold environments made it increasingly apparent that a re-evaluation of the requirements for men working in extreme heat was necessary. Subsequent studies (Consolazio *et al.* 1960, 1961) have shown that the energy requirements were actually increased in a hot environment (Table 6). Since this was a fairly controversial area, the main criticisms to be evaluated were whether the men in these studies were fully acclimatized to the heat, and whether the increased requirement was due to insufficient training prior to the beginning of the studies. In a third study, designed to re-evaluate these two factors, energy expenditure was measured at three work levels and at three strictly controlled temperatures of 70°, 85°, and 100°F (Consolazio *et al.*, 1963c). This study again demonstrated that the oxygen uptakes were significantly increased at the higher environmental temperature. The increases averaged 11.4, 13.3, and 11.7% for light, moderate, and fairly heavy physical work, respectively (Table 7).

In general agreement with these results (Consolazio *et al.*, 1963c) are the recent findings of Durnin *et al.* (1966). In this study on British troops it was reaffirmed that energy expenditures in hot environments

TABLE 6 ENERGY REQUIREMENTS IN HOT ENVIRONMENT
(AVERAGES OF EIGHT MEN PER DAY)

	Period 1 Hot sun	Period 2 Hot shade	Period 3 Cool shade
Food consumption (Cal)	3560	3516	3156
Body weight change (g)	+ 62	+ 36	+ 17
Water balance (g)	+ 120	+ 121	− 55
Weight change not due to water retention or loss (g)	− 58	− 85	+ 38
Protein balance (N × 6.25) (g)	− 2.7	− 4.2	+ 8.6
Weight change not due to water or protein (due to fat) (g)	− 55	− 81	+ 47
Caloric equivalent of this weight change (Cal/g)	− 498	− 729	+ 423
Energy requirement	4058	4243	2733

[a] Energy requirement if weight change is assumed to be glycogen: (period 1) 3780, (period 2) 3840, (period 3) 3334.

TABLE 7 ENERGY COST DURING REST, MODERATE, AND HEAVY PHYSICAL ACTIVITIES (CAL/MIN)[a]

Activity	Environmental temperature			Percentage increase vs. 100°F
	70°F	85°F	100°F	
Rest	1.36	1.41	1.52	11.4
Moderate	2.61	2.62	2.95	13.3
Heavy	7.11	7.02	7.85	11.7

[a]Mean energy expenditure of seven men during each phase.

were significantly increased by 5–9% with no significant difference between hot–wet and hot–dry conditions. The three temperatures utilized were approximately 22.2° (temperate), 37.8° (hot–wet), and 44.4°C (hot–dry). Significant differences were also observed in heart rates, rectal temperatures, sweat rates, and pulmonary ventilation. On the basis of these studies it was concluded that the energy metabolism was increased in a hot environment and that the increase was not due to either the effects of training or to acclimatization. It was also suggested that the increase in energy metabolism was the factor that led to an increase in food requirements of men living and working in hot environments. The 1974 revision of the calorie allowances published by the NRC now suggests that the food requirements are increased rather than decreased for men performing prescribed work at high environmental temperatures. The daily allowances are unchanged between temperatures of 20–30°C, but are increased by at least 0.5% for each degree increase in temperature between 30–40°C. In essence, the food allowances in a hot environment have changed from a decrease of 9% to an increase of 5% or an overall increase of 14%.

7. SALT

Salt and water requirements are closely interrelated and are an essential factor to be considered in the development of rations. The allowances are dependent, to a considerable extent, upon the ambient environmental temperatures and the physical activity of the individuals (heat load and work load). The NRC (1974) recommended 5 g/day of salt as a liberal allowance in a temperate environment and under conditions of minimal sweating, but the intake can be as high as 10–15 g/day even when the fluid intake is below 4000 g/day. It has been shown that an intake of salt between 15–20 g/day is sufficient for most men in a hot environment, although an intake of 20 g/day of salt is not uncommon under conditions of profuse sweating in a hot environment. During heat acclimatization, the salt requirements are greatly increased due to the high concentrations in sweat, but after acclimatization (between 6–10 days), the salt requirements are reduced since the sweat concentration decreases with acclimatization. The daily salt intake must reflect the body sweat losses. The best system of salt supplementation is by its addition to food as a first choice and to water as a second choice. The quantity added to water should never exceed one part in 1000, or an 0.1% solution (Consolazio et al., 1963a).

Taylor et al. (1943) have observed that a salt intake of 15 g/day was adequate for men working in extremely dry, hot environments. When the salt intake was decreased to 6 g/day, the men drank much less water, sweated less, but lost twice as much of their body weight. These individuals had increased body temperatures, heart rates, and poorer cardiovascular adjustments. Twenty-five percent of the subjects on low salt intakes collapsed. Others showed signs of dehydration, nausea, vomiting, tachycardia, hypotension, and vertigo. Only 2.5% of the men on the higher salt intakes collapsed. The maintenance of salt and water balance even after acclimatization to extreme heat is very essential for maximum performance.

A few words of caution should be voiced on the detrimental effects of a high salt intake, especially under conditions where the water supply is limited or where the troops are not losing excessive salt due to sweating. The US meal individual combat (also called the C-ration), and other packaged field rations, have been notorious for their high salt content (up to 30 g/day) which is used for its satiety factor and for long-term preservation. Baker et al. (1963) have thoroughly investigated the effects of high salt intakes on water requirements and have shown that a ration containing 22 g of salt per day would require a fluid intake of 4.69 l/day for a 70 kg sedentary man living in a warm environment. This calculation was based on the assumption that "the smallest quantity of water required to prevent overloading with salt is that which is sufficient to dilute the salt ingested to the same level as sodium and chloride normally occurring in the water of blood plasma" (Baker et al., 1963). One can see that excessive salt intakes (from survival or other rations), under conditions where the water supply is limited, should be avoided since it does increase the water requirements. In other instances it could also cause intestinal disturbances.

8. WATER

In the development of survival rations, precautions should be taken in selecting the food components which will not increase water requirements. Although the availability of water is not an immediate one, in a survival situation it is known to be more important than food. Man can live for 30 days without food, but the survival time without water may be very limited. Stevenson (1958) has estimated the survival time of men living in an environment of 39°C with one pint of water per day (500 ml) (Table 8). Under these conditions, the survival time of men wearing dry clothes is only 5 days. In an environment of 30°C, where the individual has only a total of 5 pints of water, his maximal survival time is again 5 days. Gamble (1946–7) reports that living in a temperate environment, a normal healthy adult weighing 70 kg (including 45 kg of water) will lose 1500 g of water per day from all his body sources. If he loses 9kg or roughly 20% of his body water, he is expected to die within 6 days. Gamble (1946–7) has recommended that the minimal daily fluid requirements in a temperate environment should be 700 g (which is considerably less than the normal daily consumption of 2500 g or more) and is dependent on physical activity and ambient temperature.

TABLE 8 ESTIMATED SURVIVAL TIME (STEVENSON, 1958)[a]

	One pint of water per man per day at 39°C			Five pints of water, total supply per man at 30°C		
	No shade (days)		Shade (days)	No shade (days)		Shade (days)
	Dry clothes	Wet clothes	Wet clothes	Dry clothes	Wet clothes	Wet clothes
20% body weight loss (limit of survival)	5	14	20	5	11	13.5
10% body weight loss (limit of ability to work)	2.5	7	10	3	6.5	8

[a] Previous dehydration will greatly shorten the survival times; 20% body water losses may be fatal in some instances.

Water requirements are increased with an increase in environmental temperature due to the increased heat load caused by sweating, physical activity, and the increased respiratory water loss. In a mild desert environment, with a minimal amount of activity, and an increased environmental temperature of 37.8°C, with heavy physical activities, a minimum of 12 kg of water per day is required to have troops maintain maximal efficiency (Ladell et al., 1944).

In a desert environment, Adolph and Dill (1938) have observed evaporative water losses as high as 1600 g/h and it is no wonder that under these conditions the water requirements are increased by three to six times. Ladell et al. (1944) reported studies of soldiers in Iraq during World War II living in environments averaging 46.1°C, who required approximately 7.5 kg of water per day to maintain water balance. It was recommended that the troops should drink sufficient quantities of water to produce at least 900 g per day, since a low urine excretion was indicative of an early symptom of collapse from a consistent negative water balance (Ladell et al., 1944). In a hot environment with water restriction, man becomes incapacitated and then exhausted within a few hours. This "dehydration exhaustion syndrome" reported by Adolph (1947) and Johnson (1943) is accompanied by an increased body temperature and heart rate, restlessness and insomnia, muscular fatigue, anorexia, extreme lassitude, and are all apparently due to the decrease in blood volume and impaired circulation. Many investigators (Adolph, 1947; Saltin, 1964; Consolazio et al., 1965; Pitts et al., 1944b) have shown that body hypohydration, even with moderate physical activity, results in a decrease in performance (Fig. 1). A portion of the daily water requirement is available from

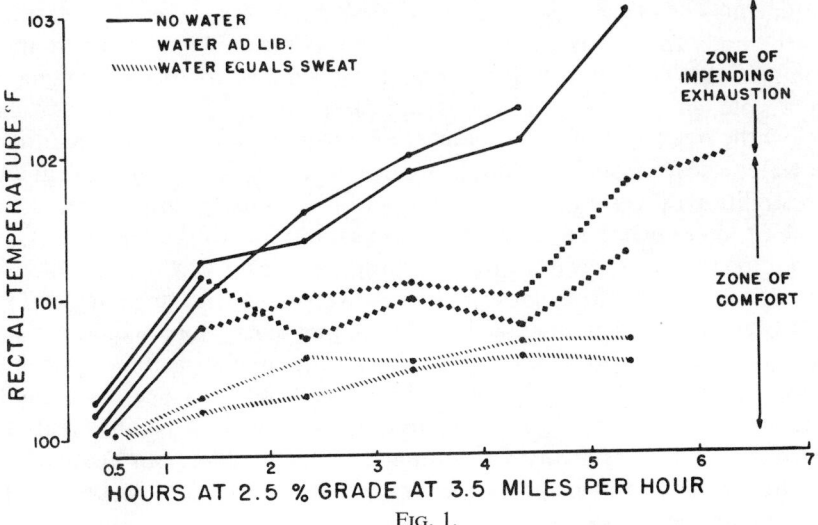

Fig. 1.

metabolic water, which is produced by the body from the oxidation of protein, fat, and carbohydrate in foods.

Water requirements are greatly influenced by the nutrient composition of a ration. It has been shown that protein intake increases the water requirements by increasing the osmotic intake, which in turn requires more water to eliminate the nitrogen byproducts (especially urea) in the urine. On the other hand, fat and carbohydrate, which both yield considerable quantities of water on oxidation, will decrease water requirements.

The maintenance of water balance is essential in maintaining optimal efficiency, and it is extremely necessary to be certain that water is ingested *ad libitum* at all times, especially under conditions of profuse sweating. The osmotic balance critically affects the water balance and, under conditions where too little osmotically active material is ingested, the body cannot retain water because the kidney cannot function efficiently. When large quantities of osmotically active material is ingested, excessive fluid must be excreted by the kidney to get rid of the excess. Sargent and Johnson (1957) feel that under conditions of limited fluids the small osmotic intake actually accentuates dehydration.

In a cold environment, although the problem of water requirements may not appear to be as critical as they are in a hot environment, the exposure to cold does have a significant diuretic effect on troops. Under these conditions, the blood volume is decreased and the skin and subcutaneous body tissues become dehydrated, which is a protective measure by the body to prevent the freezing of skin (Frazier, 1945). Sargent and Johnson (1957) recommended minimal water intake of 1000–2000 g/day in a cold environment, which is increased as the temperature drops below the freezing level. The colder the environment, the greater quantity of water is lost through the lungs. A word of caution concerning the great possibilities of voluntary water restriction in a cold environment. In general, there may be a restricted water supply due to the limitations of fuel to melt ice or snow for water consumption. The procedure for obtaining drinking water from snow and ice is fairly slow, and tiresome, and it has been observed frequently in field studies that troops would rather become voluntarily dehydrated than spend the time in melting sufficient snow for their daily requirements. Water restriction (a decreased fluid intake) in the cold could be disastrous due to the increased daily sweating from the wearing of the heavy clothing and boots, from poor ventilation of the clothing, and from the respiratory water losses from breathing the dry air (Hulse, 1956).

The Department of the Army TB MED 175 (1969) specifically states the following on water requirements in a hot environment: "(a) These sweat losses must be replaced or rapid decrease in the ability to work, a rise in body temperature, heart rate, deterioration of morale, and heat exhaustion will occur. Water loss should be replaced preferably by periodic intake of small amounts of water throughout the daily work period. (b) The belief that men can be taught to adjust to decreased water intake is incorrect."

For continued maximal physical and mental efficiency it is the duty of every field commander constantly to emphasize the deleterious effects of water deprivation in man. Adequate hydration is indispensable for maximal efficiency.

9. KETOSIS

The prevention of ketosis by consumption of a survival ration is a primary prerequisite. High concentration of ketone bodies (acetone, acetoacetate, beta-hydroxybutyric acid) are injurious to brain function, and they will markedly impair the acid–base balance. A diet containing adequate total calories, including a reasonable quantity of carbohydrate, will prevent ketosis. A diet deficient in calories, such as in semistarvation and starvation, or a diet low in carbohydrate and high in fat, will produce ketosis. In some instances, a high-fat/high-protein diet may be highly ketogenic in a cold environment and much less so in a hot environment, but, in general, the greatest ketogenicity is observed with large calorie deficits as in starvation.

10. RATIONS

In the planning and development of rations for optimal utilization of foods, acceptability and palatability are of primary importance in fulfilling military requirements. Prior to and at the beginning of World War II, the concept for these requirements was that the food components should provide the greatest nutritive value and have the least weight and least bulk. In some instances, acceptability was secondary, and at one time soybeans were actually considered as a meat replacement. Although the ration provides a liberal allowance of all the nutrients essential in the diet, the adequacy is highly dependent on the extent to which the individual consumes some or all components of the diet. If the troops do not eat specific items of the ration issued, their intake over a period of time may be deficient in one or more of the essential nutrients. As an example, in the United States fish, liver, lima beans, kidney stew, spinach, etc., which contribute many of the essential nutrients, are disliked and usually consumed in small quantities. In essence, the individual must be indoctrinated in the importance of eating protective foods. The acceptability and nutritional adequacy of the ration is also highly dependent on good food preparation by the cooks. It is essential that the cooks should be well trained in all phases of food preparation especially in matters of nutrient conservation, and, above all, they should have a great interest in the final acceptability of the product. An unacceptable food item, regardless of the cost or nutrient composition, is of no use if it is badly prepared and is not eaten by the troops.

One must also remember that considerable quantities of vitamins are lost during cooking in the military mess halls (Table 9). The greatest losses have been reported for thiamine, i.e. 35% for fresh meats, 60% for canned meats, 40% for leafy green and yellow vegetables, and 40%

TABLE 9 PERCENTAGE COOKING LOSSES AS OBSERVED IN THE US ARMY MESS HALLS (TM 8–501) (1961)

	Thiamine	Riboflavin	Niacin	Ascorbic acid
Meats, fresh	35	20	25	
Meats, canned	60	20	25	
Eggs	25	10		
Cereals	10		10	
Legumes	20			
Vegetables (leafy, green, and yellow)	40	25	25	60
Vegetables, tomatoes	5	5	5	15
Vegetables, potatoes	40	25	25	60
Vegetables, other	25	15	25	60

for potatoes. The cooking losses for riboflavin and niacin are also quite large for the same food items. Very high losses of 60% of the ascorbic acid have been observed in vegetables, including potatoes.

Edible food losses in US military messes are also quite high, averaging between 8.4 and 15.3% of the total calories served. The lowest edible wastes of 8.4% were observed during Ranger training at Fort Benning, Georgia, where the daily energy expenditure averaged 4800 Cal/day

(Consolazio *et al.*, 1966). The field of garrison ration should provide sufficient quantities of all the nutrients to allow for the cooking losses.

Armstrong (1951) described the four basic characteristics of a ration to be utility, acceptability, stability, and its nutritional value. The utility requirements become highly essential especially under conditions that are far removed from the main sources of supply. These requirements include the minimal weight and cubage which can be decreased by reducing the water content of a ration and by the use of dehydrated precooked foods. The components of the ration should have the highest possible acceptability to maintain morale in the troops. Appetite is greatly affected by the various psychological and physiological factors such as fatigue, mental stress, excitement, and extreme cold, heat, and altitude. The nutritional value of the ration in the United States is based on the recommended dietary allowances of the NRC, whenever it is practical (1974). The final characteristic is the development of the ration for stability. These requirements include long-term storage under extreme environmental conditions ($-56°C$ to $+43.2°C$ range), and the prevention of bacteriological, physical, and chemical changes which would make the foods toxic and unacceptable (Armstrong, 1951).

11. HISTORY OF US ARMY FEEDING

In the early years of the American Revolution, the feeding of a rapidly growing army became such a great logistical problem that on 4 November 1775 the Continental Congress passed a resolution that provided for a ration allowance for the troops (Table 10A). The initial ration actually provided more calories, twice the quantity of the daily protein allowance, and a more adequate supply of minerals and vitamins (except vitamins A and C) than the present-day dietary allowances. The Congressional resolution read as follows:

> Resolved that a ration consists of the following kinds and quantities of provisions: 1 pound[†] of beef or 3/4 of a pound of pork or 1 pound of salt fish per day; 1 pound of bread or flour per day; three pints of peas or beans; 2 pints of milk/man/day or at the rate of 1/72 of a dollar; 1/2 pint of rice or 1 pint Indian meal/man/day; 1 quart of spruce beer or cider/man/day, or 9 gallons of molasses/company of 100 men/week; 3 pounds of candles/100 men/week for guards; 24

[†] 1 US pound = 454 g.

TABLE 10A EARLIEST US ARMY RATIONS[a]
(GRAMS ISSUED PER DAY PER MAN)

Ration items	1775	1812	1838	1860–5
Beef	454	570	570	570
Flour	454	513	513	627
Milk	454	—	—	—
Beer, spruce	908	—	—	—
Peas	194	—	—	—
Rice	40	—	—	—
Soap	5.2	18	20	18
Candle	2.0	7	5	7
Rum	—	113	—	—
Vinegar	—	113	19	41
Salt	—	18	18	18
Beans, dried			70	76
Sugar			55	68
Coffee, green			27	46
Potatoes				200
Yeast				1.3
Pepper				1.3

[a] The first Army ration was fixed by legislation on 4 November 1775.

pounds of soft or 8 pounds of hard soap/100 men/week. [QM Corps OQMG, 1949].

In 1785 the US Army ration was supplemented with 4 oz of rum (113 g), and additional items included small quantities of salt and vinegar. The rum ration was considered too high, and in 1790, by Presidential decree, it was reduced by one-half (57 g) with the exception of those troops in frontier areas. By 1795 the supplemental rum ration was completely abolished for troops in the western frontiers by an Act of Congress; in 1832 the complete rum ration was eliminated and substituted with coffee and sugar. The Congressional Act of 1846 again instituted a monetary allowance for the purchase of liquor for soldiers who were engaged in heavy construction, but by 1865 a General Order from the War Department finally discontinued the liquor ration (OQMG, 1949).

The food allowance had gradually changed by the year 1812 with the elimination of the peas, rice, milk, and spruce beer. Although this ration had a reduction in total calories, it contained adequate quantities of protein, calcium, niacin, and thiamine, but was deficient in vitamins A and C, and riboflavin (Table 10B). After many years of experimentation with the various procedures of purchasing and supplying food to the troops, the Congress in 1818 finally passed a bill making it the respon-

TABLE 10B NUTRIENT COMPOSITION OF THE EARLIEST US WARTIME RATIONS [a]

Nutrient	Revolution 1775	War of 1812	Mexican war 1838	Civil war 1860–5	Spanish American war 1898
Calories	4081	3238	3614	4172	4054
Protein (g)	212	168	183	206	192
Calcium (mg)	900	261	350	445	400
Vitamin A (IU)	1443	—	—	39	90
Thiamine (mg)	5.00	3.36	3.77	4.82	4.27
Riboflavin (mg)	2.85	1.42	1.58	1.87	1.77
Niacin (mg)	62	55	69	81	75
Ascorbic acid (mg)	4.5	—	13.5	23	51

[a] From QM Corps, 1949.

sibility of the Commissary General and his staff for purchasing and issuing provisions. Although vitamins A and C were still inadequate, by the year 1832 the ration was an improvement since it had adequate calories and was a good source of the other vitamins. Prior to the beginning of the Civil War, the variety of foods was appreciably increased from 9 to 12 items. The flour allowance was increased by 113 g (4 oz), and the ration was supplemented with potatoes, yeast powder, and pepper (Table 10 A). The nutritional adequacy of the ration was greatly improved at this time. The period between the Civil and Spanish wars showed little change in the daily allowances; mainly the flour ration reduced by 113 g, decreased dried beans, and an increased potato ration. The yeast was replaced by baking powder. This resulted in only minor nutritional changes in the rations. At the beginning of World War I (Table 10C), the sugar ration was increased, and new items such as butter or margarine, lard and a flavoring extract were included in the ration. The ration items had now increased to 17, but as in the past, the daily ration was still deficient in vitamin A (OQMG, 1949).

For many years it had been observed that the Mexican and Indian raiders, who generally foraged for food, carried dried rations that consisted primarily of "jerked" beef and pinole. The beef had been cut into small strips of lean beef that had been sun-dried in desert-type environments. The pinole consisted of parched and ground wheat and corn. The first of the US Army field emergency rations was authorized in 1907, and it contained dried beef, parched corn and wheat, with small quantities

TABLE 10c US ARMY RESERVE RATION[a]

Ration item	g/day
Corned beef	454
Hard bread	200
Coffee	32
Sugar	68
Salt	4.6

[a] Used at the beginning of World War I. This ration was "reserved" for use only if field ration supply lines failed, in the event any troops outdistanced them. The bread was very hard and quite unpalatable. Later modifications of this ration showed the bread component to be decreased. (QM Corps, 1949).

of sweetened chocolate, and salt and pepper for seasoning. Each tinned ration weighed one pound (454 g) (Table 11). In 1922 the War Department finally approved and authorized a reserve ration (canned) that consisted of 454 g of meat, 400 g of hard bread, 69 g of sugar tablets, and 17 g of a soluble coffee extract (Table 11). The authorization of these canned foods began an era of field ration development for the Armed Forces (OQMG, 1949).

Prior to World War II, two of the very well-known American rations (field ration D and C or combat ration) were developed. The D ration, for emergencies, was developed between the years of 1933 and 1937 by Col. Paul Logan, and it was made up of a chocolate bar that had been

TABLE 11 EARLIEST US ARMY EMERGENCY RATION[a]
(grams issued per day per man)

Food item	Emergency ration, 1907	Food item	Reserve ration, 1922
Beef, dried, powdered	454	Meat	454
Parched wheat	454	Bread, hard	400
Cooked wheat	454	Sugar, granulated tablet	69
Sweet chocolate (small quantity)		Coffee, soluble extract	17
Salt for seasoning			
Pepper for seasoning			

[a] These two rations were the beginning of the US Army canned rations. The original 1907 ration was a mixture that weighed 1 lb (454 g) (QM Corps, 1949).

stabilized to a high melting point by the addition of oat flour. The ration consisted of three chocolate bars weighing 4 oz (113 g), containing 600 Cal each, for a total of 1800 Cal. This emergency ration was designed to relieve the hunger caused by missing a single meal. During World War II, the D-bars were widely used as supplements to the field rations, and although millions were produced and utilized, they were reported to induce nausea and to be thirst-provoking.

Development of the original US combat ration began in 1938, and by 1939 it was authorized for military use in the field. This was the forerunner of all the C or combat rations in which a full day's ration was contained in six cans (three cans of meat and vegetables, three cans of crackers, and soluble coffee and sugar). The daily ration contained an adequate supply of vitamins and minerals, 114 g of protein, and 2974 Cal/man (Table 12).

TABLE 12 US ARMY FIELD RATION C (1944 PACK)[a]

Ration items	g/man/day	Cal
Breakfast		
Biscuits, type C	74	305
Coffee, soluble	5	18
Candy, hard	17	66
Sugar (3 tablets)	17	67
Meat and beans	342	387
Can opener	1 each	
Cigarettes	3 each	
Lunch		
Biscuits, type C	74	305
Cocoa beverage, powder	43	167
Candy, hard	17	66
Stew, meat and vegetables	340	396
Can opener	1 each	
Supper		
Biscuits, type C	74	305
Lemon juice powder (synthetic)	7	27
Caramels	17	73
Sugar, granulated (6 tablets)	34	135
Meat and spaghetti	342	477
Can opener	1 each	
Cigarettes	3 each	
Matches	1 book	

[a] This ration contained an average of 2794 Cal/day. The ration consisted of three meat units and three B units per man per day.

This authorization of the War Department in 1939 resulted in a precooked ration that did not require refrigeration which could be consumed by the individual combat soldier either hot or cold in any extreme environment. The original concept was that this ration would be carried by the individual soldier and would have the highest caloric density for maximal nourishment. (This may have been true for the World War II and Korean conflicts, but the present-day guerilla combat situations have led to drastic modifications in combat type rations. This point will be discussed later.) Other requirements of a combat ration are that they (a) be stable for at least 2 years under extreme environmental conditions, (b) be rapidly prepared for issue and consumption in the field, (c) have sufficient variety to be palatable and acceptable for indefinite periods, and (d) shall conform with the nutritional requirements as established by the Office of the Surgeon General so that their consumption for extended periods of time would cause no detrimental effects.

By the end of 1943, the variety of food items in the C ration had changed drastically, and after two more field trials at Fort Carson, Colorado (Johnson, 1947), and Prince Albert, Saskatchewan, in 1944 (Kark and McCreary, 1944), many new modifications were suggested and implemented in later rations. In both of these studies, the troops performed very heavy physical work that included long marches with full field equipment over rough terrain and in pulling fully loaded toboggans over wet snow. Although it was shown that the ration was monotonous and lacked variety, it seemed to provide adequate nutrition for the heavy, physical, activity maneuvers. The advantages observed were the ease in preparation of the foods, the simplicity in distribution and division of the ration, the accessibility by simply opening tins, and the provision for a variety of hot beverages at each meal. The disadvantages incurred were that the ration was monotonous and lacked variety, was fairly heavy and bulky to carry, and it contained too much food which contributed to large wastes. It was recommended that the ham, egg, and potato item be eliminated due to its very low acceptability. On the basis of these recommendations, the C-ration was later modified and utilized until 1954 when the US Army Individual Combat Ration was developed (Table 13).

The French individual combat ration is comparable to the US ration in many ways. The main differences are that the French have two rations: one for the non-Moslem personnel, and one for all other religions. In addition, these rations have a lower fat content than US rations, averaging 29.2% versus 38% of the calories from fat.

TABLE 13 US ARMY RATION INDIVIDUAL COMBAT (1954)[a]

Ration item	g/unit	Cal
Menu 1		
Pineapple	227	213
Beans with frankfurters	340	503
Hamburgers w/gravy	234	805
Meat and spaghetti	340	463
Pecan roll	113	483
Menu 2		
Fruit cocktail	227	186
Chicken and vegetables	326	554
Hamburger w/o gravy	234	805
Beans and meat	340	412
Pecan roll	113	483
Menu 3		
Fruit cocktail	227	186
Beefsteak with potatoes	340	313
Meat balls with beans	340	463
Tuna with noodles and vegetables	326	548
Fruit cake	142	561
Menu 4		
Applesauce	227	191
Beef stew	340	289
Chicken with noodles	326	479
Pork sausage patties	234	936
Pound cake	62	309
Menu 5		
Fruit cocktail	227	186
Beans with pork	340	412
Ham and potatoes	340	486
Beef, macaroni with cheese	340	589
Fruit cake	142	561
Menu 6		
Beans with frankfurters	340	503
Beef and peas	340	405
Meat and noodles	340	486
Apricots	227	188
Pound cake	62	309
B-1 Unit		
Crackers (5)	49	216
Cocoa beverage powder	57	218
Jam	42	122
B-2 Unit		
Crackers (5)	49	216
Candy component, one of the following:		
Vanilla cream disk	49	223
Chocolate fudge disk	50	215
Sweet chocolate disk	57	303

[a] Each of the above menus are supplemented with one B-1 unit, one B-2 unit, and an accessory packet. The average ration contains 3824 Cal with 145.9 g of protein, 152.0 g of fat, and 469.2 g of carbohydrate.

12. K-RATION

In 1941 it became apparent that there was a great need for a ration for use in mobile type warfare. Since the C-ration was not applicable, development began on a ration for troops in airborne, tank crops, motorcycle, and other mobile units. This ration was designed and adopted in 1942, and named "Field Ration Type K" (originally called the Parachute Ration (Table 14). Although the ration contained 3300 Cal/day with

TABLE 14 US ARMY K-RATION (COMBAT RATION)[a]
ORIGINAL RATION 1941–2
(CALLED PARACHUTE RATION)

Food item	Total weight (g)
Breakfast	
Pemmican biscuit	115
Gum	1 stick
Malted milk tablets	28
Veal loaf, canned	114
Coffee, soluble, tablets	5
Sugar, cubes (2)	23
Lunch	
Pemmican biscuit	115
Gum	1 stick
Dextrose tablets	57
Ham spread, canned	114
Bouillon cube	11
Supper	
Pemmican biscuit	115
Gum	1 stick
Cervelat sausage	114
Lemon powder	7
Sugar, cubes (2)	23

Total daily caloric content averaged 3300 Cal/day with 99 g of protein.

[a] There have been many modifications of this ration.

99 g of protein, it was still slightly below the recommended vitamin and mineral allowances adopted by the NRC. Some of the good features of this ration were the compact packaging for airborne and assault missions, the ease of issuing, the convenience of carrying, and the high caloric density. In subsequent cold weather field studies (Kark and McCreary,

1944), it was observed that although nutritionally adequate, it was relatively unpalatable, especially under conditions when the ration was used for longer periods than it was designed (3 days). The low water content of the ration was one of the main criticisms, and whenever the water supply was limited, troops experienced great difficulty in preparing and consuming the concentrated foods in the K-ration.

The greatest complaints were the biscuits, which were too hard and produced sore gums; the bouillion, which was too salty; the malted milk tablets, which were disliked; and the excessive quantity of cheese at the noon meal. In addition, the ration was high in fat and was also thirst-provoking. Although revisions were made in 1945 to increase palatability, the ration was still inferior to the modified C-ration. It was shown that the higher caloric density (4.0 Cal/g) decreased the acceptability, so improvements in the ration resulted in increased acceptability with decreased caloric density (2.3 Cal/g). Since the only advantage of the K-ration was that it was not damaged by free aerial drop, this ration was eventually discarded in favor of the modified C-ration.

13. RATIONS AND FOOD PACKETS (TM 8-501, 1961)

13.1. RATION

A ration is the daily food allowance for one man as prescribed by military regulations, and in most instances it provides a liberal allowance of all essential nutrients. This would make it nutritionally adequate so that when completely consumed it would maintain troops in maximal physical efficiency.

13.2. RATION SUPPLEMENT

A ration supplement is a collection of foods, beverages, condiments, tobacco, and toilet articles that are designed to increase the nutritional value of a ration, to enhance the morale of the troops, or to increase the acceptability of a ration. This is not considered to be a complete ration but is a supplement to a ration (Dept. of Army, 1961). The US Ration Supplement Sundries Pack is a good example of a ration supplement, and is actually a front line post exchange used primarily with the B-ration before normal facilities are available. This pack is designed to meet the daily requirements for 100 men, and contains a tobacco pack, a toilet article pack, and a confection pack.

13.3. FOOD PACKETS

Food packets are a source of nourishment for short periods of time for use under unusual operational and environmental conditions. They are composed primarily of precooked or prepared foods that can be consumed either hot or cold. The food packet should be designed for maximal nutritional content, acceptability, have minimum bulk and weight, and—most important—it must be small enough to be carried by the troops until a planned re-supply can be established. Since this may not be a complete ration, the caloric content may not be necessarily high. An example of the food packet is the US Individual Assault Pack which is designed to be utilized for a period less than 30 h. The lightweight ration provides food for the individual man in the initial stages of combat, including initial phases of amphibious assault, airborne assault, patrol action, or other similar situations. Each of the eight menus contain approximately 800 Cal, and consist of a canned meat item, a bread type unit, and an accessory packet containing a candy bar, coffee, sugar,

TABLE 15 US FOOD PACKET, INDIVIDUAL ASSAULT (PRESENT RATION)[a]

Menu	Ration item / Meat units	Total weight (g)	Cal
1	Beef and corn	156	234
2	Beefsteak	170	381
3	Ham and eggs	156	329
4	Hamburgers with gravy	128	378
5	Boned chicken, solid	163	318
6	Pork with beans	184	243
7	Sausage patties	128	454
8	Pork steaks	170	471
Accessory pack			
	Candy bars	46	202
	Gum	3.4	10
	Coffee	5	6
	Sugar	12	48
	Cream, dry product	8	41
B–Unit			
	Oatmeal–chocolate chip	14	69
	Crackers (3)	30	135

[a] Each assault food packet is made up of a meat unit, one can of a B-unit, and one accessory pack. The average caloric content is 862 Cal with 34.2 g of protein, 39.2 g of fat, and 93.2 g of carbohydrate.

cream, cigarettes, matches, toilet paper, etc. The food items can be eaten either hot or cold (Table 15).

13.4. GARRISON RATIONS

The garrison ration is the food allowance for one man per day that is based on a monetary allowance for subsistence rather than based on an issued ration, and is prescribed at military installations in a peace-time situation. This ration may be procured locally, and is used primarily in hospitals and small isolated areas where it is impractical to use a field ration. The acceptability and nutritional adequacy of this ration is highly dependent on good food preparation by the cooks.

In the United States, the Food Service Division of the Office of the Quartermaster General is responsible for the inspection of the messing areas for cleanliness, food preparation, cooking, storage, and for the preparation of the entire Army's master menu. This menu, which is

TABLE 16 US ARMY GARRISON RATION [a]

Ration item	g/man/day	Ration item	g/man/day
Bacon	57	Coffee, roasted, ground	57
Beef, fresh	285	Cocoa	57
Chicken, fresh	57	Tea	1.4
Pork, fresh	114	Milk, fresh	228
Egg (1)	50	Milk, evaporated	28
Beans, dry	14	Lard	18
Rice, dry	17	Lard substitute	18
Rolled oats	42	Butter	57
Vegetables, fresh, canned		Flour, wheat	342
String beans, canned	57	Baking powder	2.6
Corn, canned	57	Macaroni	7
Peas, canned	57	Cheese	7
Potatoes, fresh	285	Sugar	142
Tomatoes, canned	57	Cinnamon	0.4
Fruit		Flavoring extract	0.6
Apples, canned	42	Pepper, black	1.1
Jam or preserves	14	Pickles, cucumber	4.6
Peaches, canned	34	Salt	14
Pineapple, canned	34	Syrup	14
Prunes	9	Vinegar	4.6

[a] Continental United States.

published monthly, is based on procurable food items, and is distributed to military posts, camps, and stations 4 months in advance of the actual ration period. Local menu boards are authorized to make some modifications that may be necessary to meet local unavailability of specific food items. A typical example of a US Army garrison ration, based on the master menu, is represented in Table 16. In a 12-month period, the master menu issue averaged 4027 Cal/man/day (1967). The other nutrients are presented in Table 17.

TABLE 17 CALCULATION OF THE NUTRIENT CONTENT OF FIELD RATION A (MASTER MENU)[a]

Nutrient	Army basic allowance garrison ration	Master menu (average/day)
Calories	3600	4027
Protein (g)	100	125
Fat (g)		188
Carbohydrate (g)		445
Calcium (g)	0.7	0.98
Iron (mg)		24.0
Vitamin A (IU)	5000	14534
Thiamine (mg)	1.7	1.92
Riboflavin (mg)	2.0	2.65
Niacin (mg)	16.0	26.5
Vitamin C (mg)	75	117

[a] Monthly average for 12 months of Master Menu (QMC, 1967).

In the British Army, the feeding of troops is the responsibility of the Director of the Army Catering Corps. This responsibility is shared by the Director-General of the Army Medical Services who, in addition to evaluating the nutritional adequacy, cleanliness, and hygienic handling of food, also gives advice and supervision to the other nutritional problems (Skinner and Mann, 1963).

An excellent detailed review of the history of troop-feeding in the British Army has been published by Skinner and Mann (1963). In this article the first British ration scale was traced back to 1587, during the Holland campaign.

The responsibility for preparing the daily dietary allowances and feeding the Indian troops, after independence, was designated to the

Defence Food Advisory Council. This group recommended a daily allowance that provided 3900 Cal/day for Army troops and 4100 Cal/day for the Air Force and Navy personnel (Rao et al., 1966a). The reasons for the increased allowances for the latter services are unclear, but one finds the same situation in the US Navy, which also has an increased daily allowance over the Army personnel.

In the British Commonwealth countries, the system of menu planning for the garrison ration is not done at the headquarter's level but at the local command level, down to the company-size mess hall. It is the responsibility of the mess officers and cooks to select food items from a standard list when preparing the weekly menus. The daily British allowance for the garrison ration is 2800 Cal/man, which is considerably lower than the Australians at 4100 and the Canadians at 4650 Cal/day. Each of these groups also receive a small monetary allowance. However, the British also allocate an additional 500 Cal for troops performing heavy physical activities. The decrease in calories in the British ration may be a reflection of the British postwar economic situation, but it should be emphasized that the British spend a considerable quantity of their military budget in training cooks, with the result that the edible food wastes are decreased in comparison to other countries (Greene, 1952).

TABLE 18A GERMAN PARATROOPER RATIONS

Supplemental, World War II [a]			After parachute drop, World War II [b]	
Food item	Jump day (g)	Long flights (g)	Food item	Quantity
Bread	318	—	Sausage	2 cans
Crackers	113	113	Cheese	2 cans
Butter	27	18	Chocolate	1 bar
Milk	227	—	Crackers	1 package
Fresh egg	1 each	—	Chewing gum	6 packages
Fruit crystals	—	73	Lemonade powder	1 package
Sugar	—	27	Coffee with sugar	1 package
Chocolate bar	—	1 each	Fuel, solid, white	1 tablet

[a] Ration 1 was usually given on the day that a man jumped. Ration 2 was taken during flights that took 2 h or longer. The Germans used these rations for building morale and for "increasing the stamina of the troop".

[b] This "iron" ration was the total for a 3-day period during operations where the man was selfsufficient. He could prepare a hot beverage, using the solid smokeless fuel, and still maintain security precautions.

TABLE 18B GERMAN RATIONS, WORLD WAR II

Tank crew, supplement ration			Infantry front-line assault ration	
Food item	g	Cal	Food item	Cal
Fruit bar	160	664	Chocolate bars	200
Confection, tartaric acid	110	475	Fruit bars	310
Chocolate bar	100	520	Orange candy	190
			Chocolate caramels	50
			Biscuits	316
			Cigarettes	6 ea

Nutrient composition, complete ration (2-day supplement)

		Comparison with other rations		
		German above	US Army D-ration	Assault
Calories	1659	Calories, total	1086	1775	685
Protein (g)	19	Protein (g)	13	30	8
Fat (g)	55	Fat (g)	15	95	16
Carbohydrate (g)	275	Carbohydrate (g)	223	190	124
Vitamin A (mg)	0.42	Vitamin A (mg)	0.22	0	0.30
Thiamine (mg)	0.22	Thiamine (mg)	0.32	1.77	0.35
Riboflavin (mg)	1.6	Riboflavin (mg)	1.26	1.10	1.03
Niacin (mg)	4.9	Niacin (mg)	4.1	2.4	4.7
Vitamin C (mg)	0	Vitamin C (mg)	0	0	0

TABLE 19 CHINESE NATIONALIST ARMY RATIONS

Daily ration allowance		Regulation pack ration[a]		Army combat ration, 1960[b]	
Item	g/day	Item	g/day	Item	g/day
Brown Rice[c]	467	Beef, 8 units	200	Menu A	
Flour	252	Vegetables, 8 units	125	Beef, canned	120
Soybeans	62	Bouillion, 8 units	32	Crackers	190
Edible oil	20	Pepper bean sauce	15	Chocolate	32
Salt	15	Garlic extract	4	Orange drink, dehyd.	18
Sugar	25	Ginger extract	2	Vitamin tablet	1 each
Soy sauce	20	Tea leaves	32		
Pork, canned	33	Ginger candy	100	Menu B	
Fish, canned	33	Cigarettes	16	Fish paste	20
Vegetables	460	Paper	4	Crackers	255
Sweet potatoes	200			Ginger candy, hard	16
Condiments	200			Orange drink, dehyd.	16
		Calories, total	1887	Calories, total	2558
		Protein (g)	128.6	Protein (g)	77.5
		Fat (g)	60.4	Fat (g)	23.9
		Carbohydrate (g)	207.2	Carbohydrate (g)	360
		Total weight (g)	478		

[a]Field ration for one man for 4 days.
[b]Packaged in two units or meals/man/day.
[c]62 g of rice extra for basic trainees.

TABLE 20 ROYAL THAILAND ARMY RATION

Daily army allowance		Army combat ration	
Food item	g/man/day	Food item	
Rice, regular or glutinous	1000	Fried rice and meat	
Beef, pork, fish, or poultry	150	Fried rice and tomato sauce	
Vegetables (fresh)	500	Fried rice, shrimp paste and meat	
Fish sauce	82	Salt	
Lard	17	Spoon, 1 each	
Shrimp paste	2.5	Tissue	
Coconut sugar	11.6	Tooth picks	
Vinegar	10	Nutrient composition	
Coconut, shredded	59	Calories, total	1900 per day
Tumarin pulp	7.6	Protein (g)	70.8
		Fat (g)	51.8
		Carbohydrate (g)	288

The garrison rations of the American, British, Canadian, and Australian armies all compare quite favorably with the average civilian-type diet that is found in these respective countries. The differences between the types of foods eaten by the armies (United Kingdom, Canada, Australia, and the United States) are quite small, but in some instances they are quite revealing. The U.S. troops use coffee exclusively, while the UK troops prefer tea. The British eat liberal quantities of liver and kidneys, while the Americans demand and receive a great variety of good cuts of meat—preferably beef. For dessert, the Americans select ice cream, while their counterparts prefer cake, custard, or pudding. In general, the Australian and Canadian troops' tastes lie between the tastes of the Americans and the British.

Individual food preferences of the various countries are also quite prominent in their packaged rations. The German preferences are quite similar to the Western group, and contain items such as sausage, cheese, and candy (Tables 18A and B); the Chinese Nationalist troops prefer items such as rice, soybean milk and sauce, ginger candy, and fish paste (Table 19); the Royal Thailand Army ration contains primarily fried rice mixtures with meat, tomato sauce, shrimp paste and meat (Tables 18–20).

13.5. FIELD RATIONS

A field ration is the food allowance in which all of the subsistence items are issued. This ration is usually prescribed in time of war, national emergencies, or at any time by an Executive Order of the President of the United States.

The basic concept of troop feeding in the field has not changed significantly during the past 100 years. In the United States and other countries, this Army field ration is a replacement of the normal garrison ration that provides no changes in the daily monetary allowances. The ration which is usually supplied from foods found locally is very similar to the garrison ration. It is made up of the finest available foods for troop feeding, under conditions where modern conveniences such as organized kitchens with kitchen personnel and refrigeration are available.

In the United States, the basic Army field ration is designated as Field Ration A, and contains a maximal number of grocery store type perishable items (approximately 200) such as meats, fish, poultry, fresh fruits, and vegetables, supplemented with a variety of canned foods and

TABLE 21A JAPANESE FIELD RATION (PRIOR TO WORLD WAR I)

Food item	g	Cal
Rice *or*	1020	3604
Bread, hard	480	
Fresh meat *or*	68	102
Salted meat, dried	51	
Pickled fruit	26	
Salt	5.1	137
Sugar	5.1	
Tea	1.7	
Total Cal/day		3845

TABLE 21B RUSSIAN FIELD RATION (PRIOR TO WORLD WAR I)[a]

Food item	g	Cal
Fresh meat	396	
Black rye bread	907	
Cereals or fruits and vegetables	85–113	
Tea and sugar	(As available)	
Total		4180 per day

[a] In emergencies the quantities, especially meats, are often reduced. This ration contains 150 g of protein and 450 g of carbohydrate.

condiments. Menu changes and substitutions of the food components are only authorized by Headquarters, Department of the Army. Although these foods must be nutritionally adequate to maintain maximal efficiency of the troops, they must contain a great majority of items that are readily acceptable for troops of a given country. As a result, the food items usually represent very closely the present-day national diet or food habits of a specific country, and could be either frozen, canned, or dehydrated foods.

The nutrient distribution of foods in the diet vary with the individual countries, and in most instances are a matter of food habit, food preparation, and economic status. North Americans, and some of the Western European countries, are accustomed to and enjoy consuming a high fat diet which includes the high consumption of meat, butter, and oils (40% of the calories consumed). This may be due to the higher economic levels of these countries, but in countries of lower economic status the general diet usually consists of a high-carbohydrate, low-fat intake. This could

TABLE 22 TYPICAL VIETNAMESE RATIONS (FIELD)[a]

Ration item	Unit 1 (g/day)	Unit 2 (g/day)
Bread	125	70
Sugar	21	35
Curry	1.3	—
Beef	68	—
Pork	95	—
Fish	30	76
Rice	476	608
Salt	25	21
Oil	32	22
Green onions	7	3
Limes	13	—
Tamarind	12	—
Red chili pepper	28	3
Sweet potatoes	40	—
Vinegar	6.5	—
Bean sprouts	49	—
Celery	—	160
Squash	43	118
Nuoc mam	70	58
Bananas	144	—
Chicken	—	71
Onions, mature	—	3

[a] These rations averaged 3150 Cal/man/day.

be related to the fact that rice, corn, and grain products (all excellent items) are fairly inexpensive, and as a result make up a considerable quantity of the daily diet. The ultimate in a field ration (world wide) would be one that is acceptable to troops of all nations, but it is obvious that food preferences are a deciding factor in the planning and development of a ration. Some of these food preferences include (a) the use of liver and kidney stew in the British rations, which is not tolerated by the North and South American troops (b) rice and hot spicy foods (highly seasoned) which are preferable in the Middle and Far East, and in Central and South America, (c) in Taiwan and Japan, rice and soybean products which are mainstays of the oriental diet; in Russia the troops prefer black rye bread, and (d) in Thailand, Vietnam, and Korea, rice, fish sauce (nuoc mam), and at least 10 condiments that are preferred and used with each meal (Tables 21A, 21B, and 22).

13.6. OPERATIONAL RATIONS

An operational ration is the food allowance for a man performing operational duties away from the normal field supply system. These rations are designed to satisfy the feeding requirements of large (organizational type) or small groups of troops. During World War I the American operational ration was called the "reserve ration". This indicated that the ration was reserved for use only when the normal supply system failed or if the messing areas were out of distance of the troops (Dept. of Army, 1961).

In the United States, one basic ration—operational or otherwise—is used to feed all troops, but in India the use of a standard ration is impractical due to the various population groups. One observes great differences in the food habits and food preferences of Indian troops that include (a) vegetarians and nonvegetarians, (b) rice and wheat eaters, and (c) soldiers from the north and south (Rao and Vijayaraghavan, 1966).

The feeding problems of British troops in the Middle East during World War II were great since the Army had troops from many different countries (race, creed, and environment). The daily basic Middle East field service ration was 4000 Cal/day, and included such items as meat, bacon, cheese, eggs, and milk for the protein source; flour, bread, potatoes, oatmeal, and pulses for carbohydrate; and margarine and other cooking fats with vitamin supplements. This ration was nutritionally adequate, and prevented nutritional deficiencies in the troops.

Substitutions were provided for those units in the Indian Army who did not like the standard British ration. These items included dal, atta, ghee or nut oil, and a variety of Indian condiments (Rao and Vijayaraghavan, 1966).

The Indian Army, although under the British Command, did not have a ration scale prior to World War I, but each man received a cash allowance to purchase the food he could afford and preferred. As expected, this resulted in an outbreak of scurvy and beriberi in Mesopotamia in 1916 (Rao et al., 1966; Rao and Vijayaraghavan, 1966); thus the system was changed and the troops were then issued the basic food commodities including rice, atta, dal, sugar, potatoes, and salt. After the war, the Indian Army established two ration scales which were utilized until the beginning of World War II. The ration scale for peace areas, which included the basic food commodities, also offered a meat (or substitute) on alternate days, and fresh fruit three times a week (Rao et al., 1966).

The present-day operational rations for the Indian Army include the composite eight-man pack containing 4000 Cal/day, the composite 10-man pack with 3800 Cal, the individual pack with 3500 Cal/day, and the emergency ration containing 1200 Cal/day.

Some of the Japanese rations used during World War II are summarized in Table 23. The Compressed and Special Emergency rations are quite similar to the US K-ration; the Compressed Special No. 1 ration is comparable to the US D-bar, and the Emergency ration is most similar to the US Pemmican ration.

In the United States, the operational B-ration, which conforms with the nutritional allowances as established by the OTSG, was designed for feeding large groups. This ration is the best substitute for the US Field Ration A, and provides a food allowance under conditions where refrigeration is not available but where kitchen and cooking facilities are available. The perishable food items have been replaced by canned foods such as meats, canned fruits and vegetables, milk products, cereals and cereal products, dehydrated fruits, vegetables, milk, and eggs. Occasionally in combat situations, whenever permissible, this ration provides hot meals for the troops. The menu is prepared on a 15-day cycle and averages 3900 Cal/day. Although these rations may be lower nutritionally than the fresh food items, they must be used under special conditions over limited periods of time without any significant impairment of performance. A typical three-meal B-ration menu is presented in detail in Table 24.

Although the components of the ration, operation-B and packaged

TABLE 23 JAPANESE RATIONS—WORLD WAR II

	Compressed ration[a]	Compressed special No. 1[b]	Pemmican type[c]	Emergency ration[d]	Special emergency ration (2 meals)[e]	Navy emergency ration[f]	Navy ration tropical (one unit)[g]
Calories, total	927	753	1471	1329	1548	1210	190
Protein (g)	35.7	28.6	41.0	41.0	38.0	81.6	1.9
Fat (g)	5.8	1.0	31.0	61.0	5.2	5.8	3.1
Carbohydrate (g)	182.8	157.4	257.0	153.0	338.0	208.3	38.7
Thiamine (mg)	0.02	0.05	0.05	—	0.26	0.18	.03
Riboflavin (mg)	0.02	0.11	0.48	—	0.27	0.30	.03
Niacin (mg)	10.8	4.0	3.1	—	4.8	5.2	1.00
Calcium (mg)	—	968	360	—	—	—	—
Total weight (g)	260	200	360	300	440	250	50

[a] Comparable to US K-ration. Made up of powdered sugar, fish, plums, and cereal.
[b] Comparable to US D-ration. Made up of bonito, tuna, and cooked rice pressed together.
[c] This ration has the consistency of American cream cheese. The United States does not have a similar ration.
[d] Comparable to US pemmican. Made up of six compressed blocks. The main ingredients consisted of toasted rice, fats, dried baked meats, and dried vegetables.
[e] This ration has two components—a rice cereal and a compressed meat and vegetable bar. This ration is comparable to two meals of the US K-ration.
[f] This ration contains 180 g of rice crackers, 50 g of dried tuna fish, and 20 g of grape sugar.
[g] This unit is similar to the common American caramel with sesame seeds.

TABLE 24 STANDARD US ARMY B-RATION[a]

Typical menus

Breakfast	Dinner	Supper
Orange juice	Tomato or vegetable soup	Grilled corned beef
Hot wheat cereal	with crackers	Mustard
Griddle cakes with hot maple syrup	Baked chicken and rice	Lyonnaise potatoes
	Cranberry sauce	Stewed tomatoes
Bacon	Buttered green beans	Cabbage and green pepper salad
Bread	Sweet pickles	
Margarine	Bread	Cornbread
Jelly	Margarine	Margarine
Coffee	Yellow cake/chocolate cream icing	Jam
		Apple crisp
	Coffee	Coffee

Gross weight per ration	4.325 lb (1.97 kg)
Net weight per ration	3.350 lb (1.52 kg)
Gross cube per ration	0.120 ft^3 (0.358 cm^3)
Calories per ration	3900 approx.

[a] The Standard B-ration is the field ration which is used for mass feeding in areas where kitchen facilities, with the exception of refrigeration, are available. The ration consists of approximately 100 nonperishable items—mainly canned and dehydrated—and is supplied in bulk. Hot meals furnishing approximately 3900 Cal/man/day are prepared using a 15-day cycle of menus. Caloric content may be varied to meet requirements of varying climatic conditions or degree of physical activity of the troops as determined by the local medical authority.

rations are referred to as nonperishable, many of these items undergo deterioration when stored in high temperature, such as occurs in the tropics or in hot desert areas. This deterioration, commonly called "browning reaction", adversely affects the acceptability of the ration and reduces its nutritive value. For this reason, the rations should be stored in the coolest place possible and protected from the sun. Caves or dugouts may be utilized for this purpose. If buildings or tents are used as shelters, adequate ventilation should be provided. Powdered whole milk, bread, and eggs are particularly susceptible to this "browning" reaction, even with vacuum packing, and they rapidly become inedible when stored at high temperatures. If at all possible, powdered eggs and milk should be treated as perishable products and stored at a temperature below 50°F (Dept. of Army, 1961). Canned items may become tiresome when consumed over long periods of time. Under these conditions the food intake will be decreased with a subsequent decrease in operational efficiency of the troops. To reduce monotony, extreme care should be made in the selection of a variety of foods that are acceptable for indefinite periods. It is antici-

TABLE 25 MEAL, UNCOOKED, 25-MAN RATION

Typical menus

Breakfast	Dinner
Grapenuts/milk	Green pea soup
Apple juice	Crackers
Beef and potato hash	Breaded cube steaks
Bread	Rice, Spanish
Jam	Corn
Military spread	Bread
Coffee	Military spread
Cocoa	Jam
Cream, sugar	White cake with chocolate icing
	Coffee
	Cream, sugar

Supper
Breaded pork chops
Cream gravy
Mashed sweet potatoes
Green beans
Bread
Military spread
Apple sauce
Coffee
Cream, sugar.

pated that the B-ration will be replaced by the newly developed meal, uncooked, 25-man ration, made up primarily of dehydrated foods (Table 25).

The British equivalent of the US Army B-ration is the "compo", a canned equivalent to the fresh garrison ration. This ration contains seven menus, can be eaten cold, has a shelf-life of 2.5 years in any extreme environment, and only requires the use of a stove for heating and cooking, and a container for boiling water. This ration consists of a cooked breakfast, a main meal of two or three courses, and a snack (Skinner and Mann, 1963).

13.7. COMBAT RATIONS

The combat ration is designed to provide the troops with a readily carried ration, which can be used in active combat, particularly assault. The ration should be prepared so that it can be eaten either hot or cold, and must be acceptable to the troops to ensure that the soldier will consume sufficient calories to remain in energy balance. Otherwise, troops might deteriorate rapidly and become operationally incapacitated within a short period of time.

13.8. COMBAT INDIVIDUAL RATIONS

The feeding of troops in a cold environment may in some instances be very difficult. For maximal efficiency, the troops should be provided with hot meals and with sufficient water for drinking and cooking. Hot drinks and hot foods are essential for maintaining body warmth and in preventing the loss of physical efficiency as a result of the cold weather. Additionally, frequent feeding is very beneficial in maintaining body heat and providing quick sources of energy. Snacks such as candy bars, fruit, or biscuits could be distributed to the troops for in-between-meal consumption that can be eaten "while on the march" and would not interfere with the military operation. Some of these food items are part of the "assault packets" (Keys *et al.*, 1944), and the US Army Ration, Individual, Trail, Frigid (Table 26). Under extremely cold conditions the fuel consumption for cooking purposes will increase proportionally

TABLE 26 US ARMY RATION, INDIVIDUAL, TRAIL, FRIGID[a]

Ration items	Total g	Ration items	Total g
Breakfast		Supper	
Cereal bar	42	Soup	113
Fried ham, canned	156	Meat bar	113
Crackers	49	Soup and gravy base	7
Coffee	2.5	Onions, dehydrated	10
Cream, dry	3	Chili powder seasoning	3
Sugar	6	Tea	0.65
Lunch		Cream, dry	3
Cheese	160	Sugar	6
Mixed candies	52	Crackers	49
Fruitcake bar	142	Accessory items:	
Cocoa beverage	57	Gum	3.4
Sugar	6	Chocolate raisins	28
		Chocolate bars	57
		Imitation beverage base	7
		Matches, book	
		Cigarettes	
		Toilet paper	
		Nonwoven fabric	
		Can opener	
		Plastic bag	

[a] This ration containing a minimum of 4410 Cal is designed for cold environment feeding.

with a decrease in environmental temperature. As a result, the cooking and heating time of food will increase. To conserve fluid when field kitchens are unavailable, small group feedings of five men is highly desirable. The US Army Ration, Individual, Trail, Frigid, was specifically designed for this purpose.

Dehydrated rations may not be applicable for troop feedings in cold environments due to the anticipated water shortages. Canned foods are more practical since they already contain sufficient water and are easily prepared for consumption. However, under conditions of combat patrol, where the soldier must carry his food supply and equipment for periods of 2–10 days, it is necessary to sacrifice the convenience of canned foods for the light weight, less bulky, pre-cooked dehydrated rations. These food items may not be too acceptable to unseasoned troops, and under conditions of long-term usage may result in anorexia or voluntary caloric restriction. This results in a loss of morale, physical deterioration, and insufficiency. Kark and McCreary (1944) have shown this to happen under conditions of decreased food and water intakes.

Under conditions of heavy physical activity in a cold environment, the British Mountain Arctic Ration Pack (Table 27) was observed to be nutritionally adequate, but the men still complained of insufficient food

TABLE 27 BRITISH MOUNTAIN ARCTIC RATION PACK, 1944[a]

Ration item	g/man/day	Ration item	g/man/day
Pemmican	171	Tea, sugar, milk mixture	71
Biscuits	228	Ascorbic acid tablets	2 each
Cheese, processed	121	Salt	15
Margarine	57	Miscellaneous items:	
Oatmeal	64	Flare matches	3 each
Bacon, chopped	114	Latrine paper	
Raisin chocolate bars	171	Solid fuel, stove lighters	
Boiled sweets (hard candy)	57	Instruction sheet	
Sugar	57		

[a] This ration contained an average of 5100 Cal/day.

and the fairly long time (45 min) required to prepare the food. The pemmican, as in most field studies, was unacceptable and extremely disliked. The men felt sickened, complained of the bitter taste, and had difficulty digesting the food (Kark et al., 1945).

The field test of the British 24-h Ration Pack (Table 28) showed conclusively that what may be acceptable to the British troops may not be true for Canadians, who tested this ration in an extremely cold environ-

TABLE 28 BRITISH 24-HOUR RATION PACK, 1943[a]

Ration item	g/day
Meat block	113
Meat extract cubes	14
Biscuits	256
Sugar	7
Hard candy	14
Chewing gum	8 tablets
Oatmeal blocks	100
Chocolate with raisins	114
Chocolate, plain	57
Tea, milk, sugar mixture	57
Salt	7
Latrine paper	
Instructions for use	

[a] The average daily ration contained 4100 Cal.

ment (Kark et al., 1945). In general, the morale was fair at the end of the test, but the men lost 2.3 kg and showed a decrease in physical performance. They did not look forward to eating this ration due to the poor acceptability of the meat items which were greatly disliked and appeared to cause nausea. Other items such as the biscuits were considered dry and tasteless; the meat extract cubes were very unpopular, and the meat blocks were practically impossible to eat without prior cooking. The general comments were: "This ration may be acceptable to the British, but not to the Canadians."

The Canadian Mess Tin ration proved to be an acceptable field ration under conditions of heavy physical activity in an extremely cold environment (Kark et al., 1945) (Table 29). The troops' morale was high at the end of the test, and physical performance was not impaired. Although the ration was nutritionally adequate, the majority of the men felt that it was thirst-provoking. Three items were unacceptable: (a) sardines, which were difficult to digest and made the men sick, (b) the sugar and milk mixture, which was difficult to reconstitute and became very lumpy on the surface, and (c) the pea soup, the most disliked item.

The field trial of the Canadian Arctic Experimental Ration (Pemmican) (Kark and McCreary, 1944) was the first in a series of studies to evaluate the acceptability and nutritional adequacy of a high-fat/high-caloric density ration. This ration contained four packets weighing 170 g each, and was composed of dehydrated prime beef with suet added in which

Table 29 Canadian Mess Tin Ration, 1943[a]

Ration item	g/man/day	Ration item	g/man/day
Pork loaf	86	Milk and sugar mixture	42
Beef, spiced	86	Candy	4 pieces
Cheese	42	Chocolate bar	57
Sardines	100	Chewing gum	3 pieces
Sugar	7	Miscellaneous items:	
Butter	57	Matches	1 book
Jam	42	Fork, wooden	1 each
Chocolate drink	42	Spoon, wooden	1 each
Biscuits	258	Cardboard caps for jam and butter	
Pea soup, dehydrated	57	Can opener	1 each
Tea	2 bags	Cigarettes	10 each
Coffee, soluble	5	Ascorbic acid tablets	2 each
Salt	7		

[a] Each daily ration averaged 3750 Cal/man.

Table 30 Canadian Arctic Experimental Ration (Pemmican)

Ration items	Quantity
Dehydrated prime beef with added suet (4 packages)[a]	681 g
Tea bags	6
Cigarettes	10
Matches, folders	2
Matches, box, waxed	1

[a] This ration contained 1250 Cal/package or 5000 Cal/day. 70% of the calories were from fat.

This ration was consumed for only 3 days since it produced ketonuria, caused nausea, and resulted in a very poor physical performance by the men. Supplementation with 142 g rolled oats, 284 g crackers, 85 g of sugar, and 142 g of milk was very beneficial in the rapid rehabilitation of the same troops.

70% of the calories were from fat and 30% from protein. Each packet contained 1250 Cal, totalling 5000 Cal/day for four packets. Other items included six tea bags, cigarettes, and matches (Table 30). Although the instructions specifically stated that the ration could be eaten without cooking, it was soon discovered that this was practically impossible. It took 40 min to reconstitute this product with water and there was still a separation of fat and protein. In this study (Kark and McCreary, 1944), a platoon of troops in excellent physical condition bivouacked in a very cold Canadian environment, working at an expenditure of 4500 Cal/day. Within 3 days the men could not tolerate eating this product since it induced nausea, indigestion, and ketonuria, which resulted in the deterioration of their morale and physical fitness. They became completely incapacitated operationally. Other troops, working at the same rate and consuming different field rations, showed no signs of these abnormalities. The demoralized troops were brought back to camp and rehabilitated with a diet supplemented with high carbohydrate foods. On the basis of clinical and biochemical evaluation prior to rehabilitation, the troops had (a) severe calorie deficiency associated with severe ketosis, (b) indications of involuntary hypohydration, (c) severe mineral, and (d) vitamin C depletion. The main causes for the rapid deterioration were the first two factors described above, and rehabilitation with a high carbohydrate diet showed morale, physical fitness symptoms, and ketosis to be practically eliminated within 12 h. This study showed conclusively the adverse effects of an undesirable high-fat diet with heavy physical activity. The high-carbohydrate foods utilized included 142 g of rolled oats, 285 g of pilot biscuits, 85 g of sugar, and 142 g of canned milk. These items were mixed with two pemmican meat bars and prepared as a fairly acceptable gruel. The men returned to the field where they were able to finish the study with a fairly high morale and minimum of complaints. On the basis of this study, all of the future rations containing pemmican were supplemented with high-carbohydrate items. Pemmican was also shown to be unacceptable in a temperate environment (Consolazio and Forbes, 1946).

14. COMBAT RATIONS FOR GROUP FEEDING

Special rations have been developed by the military for feeding small groups under conditions where field kitchens are impractical. This would include the feeding of troops during combat and emergency situations such as gun and armored vehicle crews, combat patrols, small tactical units, etc. These rations were not to be combined of multiples of 4, 5, or 10 units from the individual's rations since this would defeat the purpose of increasing the variety and acceptability. This was done by replacing the mixed meat and vegetable items (stews, hash) with individual canned items such as meats, vegetables, etc., without increasing the weight or cubage of the new ration.

TABLE 31 US ARMY RATION, SMALL DETACHMENT, FIVE PERSONS[a]

Ration item	g/unit	Cal/five men/day
Menu 1		
Peaches	822	641
Pineapple	822	608
Tomatoes	454	86
Peas	907	528
Potato sticks	156	850
Beef with gravy	822	1439
Ham and eggs	851	1820
Tuna fish	737	1291
Bread, white, canned	765	2434
Cereal blocks	213	925
Pound cake	326	1594
Cheese spread	163	667
Jelly, apple	170	429
Jam, grape	170	473
Peanuts, roasted, shelled	227	1324
plus		
Uniform components		2840
Total		17949
Average/man		3590
Menu 2		
Fruit cocktail	851	646
Beans, green	439	56
Beans, white with tomato sauce	879	1186
Corn, whole	680	578
Bacon, sliced	680	1520
Ham and gravy	822	1825
Meat balls with spaghetti and sauce	1701	2279
Vegetable soup with beef cond.	595	452
Bread, white	765	2434
Fruit cake	397	1516
Cheese spread	163	667
Jam, peach	170	473
Peanut butter	170	1009
Candy, chocolate disk	283	1437
Uniform components		2840
Total		18918
Average/man		3784
Menu 3		
Apple sauce	464	413
Apricots	851	731
Beans, kidney, and ham	1701	2500
Potato sticks	156	850
Frankfurters	850	1397
Luncheon meat	680	1619

TABLE 31 (*Cont'd*) US ARMY RATION, SMALL DETACHMENT, FIVE PERSONS

Ration item	g/unit	Cal/five men/day
Soup, cream of tomato	595	536
Bread, white	765	2434
Cereal, block	213	861
Fruitcake	340	1320
Cheese spread	163	667
Jam, peach	170	473
Jam, cherry	170	473
Candy, chocolate disks	269	1233
Uniform components		2840
Total		18347
Average/man/day		3669
Menu 4		
Apple sauce	454	413
Peaches	822	641
Lima beans	464	296
Beans, white with pork	879	1186
Corn, whole grain	680	578
Beef with gravy	822	1439
Pork with gravy	822	1661
Sausage links, pork	850	1839
Bread, white	765	2434
Cereal blocks	213	863
Cookie sandwich	151	773
Cheese spread	163	667
Jam, grape	170	473
Peanut butter	170	1009
Candy chocolate disks	269	1233
Uniform components		2840
Total		18345
Average/man/day		3669
Menu 5		
Pears	822	625
Beans, green	439	56
Beans, white with pork	879	1081
Potato sticks	156	850
Bacon, sliced	680	1520
Beef and vegetables with gravy	1701	1837
Chicken, boned	822	1472
Chicken noodle soup, concentrated	595	387
Bread, white	510	1623
Pecan cake roll	269	1158
Pound cake	326	1594
Jelly, blackberry	170	429
Jam, pineapple	170	473

TABLE 31 (Cont'd) US ARMY RATION, SMALL DETACHMENT, FIVE PERSONS

Ration item	g/unit	Cal/five men/day
Peanut butter	170	1009
Candy, chocolate disk	283	1437
Uniform components		2840
Total		18391
Average/man/day		3678
Uniform components		
Candy bars: one of the five are issued with the five menus:		
Starch jelly bars	283	1015
Caramel nougat	213	878
Chocolate fudge	248	1064
Cocoanut	213	925
Vanilla cream	248	1079
Average of five candy bars	241	992
Each of the following are issued daily with menus 1–5:		
Cocoa beverage powder	213	770
Gum, candy coated	51	146
Salt, table	28	—
Sugar	120	462
Cream, dry (for coffee)	80	406
Coffee, instant	50	64

[a] The average content of the five menus was 3678 Cal with 141.6 g of protein, 161.2 g of fat, and 438.4 g of carbohydrate.

The US 5-in-1 ration and the British and Canadian five-man packs are all quite similar for small group feeding (Tables 31–33A). These rations have five daily menus consisting of a fairly acceptable variety of foods which tend to avoid monotony. Although the French Army also has a five-man combat ration, the macro nutrient composition is quite different from the US 5-in-1 ration (Table 33B). The differences are in the ration's fat content: 27% in the French ration and 39.4% of the calories in the US ration. The higher fat content in the US ration is not unusual since the American population has been known to prefer a higher fat intake.

The US 5-in-1 ration is the first ration in which the caloric density was sacrificed in favor of higher acceptability foods. The caloric density was reduced to 1/3 Cal/g by including fruit juices, canned fruits, and vegetables. This resulted in a fairly heavy duty ration averaging 5.8 lb/man (2.63 kg). Other US rations for small group feeding consisted of a

TABLE 32 BRITISH FIVE-MAN RATION. EXAMPLE OF DAILY RATION

Commodity	Weight (oz)	Menu A	Commodity	Weight (oz)	Menu A
Breakfast			Sundries		
Oatmeal block	5 × 1	1	Chocolate biscuits and fruit	2	5
Sausage	15	1	Sweets, boiled	$2\frac{1}{2}$	$2\frac{1}{2}$
Sausage	$7\frac{1}{2}$	1	Cans for above:		1
Main Meal			5 bars Chocolate $2\frac{1}{2}$ oz sweets or clear gums		
Soup powder	3	1	Salt	1	1
Corned beef	12	3	Matches		1
Dried, mixed vegetables	10	1	Sweets, boiled	$2\frac{1}{2}$	$2\frac{1}{2}$
Potato mash, powder	6	1	Cans for above:		1
Mixed fruit pudding	14	1	1 salt dispenser		
Mixed fruit pudding	7	1	1 box matches		
Tea			$2\frac{1}{2}$ oz boiled sweets or clear gums		
Salmon	16	1	Reclosure lids		2
Cheese	8	1	Soap, G.P.		1
Jam	9	1	Cases, complete		1
Tea	$3\frac{3}{4}$	1	Contents list		1
Sugar	$14\frac{1}{2}$	1	Toilet paper		50
Milk, instant	$2\frac{1}{2}$	2	Can opener		1
Margarine, HC.	$7\frac{1}{2}$	1	Kraft bag satchel		1

TABLE 33A CANADIAN FIVE-MAN RATION PACK RP-1

Ration item	Net weight (g) or quantity per unit	Menu 1	Menu 2	Menu 3	Menu 4	Menu 5
Almonds	71	5		5	5	
Apricots	242	5				
Bacon	128	5		5		5
Bacon, chopped	93					5
Beef, corned	93		5		5	
Beefsteak with onions	200				5	
Cake, steamed fruit	185		5		5	
Chicken, boneless	200					5
Fruit cocktail	242			5		
Ham, spiced	93	5	5			
Hamburgers with gravy	200	5				
Honey	114			5		
Jam, raspberry	114		5		5	
Jelly, grape	114	5				5
Menu	1 menu	5	5	5	5	5
Peaches	242					5
Pork chops	200		5			
Potatoes, mashed, dehydrated	28	5	5		5	
Raisins	71		5		5	
Sausage, pork	114		5			
Soup, chicken, dehydrated	23		5	5		
Soup, pea, dehydrated	28	5			5	
Soup, vegetable, dehydrated	28					5
Weiners and beans	313			5		
Beverage, fruit	8				1	
Biscuits, plain	97				1	
Biscuits, sandwich	85				1	
Candy, hard	28				1	
Cheese, process	85				1	
Chocolate disks, pan-coated	71				1	
Cigarettes	20 each				1	
Cocoa beverage	43				2	
Coffee, soluble	2.5				2	
Cream, dry, coffee type	4				6	
Gum, chewing	6 each				1	
Matches	20 each				1	
Oatmeal block	85				1	
Reclosure cap	1 each				1	
Salt	6				1	
Spoon, plastic	1 each				1	
Sugar	85				1	
Tablets, water sterilizing	6 each				1	
Tea, bag	2 each				1	
Paper, toilet	10 sheets					
Soap paper	1 sheet				1	
Towels, paper	6 towels					

[a] The standard assembly was issued daily to each man.

TABLE 33B FRENCH ARMY RATIONS, 1966

5-in-1 combat ration No. 21
   This combat ration contains five individual combat rations in one package. The food items included in the individual combat ration No. 20 are utilized as far as possible in the ration No. 21. It also provides two types of menus:
      E includes eight menus for non-Moslem soldiers, only.
      M includes four menus for soldiers belonging to any religion.
   Ration No. 21, including bread or biscuits, provides an average of 4000 Cal/men and the following macro nutrients:

	g	Cal	% Cal
Protein—120 g		480	12.0
Fat—120 g		1080	27.0
Carbohydrate—610 g		2440	61.0

The average energy characteristics of E and M rations are as follows:

$$\frac{\text{Protein calories}}{\text{Non-protein calories}} = \frac{1}{7.3}$$

$$\frac{\text{Fat calories}}{\text{Total calories}} = \frac{1}{3.7}$$

The 27% of calories from fat are low for US troops. The US 5-in-1 ration contains 39.4% of the calories from fat sources.

variety of precooked foods that were easily prepared for high altitude operations. These rations were compact, with a caloric density of 4.3 Cal/g and included some slowly digestible food items that attempted to provide satiety. The jungle ration had a slightly lower caloric density of 3.8 Cal/g.

The US 10-in-1 ration, which is quite similar to the British 14-man ration, eventually replaced the mountain and jungle rations (Tables 34 and 35). In this ration's planning and development, the prime objectives were acceptability and utility. This ration had more calories, was more compact, and contained a greater variety of food items than the 5-in-1. If any nutritional deficiencies existed, food supplements were available. The 10-in-1 was designed for consumption over long periods of time, and was eventually the principle US ration for troop feeding in all environments. It was used in advance to the field kitchens just prior to engaging in actual combat for small groups of isolated troops and highly mobile troops. Some of the outstanding developments of the 10-in-1 were the replacement of the biscuits with canned bread, the increased cocoa and coffee issue, a greater variety of highly acceptable "chunk" meats,

TABLE 34   US Army 10-in-1 Ration,[a] 1944

Ration item	Quantity per 10 men (g)	Ration item	Quantity per 10 men (g)
Menu 1		Egg product (K-ration)	1069
Pineapple-rice pudding	1140	Candy, hard	392
Pork sausage	1938	Lemon juice powder, synthetic	70
Tomatoes	1083		
Cheese (K-ration)	1140	+ Ration K, menu 4	
Beans, baked, dehydrated	1140	Menu 5	
+ Ration K, menu 1		Bacon and eggs	1710
Menu 2		Beans, lima	1140
Sliced bacon	1368	Hash corned beef, dehydrated	740
Beans, snap	1083	Egg product (ration K)	1069
Stew, English style	1710	Grape juice powder (synthetic)	30
Cheese (ration K)	1140		
Fruit bars	570	Ration-D bar	570
+ Ration K, menu 2		+ Ration K, menu 5	
Menu 3		All menus contained the following:	
Beef, corned	1368		
Ham and eggs	1710	Army spread	214
Peas	1140	Coffee product, soluble	114
Meat (K-ration)	1069	Jams	627
Fruit bar	570	Milk, evaporated	342
Orange powder, synthetic	70	Biscuit C square	1824
+ Ration K, menu 3		Cereal pre-mixed	570
Menu 4		Salt	57
Bacon	1368	Cigarettes, 10 × 10	
Beef, roast	1368	Halazone tablets	100 each
Corn, sweet	1140	Matches	200 each
		Opener, can	2 each
		Paper toilet	250
		Soap, toilet	4
		Towels, paper	20

[a] This was a canned ration containing an average of 3927 Cal/man/day

Nutrient Composition, Average/man/day

	Total weight (g)	Cal	Protein (g)	Fat (g)
Menu 1	1114	3675	127.3	151.6
Menu 2	1174	4183	96.3	214.8
Menu 3	1212	3720	137.0	141.0
Menu 4	1121	4004	106.2	183.3
Menu 5	1157	4053	155.1	165.4
Mean all menus		3927	124.4	171.2

TABLE 35 BRITISH COMPOSITE, 14-MAN RATION, 1943[a]

Ration item	Quantity per 14 men per day (g)	Ration item	Quantity per 14 men per day (g)
Menu A		Menu G	
Steak and kidney pudding	5016	Meat and vegetable with	
Sausages	1596	beans	6348
Pork and beans	1368	Sausages	1596
Potatoes	1196	Concentrated soup (beef stew)	1710
Vegetables	570	Treacle pudding	2109
Peaches	1710	Biscuits	3420
Biscuits	3420	Menu No. 1 (no biscuits)	
Menu B		Corned beef	4768
Stewed steak	4560	Sardines	800
Bacon	1368	Concentrated scotch broth	1710
Beef stew	1596	Spiced pork	1026
Vegetables	1596	Carrots, whole	1681
Date pudding	2023	Potatoes, diced	800
Biscuits	3420	Fruit pudding	1539
Menu C		Vegetable salad and	
Meat and vegetables with		mayonnaise	1824
beans	3648	Sultana pudding	454
Meat and vegetables without		Processed cheese	484
beans	2736	Menu No. 2 (no biscuits)	
Sausage	1596	Stewed steak	4540
Concentrated soups	1710	Salmon	1938
Sultana pudding	2109	Bacon, sliced	1282
Cheese, processed	6840	Pork and beans	1762
Menu D		Potatoes	1596
Stewed steak	4560	Peas, canned	860
Bacon	1368	Apricots	1653
Sardines	800	Menu No. 3 (no biscuits)	
Vegetables	1824	Meat and vegetables with	
Soup	860	peas	3648
Rice pudding	2223	Meat and vegetables with	
Biscuits	3420	beans	2736
Menu E		Pork sausage	1539
Oxtail stew	5472	Pork and beans	860
Sardines	800	Beans without pork	912
Sausages	1596	Soup (beef stew)	1710
Vegetables	1026	Marmalade pudding	2023
Marmalade pudding	2023	Jam	598
Processed cheese	456	Margarine	454
Biscuits	3420	Tea, sugar, milk mixture	940
Menu F		Chocolate	800
Corned beef	4104	Boiled sweets	454
Prem (luncheon meat)	1026	Salt	57
Salmon	1368	Matches	5 packets
Concentrated scotch broth	1710	Cigarettes	10 per man
Potatoes	1596	Soap	71
Vegetable salad	912	Latrine paper	
Mixed fruit pudding	1996		
Biscuits	3420		

[a] Rations A to G averaged 3590 Cal/man/day; menus 1 to 3 averaged 3520 Cal/man/day.

individual cans of vegetables, the addition of canned sweet and white potatoes, the use of a better cheese spread, and more acceptable canned soups.

TABLE 36 UNITED KINGDOM 10-MAN COMPOSITE RATION PACK,[a] 1950

Menus	
Menu A	Cheese, processed
Rolled oats	Margarine
Bacon	Jam, various
Sausage	Milk, condensed
Tea	Matches
Peas	Water sterilizing outfits
Carrots	Salt
Potato, mashed, powder	Mepacrine
Preserved meat	Latrine paper
Fruit, various	Paper bags
Rich cake	Can opener
Chocolate	List of contents
Sweets (hard candy)	Soap
Sugar	Menu C
Cheese, processed	Rolled oats
Margarine	Bacon
Jam, various	Sausage
Milk, condensed	Tea
Matches	Peas
Water sterilizing outfits	Carrots
Salt	Potato, mashed, powder
Mepacrine	Steak and kidney
Latrine paper	Fruit pudding
Paper bags	Treacle pudding
Can opener	Salmon
List of contents	Chocolate
Soap	Sweets (hard candy)
Menu B	Sugar
Rolled oats	Cheese, cheddar
Bacon	Margarine
Sausage	Jam, various
Tea	Milk, condensed
Peas	Matches
Carrots	Water sterilizing outfits
Potato, mashed, powder	Salt
Stewed steak	Latrine paper
Fruit pudding	Paper bags
Treacle pudding	Can opener
Rich cake	List of contents
Chocolate	Soap
Sweets (hard candy)	Mepacrine
Sugar	

[a] These menus averaged 4050 Cal/day.

In a field test conducted in an extremely cold environment (Kark and McCreary, 1944), the US 10-in-1 ration was nutritionally adequate since the men ate well and their morale was maintained. The major complaints were the excessive salt in the bacon and pork sausage which provoked thirst. The majority of the men complained about bloating, with excessive belching and flatus, and a few men reported incidences of abdominal cramps, which may have been caused by the chopped ham and egg mixture, and the beans.

In the same field trial (Kark and McCreary, 1944), the acceptability of the British Composite Pack was high, and the ration nutritionally adequate (Table 36). As in the American 10-in-1 ration, the bacon was salty, and the margarine was rather tasteless and difficult to spread, thus unacceptable. The major complaint was that the caloric density was low,

TABLE 37 AUSTRALIAN 24-HOUR OPERATIONAL RATION[a]

Ration item	Menus (g)		
	A	B	C
Bacon and beans		142	
Chopped bacon			142
Beef, corned, with jelly			142
Beef and egg, ground		142	
Beef loaf and cereal			142
Beef preserved	142		
Biscuits	256	256	256
Boiled sweets	114	114	114
Can opener	1 each	1 each	1 each
Chewing gum	4 tablets	4 tablets	4 tablets
Chocolate bar	57	57	57
Fruit and cereal block	114	114	114
Ham and egg spread	142		
Luncheon meat		142	
Matches	20 each	20 each	20 each
Milk, sweetened, condensed	57	57	57
Oatmeal blocks	57	57	57
Plastic bag fastener	1 each	1 each	1 each
Salt	6 tablets	6 tablets	6 tablets
Sausage and beans	142		
Sugar	85	85	85
Tablets, paludrine	1 each	1 each	1 each
Tea	21	21	21
Toilet paper	10 sheets	10 sheets	10 sheets

[a] This ration contained an average of 3500 Cal/man/day. This ration is based on the British ration but has modifications to suit the Australian taste.

and certain items should be concentrated to reduce the weight and to decrease the heating and cooking time of food. It was recommended that the bacon be soaked in water for longer periods of time prior to cooking, which would reduce the saltiness.

The Australian 24-h (one-man) ration pack has a lower caloric density per gram than the Canadian One-man Pack, averaging 2.96 and 3.20 Cal/g, respectively (Tables 37 and 38). Although it appears that a considerable variety of meat items are provided in the ration, three were very similar to canned beef, and two others were closely associated to luncheon meats (Ballantyne *et al.,* 1958). This ration closely resembles the British rations, but has been modified to suit the Australian tastes. This ration was not suitable for tropical (jungle) fighting because it was fairly heavy and bulky and did not contain a sufficient variety of food items. An experimental ration was planned and developed to contain the following specifications: less weight and cubage, longer storage, easy transportability, and an adequate salt and protein content. Modifications in the experimental ration included a dessert, compressed oatmeal, fruit, and cereal blocks, which reduced the weight. Provisions were made for increased quantities of condensed milk, sugar, and tea, thus enabling the troops to prepare tea whenever required and permissible. Tea is a great morale factor for the "Aussies" who are renowned tea-drinkers. In addition, chocolate, fruit tablets and barley sugar supplements were made available for in-between-meal snacks.

The jungle field test of the Indian Army eight-man composite ration was conducted at Mohand, United Provinces, India, in 1945 using Gurkha troops (Kark *et al.,* 1945). This ration contained 4000 Cal/day, and consisted of a variety of canned and dried food items, including biscuits, canned milk, salmon, almonds, cheese, confection, and beverages. The daily physical activity was moderately heavy, and the terrain a relatively dense jungle where the temperature ranged from 40° to 85°F with 50% relative humidity. This ration proved to be nutritionally adequate since the men ate well and showed no significant body weight changes in 21 days. Military efficiency, physical performance, and physical well-being all improved, indicating that the men could operate quite efficiently in a jungle, under conditions of a high-energy expenditure rate.

During World War II, the Canadians and Australians had no operational rations because of their relatively small standing armies and their comparatively small military research and development agencies. The units of these countries were always integrated as part of the British Army and, as a result, were fed the same British rations, including the

TABLE 38 CANADIAN RATION PACK, ARCTIC ONE-MAN (RPX 3B), 1952

Ration item	g	Cal	Ration item	g	Cal	Ration item	g	Cal
Menu 1			Menu 2			Menu 3		
Oatmeal block	85	390	Oatmeal block	85	390	Oatmeal block	85	390
Liver and bacon	92	296	Bacon	92	213	Corned beef	92	199
Biscuits	97	405	Biscuits	97	405	Biscuits	97	405
Raspberry jam	85	217	Peanut butter	85	477	Strawberry jam	85	217
Coffee	5		Coffee	5		Coffee	5	
Cheese	85	316	Cheese	85	316	Cheese	85	316
Almonds	57	337	Almonds	57	337	Almonds	57	337
Chocolate bar	71	351	Chocolate bar	71	351	Chocolate bar	71	351
Hard candy	28	107	Hard candy	28	107	Hard candy	28	107
Cocoa beverage	85	339	Cocoa beverage	85	339	Cocoa beverage	85	339
Cookies	85	418	Cookies	85	418	Cookies	85	418
Tea	9		Tea	14		Tea	14	
Pea soup	28	82	Chicken soup	28	90	Bean soup	28	107
Meat bar	85	540	Meat bar	85	540	Meat bar	85	540
Potatoes	28	100	Potatoes	28	100	Potatoes	28	100
Raisins	71	190	Raisins	71	190	Raisins	71	190
Orange beverage	8	24	Grape beverage	8	24	Lemon beverage	8	24
Onions	14	51	Onions	14	51	Onions	14	51
Milk powder	57	240	Milk powder	57	240	Milk powder	57	240
Gum	7	46	Gum	7	46	Gum	7	46
Chili powder	3		Gravy base	28	5	Barbecue sauce	42	111
Sugar	34	134	Sugar	34	134	Sugar	34	134
Total		4583	Total		4773	Total		4622

British 24-h ration and 10-man composite ration. In many instances, these troops also used the US Army C and 5-in-1 rations, which were quite comparable to the two British rations.

Although an increased food variety increases the acceptability of the ration, it is very important to keep the number of items at a minimum, under operational conditions, since an excessive number of items could lead to great administrative nightmares and impossible supply situations. Under any field condition, fresh food commodities such as bread and potatoes are preferable to such items as canned fish or dehydrated potatoes. Greene (1952) observed that the British troops are highly suspicious of overly spiced foods or items, the names of which are unfamiliar to them or their country. Although they will eat the American ration with relish, after a time, eventually they will revert back to their own ration. The British, American, Canadian, and Australian operational rations are similar enough to be interchangeable for a limited period of time (Greene, 1952), with the exception of the beverages.

Comparisons of some of the food categories of the four UK forces' rations and one US ration of the 1950s are presented in Table 39. These rations included the British and Australian 24-h, the British Snow, the Canadian Arctic One-man, and the US Army Individual Trail Frigid. Although the Australian ration mainly contains beef, both the Canadian and US have utilized the improved meat bar in their cold weather ration. In the cereal and baked products category, the Australians have a fruit and cereal bar; the British have rice, treacle, and mixed-fruit pudding; the Canadians have cookies; and the American ration contains crackers, a fruit cake bar, and a cereal bar. Other food comparisons are tabulated categorically in Table 39.

Comparisons of other UK and US rations, including the Australian and British 10-man composite, the Canadian 5-man arctic, and the US 5-in-1, are detailed in Table 40. In these rations, the Canadian and American rations contain five different menus, the British contain four, and the Australian contain three. In the meat category, the Australians prefer beef; the British have variety in the use of luncheon meats, salmon, and sardines; the Canadians achieve variety by using luncheon meats, salmon, chicken, spiced ham, and sausages and beans; and the Americans go all out with 12 meat items, including ham and gravy, bacon, meatballs and spaghetti, frankfurters and beans, chicken, beefsteak, beefsteak with potatoes, etc. Other comparisons of these rations are detailed in Table. 40.

It can be readily seen that field rations must be tested under simulated

TABLE 39 COMPARISONS OF MILITARY OPERATIONAL RATION[a]

Food category	Australian 24-hour	British 24-hour	British snow ration	Canadian Arctic, one man	United States ration, individual, trail, frigid
Meats	Majority of beef			Improved meat bar	Improved meat bar and ham
Cereal and baked products	Fruit and cereal bar	Treacle and mixed fruit puddings		Cookies	Crackers, fruit cake bar, cereal bar
Dairy products	Replaced by more beef	Cheese	Cheese, powdered milk	Powdered milk, cheese	Cheese, dry cream (for coffee)
Fruits and vegetables	Cereal and meats	Potato salad, vegetable salad, and tomato sauce			Onions, dehydrated
Beverages	Tea	Tea	Tea	Coffee, cocoa, tea, and fruit beverage	Coffee, tea, soup, and cocoa
Sweets	Candy, chocolate bars	Candy, chocolate bars		Candy, chocolate bars	Chocolate, raisins, candies, chocolate bars
Miscellaneous		Jam and marmalade		Jam, peanut butter	
Total calories per ration	3700	4000	4250	4250	4400

[a] Three of these rations are used in a cold environment.

TABLE 40 COMPARISONS OF MILITARY OPERATIONAL RATION[a]

Food category	Australian 10-man	British 10-man	Canadian 5-man Arctic	United States small detachment, 5-person
Meats	Primarily beef supplemented with rabbit	Luncheon meat, salmon, sardines	Chicken, luncheon meat, salmon, spiced ham, sausages, and beans	Twelve meat items, some with vegetables
Cereals and baked products	Puddings, cakes	Puddings, cakes	Biscuits, cookies	Bread, cakes
Dairy products	Butter concentrate	Margarine	Vegetable fat, biscuit spread, and milk powder	Cheese spread, cream dry (for coffee)
Beverages	Tea	Tea	Tea, coffee, coffee fruit beverage	Coffee, cocoa, and soup
Caloric content per day	3600	3600	4800	3600

[a] Bread and biscuits are issued separately to Australian and British troops using the 10-man composites.

field conditions for acceptability, nutritional adequacy and composition, water requirements, physical performance, caloric density, and packaging. On the basis of these studies, modifications are made in the ration to include deletions and substitutions of food items.

15. LIMITED WARFARE RATION (2000 CAL)

The marked increase in the importance of limited warfare (guerilla war, combat patrol) situations has created new problems in providing food for combat personnel. Heading the list of these problems is the impossibility in some instances of food resupply for 10–14-day periods. Both the American and Allied soldier must frequently carry his own food and equipment for these 10–14 days. First, because of ration weight and bulk, and, second, because of the diversity of food acceptability between American and Allied personnel, there is a serious doubt that the present-day US meal-type combat rations are the most suitable for many of the guerilla-type situations in limited warfare. Within American and Allied military commands, e.g. in Southeast Asia, there are many diverse opinions on the suitability of various rations, but scientifically acceptable data under combat or simulated field conditions was unavailable.

On the basis of this concept, a study was conducted concerning the nutritional adequacy and acceptability of limited warfare combat rations designed for non-resupply situations of approximately 10 days. Four US rations, and two commercially procured food products were evaluated (Consolazio *et al.*, 1965). These fairly high caloric density rations were issued to highly trained troops maneuvering in mountainous terrains at high energy expenditure levels for 10-day periods. These rations, issued at the approximate 2000 Cal/day level, included (a) the US Food Packet All-purpose Survival, (b) the Ration Supplement Aid Station (a liquid ration), (c) the US Long Range Patrol (a dehydrated ration), (d) the US Meal Combat Individual MT (served at the 2/3 daily level), (e) a commercial liquid product, and (f) a commercial fruit and vegetable bar (Tables 41–44).

The primary purpose of this field test was to provide food in a form that could be easily prepared and consumed in the field. It was concluded that a motivated soldier can and will eat any reasonable form of food for a limited period of 10 days, since practically all of the issued rations were consumed (Consolazio *et al.*, 1965). One of the unexpected findings was the high daily consumption of the two liquid rations even though they

Nutritional and Physiological Basis

TABLE 41 US ARMY FOOD PACKET, SURVIVAL[a]

Ration item	g/unit	Cal
Fruit cake	52	193
Chocolate fudge	28	221
Cornflake bar	30	253
or		
Rice-cornflake bar	30	253
Chicken-flavored bar	34	106
Cheese-potato bar	30	134
Four of the six food bars above are issued randomly with each ration		
Coffee, instant	2.5	
Sugar	6	24
Chicken soup and gravy base	7	19
Can opener	1 each	
Instructions		

[a] This ration contains 950 Cal/packet.
This ration is designed to be used in any survival situation under all extreme environments.

TABLE 42 US ARMY RATION SUPPLEMENT, SPECIAL ITEM PACK, AID STATION[a]

Ration item	Total quantity
Cocoa beverage powder	10 cans, 454 g each
Soluble coffee	12 cans, 113 g each
Dry modified sweetened milk	9 cans, 227 g each
Soluble tea	1 can, 142 g
Sugar, granulated	3 packages, 908 g each
Plastic sippers	3 each
Toilet paper	125 sheets
Can opener, folding	2

Nutrient composition	Per 114 g	Per lb (454 g)
Calories	553	2213
Protein (g)	25.6	103.1
Fat (g)	26.2	104.8
Carbohydrate (g)	53.5	214.2

[a] This supplement provides a variety of hot, stimulating beverages (coffee, tea, or cocoa) for combat zones, casualties at aid or clearing stations.

TABLE 43 US ARMY PACKET, SUBSISTENCE, LONG-RANGE PATROL (DEHYDRATED)[a]

Ration item	Cal	Ration item	Cal
Menu 1		Menu 5	
Beef hash	771	Chicken stew	551
Cereal bar	174	Fruit cake bar	234
Cocoa	154	Cocoa	154
Coffee, cream, sugar	46	Coffee, cream, sugar	46
Total	1145	Total	985
Menu 2		Menu 6	
Chili con carne	814	Meat balls with beans	875
Chocolate bar with almonds	298	Chocolate fudge bar	212
Coffee, cream, sugar	46	Coffee, cream, sugar	46
Total	1158	Total	1133
Menu 3		Menu 7	
Spaghetti with meat sauce	752	Beef stew	587
Cocoanut candy bar	185	Vanilla cream bar	216
Coffee, cream, sugar	46	Cocoa	154
		Coffee, cream, sugar	46
Total	983	Total	1003
Menu 4		Menu 8	
Beef with rice and onion gravy	832	Chicken with rice	577
Cereal bar	174	Starch jelly bar	203
Cocoa	154	Cocoa	154
Coffee, cream, sugar	46	Coffee, cream, sugar	46
Total	1206	Total	980

[a] All the meat items in these rations are dehydrated.

TABLE 44A US ARMY RATION, INDIVIDUAL, COMBAT, MEAL TYPE [a]

Ration item	g/unit	Cal
Menu 1		
Boned chicken	163	330
Fruit (average)	170	139
B-1 unit	141	723
Beverage and gum	16	60
Menu 2		
Beef steaks	156	284
Fruit	170	139
B-1 units	141	723
Beverage and gum	16	60

TABLE 44A (*Cont'd*) US ARMY RATION, INDIVIDUAL, COMBAT, MEAL TYPE[a]

Ration item	g/unit	Cal
Menu 3		
Ham and eggs	156	324
Fruit	170	139
B-1 units	141	723
Beverage and gum	16	60
Menu 4		
Turkey loaf	170	326
Fruit	170	139
B-1 units	141	723
Beverage and gum	16	60
Menu 5		
Frankfurters and beans	340	544
Dessert (average)	88	402
B-2 units	69	323
Beverage and gum	16	60
Menu 6		
Beef and peas with gravy	340	405
Dessert	88	402
B-2 units	69	323
Beverage and gum	16	60
Menu 7		
Ham and potatoes with gravy	340	510
Dessert	88	402
B-2 units	69	323
Beverage and gum	16	60
Menu 8		
Tuna and noodles with vegetables	326	552
Dessert	88	402
B-2 units	69	323
Beverage and gum	16	60
Menu 9		
Beef spiced with sauce	156	383
Bread	50	160
B-3 units	164	665
Beverage and gum	16	60
Menu 10		
Ham, fried	156	237
Bread	50	160
B-3 units	164	665
Beverage and gum	16	60
Menu 11		
Beef steak	156	284
Bread	50	160
B-3 units	164	665
Beverage and gum	16	60
Menu 12		
Pork steak	156	271
Bread	50	60

TABLE 44A (Cont'd) US ARMY RATION, INDIVIDUAL, COMBAT, MEAL TYPE[a]

Ration item	g/unit	Cal
B-3 unit	164	665
Beverage and gum	16	60
Beverage and Gum Component for all menus 1–12		
Coffee	2.5	4
Sugar	6.0	24
Cream, dry	4.0	21
Gum	3.4	11
Fruit items, one, menus 1–4		
Apricots	170	151
Peaches	170	128
Pears	170	128
Pineapple	170	148
Dessert item, one, menus 5–8		
Pecan roll	113	494
Pound cake	62	310
B-1 unit, menus 1–4		
Crackers (5)	49	220
Peanut butter	43	267
Candy disk (average)	50	240
Candy disks, B-1 unit, one of the four in menus 1–4		
Cocoanut disks	43	208
Chocolate fudge disk	50	223
Sweet chocolate disk	57	307
Vanilla cream disk	50	223
B-2 unit, menus 5–8		
Crackers (3)	30	132
Cheese spread	39	191
or		
Jam	43	122
B-3 Units, menus 9–12		
Jam	43	122
Cocoa beverage powder	57	218
Vanilla	65	326
or		
Chocolate sandwich	65	324

[a] The average caloric intake of the 12 menus was 1212, containing 51.9 g protein, 51.0 g of fat, and 136.3 g of carbohydrate. Three of the menus are issued daily to each man.

were very monotonous and lacked variety. These rations were easily reconstituted using either hot or cold water, depending on the environmental temperature during the patrols.

TABLE 44B FRENCH ARMY RATIONS

The individual combat ration No. 20:
   The individual French combat ration is available in two types (E and M), and consists of eight menus. Type E is for the non-Moslem soldiers, and includes pork items and alcohol; type M does not have any pork or alcohol, and is available and acceptable for all religions. These rations, which include bread and biscuits, have an average caloric content of 3700 Cal/day. The macro nutrients include:

	g	Cal	% Cal
Protein—115 g		460	12.4
Fat—120 g		1080	29.2
Carbohydrate—540 g		2160	58.4

Although the French think that this ration is a little bit too high in fats, they feel that the excess is not a major problem taking into account the way in which it is used. The average energy characteristics of E and M rations are as follows:

$$\frac{\text{Protein calories}}{\text{Non-protein calories}} = \frac{1}{7}$$

$$\frac{\text{Fat calories}}{\text{Total calories}} = \frac{1}{3.46}$$

Comparisons with the US individual combat ration show the US ration contains 38% of the daily calories from fat. This is a normal US intake which is normally high in fat.

The Long Range Patrol dehydrated ration was highly acceptable even though it required water for reconstituting. It was very difficult for the troops to decide which item in this ration was the least acceptable. During the first few days on patrol, the men indicated that the two meals of the Long Range Patrol ration were more than they could eat, but after day 4 most of the men indicated that they could have easily consumed a third ration. This ration, with some minor modifications (a decrease in calories with each packet), was highly recommended for combat patrol since it was easily reconstituted (20 min), very acceptable, and fairly light to carry.

The US Army Meal Combat Individual Ration (MT), the present-day C-Ration, is an excellent field ration, mainly because of the great variety of food items that are repeated at 4-day intervals. Only two items are relatively unacceptable in this ration—ham and lima beans, which have a high fat content, and the date pudding which is very dry. In its present form, this ration would be impossible to carry on a 10-day patrol due to its great weight and bulk. The MT ration is one of the best field rations ever developed for US troops. The variety is great, the acceptability of the various food items is excellent, but this ration (10-day supply) was not developed to be carried on a 10-day patrol. In one phase, the men were issued a 10-day supply of the ration (51 lb) (23.2 kg) in addition to full field gear and radio equipment. It was practically impossible to carry this weight over fairly difficult terrain. As a result, within a day, every man on the team had a seriously bruised back. It was quickly decided that the men consuming the MT ration would only carry a 3-day food supply (maximum), and be resupplied at intervals. In a study by Archer in Malaya (1958) it was also observed that weight was a limiting factor on patrol activities. The troops could only carry a 5-day supply of tinned packaged rations without excessive fatigue and risk of complete

TABLE 45   AUSTRALIAN 24-HOUR TROPICAL RATION—EXPERIMENTAL, OPERATIONAL[a]

Ration items	Menus (g/day)		
	A	B	C
Apricot and cereal	57		
Barley sugar	28	28	28
Biscuits	200	200	200
Can opener	1 each	1 each	1 each
Cheese	28	28	28
Chocolate bar	57	57	57
Condensed milk	171	171	171
Corned beef	114		
Currants and cereal			57
Fish loaf			114
Fruit tablets	28	28	28
Ham and eggs		114	
Luncheon meat		114	
Matches	20 each	20 each	20 each
Meat and cereal	114		
Nut food			114
Oatmeal block	57	57	57
Paludrine tablets	1 each	1 each	1 each
Salt tablets	6 each	6 each	6 each
Sugar	85	85	85
Sultanas and cereal		57	
Tea	21	21	21
Tuna fish			114
Vienna sausage	114		
Wooden spoon	3 each	3 each	3 each
Toilet paper, sheets	10 each	10 each	10 each

[a] Average caloric content is 3500/man/day.

exhaustion. The resupply of food by plane at 5 days could lead to a dangerous situation for the men since it would reveal their position (Table 45).

The six rations issued and consumed at the 2/3 level allowance all seemed to be adequately equal in maintaining top physical efficiency, as observed by the bicycle maximum performance test and the 14-mile contest marches conducted at the end of each 10-day patrol. This can be interpreted that 2000 Cal/day, in any reasonably acceptable form, will maintain physical efficiency and performance during a 10-day combat patrol.

The use of dehydrated rations for combat patrols are excellent since they greatly reduce the weight that an individual must carry, but sufficient water must be available, and the troops must be well indoctrinated in the use of sufficient water to hydrate these items. These rations cannot be compared with the US Meal Type Combat Rations which require no extra water. A ration providing 2000 Cal/day, as Sargent and Johnson (1957) suggested, is quite adequate for limited warfare.

16. LIMITED WARFARE RATIONS: 10-DAY STARVATION AND CALORIC RESTRICTION BELOW 1000 CAL/DAY

During complete fasting, significant metabolic stresses will develop that may eventually result in serious abnormalities. Under fasting conditions, both body fat and protein stores are utilized as energy sources since the maintenance of normal carbohydrate levels in the blood requires a known quantity of protein breakdown. A large increase in fat metabolism occurs during starvation, and produces both acidosis and ketosis. In the reexamination of the pressures of war, many abnormalities are associated with long-term starvation and semistarvation. Canadian POWs were on restricted intakes in Singapore and Hong Kong camps during World War II and were studied more than 10 years after being released (Coke, 1961). Some of the most frequent symptoms observed included: easy fatiguability, profuse sweating for no apparent reason, numbness and cramps in the calf muscles, loss of ambition, poor vision, edema, dyspnea on even the slightest exertion, depression, tachycardia, anorexia, nausea, restlessness, irritability, and insomnia. The evidence of these symptoms were higher than one observes in the same population who were not POWs.

Recent emphasis on the importance of warfare situations involving prolonged combat patrol activities, air-drop operations, limited amphibious operations, and other operations where resupply is difficult, have created new problems in providing sufficient food and water for combat personnel to maintain adequate performance. The soldier in combat or on combat patrol for periods of up to 10 days must carry his field pack, radio equipment, weapons, and an adequate food and water supply, which is usually quite heavy and bulky. The question has arisen time and time again as to the minimal food intake necessary to permit the individual combat soldier to effectively perform his duties for periods of 3, 7, and 10 days.

Many US investigators (Bloom, 1959) have been advocating acute starvation as a means of body weight loss in obesity for long periods of time, but these studies are primarily being conducted on abnormal individuals. As a result, recent studies have been initiated in six normal adults on complete starvation, with water *ad libitum*, for 10 days (Consolazio *et al.,* 1967b, c) working at an expenditure of 2800 Cal/day. Three undesirable problems related to fasting were encountered: (a) the great body water loss resulting in body hypohydration, (b) the fairly large urinary nitrogen excretion showing that body protein was being catabolized, and (c) the fairly large mineral losses concomitant with the large body water loss. Also, abnormalities in all electrocardiograms and one electroencephalogram were observed during the latter stages of starvation. These factors, reflecting severe stress, could eventually lead to greatly impaired mental and physical efficiency.

At the end of 10 days of starvation, the men were in very poor condition, both physically and mentally. There appeared to be increased weakness and apathy toward mental and physical work. They had frequent memory lapses, were tired, pale, and haggard, and had indications of muscle cramps, which may have been due to salt restriction and body stores depletion.

It is suggested in the conclusions that complete fasting without mineral or vitamin supplementation should not be recommended either for a soldier on combat patrol or for a reducing diet. Although the men appeared to be in fairly good physical condition at the end of the third day of fasting, starvation could not be recommended for this period of time, since there might be an occasion when the period would be extended (Consolazio *et al.,* 1967b).

These findings are not unusual since both the body fat and protein stores must be utilized as energy sources. The maintenance of normal blood carbohydrate levels require a known quantity of protein breakdown. As a result, it was suggested that low calorie antiketogenic diets and adequate mineral supplementation could prevent the marked ketosis, minimize protein catabolism, maintain fluid balance, and decrease the electrolyte excretion. Gamble (1946–47), in concluding his studies on the nitrogen and sodium sparing effects of glucose, suggested the use of 400 Cal/day of carbohydrate. He observed that 100 g of carbohydrate reduced the loss of body protein by one-half as much as in fasting (from 80 to 40 g of protein per day), with a subsequent reduction in the body water deficit, attributable to the sparing action of body protein. The beneficial effects of small quantities of carbohydrate in retaining water have also been confirmed by others (Winkler *et al.*, 1944; Hervey and McCance, 1953; Rogers *et al.*, 1965) in a 3-day subarctic survival study, has shown that 500 Cal of carbohydrate with mineral supplementation, was also beneficial in retaining water.

In another study (Consolazio, 1967a), the effects of short-term caloric restriction and its relationship to body hypohydration and to mineral and nitrogen balances were investigated. A 400 Cal/day carbohydrate diet was fed to two groups of subjects for 10 days; one group received only the carbohydrate, and the other group received the carbohydrates plus mineral supplementation.

These studies were another attempt to evaluate the effectiveness of military troops operating in the field with limited food intakes but with water available *ad libitum*. The body weight losses of 8.0 and 5.9% of the initial body weight were in the same range observed by Taylor (1957), whose subjects averaged a 7% weight loss on an intake of 580 Cal/day for 12 days. These data indicated some beneficial effect of water retention on a limited carbohydrate diet alone. This is contrary to Sargent and Johnson (1957), who concluded that all-carbohydrate rations contain very little osmotically active material that actually accentuates hydration. In addition, mineral supplementation had beneficial effects in retaining water since the mineral supplemented group lost less body weight than the control group during the caloric restriction period, and regained much less body weight during the 8 days of rehabilitation.

Nitrogen balances, which included estimates of the sweat losses, were again highly negative for both groups during the entire caloric restriction period. Quinn *et al.* (1954) also observed no beneficial effect or improvement of nitrogen balances of intakes up to 900 Cal/day. These subjects showed a negative nitrogen balance of 7.3 g/day for the 9-day study, equivalent to 45.6 g of protein loss per day. Although the supplemented group had slightly lower values than the control group, it appeared that both limited carbohydrate alone with mineral supplements did prevent some body catabolism of protein.

The great losses of total nitrogen, urea nitrogen, and uric acid in urine, during caloric restriction, are all indicative of catabolism of body protein for gluconeogenesis and energy. The subsequent small decrease in the excretion of these substances toward the end of the 10-day period indicate some adaptive mechanisms for conserving body protein. Animal studies have shown the availability of the labile stores of body protein or protein reserves that may be readily lost during adaptation to low protein or low caloric diets.

In the conclusion of this study on fairly active troops it was observed that although limited calories without mineral supplementation appeared to be more beneficial than complete starvation, some major abnormalities were still present, including fairly large hypohydration during days 1 and 2, and large negative nitrogen balances. Although EEG changes were all abnormal in the unsupplemented group during caloric restriction, these men were back to normal within 2 days of rehabilitation.

Mineral supplementation and limited carbohydrate calories greatly reduced the water deficit and hypohydration effect, prevented ketosis and abnormal EEG changes, but had practically no effect in decreasing protein catabolism. Mineral supplementation with limited carbohydrate was beneficial in comparison to limited calories alone, but the great body catabolism under these conditions suggest that this type of restricted diet with supplementation could not be recommended for limited warfare (combat patrol). One must keep in mind that these men were fairly active, expending 3200 Cal/day.

17. SURVIVAL RATIONS

Survival ration development has always been a major problem. The early ration developers followed the theory that an emergency ration should not be palatable because the troops then would eat the ration rather than carry it until the emergency arose. They did not take into consideration that if not palatable, the soldier would discard it rather than carry it. Contrary to popular belief, man will not eat anything when he is hungry under survival conditions. Field studies have shown that individuals will permit themselves to become ill and physically inefficient rather than eat an unpalatable ration (Pate, 1955), and in some instances men have chosen to die rather than eat food that they considered "unfit to eat" (Tiira, 1955).

The primary prerequisite of a survival ration is to keep the daily water requirements at a minimum. Under these conditions, the limited food supply is to keep up morale, motivation, and to ameliorate the long-term after-effects of semistarvation, such as ketosis, hypohydration, and decreased physical efficiency. Calloway and Spector (1954), in their nitrogen balance studies as related to calorie and protein restriction, observed that on intakes of 1500 and 2000 Cal (15–30% protein calories), the negative nitrogen balance could be improved, but a positive balance could not be achieved until the protein intake was 160 g/day. This high protein intake will produce larger quantities of urea and will increase the renal water requirements quite substantially, but a fourfold increase in the obligatory urine volume is not a physiological bargain, especially under conditions where water may be limited. Based on these conclusions, these authors recommend protein intakes of only 7–8% of the calories.

There is no convincing evidence available that a total deficiency of vitamins (with the exception of thiamine) or minerals such as calcium, phosphorus, or potassium will lead to deterioration in a 4-week period; however, sodium chloride (2 g per 1000 Cal) is required since it prevents great body water losses when water is limited, and it helps maintain physical efficiency in the heat when food is limited.

Recent studies (Consolazio et al., 1963b, d) have shown that there is an increase in minerals and nitrogen excretion in sweat with increased environmental temperature, and increased physical activity, and a subsequent increase in sweat rate. When sweat losses were included in nitrogen balance studies, the balances were highly negative. The possibility of increased protein requirements under conditions that produce profuse sweating should be re-evaluated, especially in individuals living and working in extremely hot environments, and who are consuming low-to-marginal protein diets. These sweat losses of nitrogen (13–14% of the total intake) observed in individuals consuming a normal American intake may be quite significant in individuals consuming low intakes of 25 g of protein per day. It has been shown that these losses are not compensated by decreased losses of these nutrients from the kidneys and alimentary tract.

The physiological requirements for survival are quite different in the desert, tropics, extremely cold environments, shipwreck at sea, and other isolation conditions. During survival in these uninhabitable areas, the individual must quickly decide whether he should leave the accident area to get food and water, or remain at the scene and await rescue. If he chooses to remain and becomes relatively sedentary, he may be able to survive for many days providing he has sufficient drinking water. Food is not the major consideration in survival; in fact it has a low priority on the list of major essentials. The most important factor is to adapt to the environment so that he does not die of exposure (Stevenson, 1958), but sooner or later long-term undernutrition and malnutrition, including severe water depletion, will result in deterioration, sickness, or even death, especially in extreme hot or cold environments. The survival ration at best can only minimize deterioration and protect the individual's chances for survival (Sargent and Johnson, 1957). Undernutrition can affect every organ and function of the body, and undoubtedly affect the incidence and course of most diseases. A negative calorie balance is produced by most serious illnesses, and many chronic diseases can result in a serious state of malnutrition. One must remember that a daily negative balance of only 100 Cal/day amounts to a loss of approximately 10.5 lb (4.75 kg) of body weight in a year. A moderate caloric deficit in normal individuals for a relatively long period of time will greatly decrease work performance. This was conclusively shown in the Minnesota study (Keys *et al.,* 1950) during World War II, where physical fitness performance was measured before and during semistarvation, and during rehabilitation. Maximum performance dropped from 4400 kg/m work to approximately 1000 kg/m work after 24 weeks of semistarvation. A 20-week rehabilitation period was necessary before the subjects returned to their normal control values of 4400 kg/m work. Some situations are impossible for survival, and these include the flier who has crash-landed in the Arctic's cold icy waters (death from exposure usually occurs in less than an hour), the inadequately clothed individual who is exposed to extremely cold and freezing weather, and the unindoctrinated individual trying to survive in the desert.

On the other hand, an adequately clothed man isolated in the same cold environment may survive for some time if he builds a shelter or snow cave, keeps his clothes dry, reduces activity so that he does not sweat excessively, ventilates his clothing by loosening his clothing at the wrist and neck, and prevents snow blindness. In a hot environment, he must prevent sunburn by keeping sheltered; prevent great body water loss, and be protected from insects by using antimalarial drugs, and avoid poisonous plants. In a life raft, the most important factors for survival are the availability of the emergency gear (medical items, signal equipment, etc.), protection from the sun, and the ability to stay afloat.

Other factors that a man must conquer are fear, location of an adequate water supply, replacement of salt losses, and, finally, he must have access to some food. Food could eventually be a significant fact in survival, since it would greatly enhance morale and mental efficiency, and could influence the individual's ability to make the right decision (Johnson and Kark, 1947a). Stevenson (1958) has published an excellent review on problems related to survival feeding.

A survival ration should contain energy in sufficient quantities to minimize the breakdown of body tissue, but all of the present-day survival rations will still produce fairly large negative nitrogen balances of approximately 5–7 g/day. It is generally agreed that a survival ration should provide between 400–1500 Cal/day, but these quantities are usually dependent on the anticipated food supply.

In planning and developing a compact survival ration, the use of fat at 9 Cal/g would be an ideal nutrient, but it has been shown repeatedly (Johnson and Kark, 1947b; Kark *et al.*, 1945) that fat without any carbohydrate will produce ketonuria. This subsequently results in an increased urine excretion with a loss of calories and would be detrimental under conditions of water deprivation. To prevent ketonuria, the most desirable fat–carbohydrate combination is when the fat composition is less than 50%. Protein would also appear to be an ideal nutrient as a survival ration component, since the primary reason for calorie consumption is to prevent a breakdown of body tissue. This reasoning does not follow because at low intake levels nitrogen is not utilized to replace the body tissue losses. It has been shown that nitrogen from amino acids is converted to urea, which is rapidly excreted in the urine. This results in an increased urinary excretion which also would be detrimental under conditions of a limited drinking water supply. Food items containing protein should be restricted as a survival ration component if the water supply is limited. The US Army (1961) recommends that the use of protein, as a survival ration component, is inadvisable on intakes below 1000 Cal, but on 1000–1500 Cal intakes the addition of some protein will tend to increase the nitrogen retention above that produced by carbohydrate.

Although Sargent and Johnson (1957) do not agree with this concept, carbohydrate is the most practical nutrient for a survival ration since it is readily utilized and completely oxidized to carbon dioxide and water without increasing the water requirements. Gamble (1946–7) showed conclusively that 100 g of carbohydrate reduced the body weight loss by one-half the quantity observed during fasting, and an even greater

TABLE 46 US FOOD PACKET, CARTON, ABANDON SHIP—SURVIVAL AT SEA[a]

Ration item	Quantity
Starch jelly bars	2 ea
Sugar tablets, compressed	4 ea
Chewing gum	2 ea
Matches	Book
Cigarettes	Package
Total Cal/day	466

Components with maximal stability are used in this packet. Must withstand great environmental changes. The ration allowance is one packet per day.

TABLE 47 US FOOD PACKET, LIFE RAFT, AIRCRAFT

Ration item	g/unit
Sucrose—citric acid tablets	20
Sucrose—malted milk	19
Sucrose–lipid–citric acid tablet	30
Vitamin tablets	2 ea
Candy coated gum	2 ea
Total Cal	306

Miscellaneous Items
    Waterproof bag
    A length of twine
    An instruction sheet
    A can opener

[a] This ration is made up of tablets and used for survivors in Naval emergencies. The ration is designed not to provoke thirst.

decrease of urine water which resulted in a decrease in the minimal water intake of about 100 ml. This prevented the development of ketosis and permitted a decreased urine volume and excretion. Since a minimal intake of 400 Cal/day is the lower limit of calories that may have any significant sparing effect on the tissues, the ideal survival ration nutrient at less than 1000 Cal/day should be mainly carbohydrate under any environmental conditions. Since protein may cause a diuresis, this nutrient should be

Nutritional and Physiological Basis

TABLE 48 US FOOD PACKET SURVIVAL, ST (FOR AIR CREWS)[a]

Ration item	g/unit	Cal
Starch jelly bars (7 each)	200	800
Soluble coffee (3 packages)	15	12
Soluble tea (3 packages)	4.8	
Chewing gum, tablets, (6 each)	12	18
Sugar cubes (4 each)	20	80
Cigarettes (8 each)		
Book matches (2 each)		
Water purification tablets (12 each)		
Survival instruction pamphlet		
Total Cal		910

This survival ration is for air crews operating in tropical environments. Each unit contains food for 3 men/day or 1 man/3 days. With a minimal recovery time, this ration would sustain life.

TABLE 49 CANADIAN (RCAF) SURVIVAL FOOD PACKET, AFFP-3, 1958[a]

Ration item	g/unit
Chocolate disks	36
Starch jelly candy (12)	136
Chicken soup (3 units)	21
Fruit cake	89
Coffee (3 units)	10
Sugar (4)	22.5
Salt	6
Water sterilization tablets	10 ea
Total Cal/packet	1235

[a] The gross weight/packet is 444 g. The ration contained 2% protein, 23% fat, and 75% carbohydrate. The issue as three packets (3705 Cal) for a 10-day period.

limited in the rations using reduced salt and water. In general, most of the present-day survival rations contain a very high percentage of carbohydrate (Tables 46–54).

An ideal survival ration should be suitable under all environmental

TABLE 50 Canadian RCAF Survival Food Packet[a] AFFP-2, 1959

Ration item	g/unit
Starch jelly candies (33)	407
Vitamin tablets (12)	100 mg Vit C/Tablet
Polyethylene bag	1 ea
Total Cal	1628

[a] The instructions on this ration were as follows: on day 1 of survival no food or water if the water is limited. Each packet should last for at least 4 days (8 pieces of candy/day). Vitamin pills should be taken twice a day.

TABLE 51 US Food Packet, Individual, Survival, SA—Arctic Areas Survival[a]

Ration item	g/unit
Compressed cereal bars (3 each)	126
Compressed fruit bars (3 each)	126
Compressed nut bars (3 each)	126
Starch jelly bars (2 each)	57
Cigarettes (3 each)	
Chewing gum	
Bouillion powder	
Halazone tablets (water purification)	1 packet
Soluble tea	0.65
Soluble coffee	2.5
Soluble cream	3
Matches, book	
Polyethylene bag	
Survival instructions for cold environments	

[a] The nutritional content of this ration is designed for minimal water consumption (1 quart/man/day) (0.908 l).

conditions; should have the highest possible acceptability to be certain of continued use; should be lightweight (less than 500 g); be compact for carrying on one's person permanently; be easily opened; have a long storage life; must not be thirst-provoking and can be digested slowly; must contain a maximum of calories; should not produce ketonuria or impede renal function; minimize body weight loss; and should not cause the survivor any detrimental physiological effects (Kark *et al.,* 1945).

TABLE 52 US Ration, Survival, Individual, Pemmican Ration[a]

	Nutrient composition		
Ration item	Weight (g)	Cal	Protein (g)
Meat—food products bars	86	515	25.0
Fruitcake bar	52	234	3.2
Cereal bar	43	174	4.6
Onion powder	3		
Chili powder seasoning	3		
Soluble coffee	2.5		
Soluble tea	0.65		
Sugar	7		
Recipe sheet			

[a] This ration contains 3460 Cal.

TABLE 53 Canadian Survival Life Pack Food Kit, 1958[a]

Ration item	g/unit
Can No. 1	
Biscuits (4)	31
Chocolate pieces (7)	99
Pemmican (1)	100
Can No. 2	
Biscuits (9)	72
Chocolate malted-energy tablets	101
Water (4 cans)	1244

[a] The chocolate bar was specifically made for tropical use. The pemmican contained raisins, peanuts, dried apples, dextrose, soyoil, shortening, vanilla extract, and salt.

Calloway (1960), on the basis of her studies, has suggested requirements for an all-purpose survival ration to meet these criteria. The nutrient composition of this ration, to assure that the components will not impair water economy, should contain a maximum of 7–8% of protein and a minimum of 75–100 g of carbohydrates. Browe (1962) developed an experimental bomb-shelter ration based on Calloway's (1960) recommendations which consisted of crackers made of wheat, corn and soya flours, sugar, corn sugar, partially hydrogenated cottonseed oil, salt,

TABLE 54   CANADIAN FOOD PACKET, SURVIVAL, SEAT PACK[a]

Ration item	Menu A		Menu B		Menu C	
	g/unit	Cal	g/unit	Cal	g/unit	Cal
Meat bars	341	2166	—	—	—	—
Biscuits	142	635	—	—	—	—
Tea	6.4	12	—	—	—	—
Sugar	45	176	—	—	—	—
Chewing gum	13.6	63	55	252	—	—
Jelly candy	—	—	426	1501	75	268
Hard candy	—	—	114	478	50	204
Fruit beverage	—	—	—	—	—	84
Total		3052		2231		556

[a] Food packets A and B or B and B (5283 and 4462 Cal, respectively) are adequate for survival for a 10-day period during a Canadian summer.

ammonium and sodium bicarbonate, and water. This ration contained 2000 Cal/day, including 8% protein, 17% fat, and 75% of the calories from carbohydrate.

A survival ration containing 1500 Cal, with 5–10% protein calories, will minimize the deterioration and breakdown of body tissue, and in addition it will allow the individual to do a limited amount of work. For each 1000 Cal, 2 g of sodium chloride should be added to the food. This is a protection in retaining body water when water is limited (Dept. of Army, 1961).

In extensive studies, Sargent and Johnson (1957) have in essence resolved the problem of an all-purpose survival ration suitable for the healthy young male in all environments to include heat and cold, and based on the same criteria that (a) all-purpose survival rations should

TABLE 55   CHINESE ARMED FORCES, EMERGENCY RATION, 1960[a]

Ration item	g/meal
Biscuits	250
Fish velvet	20
Sour plum berry, dried	2 ea
Gingered Compressed Candy	16
Total Cal/meat	1032

[a] This ration contains 34.4 g of protein, 8.4 g of fat, and 204.8 g of carbohydrate.

contain 2000 Cal/day and consist of 15% protein calories, 52% from carbohydrate, and 33% from fat; (b) the osmotic intake of 0.7 osmoles/day from protein and minerals be optimal; (c) the fluid intake should never be less than 1 l/day and 3 l/day in a hot environment, but in general the water intake should be as liberal as possible; (d) within limits the ration should be set by the recommended proportions of protein, carbohydrate, fat, minimal ketogenicity, minimal specific dynamic action, and maximal water of oxidation. Under some instances, a nutritionally unsound ration will actually produce deterioration faster than starvation, especially under limited water supply conditions. This is the main reason that these authors do not recommend the use of either the high fat meat bar or only carbohydrate (Sargent and Johnson, 1957). Both of these rations appear to have intrinsically undesirable effects on the body's organic functions and total efficiency in comparison to the minimal effects of their proposed survival ration. A low-calorie ration cannot prevent deterioration entirely but can minimize the onset of deterioration in survival conditions.

The composition of the US, French, and Canadian survival rations are primarily based on the works of Gamble (1946–7), Calloway and Spector (1954), and Johnson and Kark (1947a), the general trend being a high carbohydrate ration for survival in practically all environments except extreme cold, and the major source of calories in the cold being

TABLE 56A GERMAN ARMY EMERGENCY RATION—PEMMICAN (WORLD WAR II ITEM)

Nutrient composition	
Calories	2094
Protein (g)	168
Fat (g)	158
Carbohydrate (g)	0
Ash (g)	6
Calcium (mg)	88
Iron (mg)	23
Thiamine (mg)	0.32
Riboflavin (mg)	0.81
Niacin (mg)	15.8

This 12 oz bar consisted of dehydrated beef and pork products with added butter fat. The composition is somewhat similar to the American meat bar (pemmican).

the meat bar (pemmican) supplemented with high-carbohydrate foods to prevent ketosis.

For example: three of the US survival rations, (a) Abandon Ship, (b) Air Crews, and (c) Life Raft, and the two Canadian food packets, AFFP 2 and 3, are principally carbohydrate made up of starch jelly bars (Tables 46–50). The US ration for Arctic Survival (Table 51) is designed for a minimal water consumption of 1000 g/day, is also high in carbohydrate, and consists of compressed cereal, fruit-nut bars, and starch-jelly bars.

On the other hand, the Canadian Arctic Experimental Ration (Table 52) field tested during World War II was made up of only pemmican, the high-fat, high-protein meat bar. This ration caused the complete breakdown of troops within 3 days (Dept. of Army, 1961). Although the American Ration, Survival Pemmican, has large quantities of the meat bar, it also contains liberal quantities of cereal and fruit-cake bars for the carbohydrate source (Table 52). The newer Canadian survival rations, Life Pack Food Kit and Sea Pack, are greatly improved, and comparable to the American ration since they contain the pemmican with fairly large

TABLE 56B FRENCH ARMY SURVIVAL RATION

French Army Survival Ration
  The French survival food packet was designed to be used in an emergency situation for periods up to 24 h. Long-term use is not advisable. This ration, as in most survival rations, contains less than 10% of the calories from protein; approximately 60% of the calories are from carbohydrates (1056 Cal.).

Composition of ration

	Cal	% Cal
Protein—26 g	104	9.8
Fat—36 g	324	30.7
Carbohydrate—157 g	628	59.5

quantities of biscuits, candy, and chocolate as the high calorie source (Tables 53 and 54). Chinese, German, and French rations are presented in Tables 55, 56A, and 56B.

18. SURVIVAL AT SEA

In survival at sea, certain precautions should be taken if at all possible (Stevenson, 1958). Prior to abandoning ship, a man should try to drink as much water as possible, and then restrict water for a 24-h period after leaving the ship unless he gets very thirsty. Fasting, in association with a negative water balance from water deprivation, is additive. It has been recommended that under conditions of minimal exertion and negligible seasickness, 500–1000 g of water per day will prevent dehydration in food-restricted survivors on life boats or rafts in a tropical environment (Futcher et al., 1944).

It has been consistently reported that drinking significant quantities of sea water accelerates the increase of total osmotic pressure of the human body. There is no question that an apparent improvement in water balance initially occurs after drinking sea water, but in time the apparent gain in water balance is replaced by an osmotic diuresis, which could be quite puzzling. Hervey and McCance (1952) inferred that an increased osmotic pressure in body fluids occurred when 150 g of sea water and 350 g of distilled water were consumed daily over a period of time. These investigators (1952) strongly recommended against drinking sea water, even in small quantities, because evidence indicates that it is extremely harmful.

Some individuals have suggested that shipwreck survivors use fish as a source of water supply in an emergency. The problem of pressing enough water out of fish muscle is too difficult to warrant the effort, and the whole fish has only sufficient fluid to mediate the excretion of metabolized nitrogen from the fish protein. None of the water of the ingested fish is retained, and the subject's own water loss is not impeded. In addition, when water is limited, ingestion of high-protein foods are definitely undesirable (Hervey and McCance, 1952), since this will only increase the water requirement.

The US Navy recommends only food items that will not cause seasickness. The ration should be able to float in salt or fresh water in an emergency, and should be a bright yellow color to facilitate the location and recovery of personnel. In addition, the ration should contain 300 Cal/day made up primarily of carbohydrate with a small quantity of fat that is consistent with acceptability (Calloway, 1960). The RAF, in designing their life-raft ration for survival (Stevenson, 1958), provided for the immediate protection against the environment, for rapid location and rescue, for food, water, and the aids. These aids included a first-aid kit, a knife, matches, fishing net, torches or flares, candles, and sharpening hone. The other characteristics of the ration included acceptability, long-term storage, nutritional adequacy, and field practicability. Stevenson (1958) has recommended that the desirable emergency ration for sustaining life on a life-raft is a 350 Cal/man/day maximum. This

TABLE 57 RECOMMENDED EMERGENCY RATION (SURVIVAL), STEVENSON 1958

Ration item	g/five men/day	Cal/Man
The desirable ration		
Water	4000	
Boiled sweets	500	400
Toffee (30% fat)	500	500
Condensed sweets, Milk	500	350
Biscuits	500	480
Cigarettes	10	
Total/man		1730
The compromise ration		
Water	2500	
Boiled sweets	500	400
Toffee (30% fat)	500	500
Condensed sweet milk	500	350
Cigarettes	10	
Total/man		1250
The minimal ration		
Water	2000	
Boiled sweets	750	600
Total/man		600

ration included 800 g of water, 60 g of carbohydrate in the form of sweets, and 20 g of biscuits (Table 57).

For survival, it is imperative that troops are constantly reminded of the deleterious effects of water deprivation in man. No amount of acclimatization or discipline will enable a soldier to remain physically fit if he does not drink as much water daily (preferably replaced hourly) as is lost from his body (Dept. of Army, 1961). One must keep in mind that thirst is not a reliable index of water requirements because an individual's thirst may be satisfied by drinking water long before the sweat losses have been replaced (Hulse, 1956). Adequate hydration is indispensable with maximal efficiency.

19. FUTURE CONCEPTS OF MILITARY FEEDING

As plans for tactical operations change, new feeding and logistical requirements for the military services will develop. Closer liaison with the food industry, and their increasing industrial skills in food technology, the development of highly acceptable individual, interchangeable meals rapidly prepared for field use. These rations, to be carried for 10-day periods, for guerilla-type warfare, must be compact, lightweight (approximately 1 lb/day (454 g)), have great variety, and contain no more than 700 Cal per individual packet. Many areas have been investigated and include the use of (a) dehydrated foods when water is available, (b) high energy compounds exclusive of fats that can be designed and synthesized such as 1.3 butanediol with a 7.5 Cal/g caloric density, (c) irradiated foods for long-term preservation, and (d) the great future water problem which lies in the realm of desalting sea water.

One example of future feeding is the 25-man, uncooked ration which has been designed to replace the B-ration for normal feeding in the support section and combat area except when prohibited by the tactical situation. This ration consists of factory assembled, nonperishable foods, packaged in 25-man modules, making maximal use of present-day dehydrated foods and lightweight packaging. The weight per unit will be under 25 lb (11.3 kg), exclusive of the bread and cakes which will be provided separately. Although only 18 menus for a 6-day cycle are now available, ultimately this ration will contain 30 different meals for a 10-day cycle. This ration is being designed to simplify provision of kitchen-prepared meals in future operations, since it will greatly reduce the number of food service personnel and kitchen personnel required for food preparation. It will also reduce the requirements for transportation, storage areas, handling equipment, and supply personnel. The meals are used interchangeably with other packaged meals as the tactical situation changes. This ration, supplemented with bread and cake, will be nutritionally adequate, acceptable, and stable for maintaining the physical efficiency of combat troops without any other food supplements (QMF and CI, 1951). Plans have already been initiated to field test this ration for a 35-day period, for acceptability and performance evaluation.

20. NEW FEEDING SYSTEMS

Due to the changing needs of the military, there is a continuing necessity to evaluate the capability of current and newly developed rations (both freshly prepared and as altered by varied storage conditions) to provide adequate nutrition to the soldier under a variety of duty requirements and environmental situations. The nutritional basis of the present ration system used by the US military is adequate for garrison training duty on a current basis, but may not be optimum for the various phases of military life to which the man is exposed. In addition, several new innovations in military feeding (i.e. "short order" or "snack line", specialty houses, and a greater variety of food items available through the new procurement system) require that close attention be devoted to the nutritional status of the man. Longitudinal evaluation of the nutrient status, body composition, work performance and capacity of the person is essential to insure that his effective military performance is not impaired by improper nutrition during his duty career. Such impairment could limit the capability of the military at a time when instant readiness is mandatory. Previous studies, though helpful, provide only some of the necessary answers.

The efforts of all three branches of service to make the service operated dining halls and the military subsistence more appealing to the young military member coincides with the incorporation of many new food items which have not been thoroughly studied for nutritional quality or nutrient content. In addition, the incorporation of new foods and feeding systems has adversely stimulated various concerned elements of the established food production industry to question the nutritional adequacy of the new feeding systems. To adequately respond to these criticisms more information is required and it can be supplied through surveys of the more advanced DOD dining halls.

It has been estimated that the feeding of personnel costs the Department of Defense approximately $6 billion per year when food procurement, transportation, equipment and personnel involved are all considered. Despite this large monetary outlay it has been demonstrated that utilization of the DOD dining facilities ranges only from 45 to 68% by the authorized personnel. A great deal of concern is expressed as to the consumption outside of the dining facilities by the various service members. This consumption has been observed to include many items of questionable nutritional value and may have negative influence upon the nutritional status of the individuals. Unfortunately, the consumption outside of the dining facilities has not been properly documented nor studied to adequately interpret the nutrient intake and the selectivity of the individuals.

Military feeding systems are of such large scope and have such a close relationship to the varied military training and tactical situations that they have no commercial counterpart. Because of this situation, the US Army Natick Laboratories (NLABS) were charged with developing and maintaining an operations research/systems analysis (OR/SA) study to be applied to military feeding systems to identify causes of non-utilization of the systems by the consumer in order to correct these situations, improve efficiency in the various operations conducted within the feeding systems, reduce cost, and reduce manpower requirements. The NLABS OR/SA Program came into existence in FY 71 when effort was concentrated on identifying the causes for non-utilization. Emphasis was placed upon food preference. Feeding systems were studied to identify the feasibility of consolidating food preparation activities in a central area for the purpose of serving smaller feeding facilities and for consolidating smaller feeding facilities into larger feeding facilities.

a. Based on the data obtained during FY 71, it was determined that it was feasible to study the effectiveness of the central preparation system utilizing menus developed from the OR/SA acceptance tests.

The Centralized Army Feeding System (CAFE) was designed to improve the performance of military feeding systems by increasing the meal attendance of personnel. Another objective of this system was to reduce costs and manpower to a minimum, and to design a feeding system that would be a model of efficiency and performance. This new system might eventually be used in all large Army garrison installations.

An experimental feeding system involved a central food preparation and transportation area for distributing pre-cooked (frozen) foods to satellite dining halls for reconstitution (heating) and serving. A centralized sanitation unit of all dishware was also an integral part of the study.

b. Another new feeding system was designed to provide information on the quantity, acceptability and nutritional quality of the food consumed from the "short order" or "snack line" in comparison to the regular "full meal line". A greater objective was to evaluate whether the use of short order lines would increase meal attendance of personnel.

The introduction of the "short order" or "snack bar" line in military dining halls was intended to provide an opportunity for the consumer to obtain food items in keeping with his previous eating practices and habits (hamburgers, franks, chili, French fries, carbonated drinks, etc.). The US Air Force has been a pioneer within DOD with this type of feeding and has developed experience and expertise while maintaining their expenditures within established monetary limitations.

c. Another system being evaluated is a complete civilian catering system, where the contractor is responsible for the procurement, distribution, preparation, serving of food, and the subsequent clean up of the dining hall facilities. This catering system was instituted as a means of improving the military feeding system by increasing the efficiency of the various operations within the system, reducing the costs and military manpower requirements, and by increasing the acceptability of the foods being served.

The "McDonald" type hamburger and chicken stand has also been investigated and shows some possibilities as a feeding system for the military. In this system, the individual may drive up to the stand and order what he wants. The items are boxed so that he can eat in his car or take it home.

d. Although these systems are all designed to increase the dining hall attendance of military personnel, preliminary information indicates that authorized military personnel still eat considerable quantities of food from sources outside the military dining halls. This has led to new studies that will evaluate the feeding habits of military personnel under conditions where the individuals receive the monetary ration allowance. The men are still authorized to eat in the dining halls, and only pay for whatever they choose. Preliminary information suggests that the dining hall attendance is drastically reduced. There is no question that costs and military personnel will be greatly reduced under this system, however the nutritional adequacy of the ration being consumed may be debatable.

21. SUMMARY

An attempt has been made to present some of the major problems related to ration planning and development. The primary prerequisite is that the "fighting man" must and should have the best possible food available with a great variety and the best means of food preparation. The foods, whether in garrison or packaged rations, must be palatable, highly acceptable, and nutritionally adequate to maintain the troops in maximal physical and mental efficiency, high morale, and to provide an incentive for motivation. Foods are useless if they are not consumed in sufficient quantities to prevent nutritional deficiencies. There is no question that packaged food can never replace fresh foods, and that a hot meal for the troops in the field will always be the first priority.

Some of the basic requirements for ration development should include (a) the incorporation of foods that will not increase water requirements such as high salt, high protein, etc., (b) the use of antiketogenic foods with fat below 50% of the calories, (c) the use of dehydrated and high density foods under conditions where water is available (lightweight, etc.), and (d) adequate planning time in the development of rations for acceptability, etc. Above all, the troops must be well indoctrinated in the well-established principles of water, salt, and calorie allowances.

REFERENCES

ADOLPH, E. F. and DILL, D. B. (1938) *Am. J. Physiol.* **123**, 369–378.
ADOLPH, E. F. *et al.* (1947) *Physiology of Man in the Desert,* Interscience, New York, NY.
AR 40–25 (1972) *US Army Regulation, Medical Service, Nutrition,* Department of Army, US Government Printing Office, Washington DC.
ARCHER, T. C. R. (1958) *Royal Army Medical Corps* **104**, 1.
ARMSTRONG, J. G. (1951) *A Study of Food Problems of the Armed Services Undertaken by the Defence Research Board,* Defence Research Board, Toronto, Canada.
ASTRAND, P. (1967) *Fedn. Proc.* **26**, 1772.
BAKER, E. M., PLOUGH, I. C., and ALLEN, T. H. (1963) *Am. J. clin. Nutr.* **12**, 394–398.
BALLANTYNE, R. M., GALBRAITH, J., HULSE, J. H., SMITHIES, W. R., and STACEY, N. E. (1958) *Fd Technol.* **12**, 470–472.
BERGSTROM, J., HERMANSEN, L., HULTMAN, E., and SALTIN, B. (1967) *Acta physiol. scand.* **71**, 140.
BLOOM, W. L. (1959) *Metabolism* **8**, 214.
BRANSBY, E. R., MAGEE, H. E., HUNTER, J. W., MILLIGAN, E. H., and ROGERS, T. S. (1944) *Br. med. J.* **1**, 77.
BRITISH RECOMMENDED INTAKES OF NUTRIENTS FOR UK (1970) Dept. of Public Health and Social Security 120, London, Her Majesty's Stationery Office.
BROWE, J. H. (1962) *Hlth News* **39**, 4–13, New York State Department of Health, Albany, NY.
CALLOWAY, D. H. (1960) *US Armed Forces J.* **11**, 403–417.
CALLOWAY, D. H. and SPECTOR, H. (1954) *Am. J. clin. Nutr.* **2**, 405–411.
CHRISTENSEN, E. H. and HANSEN, O. (1939) *Acta physiol. scand.* **8**, 137.
COKE, L. R. (1961) *Med. Servs. J. Can.* **17**, 313.
CONSOLAZIO, C. F. and FORBES, W. H. (1946) *J. Nutr.* **32**, 195–211.
CONSOLAZIO, C. F., POLLACK, H., CROWLEY, L. V., and GOLDSTEIN, D. R. (1956) Studies on Nutrition in the Far East: V. Calorie cost of work and energy balance studies. *Metabolism* **5**, 259–271. (H. Pollack, ed.), Grune & Stratton, New York, NY.
CONSOLAZIO, C. F., KONISHI, F., CICCOLINI, R. V., JAMISON, J. M., SHEEHAN, E. J. and STEFFEN, W. F. (1960) *Metabolism* **9**, 435.
CONSOLAZIO, C. F., SHAPIRO, R., MASTERSON, J. E., and MCKINZIE, P. S. L. (1961) *J. Nutr.* **73**, 126–134.
CONSOLAZIO, C. F., JOHNSON, R. E., and PECORA, L. J. (1963a) *Physiological Measurements of Metabolic Function in Man,* Blakiston Divison, McGraw-Hill, New York, NY.
CONSOLAZIO, C. F., MATOUSH, L. O., NELSON, R. A., HARDING, R. S., and CANHAM, J. E. (1963b) *J. Nutr.* **79**, 407–415.
CONSOLAZIO, C. F., MATOUSH, L. O., NELSON, R. A., TORRES, J. B., and ISAAC, G. J. (1963c) *J. appl. Physiol.* **18**, 65–68.
CONSOLAZIO, C. F., NELSON, R. A., MATOUSH, L. O., HARDING, R. S., and CANHAM, J. E. (1963d) *J. Nutr.* **79**, 399–406.
CONSOLAZIO, C. F., MATOUSH, L. O., and HARRIS, C. W. (1965) US Army Medical Research and Nutrition Laboratory Report No. 288, Fitzsimons General Hospital, Denver, Colorado.

CONSOLAZIO, C. F., MATOUSH, L. O., NELSON, R. A., HARDING, R. S., and CANHAM, J. E. (1966) US Army Medical Research and Nutrition Laboratory Report No. 291, Fitzsimons General Hospital, Denver, Colorado.

CONSOLAZIO, C. F., MATOUSH, L. O., JOHNSON, H. L., KRZYWICKI, H. J., ISAAC, G. J., and WITT, N. F. (1967a) US Army Medical Research and Nutrition Laboratory Report No. 312, Fitzsimons General Hospital, Denver, Colorado.

CONSOLAZIO, C. F., MATOUSH, L. O., JOHNSON, H. L., NELSON, R. A., and KRZYWICKI, H. J. (1967b) *Am. J. clin. Nutr.* **20**, 672–683.

CONSOLAZIO, C. F., NELSON, R. A., JOHNSON, H. L., MATOUSH, L. O., KRZYWICKI, H. J., and ISAAC, G. J. (1967c) *Am. J. clin. Nutr.* **20**, 684–693.

DARLING, R. C., JOHNSON, R. E., PITTS, G. C., CONSOLAZIO, C. F., and ROBINSON, P. E. (1944) *J. Nutr.* **28**, 273–281.

DEPARTMENT OF THE ARMY SUPPLY BULLETIN SB 10–260–1 (1967) *Recapitulation of Master Menu*, Department of Army and Air Force, US Government Printing Office, Washington DC.

DEPARTMENT OF ARMY TECHNICAL MANUAL TM 8–501 (1961) *Nutrition Headquarters*, Department of the Army, US Government Printing Office, Washington DC.

DURNIN, J. V. G. A., HAISMAN, M. F., PETERS, D. W. A., and ZURICK, L. (1966) Army Personnel Research Establishment Memo N/3, England.

FRAZIER, R. G. (1945) *Proc. Am. phil. Soc.* **89**, 249–255.

FRENCH ARMY RATIONS (1966) Republic of France.

FUTCHER, P. H., CONSOLAZIO, W. V., and PACE, N. (1944) *War Med.* **5**, 203–206.

GAMBLE, J. L. (1946–47) *Harvey Lecture Series* **42**, 247.

GONTZEA, D. (1965) *Int. Z. angew. Physiol.* **21**, 1–2.

GREENE, A. H. M. (1952) *Rations of the Commonwealth Nations, Activities Report* **4**, 181–211, Research and Development Association, Armed Forces Food and Container Institute Inc., Chicago, Ill., Office Quartermaster General, Washington DC.

HERMANSEN, L. E., HULTMAN, E., and SALTIN, B. (1967) *Acta physiol. scand.* **71**, 129.

HERVEY, G. R. and MCCANCE, R. A. (1952) *Proc. R. Soc. Lond.* B, **139**, 527–545.

HULSE, J. H. (1956) Canada Food Industries, Quebec, Canada.

JAKOVLEV, H. (1961) *Physculture and Sport*, Moscow, Russia.

JOHNSON, R. E. (1943) *Gastroenterology* **1**, 832–840.

JOHNSON, R. E. (1947) *Test of Operational Ration Type "E" Regarding Acceptability and Nutritional Adequacy, Camp Carson, Colorado*, US Army Medical Nutrition Laboratory, Chicago, Illinois, Office Quartermaster General, Washington DC.

JOHNSON, R. E. and KARK, R. M. (1947a) *Feeding Problems in Man as Related to Environment*, QM Food and Container Institute, Research and Development Branch, Office of Quartermaster General, Chicago, Illinois, Office of Quartermaster General, Washington DC.

JOHNSON, R. E. and KARK, R. M. (1947b) *Science* **105**, 378.

KARK, R. M., AITON, H. F., and PEASE, E. D. (1945) Report No. C6191 to Associated Committee on Army Medical Research, National Research Council, Canada.

KARK, R. M. and MCCREARY, J. F. (1944) *Cold Weather Operational Trials of Rations, Prince Albert, Saskatchewan, January–March 1944*, a report to the Standing Committee on Nutrition, Department of National Defence, Toronto, Canada.

KARK, R. M., JOHNSON, R. E., and LEWIS, J. S. (1945) *War Med.* **7**, 345–352.

KARPOVICH, P. V. and MILLMAN, N. (1942) *New England J. Med.* **226**, 881.

KEYS, A., BROZEK, J., HENSCHEL, A., MICKELSEN, O., and TAYLOR, H. L. (1950) *Biology of Human Starvation*, University of Minnesota Press, Minneapolis, Minnesota.

KEYS, A. and HENSCHEL, A. (1942) *J. Nutr.* **23**, 259–269.

KEYS, A., HENSCHEL, A., MICKELSEN, O., BROZEK, J. M., and CRAWFORD, J. H. (1944) *J. Nutr.* **27**, 165–178.

LADELL, W. S. S., WATERLOW, J. C., and HUDSON, M. F. (1944) *Lancet* **ii**, 491–497 and 527–531.

NATIONAL RESEARCH COUNCIL (1974) *Recommended Dietary Allowances*, 8th rev. edn., National Academy of Sciences, Washington, DC.
PATE, L. W. SGT. (1955) *Reactionary*, Harpers, New York, NY.
PITTS, G. C., CONSOLAZIO, C. F., and JOHNSON, R. E. (1944a) *J. Nutr.* **27,** 497–508.
PITTS, G. C., JOHNSON, R. E., and CONSOLAZIO, C. F. (1944b) *Am. J. Physiol.* **142,** 253–259.
QM CORPS (1949) *Conference Notes, Rations*, QM School for the Quartermaster General, Chicago, Illinois, Office of Quartermaster General, Washington DC.
QM FOOD AND CONTAINER INSTITUTE FOR THE US ARMED FORCES (1951) *Conference on All-purpose Survival Rations for use by the Army, Navy, and Air Force*, Activities Report 3, DRB 53/1394, Chicago, Illinois, Office of Quartermaster General, Washington DC.
QUINN, M., KLEEMAN, C. R., BASS, D. E., and HENSCHEL, A. (1954) *Metabolism* **3,** 68–77.
RAO, N. A. N. and VIJAYARAGHAVAN, P. K. (1966), *Indian J. Nutr. Diet.* **3,** 75–78.
RAO, N. A. N., SARMA, M. L., and VIJAYARAGHAVAN, P. K. (1966), *J. Nutr. Diet.* **3,** 85–99.
ROGERS, T. A., SETLIFF, J. A., and BUCK, A. C. (1965) Arctic Aero Medical Laboratory, Aerospace Medical Division, Ft. Wainwright, Alaska.
RYER, R. III, GROSSMAN, M. I., FRIEDEMANN, T. E., BEST, W. R., CONSOLAZIO, C. F., INSULL, W., JR., and HATCH, F. T. (1954) *J. clin. Nutr.* **2,** 179–194.
SALTIN, B. (1964) *J. Appl. Physiol.* **19,** 1114–1118.
SARGENT, F. II and JOHNSON, R. E. (1957) *Physiological Basis for Various Constituents in Survival Rations*, Part IV WADC Technical Report 53–484, US Air Force, Wright-Patterson AFB, Ohio.
SIMONSEN, E., BAER, A., and ENZER, N. (1942) *Fedn Proc.* **1,** 81.
SKINNER, H. G. and MANN, G. M. (1963) Nutrition in the British Army, *Proceedings of the VIth International Congress of Nutrition* (C. F. Mills and R. Passmore, eds.), Livingstone, Edinburgh, Scotland.
STEVENSON, J. A. F. (1958) *Survey of Survival Feeding*, Defence Research Board Report No. DR 125, Department of National Defence, Toronto, Canada.
TAYLOR, H. L. (1957) *Conference Notes, Coordination Meeting of the Assignment to the Army of Primary Responsibility for Research and Development in the Field of Food, Natick, Mass., 21–22 May 1957*, Office of the Quartermaster General, Washington DC.
TAYLOR, H. L., HENSCHEL, A., MICKELSEN, O., and KEYS, A. (1943) *Am. J. Physiol.* **140,** 439–450.
TIIRA, E. (1955) *Raft of Despair*, Dutton, New York, NY.
US ARMY TECHNICAL BULLETIN (MED) No. 175 (1969) *The Etiology, Prevention, Diagnosis and Treatment of Adverse Effects of Heat*, Department of the Army, US Government Printing Office, Washington DC.
WELCH, B. E., LEVY, L. M., CONSOLAZIO, C. F., BUSKIRK, E. R., and DEE, T. E. (1957) US Army Medical Research and Nutrition Laboratory Report No. 202, Fitzsimons General Hospital, Denver, Colorado.
WINKLER, A. W., DANOWSKI, T. S., ELKINTON, J. R., and PETERS, J. P. (1944) *J. clin. Invest.* **23,** 807–815.

CHAPTER 6

INDUSTRIAL FEEDING IN EUROPEAN COUNTRIES*

E. N. Bennett

Catering Consultant

CONTENTS

1. The Provision of Industrial Feeding Facilities — 315
2. Trends Affecting Industrial Feeding — 317
3. The Finance and Control of the Canteen — 319
4. Canteen Premises, Planning, and Equipment — 323
5. Hygiene — 329
6. Staffing and Training — 329
7. Canteens as an Educational Factor — 331
8. Research on Nutrition in Relation to Working Efficiency — 332
9. The Approach of the Worker Towards the Canteen Services — 335

1. THE PROVISION OF INDUSTRIAL FEEDING FACILITIES

Catering, whether commercial or part of a welfare service, reflects the social and economic pattern and needs of the life of the community. The introduction and development of industrial feeding has been promoted through the needs peculiar to different countries and to different localities within those countries. The provision of canteens and ancillary feeding services has therefore been designed to meet both local and national requirements. The background influences motivating the provision of some form of feeding service create considerable variation with regard to the extent to which in-plant feeding is provided and also the standard and sophistication of both premises and services.

Broadly speaking, the dominant influences cover two aspects:

In western Europe and in countries with few fundamental problems relating to undernutrition, feeding within the plant holds little signi-

---

*The basic data for the chapter was obtained during two assignments undertaken for FAO in 1963 and 1964.

ficance as an intentional medium for the promotion of improved feeding habits. With the exception of the Latin-speaking countries canteens have become accepted as being an integral part of the factory organization and the services are regarded as an established fringe benefit. In Latin countries the family circle is the dominant factor. Communal feeding is not accepted readily by the worker.

In eastern Europe the pattern is different. The feeding of the industrial worker is usually considered a part of the national feeding programme, but different levels of priority are set according to the economic background of the particular country.

There is no specific legislation in European countries enforcing the provision of feeding facilities for the workers. In broad principle, government and trade unions oversee the provision of such services, the determining factors being the need of the working force and the demand for in-plant feeding facilities voiced through the worker's organizations in individual places of employment.

In western Europe and in countries where general affluence negates the need for a rigid national feeding programme, it is general practice for the provision of the factory canteen to be left to the discretion of the individual plant management. It is, however, significant that in most countries the provision of in-plant feeding facilities in all large industrial units and in a high proportion of small units is taken for granted, by both factory management and by the employee.

In Great Britain, during the World War II, all industrial units employing 250 operatives or more were required by law to provide canteens. The subsequent withdrawal of the compulsory order was not followed by the closure of canteens, and in Britain today the canteen is an established part of the factory organization.

In Sweden the provision of feeding facilities in industry has also become general practice, in fact the Swedes might be said to be "industrial feeding conscious".

Both Czechoslovakia and Poland attach great importance to the value of in-plant feeding as a direct means of maintaining the health of the industrial employee and of maintaining production. The trade unions in Poland initiate the provision of canteens. If eighty employees on an industrial plant require feeding facilities, the trade unions press the factory management to provide a canteen. The Department of Gastronomic Industry, a branch of the Ministry of Inland Trade, is responsible for the policy determining the planning, organization, and finances of mass feeding on a national level. The provision and operation of canteens comes within the scope of this department, and is considered an important influence in both the industrial production programme and the national nutritional programme as a whole.

Services and the food provided in canteens reflect the pattern of the services and the food available in commercial catering establishments. In general, changes relating to physical needs take place gradually, and the catering industry as a whole has been conservative and slow to accept new practices and to break from habit and tradition. Today, social changes and economic problems have created a pressure that can no longer be ignored, and these are having a significant impact on the approach towards catering as a whole and in particular to welfare catering which includes industrial feeding.

Although social and economic backgrounds differ from country to country, and the foods served and their method of preparation reflect the food supplies and cultural pattern of the country, there are certain basic problems common to most countries today. Management is concerned not only with the changing eating patterns and varying demands of the workers and with the increasing cost of establishing and operating a food service, but also with the shortage of catering staff, in particular trained managers and skilled craftsmen.

To management, in-plant feeding often represents an uneconomic use of valuable space plus an investment in equipment which is used only a few hours a day. In addition, the employees do not expect to pay prices comparable to those charged in commercial restaurants, and strongly resist price increases. It is, however, more expensive to provide similar services within the structure of an industrial organization because the establishment operates to peak service periods linked with the factory hours of production and rest pauses. These factors are causing management to appraise the value of the canteen firstly as an influence towards good relationship with the worker, and, secondly, from an angle that to date has received too little attention—the effect of the services on productivity.

2. TRENDS AFFECTING INDUSTRIAL FEEDING

In addition to severe economic pressures and staffing problems, factory management is now faced with the need to modify both the pattern of in-plant feeding facilities and the type of meal service provided in order to meet new needs created by rapidly expanding industrialization and a changing pattern in social life.

Some of the influencing factors are as follows:

(a) The shortening of the working day by reducing the midday break is resulting in increased use of in-plant food services.
(b) Labour shortages have resulted in the employment of large numbers of foreign labourers who, lacking domestic amenities, tend to rely on the in-plant food service for one or more of their meals.
(c) Full employment has led to the employment of large numbers of women, both single and married, increasing the dependence of both men and women workers on meals at the place of work.
(d) Inadequate transportation facilities in larger centres, including those where traditional hours are still maintained, tend to break down the long-established practice of taking the noon meal at home, and to direct more and more workers toward in-plant feeding.
(e) The expansion of shift work is necessitating more than one service of substantial meals during the course of the day.

The desire of the worker to enjoy the main meal at home is predominant throughout Europe. Any reduction in the length of the midday break which results in altering this accepted pattern of eating at home or taking a leisurely meal elsewhere, is resisted. Full employment of women may, in the long run, force married couples, as well as individuals, to depend on in-plant feeding facilities or public restaurants for the main meal of the working day, or, alternatively, to take the main meal in the evening. The latter presents a contradictory element and would, of course, tend to reduce or eliminate the demand for a meal at the place of employment. In many countries the adoption of a shorter midday break is affecting the existing pattern of industrial feeding and altering the volume of trade, the type and speed of service, and the kind of food demanded by the worker, but the meal pattern of the future and the demand and needs of the workers are difficult to forecast due to a diversity of influencing factors.

Management is therefore faced with the serious problem of maintaining present standards of industrial feeding, of adjusting the services to meet changing eating patterns, and at the same time resolving the problem of increasing economic pressure and the shortage of labour.

Traditional kitchen practices are being replaced by more efficient methods and by a more widespread introduction of mechanization. Many traditional kitchen practices are now outdated due to the introduction of prepared foods. Accepted methods of service are being adapted to new conditions. Much of the personal service enjoyed in the past is being replaced by self-help and automation.

It is also inevitable that some compromise must be reached between traditional practices of food handling and the use of mass-produced products. Many large feeding services and, indeed, some governments, are investigating the use of centralized operations and simplified methods of food preparation and service; for example, the purchase of prepared foods, portioned foods, and conserved foods that are partially or fully cooked. Because it is inevitable in the interests of economy, both in money and labour, that the present duplication of basic processes must be eliminated, food must be purchased, stored, processed, portioned, and transported in large quantities. It is widely recognized that there must be control of the quality of the food handled in bulk, and the development of appropriate techniques for this purpose is essential.

Vending machines have been used in industry for some years, primarily for ancillary services such as sales of cigarettes, cartoned cordials, minerals, and confectionery. They have proved useful as a round-the-clock service, reducing direct labour cost and, in addition, have provided effective sales control.

The use of beverage vending on the factory floor is now expanding rapidly, particularly where the open break has replaced the morning and afternoon rest pause. There is a certain amount of customer resistance, but as the quality of the processed ingredients improve, vended beverages are accepted more readily. The vending of food has not progressed at the same rate although there is some indication of interest in hot-meal vending particularly for shift workers and night shifts and persons requiring a meal at off-peak periods.

3. THE FINANCE AND CONTROL OF THE CANTEEN

Industrial catering may be described as "welfare catering", a term indicating that from the financial angle services are provided and food sold for charges that only partially reimburse operational costs and overheads. Whether the factory is nationally controlled or private enterprise, it is general practice for the management of the industrial unit to assume financial responsibility for the provision and direct operation of the in-plant feeding services.

Such control is implemented in three ways:

(a) Through the direct employment of an experienced caterer who is responsible to the plant manager, generally through the personnel officer who acts as an intermediary to implement policy and to see that satisfactory services are maintained. The requirements of the workers are frequently voiced through advisory committees set up to deal with matters pertaining to the plant as a whole or set up to deal specifically with canteen matters. In such an organization the catering manager is responsible for the day-to-day buying, costing, and cash receipts, but the financial control is usually integrated with the overall plant administration. In the past it was common practice for financial results to be controlled loosely, the firm meeting the trading losses without question. It is now more general for the catering manager to operate in accordance with a predetermined budget showing a calculated trading loss, the wages and salary rates of the catering personnel and also the prices charged for beverages and meals being determined by the company and not the catering manager.

(b) Through the employment of a catering contractor: this method of control has been accepted as a means of dealing with professional services alien to the main factory operation through companies specializing in industrial catering, and in doing so relieving the plant manager of the domestic day-to-day responsibility and problems of running the canteen. At one time it was common practice for these contractors to operate on a direct contract, thus enjoying a trading profit over and above the cost of food and wages. It has not been possible to pass on the rapidly rising cost of materials and labour to the customer, and it has now become a more general practice for contractors to operate on a management fee basis. Under such circumstances the plant management stipulates the type of service required, the prices to be charged, and accepts responsibility for meeting trading losses.

(c) Through controlling committees: these committees usually consist of works and staff representatives. They either assume direct control, operating through a catering manager or employ catering contractors. It is their responsibility to see that the canteen operates within a given budget. There is usually some contribution towards running costs from plant management or from special funds set aside for this purpose.

Whatever method of control is adopted for the operation of the canteen, it is general practice for the factory unit to provide the premises, capital investment for the equipment, and the service charges for heating, lighting, and water. Firms are beginning to evaluate the returns from capital invested in expensive kitchen equipment and valuable space, neither of which can be used to capacity. This approach is resulting in an increasing interest in automation, and exploration into the possibility of simplifying services or obtaining factory-produced meals from an outside source, thereby obviating the need for the provision of kitchens planned on traditional lines. The future might well see the closure of canteens that are not well patronized, and, in consequence, becoming a heavy financial liability.

The approach towards operational costs is variable. Most concerns expect to cover the cost of food from revenue. The proportion of labour, replacement of light equipment and incidental overheads set against revenue varies considerably, and the balance that has to be met is increasing and becoming a heavy burden.

In most western European countries plant management meet the canteen operational losses from the trading profits of the enterprise. France, however, has a different system. The trade unions require employers to allocate a sum of money equivalent to a given percentage of the wages bill towards the provision of social and welfare amenities. The administration of this fund varies. It is either undertaken by the company direct or by an elected committee of workers. The cost of the canteen services is met from canteen revenue together with the proportion of this fund allocated by the committee for the provision of feeding facilities. The system of self-management in Yugoslavia produces somewhat similar results inasmuch as the responsibility for the distribution of income is at the disposal of workers organizations. The workers therefore in both France and Yugoslavia can and do opt against the provision of catering facilities, directing the funds towards the provision of other amenities.

In Poland, works funds exist in most factories. They are used for financing housing construction, paying bonuses, for providing various amenities, and for subsidizing the canteens. The revenue from the canteen is expected to cover food and labour, but sometimes a budget is granted towards labour, and this is drawn from the profit derived from kiosks from which employees may purchase foods at retail prices. In heavy industries such as mining and steelworking, the trade unions grant a special subsidy per meal towards the cost of food.

Czechoslovakia is now operating on similar lines. Prior to 1964 a contribution was granted from state means for each meal taken in the canteen. The withdrawal of this contribution resulted in a period of recession in the use of the canteens. Since January 1966, however, individual enterprises have been encouraged to improve and develop industrial feeding. A certain percentage of the gross profit of each enterprise is now directed to form a fund for the promotion of cultural and social needs. By this means the canteens are subsidized, sometimes to the extent of the cost of raw materials, from the profits of the enterprise. The result has been a favourable development in industrial feeding.

Canteens in Federal Germany and in Italy are heavily subsidized. In Italy, although there is no legal obligation to provide a canteen, there is an agreement between the confederation of industries and the trade unions whereby firms undertake to arrange a contract with the workers, either to provide a food service or to make some payment in lieu of a food service. In practice, firms appear to provide a food service and also to supplement wages. In effect, workers often obtain free meals or meals for a nominal sum.

The approach towards the subsidizing of operational costs varies not only in general principle from one country to another but in actual extent and practice from one unit to another.

It has been evident for some time that unless those responsible for administering funds are prepared to accept rapidly spiralling costs or increase selling prices quite substantially to a more economic level, there must be some alternative to the pattern of services provided. The economic situation is now such that it must be faced squarely and fully appreciated by both management and the factory worker.

Over the past few years the catering manager has been working under economic pressure. Through the promotion of careful buying, efficient staff organization, carefully designed control systems, and every facet of craft expertise, he has endeavoured to curb rising operational costs. It has been necessary for him to introduce new methods and to use convenience foods. This has altered the whole approach towards costing. A high gross profit margin is no longer a set target, the cost of labour often outweighs the cost of materials, and prepared foods—yielding a low gross margin—are used to obtain better economic results. The importance now attached to the evaluation of the cost of the labour content of the performance of any function, such as the production of a menu, or the preparation of a specific dish, is promoting a new balance of values, and this has to be taken into account in the background planning of day-to-day activities in the canteen.

Such practices, combined with the better use of mechanical equipment, the introduction of automation, and the elimination of costly and wasteful functions, need to be undertaken to reduce both operational costs and the capital investment required for the provision of canteens. The "welfare approach" may appear to be overshadowed at the moment, but greater attention to the balance and relationship of capital investment and operational costs is producing a more practical and businesslike approach towards industrial feeding.

4. CANTEEN PREMISES, PLANNING, AND EQUIPMENT

The standard of living and technological development of a country is directly reflected in her industrial feeding services. For example, in Sweden the in-plant feeding services are functional and well designed. Mechanized equipment and streamlined methods are used, and a wide variety of foods are prepared and served. In contrast, Poland was handicapped for long years following the devastation of war, and is only now planning for the rapid development and expansion of her industrial feeding. However, both Poland, Sweden, and other European countries are concerned with the same fundamental problems—the technically sound economic use of premises, the optimum use and care of equipment, and the most efficient use of skilled personnel.

It is, however, safe to generalize in that the facilities provided for in-plant feeding in all countries compare favourably in respect of design, planning, and equipment with those in other fields of catering.

Despite the fact that a disappointingly low percentage of the total population of a unit purchase meals at midday, factory management takes pride in providing well-presented and adequate meals in attractive and pleasant surroundings. If anything, there has been a tendency to err on the side of extravagance both with regard to the over-equipping of kitchens and the provision of over liberal space in both dining rooms and kitchens.

The extent to which guidance is given regarding the planning and equipping of canteens, varies from country to country. Specific legislation for the provision of in-plant feeding might have resulted in the provision of certain national standards. This is not general, but certain countries have established machinery whereby guidance can be obtained or minimal standards maintained. For example, in Sweden, under the Workers Protection Act 1949: "A suitable place shall be made available to employees at or near the place of employment in such manner as may be considered satisfactory in view of their number, the proportion of each sex, and the nature and duration of work." This Act is implemented by the Workers Protection Board. Under section 7 of the Regulations under the Workers Protection Act: "An employer who intends to construct, reconstruct or extend any workroom or staff accommodation must submit the proposal to the Labour Inspector, accompanied by such drawings and other particulars as may be required for the examination of the proposal." The Board has issued instructions concerning the provision of standards for the fixtures and equipment of personal service rooms.

Governments in eastern European countries have more direct control over the planning of canteens than those in the west, where, with the exception of Sweden, the planning is very much the direct decision of the manager of the enterprise or the experts he may engage to undertake the work.

In-plant feeding in Poland is covered by the National Feeding programme. The Department of Gastronomic Industry, a branch of the Ministry of Inland Trade, is responsible for the policy determining planning, organization, and the finances of mass feeding, both in industrial concerns and open restaurants. Because of this, basic catering problems and future developments are common to all types of catering. All catering establishments, commercial and industrial, are planned by the Bureau of Projects and based on:

(a) a schedule of areas and equipment and staffing needs drawn up by the Ministry of Internal Trade; and
(b) hygienic requirements laid down by the Ministry of Hygiene.

In Czechoslovakia, the Institute of Commercial Research, which works under the direction of the State Committee for the Co-ordination and Direction of Science and Technology, operates in an advisory capacity, and in Yugoslavia advisory bodies are available to help enterprise management.

The catering industry has been slow to use new methods and new sciences, but now the changing approach of management towards the operation of the canteens is bringing a more enlightened and professional approach towards the planning of the canteens. Planning is not now the prerogative of the architect, caterer, and engineer. Experts on work organization and ergonomics are being consulted. The industrial field is fortunate in that these sciences have for years been applied to the factory floor, and experts are readily available and are now consulted and used in respect of canteen planning and operational problems.

In the past the canteen was regarded as an adjunct to the planning of a factory rather than an essential part of the complete concept. This frequently resulted in badly sited and unsuitable premises, not readily accessible to the worker and difficult to operate, thereby causing time wastage and adding to both factory production costs and the cost of operating the canteen itself. It is desirable that a canteen should be sited so that it is within easy access from all parts of the factory and offices, thus becoming integrated with the factory work programme and providing a service within the structure of factory hours and practices without causing disruption or waste of production time.

At the same time, the canteen should be a functional unit in its own right, well ventilated and sanitary, and suitably furnished and designed to promote an atmosphere for relaxation and contrast for the worker from his place of work.

The layout and planning of a canteen must be designed to meet the specific demands of the unit, and to give efficient service.

The services required by industrial units show considerable variation influenced by locality, the type of labour employed, the balance of male and female labour, and the type of production upon which the labour is engaged together with the hours of work. Not only have the persons responsible for planning canteens to bear in mind fundamental factors such as areas required for seating, service, kitchen functions, and storage, but must relate these to the specific requirements of each individual unit taking into account the timing of break periods and the loading at any given time of service. The essential factors of service in an industrial canteen are punctuality and speed. There can be no leeway. The worker expects to enjoy the maximum proportion of his break period relaxing, not queueing for a meal, and after the break period he must return punctually to his place of work.

Planning for the ancillary services is equally as important as the planning of the canteen itself. Mid-spell break services, whether provided within the canteen, from tea bars, trolleys, or vending machines, should be a means of boosting production, but if badly organized can cost a firm dearly in wasted production time. The siting of such services, the loading of equipment, and the selection of suitable equipment is important.

The present trend in Great Britain is away from the trolley and tea bar to vending. In Germany and Holland vending is already well established, but in France the vended cup of coffee is not readily accepted. Eastern European countries have not progressed so far in this field, and few machines are provided on the factory floor.

The introduction of factory-floor vending services necessitates a new approach towards planning. The installation, siting, and area for customer movement are more closely related to factory operation than catering functions.

One of the problems of today is the adjustment of existing facilities to meet changing circumstances and at the same time retain a layout and flow of work that will maintain efficient operation. Catering practices, for so long unchanged and conservative, are altering, and the speed of change is accelerating under present-day economic pressure. It is therefore inevitable that kitchen planning will be faced with a transitional period during which experiments in new methods will bring about a reallocation of areas and the introduction of new equipment.

The canteen is a place for rest and relaxation as well as for the service of meals. The provision of comfortable, colourful, and well-furnished dining rooms, is general. New, easily cleaned fabrics and materials for walls, floors, and furnishing have added much to the appearance of these establishments as also has the use of indoor plants and modern murals. Within the last 20 years the character, appearance and comfort of industrial canteen dining rooms has changed from austerity to comfort, from drab to colourful, from the institutional and makeshift, to the outcome of careful and professional attention to design and function.

The tendency of industrial catering is to reflect the practices, services, and conditions of those to be found in commercial catering. The margin of difference between these two aspects of the catering field has narrowed. The industrial worker expects to find similar comforts, services, and choice of menu to those he would take for granted in a commercial restaurant, and management take for granted the elaborations of haute cuisine. These refinements of service have, however, added to the cost of equipping and operating the canteens, and the resulting economic problem is promoting a move towards radical changes that may well alter the structure and design of the canteen premises of the future.

Multipoint services are expensive to operate. This and the democratic approach of one service for all levels may eventually reduce the number of units with socially stratified dining rooms, but it is still general practice for the executive, and often clerical staff, to enjoy waitress service and the factory worker to use a self-help service. In western Europe in particular, much business entertainment takes place on the plant, and many visitors' dining rooms and executive rooms are elaborately furnished and equipped, even to the point of luxury.

Over a number of years the self-help service in the main hall has been changing steadily from the pre-plated composite meal to the free selection of meal components made available by cafeteria service. This has resulted in the installation of more elaborate counters with *bain-marie* fittings and showcases. Display and presentation has become an important feature. Cafeteria service is ideally adapted to meet a constant flow of customers or a service divided into several peak periods, but as the flow through is not as quick as the pre-plated method, it is unsuitable for a heavy loading of customers during a short meal-break period.

The tendency to shorten the midday meal break must influence the methods of service. Speed will be the essential factor; this, together with the shortage and increasing cost of labour, will promote the expansion of self-help services. Already the open-flow type of service is being adopted in Great Britain. Vended chilled foods and customer-operated microwave ovens are being introduced into dining areas.

If quick service and a satisfactory flow of work is to be maintained, kitchen planning must be influenced by the method of service adopted in the dining room. Pre-plated service requires early cooking in order that the food can be plated up and maintained at a temperature acceptable to the customer. This necessitates bulk production; therefore larger units of equipment are required and, in consequence, greater kitchen floor space. With cafeteria service the food need not be cooked well in advance. It can be prepared and cooked in relays as required to replenish the containers on the counter throughout the service. Smaller quantities can be cooked at a time, and the use of the storage hot closet reduced to a minimum. Large bulk boilers can be replaced by smaller units or by the introduction of more surface cooking space and boiling plates. The food can be transported directly from the stove or oven to the counter. The large central blocks of equipment can be broken down to a more flexible arrangement, with improved work flow and accessibility from preparation section to counter.

The kitchens of today reflect the predominance of cafeteria service. The kitchens of tomorrow will reflect the evolution that is taking place from present methods and traditional practices to those arising from the introduction of convenience foods, increased mechanization, and automation. Already mechanical equipment is used extensively, and has particular value in alleviating the drudgery of tasks regarded as menial, such as washing-up and preparing vegetables.

The rising cost of labour has turned attention to the use of materials that require less handling in the kitchen. Over the past few years convenience foods, either prepared or portioned, have been on the market, initially produced for domestic use, but now extensively used in the catering industry. The use of such foods is already having an impact on kitchen practice and, in consequence, kitchen design, equipment, and storage are being adjusted to a new pattern of work. In Great Britain the use of prepared vegetables, either fresh, air dried, or frozen, is steadily increasing, thus obviating the need for vegetable preparation units and eliminating an unpopular aspect of kitchen work.

Many new canteens are being designed with much reduced or even without the traditional vegetable preparation section. Large vegetable stores are not required, thus valuable space is saved. The impact of the introduction of prepared foods and consequent readjustment of kitchen work necessitates the reallocation of kitchen space for certain processes, in particular that of storage.

As the need for economy is accelerating the introduction of new methods of food preparation and conservation, the chasm between technological research and the practical application of new processes is being bridged, there is, therefore, much need for closer liaison between laboratory and the practical caterer, between research and factory food production, and processing plants and equipment manufacturers. It is evident that certain fields of catering will benefit if food can be mass produced, and it is equally evident that the mass production of cooked food will have considerable impact on kitchen design and equipment for both the production and the service unit. The mass production of cooked meals either in food factories or central production units in large industrial concerns will result in a revised pattern of kitchen work. Simplification of work on the belt system of production will necessitate maximum mechanization for large quantities of material and result in the optimum use of equipment and of craftsmen.

There is every indication that the kitchen in the factory unit itself will cease to deal with the production of the basic meal but be used only for the reconstitution of convenience foods, the regeneration of frozen or preserved cooked dishes, and the quick cooking or grilling of special dishes.

The areas required will, therefore, be much reduced, the planning streamlined and simple, consisting of a servery backed by suitable storage and specialized equipment designed for the rapid reheating of food. Equipment manufacturers are being pressed to accelerate development of suitable equipment to meet this changing pattern. The demand for microwave, forced-air convection ovens, and infrared heating equipments, is increasing.

As yet, the use of this equipment is somewhat exploratory, and the caterer is waiting for the equipment manufacturer to progress and to market equipment that will reheat large quantities of chilled or frozen food quickly and satisfactorily.

Factory produced meals will result in greater standardization of equipment, and there will inevitably be expansion in the use of expendible containers. In consequence, garbage disposal will assume importance. The use of expendible cartons and wrappings contributes much to the untidiness of our streets today, and as the use of expendible materials increase in the factory, suitable means of disposal will be essential in the interest of safety and hygiene.

5. HYGIENE

Many countries have regulations concerning hygiene. Specific requirements regarding sinks, storage, ventilation, the finish of walls and floors, and the provision of cloakroom and washing facilities for canteen staff, are laid down. Where canteens are subject to regular inspection, high standards of sanitation are maintained.

New premises reflect considerable improvement over old in the siting of kitchen equipment and the smooth flow of operations, facilities for food storage and washing-up, and the provision of effective ventilation. The extensive use of stainless steel, formica, and other materials impervious to grease and water, has not only improved the appearance of the canteens but facilitates cleaning and eases the work of the canteen staff, thus promoting pride in the job. Improved kitchen planning and the streamlining of equipment has also eased the work of cleaning, therefore eliminating hazards to the maintenance of sanitary conditions.

A further contributory factor towards improved kitchen hygiene is the attention given to the washing of crockery and cutlery and the increasing use of dish-washing machines with high temperature sterilization and the use of sterilents. The china cup, which probably provides the most persistent washing-up problem and, in consequence, health hazard, is being replaced gradually by the expendible plastic or paper container.

Food-handling in canteens reflects a national approach towards food hygiene and also the extent to which the subject has been taught and emphasized in the training colleges and promoted by training given by catering managers to their staff on the job.

6. STAFFING AND TRAINING

The problem of staffing is acute throughout the catering industry. Adverse reflection on the status of catering as a profession is slow to die, particularly with regard to the non-skilled jobs which are regarded as menial and semi-domestic. Industrial catering is further handicapped through direct competition with the hotel and restaurant trades for all levels of food service workers by means of wages and, below management and craft levels, tips and other prerogatives.

In all countries the demand for trained food service managers greatly exceeds the supply, and underlines the need for training courses specifically for the industrial and institutional field. In western Europe the stream of trained managers tends to flow directly towards hotels and restaurants, the impetus being promoted by the training schools which have a strong bias influenced by the needs of the tourist trade. Indeed, in Italy, France, and Switzerland, craft training is primarily based on the requirements of the tourist trade.

With the exception of Italy, too few people are trained in the food crafts to fill present vacancies. In Italy, France, and Sweden, few women undertake training as cooks and bakers, and men trained in hotel schools prefer employment in hotels and restaurants.

The universal lack of staff and the need for trained staff to operate efficient and economic services is causing large concerns and commercial catering organizations to develop their own training programmes; indeed, this concept is being promoted in Great Britain now that the Catering Training Board has been formed. This system should promote a higher standard at the semi-skilled and unskilled level.

In addition to the strained economic situation, the lack of staff and, in particular, those trained for skilled and managerial functions, is forcing operators of large food services to look for means of centralizing production so that expertise may be utilized to the full. This concept of centralization may alter the pattern of catering in industry. In fact, it is probable that in some countries it may alter the overall pattern of mass feeding. The mass feeding programmes in Poland and Czechoslovakia cover both commercial and industrial catering, and the conception of the bulk production and distribution of cooked foods has been under examination in both countries for several years.

Faced with establishing priorities, and left with limited training facilities and few trained teachers and experienced caterers, Poland has been examining the possibility of and is now promoting the introduction of bulk production as a means of utilizing both equipment and catering personnel to the full.

In Czechoslovakia in-plant feeding is very much part of the national programme of feeding and nutrition. This country has a well-organized structure of training for the catering industry, covering both craft and management, and a well-established industrial feeding organization. However, here a different problem is turning attention towards the establishment of central production units—the use of prepared foods and increased mechanization. The national programme for improved nutrition together with the development of mass feeding projects is not only proving costly but is absorbing an increasing number of personnel. Centralization would serve the dual purpose of reducing costs and also releasing much needed labour for other industries.

Development of centralized production will bring into being a different pattern of staffing. Large production kitchens will be highly mechanized, and it will be necessary for control and management to be in the hands of trained experts with a sound knowledge of administration, management skills, and food technology. This will create a new field where training in new methods of production, food conservation, and preservation will be essential. Staffing of the receiving units will require reliable supervisors but not necessarily craftsmen. There will be few menial tasks in these units, and it may be anticipated that such conditions will prove attractive to a different and better type of labour.

7. CANTEENS AS AN EDUCATIONAL FACTOR

There is little attempt to guide workers' eating habits by the use of canteens as a medium of education in nutrition although, of course, industrial feeding may provide a useful medium for nutrition education when carefully planned, attractively served meals are provided. Through example, foods not served at home gain acceptance and broaden the range of the workers' food preferences. Direct education through the medium of the canteen has, however, been limited. Only a few countries attempt this through well-selected posters, pamphlets, films, discussion groups, and classes for the workers. Little effort is made to relate calorie or nutritive value of the meal to the requirement of the worker in the type of work performed.

The development of cafeteria service which allows the customer individual choice of meal components reduces the chance of a well-balanced diet, the pocket and the palate of the customer direct selection. The general approach towards food education is through the home and the child at school. In time this may bear fruit, and as a result of education as a child the adult industrial worker may select a nutritionally balanced meal from the cafeteria counter. There is an awareness at national level in some countries that certain national feeding habits impair health, and these are being approached on a national basis that may eventually filter through to industrial feeding.

8. RESEARCH ON NUTRITION IN RELATION TO WORKING EFFICIENCY

A gap exists between research in the field of nutrition and its application in industrial feeding practice. This applies both to methods of food preparation and conservation on large-scale lines and to the diet of the individual.

The worker's use of in-plant feeding facilities is optional, depending to a large extent on his social and economic background and his hours of work. As a result there is no assurance that the worker's intake of food provides him with the required calories and nutrients relative to the work in which he is engaged.

The application of the principles of nutrition, of meal planning and relationship of nutrition to the efficiency of the working force appears to be of incidental concern to the average factory management and food service manager. Most catering managers provide special diets if these are ordered by the physician, but there is little or no attempt to relate the caloric or nutritive value of the meal to the requirements of the worker or the type of work performed. It is, however, general practice to provide milk for persons doing specialized work, heavy work, and those employed in coal-mining and chemicals. In German-speaking Switzerland and Poland, special provisions are made for those working in inclement weather.

Few surveys have been carried out since the World War II and little information is available regarding direct results of nutrition on working efficiency. Growing concern regarding the expense of operating in-plant feeding services may precipitate interest in this field. Investigation into the function and use of the canteen exposes the need to appraise its value and use in the promotion of production as much as in maintaining happy factory relationships.

The introduction of vending as a replacement for the traditional trolley or tea-bar service is stimulating investigation into the value of rest pauses and the need for some form of stimulant such as beverages and snacks during the mid-morning and mid-afternoon, not only during recognized break periods but when the worker himself feels the need of a stimulant. For example, in 1965 in Great Britain, the Tavistock Institute of Human Relations issued a report on investigations into the role of food, drinks, and sweets in reducing industrial fatigue. The Arhatofysiologiaka Institute of Sweden has also carried out experiments on the physiology of work.

Some of these experiments were made at the request of industrial concerns and included:

(a) the respective advantages of high carbohydrate or high fat diet as related to muscular exercise and nervous fatigue;
(b) the effect of the spread-over of work and length of work breaks on efficiency;
(c) and the advantages of effervescent saline drinks made available without charge at the place of work.

The Nutrition Institute, Prague, has also been active in the field of clinical work, physiology, nutrition, and biochemistry. Subgroups are working on food technology and the feeding of the factory worker. Studies have been made on:

(a) prevention of disease, e.g. silicosis, through controlled fat content of the diet, and the protection of workers on analine dyes through diet;
(b) nutritional control of conditions affecting health, e.g., obesity;
(c) the rhythm of eating and its effect as shown by psychological tests and by the efficiency of workers on automated processes;
(d) the effect of food processing on nutritive value, e.g. frozen foods.

Yugoslavia is also conducting extensive programmes in the field of nutrition including research on industrial feeding. Research is in progress on soya processing and the use of soya to supplement the levels of protein in the diet and a factory for soya products is being built. In order to supplement the low protein content of the diet soya fortified foods will be available in all fields of catering.

In countries where general affluence has made available a wide range of foods for all levels, the dietary intake is at the discretion of the individual both in the home and in the factory. In certain of the developing countries, where the national feeding programme covers all aspects of mass feeding, more attention is given to the caloric value of the meals and to the provision of menus designed to offset nutrient deficiency.

In Czechoslovakia the Institute of Commercial Research has compiled a recipe book which is available for all industrial feeding units. These recipes give examples of variations of cost adjustment to constant nutritional and caloric value.

In 1963 Poland prepared proposals for the provision of regenerative meals which might well alter the pattern of feeding in industry and increase the percentage using canteens. These proposals were for the introduction of four categories of meals based on the caloric requirement for:

(a) heavy industry—steelworks, mines, and buildings;
(b) medium and light industry;
(c) administration;
(d) youth organizations, schools, and universities.

It was intended to break down the caloric value of meals as follows:

Breakfasts   30% of the total number of calories per day.
Lunch   40%–45%.
Supper   20%–25%.

It was anticipated that the customers would pay full value for breakfast and supper. The majority of workers would pay for the lunch, but this meal would be provided free for those on heavy work or working under difficult conditions. The "long day" would be broken up and meals provided after 4 hours of work.

The German Federal States have also given attention to the provision of meals based on caloric requirement. The Max-Plank Institute influences industrial feeding by direct contact with the management and also through the German Nutrition Society. As a result of general research on nutrient requirements, the Max-Plank Institute recommends five meals a day for the worker, that is, 30–35% of the daily caloric requirements for the worker should be provided through the medium of in-plant feeding.

The institute strongly supports the introduction of automatic vending machines in places of work in order to ensure the provision of between-meal snacks.

The German Nutrition Society has operated for 12 years under the guidance of scientists engaged on research in connection with nutrition, internal medicine, and food chemistry. The society is partially financed by government and partially by fees paid by concerns for consulting services. Advice includes all aspects of catering particularly the planning of balanced menus and the provision of recipes which indicate quantities of ingredients and nutrient values.

The National Institute of Public Health in Sweden closely follows the results of research at the Max-Planck Institute. The institute issues literature for guidance on nutrition and has analysed the general pattern of feeding. Only four meals a day are advocated against the five recommended in Germany. There is, however, no association comparable to the German Nutrition Society to channel information to industry.

The anticipated centralization of food industries may prove to have many advantages both with regard to the economics of production and control of the nutrient value of the meal served to the customer. So often good material is spoilt through bad kitchen practice, particularly in small units employing inexperienced cooks or managers. The use of factory-produced convenience foods opens up an opportunity to apply nutritional standards. This has already been promoted in Czechoslovakia through the control of the Milk Nutrition Industry, which processes milk products, introducing a range of pre-mixes for use in mass catering. The use of these pre-mixes in conjunction with the recipes and menus issued by the Research Institute has considerable influence on the nutrient value of the meal provided in the factory canteen.

9. THE APPROACH OF THE WORKER TOWARDS THE CANTEEN SERVICES

Basically the catering services within the plant are similar in all countries in as much as they reflect the needs of the worker in relation to the hours of work and established break periods. Often industrial catering services are not well patronized, and the need for and reasons promoting the provision of canteens might well be questioned. In Great Britain the provision of a canteen, or of some form of food service, is taken for granted by industrial employees, but frequently the services are patronized by a small minority of the workers.

Possibly the approach in Yugoslavia is more realistic. The system of self-management which places the responsibility for the distribution of income at the disposal of workers' organizations is logical. The workers can and do opt to use these funds for purposes other than the operation of a canteen.

The general pattern of services is similar in most countries. For day workers this consists of a break at midday for a substantial meal and a short break morning and afternoon in which the workers are provided with light snacks such as filled rolls, sandwiches, and cakes and beverages.

In Poland the pattern is somewhat different. A "long day" is worked and the main meal is taken before or after work. This may contribute to the fact that a very low percentage take main meals in the canteens. Poland, however, offers a useful ancillary service. Kiosks are provided from which butter, bread, sausages, minerals, etc., can be purchased at retail prices, and buffets are provided for the sale of snacks on the job. Coffee and sometimes tea are provided on the factory floor. In order to encourage workers to use the canteens in Poland, it is quite general for a reduction to be allowed on the bulk purchase of meal tickets.

Investigation has shown that a high percentage of workers rely on the canteen for the first meal of the day, and in areas where the rapid growth of industrialization results in workers travelling long distances to work, there exists the very real problem of relieving fatigue in the early part of the working day. In Yugoslavia such conditions are general. Factories operate on 8-hour shifts. Workers are allowed $\frac{1}{2}$-hour breaks during this period in which substantial "breakfast meals" are served, and the percentage taking these meals is high. Main meals are served before and after work.

The provision of ancillary services in the form of tea bars, kiosks, and vending, help to provide on-the-job snacks for workers.

During the past few years the use of vending machines has increased considerably. For many years vending has been used for ancillary services such as the sale of cigarettes, confectionery, and cordials, but despite initial resistance is now becoming accepted as a replacement for the trolley or tea bar, and is particularly suitable for services where the timed mid-spell break has been replaced by the open break. Much research has been done regarding the operational efficiency of the machines and the suitability of materials for the service of hot beverages. Although the materials have not yet been perfected, the drinks available are becoming more acceptable and most important provide a standard quality of beverage served under hygienic conditions. The machines have a certain asset in as much as they provide a round-the-clock service and a choice of beverage.

In Great Britain both the consumption of coffee and of chocolate has increased as the introduction of machines has become more widespread. The service of food through the medium of machines has not progressed as rapidly as that of the beverages. This may be due to both economics and customer reaction. Machines, particularly those operating at controlled temperatures, are expensive; machine operation reduces the choice available, and possibly—most important to the customer—the element of human contact is missing.

Off-peak services are a problem in canteens where shift work, overtime, and night shifts are in operation, and the practice is developing of making use of machines for these services. Such services are difficult to operate in as much as the response of the worker is variable, and at night in particular he is very selective in his choice of food.

Despite effort on the part of management to give the worker means to avail himself of both snacks and substantial meals, the response is varied and, on the whole, disappointingly low. This is in no way a reflection on the quality of the services or the food provided, but is influenced by domestic economics and a preference on the part of the worker to partake of the main meal of the day within the family circle.

In Yugoslavia the wide variations in food habits and food preferences of the people and the rapid movement of families from rural to developing industrial areas presents a problem. The country has an extensive national programme for education on nutrition and feeding habits which should in time level out major variations in taste.

The shorter working week has necessitated an adjustment of break periods and a reduction of the midday recess. Workers who at one time were able to return to their homes for the midday meal can no longer do so. Resistance to this situation has been particularly strong in some countries. In 1963, in northern Switzerland, in order to avoid difficult labour relations, some firms, as a temporary measure, found it advisable to give their employees the option of an hour and a half or an hour lunch break.

France is also facing similar resistance in urban areas where shorter hours and transportation problems confine the worker to his place of employment at midday, thus curtailing the traditional midday leisurely meal and siesta.

Although the worker in Great Britain takes it for granted, indeed expects a canteen to be provided, the proportion purchasing main meals is usually between 30 and 35%, and experience has shown that, however attractive the menu, the worker will control his spending within the limits of a budget determined by the economics of the home.

Most modern canteens, particularly in Western countries, serve meals on the cafeteria principle which, apart from the advantage of presentation, allows the customer to select meal components according to his taste and pocket. Meals in the canteens naturally reflect the customs and practice of the country, and the dishes served are generally those to which the employees are accustomed to prepare and eat at home.

In countries where foreign labour is employed, it has been found desirable to introduce special national dishes for the benefit of these people, but, in general, they soon become accustomed to the food of the country of their adoption, and the feeding of these people does not present a major problem.

Looking at the pattern of industrial catering throughout Europe it is significant that the fundamental problems are common to most countries and that the solutions to these problems are being sought by different countries along somewhat similar lines.

Methods used in one country cannot be adopted without modification by other countries having different food habits, levels of technological development, and economic conditions.

Close co-operation, understanding, and exchange of information between factory management, caterers, equipment manufacturers, and food technologists must help to resolve these problems and direct new developments so that maximum benefits can be achieved. This concept not only applies to individual countries but might be considered to advantage on an international basis.

CHAPTER 7

ALIMENTATION IN COMMUNITIES OF OLD PEOPLE AND IN HOSPITALS

H. Gounelle de Pontanel and L. Bérard

Centre de Recherches Foch, 4 Av. de l'Observatoire, Paris, France

CONTENTS

Part I. Alimentation in Communities of Old People	340
1. The Nutritional Needs of Old People	341
1.1. Caloric Intake	341
1.1.1. Protein Intake	341
1.1.2. Fat Intake	341
1.1.3. Carbohydrate Intake	342
1.2. Mineral Intake	342
1.3. Vitamin Intake	342
1.4. Drinks	343
2. Aspects Peculiar to Old People	343
2.1. Diets	344
2.2. Organization of Meals	344
2.2.1. Kitchen Premises and Equipment	344
2.2.2. Number and Times of Meals	345
2.2.3. The Dining Room	345
2.2.4. The Problem of the Disabled	346
2.2.5. Staff	346
3. Planning the Menus	346
Part II. Alimentation in Hospitals	348
4. The Basis for Hospital Alimentation	349
5. The Normal Diet	349
5.1. Calorie Intake	349
5.2. Protein Intake	350
5.3. Vitamin Intake	350
5.4. Mineral Intake	351
5.5. Drinks	351
5.6. The Choice and Preparation of Foods	352
5.7. Scheduling of Meals	352
6. The Main Types of Diet	353
6.1. Restrictive Diets	353
6.1.1. Low Calorie Diets	353
6.1.2. Low Nitrogen Diets	353

		6.1.3. Low Fat Diets	354
		6.1.4. Restricted Sodium Diets	354
		6.1.5. Carbohydrate Restricted Diets	354
	6.2.	Supplemented Diets	357
		6.2.1. High Protein Diets	357
	6.3.	Diets with a Special Texture	357
		6.3.1. Roughage-free Diets	357
		6.3.2. Liquid Diet	357
		6.3.3. Drip Feeding	359
7.	Kitchen Premises and Equipment		359
	7.1.	Distribution	361
		7.1.1. Times of Meals	361
		7.1.2. Where to serve Meals	362
		7.1.3. Distribution	362
	7.2.	Preparation	363
		7.2.1. The Problem of the Number of Kitchens	363
		7.2.2. Relay Kitchens	364
		7.2.3. The Dietetic Kitchen	364
	7.3.	Supplies	365
	7.4.	Clearing up Eating Utensils	365
8.	Staff		366
	8.1.	Kitchen Staff	366
	8.2.	Distribution Staff	366
	8.3.	The Dietist	367
9.	Menus and Foodstuffs		368
	9.1.	Planning Menus	368
	9.2.	Foodstuffs—Advantages of the New Techniques	368

PART I. ALIMENTATION IN COMMUNITIES OF OLD PEOPLE

Communities of old people apparently include a higher proportion of occupants with nutritional disorders at present than any other sort. Knowledge of the real needs of old people is not always very definite, and has only recently engaged attention.

Moreover, old people's homes generally have only a very limited budget at their disposal, which makes it all the more regrettable that the money is not always spent to good effect, since the foods provided are not consumed by the inmates.

Psychological problems play their part: the essential process of adaptation to community life is more difficult after a certain age. The passing years attach us to our habits, and to our nutritional habits perhaps more than any others. Also, many old people, because their resources have been too minimal, or preparing their meals has proved irksome, become used to progressively more monotonous and restricted food, and only gradually re-adapt to a more normal diet. This explains why many old people enter homes in a more or less marked state of malnutrition, which must be remedied, always taking into account the usual precautions of gradual progression.

Problems of digestion and diet arise more often at this time of life than they do in younger communities.

1. THE NUTRITIONAL NEEDS OF OLD PEOPLE

All other factors being equal, the needs of the healthy old person are theoretically similar to those of an adult (indeed, how could one make a clear distinction between the two ages?). It is obviously an individual question: the stages of old age vary from one subject to another.

1.1. CALORIC INTAKE

Caloric needs diminish slightly with age. Activity in old people's homes is fairly restricted (let us emphasize, nevertheless, that participation in some form of work has proved beneficial both to health and morale). As buildings are well heated, the expenditure in thermoregulation is also low. An intake of the order of 1800–2000 Cals would thus seem sufficient.

Weight-watching is essential. Although an old person must eat enough not to lose weight, he must also take care to avoid any weight gain.

As at any other age, the total caloric intake must be correctly divided among three dietary principles.

1.1.1. *Protein Intake*

Protein intake must provide approximately 12% of the total calories, with a correct balance between animal and vegetable proteins (AP/VP ≥ 1). Priority must be given to dairy products, especially skim-milk, which is a protein food of high biological value with an attractive cost-price, and represents an important source of calcium, required in greater quantities by old people than by young adults because of a frequent assimilation deficiency.

1.1.2. *Fat Intake*

It is prudent to restrict slightly the total fat intake, and more especially the intake of animal fats. A diet over-rich in these is in fact known to be conducive to atherosclerosis—a cause of cardiovascular disorders. This implies a very limited use of fatty preparations (beef, mutton and pork products; sauces; foods fried with hard fats) and the predominant use of vegetable fats for seasoning. A small quantity of butter (10–15 g/day) may be maintained to ensure a sufficient intake of vitamin A. The least fatty protein foods should be selected. The particular suitability of skim milk should be emphasized.

1.1.3. *Carbohydrate Intake*

Carbohydrate foods should provide more than half the calories (55–60%). Cereals, flour, bread, potatoes, fruit and vegetables, sugar, and sweetened products should contribute to this. An important place must be given to green vegetables, which should be served once a day, as they help to avoid constipation by ensuring that the alimentary bolus has sufficient volume.

1.2. MINERAL INTAKE

Various aspects of this need to be watched.

Calcium: absorption is often reduced in the old, and cases of osteoporosis are not uncommon, especially in old women. Thus it is essential to ensure a relatively large intake (600–800 mg). Dairy products—skim milk in particular—are therefore of prime importance for old people. A parallel intake of vitamin D, which regulates calcium and phosphorous metabolism, would seem desirable.

Iron: cases of iron-deficiency anaemia are also common. The diet must therefore provide foods rich in iron in the forms which are most compatible with habit and budget: meats, egg-yolk, and green vegetables.

Magnesium: there are often fairly serious deficiencies here in the aged. A balanced diet providing adequately for the preceding requirements ought to ensure the necessary amounts.

1.3. VITAMIN INTAKE

Raw fruit and vegetables rich in ascorbic acid must be eaten regularly. The role of this vitamin as a stimulant and in combating infections is well known. A particular check must be kept on the intake of vitamins in the B group (if necessary, small quantities of yeast can be added to food daily), and vitamins A and D. As assimilation is less efficient in the old than in the young adult, it may be desirable in certain cases, especially when there is a decline in the subject's general condition, to envisage administering a multivitamin product.

1.4. DRINKS

Water and other liquids, e.g. soups, must be given in sufficient quantity (about one litre per day). Those who suffer from enuresis should be advised to spread the daily total more satisfactorily by reducing liquids taken with the evening meal so that they do not have to get up too often during the night.

What attitude should be adopted towards tea and coffee? It seems that national and individual habits should be considered as well as the tolerance of the subject. In the case of coffee it should be noted that the effect varies according to the caffeine content, which depends on the origin of the beans used and the method of preparation. Chicory, on its own or added to coffee, has no disadvantages.

There remains the question of the various alcoholic drinks (wine, beer, cider, etc.). Here, too, a systematic approach is difficult. When a subject has been accustomed all his life to drinking wine, cider, or beer, these drinks constitute an appetizing factor—a small pleasure to be respected. Thus it is wiser to act according to local custom, social environment, and also the financial possibilities. Of course, consumption should be moderate ($\frac{1}{4}$ to $\frac{1}{3}$ litre of wine at 10 for the men, a little less for the women, or an equivalent double ration of beer at 5°).

EXAMPLE OF AVERAGE RATION FOR 24 HOURS

Milk	0.4 l	Fruit	250 g
Cheese	30 g	Butter	15 g
Meat or equivalent	120 g	Oil	20 g
Bread	150 g	Sugar	25 g
Potatoes or equivalent	300 g	Jam	25 g
Green vegetables	300 g		

Calories: 1945
Proteins: 68 g (13% of calories)
Fats: 67.5 g (30% of calories)
Carbohydrates: 261 g (57% of calories)

2. ASPECTS PECULIAR TO OLD PEOPLE

With age, a diminishing function of the digestive processes is observed:

a decrease in the various secretions, slight atrophy of the digestive mucous membranes, a decreased intestinal activity. This explains why the old person, whose absorption and assimilation processes are less efficient, is more sensitive to an unbalanced or inadequate diet. It also emphasizes the necessity of providing dishes and preparations which are easily digested and of sufficient volume to avoid constipation.

On the other hand, the teeth of old people are rarely complete and in good order. Absence of some of the teeth, or the wearing of a clumsy or ill-fitting denture, may cause inefficient chewing with all its consequences for the digestive system. This difficulty in mastication can also give rise to alimentary unbalance, as it leads to the almost exclusive consumption of soft foods which are often constipating or inadequate.

Two other conditions well known to those who deal habitually with old people should also be mentioned: a prolonged loss of appetite or the reverse, bulimia. Both are equally tiresome and must be watched for.

2.1. DIETS

This question is obviously more likely to arise in a community of old people than in a community of adults. However, thoughtfully planned, varied, and balanced food which is relatively poor in fats and is easily digested can be adapted to suit most cases.

The most common special diets are those for diabetics (which can be managed perfectly well with the foods used for a normal diet) and saltless diets.

2.2. ORGANIZATION OF MEALS

2.2.1. *Kitchen Premises and Equipment*

We shall not spend much time on this question. The organization of the kitchen and its annexes and stores should be that of any community of healthy people and should be based on the number of inmates (generally speaking, old people's homes only cater for small or medium numbers, which makes organization easier).

We shall, on the other hand, devote more time to questions connected with the distribution of meals.

2.2.2. Number and Times of Meals

Meals must not be too copious, so that they do not require too much work from the digestive system. It is therefore preferable to plan for more and smaller meals. A light meal in the afternoon is very appropriate —it can be used to help balance out the other meals and it makes an agreeable break in the day.

Supper should not be served too early because the evenings are long for poor sleepers. It must be easily digested but sufficient to avoid heaviness or nocturnal hunger pangs, both prejudicial to sleep which is already easily broken.

At all meals the service should be relatively slow: old people, like young children, need more time to eat.

2.2.3. The Dining Room

One should aim at recreating a calm, comfortable family atmosphere for meals. The room should be light and agreeably decorated. It does not cost much to paint the walls in gay colours, put up photos or posters, provide a floor-covering which cuts down noise, and a few flowers or green plants—no more, in any case, than the cost of equivalent noisy or gloomy installations.

Small tables seating a maximum of six to eight people (round or oval if possible) are cosier than large ones. They allow the inmates to form groups by affinity. It must be understood that the places are not necessarily fixed and that they can be changed around from time to time. Similarly, if the numbers are large it is better to arrange for two adjacent dining rooms than one large refectory.

The tables should have cloths of ordinary material if laundry presents no problem; otherwise of plasticized material.

Each pensioner must have a table napkin and a knife, fork, and spoon which he finds ready at his place when he sits down to eat.

The service should be calmly carried out, and must include provisions for elementary comfort which are really nothing more than marks of respect: careful presentation of the dishes; plates changed at least once during the meal (between savouries and dessert) and preferably between each course. It is a good idea for a responsible person to act as mistress of the household in the dining room, ensuring that everyone has enough to eat—and not too much, encouraging feeble appetites and checking personal tastes.

2.2.4. The Problem of the Disabled

This cannot be passed over. The crippled, the paralysed, the haemiplegic, the bedridden—there are many in a home for old people who either cannot come to table or are unable to feed themselves (or can do so only with difficulty).

For these, special equipment must be provided: a table for the bed or at least a tray on wheels, unbreakable plates and cups, and a device to hold their table napkin in place, and they must be helped to eat.

However, meals taken in bed should be reduced to a minimum (the unwell, the totally paralysed, and some haemiplegics). To make old people get up for meals is to render them a service, for doing so regularly develops the appetite and cuts down the chance of their becoming bedridden.

2.2.5. Staff

The needs here are those of any community, with special attention to the serving of the less able, which we have just discussed, and which may occupy several people at mealtimes.

When the community is not very sizeable, a good cook is just as satisfactory as a "chef" so long as she has the necessary authority over the kitchen staff.

It is always possible to ask some of the pensioners, approaching them with all necessary tact, to take on some of the lighter work, perhaps in exchange for payment: tasks like plucking poultry, laying the table, and attending to the flowers in the dining room.

The dietist also has her place in an old people's home. If the home is too small to necessitate a resident dietist or is unable to support one, attendance once or twice weekly would suffice for the planning of balanced menus suited to the greatest number, the study of individual diets, advice and encouragement for those of the inmates in need of it, and more continuous training of the personnel.

3. PLANNING THE MENUS

We have already considered much of the content of these menus. Let us state once more that each of the two main meals should include:

> a dairy product (cheese or milk in some form);

Sample Menus for One Week

Breakfast
1. Sweetened flavoured milk (0.200 l).
   Bread or rusks; butter; jam.
   alternating with
2. Sweetened milk and cereals.
   Fresh or stewed fruit.

Other Meals

Breakfast	Lunch	Snack	Supper
1	Raw vegetable Tongue and tomato sauce Pasta Coffee, cream	Dry biscuits Fruit juice	Vegetable soup with vermicelli Cauliflower cheese Salad Stewed prunes
2	Tomato salad Cod *meunière* Buttered carrots Cheese	Vanilla cream (1 small pot)	Chervil soup with milk Fried egg Mashed potatoes Fruit
1	Sliced radishes with cream Minced steak Creole rice *Petits suisses*	Tartlet Fruit juice	Cream of lettuce soup with milk Cheese tart Mixed vegetables Fruit salad
2	Grated carrots with lemon Beef stew and vegetables Yoghurt	Flavoured milk Dry biscuits	*Consommé* with tapioca Stuffed tomatoes Individual rice moulds Fruit
1	Leeks *vinaigrette* Fillet of whiting with bechamel sauce Braised lettuce Fruit	Madeleine cakes Fruit juice	Thick tomato soup Omelette with croutons Salad Semolina pudding
2	Grated cabbage with lemon juice Escalopes Roast potatoes Cottage cheese	Rice pudding with jam	Julienne soup Ham Spinach with white sauce Fruit
1	Cheese straws Leg of lamb Haricots princesse Strawberry ice	Fruit juice	Leek and potato soup Macaroni cheese Salad Creme caramel

Note: these menus only represent examples adapted to French eating habits.

a protein food (meat, fish, eggs, or a dairy product in greater quantity);

raw fruit or vegetable (entree, salad, or fruit) which is easy to chew;

a vegetable dish, which should be either a green vegetable or a farinaceous vegetable (potatoes, pasta, rice, or dried vegetables), both types being served every day.

Protein foods of high biological value are often expensive. It is therefore necessary to be able to choose the less expensive ones which are, nevertheless, of equivalent value, in order to give sufficient protein intake without exceeding the budget. These are:

minced meat, cuts for slow cooking;
fish;
eggs;

which are better value than grilling or roasting meat. Dishes based on dairy products (gratins and various puddings) are especially valuable because of their low price, soft texture, and nutritive value. It cannot be said too often that menus must be varied. The same menu should not be repeated for several weeks (never less than three) and must never be served on the same day of the week. It is so simple to make a change, even by altering one or two of the components.

An effort should also be made in honour of special occasions: Sundays, holidays, and in smaller homes even individual birthdays and anniversaries.

Old people's homes are, indeed, for many of their inmates the only, and probably the last, family home. We should therefore do our utmost to ensure them as much joy and comfort as possible in every way, and we know the importance of food in this respect.

PART 2. ALIMENTATION IN HOSPITALS

Alimentation in hospitals is surely the most complex of all forms of collective alimentation. There are requirements specific to hospitalization. The recipients are all, in some degree, patients for whom their food is one of the main contributory factors in a rapid cure.

We know that a balanced diet is indispensable for a good state of general health. It also plays a part in resistance to infection. Moreover, in many illnesses dietetics has come to be an essential part of the treatment whether in correcting a metabolic disorder, remedying faulty nutrition—

including obesity, helping scar formation, or speeding up convalescence. In all cases, food is an integral part of the patient's comfort, whose psychological importance is no longer in question.

It seems, nevertheless, that the feeding of hospital patients is not the object of as much consideration as could be wished. The main faults are:

- the food does not correspond to the patients' real needs;
- it does not take account of their tastes or habits;
- it is monotonous;
- it is badly presented.

These facts are all the more regrettable as they mean that some or all part of the meal served is not eaten by the patient, i.e. they lead to waste. Sums of money vainly spent in this way could, with the help of good organization, be used to the patient's real advantage.

4. THE BASIS FOR HOSPITAL ALIMENTATION

This is formed by the theoretical diets, the type of diets from which the menus are made.

As the alimentation of the young is considered elsewhere, we shall not consider paediatric problems here, but simply the alimentation and diets of the adult patient.

5. THE NORMAL DIET

This forms the basis for hospital alimentation. It must be carefully compiled because from it, by suitable modifications, all possible applicable diets are derived in their final form.

Most hospital patients do not need a special diet, or need one only during a part of their stay in hospital. Nevertheless we should not forget that this 'normal' food is intended for *patients in bed* or patients getting a minimum of physical activity, living in a comfortable atmosphere at a constant temperature. It is nonsensical to base the 'normal' diet of a hospital patient, as is too often done, on the normal food of an active, healthy person.

5.1. CALORIE INTAKE

Taking into account the considerable drop in energy expenditure of a hospital patient, an energy intake slightly greater than that of the basic metabolism-2000 to 2200 Calories-would seem to be sufficient (on condition, of course, that the proposed food is in fact eaten). This intake should be correctly divided between three main dietary principles according to the classical plan:

Proteins: 12–15% of total calorie intake.
Fats: 25–30%.
Carbohydrate: 55–60%.

5.2. PROTEIN INTAKE

Protein foods of animal origin with a high biological value should constitute slightly over half the protein intake. Among these, preference should be given to dairy products (milk, cheese, and milk derivatives) which ensure a sufficient ration of calcium besides the protein intake. The very wide range of milk products makes it possible to vary the food and suit individual taste. The cost price of dairy products is often lower than that of other protein foods.

5.3. VITAMIN INTAKE

A recent survey carried out by one of the authors of this chapter, compiling the results of vitamin analyses carried out in a general medical department in a hospital, showed a lowering of the average blood vitamin levels (principally ascorbic acid and to a lesser degree thiamine and cyanocobalamin), indicating at most a mediocre supply of vitamins. This lowering of the average implies really low levels for a large percentage of the hospital population. As we are concerned, moreover, with subjects weakened by illness and often fighting infection, it is especially important to ensure a sufficient or, indeed, a raised vitamin intake. Well-balanced menus and a judicious choice of foods will provide for this. It may in certain cases prove useful to add a multivitamin preparation.

Ascorbic acid: each meal must include a sufficient quantity of a carefully selected raw fruit or vegetable. Cooked green vegetables should be served at least once a day. The fresh or tinned juice of fruits rich in ascorbic acid (citrus fruits, tomatoes, etc.) is an excellent additional source, as well as being pleasant to drink.

Retinol: this can be provided by a small amount of fresh butter given daily (with breakfast, *hors d'oeuvre,* or cheese) and by regularly including liver in the menu (at least once every two weeks).

Vitamins of the B group: the application of the above principles—an adequate intake of foods of animal origin and fresh fruit and vegetables—should ensure a sufficient supply of these vitamins.

Nevertheless, there is some value in allowing a certain "safety margin" with the regular daily addition of 5 g of yeast to various dishes (soups, purees, pasta, etc.).

5.4. MINERAL INTAKE

We have already considered one of the most important of the minerals (calcium) which the various milk and dairy products must be regularly relied upon to supply. It is all the more necessary to ensure a sufficient intake as there is often a high percentage of old people in the adult wards of hospitals and, as will be seen from the chapter dealing specifically with alimentation in communities of old people, their need for calcium is greater as their absorption is inefficient.

Adjustments must also be made for special forms of treatment: for example, low sodium diets requiring the exclusion of foods naturally rich in sodium; restricted or, on the contrary, enriched potassium diets which must take account of such foods as carrots, dried fruit, bananas, and chocolate.

5.5. DRINKS

Water remains a basic necessity (1 ml/Cal). This intake can be in the form of ordinary water, mineral water, or more complex drinks:

skim milk, which has already been mentioned as a valuable source of protein and calcium;
fruit juice;
various infusions, broths, etc.

All these drinks should preferably be served in bottles or individual portions. They should always be supplied at a temperature which makes them enjoyable to drink. As for *alcoholic drinks,* several attitudes can be envisaged:

They can be categorically forbidden; this is surely the most effective way of preventing their all-too-frequent abuse.
They may be given to the patients in moderate quantities ($\frac{1}{4}$ to $\frac{1}{3}$ litre of wine per day at 9° or 10°).
Small quantities of good quality wines may be proposed in certain cases only.

The solution adopted will depend upon the system of hospitalization (single or shared rooms), the diseases being treated, and the social background of the patients as much as on the local customs. In any case, three essential points must be respected:

> the system adopted must be followed strictly and without exceptions;
> it must be absolutely forbidden to bring alcohol in from outside;
> discreet but effective checks must be made on the rooms, cupboards, and bedside lockers, and a careful eye kept generally on all opportunities for deception.

5.6. THE CHOICE AND PREPARATION OF FOODS

Even when there are no special difficulties in this respect, lying in bed slows down the digestive processes. Therefore the alimentation, while maintaining a certain standard of taste, must nevertheless exclude, or make only moderate or infrequent use of foods and preparations which are difficult to digest:

> pork, pork products, and fat meat;
> strong-tasting vegetables (cabbage, onions, etc.);
> dried vegetables;
> cooked fats, very elaborate sauces, chipped potatoes, and fried foods;
> strongly fermented cheeses.

The foods must always be of unexceptionable quality and must conform to the strictest criteria of hygiene.

5.7. SCHEDULING OF MEALS

We shall study the question of timetables in connection with the distribution of meals later. We should like to point out now that it is necessary to provide three main meals, including a breakfast which should be as substantial as possible, taking local habit into account.

If need be, one or two snacks can be added to these main meals for patients whose appetite is feeble or erratic, or when a supplemented diet is necessary. These may be given in the morning, in the afternoon, or before going to sleep at night.

6. THE MAIN TYPES OF DIET

Type diets must be planned in relation to the 'normal' diet. It is taking this normal diet as a basis that additions or subtractions are determined which will adapt the alimentation to needs modified by illness. Whatever change is made, and especially when items are removed, it is essential to ensure that balance is maintained in order to avoid possible deficiencies. The main types are:

6.1. RESTRICTIVE DIETS

These will include smaller quantities of one or several elements of the normal diet. The principal ones are:

6.1.1. *Low Calorie Diets*

These rarely go below 600 Cal; restrictions are mainly on foods containing fat and carbohydrate. The essential nutriments must be provided in sufficient quantity: proteins (selecting the least-fat sources), vitamins, mineral salts. A low calorie diet is relatively high in protein. Normal rates of salt and water intake are maintained in most cases.

6.1.2. *Low Calorie Diets*

Apart from special diets used in certain acute cases, total suppression of protein foods cannot be envisaged, and the minimum need (0.20–0.25 g/kg of weight) must be supplied. Therefore the protein ration is rarely taken below 20–30 g per 24 h according to the weight of the subject and the seriousness of the illness under treatment.

LOW PROTEIN DIETS

Foods strictly rationed and often excluded	Foods which can be used *ad libitum*
Eggs, milk (preferably to be kept on, as these proteins are the most easily digested) Meat, offal, pork products, and poultry Fish and sea-foods, cheese Bread, dried vegetables Cakes, pastries, biscuits, etc.	Green vegetables, salads, fruits (except dried fruits) Jam, sugar, honey, dextrose Oil, butter Potatoes, rice, protein-free pasta, starch, tapioca Sweets, toffees

These diets are as far as possible hypercaloric (low nitrogen value per calorie intake), therefore rich in carbohydrates and fats. Hypercaloric preparations of small volume are very useful when the appetite is small.

A check is often kept on the sodium intake.

6.1.3. *Low Fat Diets*

When planning these diets, it is necessary to remember that fats used in seasoning represent only a part of the fat intake. The majority is incorporated in the foods (milk, cheese, meat, fish, eggs, etc.). It is therefore necessary to select non-fatty protein foods. A sufficient supply of retinol must be ensured (liver).

6.1.4. *Restricted Sodium Diets*

In hospital practice, two types of sodium restriction can be envisaged:

- Low sodium diets (2–3 g of sodium) in which cooking salt, table salt, and pork products are excluded, and ordinary bread replaced by bread made without salt.
- Strictly sodium-free diets (300 mg of sodium) in which, as well as the above restrictions, less apparent sodium sources (ordinary milk, cheese, preserves, biscuits, cakes and pastries, sweets, and vegetables naturally rich in sodium) are also excluded and replaced as far as possible by sodium-free foods which otherwise possess the same nutritional value (milk without sodium, saltless preserves, etc.). (Table 1).

Special care must be taken when preparing these diets to keep them as tasty as possible (by the use of spices and condiments and carefully selected cooking methods).

6.1.5. *Carbohydrate Restricted Diets*

The total exclusion of carbohydrates from the diet leads to acidosis through overproduction of ketone bodies (at the expense of fats, which are burnt in too great a quantity). Therefore the carbohydrate intake is never taken below 80–100 g/day. Except in cases of obesity, where this minimum intake is maintained, most low carbohydrate diets have a daily rate of about 150 g. Lastly, in the case of more or less marked faulty nutrition (wasting diabetes) or increased requirements due to a physiological state (growth, pregnancy) or a pathological state (associated

TABLE 1 RESTRICTED SODIUM DIETS

Food excluded for			Staple foods of the diet
Diet with 2–4 g Na (1)	Diet with 700–1000 mg Na (2)	Diet with 250–500 mg Na (3)	
Kitchen salt Table salt Ordinary bread Pork products Salt foods Smoked fish and meat	As for (1) plus: Offal (except liver occasionally) Preserved foods of all kinds (fruit, vegetables, meat, fish, jam, fruit-juice, etc.) Lithia water, mineral waters (except Vittel, Evian, Volvic, Contrexeville, Charrier). Cube and packet soups. Oysters; molluscs; crustaceans Ordinary milk: 0.350 l/day maximum. Cheese: 20 g/day	As for diets, (1) and (2) plus: Ordinary milk—to be replaced by saltless milk Cheese and yoghurt Dried fruits, oleaginous fruits Commercially made cakes and pastries Commercially made biscuits Pastries made with baking powder Confectionery Instant desserts and breakfast foods Salted butter, margarine Animal fat. Radishes, turnips, beetroot, salsify, dandelion, cress, spinach, sorrel, red cabbage, sauerkraut, celery, rhubarb, melon, chestnuts	Fresh meat Fish Saltless breads and rusks Green vegetables containing no sodium Fresh fruit and fruit juice Potatoes, pasta, rice, dried vegetables Butter, oil Home-made jam, home-made pastries without baking powder Egg (care should be taken with white of egg) Sodium, free milk Saltless preserves.

tuberculosis), the rate, although restricted, is higher (200 or even 300 g).

Among carbohydrate sources, two must be given priority: citrus fruits rich in ascorbic acid, and milk rich in calcium. The other foods should only be used to complement these.

Carbohydrate content of the principal foods

- 3% Cucumber, marrow, spinach, tomato, lettuce, asparagus, chard, celery.
- 5% Milk.
- 6% Whole artichoke, aubergine, green cabbage, cauliflower, haricot beans, turnip, melon, pumpkin, grapefruit.
- 8% Lemon, strawberry.
- 9% Beetroot, Brussels sprouts, carrots, celeriac, onions, leeks.
- 10% Peaches.
- 12% Artichoke hearts, salsify, apricots, raspberries, gooseberries, mandarine, oranges, plums.
- 15% Nectarine, cherry, clementine, pear, apple.
- 18% Peeled pineapple, fresh figs, grapes.
- 20% Potatoes, cooked pasta, cooked rice, cooked dried vegetables, fresh shelled peas and haricot beans, bananas.
- 50% and over: Dried and oleaginous fruits.
- 55% Bread.
- 75% Rusks.
- over 75%: Biscuits, pastries, confectionery, chocolates, jams, honey.
- 100% Sugar.

Equivalents

Vegetables: 100 g of vegetables with 20% carbohydrate can be replaced by:
- 300 g of vegetables at 6%.
- 200 g of vegetables at 9%.
- 150 g of vegetables at 12%.
- 35 g of bread.

Fruit: 100 g of fruit with 12% carbohydrate can be replaced by:
- 150 g of fruit at 8%.
- 120 g of fruit at 10%.
- 80 g of fruit at 15%.
- 70 g of fruit at 20%.

In the case of diabetics undergoing insulin treatment, it is necessary to

6.2. SUPPLEMENTED DIETS

6.2.1. *High Protein Diets*

High protein diets for the adult are those in which the protein intake is from 1.5 to 2 g/kg of weight. They are for the most part also high calorie diets, implying an increased intake of carbohydrates and fats. In the case of the latter, it is necessary to take account of the fats already present in the principal protein foods. In fact the quantity of fats used as seasoning will only be slightly increased.

Where appetite is lacking, one may fall back on so-called "enriched" products yielding a higher protein intake for the same small volume (e.g. milk enriched by skim milk).

6.3. DIETS WITH A SPECIAL TEXTURE

These are indicated in cases where chewing and swallowing are difficult, or in certain more or less painful diseases of the digestive tract.

6.3.1. *Roughage-free Diets*

These are intended to lessen the secretions and the activity of the digestive tract by limiting the mechanical, physical, and chemical stimulation caused by food. This implies a selection of:

- foods and preparations which are bland and therefore cause a minimum of digestive secretions (dairy products are useful here);
- foods and preparations which are not very irritant (this means the exclusion of raw fruit and vegetables, cooked fats, and very sweet preparations).

Care must be taken to maintain sufficient quantity and variety of foods, and also an adequate ascorbic acid intake (strained juice of citrus fruits to be given once a day). A summary is given in Table 2.

6.3.2. *Liquid Diet*

This is intended to restore and maintain the nutritional state of patients

TABLE 2 ROUGHAGE-FREE DIET

Basic foods of diet	Possible cooking methods, etc.	To be excluded
Milk and yoghurt		
Fresh cheese, hard cheese		Fermented cheese
Lean meat and poultry, liver	Grilled, roast, boiled, minced	Fat meat, or served high or with a sauce. Pork products
Non-oily fish	Grilled, baked, in its own stock	Oily fish, fish served fried or with a sauce; crustaceans and molluscs
Eggs	Boiled, hard, soft, poached, in puddings and pastries	Omelettes, fried eggs
Bread	Stale, toast, rusks.	Fresh bread, wholemeal bread
Potatoes	Most	Chipped, sauteed, or served in stews
Pasta, rice, tapioca, refined cereals		
Flour		
Dry biscuits, pastries		Cream
Fresh, cooked vegetables	Boiled, mashed, in soup	Dried vegetables, strong tasting vegetables (cabbage, cauliflower, onion, celery, sauerkraut); raw vegetables
Fresh fruit	Very ripe, peeled, cooked fruit, strained fruit-juice (preferably not on an empty stomach)	
Oil and butter	Uncooked or very slightly warmed	Other kinds of fats, all cooked fats, sauces, fried foods and mayonnaise
Sugar (care should be taken with jam and very sweet preparations)		Alcohols, aperitifs, spices, strong tea and coffee

who are unable to take solid foods, as a result either of:

particular difficulties in swallowing and chewing, or
severe anorexia.

It must provide all the nutritive elements which would have been provided by solid food suited to the state of the patient, and must respect the same precautions and exclusions.

In spite of the special form in which they are given, meals must be as varied as possible. In the case of anorexia, enriched preparations may be used.

6.3.3. Drip Feeding

This is resorted to when all forms of oral feeding prove impossible. Like the liquid diet, it must constitute the strict equivalent of the solid foods required by the patient's state.

It is essential that these diet types be thoroughly studied and standardized. However paradoxical it may appear at first sight, it is only by this basic organization that maximum individualization can be achieved. It makes it possible to harmonize the various menus and simplify the kitchen work—steps which are always accompanied by an improvement in the quality of the food served.

The mixture used for drip feeding must be completely smooth and homogeneous. The mixture shown in Table 3 must be prepared once each 24 h, and divided into 4 or 5 flasks of equal volume to be kept under refrigeration. Before each meal, the mixture is heated in a water bath to 37°C.

The liquid must be administered *slowly,* either with a funnel, or drop by drop. After each meal, the catheter is rinsed with fresh fruit juice or, possibly, vegetable broth. For some years now a number of dehydrated or freeze-dried industrial products have been available which are specially designed for drip feeding. These greatly simplify the work of preparation, and also mean that it is no longer necessary in the hospital departments where this type of feeding is frequently needed (such as Ear-Nose- and Throat for example) to have massive refrigeration space available. These products also allow better standards of hygiene.

7. KITCHEN PREMISES AND EQUIPMENT

The standard diet is the basic blueprint from which the various menus

TABLE 3 AN EXAMPLE OF A DIET FOR DRIP FEEDING AT 2200 CAL

Foods	Quantities	Protein g	Fat g	Carbohydrate g	Cal
Whole milk	0.500 l	17.5	17	25	325
Powdered skim milk	50 g	17.5	—	25	175
Homogenized meat	150 g	27	15	—	245
Eggs	1 yolk	3.5	6	—	65
Malted flour	150 g	12	3	127	585
Dextrose	70 g	—	—	70	280
Homogenized vegetables	300 g	6	—	18	95
Oil	30 g	—	30	—	270
Saline	1 soup spoon				
Yeast	1 soup spoon				
Vegetable broth	Q.S.P. 2 l				
Total		83.5	71	265	2040
For rinsing:					
Fruit juice	0.400 l	3.5	—	48	205
Total		87	71	313	2245

are compiled. But other factors of hospital organization will also affect them. We should like to discuss the installations: kitchen premises and equipment.

Only well-planned kitchens, suitably equipped, with carefully studied work and distribution circuits will allow the patients' food to be served under optimum conditions and (it should be emphasized) at the lowest cost. Of course if it is a question of adapting old premises, one must make the best of existing conditions. However, one all too often sees the same (avoidable) mistakes being repeated in new buildings. It would be highly desirable in either case for the architects to be assisted by qualified staff (chefs and dietists), and for a detailed study to be made *before* building. Indeed, although in an old hospital one is obliged to adapt the service of meals to the possibilities of the existing installations, new installations should be set up considering the best possible service of meals.

We have no space for a detailed consideration of these questions. We simply wish to demonstrate the close relationship between the different stages from the time when the provisions are received to their presentation to the patient—relationships too often passed over. We shall attempt to isolate the principal points which have occupied the specialists and put forward the solutions they have envisaged. One idea in this field, which has appeared within the last few years and seems to us of particular interest, is the new equipment designed specifically for large-scale catering, which provides a solution to many tricky problems (speed of preparation, quality of taste, distribution temperature, and lack of staff). We shall study successively the questions raised by distribution, preparation, and stores.

7.1. DISTRIBUTION

We shall begin this brief study with distribution because, as we have already emphasized, it is distribution which determines (or ought to determine) the operations preceding it.

7.1.1. *Times of Meals*

We have already shown the necessity of providing three main meals (breakfast, lunch, and supper). Timetables will be adapted to local habits, but two points remain essential:

> The patient must be given a sufficient time for each of these meals (three quarters of an hour at least).

The meals must be correctly spaced so that appetites remain good and so that supplementary snacks can be added in the morning or the afternoon if need be.

The staff timetables must be drawn up to fit in with the times when the patients are served; all too often this is not the case.

Meal-times should be times of pleasure and relaxation, to which the service should contribute (pleasant attitude of staff, help for patients who have difficulty in feeding themselves, attractive presentation of dishes, etc.) just as much as the quality of the food.

7.1.2. Where to serve Meals

A dining-room can be envisaged for serving meals. This would be difficult to do in a general hospital, but would, on the contrary, be desirable in nursing homes, convalescent homes, and sanatoriums. In a hospital, meals are distributed in the rooms or wards, the patient taking his meal in bed or at a nearby table. Thus there is a need to bring the meal to the consumer, although in all other cases the opposite (consumer-meal) applies, and this affects distribution problems.

It is in the place where he spends his day that the hospital patient must be provided with the maximum degree of comfort to eat his meal (special table for the bed or large tray on legs, with an extra pillow for support, or a suitable table and a chair of suitable height). Bandages, basins, and other objects not compatible with eating a meal must be removed from the room.

7.1.3. Distribution

The patient must receive his share of the food which has been prepared in bulk. The food must be served to him at a suitable temperature and pleasantly presented. This individualization can be achieved in several ways.

(a) *In the presence of the patient* by serving him on request as much as he wishes of the foods which are taken around in heat-retaining vessels or heated trolleys. Unfortunately, the patient does not always choose a balanced diet, and an adviser at this point would slow down a service which is already slow. Most special diets have to be served separately (double service). Less care can be taken with presentation, and it is more difficult to calculate quantities in advance.

(b) *In pantries attached to the wards* where individual trays are made up according to slips distributed from the kitchen or filled in by the patient from the hot and cold foods prepared in the central and dietetic kitchens. This structure is more economical, and the distribution is quicker and better adapted to its purpose. However, the number of stages of preparation is increased.

(c) *In the central kitchen itself* provided that equipment is available which can fully preserve the quality of the food as well as an adequate system of stacking and loading trolleys. The new materials (plastic) and the improvements in the old materials (aluminium, stainless steel, and porcelain) combine to provide individual trays which are light and pleasing to the eye, and on which foods can always be kept at the optimum temperature without spoiling the taste (red meat, grilled food, chips); there are various systems available for doing this. When the number of patients is large and the layout of the hospital permits, distribution by conveyor belt allows individual trays to be served rapidly (500–600 trays per hour per distribution chain). Control is facilitated by a system of coloured markers and cards, so that the staff stationed along the conveyor belt can serve automatically. This system, which has evolved very recently, has many obvious advantages. Distribution is simple and rapid on the wards; it requires only a small staff; planning can be completely accurate, as the patients' slips are made out according to their diet, taste, and appetite. Far more care can be taken with presentation. By cutting out subsidiary kitchens, the number of times the food is handled is reduced and hygiene improved. But it is essential to have a central kitchen which is suitably equipped and can be adapted to the rhythm of chain distribution.

7.2. PREPARATION

Here we shall discuss the kitchen and its annexes (for vegetables, cakes, and pastry, and meat preparation).

7.2.1. *The Problem of the Number of Kitchens*

Should there be a single kitchen or several independent kitchens? For a long time the idea prevailed that the number of kitchens depended on the number of patients, the figure being put at one kitchen per 300–400 patients. This system, which was desirable for maintaining a certain standard of cooking, was inconvenient because it increased the necessary number of staff.

Today (and the future will emphasise this trend) the only reason for having more than one kitchen is the layout of the building (e.g. a hospital built in separate blocks) and the distribution circuits.

In fact, kitchen equipment has also become mechanized to an ever-increasing degree, making it possible to prepare food with regularity, and in quantities, which was not possible with traditional methods, and to reduced space. For example, it is possible to prepare 1200 portions of roast meat per hour per roasting chain, 2000 portions of steamed vegetables, etc., and all of an excellent quality.

These systems of continuous preparation can be run with a small staff and can feed a regular supply to the tray distribution chains.

7.2.2. *Relay Kitchens*

The necessity for these depends on the arrangement of the premises and on the distribution system. Their advantage is that they reduce the interval between the preparation of foods such as red meats and chips, and their consumption by the patient. Suitable distribution equipment and a rapid distribution system have made these relay kitchens unnecessary or, more precisely, they have incorporated them into the central kitchen, which is differently conceived, and where work circuits differ from the traditional ones. However, these modifications only affect the order of the operations. It goes without saying that the traditional rules for efficient organization of work (that operations must succeed one another in a logical order and without intersection) and food hygiene (the paths of clean food and supposedly dirty objects and foodstuffs should never intersect) remain valid.

7.2.3. *The Dietetic Kitchen*

Its size will depend upon the number and type of diets served in the hospital. The preparations used in most of the classical diets can perfectly easily be prepared in the central kitchen. With carefully studied basic diet types and well-planned menus, low carbohydrate diets, low calorie diets, and low fat diets can include some of the preparations used in the normal diet.

Saltless preparations, even when based on foods identical to those of the normal menu, enriched preparations, and liquid preparations, must be separately prepared. These processes can also be centralized.

Thus only the special diets remain: diets for dietary balance studies or allergy tests, diets which have to be weighed out exactly, those which are subject to variation almost daily (for gradual rehabilitation), those which exclude some particular element (gluten, phenylalanine, lactose, etc.), and mixtures for drip feeding. In a general hospital these constitute only 10% of the alimentation. These diets, too, can be centrally prepared, in a place either within the central kitchen itself or immediately adjacent, so as to derive maximum benefit from chores already carried out elsewhere (plucking, pre-cooking, etc.).

With preparation, maximum centralization should preferably always be the rule. This cuts down the number of manipulations and the number of food circuits, and thus the risk of contamination on the one hand and wastage on the other. Supervision is easier, as operations are less scattered. Thus the staff requirements are smaller.

7.3. SUPPLIES

These should also be taken into consideration and sufficient storage space reserved to allow more advantageous buying and correct storage conditions.

Storage should include, notably, cold chambers whose volume, temperature, and equipment should be compatible with keeping the food under the best conditions of hygiene and making full use of modern processes such as deep-freezing (of commercial products or the hospital's own).

7.4. CLEARING UP EATING UTENSILS

Cutlery and crockery must not return to the kitchen dirty; their path must not intersect that of clean eating utensils. They must go direct to a purpose-built washing-up scullery where they must be carefully washed, disinfected, and rinsed (the available chain equipment is also of great value in carrying out these operations).

The detergents must be carefully selected for their lack of toxicity and must be carefully measured out. It is up to those responsible for hospital alimentation (and alimentation in general) to obtain from the manufacturers instructions clearly understandable by the washing-up staff about the use of these products and the quantities needed. These products, like all other maintenance products, must be kept apart in order to eliminate any risk of their being mistaken for food products. Rinsing must be absolutely thorough. The washing-up staff must be made well aware of their responsibilities, and checks must be carried out regularly. When they come to the patient, the crockery and cutlery must be in a good state of repair and perfectly clean. Whenever possible, it is preferable to use "disposable" receptacles which are used only once (aluminium foil, disposable plastic).

8. STAFF

8.1. KITCHEN STAFF

It is not always possible to recruit a sufficiently large and capable staff. Nevertheless it is essential to include among the kitchen staff a certain number of professionally qualified personnel (chef and assistant chef, possibly butcher and pastry-cook).

Automatic equipment, if fully used, cuts down the necessary number of kitchen staff and removes the necessity for specialized training beforehand. However, staff must be capable of a certain degree of care and attention, must be perfectly disciplined, and work as a team.

8.2. DISTRIBUTION STAFF

It is best if distribution is not carried out by nursing staff who are already extremely busy with their own work. Purely on hygienic grounds, this task should not be assigned to them; it is not desirable to change bandages and tend the patients in a uniform worn while distributing meals, or vice versa. Meal-distribution staff should be a special section of the general food and kitchen staff. Systems based on distribution of individual trays cut down the necessary number of distribution staff, and do not require of them any skill except the ability to read a name or a number, or any quality other than to be clean and agreeable. Between meal times this staff can be occupied with other occasional jobs, such as washing up and putting away eating utensils, preparing cold foods, etc.

In the case of both kitchen and distribution staff it is essential to ensure a good state of health and a high standard of personal hygiene and to avoid direct contact between food and possible carriers of germs.

A possible basis for necessary checks is the French legal requirement that on employment, staff should undergo:

> chest X-ray and skin reaction to tuberculin (Mantoutest);
> examination for pathogenic staphylococcus in the nasopharynx and nostrils; examination of faeces for salmonella; parasitological

examination to detect vegetative and cystic forms of dysenteric amoebae are recommended.

These examinations must be repeated on return to work after sick leave and whenever intestinal infections of an epidemic character or with symptoms apparently due to staphylococcal *infection* appear in the hospital.

8.3. THE DIETIST

The dietist is a technician trained to deal with all the problems which arise out of providing a suitable diet, special or normal. These specialized staff made their appearance in the hospital team as soon as the importance of food in the treatment of disease was demonstrated.

The role of the dietist in hospital alimentation is threefold.

(a) *In the hospital department* she works with the medical team and the nursing staff. She knows the patient, his tastes, habits, dietary needs, and the form his diet may take. Being acquainted through her training with the requirements and possibilities of a collective kitchen, she can issue precise and appropriate orders to those concerned with preparing the food. She supervises the distribution and makes a check on anything left over.

(b) *In the preparation centres* she plans the standard diets, works out the normal menus and the diet menus together with the administrative manager, sees that they are correctly carried out, that the trays are satisfactorily prepared, and trains the staff. This twofold articulation ensures permanent contact between the prescription (medicine), the realization (kitchen), and the administration of the establishment. The dietist is indispensable in ensuring that medical prescriptions about diets—including actual consumption of the food by the patient—are fully carried out, and that the sums spent on the patients' food are used to full effect.

(c) *With the patient himself* her role is no less important. If he has to follow a diet, she explains to him the conditions and the necessity of the diet. Having followed his progress in hospital and acquainted herself, with the help of the dietetic questionnaire, with his tastes, habits, and living conditions at home and at work, she can establish and explain a post-hospital diet which fits in well with all these practical considerations.

Besides establishing a particular diet, she is also important in an educative capacity. She can point out bad feeding habits, explain them, and show how they can be remedied.

She exerts her influence not only upon the patient but also upon his circle of visiting friends and family, to whom she gives the necessary advice. It falls to her to keep a tactful eye upon food brought in from the outside—too often a source of unintended modifications to the diet or even of deliberate deception.

Thus, through the intermediary of the dietician, the medical treatment is carried out in the small details of the patient's everyday life. The questions dealt with, in spite of their practical importance, do not really fall within the province of the doctor, who must concern himself with more direct medical problems and who, even if he is a discerning gourmet and a notable gastronome, does not always possess the necessary information about day-to-day cooking and the family budget.

There are not always enough dietists available in hospitals. With the exception of metabolic units, it is always preferable when a sufficient number is lacking to concentrate their action centrally on the general menu and standard diets so as to ensure food corresponding to their needs for the greatest possible number of patients.

9. MENUS AND FOODSTUFFS

9.1. PLANNING MENUS

We shall conclude with this topic. It is, as we have seen, conditioned by all the preceding factors.

In all cases, the menu of the normal diet (a balanced diet compiled from easily digestible preparations) must be such as to supply most of the diet types with only a minimum of modifications. It must include some opportunities for choice in order to ensure adaptation to individual taste. Moreover, the study of and knowledge of these tastes can contribute to the orientation of menu planning.

The food must be varied, and the same menus must not be repeated at an interval of less than 3 weeks. It is true that the population of a hospital has a more rapid turnover than that of any other institution; nevertheless, certain illnesses or treatments necessitate prolonged or repeated stays in hospital. Moreover, monotony is never a sign of good food.

9.2. FOODSTUFFS—ADVANTAGES OF THE NEW TECHNIQUES

The main factor considered by the hospital when buying supplies must be their quality and their guarantee of hygiene. Progress in the food industry has, moreover, made sweeping improvements to hospital food.

Canned foods which, among their other advantages, ensure a maximum of variety out of season in the serving of green vegetables. Let us remember that these industrially prepared products have a considerable vitamin content.

Deep-freezing which allows food to be kept in perfect condition without salt and simplifies the consumption of perishable foodstuffs such as fish. Many hospital establishments already deep-freeze their own foods, either uncooked or in ready-cooked portions, which frees the staff for holidays and weekly days off, and ensures a safety margin in case of an unexpected increase in numbers.

Processed foods: skim milk, sodium-free milk, flour, and pasta without gluten, homogenized meat, and vegetables.

Special preparations: mixtures for drip-feeding.

The hospital today is able, in its various services of nursing, surgery, and intensive care, to draw upon the most modern and delicate techniques and the most highly qualified staff. It therefore owes it to itself to be as uncompromisingly modern in the alimentation of the patients and to make use, in this field also, of all the possibilities afforded by the most advanced techniques.

CHAPTER 8

SPECIAL FEEDING: SPORTS AND ATHLETICS, MOUNTAINEERING AND OTHER EXPEDITIONS

Martti J. Karvonen

Institute of Occupational Health, Helsinki, Finland

CONTENTS

1. Nutrition and Performance	372
1.1. Criteria for Performance Capacity	372
1.2. Body Energy Stores	373
1.2.1. Carbohydrate	373
1.2.2. Fat	375
1.3. Absorption and Utilization of Nutrients	375
1.4. Nutritional Requirements in Sports	378
1.4.1. Energy Expenditure	378
1.4.2. Carbohydrates and Fats	381
1.4.3. Proteins and Amino Acids	383
1.4.4. Vitamin and Mineral Supplementation	384
1.4.5. Water and Electrolytes	389
1.4.6. Food During Training	392
1.4.7. Food for Performance	393
1.4.8. Alcohol	395
2. Nutritional Balance and Performance	396
2.1. Expeditions in Temperate Climates	397
2.2. Cold Climates	399
2.1.1. Energy Requirements	400
2.2.2. Proportions of Nutrients	401
2.2.3. Skiing or Sledging Rations	404
2.2.4. Survival Rations	406
2.3. Hot Climates	407
2.3.1. Energy Expenditure	408
2.3.2. Proportion of Nutrients	409
2.3.3. Vitamins	409
2.3.4. Water and Electrolytes	409
2.3.5. Rations for Tropical Expeditions	409
3. Food for Sea Voyages	410
4. Altitude and Nutrition	410
5. Air and Space Flights	413
5.1. Aviation	413
5.2. Space Travel	414
References	417

1. NUTRITION AND PERFORMANCE
1.1. CRITERIA FOR PERFORMANCE CAPACITY

The two salient functions of nutrition are to sustain life and to supply fuel to the working human machine. In sports, man is performing at his maximum level, whether it be the maximum of strength, of speed, of power, of endurance, or even of skill.

A sports performance, when expressed in units of length, weight, or time, serves as a rather exact measure of some facet of the human performance capacity or of a combination of capacities. When trained athletes compete, this measure is not only exact, but often also reliable in the sense that the result varies little from time to time. In fact, the test–retest repeatabililily of sports performances may be superior to that attained in laboratory experiments. An exact and reliable measure gives an excellent possibility for studying the influence of various factors on human performance capacity. Running times are sensitive to changes in air pollution (Wayne et al., 1967), and may equally well be used as indicators of dietary effects.

The metabolic requirements of different sports show a wide spectrum. A rational way to classify sports is to divide them into three groups. One of them includes such performances which last from a few seconds up to 2 min, and are characterized by a rapid development of oxygen debt. The second group comprises such performances, generally from 2 to 3 min minimum duration, in which a metabolic steady state is achieved. The third group consists of endurance events of more than 30 min duration, in which metabolic changes gradually break the steady state (Christensen, 1958; Jakovlev, 1961).

Studies of dietary effects on performance have been carried out more often in the laboratory than on the sports field. The subjects have been tested for mechanical efficiency, for maximum aerobic or anaerobic power or for endurance on a bicycle ergometer or on a treadmill. Dynamometers have been used for measuring muscle strength and psychomotor tests for complex neuromotor functions. Another approach for studying the influence of diet is to look for deviations from the homeostasis of body chemistry, and to relate them to changes in performance capacity. Blood glucose, muscle and liver glycogen, blood free fatty acids, and ketone bodies are of obvious interest as sources of fuel to the working muscles and to the central nervous system, which directs and controls the human machine. Also other homeostatic mechanisms may become heavily taxed in some sports events, notably the water and electrolyte balance as affected by sweating.

In order to be able to perform, an athlete has to train. It is natural to ask whether the training process may be influenced by dietary measures. While adequate information has not been easily accessible, various fads have enjoyed popularity among some athletes and their coaches.

In the provision of food for expeditions, the functional requirements may vary between the extremes of keeping a parachuted pilot alive resting, up to supporting a mountaineer climbing Mount Everest. Recommendations have been based to a large part on empirical knowledge gained over centuries, but recently also on laboratory experimentation. Obviously, when testing survival rations for man, some criterion other than survival must be used as a basis for evaluation.

1.2. BODY ENERGY STORES

The resting man derives his energy from the oxidation of carbohydrate, fat, and protein. As man starts to work, he covers the increased energy expenditure by oxidizing more carbohydrate and fat, while the use of protein remains at the resting level. This basic observation was made a hundred years ago by von Pettenkofer and Voit (1866).

The maximum rate of the release of energy may be limited by the total amount of its immediate sources—adenosine triphosphate and creatine phosphate. Their total amount is too small to be considered in calculating the energy balance except in very short performances, in which they contribute to the alactic oxygen debt; this rises up to $4 l\, O_2$, corresponding to 20 Cal.

The other component of the oxygen debt is associated with the anaerobic breakdown of muscle glycogen into lactic acid. The maximum lactic phase of the oxygen debt is of the order of $8 l\, O_2$, equivalent to 40 Cal; it is individually variable and generally larger in athletes who practise sports with a marked anaerobic component.

1.2.1. *Carbohydrate*

Carbohydrate exists in the body as glucose and glycogen. The total amount of glucose in the extracellular space is approximately 10–15 g, which corresponds to 40–60 Cal only. The glycogen reserves are much larger. The average normal muscle glycogen content is some 1.6 g per 100 g wet tissue (Bergström and Hultman, 1966), but may rise up to 4 g per 100 g (Saltin and Hermansen, 1967). In exercise with large muscle groups, some two-thirds of the muscles of body, approximately 20 kg of muscle tissue, are involved. The maximum available muscle glycogen store would thus be $20 \times 4 \times 10 = 800$ g (Saltin and Hermansen). Previous investigators have reported maximum values of the order of 450–500 g (Hedman, 1951). In terms of aerobic energy, 500 g of glycogen corresponds to 2000 Cal, i.e. to an amount sufficient for 2 h at the realistic energy expenditure level of 15 Cal/min. In anaerobic work, however, lactic acid produced from glycogen yields only 0.25 Cal/g (Cerretelli et al., 1969).

Factors influencing the storage of carbohydrate have been studied by Saltin and Hermansen by using muscle biopsy. A change from mixed diet to a diet rich in carbohydrate increases the muscle glycogen content in 2 or 3 days up to approximately 2.5 g per 100 g muscle. Prolonged vigorous exercise, on the other hand, depletes the muscle glycogen. However, if man is subjected first to prolonged exercise with consequent depletion of muscle glycogen and subsequently to a carbohydrate diet, an overshoot phenomenon is observed, with muscle glycogen content reaching 3 g per 100 g muscle. The overshoot may further be increased by prolonging the antecedent depletion phase to 2 or 3 days with the aid of a fat–protein diet. The relations between the degree of muscle glycogen depletion, its duration, the supply of carbohydrate, and the time relations and level of the overshoot—which is limited to the exercised muscles—have recently been under intense study (e.g. **Hultman, 1967, 1969**).

In the human liver, the average glycogen content on a mixed diet is 100 g. Carbohydrate-rich meals may increase the glycogen content of the liver up to 10% of the liver weight, corresponding to a total of 180 g, i.e. to less than one-fifth of the body total maximum carbohydrate store.

The contribution of liver to the supply of glucose during heavy exercise (10–12 Cal/min) has been determined by Rowell et al. (1965). After a fast of 15–18 h, the average splanchnic glucose production was 0.3 g/min as against a resting level of approximately 0.1 g/min. At this intensity of exercise, the release of glucose from the splanchnic organs accounted for 10% of the total energy expenditure. While the contribution of liver to the total carbohydrate utilization is modest, it still plays a key role in the regulation of blood glucose, and hence of the supply of energy to the central nervous system.

Such total carbohydrate stores which may be readily mobilized in untrained subjects are limited to 100 or 200 g (Passmore and Swindells, 1963; Passmore, 1964). With a diet rich in carbohydrate, another 300–600 g could be added to the stores. With trained athletes higher values may be achieved.

1.2.2. Fat

Fat is the main energy store. One kilogram of fat is equivalent to 9000 Cal, and 1 kg of human fat tissue to approximately 7500 Cal. The amount of fat in the human body is very variable indeed; the Reference Man as defined for the purposes of assessing calorie requirements—(FAO, 1957) and weighing 65 kg has some 9 kg of fat in his body. Many people have more. At a daily energy expenditure of 3200 Cal, as assigned to the Reference Man, he could theoretically carry on some 25 days solely by utilizing his fat calories; or even longer, as his daily energy expenditure would diminish with the reduction of body weight.

The fat stores are mobilized for exercise. In protracted aerobic exercise, the main source of fat is the adipose tissue, and the intramuscular fat plays a secondary role (Paul and Issekutz, 1967; Issekutz and Paul, 1968). Rowell et al. (1965) have determined the contribution of liver to the lipid supply during exercise. While ketone bodies were released in the splanchnic vascular bed at the average rate of 0.02 g/min, there was no net supply of triglycerides and phospholipids, and an uptake of free fatty acids occurred at the average rate of 64 µm/min. The release of lipid substrate from the liver thus accounted for less than 5% of the total energy expenditure.

Training appears to have little effect on the fat content of muscles (Pařízková et al., 1966), although it generally tends to reduce the total fat content of the body (Behnke et al., 1942; Welham and Behnke, 1942; Pařízková, 1966). Swimming is an exception, and long-distance swimmers in particular have ample subcutaneous fat tissue (Pugh and Edholm, 1955). However, it does not serve primarily as an energy store but rather as thermal insulation, and increases the buoyancy.

1.3. ABSORPTION AND UTILIZATION OF NUTRIENTS

Indigestion is often reported by sportsmen, and vomiting may occur if a copious meal has been eaten a short time prior to the competition. It is of practical importance whether food eaten immediately before or during an endurance event can still be utilized for it in the normal way.

As presented in § 1.2, carbohydrate stores may become a limiting factor even in relatively short sports performances, within some 2 h, while a depletion of fat and protein is likely to limit the performance capacity only as a result of protracted starvation or malnutrition. The possibility of refilling or supporting the body carbohydrate stores during exercise thus assumes practical importance.

In experiments where the subjects exercised for 1 h at the rate of 64–78 % of their maximum oxygen uptake, the gastric emptying of a solution containing 13.3% glucose and 0.3% sodium chloride was found to be unaffected by the exercise (Fordtran and Saltin, 1967). The composition and amount of the solution had been selected to replace losses calculated for a similar exercise load. Fluid was drunk in portions of 150 ml at the start of the exercise and every 10 min.

At rest glucose may be absorbed from the intestine at the maximum rate of 120 g/h, corresponding to 8 Cal/min. The intestinal absorption of test solutions containing a non-absorbable marker has been studied during exercise by using a triple-lumen tube (Fordtran and Saltin, 1967). Neither in the jejunum nor in the ileum was the absorption of glucose, water, sodium chloride, potassium, or bicarbonate affected in any consistent way by the exercise.

Exercise may cause marked reduction in the portal blood flow. Rowell et al. (1964, 1966) have determined the splanchnic blood flow with the aid of the indocyanine green clearance at rest and up to maximum exercise. While the flow at rest was on an average 1.6 l/min, the flow rates recorded at various intensities of exercise ranged from 0.4 to 0.8 l/min.

Even if the reduction in splanchnic blood flow would restrict the absorptive capacity, it should be noted that in exercise at the rate of 15 Cal/min, with the supply of 50% of energy from carbohydrate, the absorption of glucose at half the normal rate could still cover approximately half of the need for carbohydrate.

The utilization of ingested sugar solutions has been studied by following the changes of the blood glucose and of the respiratory quotient (RQ) (Douglas and Koch, 1951). When 50 g of glucose was given in divided doses of 10 g at equal intervals during a 10-mile walk at the speed of 3.5 or 4 miles/h, both the blood glucose level and the RQ tended to remain unaltered and post-exercise ketonuria did not occur. These observations were interpreted to show that glucose intake increased the carbohydrate utilization during the exercise. However, if 60–70 g of glucose is ingested 70 min or immediately prior to the start of exercise, it remains without effect on the carbohydrate utilization.

The preferred substrate of the working muscle is, however, muscle glycogen, and the administration of glucose during performance is only able to retard moderately the depletion of muscle glycogen (Hultman, 1969). In experiments on fasted dogs, glucose or protein was unable to prolong running time in exhaustive treadmill work in spite of a rise in RQ (Young et al., 1960).

The experimental findings of Fordtran and Saltin contradict the results of some earlier studies, where more indirect evidence suggested that exercise might limit the absorption of nutrients in the gastrointestinal tract (Campbell *et al.*, 1928; Hellebrandt and Tepper, 1934; Williams *et al.*, 1964).

Glucose ingestion immediately prior to vigorous exercise may, after a primary rise of the blood glucose, occasionally be followed by a deep hypoglycaemic phase, with consequent symptoms and reduction of performance capacity (Bøje, 1936).

The regulation of the blood glucose level is intimately geared together with glycogen stores and gluconeogenesis in the liver. An increased concentration of glucose in the portal blood coming from the gastrointestinal tract to the liver causes an increased storage of glucose as liver glycogen, and vice versa. Insulin and other hormones are able to influence this basic mechanism. An essential feature is that the liver cells are not exposed to the arterial glucose level, as are the cells of the central nervous system and the insulin-secreting cells of the pancreas, but rather to the portal venous blood, in which the glucose level is affected by four factors:

(1) the arterial blood glucose level;
(2) the rate of absorption of glucose from the intestine;
(3) the rate of utilization of glucose by the organs from which the portal blood is derived;
(4) the portal blood flow.

Of these factors, the rate of absorption is obviously nil when no carbohydrate has been ingested.

A reduction of splanchnic blood flow evidently has divergent effects on the portal glucose level depending on the absorptive state. If no glucose is being absorbed, only utilization occurs in the gastrointestinal tract, and the portal blood glucose level becomes, during exercise, further decreased from the arterial level. On the other hand, during absorption, as the splanchnic flow is reduced relatively more than the rate of absorption, the portal glucose level becomes more elevated during exercise than at rest. When absorption occurs during exercise, the liver cells may thus be "fooled" into storing glucose as glycogen in spite of a relatively low level of glucose in the general circulation if no other regulatory mechanism interferes.

The discrepancy between changes in the rate of absorption and the portal flow may thus offer an explanation to some anomalies in the regulation of the blood glucose level during exercise.

In competitions lasting for several days, a weight loss is generally experienced. Similarly, in a competition of two full and two half working days of lumber work, the competitors ate more on the half days, the difference being 487 Cal/day (Karvonen and Turpeinen, 1954).

1.4. NUTRITIONAL REQUIREMENTS IN SPORTS

1.4.1. *Energy Expenditure*

The concept "sports" includes a wide variety of leisure activities; some of these are also being pursued as a profession. The energy expenditure in "sports" correspondingly shows a range from a level characteristic of sedentary activities to the maximum humanly attainable.

A substantial body of energy expenditure determinations in various sports activities exists. The results are based mostly on determinations of the oxygen uptake and carbon dioxide production. Gasometric methods are not applicable at "real" competitions and games. In protracted activities, like a football game, the average energy expenditure may be assessed from a rise of the body temperature; as the relation between energy expenditure and the rise of body temperature is individually variable, each subject should be "calibrated", e.g. with the aid of work carried out on an ergometer at different loads. Similarly, a telemetrically recorded heart rate may serve as an indirect measure of the energy expenditure. Again, individual calibration is required.

Some sports events last only a few seconds, and the required energy may be obtained entirely anaerobically. With performances lasting a few minutes both the aerobic and anaerobic energy supplies play an important role. If the exercise lasts longer than 5 min, even the maximum energy available from anaerobic processes becomes proportionally unimportant. Table 1 gives a selection of published energy expenditure figures without, however, any claim for completeness.

In sports activities lasting 2 h the maximum energy expenditure may reach twenty times the basal level. For 4 min, up to fifty times the basal metabolic rate (BMR) may be expended. In a sports performance lasting less than a minute, the expenditure may be up to 200 times higher than the BMR (Seliger, 1968).

The energy cost of horizontal locomotion by running is about twice as high, approximately 1 Cal/kg/km as that of walking at the most economical speed of 4 km/h. A nomogram has been constructed for calculating the energy expenditure of running at different speeds and inclines (Margaria *et al.*, 1963).

Special Feeding

TABLE 1 ENERGY EXPENDITURE IN SPORTS
Values refer approximately to a man (M) weighing 65 kg or
to a woman (F) weighing 55 kg

Activity	Cal/min	Source
Duration 5 min or longer		
Archery	3.2–5.7	Covell et al., 1965; Edholm et al., 1955
Badminton	6.3	Widdowson et al., 1954
Basketball, M	9.0	Widdowson et al., 1954
	14.3	Seliger, 1968
Bowling, M	4.1	Garry et al., 1955
Canoeing, 8.3 km/h, M	8.4	Seliger, 1968
Circuit training	12	Durnin and Passmore, 1967
Cricket		
Batting	5–7	Fletcher, 1955
Bowling	5–8	
Cross-country running		
10.6–14.0 km/h, M	12.8–13.9	Heinonen, 1965
9.9–11.1 km/h, F	8.1–10.4	
Cycling		
3.5 km/h, M	2.5	Gräfe, 1957
8.5 km/h, M	3.3	Gräfe, 1957
10 km/h, M	6.1	Gräfe, 1957
20 km/h, M	8.6	Gräfe, 1957
Figure skating		
M	13.0	Seliger, 1968
F	10.4	Seliger, 1968
Football game, M	5–12	Durnin and Passmore, 1967
	11.7	Seliger, 1968
Golf, M	4–7	Durnin and Passmore, 1967
Gymnastics, army, M	2.5–6.5	Kennedy, 1933
Hockey	8.7	Malhotra et al., 1962
Horse riding		Geldrich, 1927
Walking	3.0	
Trotting	8.0	
Galloping	10.0	
Judo	14.6	Passmore and Draper, 1964
Rowing		
3.3 km/h, M	4.7	Liljestrand and Stenström, 1920
5.4 km/h, M	13.1	Liljestrand and Stenström, 1920
Running		
8 km/h, M	8.1	Gräfe, 1957
12 km/h, M	10.1	Gräfe, 1957
14.3 km/h, M	15.4	Klotschkow and Wassiljewa, 1934
Skating		
12.2 km/h, M	6.9	Liljestrand and Stenström, 1920
22.0 km/h, M	11.9	Liljestrand and Stenström, 1920
Skiing		
Cross-country,		
4.2 km/h, M	6.8	Christensen and Högberg, 1950

TABLE 1 (Cont'd)

Activity	Cal/min	Source
Cross-country, 14.7 km/h, M	22.1	Christensen and Högberg, 1950
Squash rackets, M	10.1–18.2	Durnin and Passmore, 1967
Table tennis, M	3.6–5.2	Covell et al., 1965
		Widdowson et al., 1954
	5.2	Seliger, 1968
Tennis	5.7–8.5	Edholm et al., 1955
Volley ball, M	3.5	Pollack et al., 1944
	6.5	Seliger, 1968
Duration 2–5 min		
Boxing, M		Seliger, 1968
Punching-bag	21	
Match	15.0	
Ice hockey, M	38	Seliger, 1968
Kayak-paddling		Seliger, 1968
500 m race, M	29	
500 m race, F	14.9	
Running, 19.5 km/h, M	37.5	Gräfe, 1964
Skiing, downhill		
M	7.2–11.2	Eigelsreiter and Schröcksnadel, 1966
F	9.3	
Sport gymnastics, F		Seliger, 1968
Parallel bars	7.7	
Balancing beams	6.0	
Horse	8.2	
Duration 1 sec–2 min		
Football, M		
Shooting	24	Seliger, 1968
Centre	21	
High jump, M	96	Seliger, 1968
Javelin throw, M	76	Seliger, 1968
Long jump, M	101	Seliger, 1968
Running, 24 km/h, M	92	Jakovlev, 1953
Shot put, M	114	Seliger, 1968
Weight-lifting, M		Seliger, 1968
Press	50	
Snatch	52	
Jerk	44	

In many sports events the oxygen transport is the limiting factor for the performance. In such a situation it is of importance that the energy value of a litre of oxygen is not identical for all foodstuffs. It is highest, 5.05 Cal/l, on a carbohydrate diet, 4.69 Cal/l on a fat diet, and 4.46 Cal/l on a protein diet. A carbohydrate diet thus may be expected to give the best performance in all such events where aerobic metabolism plays a decisive role.

1.4.2. *Carbohydrates and Fats*

During exercise, the increase of energy expenditure above that at the resting level is paid off by the utilization of carbohydrate and fat. The contribution of each fuel may be assessed by studying the RQ, i.e. the ratio of carbon dioxide produced to oxygen used in the respired air. When carbohydrates alone are used, RQ = 1.00; with fat alone, RQ = 0.7. The average resting RQ, 0.8, corresponds to the use of a mixture of both, with one-third of the calories derived from carbohydrate and two-thirds from fat. For accurate calculations, the oxidation of protein should also be considered; the RQ for protein is 0.8. At rest, approximately 10–15% of the total calories are obtained from protein. However, as the oxidation of protein does not increase during exercise, its share becomes relatively smaller when the total energy expenditure is increased. At the expenditure levels observed in many sports, above 10 Cal/min, protein may contribute only 1% of the total calories.

The relative contribution of carbohydrate and fat in exercise depends on factors such as the intensity of exercise, exercise capacity of the subject, the size of muscles used, the duration of the exercise, the carbohydrate stores, and/or supply available. With adequate carbohydrate stores, the transition from rest to moderate exercise causes no change in the RQ: the mixture of fuel used remains the same. However, if the exercise is intense, the RQ rises, indicating an increased contribution of carbohydrate calories.

A shift from the resting mixture to an increasing use of carbohydrate depends on the exercise capacity of the subject. With increasing energy expenditure, an untrained subject increases the share of carbohydrate in the fuel at lower levels than the trained athlete. However, if the level of exercise is not expressed as Cal/min but as a percentage of the total aerobic capacity of the subject, the difference between trained and untrained subjects becomes smaller.

If work is done against the same load with arm muscles and leg muscles, the RQ behaves differently; it starts rising at lighter loads in arm work than in leg work. The muscles of the arms are smaller than those of the legs: the same rate of work in terms of Cal/min is effected at a higher rate of energy expenditure per gram of muscle in arm work than in leg work. With protracted exercise, RQ tends to decrease, reflecting a shift from carbohydrate to fat as a fuel. This change does not occur as long as carbohydrate is sufficiently available either as muscle glycogen or blood glucose (cf. § 1.3).

The effect of variation in meal composition on performance may be studied in two ways, either by making the subject perform after ingestion of a meal of known composition or by feeding him a special diet to "saturate" the body with a given nutrient (Gemmill, 1942). Christensen and Hansen (1939) observed that trained subjects could work on a bicycle ergometer at the load of 1080 kg/min two to three times longer after a carbohydrate diet than after a fat diet. The fatigue could be abolished by administering sufficient glucose to raise the blood glucose level. Krogh and Lindhard (1920) demonstrated that the mechanical efficiency of bicycle ergometer work was 11% higher on a carbohydrate diet than on a fat diet. In Bierrings's (1931) studies the difference was 8.3%. As pointed out above, carbohydrate also requires less oxygen than protein or fat to yield the same amount of energy.

Carbohydrate is thus the best fuel for muscular work. This statement does not imply that the provision of extra carbohydrate would increase the performance capacity over and above that reached with adequate carbohydrate supply. The advantage of carbohydrate can also be demonstrated only in protracted hard work, where the carbohydrate stores become exhausted. Less intense work may be carried out rather long even without the supply of any carbohydrate. A group of volunteers walked approximately 50 km each day for 10 days, fasting, consuming only water. At the end there still was glycogen left in the muscles (Hultman, 1969). Gluconeogenesis from other substrates, mainly from protein, is stimulated and supplies sufficient carbohydrate. The use of fat is also activated in fasting.

Fat is an important source of energy for exercise. Its role becomes proportionally more important in protracted exercise and with limitation of carbohydrate supply. However, the body has ample fat to cope with all athletic performances, and there is no need to include it therefore in the diets of sportsmen. The main virtues of fat in the diet are that they provide energy in a compact form, add to the palatability of the diet, and have a great satiety value. Of these considerations the first one is of particular importance to the training sportsman. Many diets based on carbohydrate tend in the temperate climate to have an energy/weight ratio of 1 Cal per 1 g of food corresponding to the intake of approximately 25% solids and 75% water. At the realistic energy expenditure level of 5000 Cal/day for a training athlete, the accommodation of 5 kg food per day would be a serious handicap. The inclusion of 200 g fat in the daily diet would decrease its bulk by 1.5 kg and thus bring it to an easily manageable volume.

1.4.3. *Proteins and Amino Acids*

It is a common belief among coaches that athletes need much meat for the building and upkeep of strong muscles. This belief dates back as far as the fifth century BC to the Ancient Greek culture. Up to that time, the athletes had used the traditional, chiefly vegetarian, Greek diet; the change of diet is recorded as having been introduced by two known athletes in order to increase body bulk and weight (Christophe and Mayer, 1958).

Exercise does not increase the catabolism of protein when sufficient carbohydrate is available. Thus protein supplementation is not necessary or useful for a sports performance.

Muscle strength is directly proportional to the cross-section of the muscles. In order to build up strength, muscle tissue has to be accumulated. In principle it thus appears that protein supplementation might be needed during strength training. However, most diets probably contain an adequate amount of protein also for this purpose.

Yoshimura (1961) has studied the effects of critical protein intake during a training programme in young men. In spite of a positive nitrogen balance, anaemia and hypoproteinaemia developed after about 10 days' training. Yoshimura was led to recommend a protein intake of 2 g/kg/day provided that about 25% is animal protein. This is more than twice as much as the current FAO–WHO recommendation. Yoshimura's views are not generally accepted, but the problem requires further study.

When rats kept on protein intakes low enough to stunt growth are trained to run on a treadmill, they develop an endurance far superior to that of rats given an adequate diet (Fuge *et al.*, 1968). This observation ties up to the early uncontrolled experiment by Chittenden (1904) where he observed a gradual improvement of strength over 5 months on a low protein intake, 50–60 g/day. However, in a later study of 2 months' duration at two levels of protein intakes, 50–55 g/day and 160 g/day respectively, no difference in performance was observed (Darling *et al.*, 1944).

Some amino acids and proteins have been used as doping agents; glycine, the glycine-rich protein gelatine, and potassium–magnesium–aspartate. While the doping effects of glycine and gelatine have not stood critical testing (e.g. King *et al.*, 1942), potassium–magnesium–aspartate on the contrary has been able to prolong the capacity for protracted exercise. In the experiments of Ahlborg *et al.* (1968) its administration increased the time of standard bicycle ergometer work until exhaustion from an average of 85–128 min. No effect on muscle strength has been observed (Consolazio *et al.*, 1964b). It appears probable that aspartate interferes with mechanisms responsible for fatigue rather than acting as a nutrient.

1.4.4. *Vitamin and Mineral Supplementation*

Vitamin supplements have been extensively used in the preparation of athletes for performance. This is based partly on inference from the symptoms of specific vitamin deficiency diseases and partly on evidence derived from experiments in which physiological changes or an improvement of performance have been observed after vitamin administration. However, later attempts to confirm such results have often failed to substantiate the initial claims. In particular, no vitamin appears to have established itself as an effective doping agent if subjected to the crucial test of a double-blind experiment.

Obviously the results of vitamin supplementation may be expected to vary according to the pre-experimental level of supply. In frank vitamin deficiencies, the reduction of performance capacity is adequately documented and reparable through vitamin supplementation (Archdeacon and Murlin, 1944; Berryman *et al.*, 1947; Barborka *et al.*, 1943; Wilson *et al.*, 1949).

On the other hand, a vitamin administered to subjects receiving a diet already rich in the same vitamin may be looked upon solely as a doping agent. However. there is a "twilight zone" in between manifest vitamin deficiency diseases and ample vitamin supply, where vitamin supplements may be postulated to improve the performance capacity.

1.4.4.1. Ascorbic Acid

The administration of ascorbic acid supplements to athletes is based on three kinds of evidence: (a) on the depletion of body ascorbic acid stores during exercise, (b) on the deterioration of performance capacity in "sub-clinical" ascorbic acid deficiency, and (c) on reports of improved performance capacity as a result of ascorbic acid supplementation.

A decrease in the *blood ascorbic acid level* during a march of 30 km from 0.88 ± 0.25 by 0.29 ± 0.11 mg per 100 ml ($p < 0.001$) was observed by Borgmann (1940). After having supplemented the diet with 50 mg/day during one week in another group, the starting level was brought up to 0.91 ± 0.19 mg per 100 ml; the same performance now caused a decrease by 0.38 ± 0.07 mg per 100 ml ($p < 0.001$). The drop of the blood ascorbic acid after supplementation was significantly greater ($p < 0.05$).

A decrease of blood ascorbic acid during exercise has later been confirmed by several investigators and is considered a part of the acute stress syndrome. (For reference, see, e.g. Prokop, 1960b.)

Emotional tension may also cause a decrease of the blood ascorbic acid concentration. Thus a jet flight was reported to cause a decrease in the plasma ascorbic acid level from 0.40 ± 0.03 to 0.23 ± 0.015 mg per 100 ml while no change was observed in control experiments (Arutyunov et al., 1962).

The urinary excretion of ascorbic acid is increased during exercise. The excretion increases, of course, with a rise in the plasma ascorbic acid level, but it has also been reported that the urinary excretion of ascorbic acid is greater in trained athletes than in non-trained subjects. Correspondingly, a diet deficient in ascorbic acid leads to symptoms of scurvy in previously trained guinea-pigs earlier than in non-trained animals (Jakovlev, 1953). On the other hand, 24 h urinary excretions of ascorbic acid, as well as those of thiamine, riboflavin, N-methylnicotinic acid, and 4-pyridotinic acid have been reported to decrease in connection with flying stress (Arutyunov et al., 1962).

The *deterioration* of performance capacity in ascorbic acid deficiency has been studied on one subject by Crandon et al. (1940). Weakness and easy fatigue appeared by the end of the third month; clinical symptoms of scurvy appeared later, during the fourth month. The "aerobic" performance capacity in walking and running to exhaustion on a treadmill decreased, but the capacity for "anaerobic" work as studied using a hand ergograph, was unaffected. The complaints of fatigue and decreased work output were confirmed by Farmer (1944), especially during the sixth and seventh month of ascorbic acid depletion. Johnson et al. (1945) reported easy fatigue as the first sign of deterioration, at the end of 2 months of a diet free of ascorbic acid.

Studies on the effects of ascorbic acid *supplementation* range from isolated organs to athletic competitions. In an isolated frog-muscle preparation, the addition of 0.05–0.1 mg per 100 ml ascorbic acid to the Ringer bath (Sievers, 1939) has been reported to prolong the contracting ability. In guinea-pigs, supplementing the diet with tangerine-juice has been observed reversibly to improve working capacity and to prolong the ability to work. This change was not accompanied by any change in the glycogen content of the muscles. Moreover, the ascorbic acid supplementation accelerated the improvement of performance during training; this change was associated with increased muscle glycogen storage (Jakovlev, 1941).

In laboratory experiments with placebo controls on sixty subjects, Prokop (1960b) administered 100 mg of ascorbic acid in orange juice one hour before a standard bicycle ergometer test. Ascorbic acid effected a significant decrease of the oxygen debt, of the rise of heart rate, and of systolic pressure during work as compared with no medication. However, juice also caused a significant decrease in the circulatory changes during exercise. Somewhat more marked effects were observed when the same amount of ascorbic acid was administered as an orange-juice concentrate. The effects were independent of the blood ascorbic acid level.

The administration of 200 mg of ascorbic acid to athletes before competition has been reported to improve their performance (skiers and gymnasts) as against that of control subjects (Jakovlev, 1953). A daily ascorbic acid supplementation of the diet of students of physical education was also reported to improve the performance capacity as against a control group (Jakovlev, 1953).

Against these reports, which have been publicized by those with commercial interests, several critical studies have failed to confirm an improvement of performance capacity by ascorbic acid (e.g. Margaria *et al.*, 1964). Thus, variations in the ascorbic acid intake from 40 to 540 mg/day had no effect on work performance, endurance, psychomotor ability, or the incidence of heat exhaustion in controlled laboratory experiments with slow walking on a treadmill at temperatures up to 50°C (Henschel *et al.*, 1944). In a review of nutrition and athletics, Mayer and Bullen (1964) concluded that there was no evidence that athletic performance is improved by supplementing a nutritionally adequate diet with ascorbic acid.

It has been claimed that post-exercise muscular soreness is reduced by an ascorbic acid supplement of 100 mg/day to the diet (Staton, 1952). However, the evidence is not fully convincing.

1.4.4.2. THIAMINE

The increased need for thiamine in exercise is based on the accepted observation that physical activity increases its utilization. The effects of thiamine *depletion* on performance capacity have been studied by several investigators. Johnson *et al.* (1942) observed that the urinary excretion of men who performed exhaustive physical work indicated a depletion of body thiamine stores in 7 days of a thiamine-free diet, while this took considerably longer in sedentary men (Williams *et al.*, 1940). Foltz *et al.* (1944) found a reduction in work output within 4 weeks in subjects whose thiamine intake was adjusted to 0.17–0.21 mg per 1000 Cal. Keys *et al.* (1943) conducted an extensive series of experiments at various intake levels down to 0.23 mg thiamine per 1000 Cal. No difference was observed between the subjects and their controls in laboratory tests of muscle strength, of brief exhausting work, and of prolonged severe work and recovery. In another series, four subjects were given a diet with an intake of 0.185 mg thiamine per 1000 Cal over 161 days. The work response of the subjects and of their controls showed no difference, although an increase of the blood pyruvate level indicated a borderline deficiency of thiamine. A further decrease in the intake of B-complex vitamins, with 0.008 mg thiamine per 1000 Cal, led in 8 days to a deterioration of speed and co-ordination, and to loss of endurance.

In treadmill training of rats, Jakovlev (1953) reports an increase of time run by rats which receive a thiamine *supplement*. In students of physical education, who took part in a skiing contest, the administration of thiamine before competition had no effect on their performance. However, daily thiamine supplementation resulted in an improvement of skiing results as compared with those of a placebo-treated control group. Vytchikova (1958) has pleaded for a supplementation of the athletes' diet with 10–20 mg/day of thiamine, as this will reduce the pyruvate levels after vigorous activity to those found in manual workers engaged in moderate exercise.

A joint FAO–WHO Expert Group (FAO–WHO, 1967), admitting the lack of direct evidence, inferred that the increase in caloric requirement in physical activity leads to a corresponding increase in the requirements of thiamine with no change in the thiamine–calorie ratio. It recognized that a marked increase in physical activity precipitates symptoms of thiamine deficiency in those subsisting on an inadequate diet. However, this does not indicate a need to modify the recommended thiamine—calorie relationship of 0.40 mg per 1000 Cal in situations of heavy physical activity.

1.4.4.3. TOCOPHEROL

Vitamin-E preparations have enjoyed some popularity as nutritional supplements to sportsmen. The impetus for this was evidently given by the well-known development of muscle dystrophy in animals as a consequence of vitamin-E deficiency. Beneficial effects on athletic performance have been claimed in man (Percival, 1951) and in race horses (Darlington and Chassels, 1956, 1957, 1958). Prokop (1960a) observed a decrease in oxygen debt, and Novosadova and Jirka (1966) have reported diminished oxygen uptake for standard ergometer work.

Cureton (1954, 1959–60, 1970) and Cureton and Pohndorf (1955) observed significant improvement in endurance when running to exhaustion in 2–6 min and in some cardiorespiratory measurements as a result of the ingestion of wheat germ oil containing tocopherol. However, other investigators (Thomas, 1957; Sharman et al., 1971) have been unable to confirm the claims for an improvement, even when using either substantially larger doses of vitamin E or wheat germ oil.

1.4.4.4. OTHER VITAMINS

Exercise reduces the intestinal absorption of vitamin A (Schjøth, 1965), but little is known about the effect of this vitamin on performance capacity. With ultraviolet irradiation, increase in the muscle strength of untrained subjects have been observed, but this effect cannot be reproduced with vitamin-D administration.

The belief that the catalysers of important biochemical reactions might become critical factors has encouraged the use of several members of the vitamin-B group as doping agents. In addition to thiamine, this applies to riboflavin, nicotinic acid, pantothenic acid, pyridoxine (B_6), cyanocobalamine (B_{12}) and to thioctanic acid which, however, is not a vitamin.

The recommended intake of riboflavin (FAO–WHO, 1967) is adjusted according to the energy expenditure at 0.55 mg per 1000 Cal. The same applies to niacin (FAO–WHO, 1967); the recommendation is 6.6 niacin equivalents (corresponding to 6.6 mg niacin) per 1000 Cal.

There is no critical evidence that extra supplementation of these vitamins above the recommended allowances would be of any benefit in sports (see, for example, Ariëns, 1965).

Water-soluble vitamins are readily excreted through the kidneys and are therefore probably harmless as doping agents. The fat-soluble vitamins, however, may be able to cause serious derangements in body chemistry, and should not be used as doping supplements.

1.4.4.5. IRON

The bulk of the iron in the organism is in the haemoglobin molecule. An increased total blood volume and total amount of haemoglobin are intimately associated with training changes of the cardiovascular system. Close correlations have been demonstrated between blood volume and total haemoglobin, on one hand, and the maximum oxygen uptake and roentgenological heart volume, on the other (Kjellberg et al., 1949). Moreover, the amounts of myoglobin and cytochrome in the body increase as a result of training (Vanotti, 1959). Consequently, during intense training additional iron may be needed for the formation of the extra haemoglobin.

The possibility of an increased loss of iron among athletes has also been studied. After a soccer match, the content of free haemoglobin in plasma may rise markedly (Vanzetti and Valante, 1965), but only minimal increases of intravasal haemolysis have been observed after a ski run of 94 km or 4 days' cycling competition (Vuori, I., personal communication). Sportsmen may sweat as much as 8–9 l/day (Král et al., 1963). The elimination of iron in sweat during exercise increases, but still is not likely to cause iron deficiency except as an aggravating factor at critical levels of supply (Vuori et al., 1966). Sweat as elicited by exercise has been reported to contain from 0.11 to 7 mg iron per litre (Mitchell and Hamilton, 1949; 1–2 mg/l; Adams et al., 1950: 0.64–7 mg/l; Johnston et al., 1950: 0.24–0.28 mg/l; Foy and Kondi, 1956: 0.3–6.5 mg/l; Vuori et al., 1966: 0.18 ± 0.11 mg/l).

The haemoglobin concentration in the blood of physically active people has been reported as the same—slightly higher or slightly lower than that of sedentary control subjects (Karvonen and Kunnas, 1952). An intense training programme for a rugby game has been shown to cause a significant decrease in the erythrocyte count and in the total haemoglobin content (Yamada, 1958). However, in bicycle-racing champions, training caused no anaemia (Yoshimura, 1966).

In the course of a long training season, the haemoglobin concentration of endurance runners and skiers has a tendency to decrease. This decrease is partly independent of the iron supply, but iron deficiency often contributes to the fall. Iron supplementation is required if the diet does not supply sufficient amounts (cf. FAO–WHO, 1970).

1.4.5. *Water and Electrolytes*

Physical activity entails a loss of water at the cellular level: glycogen is stored in the cells with water, and a loss of body glycogen stores causes a parallel loss of weight, maximally 2.5–3.5 kg (Olsson and Saltin, 1970). This is well known from the weight loss effected within a few days on transition from a carbohydrate-rich diet to a protein-fat diet.

At the level of the entire organism, the loss of weight during athletic performances is determined essentially by the requirements of the heat balance and by the consequent sweating. Table 2 indicates the magnitude of weight loss during various sports activities. In hot climates, sweat loss is greater.

TABLE 2 WEIGHT LOSS IN SOME SPORTS PERFORMANCES (JAKOVLEV, 1956)

Event	Weight loss in kg
100 m run	0.15
10,000 m run	0.9–1.5
Marathon	4.0
Cycling	
7.5 km	0.8–1.0
50 km	1.5–3.0
Skiing, cross-country	
10 km	0.8–1.0
20 km	1.1–1.2
30 km	1.1–2.0
50 km	2.5–3.5
Rowing	
2000 m	0.8
25 km	1.5–3.0
Riding	0.9–1.0
Gymnastics	0.4–0.7
Fencing	1.0
Soccer	0.9–3.0
Boxing	0.8–1.8
Wrestling	0.4–1.8
Shooting	0.2–0.8

Sweat is hypotonic in relation to the body fluids. If the losses of water and electrolytes are not replaced, the osmotic pressure of the body fluids tends to rise. This leads to the secretion of antidiuretic hormone from the posterior pituitary. If large amounts of water are drunk in this situation, it may be absorbed more rapidly than the effect of the antidiuretic hormone disappears, and extracellular fluid becomes diluted and "water intoxication" ensues. Secondarily water is transferred into the cells, and causes some cellular swelling. The swelling of the brain causes a rise of the intracranial pressure, with consequent symptoms of fatigue, malaise, headache, sometimes vomiting, and even convulsions.

It is advisable, therefore, to drink water only in small portions in all such situations in which the urine flow has ceased as an effect of the antidiuretic hormone. Liberal amounts of water may be drunk when urine flow again has been established. This generally takes approximately half an hour from the beginning of the rehydration.

Not only water but also the electrolyte loss has to be replaced. Drinking water without electrolytes causes a mild "water intoxication", which shows characteristic symptoms of fatigue and persistent thirst. Moreover, the taste threshold for salt changes: a 0.2–0.5% NaCl solution which normally has an objectionable salty taste, is in such a situation accepted as a tasty drink.

In an unacclimatized subject, sweat excreted during exercise corresponds osmotically to a solution of 0.2–0.3% NaCl with wide individual variation. Exposure to a hot climate causes an adaptation, and the sweat becomes more diluted, corresponding to as little as 0.1% NaCl. Salt supplementation, either as salt tablets or as an addition to the drinking water, fruit-juices, etc., or by offering skim milk as a drink, is of particular importance during the first days of heat exposure. After approximately a week, adaptation generally has advanced far enough to make salt supplementation unnecessary (Toor et al., 1959). Physical training by itself causes no corresponding decrease of the sweat electrolyte concentration (Král et al., 1966).

In protracted exercise with a copious sweat loss, thirst is not an adequate guide for the replacement of the losses (Adolph, 1964). It has been recommended that conscious programmed drinking at frequent intervals over and above the amounts dictated by thirst would be the best procedure for preventing dehydration with consequent deterioration of the performance capacity (Lehmann and Szakáll, 1937, 1939, 1940). The body temperature rises more with water restriction. Dehydration also causes changes in behaviour: men become morose and difficult to handle.

In a practical experiment on sixty men marching 29 km, those offered water *ad libitum* run a water deficit of 2.9% of their body weights as against 4.8% in men allowed only 1 l of water; the sweat loss was 4.5 l in both groups. Seven of the thirty men with water restriction collapsed or fell out because of exhaustion, while this occurred to one man only in the *ad libitum* group (Strydom et al., 1966). Carbohydrate may suitably be provided at the same time. For practical purposes, adequate secretion of urine would be a better guide than the sensation of thirst. If the water loss is not replaced on frequent occasions, copious drinking should be avoided during exercise: the performance capacity is affected less by moderate dehydration than by a sudden rehydration leading to symptoms of water intoxication. A water loss up to about 2.5 l is generally without significant physiological or psychological effects (Ladell, 1955, 1957).

Electrolytes with a cation excess have been administered to athletes in order to produce alkalosis and, with it, a doping effect. Dennig *et al.* (1940) used sodium bicarbonate, sodium succinate, and potassium citrate, and observed a prolongation in submaximal bicycle ergometer work capacities as against the acidifying salt ammonium chloride or placebos. A tendency to improvement in running (1600–3200 m) and swimming (200–400 m) times was also observed.

1.4.6. Food During Training

The diet of athletes during training may be approached from two angles—from the purely observational one describing the actual food habits, or from the normative one telling what the athletes should eat.

Observational studies have been carried out and recorded ever since the ancient Greek athletes (Harris, 1966). In an individual balance study of the modern Olympic skiers, the mean daily food consumption was found to be practically the same in men and women—on an average 4900 Cal (range for seven men, 4500–5250 Cal; for five women, 4700–5000 Cal). The total energy expenditure, as based on a time and motion study, correspondingly gave an average of 5200 Cal/day for the men (Namyslowski, 1967). Although skiers are sportsmen in whom the largest aerobic capacities have been observed, their energy expenditure during training, nevertheless, does not exceed that of the heaviest forms of occupational labour such as forest work. In some other sports, the energy spent in training may remain considerably lower.

Jakovlev (1956) gives values of daily energy expenditure per kilogram body weight ranging from 60 Cal for sprinters, jumpers, throwers, gymnasts, shooters, and alpine skiers, up to 90 Cal for long-distance cyclists.

As the athletes' energy expenditure is rather large, it is advisable to divide it into several portions. In a study among Finnish athletes 21% ate six meals, 40% five, 31% four, and 8% three meals a day (Pellervo-Seura, 1968). The Finnish sportsmen favoured meat, milk, vegetables, fruit, and eggs, but avoided fat and "heavy" fried foods. They were keen to have sufficient vitamins and iron.

For muscle growth, an extra supplement of protein above the physiological minimum is required, and extra iron is necessary when building up a larger total blood volume. Otherwise there is no physiological basis for any benefit to the training process to be derived from specific dietary modifications.

A critical analysis of the physiological background of sports performances would thus justify only the recommendation of a "normal", adequate diet for the training sportsman, in amounts adjusted to the intensity of training to avoid undesirable weight changes. Nevertheless, long treatises have been written and detailed advice given recommending specific dietaries for each branch of sports (e.g. Jakovlev, 1953; Gräfe, 1964). The entire field of sports has been covered up to professional golf (Ebbetts, 1966). Gräfe's norms range from 4600 Cal/day in the lightest sports to 7000 Cal for hammer and discus throwers and shot putters.

Detailed dietary recommendations for sportsmen may, nevertheless, be justified insofar as the "normal" diet in many parts of the world is not adequate, and particularly because the sportsmen and their coaches may sometimes have scientifically quite unfounded ideas and fads about the optimum diet. They may also be useful as conducive to regular life habits.

1.4.7. Food for Performance

In planning the diet of an athlete for the period immediately preceding a competition, consideration is to be given to the digestive and to the metabolic processes. Obviously, a stomach full of food is a mechanical handicap in many sports; furthermore, heavy exercise after a copious meal often elicits vomiting. Fat foods tend to remain long in the stomach, and therefore should be avoided. As the emptying of the stomach may be delayed by heavy exercise (Hellebrandt and Tepper, 1934; Rose and Fuenning, 1960), there is, indeed, no reason to eat immediately before a sports event. When athletes prepare for an important competition, the emotional stress may manifest itself also through various dyspeptic symptoms. When competing abroad, the exposure to foreign foods contributes to disturbing the functions of the gastro-intestinal tract. Many travelling sports teams equip themselves with a supply of foods customary to their own country. Although this practice generally has no nutritional justification, it may be a valuable contribution to morale.

At the 1948 Olympic Games in London, the food eaten by twenty-eight athletes of nine nations was studied (Berry et al., 1949). A great variety of food habits was observed among the competitors. At the 1952 Helsinki

Games, the following experiences were gained in catering for the athletes (Kolkka, 1955):

> in great demand were beef, mutton and chicken;
> foods fried in fat were avoided;
> little fish was eaten;
> the most popular dessert was ice-cream;
> wheat and graham bread were popular;
> much milk, butter, fresh vegetables and fruit were consumed;
> honey, maltose, and glucose were eaten by many;
> tinned uncooked foods were avoided;
> along with milk, favoured beverages were iced water, fruit-juices, and light beer.

Among metabolic factors, the supply of carbohydrate has been given most attention. As discussed in §1.2, it has to be examined separately in three situations:

(1) in short events which do not essentially tax the carbohydrate stores;
(2) in protracted events which the carbohydrate stores may become exhausted;
(3) in protracted events in which the use of carbohydrate exceeds the maximum capacity of the body stores.

The rationale in giving carbohydrate before a short-term exercise is either to prevent a fall of the blood sugar, with concomitant deterioration of the performance, or to expect an improvement of the performance capacity, i.e. a "doping effect". The blood glucose level during exercise has been studied by several investigators (e.g. Christensen, 1931; Douglas and Koch, 1951; Meythaler and Droste, 1934; Naegeli *et al.*, 1961). The normal response is a rise in the blood sugar level. Gebhardt (1966) determined the blood glucose before and at the end of running distances from 400 to 5000 m; the average rise of glucose at the end of the race increased with the distance from 20 to 48 mg per 100 ml. The oral administration of 50 g of glucose in tea 30 min before performance increased the blood glucose further by 19 mg per 100 ml at the end of the 400 m run, but had no effect on blood sugar after performances of longer duration. If the blood sugar rises during the sporting event, administration of glucose obviously is not needed for preventing its fall. Furthermore, after performances lasting longer than approximately a minute, the previous administration of glucose had no effect whatsoever on the blood sugar. Glucose has enjoyed quite a lot of popularity as an "ergogenic aid", i.e. as a harmless doping agent. There is no scientific basis for this use for short performances.

In protracted events, in which the carbohydrate stores may become exhausted, the rational approach is to fill the stores in advance as much as possible, after a preceding depletion, with the aid of exercise and dietary manipulations. This is described in §1.2.

In such performances, where the use of carbohydrate exceeds the capacity of body stores, i.e. in Marathon running, 30–50 km skiing, long-distance cycling, and the like, the competitor has to be fed during the performance. For the cyclists, an allowance of 1000 Cal/h of cycling time has been found applicable (Hamley, 1964). A solution of glucose is rapidly absorbed, and therefore much used. It is advisable to use a 5% (10% at maximum) solution, since more concentrated solutions remain unduly long in the stomach and may cause vomiting. A dose of 0.1–0.3 l of 5% glucose every 10 or 15 min makes it possible to administer 1–1.5 l water and 50–60 g glucose per hour (Olsson and Saltin, 1970). Large quantities of cold drinks frequently cause vomiting and gastric distress. The temperature should be 15–25°C. Many sportsmen prefer a flavoured drink: citrus flavour is much used.

The dietary provision of athletes on the day of competition has been dealt with in a monograph by Jakovlev (1956). He recommends a substantial breakfast with plenty of easily assimilable carbohydrate. An interval of $2\frac{1}{2}$–3 h should be left between a meal and competition. However, Rönnholm and Karvinen (1964) found no difference in the amount of bicycle ergometer work at stepwise increased loads carried out until exhaustion, whether a substantial porridge and milk breakfast or tea only were taken 1 h 45 min before the tests. Similar results have been obtained by Naegeli *et al.* (1961). With a very uneven distribution of meals, like that practiced during the Ramadan, the results of timed races become poorer than at a time of the year when three meals are consumed (Causeret, 1957).

1.4.8. *Alcohol*

The oxidation of ethyl alcohol in the body is initiated in the liver. Thus the rate of oxidation is essentially unaffected by exercise and, in fact, by most physiological factors. The metabolites of ethyl alcohol can be oxidized further by the peripheral tissues, including muscle, and in this sense alcohol can serve as fuel for exercise and replace other carbohydrate or fat. Approximately 7 g of alcohol is oxidized in an hour releasing approximately 50 Cal energy. This is almost sufficient for absolute rest, but only a small portion of the energy expenditure levels observed in many sports.

The well-known effects of alcohol on the central nervous system have encouraged athletes to use it as a doping agent. However, critical studies have not shown any improvement of the performance capacity. On the contrary, a deterioration of performance has been reported even after relatively small doses of alcohol. Jakovlev (1953) reports a mean increase of 0.4 sec in the time for a 100 m run, and of 1–2 sec in 100 m swimming, when a moderate dose of alcohol was consumed immediately prior to the performance. In mountaineering, the intake of 1 l of beer reduced the climbing performance by 20% while the energy expenditure increased by 14%.

In laboratory experiments, small doses of alcohol, 0.46 g per kg body weight, have been shown to cause no change in muscle strength, a 10% decrease in running speed, and a 6% decrease in jumping power, a significant deterioration of the neuro-musclar coordination of vertical posture, and a considerable increase in heart rate during standard bicycle ergometer exercise (average 23 beats/min) (Hebbelinck, 1959, 1961).

2. NUTRITIONAL BALANCE AND PERFORMANCE

In planning diets for many expeditions, one of the crucial problems has been, particularly in the past, to what extent man may depend on his body stores of nutrients and what food must be included in his provisions. Table 3 gives a list of the sequence of deficiency syndromes in men exposed to complete deprivation of one or more of the important nutrients. Easy fatigue is a main early symptom of nutrient deprivation (cf. Young and Spector, 1957). The members of expeditions must often be able to do vigorous physical exercise; a situation seldom occurs where mere survival means success. Starvation for 10 days is compatible with normal daily activity (Brown and Pulsifer, 1965) or even with marching 50 km each day (Hultman, 1969).

In under-nutrition, caloric and otherwise, endurance deteriorates fast while strength is remarkably resistant (Keys, 1946). The large muscles are proportionally more affected than the small ones. Pronounced deterioration in strength (as measured with the hand dynamometer) and in aerobic capacity occur when 10–16% of weight has been lost (Taylor et al., 1957).

TABLE 3 RATE OF ONSET OF DEFICIENCY SYNDROMES IN WORKING MEN
EXPOSED TO COMPLETE DEFICIENCY OF ONE OR MORE NUTRIENTS
(Modified from Johnson, 1943; cf. Mayer and Bullen, 1960).

Nutrient	Time before earliest deleterious effects	Earliest deficiency syndromes and results
Water	A few hours	Easy fatigue, poor performance. Eventual exhaustion or dehydration
Food energy	Two or three days	Easy fatigue, poor performance
Sodium chloride	Several days	Easy fatigue, poor performance. Eventually, heat cramps
Carbohydrate	Several days	Easy fatigue, poor performance. Eventually, ketosis
Thiamine	Days to weeks	Endurance decreased. Eventually, beri-beri
Ascorbic acid	Several weeks	Easy fatigue, poor performance. Eventually, scurvy
Protein	Probably several weeks	Earliest effects not known; late result, nutritional oedema
Riboflavin	Several months	Skin and mucous membranes affected
Vitamin A	Several months	Night blindness
Fats	Many months	Earliest effects not known.

An obese subject stands fasting better than a lean one: subjective symptoms—irritability, easy fatiguability and gastritis—are less severe (Brown and Pulsifer, 1965). The lean and the obese also show different metabolic responses: the lean ones have more tendency to develop ketosis during fasting (Bloom *et al.*, 1965).

When sufficient food is not made available, the performance capacity may be affected by the type of diet prior to the expedition. In rats, a high fat diet (80% of energy) led to longer survival during subsequent fasting and the ability to do greater amounts of work until exhaustion than an equicaloric high carbohydrate or high protein diet (Samuels *et al.*, 1948).

The effects of vitamin deprivation on performance capacity have been reviewed by Mayer and Bullen (1960). As multi-vitamin preparations have become commonplace, such effects should now be of historical interest only. Lack of water causes deterioration faster than lack of food.

2.1. EXPEDITIONS IN TEMPERATE CLIMATES

Providing expeditions with food is an art which has been cultivated for thousands of years by civilians and the military with varying success.

For an expedition it often is essential to be as independent as possible from fixed supplies. Roman historians describing the war waged by Septimius Severus in Caledonia—now Scotland—tell us that the Caledonians were capable of enduring hunger, thirst, and hardships of every description. "When they are in the woods they survive on bark and roots; and they prepare for all emergencies a certain kind of food, of which if they eat only so much as the size of a bean they neither hunger nor thirst" (Morton, 1958).

The range of needs to be considered extends from the provision of a diet with an energy content adequate for action to rations for mere survival (cf. Edholm and Bacharach, 1965b). Skinner and Mann (1964) give an elucidating description of the history and modern rations of the British Army; the operational rations have been described by Smith (1954). Before the development of modern food technology, protein foods and the lack of knowledge about vitamins were the main sources of difficulties. Dried meat (biltong) and the various pemmicans were convenient to take along, although not generally considered tasty (Kark et al., 1945; Lewis et al., 1957).

With modern food technology, most of these problems have disappeared: modern expeditions may choose a wholesome diet from canned, frozen, and freeze-dried products. Skill, practical issues of weight, package size, available transports, means for reconstitution, and the like have to be negotiated to fit the needs of each expedition. When weight becomes a consideration, and water will be available for reconstitution, condensed and dried foods are the choice. Some examples of the nutrient content and energy values of dried prepared foods marketed specifically for the rucksack are given in Table 4 (cf. also de Jong, 1965). Emergency rations

TABLE 4 NUTRIENT CONTENT AND ENERGY VALUE OF SOME DRIED FOODS MARKETED FOR EXPEDITIONS (PARTIOAITTA LTD.)

Food	100 g contains			
	Protein (g)	Fats (g)	Carbohydrate (g)	Energy (Cal)
Chocolate drink	14.6	18.0	60.2	550
Semolina gruel	18.8	21.7	49.4	440
Oatmeal gruel	19.2	20.6	46.5	446
Fruit jelly	1.0	0.2	88.0	339
Pea soup	19.6	1.7	55.0	304
Potato soup	8.4	2.0	63.1	300
Macaroni soup	10.1	0.9	69.6	335

may have to keep men fit enough for marching and fighting, or for survival only whilst waiting for rescue.

The available space and weight often are critical considerations, and, similarly, the "shelf life" of the foods included. Much study has been devoted to the physiological requirements (Sargent et al., 1953; Hervey and McCance, 1954; Whittingham, 1954, 1965). A diet of 1000 Cal/day has in practical experiments proved sufficient for allowing marching for 4 days at the daily energy expenditure of 5000 Cal. The concurrent loss of weight was 4 kg. Several measures of performance capacity showed no deterioration over and above such subjects who received food *ad libitum*. At the energy expenditure of 5000 Cal/day, the dietary intake did not generally exceed 3000 Cal/day (Øyen, 1967). Keys *et al.* (1958) have shown that at the daily expenditure of 2700 Cal, a 1010 Cal diet was well tolerated for 24 days, with only slight mental symptoms.

Water supply is, of course, essential. In temperate climates, man survives without water intake 10–14 days. The daily water production from metabolism is from 300 to 500 ml. Losses of water are totally balanced by a daily intake of 1.2–1.5 l.

In the composition of the emergency rations, acceptability and satiety value are to be considered. Roth (1948) was an early advocate of pure carbohydrate as a universal item. American and Canadian recommendations have generally followed this line (Wickett and Bliss, 1952). The British have, for reasons of acceptability, adopted a mixture of protein, fat, and carbohydrate in the ratio of 1:2.5:5.1 for a ration giving 4771 Cal, and of 1.5:2.5:5.1 for a ration of 6805 Cal. In experiments simulating the practical survival situation, a wide range of nutrient proportions has been found compatible with the preservation of physical efficiency (Whittingham, 1954).

2.2. COLD CLIMATES

In a cold climate the critical factor for survival is the avoidance of body cooling. This may be achieved by two means—by reducing heat loss with the aid of insulation or by increasing heat production. Present day technology offers possibilities for controlling heat loss within wide limits. For increasing heat production, on the other hand, the main method is exercise. In subjects trained for endurance, exercise is able to increase heat production over several hours by a factor of 10, while in untrained men the corresponding factor remains at approximately 5.

2.2.1. Energy Requirements

It may be inferred that people in a cold climate who have adequate shelter and clothing, modern transport facilities, and access to imported foods, have no specific dietary problems. This has also been demonstrated. Easty (1967) made a study of food intake in Antarctica. The mean calorie intake, 3600 Cal/day, was equivalent to that of a moderately active worker living in a temperate climate (cf. also Milan and Rodahl, 1961).

The early explorers were facing quite another situation. The energy for locomotion was provided by the explorers themselves and by their sledge dogs, and this energy had to be derived from food carried by the team.

The energy expenditure of locomotion in a cold climate is affected by the depth and consistency of the snow cover, by the type of footwear, and by heavy clothing (Gray et al., 1951; Welch et al., 1958). The energy expenditure of walking is much increased by a layer of soft snow. A depression of 10 cm in the snow increases the calorie cost of walking by a factor of 2.2 (to 1.4 Cal/kg/horizontal metre), of 20 cm by 4.1, of 30 cm by 8.8, and of 40 cm by 12.8 times the cost of walking on firm ground (Heinonen et al., 1959).

Snow-shoes and skis increase the bearing surface, and skis may glide on the snow. Thus the efficiency of locomotion is improved (cf. Rennie, 1958). Skiing involves several muscle groups, and as the energy expenditure is distributed to a large muscle mass, high rates of expenditure are attained with relative ease (Christensen and Högberg, 1950). It is reasonable to expect energy expenditures of the order of 10 Cal/min during several hours of skiing; in trained cross-country skiers even 15 Cal/min is quite a realistic energy expenditure.

In sledging, an expenditure of 500 Cal/h has been recorded for 8 h (Edholm and Goldsmith, 1966). The energy expenditure of sledge dogs is quite large, at base 1600 Cal/day and sledging 2500–3500 Cal/day for dogs with a mean weight of 32 kg (Masterton et al., 1957). The energy expenditure while resting is slightly increased by an exposure to cold: a rise by 140 Cal during 12 daytime hours was observed by Iampietro et al. (1958).

An element in the know-how of the arctic traveller is to adapt his pace of locomotion and energy expenditure according to the thermal requirements, and to keep the body heat load constant with minimum sweating.

The proportion of time spent in a shelter and actively exercising is the main determinant of the daily energy expenditure in a cold climate. In fact, such clothing which is comfortable to wear during exercise has not sufficient insulation to allow resting outdoors at low temperatures. With this background it is understandable that rather varying energy expenditures have been reported in different studies. The generalization made by Johnson and Kark (1947) that for every degree (°F) fall in temperature there is an increase in daily calorie intake, can be valid only in some situations.

In Arctic and Subarctic military exercises, the calorie requirement in cold climates has been assessed at 5500–6000 Cal/day (Johnson *et al.*, 1949; Swain *et al.*, 1949). For a self-sufficient mobile military unit in the Arctic, 4500 Cal/day were found adequate except for the most strenuous 1–5 day work situations (Welch *et al.*, 1957). The energy expenditures recorded during sledging on civilian expeditions have been found to be of a similar magnitude, from 4400 to 6900 Cal (Orr, 1965; Edholm and Goldsmith, 1966). With such high energy expenditures, weight loss is usual in spite of adequate availability of food.

Rather high energy expenditures have also been reported by Johnson and Kark (1947) and by Kark *et al.* (1948–9) who made observations on a mobile force travelling in motorized vehicles over 5500 km in Northern Canada. Expenditures of 4000–5000 Cal/day have also been published for the Soviet Arctic (Ponomarev and Sokolova, 1959). On the other hand, Rodahl (1949) observed that European trappers in Greenland maintained constant body weight with as low an average intake as 3000 Cal/day. In military personnel living in Alaska, food intake equalled 3000–3200 Cal/day (Rodahl, 1954b, 1958).

A meal increases the resting energy expenditure. Eating just prior to retiring to sleep in the cold helps to retain normal body temperature and to provide better rest (Kreider and Buskirk, 1957).

2.2.2. *Proportions of Nutrients*

For reasons of local availability and of economy of transport, fat has been a dominant source of calories to the inhabitants and early explorers of the cold parts of the world. Fat is a highly concentrated source of calories; fat-foods generally carry little water, and no reconstitution with water before cooking is necessary. Observation of circumpolar diets stimulated the belief that a diet rich in fat should also physiologically be particularly suitable during exposure to a cold climate.

Animal experiments have given diverging results. For instance, Giaja and Gelineo (1934) reported that rats survived at temperatures from $-14°$ to $-4°C$ 8.5 days when on a carbohydrate diet, 6 days on fats, 2.5 days on proteins, and 2 days while fasting. On the other hand, Dugal *et al.* (1945), observed that in guinea-pigs exposed to – 2°, mortality was lowest in animals on a diet rich in fat.

Human experiments in men exposed during 8 h daily to +16°C in minimum clothing, with restricted activity, have shown that an adequate diet rich in fat was most favourable for cold tolerance, as indicated by the decrement of rectal temperature and of various psychomotor test performances. However, no difference was observed between the effects of meals rich in fat or carbohydrate, respectively, when these were eaten not during but immediately prior to the exposure. Similarly, if the interval of the meals during the exposure was reduced from 4 to 2 h, the difference between fat and carbohydrate disappeared (Mitchell *et al.*, 1946). A diet rich in proteins proved distinctly inferior in similar experiments. Although the specific dynamic action of the protein-rich meals was 50% higher than on the carbohydrate diet, the difference in heat remained equivalent to a very minor degree of muscular activity and played no role in the overall response (Keeton *et al.*, 1946).

Diets rich in fat and protein have proved feasible on actual expeditions and have been eloquently recommended (Stefansson, 1957). On the other hand, when a liberal choice of foods is available, not all populations living in cold climates give a preference to fat; its percentage in the diet does not, as a rule, exceed that in the diets of otherwise comparable populations living in temperate climates, and seasonal variations in fat intake remain small (cf. Rodahl, 1960).

2.2.2.1. VITAMINS

Animal experiments have suggested that ascorbic acid supplements may increase cold tolerance. Dugal and Therien (1947) demonstrated that among rats exposed to $-4°C$, the tissue concentrations of ascorbic acid decreased in such animals which failed to adapt to cold. When guinea-pigs, which resemble man in not being able to synthesize ascorbic acid, were exposed to $-8°C$, they survived only if a daily supplement of 75 mg ascorbic acid was given. Laboratory experiments on man obviously cannot use survival as a criterion. Glickman *et al.* (1946) made an extensive study in which men were exposed daily during 8 h to temperatures of $+16°C$ (with minimum clothing on) to $-29°C$ (with protective clothing); the experiment lasted 89 days. The amount of ascorbic acid in the basic diet was 33 mg/day. Supplementation of the diet with a mixture of vitamins including 200 mg/day ascorbic acid had no effect on the skin or deep temperatures, or on a battery of neuromuscular and psychological tests.

Determinations of the ascorbic acid intake of circumpolar populations have also given no support for an increased need of ascorbic acid. Arctic travellers, trappers, and Eskimos have been shown to subsist on ascorbic acid intakes of less than 15 mg daily without clinical manifestations of deficiency (Rodahl, 1954a, b, 1960).

An increased requirement for thiamine has been demonstrated in animals exposed to low temperatures (Ershoff, 1950a), and an increased requirement for vitamin A has also been reported (Ershoff, 1950b, 1952; Ershoff and Greenberg, 1950). However, human experiments have failed to substantiate an increase of cold tolerance by vitamin supplementation (Keys, 1947).

Divergent opinions on the usefulness of vitamin supplementation in cold climates nevertheless persists. Soviet authors are in favour of generous supplements. The problem has been covered by a recent monograph (Pushkina, 1961). The requirements for ascorbic acid have been assessed as high as at 200–250 mg/day for men involved in vigorous activity. Low arterial pressure, hypercholesterolemia, and neurotic reactions have been described as manifestations of deficiency (Efremov, 1966). Also the need for thiamine is considered to be increased; a daily intake of 5 mg is recommended. (This is approximately three times more than the FAO–WHO recommended intake of 0.33 mg per 1000 Cal; FAO–WHO, 1967). For other vitamins, the intake is recommended to exceed that in temperate climates by 30–50%.

2.2.2.2. WATER AND ELECTROLYTES

During a cold exposure the water and electrolyte metabolism is affected by the cold itself. Cold causes a transient increase in urinary volume resulting in a decrease of the plasma volume and haemoconcentration (Bazett *et al.*, 1940; Eliot *et al.*, 1949).

The cold environment, on the other hand, makes the replacement of fluid losses a major effort when water is available only from ice or snow. In the practical situation secondary effects of dehydration may be superimposed on the primary effects of cold.

From May to September there are usually ample accumulations of fresh water on the polar ice of the Arctic. Melting snow produces water which is as devoid of minerals as any distilled water and equally tasteless. Melting requires constant attention because of the large volumes of snow needed. Freshwater ice is an ideal source for water. However, also sea ice may be used; although newly formed ice contains from 0.5 to 1.5% salt, the process of melting and refreezing gradually decreases the salt content of the ice (Rodahl, 1954a).

The simplest method to melt snow or ice is to use the metabolic heat, either by eating snow or ice, or by carrying it in water-tight bags close to the body. In order to melt and warm 1 kg of ice from $-13°C$ to $37°C$, $50 + 80 = 130$ Cal is required. This is only one-quarter of the metabolic heat released during one hour of heavy exercise. However, a mouthful of cold snow or ice is a painful experience, and has been advised against repeatedly. For a resting man, the intake of warm beverages is to be preferred, as they counteract body cooling and are a potent booster to the morale. However, during exercise, not too cold snow in very small amounts may be melted in the mouth without untoward effects. The Eskimos hunting on the sea ice produced their drinking water by melting snow in bags of walrus intestines carried underneath their parkas. Rubber or plastic bags serve equally well (Rodahl, 1954a).

Melting ice or snow in conventional cooking utensils requires much time and effort. Thus, in operation "Musk Ox", procuring water and eating took 3 h or longer daily; nevertheless, water was difficult to obtain in adequate quantities, and thirst was common. The average consumption of fluids was 1.2 l (range 0.7–3.4 l) (Kark et al., 1948; see also Slauta, 1956). When water is easily available, its intake is the same in cold as in temperate climates, 1.5–2.0 l/day (Welch et al., 1958).

2.2.3. Skiing or Sledging Rations

The criteria for a skiing or sledging ration are: (1) high calorie yield, (2) low weight, (3) small bulk, (4) strong, easy-open, low-weight packaging, (5) palatability, (6) variety, and (7) acceptability also without cooking (Lewis and Masterton, 1958).

Most parts of the world with a cold climate offer rather meagre resources for "living from the land". On the other hand, cold climate is ideal for the preservation of most foods. However, insofar as economizing in transports is necessary, dried foods are to be given preference. Water for reconstitution has to be obtained mostly from snow or ice. Modern freeze-drying food technology offers a wide variety of foods to the explorer. In the past, however, he had less choice. Dried meat, known under the names of pemmican or biltong, was a staple food of trappers and explorers. The early pemmicans consisted of dried meat and animal fat. However, since the 1930s, other ingredients, e.g. cereals, have been introduced. Typical figures for the composition of pemmican are: protein 25–46%, fat 43–47%, carbohydrates 0–25%, water, and minerals (Hannon et al., 1960).

Stefansson (1957), an ardent believer in diets rich in fat, fared well when crossing the American Arctic in 1906, living on a meat and fish diet like the primitive Eskimos (Abs, 1959). Most nutritionists and many expedition members, however, have found a pemmican diet less acceptable. Lockhart (1945) has discussed in detail the problems encountered with the preparation and use of pemmicans.

Compilations of rations carried during the last hundred years by several polar expeditions have been published by Lockhart (1945) and by Bertram (1954, 1964).

The British North Greenland Expedition of 1952-4 used the following basic ration (Lewis and Masterton, 1958):

	g	Cal
Butter	160	1261
Pemmican	160	890
Biscuits	122	555
Chocolate	68	392
Sugar	85	339
Porridge oats	65	264
Dried milk	45	238
Potato powder	45	124
Cocoa	11	51

Total weight: 761 g/man/day.
Total energy: 4164 Cal.

This ration has been further developed by replacing pemmican with dehydrated meat and by adding sweets, cheese, dehydrated soups, sultanas, and—for palatability—curry powder, marmite, salt, and pepper, tea, and coffee powder. The additions increased the calorie content to 4800 Cal per ration (Lewis and Masterton, 1958). Earlier rations did not reach the same degree of compactness; their average has been 4500 Cal per ration of 900 g.

Chocolate bars are a popular item in excursion diets. However, during skiing or sledging, they become less acceptable; as cold air enters the mouth, the chocolate fat tends to harden on the mucosa, salivation is often meagre because of dehydration, and taking snow into the mouth only aggravates the hardening of the chocolate. Tablets containing multiple vitamins have become a standard item in the diet of expeditions. In a normal sledge-load the weight of dog food exceeds the weight of human food by 4 to 1 (Bertram, 1954). The optimum salt intake, under a wide variety of conditions, has been found to be 0.7 osmoles a day (Johnson and Sargent 1958).

2.2.4. Survival Rations

The history of polar expeditions has no dearth of tragic events, when men had to fight their way against the perils of nature and survive on semi-starvation diets or starve outright. Planned semi-starvation under Arctic conditions is of recent origin. The need for a ration allowing survival with rather limited physical activity has arisen, as it has become possible to rescue aircrews with the aid of helicopters from the spot where they have landed. The survivors of an emergency landing or of a parachute descent construct a shelter and wait for rescue. It is expected that this will occur within a maximum of 10 days. Under such conditions a daily energy expenditure of 2000–2300 Cal/m^2 has been observed (Rogers et al., 1964). The rations should be able to protect against the life-endangering effects of starvation and to boost up the morale, whereas the issue of calories is of secondary importance; they may be drawn from the fat tissue.

The three major effects of semi-starvation to be guarded against are decrease of blood glucose, ketosis, and disturbances in the water and electrolyte balance. All of them may contribute to functional deterioration, lethargy, and death. During cold exposure, the tendency of body temperature to fall on diets deficient in calories adds to the deterioration.

The results of an extensive study of the interrelations of calorie deprivation, water deprivation, exercise, and climate have been reported by Johnson and Sargent (1958). The combinations of experimental conditions extended from starvation with 910 g water per day all the way to unlimited fresh and frozen foods with unlimited water. The results have been presented in the form of a series of nomograms.

In semi-starvation diets, carbohydrates play a special role for two reasons—they are antiketogenic and they tend to prevent a reduction of the extracellular fluid space. Both these factors are important in cold climates.

According to Johnson and Sargent, the ketogenicity of any diet is increased with decreasing temperature. Cold itself causes an increased urinary flow, and semi-starvation will accentuate the sodium deficit and the contraction of the extracellular volume. This, particularly the decrease of blood volume, reduces the exercise tolerance of the cardiovascular system and may predispose to peripheral cold injury, syncope, lethargy, and to phlebothrombosis (Rogers et al., 1964).

It is of interest that whereas sodium intake has no effect on weight loss during fasting in a temperate climate, it effectively reduces the weight loss of fasting subjects exposed to cold. A supplement of 230 meq. of sodium, corresponding to 1.1 l of extracellular fluid, was observed to reduce the weight loss by 1 kg (Rogers and Setliff, 1964).

The ability of carbohydrates to keep up the blood sugar level, and to counteract ketosis and the water and electrolyte loss, makes them an obvious choice for survival rations. Survival packs have been developed with only carbohydrate foods—sugar and sweets—in amounts calculated to provide a daily intake of 500–1000 Cal over a few days. On the other hand, proteins and fat have higher satiety value than sugar, and for reasons of morale their inclusion in palatable form appears justified. Another practice is the use of pemmican alone in survival rations. Simulated survival experiments at an intake level of 500 Cal/day over 7 days have shown that pemmican is less acceptable to the subjects than sucrose (Rogers et al., 1966). The isocaloric substitution of pemmican with sucrose up to 80 g/day on a 1000 Cal/day diet over 5 days increased the fasting blood glucose and reduced ketosis (Drury et al., 1959; Vaughan et al., 1959). Nevertheless, sucrose supplementation at this level had no influence on changes in the plasma sodium, magnesium, calcium, chloride, and phosphate levels (Hannon et al., 1960). Although ketosis was observed with the pemmican diet, the levels with or without sucrose supplement were too low to produce manifest deleterious effects. Furthermore, no subjective differences were attributable to variations in the blood glucose level (Drury et al., 1959).

At the level of an intake of 500 Cal/day, a ration of sucrose with 150 meq. of sodium as chloride on the first day and as bicarbonate on the subsequent days has proved superior to fasting, to pemmican alone, and to the electrolyte alone, using as indications weight loss, sodium balance, serum glucose, and ketone excretion. Although the differences between sucrose alone and as supplemented with electrolytes were not large, an electrolyte supplement appears useful on the basis of the fasting experiments (Rogers et al., 1966).

While protein deprivation over a few days does not affect the physical working capacity in a temperate climate, it may cause marked deterioration of the work capacity in a cold environment. In experiments at $+8°C$, at an energy expenditure of appr. 3000 Cal/day, with a calorically adequate protein-free diet, the treadmill running time was markedly shortened. Cold exposures with low-calorie and/or low-protein diets were associated with painful cold injury in extremities (Rodahl et al., 1962).

2.3. HOT CLIMATES

In a hot climate man has to cope with an environmental heat load added to the metabolic generation of heat. His ability to keep the body temperature constant is largely dependent on evaporative heat loss, sweating, and the replacement of the body water and electrolyte losses. Exercise increases the heat load and the sweat losses. In many hot regions of the world, water is scarce, and its supply becomes the critical factor (Johnson and Sargent, 1958). Another major effect of heat exposure on man is a reduction of appetite, with ensuing negative calorie balance. During a stay of 12 days in a tropical climate, the food intake of men decreased by 25%, and the negative balance was confirmed by a mean weight loss of 1.1–2.5 kg in the groups studied (Edholm and Goldsmith, 1966). Protein may increase appetite, and is therefore recommended to be used at levels above the minimum requirements (Platt and Fox, 1954). The theoretical objections against a high protein diet in hot environments, particularly in hard work, because of its high specific dynamic action, have been found unjustified. Protein intakes varying from 75 to 150 g/day have no effect on the ability to perform intermittent work in the heat (Pitts *et al.*, 1944a).

2.3.1. *Energy Expenditure*

In hot climates man tends to avoid strenuous exercise and hence his energy expenditure is reduced. Actual determinations on populations living in hot climates have confirmed this, and the recommendation has accordingly been to reduce the food allowance by 5% for every 10°C above the base temperature of $\pm 10°C$ (FAO–WHO, 1957).

In experiments with exposure to heat, opposite results have been obtained. When men were subjected to such climatic conditions where the daily sweat rates varied from 2.1 to 6.4 l, the energy requirements increased from 2733 to 4058 Cal/day, parallel to the intensity of the exposure (Consolazio *et al.*, 1961). The increase applies both to the resting metabolism (Welch *et al.*, 1956; Shapiro and Consolazio, 1959) and to the energy cost of standard exercise (Consolazio *et al.*, 1961; Durnin and Haisman, 1965). Varying results have been published from no increase up to 27% above the total energy expenditure of the same work in a cool environment (Nelson *et al.*, 1948; Consolazio *et al.*, 1963; Strydom *et al.*, 1966).

The *Recommended Dietary Allowances* of the US National Research Council have taken cognizance of these observations and state that under conditions of increased physical activity it is desirable to increase calorie allowances by at least 0.5% for every degree rise between 30° and 40°C.

2.3.2. Proportion of Nutrients

Carbohydrates appear as the food of choice for hot climates as they have the lowest specific dynamic action, and hence do not increase the metabolic heat load as much as fats and, particularly, proteins. In addition, carbohydrates contribute more metabolic water per calorie than other foods, which is useful in arid hot areas.

The loss of nitrogen in sweat has been considered an extra load to the nitrogen balance. Whereas in short-term experiments, significant losses of nitrogen through sweat may accrue, the concentration of nitrogen in the sweat of completely acclimatized subjects is very low, 0.2 mg/g, and fully compensated by a decrease of nitrogen loss in urine (Ashworth and Harrower, 1967).

2.3.3. Vitamins

There is no evidence that exposure to heat would increase the requirement for any vitamins. Their losses in sweat are quite small (e.g. Fox, 1958). Vitamin supplementation over and above physiological needs does not improve performance in a hot climate (Kark *et al.*, 1947).

2.3.4. Water and Electrolytes

The amount of sweat secreted for evaporative cooling may exceed 20 l/day (Adolph, 1947). Acclimatized young men are able to keep up a sweating rate of 1 l/h, but with more severe conditions the subjects become progressively incapacitated. When water is available *ad libitum*, thirst causes the replacement of some two-thirds of the water loss (Pitts *et al.*, 1944b). Full replacement of the water loss during work in heat requires a conscious effort. The "spontaneous" dehydration may cause a marked deterioration of the performance capacity. It is thus advisable to drink more than thirst indicates and to use the excretion of an adequate amount of urine, some 700–900 ml/day, as a guideline (Adolph, 1947; Strydom *et al.*, 1965).

2.3.5. Rations for Tropical Expeditions

In planning rations for tropical expeditions, tables of energy and nutrient values of foods commonly used in the tropics are available (e.g. Platt, 1962). The modern food industry offers a choice of tinned and dehydrated foods to supplement those locally available, all of which may not be customary and therefore not accepted. Large water containers should be available for the main supply, and each man should carry his individual desert water-bag in which the contents are cooled by surface evaporation (Platt and Fox, 1954).

3. FOOD FOR SEA VOYAGES

The choice of foods on a modern luxury liner hardly reminds us of the diet and nutrition of sailors of the past centuries. Long periods spent offshore and the lack of fresh food made scurvy a companion of the sailor. Indirectly, these problems gave a stimulus for the science of nutrition: in 1747, a physician of HMS *Salisbury*, James Lind, discovered that scurvy could be prevented by supplementing the diet of the sailors with oranges and lemons.

Even in our modern world, shipwrecks do occur. There are also people who deliberately choose the voluntary solitude of a small boat for long ocean journeys. On a transatlantic crossing by sailing, 7–8 weeks at sea, the energy value of daily food was 2500–2800 Cal and the consumption of water 1.5–3.5 l/day. After an initial period the men adopted the habit of eating only one meal a day. The average weight loss was as high as 9 kg (Lewis *et al.*, 1964).

Survivors of shipwrecks may be exposed for unspecified times to a shortage of food and drinking water. In a 3-day experiment, the administration of 100 g carbohydrate plus 250 ml distilled water proved to retain body water better than 350 ml water alone (Hervey and McCance, 1951–2, 1954). Carbohydrate spares the body protein, prevents ketosis, and also reduces the basal metabolic rate; all these effects contribute to the preservation of water balance. Sea water has a salinity of 3.3–3.8%, while the maximum concentration of sodium chloride in urine may rise only to 2%. The supplementation of the ration of 350 ml distilled water per day with sea water causes a rise in the osmotic pressure of body fluids, with consequent osmotic diuresis and hence increases the rate of deterioration. It may be concluded that carbohydrate and water are to be the prime ingredients of sea rescue rations. Simple ion exchange equipment and/or solar stills should be provided for desalting sea water (Edholm and Bacharach, 1965a).

4. ALTITUDE AND NUTRITION

Some human populations live permanently in mountainous regions at high altitudes. Mountaineering expeditions have conquered even the highest peaks, submitting to the rigours of rarefied atmosphere, cold, and strenuous physical activity. Aviation has introduced an easier and more comfortable approach to high altitudes.

Altitude exerts its major effect on the human body through the reduced partial pressure of oxygen. This is partly compensated by an increase in the oxygen transport function of respiration and circulation. However, hyperventilation as caused by hypoxia also increases the elimination of carbon dioxide, and hence leads to hypocapnia and to an alkaline shift of the pH of the blood and extracellular fluid. Up to altitudes of some 3000 m, only slight physiological changes may be observed in the resting organism. With increasing altitudes, the capacities of the central nervous system start to deteriorate, and loss of consciousness may occur at altitudes above 5000 m. However, the exercise capacity is considerably affected already at medium altitudes, below 3000 m. With a prolonged stay at altitude, adaptation occurs. Initial adaptation over the first days is connected with an increased excretion of alkali and a normalization of the blood pH. However, a slow adaptation continues; complete adaptation has been shown to require even longer than a year.

The basal metabolic rate is not essentially affected by altitude (Grover 1963; Consolazio *et al.*, 1966). The same applies to the energy cost of standard exercise (e.g. Douglas *et al.*, 1913; Christensen, 1937). However, at the altitudes encountered on Mount Everest, the efficiency of climbing decreased with altitude. This decrease is ascribed to difficult ground, wind, the weight of boots, and the drag of heavy clothing (Pugh *et al.*, 1964).

The energy expenditure of climbing expeditions may be calculated with the aid of available data. The net efficiency of walking uphill can be taken as 28% on easy surface. The energy expenditure of walking downhill is about half of that walking uphill. In well-trained climbers, the energy expenditure during climbing varies between 7 and 13 Cal/min. In a day with 7 h climbing and 3 h downhill, the energy expenditure of climbing has been calculated to be from 5900 to 7300 Cal/day (Zuntz *et al.*, 1906; Durnin, 1955; Pugh, 1958). In converting this to dietary needs, the resting expenditure must, of course, be included.

When the supply of oxygen is restricted, carbohydrate is the preferable fuel since it gives most energy for the same amount of oxygen. When one litre of oxygen is used for the oxidation of starch, it is equivalent to 5.05 Cal, while the corresponding figure for fat is 4.69 and for protein 4.60 Cal. A high proportion of carbohydrate appears, therefore, to be indicated for diets provided at high altitudes. The favourable effects of a high carbohydrate diet on performance and clinical symptomatology have been substantiated in human experiments (Consolazio *et al.*, 1969).

Experience has shown that energy balance is not generally achieved on mountaineering excursions. When expenditure during a day exceeds 5000 Cal, even at sea level, the replacement of the calories is generally delayed to the succeeding periods (Karvonen and Turpeinen, 1954). At high altitudes the intake is further reduced by a characteristic anorexia and, during forced adaptation, often also by manifest mountain sickness (Whitten and Janoski, 1969). Weight loss is a regular phenomenon: Pugh (1954) has reported an average weight loss of 5 kg during an initial 24 day period in 1952, spent in the Himalaya at altitudes mostly over 3700 m. However, adequate attention to the palatability of food may greatly improve the acceptance of food. The favourable experiences as gained from the 1953 British expedition to Mount Everest can be ascribed partly to improvements in the diet and partly to a schedule of progressive adaptation to the altitude. In contrast to previous expeditions, on which the diet included many bulky food items and was largely composed of locally available foods, the provisioning was based on pre-packed composite rations of the type used in the armed forces. This provided a varied diet of the European type, familiar to the members of the party. For altitudes above 6700 m a special "assault" ration was designed (Table 5), consisting of vacuum-packed basic foods only. Sugar was one of the main items, providing alone 1500 Cal/day. The food eaten on the 1953 expedition provided more than 4300 Cal/day during the approach march to the base camp at 5500 m and 3200 Cal/day during the assault phase, whereas on the 1935 expedition the intake remained below

TABLE 5 "ASSAULT" RATION FOR 2 MAN-DAYS, AS USED ON THE 1953 MOUNT EVEREST EXPEDITION (PUGH, 1954)

Item	Weight (g)	Item	Weight (g)
Rolled oats	57	Cheese	57
Milk powder	170	Cocoa	28
Sugar	794	Tea	43
Jam	57	Soup powder	64
Sweet biscuits	170	Lemonade powder	624
Mint bar or banana bar	113	Salt	11

2000 Cal/day at altitudes above 5200 m and at 1500 Cal/day above 6400 m. The mean weight loss during 2 months on the 1953 expedition was only 3 kg.

The water loss due to sweating must be replaced. The daily intake of water in beverages and food has varied from 2.5 to 3.5 l on Himalayan expeditions. Exhaustion of climbing parties has been ascribed to insufficient water supplies.

Pressure cookers and well-designed stoves are important on mountaineering excursions. The provision of cooked meals and warm beverages greatly contributes to the morale and helps to overcome anorexia.

It has been suggested that potassium loss might play a role in the pathogenesis of mountain sickness (Waterlow and Bunjé, 1966). The hypothesis has been studied on a few expeditions in the Andes, at 3800–5200 m, by varying the potassium intake of the members. Although the results have not been conclusive they suggest that a generous potassium supply might be helpful against the symptoms of mountain sickness in previously unacclimatized men.

In experimental animals, vitamin-E deficiency causes increased susceptibility to hypoxia (Hove *et al.*, 1945; Taylor, 1953). However, there is no evidence that vitamin-E supplementation would increase the tolerance to hypoxia of normal subjects.

5. AIR AND SPACE FLIGHTS

5.1. AVIATION

Aviation has brought man to a new environment. Until the mid-twentieth century the aviator's physical environment was rather comparable to that met by mountaineers. Hypoxia due to the rarefied atmosphere at high altitudes was the dominant physiological factor in the environment. Attempts were consequently made for increasing the tolerance of man against hypoxia by using various means including the aviator's diet. The factors to be considered have been discussed in § 4.

The reduction of atmospheric pressure may have physiological effects also independently of the oxygen supply. According to Boyle's law, the volume of gas is indirectly proportional to the pressure. This physical law applies, of course, to all gas spaces in the human body, including the gas in the gastrointestinal tract. With an ascent, the gastrointestinal gases tend to expand, and any trapped gas causes discomfort which may even incapacitate the aviator. It has been customary to advise against the use of gas-forming foods, such as beans, peas, etc., and against carbonated drinks before and during flights. However, the gastrointestinal gas volumes appear to have an easy passage, and non-observance of the recommendation has seldom been followed by serious discomfort during ordinary flight.

In modern aeroplanes, the cabin pressure is kept higher than that of the environment, but it generally is not brought quite to the sea-level pressure. In this compromise atmosphere, the aviator is, to some extent, subject to the same environmental factors as his fore-runners in the non-pressurized planes. However, he is exposed also to a new hazard—to that of rapid decompression. If the cabin pressurization fails, the aviator is subjected in a very short time to the environmental pressure. With rapid decompression, acute discomfort is generally experienced as a consequence of the expansion of the gastrointestinal gas. Therefore, the recommendation to avoid gas-forming foods is still valid, particularly in military aviation, where losses of cabin pressure are more likely to occur whereas they have become a very rare event in civil airline operations. Nevertheless, the gastrointestinal discomfort generally is not incapacitating even in rapid decompression.

Flight feeding has been discussed from the angle of preventive medicine by Taylor and Finkelstein (1958), and recommendations on food hygiene and sanitation have been published by WHO (1960).

When the survivors of a forced landing are expected to land in their aircraft or in its vicinity, no special problems over those discussed in § 2.1, are to be foreseen. However, the aviator who leaves his aircraft by using the ejection seat, will probably land very far from the remains of his aircraft, and has only his survival kit at his disposal. A small amount of food can be provided within the space available. The aim has to be restricted to keeping up the survivor's morale for some 3–5 days until rescue operations are successful. In some air forces only carbohydrates (sugar, sweets) are supplied in the survival rations of the ejection kit, whereas others have also included foods like canned meat, milk powder, chocolate, etc., primarily as they are considered to have more satiety value and to boost up the morale better than mere sweets.

5.2. SPACE TRAVEL

The space capsules are pressurized, the Soviet spacecraft to the atmospheric pressure of 760 mm Hg with a mixture of gases, while the first US missions were flown at a pressure of one-third of an atmosphere in a pure oxygen atmosphere. Thus, neither the cosmonauts nor the astronauts are subjected to hypoxia, but the astronauts experience a change of pressure. The spacecraft atmosphere is kept constant by a continuous supply of oxygen and absorption of carbon dioxide to a lithium canister. The contamination of the air should be kept at a minimum, and therefore gas-forming foods should be avoided also in space travel.

Up to now, experiences have been gained only from simulated flights and such manned flights where pre-packaged foods have been used. However, for interstellar travel a new approach is considered necessary, with recycling of water, carbon dioxide, and nitrogen in a food-producing biological system within the closed spacecraft ecological unit.

The energy expenditure of the spacecraft crew is rather low, as may be expected. Calloway (1967) reports values from 2000 to 2400 Cal/day, as determined from the carbon dioxide absorbed into the lithium canister; since there may have been losses, the real expenditure has probably been somewhat higher, 2500–2800 Cal/day. Parin and Adamovich (1968) assess the food requirements at 2800–3000 Cal/day. Extravehicular activities, on the other hand, require a high energy expenditure; moving and work in the weightless space is in itself heavy, and the cumbersome pressure suit adds greatly to the difficulty.

In planning the diet for space travel extending over a maximum of weeks or months, the limited capsule space, the need for payload economy and weightlessness during the flight are the most obvious considerations (e.g. Adamovich *et al.*, 1968). However, these are not the only ones: a more comprehensive list is given in Table 6.

TABLE 6   SOURCES OF CONSTRAINTS IMPOSED UPON SPACE FLIGHT FEEDING SYSTEM

Biological constraints	Engineering constraints	Operational constraints
Food safety limits	Temperature tolerance	Rehydration time
Acceptability limits	Weight limitation	Handling
Gastroenterologic limits	Volume limitation	Food heating and cooling
Nutritional limits	Water for rehydration	Food residue stabilization
Dietetics	Pressure	Vehicle interface
	Relative humidity	
	Acceleration	
	Vibration	

Utmost care has to be taken to eliminate sources of food-borne infections. The established food safety standards are stricter than those developed for flight feeding (Heidelbaugh, 1966). It is important that the food should contain sufficient residue so that formed stools are regularly passed. However, defaecation should be infrequent in view of the difficulties caused by the limited spacecraft size and the pressure suit.

The effects of exposure of fresh foods to near-vacuum conditions has been studied by Cooke and Heidelbaugh (1966). Although fresh foods can be used on space missions, preference has been given to rather sophisticated food preparations.

The state-of-the-art of the US space flight feeding systems has been described by Heidelbaugh (1966). Three categories of foods are supplied: rehydratable solids, rehydratable powders, and ready-to-eat bite-size foods. The rehydratable solid foods are prepared, moulded into single-portion sizes, freeze-dried, and vacuum packaged in a clear flexible plastic package. The package is fitted at one end with a valve to receive the nozzle of a water-dispensing gun, and at the other end with a tube which is cut by the pilot after he has allowed the food to rehydrate. The food is pressed through the tube into the mouth. Approximately 10% remains attached to the container. Each pack is supplied with a bacteriostatic tablet which is inserted into the pack in order to prevent spoilage of the wet food residue. A selection of twenty-one bite-sized foods has been tested in a simulated 56 day space flight (Heidelbaugh *et al.*, 1966; Vanderveen *et al.*, 1966). The foods are supplied as cubes, with no need of reconstitution. The constitution is such that crumbling does not occur.

The consumption of the individual bite-size foods varied from 29 to 99%. They were still considered by the subjects as a survival ration—monotonous and affording little pleasure. They also produced non-formed faeces with a pungent odour, which made them unacceptable to space flight missions. The unfavourable characteristics were ascribed to the high-melting-point fat used in the coating of the foods and a consequent low apparent digestibility of fat, from 77.5 to 85.5% in the four subjects. Further development of the bite-size foods is indicated.

The actual food intake at the US spacecraft missions has varied from 420 to 2230 Cal/day (Berry, 1967; Calloway, 1967). The crew do not experience hunger; they have to be reminded to eat. A weight loss has been regularly observed during space flights, up to 4.5 kg. Much is ascribed to fluid shifts and is regained within a few days after the flight (Balakhovsky, 1967).

The immobility of the crew in the capsule and the weightlessness cause some biochemical changes similar to those observed during prolonged bed rest, notably a negative nitrogen and calcium balance. While the protein loss is probably ascribed, to a large part, to inactivity, the loss of calcium indicates a demineralization of the bones due to weightlessness. It has been suggested that an ample supply of calcium during the flight may reduce calcium loss, but the available observations are not sufficient for substantiating this hypothesis (Calloway, 1967).

A decrease of the half-life of erythrocytes has been observed on some of the US space flights. This has tentatively been ascribed to the oxygen atmosphere. An increase of the tocopherol and ascorbic acid supplies to saturation levels has been suggested in order to provide anti-oxidant protection both to lipid and aqueous systems. However, the hypothesis has not yet been subjected to an experimental test (Calloway, 1967).

Space flights have provided a powerful stimulus for developing foods and food packaging, and the experiences gained may have application also in other fields. The great variety of freeze-dried, conveniently prepared foods will obviously have uses also on several terrestrial excursions. Further impact can be expected from the techniques developed in space food production for quality assurance such as use of filtered air clean room methods (Heidelbaugh, 1966).

REFERENCES

ABS, O. (1959) *Die Eskimoernährung und ihre gesundheitlichen Auswirkungen*, VEB Georg Theme, Leipzig.
ADAMOVICH, B. A., NEFYODOV, Y. G., USHAKOV, A. S., and CHIZHOV, S. V. (1968) *Life Sci. Space Res.* **6,** 23.
ADAMS, W. S., LESLIE, A., and LEVIN, M. H. (1950) *Proc. Soc. exp. Biol. Med.* **74,** 46.
ADOLPH, E. F. (1947) *Physiology of Man in the Desert*, Interscience, New York.
ADOLPH, E. F. (1964) In *Thirst*, p. 5 (M. J. Wayner, ed.), Pergamon Press, New York.
AHLBORG, B., EKELUND, L.-G., and NILSSON, C.-G. (1968) *Acta physiol. scand.* **74,** 238.
ARCHDEACON, J. W. and MURLIN, J. R. (1944) *J. Nutr.* **28,** 241.
ARIENS, E. J. (1965) In *Doping*, p. 27 (A. de Schaepdryver and M. Hebbelinck, eds.), Pergamon Press, London.
ARUTYUNOV, G. A., ANTUFJEV, I. I., VOROBJEV, A. J., KUZNETSOV, M. I., UDALOV, Y. F. and SHIBUNEJEV, A. G. (1962) *Vop. Pitan.* **21,** 3.
ASHWORTH, A. and HARROWER, A. D. B. (1967) *Proc. Nutr. Soc.* **26,** xxix.
BALAKHOVSKY, I. S. (1967) *Life Sci. Space Res.* **5,** 111.
BARBORKA, C. J., FOLTZ, E. E., and IVY, A. C. (1943) *J. Am. med. Ass.* **122,** 717.
BAZETT, H. C., SUNDERMAN, F. W., DOUPE, J., and SCOTT, J. C. (1940) *Am. J. Physiol.* **129,** 69.
BEHNKE, A. R., FEEN, C. B., and WELHAM, W. C. (1942) *J. Am. med. Ass.* **118,** 495.
BERGSTRÖM, J., and HULTMAN, E. (1966) *Scand. J. clin. Lab. Invest.* **18,** 16.
BERRY, A. (1967) *J. Am. med. Ass.* **201,** 232.
BERRY, W. T. C., BEVERIDGE, J. B., BRANSBY, G. R., CHALMERS, A. K., NEEDMAN, B. M., MAGEE, H. G., TOWNSEND, H. S., and DAUBNEY, C. G. (1949) *Br. med. J.* **1,** 300.
BERRYMAN, G. H., HENDERSON, C. R., WHEELER, N. C., COGSWELL, R. C., JR., SPINELLA, J. R., GRUNDY, W. E., JOHNSON, H. C., WOOD, M. E., DENKO, C. W., FRIEDEMANN, T. E., HARRIS, S. C., IVY, A. C., and YOUMANS, J. B. (1947) *Am. J. Physiol.* **148,** 618.
BERTRAM, G. C. L. (1954) *Proc. Nutr. Soc.* **13,** 69.
BERTRAM, G. C. L. (1964) In *Arzt und Ernährung*. p. 2, Documenta Geigy SA, Basle.
BIERRING, E. (1931) *Arbeitsphysiologie* **5,** 17.

BLOOM, W. L., AZAR, G., CLARK, J., and MACKAY, J. H. (1965) *Ann. NY Acad. Sci.* **131**, 623.
BØJE, O. (1936) *Skand. Arch. Physiol.* **74**, Suppl. 10, 1.
BORGMANN, H. W. (1940) *Militärarzt* **5**, 229. Ref. in *Das Vitamin C im Sport. Informationsbericht VII*, Eckes Übersee-Fruchtsaft KG, Nieder-Olm bei Mainz.
BROWN, J. D. and PULSIFER, D. H. (1965) *Aerospace Med.* **36**, 267.
CALLOWAY, D. H. (1967) In *Proceedings of the 7th International Congress of Nutrition, Hamburg 1966*, Pergamon Press, Oxford.
CAMPBELL, J. M. H., MITCHELL, G. O., and POWELL, A. T. W. (1928) *Guy's Hosp. Rep.* **78**, 279.
CAUSERET, J. (1957) *Bull. Soc. scient. Hyg. aliment.* **45**, 19.
CERRETELLI, P., DI PRAMPERO, P. G., and PIIPER, J. (1969) *Am. J. Physiol.* **217**, 581.
CHITTENDEN, R. H. (1904) *Physiological Economy in Nutrition*, Stones, New York.
CHRISTENSEN, E. H. (1931) *Arbeitsphysiologie* **4**, 128, 154, 175.
CHRISTENSEN, E. H. (1937) *Skand. Arch. Physiol.* **76**, 88.
CHRISTENSEN, E. H. (1958) *Das Essen und Trinken des Sportlers*, Dr. A. Wander AG, Bern.
CHRISTENSEN, E. H., and HANSEN, O. (1939) *Skand. Arch. Physiol.* **81**, 172.
CHRISTENSEN, E. H., and HÖGBERG, P. (1950) *Arbeitsphysiologie* **14**, 292.
CHRISTOPHE, J., and MAYER, J. (1958) *J. appl. Physiol.* **13**, 269.
CONSOLAZIO, C. F., MATOUSH, L. O., JOHNSON, H. L., KRZYWICKI, H. J., DAWS, T. A., and ISAAC, G. J. (1969) *Fedn Proc.* **28**, 937.
CONSOLAZIO, C. F., MATOUSH, L. O., and NELSON, R. A. (1966) *Fedn. Proc.* **25**, 1380.
CONSOLAZIO, C. F., MATOUSH, L. O., NELSON, R. A., ISAAC, G. J., and HURSH, L. M. (1964a) *J. appl. Physiol.* **19**, 265.
CONSOLAZIO, C. F., MATOUSH, L. R. O., NELSON, R. A., TORRES, J. B., and ISAAC, G. J. (1963) *J. appl. Physiol.* **18**, 65.
CONSOLAZIO, C. F., NELSON, R. A., MATOUSH, R. O., and ISAAC, G. J. (1964b) *J. appl. Physiol.* **19**, 257.
CONSOLAZIO, C. F., SHAPIRO, R., MASTERTON, J. E., and MCKINZIE, P. S. L. (1961) *J. Nutr.* **73**, 126.
COOKE, J. P., and HEIDELBAUGH, N. D. (1966) *Aerospace Med.* **37**, 788.
COVELL, B., EL DIN, N., and PASSMORE, R. (1965) *Lancet* **i**, 727.
CRANDON, J. H., LUND, C. C., and DILL, D. B. (1940) *New Engl. J. Med.* **223**, 353.
CURETON, T. K. (1954) *Am. J. Physiol.* **179**, 628.
CURETON, T. K. (1959–60) *J. phys. Educ.* 57, nos. 2, 3, 4, 5.
CURETON, T. K. (1970) To be published in *Br. J. Sports Med.* Ref. by Sharman *et al.*, 1971.
CURETON, T. K., and POHNDORF, R. H. (1955) *Res. Q. Am. Ass. Hlth phys. Educ.* **26**, 391.
DARLING, R. C., JOHNSON, R. E., PITTS, G. C., CONSOLAZIO, F. C., and ROBINSON, P. F. (1944) *J. Nutr.* **28**, 273.
DARLINGTON, F. B., and CHASSELS, J. B. (1956) *Summary* **8**, 1. Ref. by Sharman *et al.*, 1971.
DARLINGTON, F. B., and CHASSELS, J. B. (1957) *Summary* **9**, 50. Ref. by Sharman *et al.*, 1971.
DARLINGTON, F. B., and CHASSELS, J. B. (1958) *Summary* **10**, 66. Ref. by Sharman *et al.*, 1971.
DEJONG, A. B. E. (1965) In *Exploration Medicine*, p. 378 (O. G. Edholm, and A. L. Bacharach, eds.), John Wright, Bristol.
DENNIG, H., BECKEN-FREYSENG, H., RENDENBACH, R., and SCHOSTAK, G. (1940) *Arch. exp. Path. Pharmak.* **195**, 261.
DOUGLAS, C. G., HALDANE, J. S., HENDERSON, Y., and SCHNEIDER, E. C. (1913) *Phil. Trans. R. Soc. B*, **203**, 185.
DOUGLAS, C. G., and KOCH, A. C. E. (1951) *J. Physiol.* **114**, 208.
DRURY, H. F., VAUGHAN, D. A., and HANNON, J. P. (1959) *J. Nutr.* **67**, 85.

DUGAL, L. P., LEBLOND, C. P., and THERIEN, M. (1945) *Can. J. Res.* **23**, 244.
DUGAL, L. P., and THERIEN, M. (1947) *Can. J. Res.,* Sect. E, **25**, 111.
DURNIN, J. V. G. A. (1955) *J. Physiol.* **128**, 294.
DURNIN, J. V. G. A., and HAISMAN, M. F. (1965) *J. Physiol.* **183**, 75P.
DURNIN, J. V. G. A., and PASSMORE, R. (1967) *Energy, Work and Leisure,* Heinemann, London.
EASTY, D. L. (1967) *Br. J. Nutr.* **21**, 7.
EBBETTS, J. (1966) In *XVI Weltkongress für Sportmedizin, Hannover* 12–16. *Juni* 1966. *Kongressbericht,* p. 729 (G. Hanekopf. edr.), Deutscher Ärzte-Verlag, Köln-Berlin.
EDHOLM, O. G., and BACHARACH, A. L. (eds.) (1965a) *Exploration Medicine,* John Wright, Bristol.
EDHOLM, O. G., and BACHARACH, A. L. (1965b) *The Physiology of Human Survival,* Academic Press, London and New York.
EDHOLM, O. G., FLETCHER, J. G., WIDDOWSON, E. M., and MCCANCE, R. A. (1955) *Br. J. Nutr.* **9**, 286.
EDHOLM, O. G., and GOLDSMITH, R. (1966) *Proc. Nutr. Soc.* **25**, 113.
EFREMOV, V. V. (1966) *7th International Congress of Nutrition, Abstracts of Papers,* Hamburg.
EIGELSREITER, H., and SCHRÖCKSNADEL, H. (1966) In *Sportmedizinische Ergebnisse der IX Olympischen Winterspiele* 1964 *in Innsbruck,* p. 135, Verlagsanstalt Tyrolia, Innsbruck.
ELIOT, J. W., BADER, R. A., and BASS, D. E. (1949) *Fedn Proc.* **8**, 41.
ERSHOFF, B. H. (1950a) *Archs Biochem.* **28**, 299.
ERSHOFF, B. H. (1950b) *Proc. Soc. exp. Biol. Med.* **74**, 586.
ERSHOFF, B. H. (1952) *Proc. Soc. exp. Biol. Med.* **79**, 580.
ERSHOFF, B. H., and GREENBERG, S. M. (1950) *Proc. Soc. exp. Biol. Med.* **75**, 604.
FAO (1957) *Report of the Second Committee on Calorie Requirements,* FAO, Rome.
FAO–WHO (1967) WHO Techn. Rep. Ser. No. 362, WHO, Geneva.
FAO–WHO (1970) WHO Techn. Rep. Ser. No. 452, WHO, Geneva.
FARMER, C. J. (1944) *Fedn Proc.* **3**, 179.
FLETCHER, J. G. (1955) *Lancet* **i**, 1165.
FOLTZ, E. C., BARBORKA, C. J., and IVY, A. C. (1944) *Gastroenterology* **2**, 323.
FORDTRAN, J. S., and SALTIN, B. (1967) *J. appl. Physiol.* **23**, 331.
FOX, R. H. (1958) *Proc. Nutr. Soc.* **17**, 173.
FOY, H., and KONDI, A. (1956) *Lancet* **i**, 423.
FUGE, K. W., CREWS, E. L., III, PATTENGALE, P. K., HOLLOSZY, J. O., and SHANK, R. E. (1968) *Am. J. Physiol.* **215**, 6610.
GARRY, R. C., PASSMORE, R., WARNOCK, G. M., and DURNIN, J. V. G. A. (1955) *Studies on Expenditure of Energy and Consumption of Food by Miners and Clerks, Fife, Scotland* 1952. Med. Res. Council Special Rep. Ser. No. 289, HMS Office, London.
GEBHARDT, E. A. (1966) *Sportarzt Sportmed.* **17**, 298.
GELDRICH, J. (1927) *Biochem. Z.* **188**, 1.
GEMMILL, C. L. (1942) *Physiol. Rev.* **22**, 32.
GIAJA, I., and GELINEO, S. (1934) *C. r. Séanc. Soc. Biol.* **117**, 40.
GLICKMAN, N., KEETON, R. W., MITCHELL, H. H., and FAHNESTOCK, M. K. (1946) *Am. J. Physiol.* **146**, 538.
GRÄFE, H.-K. (1957) *Theor. Prax. Körperkultur* **6**, 519; **7**, 246, 520.
GRÄFE, H.-K. (1964) *Optimale Ernährungsbilanzen für Leistungssportler,* Akademie-Verlag, Berlin.
GRAY, E., CONSOLAZIO, C. F., and KARK, R. M. (1951) *J. appl. Physiol.* **4**, 270.
GROVER, R. F. (1963) *J. appl. Physiol.* **18**, 909.
HAMLEY, E. J. (1964) *Ergonomics* **7**, 237.
HANNON, J. P., LARSON, A. M., DRURY, H. F., VAUGHAN, D. A., and VAUGHAN, L. N. (1960) *US Armed Forces med. J.* **11**, 676.
HARRIS, H. A. (1966) *Proc. Nutr. Soc.* **25**, 87.

HEBBELINCK, M. (1959) *Archs int. Pharmacodyn. Thér.* **120**, 402.
HEBBELINCK, M. (1961) *Spierarbeid en Ethylalkohol,* Arscia, Brussel.
HEDMAN, R. (1951) *Acta physiol. scand.* **40**, 305.
HEIDELBAUGH, N. D. (1966) *J. Am. vet. med. Ass.* **149**, 1662.
HEIDELBAUGH, N. D., VANDERVEEN, J. E., KLICKA, M. V., and O'HARA, M. J. (1966) *Aerospace Med.* **37**, 583.
HEINONEN, A. O. (1965) *Energy expenditure of walking and running in woodland.* Rep. Inst. Occup. Hlth. No. 14.
HEINONEN, A. O., KARVONEN, M. J., and RUOSTEENOJA, R. (1959) *Ergonomics* **2**, 389.
HELLEBRANDT, F. A., and TEPPER, R. H. (1934) *Am. J. Physiol.* **107**, 355.
HENSCHEL, A., TAYLOR, H. L., MICKELSEN, O., BROZEK, J. M., and KEYS, A. (1944) *Fedn Proc.* **3**, 18.
HERVEY, G. R., and MCCANCE, R. A. (1951–52) *Proc. R. Soc.* B, **139**, 527.
HERVEY, G. R., and MCCANCE, R. A. (1954) *Proc. Nutr. Soc.* **13**, 41.
HOVE, E. L., HICKMAN, K., and HARRIS, P. L. (1945) *Archs Biochem.* **8**, 395.
HULTMAN, E. (1967) *Scand. J. clin. Lab. Invest.* **19**, Suppl. 94.
HULTMAN, E. (1969) *Svenska Läkartidn* **66**, 241.
IAMPIETRO, P. F., BASS, D. E., and BUSKIRK, E. R. (1958) *Metabolism* **7**, 149.
ISSEKUTZ, B., JR., and PAUL, P. (1968) *Am. J. Physiol.* **215**, 197.
JAKOVLEV, N. N. (1941) *Fiziol. Zh.* **30**, 384.
JAKOVLEV, N. N. (1953) *Lebensweise und Ernährung des Sportlers,* Sportverlag, Berlin.
JAKOVLEV, N. N. (1956) *Die Ernährung des Sportlers am Wettkampftage,* Sportverlag, Berlin.
JAKOVLEV, N. N. (1961) In *Sportmedizin 1960,* p. 13 (L. Prokop, and F. Rinner, eds.), Verlag Brüder Hollinek, Wien.
JOHNSON, R. E. (1943) *Gastroenterology* **1**, 838.
JOHNSON, R. E., CROWLEY, L. V., TOTH, F., KOEHN, C. J., MONAHAN, E. P., LALANNE, G. G., PARROTT, E. M., KRZYWICKI, H. J., and MANCILLA, A. (1949) *Nutrition Surveys on Troops, Alaska, Winter,* 1948–1949, No. 59. Medical Laboratory, Chicago.
JOHNSON, R. E., DARLING, R. C., FORBES, W. H., BROUHA, L., EGANA, E., and GRAYBIEL, A. (1942) *J. Nutr.* **24**, 585.
JOHNSON, R. E., DARLING, R. C., SARGENT, F., II, and ROBINSON, P. (1945) *J. Nutr.* **29**, 155.
JOHNSON, R. E., and KARK, R. M. (1947) *Science* **105**, 378.
JOHNSON, R. E., and SARGENT, F., II (1958) *Proc. Nutr. Soc.* **17**, 179.
JOHNSTON, F. A., MCMILLAN, T. J., and EVANS, E. R. (1950) *J. Nutr.* **42**, 285.
KARK, R. M., AITON, H. F., PEASE, E. D., BEAN, W. B., HENDERSON, C. R., JOHNSON, R. E., and RICHARDSON, L. M. (1947) *Medicine* **26**, 1.
KARK, R. M., CROOME, R. R. M., CAWTHORPE, J., BELL, D. M., BRYANS, A., and MACBETH, R. J. (1948–9) *J. appl. Physiol.* **1**, 73.
KARK, R. M., JOHNSON, R. E., and LEWIS, J. S. (1945) *War Med.* **7**, 345.
KARVONEN, M. J., and KUNNAS, M. (1952) *Annls Med. exp. Biol. Fenn.* **30**, 180.
KARVONEN, M. J., and TURPEINEN, O. (1954) *J. appl. Physiol.* **6**, 603.
KEETON, R. W., LAMBERT, E. H., GLICKMAN, N., MITCHELL, H. H., LAST, J. H., and FAHNESTOCK, M. K. (1946) *Am. J. Physiol.* **146**, 66.
KENNEDY, T. F. (1933) *J. R. Army med. Cps.* **61**, 1, 108, 185, 257.
KEYS, A. (1946) *Occup. Med.* **2**, 536.
KEYS, A. (1947) *Nutr. Rev.* **5**, 129.
KEYS, A., HENSCHEL, A., MICKELSEN, O., and BROZEK, J. (1943) *J. Nutr.* **26**, 399.
KEYS, A., TAYLOR, H. L., and BROZEK, J. (1958) *Nutrition and Performance Capacity,* Quartermaster, Food and Container Institute for the Armed Forces, Chicago, Ill.
KING, E. Q., MCCALEB, L. B., KENNEDY, H. F., and KLUMPP, T. G. (1942) *J. Am. med. Ass.* **118**, 594.

KJELLBERG, S. R., RUDHE, V., and SJÖSTRAND, T. (1949) *Acta physiol. scand.* **19**, 146.
KLOTSCHKOW, L. A., and WASSILJEWA, E. S. (1934) *Arbeitsphysiologie* **7**, 62.
KOLKKA, S. (ed.) (1955) *The Official Report of the Organizing Committee for the Games of the XV Olympiad Helsinki* 1952, Werner Söderström, Porvoo, Helsinki.
KRÁL, J., KOPECKA, J., and ŽENISEK, A. (1966) In *XVI Weltkongress für Sportmedizin, Hannover* 12.-16. Juni 1966. *Kongressbericht*, p. 544 (G. Hanekopf, edr.), Deutscher Ärzte-Verlag, Köln-Berlin.
KRÁL, J. A., ŽENISEK, A., and HAIS, I. M. (1963) *J. Sport Med.* **3**, 105.
KREIDER, M. B., and BUSKIRK, E. R. (1957) *J. appl. Physiol.* **11**, 339.
KROGH, A., and LINDHARD, J. (1920) *Biochem. J.* **14**, 290.
LADELL, W. S. S. (1955) *J. Physiol.* **127**, 11.
LADELL, W. S. S. (1957) *The Influence of Environment in Arid Regions on the Biology of Man. Arid Zone Research, VIII. Human and Animal Ecology*, UNESCO, Paris.
LEHMANN, G., and SZAKÁLL, A. (1937) *Arbeitsphysiologie* **9**, 630, 653, 678.
LEHMANN, G., and SZAKÁLL, A. (1939) *Arbeitsphysiologie* **10**, 608.
LEHMANN, G., and SZAKÁLL, A. (1940) *Arbeitsphysiologie* **11**, 73.
LEWIS, H. E., HARRIES, J. M., LEWIS, D. H., and DE MONCHAUX, C. (1964) *Lancet* **i**, 1431.
LEWIS, H. E., and MASTERTON, J. P. (1958) *Proc. Nutr. Soc.* **17**, 170.
LEWIS, H. E., MASTERTON, J. P., and WARD, P. G. (1957) *Br. J. Nutr.* **11**, 5.
LILJESTRAND, G., and STENSTRÖM, N. (1920) *Skand. Arch. Physiol.* **39**, 167.
LOCKHART, E. E. (1945) *Proc. Am. phil. Soc.* **89**, 235.
MALHOTRA, M. S., RAMASWAMY, S. S., and RAY, S. N. (1962) *J. appl. Physiol.* **17**, 433.
MARGARIA, R., AGHEMO, P., and ROVELLI, E. (1964) *Int. Z. angew. Physiol.* **20**, 281.
MARGARIA, R., CERRETELLI, P., AGHEMO, P., and SASSI, G. (1963) *J. appl. Physiol.* **18**, 367.
MASTERTON, J. P., LEWIS, H. E., and WIDDOWSON, E. M. (1957) *Br. J. Nutr.* **11**, 346.
MAYER, J., and BULLEN, B. (1960) *Physiol. Rev.* **40**, 369.
MAYER, J., and BULLEN, B. (1964) In *Proceedings of the 6th International Congress of Nutrition, Edinburgh* 1963, p. 27, Livingstone, Edinburgh and London.
MEYTHALER, F., and DROSTE, A. (1934) *Klin. Wschr.* **13**, 439.
MILAN, F. A., and RODAHL, K. (1961) *J. Nutr.* **75**, 152.
MITCHELL, H. H., GLICKMAN, N., LAMBERT, E. H., KEETON, R. W., and FAHNESTOCK, M. K. (1946) *Am. J. Physiol.* **146**, 84.
MITCHELL, H. H., and HAMILTON, T. S. (1949) *J. biol. Chem.* **178**, 345.
MORTON, H. V. (1958) *A Traveller in Rome*, p. 95, Methuen, London.
NAEGELI, W., GRANDJEAN, E., BÄTTIG, K., and ROSENMUND, H. (1961) *Schweiz. Z. Sportmed.* **9**, 140.
NAMYSLOWSKI, L. (1967) In *Proceedings of the 7th International Congress of Nutrition, Hamburg* 1966, Vol. 5, *Physiology and Biochemistry of Food Components*, p. 38, Pergamon Press, Oxford.
NELSON, N. A., SHELLEY, W. B., HORVATH, S. N., EICHNA, L. W., and HATCH, T. F. (1948) *J. clin. Invest.* **27**, 209.
NOVOSADOVA, J., and JIRKA, Z. (1966) *XVI Weltkongress für Sportmedizin 1966 in Hannover* "S", Berichte, II Teil No. 189.
OLSSON, K.-G., and SALTIN, B. (1970) *Svenska Läkartidn* **67**, 4568.
ORR, N. W. M. (1965) *Br. J. Nutr.* **19**, 79.
ØYEN, O. (1967) *Nord. Med.* **77**, 4.
PARIN, V. V., and ADAMOVICH, B. A. (1968) *Life Sci. Space Res.* **6**, 27.
PAŘÍZKOVÁ, J. (1966) *Proc. Nutr. Soc.* **25**, 93.
PAŘÍZKOVÁ, J., KOUTECKÝ, Z., and STAŇKOVÁ, L. (1966) *Physiol. Bohemoslov.* **15**, 237.
PASSMORE, R. (1964) In *Diet and Bodily Constitution*, p. 59 (G. E. W. Wolstenholme, and M. O'Connor, eds.), Churchill, London.
PASSMORE, R., and DRAPER, M. H. (1964) In *Biochemical Disorders in Human Disease*, 2nd edn. (R. H. S. Thompson, and E. J. King, eds.), Churchill, London.

PASSMORE, R., and SWINDELLS, Y. E. (1963) *Br. J. Nutr.* **17,** 331.
PAUL, P., and ISSEKUTZ, B. (1967) *J. appl. Physiol.* **22,** 615.
PELLERVO-SEURA (1968) Unpublished material.
PERCIVAL, L. (1951) *Summary* **3,** 55. Ref. by Sharman, *et al.,* 1971.
PETTENKOFER, M., and VOIT, C. (1866) *Z. Biol.* **2,** 459.
PITTS, G. C., CONSOLAZIO, C. F., and JOHNSON, R. E. (1944a) *J. Nutr.* **27,** 497.
PITTS, G. C., JOHNSON, R. E., and CONSOLAZIO, F. C. (1944b) *Am. J. Physiol.* **142,** 253.
PLATT, B. S. (1962) Spec. Rep. Ser. Med. Res. Coun. No. 302.
PLATT, B. S., and FOX, R. H. (1954) *Proc. Nutr. Soc.* **13,** 53.
POLLACK, H., FRENCH, C. E., and BERRYMAN, G. H. (1944) *Bull. US Army med. Dept.* **74,** 110.
PONOMAREV, L. E., and SOKOLOVA, G. M. (1959) *Sovet. Med.* **23,** 100.
PROKOP, L. (1960a) *Neue Z. ärztl. Fortbild.* **49,** 448.
PROKOP, L. (1960b) *Sportärztl. Prax.* **1,** 19.
PUGH, L. G. C. (1954) *Proc. Nutr. Soc.* **13,** 60.
PUGH, L. G. C. E. (1958) *J. Physiol. Lond.* **141,** 233.
PUGH, L. G. C., and EDHOLM, O. (1955) *Lancet* **ii,** 761.
PUGH, L. G. C. E., GILL, M. B., LATIRI, S., MILLEDGE, J. S., WARD, M. P., and WEST, J. B. (1964) *J. appl. Physiol.* **19,** 431.
PUSHKINA, N. N. (1961) *Vitamini na Severe (Vitamins in the North),* Medgis, Moscow.
RENNIE, D. W. (1958) In *Cold Injury, Transactions of the Fifth Conference,* pp. 253–90 (M. I. Ferrer, ed.), Josiah Macy, Jr., Foundation, Madison, NJ.
RODAHL, K. (1949) *Norsk Polarinst. Skrift.* No. 91.
RODAHL, K. (1954a) *North. The Nature and Drama of the Polar World,* Heinemann, London.
RODAHL, K. (1954b) *J. Nutr.* **53,** 575.
RODAHL, K. (1958) *The Human Acclimatization to Cold,* pp. 177–252 (M. I. Ferrer, ed.), Josiah Macy, Jr., Foundation, Madison, NJ.
RODAHL, K. (1960) *J. occup. Med.* **2,** 177.
RODAHL, K., HORVATH, S. M., BIRKHEAD, N. C., and ISSEKUTZ, B., JR. (1962) *J. appl. Physiol.* **17,** 763.
ROGERS, T. A., and SETLIFF, J. A. (1964) *J. appl. Physiol.* **19,** 580.
ROGERS, T. A., SETLIFF, J. A., BUCK, A. C., KLOPPING, J. C., and MATTER, M., JR. (1966) *J. appl. Physiol.* **21,** 643.
ROGERS, T. A., SETLIFF, J. A., and KLOPPING, J. C. (1964) *J. appl. Physiol.* **19,** 1.
RÖNNHOLM, N., and KARVINEN, E. (1964) Personal communication.
ROSE, K. D., and FUENNING, S. I. (1960) *Neb. St. med. J.* **45,** 575.
ROTH, J. L. D. (1948) Tech. Rep. US Air Force No. 5740.
ROWELL, L. B., BLACKMON, J. R., and BRUCE, R. A. (1964) *J. clin. Invest.* **43,** 1677.
ROWELL, L. B., BLACKMON, J. R., MARTIN, R. H., MAZZARELLA, J. A., and BRUCE, R. A. (1966) In *Physical Activity and the Heart,* p. 69 (M. J. Karvonen, and A. J. Barry, eds.), C. C. Thomas, Springfield.
ROWELL, L. B., MASORO, E. J., and SPENCER, M. J. (1965) *J. appl. Physiol.* **20,** 1032.
SALTIN, B., and HERMANSEN, L. (1967) In *Nutrition and Physical Activity,* p. 32 (G. Blix, ed.), Almqvist and Wiksell, Uppsala.
SAMUELS, L. T., GILMORE, R. C., and REINECKE, R. M. (1948) *J. Nutr.* **36,** 639.
SARGENT, F., II, SARGENT, R. E., JOHNSON, R. E., and STOLPE, S. G. (1953) *WADC Tech. Rep.* **53,** 484.
SCHJØTH, A. G. (1965) *Scand. J. clin. Lab. Invest.* **17,** 275.
SELIGER, V. (1968) *Int. Z. angew. Physiol.* **25,** 104.
SHAPIRO, R., and CONSOLAZIO, C. F. (1959) *Fedn Proc.* **18,** 583.
SHARMAN, I. M., DOWN, M. G., and SEN, R. N. (1971) *Br. J. Nutr.* **26,** 265.
SIEVERS, J. (1939) *Pflügers Arch. ges. Physiol.* **242,** 725.
SKINNER, H. G., and MANN, G. M. (1964) In *Proceedings of the 6th International Congress of Nutrition, Edinburgh* 1963, p. 39, Livingstone, Edinburgh and London.

SLAUTA, M. (1956) *Report of Travel—Including Observations on "Operation Moosehorn",* QMR and D Command, Natick, Mass.
SMITH, G. (1954) *Proc. Nutr. Soc.* **13,** 45.
STATON, W. M. (1952) *Res. Q. Am. Hlth phys. Educ.* **23,** 356.
STEFANSSON, V. (1957) *The Fat of the Land,* Macmillan, New York.
STRYDOM, N. B., VAN GRAAN, C. H., and HOLDSWORTH, L. D. (1965) *J. occup. Med.* **7,** 581.
STRYDOM, N. B., WYNDHAM, C. H., VAN GRAAN, C. H., HOLDSWORTH, L. D., and MORRISON, J. F. (1966) *S. Afr. med. J.* **40,** 539.
STRYDOM, N. B., WYNDHAM, C. H., WILLIAMS, C. G., MORRISON, J. F., BREDELL, G. A. G., VON RAHDEN, M. J., and PETER, J. (1966) *Fedn Proc.* **25,** 1366.
SWAIN, H. L., TOTH, F. M., CONSOLAZIO, C. F., FITZPATRICK, W. H., ALLEN, D. I., and KOEHN, C. J. (1949) *J. Nutr.* **38,** 63.
TAYLOR, A. A., and FINKELSTEIN, B. (1958) *Am. J. publ. Hlth* **48,** 604.
TAYLOR, D. W. (1953) *J. Physiol. Lond.* **121,** 47 P.
TAYLOR, H. L., BUSKIRK, E. R., BROZEK, J., ANDERSON, J. T., and GRANDE, F. (1957) *J. appl. Physiol.* **10,** 421.
THOMAS, P. (1957) The effects of vitamin E on some aspects of athletic efficiency, PhD thesis, University of Southern California, Los Angeles. Ref. by Sharman *et al.,* 1971.
TOOR, M. E., WERTHEIMER, S., and MASSRY, J. B. (1959) *Harefuah* **57,** 244.
VANDERVEEN, J. E., HEIDELBAUGH, N. D., and O'HARA, M. J. (1966) *Aerospace Med.* **37,** 591.
VANOTTI, A. (1959) *Eisenstoffwechsel,* p. 58 (W. von Keiderling, ed.), Georg Thieme-Verlag, Stuttgart.
VANZETTI, G., and VALANTE, D. (1965) *Clinica chim. Acta* **11,** 442.
VAUGHAN, D. A., DRURY, H. F., HANNON, J. P., VAUGHAN, L. N., and LARSON, A. M. (1959) *J. Nutr.* **67,** 99.
VUORI, J. M., POIKOLAINEN, E., and HARTIALA, K. (1966) In *XVI Weltkongress für Sportmedizin Hannover 12–16. Juni 1966. Kongressbericht,* p. 684 (G. Hanekopf, ed.), Deutscher Ärzte-Verlag, Köln-Berlin
VYTCHIKOVA, M. A. (1958) *Chem. Abstr.* **52,** 14787.
WATERLOW, J. C., and BUNJÉ, H. W. (1966) *Lancet* **ii,** 655.
WAYNE, W. S., WEHRLE, P. F., and CARROLL, R. E. (1967) *J. Am. med. Ass.* **199,** 901.
WELCH, B. E., BUSKIRK, E. R., and IAMPIETRO, P. F. (1958) *Metabolism* **7,** 141.
WELCH, B. E., LEVY, L. M., CONSOLAZIO, C. F., BUSKIRK, E. R., and DEE, T. E. (1957) Rep. US Army Med. Nutr. Lab. 202.
WELCH, B. E., MARCINEK, J. G., MANN, J. B., GROTHEER, M. P., FRIEDEMANN, T. E., IAMPIETRO, P. F., VAUGHAN, J. A., and MACLEOD, A. (1956) *Report on Caloric Intake and Energy Expenditure of Eleven Men in a Desert Environment,* pp. 1–22, Project Report No. 190, 27 August 1956.
WELHAM, W. C., and BEHNKE, A. R. (1942) *J. Am. med. Ass.* **118,** 498.
WHITTEN, B. K., and JANOSKI, A. H. (1969) *Fedn Proc.* **28,** 983.
WHITTINGHAM, D. G. V. (1954) *Proc. Nutr. Soc.* **13,** 49.
WHITTINGHAM, P. (1965) In *Exploration Medicine,* p. 154 (O. G. Edholm, and A. L. Bacharach, eds.), John Wright, Bristol.
WHO (1960) *Guide to Hygiene and Sanitation in Aviation,* WHO, Geneva.
WICKETT, J. C., and BLISS, J. Q. (1952) Rep. Can. Def. Res. Med. Lab., IAM No. 52/4.
WIDDOWSON, E. M., EDHOLM, O. G., and MCCANCE, R. A. (1954) *Br. J. Nutr.* **8,** 147.
WILLIAMS, J. H., MAGER, M., and JACOBSON, E. D. (1964) *J. Lab. clin. Med.* **63,** 853.
WILLIAMS, R. D., MASON, H. L., WILDER, R. M., and SMITH, B. F. (1940) *Archs intern. Med.* **66,** 785.
WILSON, M., TUTTLE, W. W., DAUM, K., and RODES, H. (1949) *J. Am. diet. Ass.* **25,** 221.
YAMADA, T. (1958) *Jap. J. physical Fitness* **7,** 231, 242.
YOSHIMURA, H. (1961) *Fedn Proc.* **20,** Suppl. 7, Part III, 103.

YOSHIMURA, H. (1966) In *Physical Activity in Health and Disease*, p. 74 (K. Evang, and K. Lange Andersen, eds.), Universitetsforlaget, Oslo.
YOUNG, D. R., SCHAEFER, N. S., and PRICE, R. (1960) *J. appl. Physiol.* **15,** 1022.
YOUNG, D. R., and SPECTOR, H. (1957) *Am. J. clin. Nutr.* **5,** 129.
ZUNTZ, N., LOEWY, A., MULLER, F., and CASPARI, W. (1906) *Höhenklima und Bergwanderungen*, Deutsches Verlagshaus, Berlin.

CHAPTER 9

FOOD CONTROL: LEGISLATION, STANDARDS, HYGIENE, AND INSPECTION

L. I. Pugsley

Consultant, Food and Drug Directorate, Department of National Health and Welfare, Ottawa, Canada

CONTENTS

1. Introduction	425
1.1. Historical Development	427
2. Legislation	437
2.1. Legal Definition of Food	437
2.2. General Principles of Food Legislation	439
2.3. Trends in Food Legislation	443
3. Food Standards	444
3.1. Types of Food Standards	447
3.2. Food Additives	449
4. Hygiene	455
4.1. Raw Material Requirements	456
4.2. Plant Facilities and Operating Requirements	456
5. Inspection	461
Acknowledgement	464
References	465

1. INTRODUCTION

For centuries there has been an active interest by many countries in methods to control the production, preservation, transportation, promotion, and distribution of foods. Various levels of government, national and international organizations, professional groups, industries, and people generally have exhibited interest in providing measures to protect the health of consumers, to curtail fraudulent practices, to assure high quality, and to eliminate trade barriers.

It is related that the basic principles of food control are inscribed on a stone tablet dating back to the Hittite era some 3500 years ago, exhibited in a museum in Ankara, Turkey (Forschbach, 1963). This tablet bears the inscription which has been translated as follows:

"(a) Thou shalt not poison thy neighbour's fat.
(b) Thou shalt not bewitch thy neighbour's fat."

These two commandments express the principles of the control of foods, namely to protect the public against health hazards and fraudulent practices.

Ancient examples of the application of legislation, hygiene, inspection, and enforcement of measures to protect the people against health hazards may be found in the Old Testament of the Bible in the 11th chapter of Leviticus and the 14th chapter of Deuteronomy. In these chapters, the laws of Moses directed the people of Israel regarding the meats of animals which were clean and those which were unclean. Again, in the famous Assize of Bread in England, in 1266, provision was made for fixing the weight of various types of loaves of bread and authorizing punishment in the pillory for selling bread of false weight. In 1319 the wardens of the City of London were authorized to condemn carcasses of tainted beef found in shops (Drummond and Wilbraham, 1939).

The control of foods through the establishment of codes and statutes has far-reaching influences upon the lives and habits of the public as well as upon the agricultural and industrial life of a country. Often these statutory requirements are of considerable social and economic importance to society. They extend into the home and affect the various industries concerned with production, promotion, transportation, and distribution of food commodities.

In many countries, the business enterprises concerned with the production, promotion, and distribution of foods are conducted by people highly trained in the technical skills of the trade as well as by people without the necessary training and skills. The training, skills, experience, and motivation of the people conducting these enterprises have a marked influence on the status and quality of the commodities offered to the consuming public. Most producers, manufacturers, and dealers are deeply concerned about their reputation and the quality, safety, and wholesomeness of the foods they offer to the consuming public. Such producers, manufacturers, and dealers would not intentionally create a hazard or perpetrate a fraud on the public. On the other hand, it is well recognized that there are unscrupulous, dishonest, and ignorant individuals in enterprises concerned with the production, promotion, and sale of foods whose primary interest is to take advantage of the consuming public by offering them cheapened and debased products. These individuals are motivated towards greed and profit. Such individuals have little regard for the wholesomeness and safety of the food products offered by them to the consuming public.

The fact that food is essential for the maintenance and survival of mankind appears to offer an incentive to the unscrupulous and dishonest individuals to exploit the gullible public. In many instances, consumers are at a disadvantage in that they have no way of knowing whether the food commodities offered to them may cause injury to health from harmful or potentially injurious ingredients or are represented to them in a false, misleading, or fraudulent manner.

In business enterprises there is always competition and rivalry to be the first with a new or better product for the benefit of mankind. The incentive for capturing the market for a product, resulting in increased sales and economic gain, is inherent in trading organizations, and is undoubtedly essential to the survival of business enterprises. In order to ensure that competition, rivalry, and the incentive for gain are conducted on an equitable and fair basis, it is essential that certain basic principles or ground rules are followed.

It is the practice to express these basic principles in the form of laws or codes in order to provide a measure of protection to the public against health hazards and frauds, and in the food commodities offered to them by the various business enterprises concerned with their production, promotion, sale, and distribution. Moreover, the basic principles in the codes and laws have a salutary effect in the promotion of honesty and fair dealings among producers, manufacturers, and dealers in these commodities.

It is the purpose of this chapter to discuss the basic principles concerned with the control of foods by the development of legislation, standards, hygienic practices, and inspection.

1.1. HISTORICAL DEVELOPMENT

The development of codes for the control of individual foods can be traced far back in history and encompasses a mixture of general, ecclesiastical, trade, and professional codes, rules, or laws. In many instances these were a development of common laws or rules made by the people to regulate their daily lives. For example, a brief reference was made in the Magna Carta of 1215 to the control of foods whereby one measure was established for wine, ale, and corn throughout the country. The evolution of the regulatory control of foods follows the advancing changes in commercial and personal food standards of living down through the ages. In many respects the control of foods is reflected in the industrial, economic, and social progress of countries.

As an example of the historical development of food control laws in a well-developed country, it was considered of interest to review briefly some of the incidents which influenced the enactment of food control laws in the United Kingdom.

The impact of the commercial aspects of the control of food in this country is seen in the initiation of codes by merchant companies in London in the fifteenth century in the interests of the reputation of member companies. These companies managed to obtain official recognition of requirements aimed at suppressing adulteration and maintaining quality of the particular commodities which they handled.

In the eighteenth century the interest in food standards shifted to the excise authorities in the establishment of standards for a number of imported products, e.g. tea, coffee, cocoa, and alcoholic beverages. The establishment of these standards was more for the purpose of collecting revenue than the direct protection of the consumer (Hinton, 1960). However, in 1860, an act entitled "An Act for Preventing the Adulteration of Articles of Foods and Drink" was promulgated in England. The basic principles contained in this Act, which covered all articles of food and drink, had a considerable influence on the food legislation introduced in many English-speaking countries. The following incidents are recorded as factors influencing the enactment of this law.

In the nineteenth century, apart from the offences which occurred under the excise legislation, gross adulteration of foodstuffs became quite widespread. The detection of this adulteration was facilitated significantly by the application of the microscope. Dr. A. H. Hassell, in the mid century, examined a number of foods microscopically, and his findings were instrumental in bringing many instances of adulteration to the attention of the public and the medical profession. The editor of *The Lancet,* T. Wakley, played an important role in writing editorials on the subject, soliciting action on the part of the government to correct the situation. One of the major contributors in drawing to the attention of the public and the government some of the infamous practices of adulteration prevailing at that time was John Postgate, an apothecary in London. He reported, for example, instances of the addition of lead to wine to improve brightness without any regard to the poisonous nature of the mixture; the adulteration of bread with alum, plaster of Paris, and copper sulphate, and mustard husk coloured with red lead, venetian red, and turmeric. Postgate became known as a persistent advocate and unceasing worker in the cause of preventing the adulteration of foods and drugs (Pugsley, 1967). As a result of the untiring efforts of Postgate, Wakley, and others to promote the enactment of a general Act of Parliament to prevent the adulteration of food and drugs, a Committee of Inquiry was appointed.

In 1856 this committee reported to Parliament after investigating the situation, that "adulteration prevailed to a great extent so that not only is public health endangered and pecuniary fraud committed on the whole community, but the public morality is tainted and the high commercial character of the country seriously lowered both at home and in the eyes of foreign countries" (Pugsley, 1967).

In 1857 a Bill was brought before Parliament entitled "A Bill for Preventing the Adulteration of Articles of Food and Drink". Tremendous opposition by trading groups was encountered on the second reading of the Bill, and the Government withdrew the legislation at that time. However, the matter came to a head in 1858 when the following incident occurred. A vendor had ordered peppermint lozenges from a confectioner at 7d. (3p) per pound, the usual price being 1s. 2d. (6p) and the maker of the lozenges sent for plaster of Paris to use as an adulterant, according to the price. Unfortunately, the druggist's boy went to the wrong cask and brought back arsenic instead of plaster of Paris. The arsenic was duly mixed with the other ingredients in the manufacture of the lozenges. Upwards of 400 people ate the lozenges, of whom seventeen died within a day or two, the remainder suffered horrible agony (Pugsley, 1967). The accidental use of the wrong adulterant was seized upon by Postgate as a potent weapon in his attack to obtain laws to prevent the adulteration of foods, and, finally in 1860, the above Bill was reintroduced and passed by Parliament.

Section 1 of the Act stated: "Every person who shall sell an article of food or drink with which, to the knowledge of such person, any ingredient or material injurious to the health of persons eating or drinking such articles has been mixed, and every person who shall sell as pure or unadulterated any article of food or drink which is adulterated or not pure, shall for every offence forfeit such article and pay a penalty" (Curran, 1953). This Act also made provision for the analysis of a food suspected of causing injury to health by an official analyst.

This law marked the beginning of control of the broad field of foods as distinct from previous statutes dealing with specific food items. However, from experience in dealing with offences under this Act, it was found that it had definite limitations. In order to overcome some of these, a revision was completed in 1872 under the title "An Act to Amend the Law for Prevention of Adulteration of Food, Drink and Drugs". This Act included the following main provisions:

1. Penalties imposed on persons adulterating articles of food, drink, and drugs.
2. Penalties imposed on persons selling articles of food, drink, or drugs which they knew had been adulterated.
3. The vendor must declare a product as a mixture, if such were the case, at the time of sale.
4. The appointment of official analysts and inspectors, and the submission of reports to a central agency.

The provisions of this Act expressed certain broad principles in the control of foods. The act served as a model for the initiation of food laws in Canada in 1876 and many other countries of the Commonwealth. It also served as the basis of a federal food and drug law enacted in the United States of America in 1906.

The initiation of this first national food control law in England had, as its primary purpose, the protection of the consuming public against health hazards and frauds. It was not directly associated with the imposition of duties to increase the revenue of the country.

Parallel developments took place in a number of other countries as one of the numerous consequences of industrialization and, as further examples, the situations in Canada and the United States of America are discussed.

At the time of Confederation in 1867, Canada experienced a period of rapid expansion. Davidson (1949) reports that "saloons were doing a thriving business". With the increased demand for alcoholic beverages, a fertile market was available to "fast operators" to increase sales and profits through the adulteration of these products. "Not only was there too much liquor but a great deal of it was immature, fiery spirit, the immoderate use of which would lead men on to crime, to poverty, and to insanity." Public opinion was evidently quite concerned over the situation, and it is related that "three-fifths of the insanity and four-fifths of the cases of crime and pauperism were caused by intemperance. The gaols were overcrowded and lunatic asylums were bursting at the seams, owing to the overcrowding with alcoholics" (Davidson, 1949).

A number of petitions were submitted to members of Parliament, and it was evident that some action was demanded on the part of the Government by the people. A prohibition on the sale of alcoholic beverages, as advocated in a number of petitions, would result in a loss of five million dollars in revenue, which was a rather large sum at that time. A Special Committee of the House of Commons was appointed to study the petitions and investigate the situation with a view to recommending a solution to the problem.

The report of the Special Committee was presented to the House of Commons and confirmed many of the allegations made in the petitions. After considerable discussion, a Bill was introduced into the House of Commons entitled "An Act to Impose Licence Duties on Compounders of Spirits and to Prevent the Adulteration of Foods, Drink and Drugs". The Bill was passed in May 1874 and became effective on 1 January, 1875.

It would appear from the discussions on this Bill that the widespread adulteration of alcoholic beverages had considerable influence on the legislators to include foods and drugs in the legislation. Apart from those provisions which set up a licensing system for alcoholic beverages, the provisions of the Act contained sections dealing with the control of foods which were essentially the same as those contained in the English Act of 1872. The passage of this legislation served a dual purpose—it strengthened the laws on alcoholic beverages without loss in revenue and provided for the control of all foods in all provinces of Canada. Previous to this time there had been provincial laws dealing with a number of individual agricultural commodities.

Although food control legislation in Canada had a somewhat infamous beginning, due to its association with alcoholism, the basic principles of the legislation have remained the same during the several revisions of the Act that have taken place during the past hundred years. The basic current legislation, cited as The Food and Drugs Act, was enacted in April 1953. N. C. Wright (1960), at that time Deputy Director-General, Food and Agriculture Organization of the United Nations, in his presentation on "International aspects of pure food and pure food legislation" at the Pure Food Centenary in London, commented that the current food code in Canada "is a model of clear and concise presentation".

In the nineteenth century the United States of America was also having problems with the excessive use and abuse of alcoholic beverages, and a strong movement was pressing the Government to prohibit the sale of these products. However, during the latter part of the nineteenth century an industrial society had, to a great extent, succeeded or replaced the agricultural society that earlier had prevailed in the country. With this growing urbanization, the people became more dependent upon the general market for their food supplies. Transportation facilities improved and there were advances in manufacturing and packaging of foods. This permitted increased amounts of foods to be distributed to wide areas. Competition and the development of new products accompanied these changes, and these in turn created incentives for illegal profits through the debasement of manufactured foods and mis-labelling. In an investigation of the situation, E. F. Ladd, in 1905, reported there was a widespread use of chemical preservatives in food, such as boric acid, and extensive use of coal tar dyes. The sale of "Vermont Maple Syrup" exceeded the production capacity of the state by about ten times (Roe, 1956).

The misrepresentation, frauds, and hazardous practices, whereby chemical preservatives and dyes were used extensively in the United States, came to the attention of Dr. Harvey W. Wiley, Chief Chemist in the Bureau of Chemistry of the Department of Agriculture. The crusade and campaign conducted by Dr. Wiley from 1880 until his death in 1930 are now legend. He brought to the attention of the public and the Government the indiscriminate and fraudulent practices perpetrated by unscrupulous individuals on the public in the manufacture and promotion of foods in the United States.

Dr. Wiley conducted feeding trials on a number of currently used preservatives, using human volunteers—"The Poison Squad"—and this was an outstanding achievement and brought to light the hazards associated with the use of chemical preservatives in foods without prior toxicity testing. Wiley's pioneer work in bringing together the results of analyses of a large number of natural food products formed the basis for authentic standards of composition for a large number of food commodities. His efforts were recognized in 1906 with the passage of the first Federal Food and Drugs Act in the United States, designed to control interstate commerce in the manufacture, sale, distribution, and promotion of all foods. Dr. Wiley earned the title "Father of the Pure Food Law" (Boardman, 1956).

This Act has had a number of revisions and extensions in order to keep pace with the rapid and extensive developments of industry. The basic, current legislation, cited as the Federal Food, Drug, and Cosmetic Act, was made law in 1938, and most of the original provisions of the 1906 Act were retained and extended in it. Of special interest were the provisions in the 1938 Act for the establishment of food standards and the prohibition of added poisonous substances to food unless necessary or unavoidable, in which case authority was given to establish safe tolerances.

The development of standards for the control of foods received considerable attention after World War II with the increased trend towards city dwelling and the expansion of manufacturing industries. In the expanding industrialization taking place in many countries, the production and distribution of food were no longer a direct exchange of commodities between producer and consumer but became, of necessity, a long, economic food chain which entailed considerable food processing. National food legislation had been enacted independently in many of the highly developed countries, consisting of a national food control service with its appropriate inspectors and analytical laboratories. One of the first concerns of such national bodies was the regulation of the quality of imports to ensure that they complied with domestic standards. When drawing up national food legislation and regulations, and enforcing them, there always appears to be an attendant temptation to use them as a non-economic barrier to trade in food commodities.

Paul Martin (1950), former Minister of the Department of National Health and Welfare in the Canadian Government, drew attention to the lack of uniformity between countries in the laws governing the labelling and standards for foods. He recognized that the food habits and preferences of people varied in different countries, but considered there were a number of unnecessary and trivial variations in standards. For example, he could see no real reason why each country should have a different list of harmless food colours nor why there should be different national standards for the moisture content of cheese, which in some cases differed by only a few percentage points. He indicated that there were a large number of other differences, many of them trivial, which could be cited, and this is also true with respect to labelling and food names. It was necessary for the administrators to enforce their national laws as they were written and not interpret them in accordance with their own ideas as to what the laws should be. This resulted in the rejection of import shipments of food that technically did not comply with the national laws since the commodities failed to meet the standard in some degree. He made a strong plea for international discussions on the elimination of many of the needless legislative barriers to the flow of foods from country to country. He stated: "In a world with far too many barriers to easy communication of peoples and the convenient interchange of commodities and services, we could make a useful contribution by reconciling pointless differences in our food and drug laws", and "Is it not ironic that laws designed, in domestic trade to protect the health and the purse of the consumer should, by their lack of uniformity sometimes have the opposite effect in international trade?"

Although Martin's recommendations were followed on an informal basis to some extent in the coordination of standards for foods between Canada and the United States, it remained for the late Dr. Hans Frenzel, a former Minister in the Austrian Government, to advance, in 1953, the concept of unification of legislation on food commodities in a number of the European countries through the establishment of a Codex Alimentarius Europaeus, and the meeting of the Council of this group in 1958 was the culmination of his proposals. At the inception of the European Council, certain governments took the position that the functions relating to the Codex Alimentarius could be absorbed into the activities of existing international organizations, such as the Food and Agriculture Organization and the World Health Organization of the United Nations.

The increasing attention given to the integration of markets into regional groups, and problems arising in international trade by a growing number of organizations interested in food standard programmes, were discussed in 1960 at the First Food and Agriculture Organization Regional Conference for Europe (1961). The following statement was included in the report of this Conference: ".. a valuable step forward would be achieved if the Director-General of FAO in collaboration with the Director-General of WHO and after consultation with international governmental and non-governmental organizations active in the field could submit to the Eleventh Session of the Conference proposals for a joint FAO/WHO program on food standards and associated requirements with particular reference in the first instance to the principal foodstuffs offered for sale on the European market."

In 1961 the Council of the Codex Alimentarius Europaeus agreed to enter into an association with FAO and WHO, and in November 1961, at the Eleventh Session of the FAO Conference, consideration was given to the desirability of setting up a Joint FAO–WHO Programme on Food Standards. It was pointed out that the programme would be aimed at simplifying and integrating food standard work being carried out by many international organizations. In the discussions at the conference it was felt that these objectives could be achieved by establishing a Codex Alimentarius Commission open to all interested Member Nations of FAO and WHO, which would incorporate and take over the work of the Codex Alimentarius Europaeus. With such a commission, made up of government experts with authority to act on behalf of their countries, more rapid progress could be achieved than by individual organizations or groups. In addition, duplication of effort and publication of conflicting standards could be avoided, resulting in substantial economy of time and effort. At the conclusion of the conference, a resolution was adopted which read in part as follows (Food and Agriculture Organization, 1962c):

> The Conference
> *Considering* the rapidly growing importance of internationally accepted food standards as a means of protecting consumers in all countries whatever their stage of development, and of effectively reducing trade barriers,
> *Recognizing* the need to simplify and integrate international food standard work so as to avoid duplication and conflicting standards and to effect economies in effort and outlay.
> *Conscious* of the importance of the role of the World Health Organization in all health aspects of food standard work.
> *Decides* to establish in accordance with Article VI of the Constitution a Codex Alimentarius Commission, whose statutes are set out below.
> *Urges* all interested Member Nations to contribute to the special trust fund by which, subject to review by the 12th Session of the Conference, the program will be financed and to consult with the Director General as to the amount of their contribution,
> *Requests* the Director General:
> (a) to draw to the attention of the Director General of WHO the importance attached to an early endorsement by that Organization of the present proposals for a Joint FAO/WHO Program on Food Standards;
> (b) to implement the program as soon as sufficient funds have been received and, in consultation with the Director General of WHO to call the first session of the Codex Alimentarius Commission, if possible by June 1962.

In January 1962 the Executive Board of WHO approved the proposals to convene a Joint FAO–WHO Conference to review the program of the two agencies in the field of food standards. Accordingly, a conference was held in October 1962 in Geneva, attended by representatives of forty-four Member Nations and observers from twenty-four international organizations. At this conference the proposals to establish a Codex Alimentarius Commission, guide lines for the work, and the financing of the Commission were the main topics discussed. The proposal that a Joint FAO–WHO Codex Alimentarius Commission be established was approved, along with endorsement of the need to develop international food standards, both on a world wide and on a regional basis.

The general principles of the Codex Alimentarius were formulated. In summary, its purpose is the collection of internationally adopted food standards presented in a uniform manner. The aims of these food standards are the protection of the health of consumers and ensuring fair practices in food trade. The publication of the food standards is intended to guide and promote the elaboration and establishment of definitions and requirements for foods, to assist in their harmonization, and in so doing to facilitate international trade. The scope of the Codex is to include standards for all of the principal foods, whether processed, semi-processed or raw, for distribution to the consumer. Materials for further processing into foods are to be included, to the extent necessary to achieve the purpose of the Codex Alimentarius as defined. The Codex Alimentarius is to include provisions in respect to food hygiene, food additives, pesticide residues, contaminants, labelling and presentation, methods of analysis, and sampling.

Guidelines as to the nature of the Codex Alimentarius procedures for elaboration and acceptance of standards, priorities, and the financing of the Commission were drawn up along with a final recommendation that the first session of the Commission should be convened at FAO Headquarters in Rome in June or July of 1963. Accordingly, the first session of the Codex Alimentarius Commission was convened in Rome, June 25 to July 3, 1963, and has continued to hold annual meetings. Currently it is in the process of developing standards for some 200 commodities. When standards have particular applicability only in a given region, such as Europe, it has been the practice to have them developed by committees reporting to the Coordinating Committee for Europe, or that region. Much of the preparatory work in developing food standards had already been done by subcommittees of the Codex Alimentarius Europaeus, and it is on this foundation that many worldwide Codex Alimentarius standards are now being built.

The establishment of the Codex Alimentarius Commission, under the aegis of the Food and Agriculture Organization of the United Nations and the World Health Organization, was a milestone in the history of food laws and represents a new and distinct influence in the field of international food standards. The experience and expertise of the committees involved in the development of the standards should ensure practical standards with appropriate sampling, analysis, and other requirements.

The standards established in the Codex Alimentarius should go a long way towards eliminating misunderstandings and confusion in international trade, since buyers will be able to use a common language. They should serve as a yardstick for determining value. The standards developed are not intended to affect consumer preference in any way, but to provide the consumer with information on what he is buying.

Manufacturers, processors, producers, distributors, and consumers of foods should be deeply indebted to the foresight and the leadership of the initiators of the concept of international unification of food standards and to the development of a Codex Alimentarius. The Commission deserves wholehearted support for its efforts in the food standardization field in promoting international trade. Consumers on a worldwide basis will benefit in the protection afforded by these standards against health hazards and fraud.

The development of these codes for the harmonization of the control of food commodities, is an example of the adaptation of democratic institutions to industrial developments in food technology and the accompanying social changes.

2. LEGISLATION

The laws governing the control of foods are often referred to by the public as the "pure food laws". This is natural, because in the minds of people food should be wholesome and free from the addition to or subtraction of anything that might impair wholesomeness. Foods are, by their very nature, products of many different varieties, composition, and degrees of purity, and are subject, with respect to production, preservation, transportation, and distribution, to many different conditions which may affect quality, nutritional status, and safety of use.

In considering the scope of food legislation, a distinction is generally made between food as a commodity and products which are referred to as foodstuffs. Food commodities are usually recognized as articles of commerce, whereas foodstuffs are generally considered to include foods grown or produced for one's self and consumption in the home. The laws developed to control foods have been concerned primarily with food commodities. The dictionary meaning of the general term "food" as given in the *Shorter Oxford English Dictionary* (third edition) is: "What one takes into the system to maintain life and growth, and to supply waste; aliment, nourishment, victuals." However, in developing laws to control foods, it is essential to give a much broader meaning to the term "food" in order to include materials which do not necessarily contribute to life, growth, and nourishment. Substances are added or imparted to food which contribute to the characteristics of the food itself, and form a part of it.

2.1. LEGAL DEFINITION OF FOOD

At the meeting of the Joint FAO–WHO Codex Alimentarius Commission Conference (1966), the following definition of food was adopted: "Food means any substance whether processed, semi-processed, or raw, which is intended for human consumption, and includes drink, chewing gum and any substance which has been used in the manufacture, preparation, or treatment of food, but does not include cosmetics, or tobacco, or substances used only as drugs." The Commission indicated the above definition was intended to refer to the field of work of the Codex Alimentarius Commission and emphasized that it was not intended as a definition for governments to use in their national food legislation.

The following are examples of the terminology used in defining food in current food legislation. In Canada the term "food" is defined in section 2(g) of the Food and Drugs Act 1967 as follows: "food includes any article manufactured, sold, or represented for use as food or drink for man, chewing gum, and any ingredient that may be mixed with food for any purpose whatever." This definition is very broad and has been interpreted to include chemical additives since these are substances which are usually mixed with food.

In the United States of America, food is defined in section 201(f) of the Federal Food, Drug and Cosmetic Act 1966 as follows: "The term 'food' means (1) articles used for food or drink for man or other animals, (2) chewing gum, and (3) articles used as components of any such article." This definition is broader in scope than the definition in the Canadian law in that it includes "articles used for food or drink for man or other animals".

In England the Food and Drugs Act 1955 under section 135 (Interpretations) defines food as follows:

> Food includes drink, chewing gum and other products of a like nature and use, and articles and substances used as ingredients in the preparation of food or drink or of such products, but does not include
>
> (a) water, live animals or birds,
> (b) fodder or feeding stuffs for animals or birds or fish, or
> (c) articles or substances used as drugs.

Bigwood and Gérard (1967) report that there is no official definition of food in the food control laws in France. However, in this country foods are generally recognized by public health officials and the medical and the legal professions to include both processed and unprocessed natural products that man has empirically recognized as fit for human consumption in order to cover the caloric and "plastic" requirements of his body.

The Federal Republic of Germany defines food in the current Food Act as follows: "Food shall be all raw, prepared or processed substances which are destined to be eaten, chewed or drunk by man, as far as they are not predominantly intended for the cure, relief or prevention of disease" (Food and Agriculture Organization, 1967).

In Sweden the food control laws consider food to include "all products which are intended for human consumption and provide the body with nourishment". The definition excludes drugs for which there are special provisions (Food and Agriculture Organization, 1967).

In a translation of the definition of food in the Food Quality Control Act BE 2507 (1964) of Thailand: "food means (1) all substances consumed or drunk by man, but excluding the medicines under the law on the sale thereof, (2) substances used by man for masticating or mouthing as food, (3) substances used as ingredients for the production of food including the colours and flavour seasonings."

Basically these definitions, and other definitions given in the current legislation of other countries (Food and Agriculture Organization, 1967) controlling food for man, are intended to include the same type of commodities. They differ from the dictionary meaning and the general public's concept of food as substances contributing chiefly calories and nourishment to the body. These definitions have been developed to meet jurisdictional requirements of the law in accordance with the customs and habits of people as well as to keep pace with advances in food technology.

In some countries there is a combined food and drug law, and this has advantages in dealing with products which may be represented as foods under some circumstances and as drugs or even cosmetics in others. A combined food and drug law with an accompanying administrative organization provides for flexibility and efficient enforcement. Many of the problems and actions are common to both foods and drugs. In the Canadian law the phrases "articles represented for use as foods" and "mixed with food for any purpose whatever" have been helpful in classifying substances as foods, drugs, or cosmetics.

2.2. GENERAL PRINCIPLES OF FOOD LEGISLATION

In reviewing the historical development of food laws in different countries, it is noted that the national laws for the control of food were enacted to provide protection to the public where a combination of health hazards and frauds prevailed in the country. Although the first basic aims and benefits of a food law are for the protection of consumers, it must be realized that these aims and benefits are intimately associated with both national and international marketing practices as well as with industrial developments.

In the report of the Regional Seminar on Food Legislation for Asia and the Far East, held in Bangkok in 1962, the basic principles of legislation for the control of foods were developed (Food and Agriculture Organization, 1962a). These have been summarized in part as follows:

(1) The establishment of minimum standards should be made, below which foods should not be sold, unless specifically designated as substandard and suitable exemptions made in the law for the sale of such foods. At the same time, provision should be made for the marketing of food commodities of a quality superior to the minimum standard. This has been accomplished in many countries through a marking or grading system. These grade standards have been found important in featuring the produce of a country and thus gaining a reputation for it on world markets.
(2) A provision should be included for prohibiting the sale of food that is in any way harmful to health, adulterated, or that consists in whole or in part of any filthy, putrid, repulsive, rotten, decomposed, or diseased animal or vegetable substance, or food that is insect infested or otherwise unfit for human consumption.
(3) A provision should be made for prohibiting the sale of food commodities under unsanitary conditions.
(4) A prohibition should be included on the labelling, packaging, advertising, and sale of any food in a manner that is false, misleading, deceptive, or misbranded in any manner.
(5) To facilitate the administration and enforcement of the law there should be subsections dealing with:
  (a) definitions of such keywords as adulteration, advertisement, food, label, misbranding, package, sale, unsanitary conditions, warranty, etc., rather than rely on the common or dictionary meaning of such words;
  (b) procedures for sampling and analyses;
  (c) powers of inspection and procedures to be followed;
  (d) penalties;
  (e) warranties and guarantees;
  (f) importation of foods not complying with the law.
(6) A provision for authority to make and to amend the basic law by

regulations is necessary in order to provide for flexibility and ready implementation of its purpose.
(a) This authority should include items respecting:—
    (i) the labelling, packaging, and the offering, exposing, and advertising for sale of any food;
    (ii) the size, dimensions, fill, and other specifications of packages of foods;
    (iii) the sale and conditions of sale of any food; and
    (iv) the use of any substance in or affecting the characteristics of any food,
in order to prevent the consumer or purchaser from being deceived or misled as to its quantity, character, composition, merit, or safety, or to prevent injury to health of the consumer or purchaser;
(b) prescribing standards of identity, composition, purity, quality, or other property of any article of food;
(c) the importation of any food in order to ensure compliance with the basic law;
(d) the method of preparation, manufacture, preserving, packing, storing, and testing of any food in the interest of or for the prevention of injury to the health of consumers;
(e) the maintenance of records as are considered necessary for the proper enforcement and administration of the basic law and its regulations;
(f) the powers and obligations of inspectors and analysts in their official capacity regarding the taking of samples, instituting seizures, forfeitures, and other duties as well as prescribing methods of analysis;
(g) a provision for procedures for appeal against the results of analyses;
(h) a provision for exempting any food or ingredients in a food from all or any of the requirements of the basic law and its regulations;
(i) the additions or deletions to any of the schedules to the basic law in the interests of or for the prevention of injury to the health of the consumer;
(j) the prescribing of a tariff of fees for the analysis and inspection of foods;
(k) the prescribing of forms to be used for the purpose of the enforcement of the basic law;

(l) the prescribing for the licensing or registration of food manufacturing establishments to ensure that the premises, the qualifications of the technical staff, mode of operation, the sanitation of the premises and the hygiene of the personnel are adequate to avoid hazards to the health of consumers.

On the question of penalties it was considered desirable to set up minimum sanctions (fines and or imprisonment). It was recommended, however, that the minimum penalty should not be uniform for all violations, but should be graduated according to the nature and the gravity of the offence.

In order to maintain an efficient, effective, and flexible system for preparing regulations and amendments to the basic law, it was decided that this could be accomplished through a standing committee of the government, empowered to make regulations or amendments to the law respecting the control of the manufacture and sale of food in the country, as necessary, for the protection of public health and the prevention of deceptive and dishonest practices. To support the government committee, an advisory committee, consisting of representatives of various interested departments responsible for the administration of health, agriculture, justice, finance, customs, industry, and commerce should be established. The functions and duties of the committee would be:

(a) To advise the government respecting:
  (i) the questions of principle in the field of food legislation and control of foodstuffs;
  (ii) the drafting of food laws or amendments to the existing law and regulations in the light of processing techniques, fraud, trade practices and consumer needs.
(b) To coordinate the action of various departments of government interested in food control and the prevention of fraud.
(c) To review the implementation of the basic law from time to time.

In order that the Government Advisory Committee would be adequately informed, it was considered desirable for the basic law to provide authority to set up technical subcommittees of experts in particular fields, including representation from consumers. In order to maintain uniformity of enforcement of the control of foods, it was recommended that the authority for implementation of the food legislation should be vested in the central administrative organization. If constitutional or jurisdictional problems arose with such an organization, then recourse should be made to local authorities reporting to a central administration. In order that efficient enforcement of the law could be carried out, it was considered desirable to review and draw up annual programmes of the activities. In planning such programmes, consideration should be given to the minimum number of food control operations, including sampling, to be performed annually to provide the necessary safeguards to public health and the prevention of fraud.

It was considered advisable to have a higher priority for health hazards than for economic cheats and frauds, and the main efforts should be concentrated at the source rather than at the retail level. However, it was considered essential to maintain a surveillance at the retail level in order to meet any emergency situations that might arise and to obtain leads for national programmes.

The above proposals, providing the principles of food control legislation, are quite comprehensive, and are considered to include the basic elements of a food control law designed to protect the public against health hazards and frauds. At the same time it provides for flexibility and adaptation to domestic conditions as well as to the promotion of fair trade practices.

2.3. TRENDS IN FOOD LEGISLATION

It is becoming increasingly evident that consumer organizations are taking a more active interest in methods of food production, processing, and the marketing of foods. Some of this interest stems from the costs of food commodities, and there is much concern about the increasing number of new chemicals being used in or upon foods. Demands are being made on governments for assurance that the necessary measures for the protection of the public against possible hazards to health have been taken. As indicated above, the functions of the food law are to take whatever feasible measures are available and necessary, in the light of present knowledge, to protect the health of the public and to provide the consumer with confidence that the food distributed is safe, wholesome, and that information about it is presented in a factual manner. A number of food law enforcement agencies are establishing consumer relations' units within their organizations in order to foster communication between the agency and consumers and vice versa.

With the increased urbanization of the populations within a country, a new group of so-called convenience foods has been developed by manufacturers and producers. This has brought new problems to food law enforcement agencies. Mass production of these products is now replacing foods which were previously prepared in the home. This necessitates the establishment of more rigid specifications for foods and effective sanitation requirements for the control of such foods.

Developments in the packaging industry, with the accompanying advertising in mass media, have raised problems in the promotion of food commodities. At times it would appear that there is a tendency to confuse the outward appearance of products with inside integrity. The self-service methods of merchandizing food demand careful scrutiny of the label to ensure that the consumer is properly informed. It is essential for food control agencies to take a close look at the so-called hidden cheats in the marketing of foods. Although the display and advertising of foods in an ethical and attractive manner is essential to good merchandizing, it is the responsibility of the regulatory agency to ensure that these aims are met and consumers are able to make intelligent decisions on their choice of products.

The trend towards the harmonization of food control laws at the international level during the past few years has given a new perspective to food legislation. Undoubtedly, activities in this field will lead to improved trade relations in food commodities and better protection to people, nationally as well as internationally, against health hazards and frauds, not only in the well-developed countries but in the developing countries. In this connection, international agencies have initiated programmes designed to help developing countries establish the necessary facilities and to train personnel to conduct food control operations in their respective countries.

3. FOOD STANDARDS

In reviewing the history of the development of the control of foods, it is noted that one of the major interests of the legislators was the elaboration of standards, or yardsticks, for certain basic foods. The detection of the adulteration and of the misbranding of these foods is dependent on the standards established for them. The elaboration of standards aims at ensuring the marketing of a sound, wholesome product correctly labelled and presented in a factual and forthright manner. The standards for foods do not necessarily affect consumer preference, but they are intended to inform the purchaser or consumer just what he is buying.

The development of standards for foods is of interest, not only to the enforcement agency, but to the manufacturer or producer of the food as well, and to the consuming public. In commerce, standards promote honesty and fair dealings among manufacturers, processors, and dealers. They tend to prevent unfair competition and trade practices. Thus it is seen that caution should be exercised in the enactment of food standards to ensure that they are economically acceptable and not unduly restrictive on manufacturers and processors. Standards for foods should not be looked upon as permanent nor should they wholly rely on precedent since such an outlook would often lead to mediocre products and the suppression of technological advances.

From a legislative standpoint, the following example is cited regarding procedures used in the enactment of food standards. In the Food and Drugs Act 1967 in Canada, authority is provided under section 24(C) to make regulations for carrying out the purposes and provisions of the Act. Included in the regulation-making authority is provision for "prescribing standards of composition, strength, potency, purity, quality or other property of any article of food ...", and section 6 of the Act states: "Where a standard has been prescribed for a food, no person shall label, package, sell or advertise any article in such a manner that it is likely to be mistaken for such food, unless the article complies with the prescribed standard."

It is noted that authority is provided under this Act to prescribe, by regulations, legal standards for the control of foods. This regulation-making authority is an important aspect of Canadian food and drug legislation, and is often referred to as "delegated legislation". It is a system providing authority under the general terms of the Act for the Minister of the Department of National Health and Welfare, who is also a Member of Parliament and whose department is charged with the responsibility for administering the law, to refer recommendations on legislative matters to the Cabinet of the Government in office. After discussion in the Cabinet, the legislative matter is recommended for implementation by Order in Council under the signature of the Governor in Council, or returned to the department for further consideration. The Cabinet, which is a body of fifteen or twenty ministers of departments of the Government, can readily deal with recommendations prepared by the administrative executive in the light of government policy. This procedure permits the administrators of the Act to keep the requirements in step with the times by dealing rapidly with complex and technical matters, in fields which are under constant development. To refer such matters to Parliament as a whole would mean that the subject must take its turn in the debates along with other legislative matters.

Although the Canadian Food and Drugs Act does not obligate the administrators of the Act to inform the trade or consumers prior to the initiation of proposed new standards, or changes in existing food standards, it has been the practice of the administrators of the Act to issue information letters to the interested trade on such matters for comment. Also, the subject is usually laid before a Consumer Advisory Council of the executive organization for comment. In this way a full discussion on legislative matters is obtained with industry and consumers prior to presenting recommendations to the Minister of the Department for his consideration and presentation to the Cabinet. Legal standards enacted in this manner have the same force and effect as if they were contained in the Act. The system has been in effect for some 40-odd years in Canada and has been found to be a very practical solution to a complex problem. Naturally, in the event evidence of a hazardous situation comes to the attention of the administrators of the Act involving a food standard, or other matters coming under regulatory authority, a procedure is available to act quickly to correct the situation without consulting the trade or consumer groups.

Another example of the legislative procedure used in the enactment of food standards is given in section 401 of the Federal Food, Drug and Cosmetic Act and General Regulations 1966 in the United States of America. The following authority is provided regarding the definition of standards for food.

> Whenever in the judgment of the Secretary (of the Department) such action will promote honesty and fair dealing in the interest of consumers, he shall promulgate regulations fixing and establishing for any food, under its common or usual name so far as practicable, a reasonable definition and standard of identity, a reasonable standard of quality and/or reasonable standards for fill of containers. *Provided,* that no definition and standard of identity and no standard of quality shall be established for fresh or dried fruits, fresh or dried vegetables or butter except that standards of identity may be established for avocados, cantaloupes, citrus fruits and melons. In prescribing any standard of fill of container, the Secretary shall give due consideration to natural shrinkage in storage and in transit of fresh natural food and to the need for necessary packing and protective material. In the prescribing of any standard of quality for any canned fruit, or canned vegetable, consideration shall be given and due allowance made for differing characteristics of the several varieties of such fruit or vegetable. In prescribing a definition and standard of identity for any food or class of food in which optional ingredients are permitted, the Secretary shall for the purpose of promoting honesty and fair dealing in the interest of consumers, designate the optional ingredients which shall be named on the label. Any definition and standard of identity prescribed by the Secretary for avocados, cantaloupes, citrus fruits, or melons shall relate only to maturity and to the effects of freezing.

The general administrative provisions of this Act direct the Secretary to publish the proposed standard and afford all interested parties an opportunity to present their views orally and in writing. In addition, provision is made for a public hearing prior to the enactment of a standard where any person adversely affected by the proposed standard may file objections with the Secretary, specifying with particularity the provisions of the order deemed objectionable, stating reasonable grounds thereof, and requesting a public hearing upon such objections.

It is noted that the Federal Food, Drug and Cosmetic Act of the United States of America provides considerable detail to the administrators in proposing standards for foods. Certain fruit and vegetable products and butter are excluded, and a distinction is made between a standard of identity and a standard of quality. Provision is made for dissemination to the public and the trade of any proposed standard. This is usually done through the medium of the Federal Register, the official government publication on regulatory material in the United States of America. Although the provision made for public hearings, where objections are raised to the proposals on standards, is in keeping with democratic procedures, in the instances where such have been conducted, they have proved to be a lengthy and drawn-out process for the purpose of discussing scientific matters.

A keen interest has been taken in recent years in the elaboration of food standards as a result of the advances made in transportation facilities and in food technology, along with the marked increased interest in international trade in foodstuffs. Examples of this interest on a regional basis are seen in the activities of the Latin American Food Code, the United Nations Economic Commission for Europe, and the European Common Market. On a worldwide basis, the Codex Alimentarius commission has launched a most ambitious programme on the development of food standards.

In the Fourth Report of the Commission (1966) it is stated that the standard should specify "Product designation, definition and composition. These should describe and define the food (including its scientific name when necessary) and cover compositional requirements which may include quality criteria." Accordingly, committees have been established to draft standards for a number of food products such as sugar, fruit juices, fats and oils, cocoa and chocolate, meat and meat products, processed fruits and vegetables, etc.

3.1. TYPES OF FOOD STANDARDS

It is noted in the definition of food standards that reference is made to different types of standards and, in general, these fall into one of the following categories: (a) standards of identity, (b) standards of quality or grade standards, and (c) standards of composition.

In the case of standards of identity, a definition is given to the food commodity. For example, tea is defined in the regulations under the Food and Drugs Act 1967 in Canada as follows: "Tea shall be the dried leaves and buds of *Thea sinensis* (L.) Sims prepared by the usual trade processes." This standard identifies tea with a definite plant species. The dried leaves or buds of other plants are not considered as "tea". No reference is made to the composition or the quality of the commodity nor to the addition of any ingredients to the commodity represented as tea.

Standards of quality or grade standards are established at different levels of quality characteristics for a commodity. For example, the Canada Dairy Products Act and Regulations 1967 has established the following standards for First and Second Grade Creamery Butter:

(a) Canada First Grade Creamery Butter is creamery butter that contains not more than sixteen per cent water, not less than eighty per cent milk fat and no fat other than that of milk, has a minimum total score of ninety-two points with a minimum score of thirty-nine points for flavour and has the following characteristics:
  (i) it is clean with no objectionable flavour,
  (ii) the texture is firm, close and waxy,
  (iii) the moisture is well incorporated,
  (iv) the colour is practically true and even and is of a desirable shade,
  (v) the salt is all dissolved, and
  (vi) it is packed in clean boxes which are neatly banded, cleanly lined, solidly packed and neatly finished.
(b) Canada Second Grade Creamery Butter is creamery butter that does not qualify for Canada First Grade, contains not more than sixteen per cent water, not less than eighty per cent milk fat and no fat other than that of milk has a minimum total score of eighty-seven and a minimum score of thirty-seven for flavour and may have the following characteristics:
  (i) it is slightly unclean, or unclean in flavour, or is slightly weedy but has no stinkweed or other pronounced weedy flavours, or is slightly stale or stale, or slightly metallic or metallic, or slightly tallowy or tallowy or sour, or is bitter as a result of pronounced saltiness or other causes, or has a pronounced woody or other objectionable flavour on the surface or in the butter,
  (ii) it is weak in texture, or open, greasy, brittle or sticky,
  (iii) it has free moisture or is leaky,
  (iv) it is slightly mottled or mottled in colour, slightly streaky, or streaky, uneven or has any objectionable shade of colour, and
  (v) the salt is not all dissolved.

It is noted from a compositional standpoint the specifications are the same for first and second grade, but from a characteristics standpoint, second Grade is inferior to first grade creamery butter.

The third type of food standard is usually designated as the standard of composition. In this case the standard may list the ingredients and additives which make up the product as well as the analytical requirements which must be met. For example, the following standard is given for Canned Tomatoes in the regulations under the Food and Drugs Act (1967) in Canada.

> Canned Tomatoes
> (a) shall be the canned product made by heat processing properly prepared fresh ripe tomatoes,
> (b) may contain
>   (i) sugar, invert sugar or dextrose in dry form,
>   (ii) salt,
>   (iii) a firming agent,
>   (iv) citric acid,
>   (v) spice or other seasoning: and
> (c) shall contain not less than 50 per cent drained tomato solids as determined by the official method.

It is noted that this standard gives general specifications of the commodity and provides for optional ingredients, chemical additives, and a method of analysis to determine if the product complies with minimum specifications.

Commodities for which no standard of identity, composition, or quality has been established in food legislation are usually designated as unstandardized foods. These are often distributed under a brand name, and most countries require a complete list of all the ingredients on the label of the product. For example, a brand of a rice breakfast cereal is labelled to contain "toasted rice, sugar, salt, malt flavouring with butylated hydroxyanisole added to packaging material to help preserve freshness"

3.2. FOOD ADDITIVES

Although chemicals had been added to foods for many years as antimicrobial agents, flavouring agents, colouring agents, etc., it was only after World War II, with the marked expansion of the chemical industry, that attention was drawn to the increasing number of various chemical substances being used in foods. There were wide differences in the measures taken by food control agencies to deal with the problem. Prior to this time, principles had been developed by only a few countries to deal with this group of substances to provide consumers with protection against health hazards and frauds in their use in foods.

At the meeting of the World Health Assembly in 1953, the view was expressed that the increasing use of chemical substances in the food industry had, in the last few decades, created a new public health problem which might usefully be investigated. The question was considered by the Executive Board who recommended that the WHO in co-operation with the FAO, collect and disseminate information on selected groups of chemical additives, including laboratory techniques and relevant legislation. At the Council meeting of the FAO in September–October 1954 it was recognized "that the problem of food additives is of growing importance with respect to both food production and distribution, and requested the Director General of F.A.O. to consider the kind of work which F.A.O. could appropriately undertake in this field in association with the FAO/WHO Expert Committee on Nutrition." At the Fourth Session of this Expert Committee in October–November, 1954, the Committee suggested "that the Directors General of F.A.O. and W.H.O. consider the desirability of calling a conference of representatives of the existing groups working on the subject, together with appropriate representatives of such Member Nations as might be interested and would be prepared to send delegates."

The Executive Board of the WHO agreed to the suggestion of the Joint FAO–WHO Expert Committee on Nutrition at its meeting in January 1955, and a Joint FAO–WHO Conference on Food Additives was convened in September 1955 at Geneva (Food and Agriculture Organization, 1956).

This conference was exploratory with one of the purposes "to consider the contribution which F.A.O. and W.H.O. can appropriately make in this field and how far international consultation in connection with food additives could be coordinated within the framework of F.A.O. and W.H.O.", also "in accordance with the suggestion of the Joint FAO/WHO Expert Committee on Nutrition, consideration was to be given to the desirability of convening an expert committee which would attempt to lay down acceptable broad principles governing the use of food additives". This conference confined its discussions to food additives as "non-nutritive substances which are added intentionally to food, generally in small quantities, to improve its appearance, flavour, texture or storage properties". The conference outlined a programme for the two organizations including the convening of one or more expert committees. The following year a meeting was held in Rome under the joint auspices of the FAO and the WHO to draft general principles governing the use of food additives. These were formulated under three general headings

(Food and Agriculture Organization, 1957):

A. Technical purposes for which food additives are used:
   (i) maintenance of the nutritional quality of a food;
   (ii) enhancement of keeping quality or stability, with resulting reduction in food wastage;
   (ii) enhancement of keeping quality or stability, with resulting reduction in food wastage;
   (iii) making foods attractive to consumers;
   (vi) Providing essential aids in food processing.

B. Situations in which food additives should *not* be used:
   (i) to disguise the use of faulty processing and handling techniques;
   (ii) to deceive the consumer;
   (iii) when the result is a substantial reduction of the nutritive value of food;
   (iv) when the desired effect can be obtained by good manufacturing practices which are economically feasible.

C. Safety for use of food additives.

The Expert Committee recognized that it is impossible to establish absolute proof of the non-toxicity of a specified use of an additive for all humans under all conditions, but "critically designed animal tests of the physiological, pharmacological and biochemical behaviour of a proposed additive can provide a reasonable basis for evaluating the safety of use of a food additive at a specified level of intake".

Other matters were discussed, but from a food control standpoint, the following basic principles were recommended:

(1) Legal control of the use of food additives is essential. This is best accomplished through the use of a permitted list, which effectively prevents the addition of any new substances to food until an adequate basis of judgment of their freedom from health hazard has been established.
(2) In principle, consumers should be informed of the presence of an additive in a food. Label declaration is the most effective method of achieving this result.
(3) Regulations governing the control of food additives are useless, unless the law is enforced. This requires trained food inspectors, food control laboratories and reliable analytical methods.

Following this meeting, a number of expert committees met under the joint auspices of the FAO and the WHO and have issued the following reports entitled:

Procedures for the Testing of Intentional Food Additives to Establish

> *their Safety of Use,* Food and Agriculture Organization, 1958.
>
> *Specifications for Identity and Purity of Food Additives (Food Colours),* Food and Agriculture Organization, 1963. (Antimicrobials, Preservatives, and Antioxidants, 1962b).
>
> *Evaluation of the Toxicity of a Number of Antimicrobials and Antioxidants,* World Health Organization, 1962.
>
> *Specifications for the Identity and Purity of Food Additives and their Toxicological Evaluation: Emulsifiers, Stabilizers, Bleaching and Maturing Agents,* World Health Organization, 1964.
>
> *Specifications for the Identity and Purity of Food Additives and their Toxicological Evaluation: Food Colours and Some Antimicrobials and Antioxidants,* World Health Organization, 1965.
>
> *Specifications for the Identity and Purity of Food Additives and Their Toxicological Evaluation: Some Antimicrobials, Antioxidants, Emulsifiers, Stabilizers, Flour Treatment Agents, Acids and Bases,* World Health Organization, 1966.
>
> *Procedures for Investigating Intentional and Unintentional Food Additives,* World Health Organization, 1967.

The Codex Alimentarius Commission 1966 has established a Codex Committee on Food Additives whose responsibility it is to establish tolerances for individual food additives in specific food items and prepare lists of food additives for the guidance of the Joint FAO–WHO Expert Committee on Food Additives. Thus there will be a coordination of the work of the Joint FAO–WHO expert committees and the Codex Alimentarius Commission in the preparation of the food standards to be included in the Codex Alimentarius.

The Food Protection Committee of the Food and Nutrition Board of the United States of America, National Academy of Sciences–National Research Council (1959), issued a report on *Principles and Procedures for Evaluating the Safety of Intentional Additives in Food.* The following definition was developed for the term "food additive": A "food additive" is a substance or a mixture of substances, other than a basic foodstuff, which is present in food as a result of any aspect of production, processing or packaging." The Food Protection Committee of the above organization received requests from its Industry Liaison Panel and other sources in 1958 to undertake a project designed to produce a Food Chemical Codex, providing monographs of chemicals used as food additives, similar to the monographs for drugs in the United States Pharmacopoeia and the National Formulary. Accordingly, the task was undertaken by an Advisory Panel of the Food Chemical Codex and a

Committee on Specifications. Preliminary looseleaf parts of the text were released from 1963 to 1965 as publication 1143 of the National Academy of Sciences–National Research Council, Washington D.C., USA. The first bound edition of the *Food Chemical Codex* (1966) was issued as publication 1406 of the above organization.

This is a most useful and valuable compendium of reference standards for food additives. It provides monographs for several hundred chemicals used as food additives under their chemical or common name, with their description, specifications, tests, packaging, storage, and functional use in foods.

The following is an example of the legislative action taken in establishing requirements for food additives in the United States of America. In 1958 the Federal Food, Drug, and Cosmetic Act 1966 was amended to provide for requirements for food additives. Under this amendment, food additives were defined as follows:

> The term "food additive" means any substance, the intended use of which results or may reasonably be expected to result, directly or indirectly, in its becoming a component or otherwise affecting the characteristics of any food (including any substance intended for use in producing, manufacturing, packing, processing, preparing, treating, packaging, transporting or holding food, and including any source of radiation intended for any such use) if such substance is not generally recognized among experts qualified by scientific training and experience to evaluate its safety as having been adequately shown through scientific procedures (or in case of a substance used in food prior to January 1, 1958, through either scientific procedures or experience based on common use in food) to be safe under the conditions of its intended use; except that such term does not include—
> (1) a pesticide chemical in or on a raw agricultural commodity;
> (2) a pesticide chemical to the extent that it is intended for use or is used in the production, storage or transportation of any raw agricultural commodity; or
> (3) a colour additive; or
> (4) any substance used in accordance with a sanction or approval granted prior to the enactment of this paragraph pursuant to this Act, the Poultry Products Inspection Act (21 U.S.C. 451 and the following) or the Meat Inspection Act of March 1907 (34 Stat. 1260) as amended and extended (21 U.S.C. 71 and the following).

In addition, provision was made under the Food Additive Amendment requiring any person intending to use a food additive to file with the Secretary a petition proposing the issuance of a regulation prescribing the conditions under which such additive may be safely used. The content of such petitions is prescribed as well as the action to be taken by the Secretary on them. Petitions have been filed for several hundred food additives and a permitted list has been established in the Regulations under the Act (Federal Food, Drug, Cosmetic Act and General Regulations 1966).

The following examples are presented to indicate the variety of approaches taken by certain European countries to bring food additives under legislative control.

As indicated previously, the food law in France does not provide any specific definition for food, and this is also true for the group of substances generally recognized as food additives. Dehove (1964) reports as follows regarding the interpretation of the addition of substances to foods in France: "In addition to its usual components, specifically enumerated in its definition, a food or drink may contain added substances such as flavouring, or seasoning or colouring matters, preservatives, etc., necessary for their preparation, presentation, organoleptic qualities or storage." It would appear from the above that the "added substances" are regarded as the same type of substances which are termed food additives in a number of countries.

The Swedish Food Law 1966 defines food additive as: "any product or substance which is intended to be added, usually in small amounts, to food—without being a raw material therein—in order to affect the colour, taste, consistency or durability thereof or for any other similar purpose and which remains in the product when the latter is in its finished state." The law does not regard vitamins or water as food additives and operates on the principle of a permitted list of additives (Food and Agriculture Organization, 1967).

The Food Act 1964 in Germany differentiates between two types of additives—foreign substances and technical auxiliary materials. The "foreign substances" are defined as "substances which are converted into foods and contain no assimilable carbohydrates, fats or proteins, or natural contents of vitamins, provitamins, or aromatic or flavouring substances, or the use of which in food is not determined by the presence of such contents". On the other hand, "technical auxiliary substances" are defined as substances used in the production, preparation or processing of food, but not intended for consumption. A list of permitted residue tolerances is established for these substances or the amount must not exceed the maximum which can be technically avoided (Food and Agriculture Organization, 1967).

Following the recommendation of the Joint FAO–WHO Conference on Food Additives in September 1955, the Food and Agriculture Organization of the United Nations (1956) initiated a series of publications entitled "FAO Food Additive Control Series". These publications describe the national systems for regulating the manufacture and use of food additives in several countries. Reports have been released from

Canada (Pugsley, 1959), the United Kingdom (Hinton, 1960), the Netherlands (Meizer, 1961), Australia (Jewel, 1961), and Denmark (Uhl and Hanson, 1961). These publications provide useful background information on the control of food additives in the respective countries.

4. HYGIENE

One of the most important aspects in the control of the production of a safe and wholesome food is that concerned with sanitation and hygienic principles. Ignorance, carelessness, unethical practices, and abuse of the basic principles of hygiene and sanitation on the part of the producer, processor, or distributor of food can readily lead to unsafe and unwholesome food. Undoubtedly the most desirable form of control is one in which management is well informed and highly motivated to produce a clean, wholesome product from the standpoint of hygiene and sanitation.

In the report of the fourth session of the Committee on Food Hygiene of the Codex Alimentarius Commission (1967), agreement was reached on the following definition of food hygiene: "Food hygiene comprises conditions and measures necessary for the production, processing and distribution of foods, designed to ensure a safe, sound and wholesome final product fit for human consumption." The concept of cultural and aesthetic acceptability was considered by the Committee to be included in the definition.

In the definition of food hygiene, the Committee emphasized that the rules and methods of hygienic performance constitute a continuous process and each element is important to each other and to the whole. The Committee recognized in the application of the rules and the methods that they cannot be verified in all cases at a later point of time, and in some respects it depends on supervision, which at official levels may not always be possible. In this respect, the General Principles of Food Hygiene and Codes of Hygienic Practices were objectives to develop in legislation.

The Committee on Hygiene of the Codex Alimentarius Commission (1967) has drawn up provisional general principles of Food Hygiene to provide a basis for establishing codes of hygienic practice of individual commodities. These have been dealt with under Raw Material Requirements and Plant Facilities and Operating Requirements. The following discussion is taken from the report of the committee.

4.1. RAW MATERIAL REQUIREMENTS

Consideration was given to environmental sanitation in growing and raw food production areas, the sanitary harvesting and production of raw foods, and the transportation facilities and handling procedures.

In the growing and production areas it is essential that human and animal wastes be disposed of in such a manner that they do not contaminate the food commodities especially for products that may be consumed without heat treatment. In areas where irrigation is practised every precaution should be taken to ensure that the water used does not constitute a public health hazard to the consumer through the product. Pest control operations should be carried out by or on the recommendation of an appropriate official agency with a thorough understanding of the hazards involved including the possibility of toxic residues being retained by the crops.

In the sanitary harvesting and production of raw foods, precautions should be exercised in the containers used for the food, to ensure they do not constitute a source of contamination to the product. Containers which may be reused should be of such material and construction as will facilitate thorough cleaning before being used. Products which are obviously unfit for harvesting should be segregated and disposed of in a manner that they do not contaminate the food, water supplies, or other crops. The protection of products from contamination by animals, insects, vermin, birds, chemical, or microbiological contaminants during harvesting and storage is an essential sanitary practice. All methods and procedures used in harvesting and production should be carried out in a clean and sanitary manner.

In the transportation of the harvested raw food products, the conveyances used should be of such material and construction as will permit through cleaning and be so cleaned and maintained as not to constitute a source of contamination of the product. In the transportation of perishable products every care should be taken to prevent spoilage and deterioration. Refrigeration may be necessary in some instances, and if ice is used in contact with the product it should be of sanitary quality.

4.2. PLANT FACILITIES AND OPERATING REQUIREMENTS

In this section consideration is given to plant construction and layout, equipment and utensils, hygienic operating requirements, operating practices and production requirements, sanitation control programme, and laboratory control procedures.

The plant should be located in an area reasonably free of objectionable odours, dust, smoke, or other contaminants. It should be of such construction as to protect against the entrance and harbouring of insects, birds, or vermin, and be so designed as to permit easy and adequate cleaning. The areas where raw materials are received and stored should be separated from the areas where the final product preparation or packaging is done in order to preclude contamination of the finished product.

In addition, areas or compartments for the storage, handling, or manufacture of inedible products should be separate and distinct from those used for edible products. The food handling area should be completely separated from any part of the premises used as living quarters. An ample supply of drinkable quality cold water should be available, and hot water where necessary. Similarly, the ice used should be made from drinkable water and handled and stored to protect it from contamination. If non-drinkable water is used for such purposes as fire control, it should be carried in separate lines identified preferably by colour with no possibility of cross-contamination with the drinkable water lines.

The plumbing and waste disposal lines should be watertight with adequate traps and vents. These lines should be large enough to carry peak loads, and every precaution should be taken to prevent contamination of the drinkable water supplies.

The lighting and ventilation should be given special attention. Adequate ventilation should be provided to areas producing excessive heat, steam, obnoxious fumes, vapours, and contaminating aerosols. Without adequate ventilation there is often accumulation of moisture and mold growth on upper structures which may readily drop and contaminate the food products. Protection should be provided over light bulbs and fixtures to prevent contamination of the food in case of breakage.

Adequate toilet facilities and rooms should be provided. These should be well lighted and ventilated with self-closing doors which do not open directly into a food-handling area. Hand-washing facilities should be provided within the toilet areas and notices posted requiring persons to wash their hands after using the toilet. In addition, adequate and convenient facilities for employees to wash and dry their hands, preferably with single-use towels, should be provided wherever processes require them.

With respect to equipment and utensils, all surfaces coming in contact with food should be smooth, free from pits, crevices, and loose scale, and capable of withstanding repeated exposure to normal cleaning. The material used for the surface should be non-toxic, unaffected by food products, and preferably non-absorbent.

Stationary equipment should be installed in such a manner as will permit easy and thorough cleaning. Equipment and utensils should be designed and constructed to prevent hygienic hazards and permit ready and efficient cleaning. All equipment and utensils used for inedible or contaminated materials should be identified and not used for handling edible products.

While specific operating requirements may be necessary for certain products, the following were considered the minimal in all food production—handling, storage, and distribution. The building, equipment, utensils, and other physical facilities of the plant should be maintained in good repair, clean, and in an orderly and sanitary condition. Waste receptacles should be removed frequently from working areas during plant operations. Appropriate detergents and disinfectants should be employed and in a manner as to present no hazard to public health.

A vermin and insect control programme should be instituted, and dogs, cats, and other domestic pets excluded from areas where food is processed.

In the case of the health of the personnel, every precaution should be taken to ensure no person, while known to be affected with a disease capable of being transmitted through food, or a known carrier of such disease, or while afflicted with infected wounds, sores, or any illness, is permitted to work in any area where such person may contaminate the food or surfaces with pathogenic organisms.

Separate locked rooms or cabinets should be provided for the storage of all rodenticides, fumigants, insecticides, and other toxic substances. These should be under the direct supervision of personnel with a thorough understanding of the hazards involved in their use, including the possibility of contamination of the product.

In respect to personnel hygiene and food-handling practices, a high degree of cleanliness while on duty should be required. Suitable clean headdress appropriate to the duties should be used. Hands should be washed as often as necessary, and spitting, eating, and the use of tobacco or chewing-gum prohibited. Adequate first-aid facilities should be provided to treat minor cuts and abrasions with a suitable waterproof dressing. Where gloves are used in food-handling they should be maintained in a sound, clean, and sanitary condition.

In the operating practices and production requirements, acceptance criteria should be established for receiving raw materials. Where products are known to contain decomposed, toxic, or extraneous substances, which will not be removed to acceptable levels by normal plant procedures or sorting, they should be rejected. Raw materials stored on the plant premises should be protected against infestation and contamination and under conditions which minimize deterioration. The water used in conveying raw materials should be from an acceptable source or suitably treated so as not to constitute a public health hazard.

All raw material prior to introduction in the processing line, or at a convenient point within it, should be inspected, sorted, or culled to remove unfit materials. Only clean and sound products should be processed. In the washing of raw material to remove soil or other contaminants, drinkable water should be used and not recirculated water unless suitably treated to maintain it in a condition that will not constitute a public health hazard. In the operations leading to the finished product and the packaging operations, proper timing should be employed in order to permit expeditious handling of consecutive units in production. In this way, contamination, deterioration, spoilage, or the development of infectious or toxigenic micro-organisms are avoided.

Packaging materials should be stored in a clean and sanitary manner, and when used in the packaging operation every precaution should be taken to prevent contamination with extraneous materials. The finished packaged product should be stored or transported under such conditions as to preclude contamination with or development of pathogenic deterioration of the product or the container.

In order to maintain a high level of sanitation in a food processing plant it is desirable to designate a unit to be responsible for a sanitation control programme within the plant. This unit should be divorced from production and have the overall responsibility of the cleanliness of the plant. The staff should be well trained in the use of special cleaning tools, methods, disassembling equipment for cleaning, and the significance of contamination and the hazards involved. The unit should give specific attention to critical areas, equipment, and materials as part of a permanent sanitation schedule.

In addition to inspection and supervision during production, each plant should have access to a laboratory to control the sanitary quality of the products processed. The amount and type of laboratory control will vary with the product and naturally any product which does not conform to recognized specifications should be rejected. In the specifications set up for end product control, sampling procedures, analytical methodology, etc., should be established for particular products.

The requirements under the Food and Drugs Act 1967 in Canada are given as an example of the procedures used in bringing hygienic practices in the manufacture, distribution and sale of foods under legislative control. Section 4 of the Act states:

> No person shall sell an article of food that
> (a) has in or upon it any poisonous or harmful substance,
> (b) is unfit for human consumption,
> (c) consists in whole or in part of any filthy, putrid, disgusting, rotten, decomposed or diseased animal or vegetable substance,
> (d) is adulterated, or
> (e) was manufactured, prepared, preserved, packaged or stored under unsanitary conditions.

To provide for the enforcement of the provisions of the Act at the level of the source of the commodity, section 7 of the Act states: "No person shall manufacture, prepare, preserve, package or store for sale any food under unsanitary conditions." The following definition of unsanitary conditions is given in section 2(m) of the Act: "Unsanitary conditions means such conditions or circumstances as might contaminate a food, drug or cosmetic with dirt or filth or render the same injurious to health."

The above requirements provide full authority to deal with non-hygienic or unsanitary practices found in the manufacture, preparation, preservation, packaging, or storage of food commodities. The requirement of section 4(a), dealing with the presence of any harmful and poisonous substances in foods, permits action to be taken on such substances as bacterial toxins, and section 4(c) on the presence of insect infestation in foods, while sections 4(e) and 7 cover unsanitary conditions in general as defined in the Act. Naturally it is necessary to use the authority provided in the Act along with an educational programme to attain the maximum in hygienic conditions in the manufacture, production, and storage of foods.

It is noted that the Act covers a food which consists in whole or in part of any filthy or disgusting animal or vegetable substance. It is essential to interpret such a requirement objectively and not condemn or reject a food because of the presence of foreign matter in amounts below the irreducible minimum and which are harmless and in accordance with good manufacturing practices. In some instances, realistic administrative tolerances are established in accordance with good manufacturing and production practices. As improvements are made in production or an infestation is brought under control, the basis of the action level can be lowered. The dilution of rejected products with acceptable products to bring a lot within the administrative tolerance is not considered to be in accordance with the interpretation of good manufacturing practices.

The enforcement of the unsanitary conditions requirements of the Act on imports often presents practical difficulties, since it is not always possible to show by examination of the end product that the food was manufactured under unsanitary conditions. The detection of these conditions is primarily a supervision and inspection task at the source. In some instances, inspection of foreign manufacturing plants by officers from the importing country has been practised. However, with the increasing industrial developments, the finished food product is at the end of a long economic food chain, involving considerable processing and treatment. Under the circumstances, practical difficulties are encountered by importing countries in supervising sanitary practices followed at various processing levels. One method of overcoming these difficulties is through the use of certificates from a recognized authority in the country of origin, testifying to the sanitary practices employed in the manufacture and production of the food product. Naturally, the reliability of such certificates depends on the quality of the inspection and supervision of the commodity by the authority in the country of origin.

The presentation of shipments of food at customs for entry into the country is tantamount to offering the food for sale in the country, and action can be taken to reject shipments at the port of entry where they are found to be in violation of the sanitary provisions of the law. In some instances, contamination of the food occurs during transportation due to infestations in the carrier, and as such must be dealt with as a violation of the requirements of the Act.

5. INSPECTION

The inspection aspects of the control of foods in a country are of vital interest in providing protection to the public against health hazards and frauds. The personnel charged with this responsibility are really the eyes and the ears of the law. A country may have a good food control law in its statute books, have scientifically sound food standards, well-equipped laboratories, and qualified technical and administrative personnel, but the measures of protection afforded by the law would be quite meaningless unless the law were intelligently, effectively, and efficiently enforced.

Inspection respecting the control of foods in a country must take into account the needs of the country and its particular economic development. If a country is largely agricultural in nature and is in the process of industrial development, one of the first priorities in inspection must be related to perishable, raw food products with special emphasis for example on milk, meat, and poultry, where the principles of hygiene and sanitation are so important for the production of safe and wholesome products. In addition to the administrative organizations in the control of foods, inspection usually falls into two main units which may be designated as the outside, or field inspection unit, and the analytical or laboratory unit. Food control inspection involves the application of a number of scientific disciplines such as chemistry, physics, biochemistry, pharmacology, bacteriology, engineering, etc. Although there may be two units to food inspection from an organizational standpoint, it is essential for effective control to have complete co-ordination between the field inspection personnel and the analytical or laboratory personnel. One unit must support the other. This may be accomplished by an interchange of personnel from one unit to the other.

Since the control of foods is the application of applied sciences to the enforcement of laws, it is essential that it be supported by a research organization whose function is to contribute knowledge to all the scientific disciplines involved in the control of foods. The research organization permits the inspection activities to keep pace with or even be one step ahead of the industrial developments in this wide field of food technology.

In legislation on food control, it is the practice to provide basic principles of inspection. The Codex Alimentarius Commission has not included the principles of enforcement of the food standards other than to consider this aspect of the requirements as a responsibility of governments and to be accomplished, as far as possible, with consultation and advice from the food industry. The Commission, in the development of standards for food commodities, plans to include methods of sampling and analytical procedures in the monographs on food standards.

The provisions made in the Canadian Food and Drugs Act 1967 for food inspection are presented as an example of the type of authority utilized in this field of work. The powers of inspectors, appointed to enforce the Act, are stated as follows in section 21 of the Act:

(1) An Inspector may at any reasonable time
    (a) enter any place where on reasonable grounds he believes any article to which this Act or the regulations apply is manufactured, prepared, preserved,

packaged or stored, examine any such article and take samples thereof, and examine anything that he reasonably believes is used or capable of being used for such manufacture, preparation, preservation, packaging or storing;
(b) open and examine any receptacle or package that on reasonable grounds he believes contains any article to which this Act or the regulations apply;
(c) examine any books, documents or other records found in any place mentioned in paragraph (a) that on reasonable grounds he believes contain any information relevant to the enforcement of this Act with respect to any article to which this Act or the regulations apply and make copies thereof or extracts therefrom; and
(d) seize and detain for such time as may be necessary any article by means of or in relation to which he reasonably believes any provisions of this Act or the Regulations have been violated.

(2) For the purposes of Subsection (1) the expression "article to which this Act or Regulations apply" includes
(a) any food, drug, cosmetic or device;
(b) anything used for the manufacture, preparation, preservation, packaging or storing thereof, and
(c) any labelling or advertising material.

The section continues with subsections (3)–(8) dealing with the presentation of credentials by an inspector, assistance to the inspector by the owner, obstructing an inspector, false statements, interference with articles placed under seizure, and the storing of seized articles. Procedures for the release of seized articles are also given as well as authority for their destruction or forfeiture.

In respect to the analysis of samples from a seizure, section 23 of the Act states:

(1) An inspector may submit any article seized by him or any sample therefrom or any sample taken by him to an analyst for analysis or examination;
(2) Where an analyst has made an analysis or examination he may issue a certificate or report setting forth the results of his examination or analysis.

In addition the following authority is provided in section 24 of the Act:

The Governor in Council may make regulations for carrying the purposes and provisions of this Act into effect, and, in particular, but not so as to restrict the generality of the foregoing, may make regulations....
(i) not inconsistent with this Act, respecting the powers and duties of inspectors and analysts and the taking of samples and the seizure, detention, forfeiture and disposition of articles.

It is seen that broad powers are given to the inspectors to enforce the provisions of the Canadian Act. The right to seize and detain food commodities, at the source, where reasonable grounds are available to do so, allows immediate action to be taken, especially where there is an indication that the continued distribution might present a hazard to health. The products may be held pending confirmation by laboratory examination. The authority to review records is an important aspect of the powers of the inspectors since these may provide information on existing deficiencies in manufacture and production. Moreover, it is often important to trace the distribution channels, as shown in the records of the suspected product, in case a recall is necessary.

In reviewing the legal requirements of inspection in the control of food commodities it is noted they are designed to fulfil the obligations of the law to the consumer and to ensure that food manufacturers and processors distribute products which are clean and wholesome without hazards to health and in an honest and factual manner. There are two avenues of approach in the field of enforcement to the control of foods:

(a) the inspector can initiate the application of legal sanctions in cases where violations of the requirements are noted, or
(b) he can persuade a manufacturer to comply voluntarily and spontaneously with the legal requirements by giving him expert advice and assistance in understanding the provisions of the law and the means of complying with them.

The use of these two approaches places considerable responsibility on the inspector to be able to appraise a situation always in the light of achieving consumer protection. This requires sound technical knowledge, impartiality, and tact. The application of legal sanctions of the law alone frequently creates a state of hostility among manufacturers towards inspection, and this leads to prejudice of the enforcement of the law. On the other hand, exclusive reliance upon persuasion is open to criticism since the absence of compulsion does not guarantee uniform enforcement and tends to favour deliberate transgressors at the expense of consumers. An enforcement policy using education followed by legal action, where necessary, appears to be the desirable one to achieve good law observance. At no time should education be mistaken for leniency.

ACKNOWLEDGEMENT

The author is indebted to Dr. D. M. Smith of the Food and Drug Directorate, Department of National Health and Welfare, Ottawa, for reviewing the manuscript and making many helpful suggestions.

REFERENCES

BIGWOOD, E. J., and GERARD, A. (1967) General principles and field of application, *Fundamental Principles and Objectives of a Comparative Food Law*, vol. 1, pp. 1–128, S. Karger, Basel (Switzerland) and New York.

BOARDMAN, V. R. (1956) In *The Impact of the Food and Drug Administration on our Society*, pp. 11–13, H. Welch, and F. Martin-Ibanez, MD Publications Inc., New York.

CANADA DAIRY PRODUCTS ACT AND REGULATIONS (1967) Queen's Printer and Controller of Stationery, Ottawa.

CODEX ALIMENTARIUS COMMISSION (1966) *Report of Fourth Session*, pp. 1–135, Food and Agriculture Organization of the United Nations, Rome.

CODEX ALIMENTARIUS COMMISSION (1967) *Report of Committee on Food Hygiene*, pp. 1–10 with appendices, Food and Agriculture Organization of the United Nations, Rome.

CURRAN, R. E. (1953) *Canada's Food and Drug Laws*, Commerce Clearing House, Chicago.

DAVIDSON, A. L. (1949) *The Genesis and Growth of Food and Drug Administration in Canada*, pp. 1–117, Dept. National Health and Welfare, Ottawa.

DEHOVE, R. A. (1964) *Reglementation des Produits Alimnetaires et Non-alimentaires, Repression des Fraudes et Controle de la Qualité*, 5th edn., Commerce-Editions, Paris.

DRUMMOND, J. C., and WILBRAHAM, A. (1939) *The Englishman's Food*, Jonathan Cape, London.

FEDERAL FOOD, DRUG AND COSMETIC ACT AND GENERAL REGULATIONS (1966) US Dept. Health, Education, and Welfare, Washington DC.

FOOD AND AGRICULTURE ORGANIZATION OF THE UNITED NATIONS, (1956) *FAO Nutrition Meeting Report*, Series No. 11, Rome.

FOOD AND AGRICULTURE ORGANIZATION OF THE UNITED NATIONS (1957) *FAO Nutrition Meeting Report*, Series No. 15, Rome.

FOOD AND AGRICULTURE ORGANIZATION OF THE UNITED NATIONS (1958) *FAO Nutrition Meeting Report*, Series No. 17, Rome.

FOOD AND AGRICULTURE ORGANIZATION OF THE UNITED NATIONS (1961) *Report of First European Regional Conference*, Rome.

FOOD AND AGRICULTURE ORGANIZATION OF THE UNITED NATIONS (1962a) *Report of FAO Regional Seminar on Food Legislation for Asia and the Far East*, Rome.

FOOD AND AGRICULTURE ORGANIZATION OF THE UNITED NATIONS (1962b) *Antimicrobials, Preservatives and Antioxidants*, vol. 1, Rome.

FOOD AND AGRICULTURE ORGANIZATION OF THE UNITED NATIONS (1962c) *Report of Eleventh Session of FAO Conference*, Rome.

FOOD AND AGRICULTURE ORGANIZATION OF THE UNITED NATIONS (1963) *Food Colours*, vol. II, Rome.

FOOD AND AGRICULTURE ORGANIZATION OF THE UNITED NATIONS (1967) *Report to Codex Committee on General Principles of Food Legislation*, Rome.

FOOD AND DRUGS ACT (1955) Her Majesty's Stationery Office, London.

FOOD AND DRUGS ACT AND REGULATIONS (1967) Queen's Printer and Controller of Stationery, Ottawa.

FOOD QUALITY CONTROL ACT B. E. 2507 (1964) Government Gazette of Thailand, Bangkok.

FORSCHBACH, E. (1963) *Fd., Drug, Cosmetic Law J.* **18**, 93–96.

HINTON, C. L. (1906) FAO Food Additive Control Series No. 2, pp. 1–52, Rome.

JEWEL, W. R. (1961) FAO Food Additive Control Series No. 4, pp. 1–30, Rome.

MARTIN, P. (1950) *Fd, Drug, Cosmetic Law J.* **3**, 705–10.

MEIZER, W. (1961) FAO Food Additive Control Series No. 3, Rome.

NATIONAL ACADEMY OF SCIENCES–NATIONAL RESEARCH COUNCIL (1959) Publication 750, pp. 1–19, Washington DC.

NATIONAL ACADEMY OF SCIENCES–NATIONAL RESEARCH COUNCIL (1966) Publication 1406, pp. 1–846, Washington DC.

PUGSLEY, L. I. (1959) FAO Food Additive Control Series No. 1, Rome.
PUGSLEY, L. I. (1967) *Med. Servs. J. Can.* **23**, 387–449.
ROE, R. S. (1956) In *The Impact of the Food and Drug Administration on our Society*, pp. 15–17, H. Welch, and F. Martin-Ibanez, MD Publications Inc., New York.
UHL, E., and HANSON, S. C. (1961) FAO Food Additive Control Series No. 5, Rome.
WORLD HEALTH ORGANIZATION OF THE UNITED NATIONS (1962) World Health Technical Report Series 228, Geneva.
WORLD HEALTH ORGANIZATION OF THE UNITED NATIONS (1964) World Health Technical Report Series 281, Geneva.
WORLD HEALTH ORGANIZATION OF THE UNITED NATIONS (1965) World Health Technical Report Series 309, Geneva.
WORLD HEALTH ORGANIZATION OF THE UNITED NATIONS (1966) World Health Technical Report Series 339, Geneva.
WORLD HEALTH ORGANIZATION OF THE UNITED NATIONS (1967) World Health Technical Report Series 348, Geneva.
WRIGHT, N. C. (1960) In *Pure Food and Pure Food Legislation*, pp. 73–90, A. J. Amos, Butterworths, London.

AUTHOR INDEX

Abramson, J. H.   89, 134, 135
Abs, O.   405, 417
Abt, A. F.   208, 219
Adamovich, B. A.   415, 417, 421
Adams, C. M.   135
Adams, W. S.   174, 215, 389, 417
Adolph, E. F.   237, 311, 391, 409, 417
Advaney, M.   77, 135
Aghemo, P.   421
Agostinucci, D.   29
Ahlborg, B.   383, 417
Aiton, H. F.   312, 420
Al-Azzawee, M.   135
Albanese, A. A.   158, 213
Alejo, L. G.   139, 218
Ali, M.   135
Allen, D. I.   423
Allen, T. H.   311
Allison, J. B.   156, 213, 214
Al-Saidi, S.   135
Anderson, A. A.   218
Anderson, J. T.   423
Angel, C. R.   136
Antufjev, I. I.   417
Apodaca, A.   71, 135
Archdeacon, J. W.   384, 417
Archer, T. C. R.   209, 311
Ariens, E. J.   388, 417
Armstrong, J. G.   241, 311
Arroyave, G.   158, 159, 185, 213–15
Arutuynov, G. A.   385, 417
Ashworth, A.   409, 417
Astrand, P.   227, 311
Autret, M.   213
Aykroyd, W. R.   65, 66, 117, 135
Aylward, F.   65, 86, 91, 135
Azar, G.   417

Bacharach, A. L.   410, 418, 419, 423
Bader, R. A.   419
Baer, A.   313
Bailey, K. V.   79, 121, 122, 135
Baines, A. H. J.   125, 135

Baker, E. M.   189, 208, 216, 219, 235, 311
Balaghi, M.   216
Balakhovsky, I. S.   416, 417
Ball, S.   181, 215
Ballantyne, R. M.   279, 311
Bamba, M. D.   136
Banerjee, S.   146, 212
Barborka, C. J.   384, 417, 419
Barron, G.   136
Barry, A. J.   422
Bass, D. E.   313, 419, 420
Bättig, K.   421
Baumann, C. A.   186, 216
Beaton, G. A.   186, 216
Beaton, G. H.   187, 213–15, 217, 219
Bavly, S.   83, 85, 125, 135
Bazett, H. C.   403, 417
Beam, A. S.   215
Bean, W. B.   200, 218, 219, 420
Beard, L.   339
Bechnell, R. L.   218
Becken-Freyseng, H.   418
Becker, K.   1, 29
Begum, A.   136
Behar, M.   158, 214, 215
Behnke, A. R.   375, 417, 423
Bell, D. M.   420
Beltran, P. G.   217
Bender, A. E.   157, 213
Benites, R.   138
Bennett, E. N.   315
Bergstrom, J.   227, 311, 373, 417
Berkson, J.   212
Bernadotte, J.   136
Bernstein, D. S.   171, 214
Berry, A.   416, 417
Berry, W. T. C.   393, 417
Berryman, G. H.   384, 417, 421
Bertram, G. C. L.   405, 417
Bessey, O. A.   194, 195, 217, 218
Best, W. R.   313
Beveridge, J. B.   417
Bieri, J. C.   216
Bierring, E.   382, 417

Bigwood, E. J.   438, 465
Birkhead, N. C.   422
Black, J. G.   214
Blackmon, J. R.   422
Blake, E.   105, 136
Bliss, J. Q.   399, 423
Blix, G.   422
Blodi, F. G.   217
Bloom, W. L.   292, 311, 397, 417
Boardman, V. R.   432, 465
Bodansky, O.   216
Boek, J. K.   105, 135
Bøje, O.   377, 417
Boothby, N. M.   145, 146, 212
Booyens, J.   147, 212
Borgmann, H. W.   384, 418
Boroughs, E. D.   215
Bothwell, T. H.   175, 177, 215
Bouchard, B. S.   219
Bourne, G. H.   214, 216
Bourns, G. H.   215
Braestrup, P. W.   209, 219
Bransby, E. R.   229, 311
Bransby, G. R.   417
Braude, B.   218
Bravo, Y.   138
Bredell, G. A. G.   422
Brin, M.   188, 216
Brinkman, G. L.   136
Brise, H.   178, 179, 215
Brock, J. F.   158, 213, 214
Brockway, J. M.   147, 212
Bro-Rassmussen, F.   165, 192–4, 197, 198, 213, 217
Brouha, L.   420
Browe, J. H.   301, 311
Brown, E. M., Jr.   214
Brown, J. D.   396, 397, 418
Brown, M. L.   168, 192, 207, 209, 214, 217, 219
Brown, R. R.   166, 213
Brozek, J. M.   216, 312, 420, 423
Bruce, R. A.   422
Bryans, A.   420
Buck, A. C.   313, 422
Bulatao-Jayme, J.   139
Bullen, B.   386, 397, 421
Bunje, H. W.   413, 423
Burch, H. B.   194, 200, 217, 218
Burskirk, E. R.   313, 420, 421, 423

Caasi, P.   190, 216

Caasi, P. I.   193, 217
Callender, S.   215
Calloway, D. H.   295, 301, 303, 305, 311, 415–18
Camcam, G. A.   216, 217
Campbell, J. A.   166, 200, 213, 219
Campbell, J. M. H.   377, 418
Canham, J. E.   312
Cannon, R. O.   215
Carothers, E. L.   215
Carpenter, K. J.   200, 218
Carrasco, E. O.   136
Carroll, R. E.   423
Caspari, W.   423
Castellanos, A.   138
Caster, W. O.   216
Causeret, J.   395, 418
Cawthorpe, J.   420
Cerretelli, P.   374, 418, 421
Chalmers, A. K.   417
Chaloupka, M. M.   219
Chan, G. S.   136
Chang, Y. O.   157, 213
Charconnet-Harding, F.   205, 218
Chassels, J. B.   388, 418
Chávez, A.   107, 115, 138
Chen, J. S.   78, 135
Cheyne, G. A.   215
Chittenden, R. H.   383, 418
Chizhov, S. V.   417
Chopra, S.   135
Chow, B. F.   158, 213
Christensen, E. H.   227, 311, 372, 379, 380, 382, 394, 400, 411, 418
Christophe, J.   383, 418
Ciccolini, R. V.   311
Clark, F.   104, 115, 125, 134, 135
Clark, J.   417
Clark, P.   215
Clark, R. P.   193, 217
Cogswell, R. C., Jr.   417
Coke, L. R.   291, 311
Cole, W. H.   213
Collazos, C. C.   138
Collis, W. R. F.   86, 133, 135
Concepción, I.   136
Conn, E. E.   191, 217
Consolazio, C. F.   221, 229, 232, 235, 237, 241, 268, 284, 292, 293, 295, 311–13, 384, 408, 411, 418, 419, 422, 423
Cooke, J. P.   415, 418
Coons, C. M.   179, 215
Coryell, M. N.   217

Cosgrove, L. de G.   217
Covell, B.   379, 380, 418
Cowan, J. W.   85, 135
Crandon, J. H.   385, 418
Cravioto, J.   214
Crawford, J. H.   312
Cresta, M.   163, 213
Crews, E. L., III   419
Croome, R. R. M.   420
Crowley, L. V.   311, 420
Cruickshank, E. K.   189, 216
Culik, R.   214
Cureton, T. K.   388, 418
Curran, R. E.   429, 465
Cutbertson, D. P.   214
Cutler, J. L.   218
Czaczkes, J. W.   198, 217

Daker, E. M.   214
Dalgliesh, C. E.   218
Dalton, E.   135
D'Angeli, F.   218
Danowski, T. S.   313
Darby, M. B.   219
Darby, W. J.   72, 135, 215, 219
Darling, R. C.   226, 312, 383, 418, 420
Darlington, F. B.   388, 418
Das, M. L.   204, 218
Datta, S. P.   77, 135
Daubney, C. G.   417
Daum, K.   218, 423
Davidson, A. L.   430, 465
Davis, E. B.   217
Davis, M. V.   216
Daws, T. A.   418
De, H. N.   197, 217
Dean, E. E.   219
Decken, H. von der   29
Dee, T. E.   313, 423
Dehove, R. A.   454, 465
DeJong, A. B. E.   418
de Lange, D. J.   200, 204, 218
de León, J. F.   136
Delva, H.   136
Dema, I.   135
Demarchi, M.   85, 135
de Monchaux, C.   421
Denko, C. W.   417
Dennen, P. M.   215
Dennig, H.   392, 418
de Pontanel, H. G.   339
de Schaepdryver, A.   417

Devadas, R. P.   68, 73, 134, 135
Dhakshayani, R.   136
Dieseldorff, A.   138
Dietz, C. G.   218
Dill, D. B.   237, 311, 418
Di Prampero, P. G.   418
Donoso, G.   159, 213
Douglas, C. G.   376, 394, 411, 418
Doupe, J.   417
Down, J. L.   217
Down, M. G.   422
Draper, M. H.   379, 421
Droste, A.   394, 421
Drummond, J. C.   426, 465
Drury, H. F.   407, 418, 419, 423
Dubach, R.   174, 215
Du Bois, D.   146, 212
Du Bois, E. F.   145, 146, 212
Dugal, L. P.   401, 402, 418
Dujacquier, R.   216
Dumm, M. F.   136
Duncan, M.   200, 218
Dunn, A. L.   212
Durnin, J. V. G. A.   146-7, 212, 233, 312, 379, 380, 408, 411, 418, 419
Duval, A. M.   212

Easty, D. L.   400, 419
Easwaran, P. P.   68, 73, 134, 135
Ebbetts, J.   393, 419
Eckert, R. E.   214
Edholm, O.   375, 422
Edholm, O. G.   379, 380, 400, 401, 408, 410, 418, 419, 423
Edman, M.   164, 199, 213, 217
Efremov, V. V.   403, 419
Egana, E.   420
Eichna, L. W.   421
Eigelsreiter, H.   380, 419
Ekelund, L.-G.   417
El Din, N.   379, 418
Elgin   201
Eliot, J. W.   403, 419
Elkinton, J. R.   313
Elvehjem, C. A.   218
Enns, T.   219
Enzer, N.   313
Ershoff, B. H.   199, 217, 403, 419
Escapini, H.   216
Espinas, O. E.   136
Eva, T. C.   217
Evang, K.   423

Evans, E. R.   215, 420
Everhart, W. A.   218

Fahnestock, M. K.   419–21
Faine, S.   121, 135
Falk, K. G.   216
Farmer, C. J.   385, 419
Farnsworth, H. C.   29
Faulkner, J. A.   380, 419
Feen, C. B.   417
Feniak, E.   103, 136
Fernándes López, N. A.   136
Ferrer, I.   422
Ferrer, M. I.   422
Ferro-Luzzi, G.   121, 135
Finch, C. A.   175, 177, 215
Finkelstein, B.   414, 423
Fisher, D. S.   177, 215
Fitzpatrick, W. H.   423
Fleisch, A.   146, 212
Fleischmann, G.   217
Fletcher, J. G.   379, 419
Florentino, R. F.   139, 146, 155, 212
Flores, M.   63, 68, 72, 107, 115, 120, 124, 125, 135
Foltz, E. C.   387, 419
Foltz, E. E.   417
Forbes, W. H.   268, 311, 420
Ford, Z. W.   198, 218
Fordtran, J. S.   376, 377, 419
Forschbach, E.   425, 465
Fougere, W.   136
Fox, R. H.   408, 410, 419, 421
Foy, H.   174, 215, 389, 419
Franklyn, M.   218
Frazier, R. G.   202, 238, 312
French, C. E.   136, 421
Frenchman, R.   215
Friedemann, T. E.   202, 313, 417, 423
Friend, C. J.   186, 215
Fruton, J.   191, 216
Fry, P. C.   72, 121, 136
Fuenning, S. I.   393, 422
Fuge, K. W.   383, 419
Futcher, P. H.   305, 312

Galbraith, J.   311
Gamble, J. L.   236, 293, 297, 303, 312
Garbers, C. F.   182, 215
Garry   379
Gebhardt, E. A.   394, 419

Geldrich, J.   379, 419
Gelineo, S.   401, 419
Gemmill, C. L.   382, 419
Gérard, A.   438, 465
Giaja, I.   401, 419
Gibbens, J.   218
Gill, M. B.   422
Gillman, J.   215
Gilmore, R. C.   422
Glickman, N.   402, 419–21
Goldberger, J.   200, 201, 218
Goldsmith, G.   192, 216, 217
Goldsmith, G. A.   199–202, 218, 219
Goldsmith, R.   400, 401, 408, 419
Goldstein, D. R.   311
Gontzea, D.   226, 312
Goodhart, R. S.   215, 218
Gopalan, C.   204, 213, 218
Gopalan, T. K.   135
Gordon, J. G.   218
Grafe, H.-K.   379, 380, 393, 419
Grande, F.   423
Grandjean, E.   421
Grant, F. W.   65, 105, 118, 136
Gray, E.   400, 419
Graybiel, A.   420
Greaves, J. P.   134, 136
Greenberg, S. M.   419
Greene, A. H. M.   253, 281, 312
Gronowska-Senger, A.   186, 215
Groom, D.   65, 105, 118, 136
Gross, F.   215
Grossman, M. I.   313
Grotheer, M. P.   423
Grover, R. F.   411, 419
Grundy, W. E.   417
Guggenheim, K.   198, 217
Guha, B. C.   218
Guri, C. D.   214
Guyton, A. C.   169, 206, 214, 219

Haffron, D.   218
Hahn, P. F.   179, 215
Hahn, W.   29
Hais, I. M.   420
Haisman, M. F.   312, 408, 419
Haldane, J. S.   418
Hallberg   178, 179, 215
Halley, H.   98, 136
Hamilton, T. S.   389, 421
Hamley, E. J.   395, 419
Handler, P.   214, 219

Hanekopf, G.   419, 420, 423
Hanks, J. R.   65, 136
Hannan, R. S.   165, 213
Hannon, J. P.   404, 407, 418, 419, 423
Hansen, J. D. L.   155, 213, 214
Hansen, O.   227, 311, 382, 418
Hanson, S. C.   455, 466
Harding, R. S.   312
Harper, A. E.   164, 165, 213
Harries, J. M.   421
Harris, C. L.   214
Harris, C. W.   311
Harris, H. A.   392, 419
Harris, P. L.   420
Harris, S. C.   417
Harrison, H. C.   168, 214
Harrison, H. E.   168, 214
Harrower, A. D. B.   409, 417
Hartiala, K.   423
Harvey, C. C.   218
Hatch, F. T.   313
Hatch, T. F.   421
Hauck, H. M.   65, 136
Hawkins, W. W.   179, 215
Hawthorne, B. E.   216
Heard, C. R. C.   215
Heath, C. W.   174, 215
Hebbelinck, M.   396, 417, 419
Hedman, R.   374, 419
Hegsted, D. M.   156, 157, 168, 213, 214
Heidelbaugh, N. D.   415–19, 423
Heinomen, A. O.   379, 400, 420
Hellebrandt, F. A.   377, 393, 420
Henderson, C. R.   417, 420
Henderson, L. M.   205, 218
Henderson, Y.   418
Henry   165
Henschel, A.   229, 313, 386, 420
Henschel, A. F.   216
Herbert, J. W.   186, 215
Hercus, C. E.   121, 135
Hermansen, L.   311, 373, 374, 422
Hermansen, L. E.   227, 312
Hervey, G. R.   293, 305, 312, 399, 410, 420
Hickman, K.   420
High, E. G.   182, 215
Hilker, D. M.   191, 216
Hinton, C. L.   428, 455, 465
Högberg, P.   379, 380, 400, 418
Holdsworth, L. D.   422
Hollingsworth, D. F.   69, 99, 125, 134–6
Holloszy, J. O.   419
Holman, R. L.   157, 213

Holt, L. E., Jr.   160, 164, 203, 213, 217, 218
Horvath, S. M.   422
Horvath, S. N.   421
Horwitt, M. K.   189, 192, 195, 197, 200–2, 217, 218
Houry, G.   135
Hove, E. L.   412, 420
Huang, C. S.   78, 135
Hudson, M. F.   312
Huenemann, R. L.   138
Huff, J. W.   200, 218
Huff, T. W.   200, 218
Hughes, D. E.   204, 218
Hulse, J. H.   238, 306, 311, 312
Hultman, E.   311, 312, 373, 374, 376, 382, 396, 417, 420
Hume, E. M.   183, 215
Hunter, J. W.   311
Hursh, L. M.   418
Hussain, R.   178, 215
Hutley, M. H.   219
Hytten, F. E.   175, 215

Iampietro, P. F.   400, 420, 423
Iliff, A.   212
Insull, W.   147, 212
Insull, W., Jr.   313
Intengan, C. Ll.   139
Isa   135
Isaac, G. J.   312, 418
Issekutz, B.   375, 421
Issekutz, B., Jr.   375, 420, 422
Ivy, A. C.   417, 419

Jackson, R. L.   215
Jacobson, E. D.   423
Jakovlev, H.   225, 312
Jakovlev, N. N.   372, 380, 385, 387, 390, 392, 393, 395, 396, 420
Jamison, J. M.   311
Janoski, A. H.   412, 423
Jekat, F.   164, 213
Jewel, W. R.   455, 465
Jirka, Z.   388, 421
Joffe, N. T.   101, 136
Johns, G. A.   217
Johnson, B.   103, 136
Johnson, H. C.   417
Johnson, H. L.   312, 418
Johnson, O. C.   148, 212

Johnson, R. E.   217, 222, 223, 230–2, 237, 238, 246, 291, 293, 296, 297, 302, 303, 312, 313, 385, 386, 397, 401, 405, 406, 408, 418, 420–2
Johnston, F. A.   174, 175, 215, 389, 420
Jones, G. T.   79, 136
Jones, M. E.   199, 218
Jong   398
José, F. R.   136
Joubert, C. P.   200, 204, 218
Jyothi, K. K.   77, 136

Kalinsky, H.   216
Karger, S.   214
Kark, R. M.   222, 230–2, 246, 248, 265–7, 278, 279, 297, 300, 303, 312, 398, 401, 404, 409, 419, 420
Karpovich, P. V.   229, 312
Karrer   205
Karvinen, E.   395, 422
Karvonen, M. J.   371, 378, 389, 412, 420
Karvonen, M. K.   422
Katasura, E.   187, 216
Katayama, M. C.   165, 213
Kaumvakali, T.   98, 136
Kaunitz, A.   195, 217
Keeton, R. W.   402, 419, 420, 421
Kennedy, H. F.   420
Kennedy, T. F.   379, 420
Keys, A.   145, 149, 189, 212, 216, 229, 264, 296, 312, 387, 396, 399, 403, 420
Khamis, S. H.   30
King, C. G.   205, 207, 209, 218, 219
King, E. J.   421
King, E. Q.   383, 420
King, K.   136
Kjellberg, S. R.   389, 420
Kleeman, C. R.   313
Kleevens, J. W. L.   133, 136
Kleiber, M.   147, 212
Klicka, M. V.   419
Klontz, C. E.   136
Klopper, A. I.   215
Klopping, J. C.   422
Klotschkow, L. A.   379, 420
Klumpp, T. G.   420
Koch, A. C. E.   376, 394, 418
Kodicek, E.   199, 200, 204, 218
Koehn, C. J.   420, 423
Kofrányi, E.   164, 213
Kolkka, S.   394, 420
Kon, S. K.   165, 218

Kondi, A.   174, 215, 389, 419
Konishi, F.   311
Kopecka, J.   420
Koshi, R. E.   218
Koutecký, Z.   421
Král, J.   391, 420
Král, J. A.   389, 420
Krebs, H. A.   183, 215
Krehl, W. A.   199, 204, 218
Kreider, M. B.   421
Kreisler, O.   217
Krisch, K.   219
Krogh, A.   145, 212, 382, 421
Krzywicki, H. J.   312, 418, 420
Kung, H. C.   218
Kunnas, M.   389, 420
Kutty, V. J.   135
Kuznetsov, M. I.   417

Ladell, W. S. S.   237, 312, 392, 421
Lalanne, G. G.   420
Lambert, E. H.   420, 421
Lange Andersen, K.   423
Larson, A. M.   419, 423
Last, J. H.   420
Latiri, S.   422
Layrisse, M.   215
Lea, C. H.   165, 213
Leblond, C. P.   418
Lehmann, G.   391, 421
Leitch, I.   168, 214
Leonhauser, S.   219
Leslie, A.   215, 417
Levin, M. H.   215, 417
Levy, L. M.   313, 423
Lewis, D. H.   421
Lewis, H. E.   398, 404, 405, 410, 421
Lewis, J. M.   182, 216
Lewis, J. S.   312, 420
Lewis, R. C.   146, 212
Liebert, E.   217
Liljestrand, G.   379, 421
Lind   205
Lindhard, J.   382, 421
Lockhart, E. E.   405, 421
Loewy, A.   423
Lohmann, K.   187, 216
Lojkin, M. E.   201, 203, 204, 218, 219
Lombardo, E.   213
Longenecker, J. B.   155, 213
Louhi, H. A.   188, 216
Love, O. H.   217

Lowry, O. 218
Lowry, O. H. 217
Luna, Z. G. 216
Lund, C. C. 418
Luyken, R. 159, 213
Luyken-Koning, F. W. M. 159, 213

MacBeth, R. J. 420
McCaleb, L. B. 420
McCance, R. A. 174, 215, 293, 305, 312, 399, 410, 419, 420, 423
McCance, R. D. 147, 212
McClellan, G. S. 215
McCreary, J. F. 246, 248, 265–7, 278, 312
McDaniel, E. G. 216
McGuire, C. J. 216
McHenry, E. W. 187, 213–17, 219
MacKay, J. H. 417
McKinley, P. 135
McKinzie, P. S. L. 311, 418
McLaren, D. S. 216
Macleod, A. 423
McMillan, F. J. 215
McMillan, T. J. 420
Macy, I. C. 217
Magee, H. E. 311
Magee, H. G. 417
Mager, M. 423
Mahoney, E. B. 213
Malhotra, M. S. 379, 421
Mancilla, A. 420
Mann, G. M. 252, 263, 313, 398, 422
Mann, J. B. 423
Marcinek, J. G. 423
Margaria, R. 378, 386, 421
Martin, M. 215
Martin, P. 433, 434, 465
Martin, R. H. 422
Marzan, A. M. 217
Masek, J. 182, 216
Mason, H. L. 188, 216, 217, 423
Masoro, E. J. 422
Massry, J. B. 423
Masterson, J. E. 311
Masterton, J. P. 400, 404, 405, 418, 421
Mathews, J. 186, 213, 216
Matoush, L. O. 312, 418
Matoush, L. R. O. 418
Matter, M., Jr. 422
Mayer, J. 383, 386, 397, 418, 421
Mayfield, H. L. 186, 216
Mazzarella, J. A. 422

Medairy, G. C. 217
Meizer, W. 455, 465
Melinick, D. 188, 189, 216
Mellbin, T. 98, 136
Mendez, J. 215
Meythaler, F. 394, 421
Michell, H. S. 101, 136
Mickelsen, O. 204, 218, 313, 420
Mickelson, O. 188, 216
Milan, F. A. 400, 421
Milledge, J. S. 422
Miller, C. 98, 136
Miller, D. S. 157, 159, 213
Miller, O. N. 218
Milligan, E. H. 311
Millman, N. 229, 312
Mills, C. F. 214, 313
Mills, C. G. 166, 213
Milne, H. 104, 137
Milner, M. 213
Mitchell, G. O. 418
Mitchell, H. H. 157, 164, 199, 213, 217, 389, 402, 419–21
Mitchell, H. S. 136
Mitchell, K. G. 218
Mohanty, M. 135
Monahan, E. P. 420
Moore, C. V. 173, 215
Moore, T. 181, 216
Morgan, A. F. 186, 215
Morley, N. H. 200, 218
Morrison, J. F. 422
Morse, E. H. 217
Morton, H. V. 398, 421
Morton, R. A. 181, 215
Moscoso, I. I. 138
Mueller, J. F. 219
Muller, F. 423
Munro, H. N. 165, 167, 214
Munro, J. N. 165, 214
Murlin, J. R. 384, 417
Murray, J. 105, 136

Naegeli, W. 394, 395, 421
Naiken, L. 1
Naismith, D. J. 159, 165, 213, 214
Najjar, V. A. 192, 198, 217
Namyslowski, L. 147, 212, 392
Neal, R. A. 189, 216
Needman, B. M. 417
Neff, R. 213
Nefyodov, Y. G. 417

Nelson, N. A. 408, 421
Nelson, R. A. 312, 418
Newberger, A. 218
Niccum, W. L. 177, 215
Nichol, C. A. 214
Nickelson, J. T. 214
Nicolas, G. 136
Nilsson, C.-G. 417
Nordin, B. E. C. 171, 214
Novosadova, J. 388, 421
Nunes, W. T. 217

O'Connor, M. 421
O'Hara, M. J. 419, 423
Oke, O. L. 178, 215
Olcott, H. S. 136
Oldham, H. G. 188, 196, 216, 217
Oliveros, S. B. 136
Olmedo, R. 137
Olsson, K.-G. 389, 395, 421
Omololu, A. 135
Oomen, H. A. P. C. 180, 186, 216
Orr, N. W. M. 401, 421
Orto, L. A. 213
Oshima, H. T. 76, 133, 136
Ostashener, A. S. 216
Øyen, O. 399, 421

Pace, N. 312
Palma, E. M. 136
Pardini, R. S. 216
Pargaonkar, V. U. 194, 197, 217
Parin, V. V. 415, 421
Pařízková, J. 375, 421
Parkinson, S. 73, 121, 136
Parrott, E. M. 420
Pascual, C. R. 139
Pascual, S. B. 136
Passmore, R. 146–9, 212, 214, 313, 374, 379, 380, 418, 419, 421
Pate, L. W. Sgt. 294, 313
Patek, A. J., Jr. 174, 215
Pattengale, P. K. 419
Patwardhan, V. N. 154, 178, 212, 215
Paul, P. 375, 420, 421
Payne, P. R. 157, 213
Pearson, W. N. 188, 189, 199, 216, 219
Pease, E. D. 312, 420
Pecora, L. J. 311
Peden, J. C., Jr. 174, 215
Peisach, M. 215

Pellervo-Seura 392, 421
Pelletier, O. 200, 219
Percival, L. 388, 421
Périssé, J. 86, 136, 213
Perlzweig, W. A. 200, 218
Peter, J. 422
Peter, O. F. 191, 216
Peters, D. W. A. 312
Peters, J. P. 313
Peterson, J. C. 215
Pettenkofer, M. 373, 421
Piiper, J. 418
Pike, R. L. 168, 192, 207, 209, 214, 217, 219
Pirzio-Biroli, G. 177, 215
Pitts, G. C. 226, 237, 312, 313, 408, 418, 421
Platt, B. S. 159, 214, 215, 408, 410, 421
Plough, I. C. 118, 136, 214, 311
Pohndorf, R. H. 388, 418
Poikolainen, E. 423
Pollack, H. 311, 380, 421
Pollard, M. 135
Ponomarev, L. E. 401, 422
Porter, T. 217
Powell, A. T. W. 418
Powell, R. C. 159, 214, 217
Price, D. C. 177, 215
Price, J. M. 213
Price, R. 423
Prokop, L. 385, 386, 388, 420, 422
Pugh, L. G. C. 375, 412, 422
Pugh, L. G. C. E. 411, 422
Pugsley, L. I. 425, 429, 455, 466
Pulsifer, D. H. 396, 397, 418
Pushkina, N. N. 403, 422

Quin, P. J. 92, 136
Quinn, M. 293, 313
Quiogue, E. 124, 125, 136
Quiogue, E. S. 78, 80, 133, 136

Ramaswamy, S. S. 421
Ramos, V. 136
Rao, B. R. H. 69, 136
Rao, K. V. 70, 136
Rao, M. V. R. 125, 136
Rao, N. A. M. 253, 259, 260, 313
Rao, N. R. 135
Rao, P. S. S. 136
Ray, S. N. 421

Register, U. D. 218
Reh, E. 31
Reichstein 205
Reid, B. L. 136
Reid, D. D. 146, 212
Reinecke, R. M. 422
Rendenbach, R. 418
Rennie, D. W. 400, 422
Reynolds, M. S. 213, 219
Richardson, L. M. 420
Rinner, F. 420
Rittenberg, D. 156, 214
Roberts, L. J. 136, 216
Roberts, N. R. 214
Robertson, E. C. 103, 136
Robertson, J. D. 146, 212
Robinson, P. 420
Robinson, P. E. 312
Robinson, P. F. 418
Rodahl, K. 199, 214, 217, 400–4, 421, 422
Roderuck, C. 196, 217
Rodes, H. 423
Roe, R. S. 432, 466
Roehm, R. A. 186, 216
Roels, D. A. 185, 216
Roels, O. A. 181, 216
Rogers, T. A. 293, 313, 406, 407, 422
Rogers, T. S. 311
Rogers, W. E., Jr. 186, 216
Rohdenburg, E. L. 214
Rönnholm, N. 395, 422
Rose, K. D. 393, 422
Rosen, F. 166, 214
Rosenberg, H. R. 164, 214
Rosenmund, H. 421
Rosenthal, H. L. 218
Roth, J. L. D. 399, 422
Rothwell, W. S. 218
Rovelli, E. 421
Rowell, L. B. 374–6, 422
Roy, J. K. 197, 217
Rudhe, V. 420
Ruosteenoja, R. 420
Ryer, R. III. 230, 313

Sadowsky, N. 214
Sai, F. T. 91, 136
Said, E. E. 30
Salcedo, J., Jr. 79, 136
Saltin, B. 237, 311, 312, 373, 374, 376, 377, 389, 395, 419, 421, 422
Salvosa, C. B. 136
Samuels, L. T. 397, 422
Sánchéz, M. 137
Santiago, L. C. 136
Sarett, H. P. 199, 200, 205, 218, 219
Sargent, D. W. 146, 212
Sargent, F. II. 222, 238, 291, 293, 296, 297, 302, 303, 313, 399, 405, 406, 408, 420, 422
Sargent, R. E. 422
Sarma, M. L. 313
Sarma, P. S. 218
Sassi, G. 421
Sauberlich, H. E. 187, 216, 217, 219
Sauberlich, H. F. 216
Schaefer, A. E. 193, 217
Schaefer, N. S. 423
Schendel, H. E. 158, 214
Schjøth, A. G. 388, 422
Schneider, E. C. 418
Schostak, G. 418
Schröcksnadel, H. 380, 419
Schuching, S. V. 219
Schulman, Irving 177, 215
Schulte, W. 1, 29
Schulz, J. 177, 179, 215
Schuster, P. 187, 216
Scott, J. C. 417
Scrimshaw, N. S. 158, 199, 214, 215, 218
Sebrell, W. H. 118, 136
Seeley, R. D. 213
Seliger, V. 378–80, 422
Sen, R. N. 146, 212, 422
Setliff, J. A. 313, 407, 422
Severinghaus, E. L. 136
Shank, R. E. 419
Shapiro, R. 311, 408, 418, 422
Sharman, I. M. 388, 418, 422, 423
Sheehan, E. J. 311
Shelley, W. B. 421
Sheppard, C. W. 215
Shibunejev, A. G. 417
Shift, B. B. 217
Shimazono, N. 187, 216
Sievers, J. 385, 422
Simmonds, S. 191, 216
Simonson, E. 229, 313
Sinclair, H. M. 72, 102, 137
Sjöstrand, T. 420
Skinner, H. G. 252, 263, 313, 398, 422
Slanetz, C. A. 217
Slanta, M. 404, 422
Slome, C. 135
Smit, C. P. G. J. 29
Smith, B. F. 217, 423

Smith, E. L. 214, 219
Smith, G. 398, 422
Smith, N. J. 177, 179, 215
Smith, S. C. 136
Smithies, W. R. 311
Smuts 160
Snyderman 164
Sokolova, G. M. 401, 422
Spector, H. 295, 303, 311, 396, 423
Spencer, M. J. 422
Spicer, E. H. 135
Spinella, J. R. 417
Sprinson, D. B. 156, 214
Srikantia, S. E. 194, 197, 217
Srikantia, S. G. 204, 213, 218
Stacey, N. E. 311
Staňková, L. 421
Stars, F. J. 214
Staton, W. M. 386, 422
Staudinger, H. 207, 219
Stearns, G. 215
Stefansson, V. 402, 422
Steffen, W. F. 311
Stenström, N. 379, 421
Stephen, J. M. L. 214
Stevenson, J. A. F. 222, 236, 296, 304–6, 313
Stewart, J. J. C. 215
Stolpe, S. G. 422
Stompfel, S. J. 219
Storvick, C. A. 216, 218
Strong, F. M. 199, 218
Strydom, N. B. 391, 408, 409, 422
Stumpf, P. M. 191, 217
Sunderman, F. W. 417
Sure, B. 198, 218
Swain, H. L. 401, 423
Swaminathan, M. C. 136
Swendseid, M. E. 156, 214
Swick, R. W. 186, 216
Swindells, Y. E. 374, 421
Synderman, S. E. 213
Szakäll, A. 391, 421
Szent-Györgyi 205

Tai, M. 216
Taylor, A. A. 414, 423
Taylor, C. E. 218
Taylor, D. W. 413, 423
Taylor, H. L. 235, 293, 313, 396, 420, 423
Teply, L. S. 218
Tepper, R. H. 377, 393, 420

Therien, M. 402, 418
Thomas, H. M. 90, 137
Thomas, P. 388, 423
Thomason, M. J. 65, 137
Thompson, R. H. S. 421
Thompson, S. T. 214
Tiira, E. 295, 313
Tilden, N. W. 218
Tobar, R. 137
Toor, M. E. 391, 423
Torres, J. B. 311, 418
Toth, F. 420
Toth, R. M. 423
Townsend, H. S. 417
Trenholme, M. 104, 137
Trout, M. 216
Tulane 201
Turner, J. B. 204, 218
Turner, M. D. 215
Turpeinen, O. 378, 411, 420
Tuttle, S. G. 214
Tuttle, W. W. 423

Udalov, Y. F. 417
Uhl, E. 455, 466
Unglaub, W. G. 218
Ushakov, A. S. 417

Valante, D. 423
Valenzuela, J. S. 219
Valenzuela, R. C. 136
Vanderveen, J. E. 416, 419, 423
van Graan, C. H. 422
Vanotti, A. 389, 423
Vanzetti, G. 389, 423
Vargas, C. 137
Vaughan, D. A. 418, 419, 423
Vaughan, J. A. 423
Vaughan, L. N. 419, 423
Venkatachalam, P. S. 136
Venkataraman, A. 135
Vijayaraghavan, P. K. 259, 260, 313
Villavieja, G. M. 136
Vilter, R. W. 199, 200, 219
Viteri, F. 155, 214
Vivian, V. M. 200, 213, 219
Vogelius, H. 146, 212
Voit, C. 373, 421
von Keiderling, W. 423
von Rahden, M. J. 422
Vorobjev, A. J. 417

Vuori, J. M.   389, 423
Vytchikova, M. A.   387, 423

Wadsworth, G. R.   177, 215
Wald, G.   181, 216
Walker, A. R. P.   68, 138, 214
Walker, R. B.   215
Walker, R. P.   170
Wallace, W. T.   219
Ward, M. P.   422
Ward, N. T.   135
Ward, P. G.   421
Waring, P. P.   217
Wassiljewa, E. S.   379, 420
Waterlow, J. C.   155, 158, 214, 312, 413, 423
Waugh   205
Wayne, W. S.   372, 423
Wayner, M. J.   417
Wehrle, P. F.   423
Welch, B. E.   232, 313, 400, 401, 404, 408, 423
Welham, W. C.   375, 417, 423
Wertheimer, S.   423
Wertz, A. E.   218
Wertz, A. W.   200–4, 219
West, J. B.   422
Whedon, G. D.   171, 214
Wheeler, G. A.   200, 218
Wheeler, N. C.   417
Whipple, G.   213
White, A.   209, 219
White, A. P.   214
White, H. S.   109, 138, 173, 215
White, P. L.   138, 173, 215
Whiteman, J.   121, 122, 135
Whitten, B. K.   412, 423
Whittingham, D. G. V.   399, 423
Whittingham, P.   423
Wickett, J. C.   399, 423
Widdowson, E. M.   174, 215, 379, 380, 419, 421, 423
Wiegsinger, H.   217

Wilbraham, A.   426, 465
Wilder, R. M.   217, 423
Williams, C. G.   422
Williams, H. H.   217
Williams, J. H.   377, 423
Williams, R. A.   187
Williams, R. D.   187, 188, 216, 217, 387, 423
Williams, R. R.   216, 217
Wilson, D.   215
Wilson, E. M. R.   214
Wilson, M.   384, 423
Wilson, P. W.   204, 218
Windmueller, H. G.   193, 218
Winkler, A. W.   293, 313
Witt, N. F.   312
Wittman, P.   217
Wohl, M. G.   215, 218
Wolf, G.   186, 215
Wolkskill, S. J.   219
Wolstenholme, G. E. W.   421
Wood, M. E.   384, 417
Woodruff, C. W.   205, 219
Worcester, J.   157, 213
Wright, N. C.   431, 466
Wyndham, C. H.   422

Yamada, T.   389, 423
Yoshimura, H.   158, 166, 214, 383, 389, 423
Youmans, J. B.   417
Young, D. R.   376, 396, 423
Yousif, M.   88, 138
Yu, H. H.   216

Zarkovich, S. S.   30
Zavattaro, D. N.   213
Ženisek, A.   420
Ziporin, Z. Z.   189, 217
Zubiran, S.   107, 115, 138
Zuntz, N.   411, 423
Zurick, L.   312

SUBJECT INDEX

Additives, food control 449–55
Adolescents 106
  caloric requirement 153
  iron requirement 177
Adulteration of foodstuffs 428
Afghanistan 82
Africa
  calorie intake 92–3
  climate 87
  cooking 92
  cultivators 88
  diet 96
  diet modification 89
  east 89
  food patterns 73, 86–96
  livestock 88
  nutrient intake 92–3
  pastoralists 88
  racial types 88–9
  soutn 95, 134
  southern 91
  west 90
Agricultural Commodity Projections 1970–1980 3
Alaska 102
Albumin/globulin ratio 158
Alcohol 430–1
  hospitals 351–2
  in sports 395–6
  old people 343
  role of 55
Altitudes 410–13
America
  central 72, 106–9
  diets 117
  food patterns 102–17
  Middle 106
  North 102
  South 109, 111
Amino acids 155, 156, 163–6, 204
  in sports 383
Anemia 86, 93, 109, 166, 173, 207, 342

Arab countries 81
Arabian peninsula 84
Arctic Ground Willow 103
Arepa 111
Argentina 109–14
Ascorbic acid 198, 205–11, 350, 384–6, 402, 403
  food sources 205
  roles 206–7
Ascorbic acid requirements 207–11
  estimation 207–8
  recommended dietary allowances 209–11
Atmospheric pressure 413, 414
Australia, calorie requirements 154
  diets 122
  food patterns 120–1
Austria 99
Aviation 413

Baltic countries 97
Bamboo shoots 78
Basal metabolic rate 146
  children 160
Basal metabolism 145–6, 149
Beans 107
Beef 110
Beri-beri 79, 187, 189, 260
Beverages 51, 92, 336
Biological value 157
Blood flow 376, 377
Blood pyruvic acid 188
Body protein, synthesis of 156
Bolivia
  calorie and nutrient intake levels 125
  diets 116
  food consumption by food groups 124
  food patterns 109–12, 114
Bouake Ivory Coast 89
Brazil 109–12, 116, 117
Bread 98
Bulgaria 96, 97

479

Calcium 79, 167–73, 342
  absorption from intestine 168
  dietary allowances 171
  food sources 167
  plasma 169
Calcium deficiency 170
Calcium requirements 169–73
  estimation 169–71
  recommendations 171–3
  standards 171
Calcium roles 168
Calorie content 14, 32, 34
Calorie deficiency 108, 112, 123
Calorie intake 58, 79, 92–3, 112, 150
  hospitals 349
  in food groups 133
  military rations 224
  old people 341
Calorie requirements 47, 56, 58, 145–55
  adolescents 153
  age variation 151
  Australia 154
  average daily 14
  Canada 154
  children 152
  India 154
  Japan 154
  military rations 232
  Philippines 154
  standards 150
  total 149–55
  United Kingdom 154
Calorie sources 16
Calorie value, calculation 12
Canada
  calorie requirements 154
  food control 445–9, 460, 462, 463
  food patterns 102, 103
  nutritional requirements 143
Canteens 316, 317
  adjustment to meet changing circumstances 326
  ancillary services 325
  as educational factor 331–2
  cafeteria service 327, 331–2, 337
  development of centralized production 331
  facilities provided 323–9
  finance and control 319–23
  garbage disposal 329
  hygiene 329
  kitchen 327, 328, 329
  layout and planning 325

  management approach 324
  new equipment 328
  off-peak services 337
  planning and equipping 323
  self-help service 326
  services required 325
  staffing and training 329–31
  worker approach towards 335–8
Carbohydrate diet 380
  in sports 381–2, 394
Carbohydrate intake, old people 342
Carbohydrate requirements, military rations 227
Carbohydrates 123, 165, 198, 268, 293, 297–9, 301, 303, 305, 356, 373–4, 406, 409, 410, 411, 414
CARE 12
Caribbean Islands
  diets 119
  food patterns 74, 117–19
Carotene 166, 184–6
Caspian Sea 83
Cassava 90, 91
Catering. *See* Industrial catering
Cazuela 112
Central America. *See* America
Cereals 15, 49, 89, 90, 93, 97, 104, 109, 112, 133, 199
Ceylon 78
Chaga tribe 88
Children
  basal metabolic rate 160
  caloric requirement 152
  iron requirement 176–7
  nicotinamide requirement 203
  protein requirement 162
Chile
  calorie and nutrient intake levels 125
  diets 116
  food consumption by groups 124
  food patterns 109–12
China 76, 77
Classification of foods and food products 49–51, 60, 68
Cocarboxylase 187
Codex Alimentarius Commission 434–8, 452, 455, 462
Coenzymes 187
Cold climates
  electrolytes 403–4
  energy requirements 400–1
  expeditions 399–407
  military rations 401

Cold climates (*cont.*)
  nutrient requirements 401
  survival rations 406–7
  vitamin requirements 402
  water requirements 403–4
Colombia
  calorie and nutrient intake levels 125
  diets 116
  food consumption by food groups 124
  food patterns 109, 111–14
Commodity coverage of food balance sheets 6–7
Communications effects on food patterns 75
Congo 86, 89, 92
Contamination, protection against 456
Convenience foods 327–8, 443
Cook Islands 121
Cost of living indices 43
Costa Rica 107, 108
Costs in food consumption surveys 49
Cotton 82
Creatinine excretion 159
Cultural aspects in food patterns 93–4
Cultural factors
  in food consumption surveys 46
  in food selection 65–7
Curries 78
Czechoslovakia 316, 321, 324, 330, 333, 335

Dairy products. *See* Milk and milk products
Deep-freezing 369
Dehydration 305
Denmark
  diets 101
  food patterns 97
Deserts 88
Developing countries 33
Developing market economies 14
Dietary levels, world 123–35
Dietist, hospital 367–8
Diets
  Africa 96
  America 117
  Australia 122
  Bolivia 116
  Brazil 116
  carbohydrate 380–2, 394
  carbohydrate restricted 354
  Caribbean Islands 119
  Chile 116
  Colombia 116

Denmark 101
drip feeding 359
Ecuador 116
Ethiopia 95
Europe 102
expeditions 396
Far East 79
formulation of 150
Guatemala 115
high protein 357
hospital 349, 353–9, 364
India 134
Iran 85
Iraq 85
Israel 85
Italy 101
Lebanon 85
Libya 95
liquid 357
low calorie 353
low fat 354
low nitrogen 353
low protein 353
Mexico 115
Near East 86
New Guinea 122
Nigeria 95
Norway 101
nutrient intake 133
nutritive value 126
oceanic islands 123
old people 344
Pakistan 80
Panama 115
Philippines 80
restrictive 353
roughage-free 357
Rumania 101
sodium restricted 354
South Africa 95, 134
South America 111
Spain 101
special. *See* Aviation; Expeditions; Hospitals; Military rations; Old people; Space travel; Sports, etc.
special texture 357
supplemented 357
Taiwan 80
Thailand 80
United Kingdom 134
United States 115, 134
Disabled persons, organization of meals 346

Diseases 79, 93. *See also under specific diseases*
Dominican Republic 117
Doping agents 383, 396
Drinks
  hospitals 351
  old people 343
  See also Alcohol; Water requirements
Drip feeding 359

Economic classes and regions, classification of countries by 14
Economic factors in food selection 67–70
Economic status in food consumption surveys 44–5
Ecuador 109–12, 114, 116
Education in nutrition 331
Eggs 16, 92, 133
Egypt 86, 91
Electrolytes
  in cold climates 403–4
  in hot climates 409
  in sports 389–92
El Salvador 107
Energy cost of activities 146–9
Energy expenditure 145, 381
  climbing expeditions 412
  hot climates 408
  hot environments 233
  sports 378–80, 392
Energy requirements 56
  military rations 226
  population groups 400–1
  pregnancy 152
Energy source 16
Energy stores 373, 375
England 97
  calorie and nutrient intake levels 125
  food consumption by food groups 124
Enzymes 166
Erythropoeisis rate 179
Eskimos 72–3, 102
Ethiopia
  calorie and nutrient intake levels 125
  diets 95
  food consumption by food groups 124
  food patterns 86, 89–92
Europe
  climate 96
  diets 102
  eastern 97, 98, 316, 324
  food patterns 96–102
  northern 98, 99
  southern 98
  topography 96
  western 98, 316, 321, 326
Expeditions 373
  cold climates 399–407
  diets 396
  hot climates 407–9
  Mount Everest 412
  mountaineering 410
  survival rations 406–7
  temperate climates 397–9
  tropical climates 409
Exports 9
Extraction rate 11

Family food consumption surveys 35
Far East
  diets 79
  food patterns 76–9
Fasting 291, 305
Fat content 12, 14
Fat intake, old people 341
Fats 15, 17, 51, 86, 103, 165, 185, 198, 226, 341, 375
  in sports 381–2
  source of 17
Federal Food, Drug, and Cosmetic Act 432, 438, 446, 447, 453
Feed 9
Finland 97, 98
Fish 16, 90, 91, 93, 98, 110, 133, 191
Fishing 76, 97, 111
Flavine mononucleotide 191
Flavineadenine dinucleotide 191
Flavo-proteins 195
Food, legal definition 437–9
Food accounting technique 36, 37
Food Additive Amendment 453
Food and Agriculture Organization 434, 437, 450–2
  food balance sheets 2, 6–7, 18
  Reference Man and Woman 150, 153
Food and Drugs Act 438
Food balance sheet 32, 33
  accuracy 5–6
  commodity coverage 6–7
  concepts used 6–7
  definitions used 6–7
  FAO 2, 6–7, 18
  forms of 18–20
  history and development 1–4

Food balance sheet (*cont.*)
  supply and utilization elements 7–12
  what they are and how they can serve 4–5
Food Chemical Codex 452, 453
Food classification 49–51, 60, 68
Food composition factors 12
Food composition tables 52–3
Food consumption by food groups 123
Food Consumption Levels in the United States, Canada and the United Kingdom 2
Food consumption surveys 5, 31–62
  additional tabulations and useful information 61–2
  adjustments for food obtained and eaten away from home and food eaten by visitors in the home 57–8
  classification of foods 49–51, 60, 68
  comparisons of intake with requirements 58
  cost or money value of foods 49
  cultural factors 46
  economic status 44–5
  environmental conditions 46–7
  equipment 43
  family 35
  farm-nonfarm and urbanization status 45–6
  food sources 47–8
  food wastage 48
  household characteristics 34, 43–5, 60–2
  information needed 34
  interview technique 37
  methods 36
  pilot surveys 42
  population characteristics 46–7
  population groups 59
  population unit 35–9
  random sampling 41
  religion in 46
  reporting period 41–2
  sampling methods 39
  scope of data collected 43
  statistics to be shown 59–60
  tabulation of results 58–62
  time coverage 40–1
  training of investigators 42
  types 35–9
  what they are and how they can serve 32–3
Food control 425–66
  additives 449–55

growing and production areas 456
historical development 427–37
hygiene 455–61
inspection 461–4
legislation 437–44, 462
  general principles 439–43
  trends 443–4
plant facilities and operating requirements 456–61
raw material requirements 456
standards 428–30, 433–7, 444–55
types 447
Food description 53
Food (gross) 11
Food groups
  calorie intake 133
  food consumption 123
  protein intake 130, 133
Food losses 56–7
  military messes 240
Food (net) 11
Food patterns
  Africa 86–96
  America 102–17
  Australia 120–1
  Caribbean Islands 117–19
  communications effects 75
  cultural aspects 93–4
  differences in 65
  Europe 96–102
  Far East 76–9
  industrialization effects 74
  Near East 79–86
  New Zealand 121
  oceania 120–3
  religion in 91, 93
  role of agricultural extension in improvement 73
  social events effect 75
  static and dynamic aspects 70–5
  world 75–123
Food selection
  cultural factors 65–7
  economic factors 67–70
  factors involved 64–70
  geographical location factor 64–5
  religion in 67
Food science and technology, advances in 75
Food sources in food consumption surveys 47–8
Food supplies, global levels and trends 12–17

Food wastage 5, 10–11, 48
France 96, 97, 321, 325, 330, 438, 454
Freeze-dried foods 369
Fruits 16, 82, 83, 97, 98, 104, 110, 111, 206

Gastrointestinal disturbances 179
Geographical location factor in food selection 64–5
Germany 96, 97, 99, 322, 325, 334, 335, 439, 454
Ghana 86, 88
Glucose 373, 374, 376, 377, 394–5
Glycine 383
Glycogen 373, 374, 376
Goitre 109
Grains 90, 92
Grapes 97, 111
Great Britain
  food patterns 98, 99
  industrial feeding 316, 325, 327, 328, 330, 335–7
Greece 97, 98
Guatemala
  calorie and nutrient intake levels 125
  diets 115
  food consumption by food groups 124
  food patterns 73, 107, 108
Guianas 111
Guinea 86, 89

Haiti 118
Handbook for the Preparation of Food Balance Sheets 2
Harvard step test 229
Health hazards, protection against 426–7, 456
Hemoglobin 157, 158, 174
Hemosiderosis 93
Holland 97, 325
Honduras 107
Hospitals 348–69
  alcohol 351–2
  basis of alimentation 349
  calorie intake 349
  choice and preparation of foods 352
  dietist 367–8
  diets 349, 353–9, 364
  distribution staff 366
  drinks 351
  food distribution 361
  foodstuffs 368
  hygiene 369
  individualization of food 362–3
  kitchen arrangements 363–5
  kitchen equipment 364
  kitchen premises and equipment 359–66
  kitchen staff 366
  menus 368
  mineral intake 351
  place of serving meals 362
  preparation of food 363–5
  protein intake 350
  scheduling of meals 352
  staff 366–8
  staff medical checks 366–7
  supplies 365, 368–9
  times of meals 361
  vitamin intake 350
  washing-up procedure 365
  water requirements 351
Hot climates
  electrolytes 409
  energy expenditure 408
  expeditions 407–9
  nutrient requirements 409
  vitamin requirements 409
  water requirements 409
Household characteristics in food consumption surveys 34, 43–5, 60–2
Hungary 97
Hydrogen cyanide, removal of 92
Hygiene 366
  canteens 329
  food control 455–61
  hospitals 369
Hypohydration 293, 294

Iceland 97
Imports 9
India 76, 77, 180
  calorie and nutrient intake levels 125
  calorie requirements 154
  diets 134
  food consumption by food groups 124
  food patterns 76, 77
  nutritional requirements 180
Indians 102, 106–8
Indicative World Plan for Agricultural Development 4
Indonesia 79, 180
Industrial catering 315–38
  ancillary services 336
  approach towards operational costs 321

Subject Index

Industrial catering (cont.)
  convenience foods 327–8
  food preparation and conservation 328
  multipoint services 326
  nutrition in relation to working efficiency 332–5
  provision of facilities 315–17
  trends affecting 317–19
  See also Canteens
Industrialization effects on food patterns 74
Injera 90
Input and output 8
Inspection in food control 461–4
Iran 82–5
Iraq 82, 85
Ireland 97
Iron 100, 119, 173–80, 342, 388
  access to body 174
  role 173
Iron absorption 174, 177–80
Iron deficiency 86, 173
Iron loss 174–5
Iron requirement 175–7
  adolescents 177
  children 176–7
  lactation 175
  pregnancy 175
  recommendations 180
Iron stores 177
Israel
  calorie and nutrient intake levels 125
  diets 85
  food consumption by food groups 124
Italy 96, 97, 101, 322, 330

Jamaica 117
Japan 79, 154
Jordan 82

Kenya 89
Ketosis prevention 239
Kitchens. See Hospitals; Industrial catering
Korea 76
Kwashiorkor 185

Lactation
  iron requirements 175
  nicotinamide requirements 203
  riboflavin requirements 196
Ladinos 72

Lapps 98
Latin America 73, 105, 111, 447
Lebanon
  calorie and nutrient intake levels 125
  diets 85
  food consumption by food groups 124
  food patterns 79, 82, 83
Legislation. See Food control
Libya, diets 95
Living costs 43, 45
Living standards 75

Magnesium 342
Maize 112, 203–4
Maize tortilla 107
Malaysia 78
Malnutrition 105–6, 118, 123
Mandioca 110
Manioc 92
Manufacture for food and for industrial use 10
Margarine 100
Marginal hypo-albuminaemia 158
'Mate' 111
Meat 16, 91, 99, 133
Melanesian Islands 121
Mestizo group 109
Mexico 105, 106–8, 115
Military rations 221–311
  acceptability and palatability 239, 294
  Australian 24-hour (one-man) pack 279
  Australian 24-hour tropical ration 290
  basic characteristics and requirements 241
  British Army 230
  British Composite Pack 278
  British five-man pack 271
  British Mountain Arctic Ration Pack 265
  British 24-hour Ration Pack 265
  browning reaction 262
  C ration. See combat (below)
  calorie intake 224
  calorie requirements 232
  Canadian Arctic experimental 266, 304
  Canadian five-man pack 271
  Canadian food packet, survival, seat pack 302
  Canadian Mess Tin ration 266
  Canadian one-man pack 279
  Canadian (RCAF) survival food packet 299, 300

Military rations (*cont.*)
  Canadian survival life pack food kit 301
  carbohydrate requirements 227
  Chinese armed forces emergency ration 302
  cold climates 401
  combat rations 245–6, 263–4
    group feeding 268–84
    individual 264–8
  comparison of operational rations 281–4
  D-ration 244
  definition of ration 249
  deterioration 262
  developments 306–8
  energy requirements 226
  extreme conditions 232
  field rations 256–9
  food packets 250
  French Army five-man ration 271
  French Army survival ration 304
  garrison rations 251–6
  German Army emergency ration 303
  Indian Army eight-man composite ration 279
  K-ration 248–9
  life-raft survival 305
  limited warfare, 10-day starvation and caloric restriction below 1000 cal/day 291–4
  limited warfare (2000 cal) 284–91
  Long Range Patrol 289
  maintenance of physical efficiency 230–2
  nutrient requirements 230
  nutritional adequacy 222–30
  operational rations 259–63
  optimal allowances 230
  planning and development 239
  protein intake 225–6
  ration supplement 249
  salt requirements 234–5
  survival 294–304
  survival at sea 304–6
  U.S. Army 222–3, 241–7
  U.S. Army individual combat ration 246
  U.S. Army meal combat individual ration (MT) 289
  U.S. Army ration, individual, trail, frigid 264
  U.S. 5-in-1 ration 271
  U.S. food packet, carton, abandon ship-survival at sea 298
  U.S. food packet, individual survival, SA-Arctic areas survival 300
  U.S. food packet, life raft, aircraft 298
  U.S. food packet survival, ST 299
  U.S. ration, survival, individual, pemmican ration 301
  U.S. 10-in-1 ration 274
  vitamin requirements 227–30
  water requirements 236–9
Milk and milk products 16–17, 51, 83, 84, 91, 97, 98, 100, 110, 133, 167
Mineral deficiency 295
Mineral deposits 121
Mineral intake
  hospitals 351
  in sports 384–9
  old people 342
  sources of 16
Mount Everest expedition 412
Mountaineering expeditions 410

Navaho Indians 71
Near East
  diets 86
  food patterns 79–86
Net Protein Utilization 157
Netherlands 99
New Guinea 121, 122
New Mexico 71
New Zealand, food patterns 121
Niacin 240
Nicaragua 107, 108
Nicotinamide 166, 198, 199–205
Nicotinamide absorption 204
Nicotinamide adenine dinucleotide (NAD) 199, 200
Nicotinamide adenine dinucleotide phosphate (NADP) 199
Nicotinamide requirements
  children 203
  estimation 199–205
  factors affecting 203–5
  lactation 203
  minimum 201
  pregnancy 203, 204
Nicotinamide roles 199
Nicotinic acid. *See* Nicotinamide
Nigeria
  calorie and nutrient intake levels 125
  diets 95
  food consumption by food groups 124
  food patterns 86, 88
Nitrogen 155, 157

Subject Index

Nitrogen balance 163, 165, 166, 293, 295
Nitrogen requirements 159–60
N'methyl nicotinamide (NMN) 200, 204
Norway 96–8, 101
Nutrient content 32, 34
Nutrient intake 58, 92–3, 133
Nutrient inter-relationships 143
Nutrient losses 56–7
Nutrient requirements 56, 58, 139–219
    cold climates 401
    environmental factors 144
    formulation 144
    hot climates 409
    optimum 141
    See also Nutritional requirements
Nutrients
    absorption and utilization 375–8
    essential 142
Nutrition
    and performance 370–96
    education in 331
    global levels and trends 12–17
    in relation to working efficiency 332–5
Nutritional balance and performance 396–409
Nutritional requirements 32, 34, 43, 55, 139–219
    estimating 142
    factors affecting 142–3
    in sports 378–96
    minimum requirement 141
    old people 341
    safety allowance 142
    standard range 143
    See also Nutrient requirements
Nutritive value 52, 126
Nuts 16, 112

Obesity 292
Oceania, food patterns 120–3
Oceanic islands, diets 123
Oil-exporting countries 82
Oils 17, 51, 79, 86, 97, 108
Old people and old people's communities 340–8
    alcohol 343
    aspects peculiar to 343
    average ration 343
    calorie intake 341
    carbohydrate intake 342
    diets 344
    drinks 343
    fat intake 341
    menus 346–8
    mineral intake 342
    nutritional requirements 341
    organization of meals 344
    protein intake 341
    staffing 346
    vitamin intake 342
    water requirements 343
Olives 97
Output and input 8
Oxidation-reduction systems 206
Oxygen restriction 411

Pakistan 79, 80, 180
Panama
    calorie and nutrient intake levels 125
    diets 115
    food consumption by food groups 124
    food patterns 74, 106–8
Paraguay 110
Parasitic infestations 93
Parathyroid hormone 168, 169
Pemmican 266, 303, 407
PER 163
Per caput food supplies 4, 5, 11–12
    calorie content 14
    fat content 14
    protein content 14
    quantity 14
Performance
    and nutrition 370–96
    and nutritional balance 396–409
    dietary effects on 372
Performance capacity 375
    criteria for 370–1
Peru 109–12, 114
Pestle and mortar 92
Petroleum 82, 117
Philippines
    calorie and nutrient intake levels 125
    calorie requirements 154
    diets 80
    food consumption by food groups 124
    food patterns 77–9
Phosphorus 178
Physiology of work 333
Phytates 178–9
Pilot surveys 42
Plasma calcium 169
Plasma proteins 157
Poland 97, 316, 321–4, 330–6

Polygamy 94-6
Polynesian Islands 72, 73, 121
Pork 91
Portugal 96
Potassium intake 413
Potatoes 97
Poultry 98
Pregnancy
  energy requirement 152
  iron requirement 175
  nicotinamide requirement 203, 204
  protein requirement 162
  retinol requirement 183
  riboflavin requirement 196
Prepared dishes 48
Preservatives 432
Processed foods 48, 369
Production 7-8
Production Yearbook 3
Protein content 12
  per caput food supplies 14
Protein deficiency 108, 112, 155
Protein efficiency ratio 157
Protein intake 113, 114
  hospitals 350
  in food groups 130, 133
  military rations 225-6
  old people 341
Protein-mineral interrelationship 166
Protein-nutrient interrelationships 165
Protein quality, assessment of 164
Protein requirements
  average daily 14
  bases of 156-9
  children 162
  estimation of 159-63
  factors affecting 163-7
  pregnancy 162
  standards 162-3
Protein reserves 166
Protein sources 16, 133
Protein-vitamin interrelationship 165
Proteins 155
  dietary roles 155
  in sports 383
  nutritional quality 157
  urinary excretion 158
Puchero 112
Puerto Rico 105, 117, 118
Pulses 16, 77, 82, 84, 133
Pumpkins 78
Pyruvic acid, blood 188

Red cell riboflavin stores 194
Red cell transketolase activity 188
Reference Man 150, 153
Reference Woman 150, 153
Reindeer 98
Religion
  in food consumption surveys 46
  in food patterns 91, 93
  in food selection 67
Respiratory quotient 376, 381
Retinol 180-7, 350
  assessment 181-2
  relation of infection to 186
  role of 181
  sources of 181
Retinol deficiency 182, 185
Retinol requirement 182-7
  age variation 184
  estimation 182-4
  factors influencing 184-7
  lactation 183
  pregnancy 183
Retinol terminology 182
Riboflavin 109, 119, 191-9, 240
  intestinal synthesis 197
  urinary excretion 192
Riboflavin requirement 194-205
  assessment 192-4
  effect of protein and other vitamins 198
  estimation 196
  factors affecting 197
  lactation 196
  minimum 193
  pregnancy 196
  recommended dietary allowances 196
Riboflavin stores, red cell 194
Riboflavin tissue saturation 194
Rice 76-7, 79, 82, 90, 97, 107, 204
Rickets 103
Roots 86, 93
Ruands 90
Rumania 97, 101
Rye bread 98

Safety allowances 142
Sahara 88
Salt requirements in military rations 234-5
Sampling methods in food consumption surveys 39
Sauces 90, 91
Saudi-Arabia 82

Subject Index

Scurvy 205, 207, 260, 410
Sea voyages 4–10
Seasickness 305
Seasoning 78
Second World Food Survey 3
Seed 10, 16, 89, 90, 98
Senegal 89
Senile osteoporosis 171
Serum albumin 158
Serum protein 158
Shipwrecks, survival rations in 410
Sierra Leone 90, 91
Skiing 404
Sledging 404
Social events, effect on food patterns 75
Socio-economic conditions 34
Sodium restriction 354
Somalia 89
Space travel 414–17
Spain
  calorie and nutrient intake levels 125
  diets 101
  food consumption by food groups 124
  food patterns 96–8
Special feeding 371–423
Specific dynamic effect 148, 149
Spices 107
Sports
  alcohol in 395–6
  amino acids in 383
  carbohydrates in 381–2, 394
  electrolytes in 389–92
  energy expenditure 378–80, 392
  fats in 381–2
  influence of dietary measures 373
  metabolic requirements 372
  minerals in 384–9
  nutritional requirements 378–96
  performance diets 393–5
  proteins in 383
  training diet 392–3
  vitamins in 384–9
  water requirements 389–92
  weight loss in 390
  See also Performance
Standard metabolism 145
Staple food, static mechanism of 71
Starches and starchy roots 16, 49, 78, 111
Starvation 291, 292, 406
Statistics, accuracy of 5–6
Stocks, changes in 8
Sucrose 407

Sudan 86
Sugar and sweets 16, 49, 83, 112
Sugar beets 97
Supply elements 9
Survival rations
  aviation 414
  cold climates 406–7
  shipwrecks 410
Sweat loss 390, 413
Sweden 96–8, 316, 323, 330, 333, 454
Sweets. *See* Sugar and sweets
Switzerland 96, 97, 330, 332, 337
Syria 82

Taiwan 77, 78, 80
Taro 121
Teeth 168, 344
Teff 90
Temperate climates, expeditions in 397–9
Thailand
  diets 80
  food consumption by food groups 124
  food control 439
  food patterns 76, 77
Thiaminase 191
Thiamine 109, 119, 187–91, 198, 240, 386–7
Thiamine pyrophosphate 188
Thiamine requirement 187–91
  estimation 187–90
  factors affecting 190
Third World Food Survey 3, 14
Tocopherol 387
Transketolase 188
Trinidad 117
Tropical climates, expeditions in 409
Tryptophan 166, 199, 203, 204
Tubers 78, 93
Turkey 79

Uganda 89, 90
Undernutrition 14
United Kingdom
  calorie requirements 154
  diets 134
  food patterns 99
United States
  calorie and nutrient intake levels 125
  dietary allowances 142
  diets 115, 134

United States (*cont.*)
  food consumption by food groups 124
  food control 438, 446, 447, 453
  food patterns 102, 104–5
United States Army
  history of feeding 241–7
  military rations 222–3, 241–7, 264, 271, 289
UNRRA 12
Urinary sulfate sulfur/creatinine ratio 159
Uruguay 109–14

Vegetables 16, 77, 82, 90, 91, 104, 110, 167, 178, 206
Vending machines 319, 325, 332, 336
Venezuela 109–13, 118
Vietnam 77, 78
Vitamin active compounds 185
Vitamin deficiency 295
Vitamin intake
  hospitals 350
  old people 342
Vitamin interrelationship 186
Vitamin requirements
  cold climates 402
  hot climates 409
  military rations 227–30
Vitamins 99, 142, 165, 181, 184, 240, 350
  A 79, 84, 93, 100, 108, 119
  B 93, 207, 351
  C 79, 84, 100, 123, 205, 208
  D 86, 103, 168, 169, 171, 388
  E 387
  in sports 384–9
  sources of 16

Wastage 5, 10–11, 48
Water balance 305
Water deprivation 306
Water loss due to sweating 390, 413
Water requirements 295, 306
  cold climates 403–4
  hospitals 351
  hot climates 409
  military rations 236–9
  old people 343
  sports 389–92
Water supply
  emergency 305
  in expeditions 399
  limited 297
Weighing of food items 36–8
Weight loss 292, 293, 378, 390
Wheat 81, 82, 97, 98, 110
Wine 97, 111
Women, employment of 75
Work, physiology of 333
Worker approach towards canteen 335–8
Working efficiency, nutrition in relation to 332–5
World Food Surveys 3
World Health Organisation 434, 437, 450–2

Yemen 82
Yoghurt 97
Yugoslavia 96, 97, 321, 324, 333, 335–7